using computers today

today

with applications for the IBM® PC

using computers today

with applications for the IBM® PC

David R. Sullivan
T. G. Lewis
Curtis R. Cook
Oregon State University

Houghton Mifflin Company   **Boston**
Dallas   Geneva, Illinois   Lawrenceville, New Jersey   Palo Alto

Library of Congress Catalog Card Number: 85-80895

ISBN: 0-395-41066-5

BCDEFGHIJ-RM-89876

contents
in brief

contents

preface

This book teaches the fundamentals of using computer systems effectively. It combines a comprehensive treatment of how to use productivity software with the material found in a traditional introduction to data processing course. In addition, it includes a unified treatment of the entire spectrum of computers—from the microcomputers used for personal computing to the supercomputers used to solve difficult scientific and business problems—and thus provides a balanced view of computing and data processing.

We believe the content and organization of *Using Computers Today* are well suited to a variety of introductory courses in computing. The book can be used in a modern course on data processing fundamentals; a campus-wide computer literacy course for nontechnical as well as technical students; and as a course prerequisite to advanced topics in business, engineering, science, liberal arts, and the humanities.

Coverage of Personal Computing

Whenever possible we have used personal computing as a vehicle to introduce and explain general computing concepts. In the last ten years personal computing has grown from a hobbyist activity—a mere curiosity in the field of computing—to a discipline worthy of serious study. Personal computers today are small, affordable, powerful, and understandable. They make an ideal vehicle for presenting general data processing concepts that may otherwise seem obscure and intangible. By now, nearly all important information-processing activities have a counterpart in the field of personal computing. Thus we are able to use personal computers to explain how *all* computers work.

Productivity Software

The need to know about productivity software has grown so quickly that many textbooks have not kept pace. Productivity software has changed the way professionals approach everyday tasks. Writers find that word processing changes the way thoughts are translated into words. Analysts find that spreadsheet programs open up new ways to experiment with numbers. Data management programs provide new ways to extract information from large amounts of data. The list goes on and on, and it leads to one conclusion: From a user's perspective it has become more important to know how to use and select software than to understand in great detail how computers work or how programs are written. This book addresses the needs of the user rather than the professional programmer or electrical engineer. Technical issues are not avoided, but they are discussed in the context of how they affect the user.

There are thousands of programs available. Each has its own characteristics, command structure, and user interface. It was a challenge to see beyond the superficial differences among programs and find the essence of word processors, spreadsheets, and other productivity software. For example, moving a paragraph is conceptually identical in all word processors; organizing a file of data is conceptually similar in different data management systems. Knowing these concepts will serve you well no matter which word processor or data management system you choose to use. In addition, familiarity with these concepts builds a basis for learning to use a program and understanding computing in general.

Organization of the Book

Using Computers Today is designed to accommodate a variety of course formats. The book's parts have been kept as independent as possible. After completing Part I, the remaining parts can be studied in any order.

Part I describes the basics of computing. The use and importance of computers are discussed in Chapter 1. Chapters 2 and 3 describe the inner workings of computers from their central processing engines to their input and output devices. Finally, Chapter 4 describes how to operate a computer by explaining the purpose and function of an operating system and by illustrating the use of visual and textual user interfaces.

Parts II, III, and IV deal with the concepts underlying word processors, spreadsheets, and data management systems. Part II fully describes the most pervasive use of computers: word processing. Chapter 5 gives an elementary introduction to word processing, and Chapter 6 provides more advanced instruction. In this part the reader not only learns a valuable skill, but also gains insight into the most popular of all software.

Part III covers the second most important productivity software area in contemporary computing: spreadsheet analysis. Chapter 7 introduces the concept of an electronic worksheet and explains how it is used to store numbers, text, and formulas. Chapter 8 covers more advanced features of spreadsheet programs leading into the realm of modeling and the development of professional-quality spreadsheet templates.

Part IV concludes the presentation of the three most widely used productivity software areas by discussing data management. Chapter 9 describes the use of record management programs, the simplest form of data management software. Chapter 10 extends the ideas presented in Chapter 9 to include the database management systems used on mainframes, minis, and micros. Database management connects productivity software to the world of data processing, applications, and a diversity of uses of computers.

Part V examines applications of computing in the burgeoning fields of communications, graphics, and special-purpose application software. Chapter 11 discusses communications technology and computer networking. Chapter 12 shows how the graphical capability of computers can be used to make bar charts, line graphs, and other types of presentation graphics. It also discusses the powerful graphics systems used to design airplanes, computers, and buildings in what is called CAD/CAM (computer-aided design and computer-aided manufacturing). Chapter 13 surveys the entire field of application software; it includes examples from home budgeting, accounting, education, nutrition analysis, and entertainment.

Part VI includes the most technical material in the book: how to design, program, and acquire new systems. Chapter 14 covers the system analysis approach to defining and solving data processing problems. Modern structured analysis techniques are described, complete with data flow charts and structured design methodology. Chapter 15 is an overview of programming. The different types of systems and languages are discussed including a brief comparison of programming language features. This chapter should be read before Appendix C, Programming in BASIC, is studied because it shows how to apply structured programming techniques to BASIC and Pascal programs. Finally, Chapter 16 describes the issues you should consider when you buy personal computer hardware and software.

Part VII examines the evolution of computers and the influence they have on people and society. Chapter 17 traces the computer revolution from its roots to contemporary society. It provides the usual coverage of the generations of mainframe computers and also includes a unique treatment of the development of personal computers. Chapter 18 extends the discussion by raising grave issues concerning privacy, pirating of software, and security.

The first two appendixes may be studied at any point in the course; they describe how computers process information and careers in computing. The later appendixes differ depending on which version of the book you purchased.

The Book's Three Versions

Using Computers Today is available in three versions: a generic version, a version for use with IBM® Personal Computers, and a version for use with Apple® II computers.* The versions differ only in the way they cover BASIC programming and in their treatment of TriPac™, an integrated software package designed specifically to give students hands-on experience with productivity software.

All three versions include a substantial appendix on programming in BASIC. The BASIC appendix in the generic version can be used to teach programming on either a mainframe, mini, or microcomputer equipped with standard BASIC. For both the Apple and IBM versions, a BASIC appendix has been written to match the appropriate implementation of BASIC.

TriPac is an integrated program that provides hands-on instruction in word processing, electronic spreadsheet, and data management applications. Consequently, the TriPac appendix is divided into an introductory section followed by three stand-alone sections—one for each application—and the applications can be studied in any order. The TriPac application programs are easy to use, share a command structure, and support ''cutting and pasting'' of data from the data management and spreadsheet applications to word processed documents. Because the TriPac program only runs on Apple IIs, IBM PCs, and IBM PC compatibles, the generic version does not contain an appendix on TriPac.

Supplementary Materials

Supplements have been prepared to make *Using Computers Today* a complete learning and teaching package including

- A study guide
- A combined Instructor's Manual and Test Bank
- A set of overhead transparencies
- TriPac software from Houghton Mifflin
- Computerized Test Bank for Apple, IBM, and TRS-80 computers
- Computerized Study Guide with BASIC Programs
- Grade Performance Analysis
- Abridged DoMore™ Software

---

*IBM is a registered trademark of International Business Machines Corporation. Apple is a registered trademark of Apple Computer, Inc. TriPac and DoMore are trademarks of Houghton Mifflin Company.

Acknowledgments

We would like to thank the following reviewers:

Robert M. Stewart, Iowa State University

R. E. Coursin, Tampa College

Jeane A. Schildberg, Chaffey College

George Farrimond, Southern Oregon State University

Tim Sylvester, College of DuPage

Sharon Szabo, Schoolcraft College

George Fowler, Texas A & M University

Richard M. Dean, California State Polytechnic University Pomona

Sharon Clark, Texas Christian University

Robert Schuerman, California Polytechnic State University

George L. Miller, North Seattle Community College

Marion G. Ben-Jacob, Mercy College

Donald B. Distler, Jr., Belleville Area College

Donald L. Henderson, Mankato State University

Mike Michaelson, Palomar College

Andrew M. Suhy, Ferris State College

Susan C. Traynor, Clarion University

C. Gardner Mallonee II, Essex Community College

Megan Roberts, Northwestern Michigan College

Gary Armstrong, Shippensburg University

Gary Klotz, Milwaukee Area Technical College

Mohaninder Gill, University of Wisconsin Platteville

Robert L. Horton, University of Wisconsin Whitewater

Estelle M. Sherry, Greater Hartford Community College

Francis Whittle, Dutchess Community College

Bryan J. Carney, University of Wisconsin

Thomas Dwyer, University of Pittsburgh

Rod Southworth, Laramie County Community College

Roger Cook, Southern Illinois University

Devern Perry, Brigham Young University

Patricia Milligan, Baylor University

Gregory L. Smith, Colorado State University

Roy Alvarez, Cornell University

Peter G. Bryant, University of Colorado at Denver

Norbert Enrick, Kent State University

David R. Lee, San Jose State University

Vincent Marchionni, Pennsylvania State University

William O'Neill, Villanova University

James Rainey, Michigan State University

John B. Lane, Edinboro University of Pennsylvania

Leonard Presby, William Patterson State College of New Jersey

William O'Hare, Prince George's Community College

Seth Hock, Columbus Technical Institute

Karen Watterson, Shoreline Community College

D.R.S.
T.G.L.
C.R.C.

using computers today

with applications for the IBM® PC

PART ONE

the world of computing

Our times have been called the Computer Age because ours is a high-speed, information-laden society. The name has long conjured up images of a stern, impersonal world—a world where decisions are made by balancing a mathematical formula, and people are counted, sorted, and processed on punched cards. But the Computer Age has given birth to a host of new tools that help us with everyday tasks, such as writing, planning, graphing, and communicating. Thanks to these tools, the idea that computers are cold and calculating machines governing our everyday lives is a fading myth.

Meanwhile, relentless declines in cost and improvements in performance have moved computers and machine intelligence from data processing centers to homes, offices, shopping centers, and even cars. Never before has the average person had within reach such a powerful agent for change. But what are people going to do with these easily available computers? Two facts are clear: computers are pervasive, and they are capable of revolutionizing nearly every area of life.

The pervasiveness of computers presents a problem: how should you learn to use them? Our answer is to introduce you to the world of computing through close examination of a few very important applications as well as methods for developing the instructions that control computers. Specifically, we will explain the applications and methods known as word processing, modeling with spreadsheets, storage and retrieval of database information, graphics, communications, systems analysis and design, and programming.

Mastery of the concepts presented with these explanations will guarantee success in using a computer in your own specialty.

Part I takes the first step in preparing you to understand the computer world by teaching some basic computer concepts. In Chapter 1 we survey the uses of computers, define terms common to all of computing, and illustrate how to use a computer. Next we look at how a computer works, because learning about computers is similar to learning how to drive a car: the more you know about the machine, the better operator you become. Chapter 2 explains how the thinking part of a computer—the central processing unit—and storage devices work together to execute the series of instructions known as a program. Chapter 3 discusses the various devices for communicating with the computer. Then in Chapter 4 we discuss computer programs, emphasizing the operating system, which is the master control program that manages the computer.

Rarely in history has anyone been privileged to witness the introduction of such startling inventions as atomic power, space travel, and genetic engineering. Incredibly, all of these have been introduced within the last 50 years. Computing ranks with the most profound inventions of our time, and goes even beyond the others in one respect: it allows the ordinary citizen to participate in revolutionary discovery. Part I is your first step into the rapidly evolving world of computing.

introduction 1
to computers

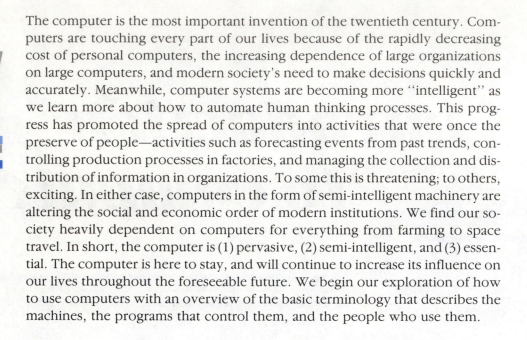

The computer is the most important invention of the twentieth century. Computers are touching every part of our lives because of the rapidly decreasing cost of personal computers, the increasing dependence of large organizations on large computers, and modern society's need to make decisions quickly and accurately. Meanwhile, computer systems are becoming more "intelligent" as we learn more about how to automate human thinking processes. This progress has promoted the spread of computers into activities that were once the preserve of people—activities such as forecasting events from past trends, controlling production processes in factories, and managing the collection and distribution of information in organizations. To some this is threatening; to others, exciting. In either case, computers in the form of semi-intelligent machinery are altering the social and economic order of modern institutions. We find our society heavily dependent on computers for everything from farming to space travel. In short, the computer is (1) pervasive, (2) semi-intelligent, and (3) essential. The computer is here to stay, and will continue to increase its influence on our lives throughout the foreseeable future. We begin our exploration of how to use computers with an overview of the basic terminology that describes the machines, the programs that control them, and the people who use them.

■ The Omnipresent Computer

Who Uses Computers?

Everyone in the industrialized world uses computers today. When you cash a check, pay a bill, or use a credit card, the transaction is quickly converted into an electronic form that is processed by a computer. Every year millions of Americans depend on computers operated by the Internal Revenue Service to process income tax returns. Figures 1.1–1.3 show some of the other ways computers are used today. Without large, powerful computers running 24 hours a day, banking would be impossible, the stock market would fail, and international trade would come to a halt.

We find computers close to home as well. The use of computers in everyday life is increasing. Only a few short years ago all grocery stores manually processed sales at the check-out stand. Now an electronic scanner reads the price of goods directly from labels on the products. Modern cars are controlled by one or more tiny computers that adjust the flow of fuel, provide safe braking, and display information about operating status on the dashboard. More and more people cook in microwave ovens controlled by computer, watch video tapes that were recorded automatically while they were asleep, and wake up to the sound of music and the aroma of fresh coffee activated by digital clocks.

Computers are also making communication easier and faster. For many years people throughout the world have been able to communicate with one

Figure 1.1 *Personal computers are used extensively in schools to teach everything from arithmetic to history.*

Figure 1.2 *Stockbrokers get the latest quotations through personal computers that double as word processors and calculators.*

Figure 1.3 *Personal computers are often used as word processors; that is, they are used to prepare reports, memos, and other documents. Editing is easier with a word processor than with a typewriter, because it is easier to move characters on a screen than it is to move them on paper.*

another through telephones controlled by computers. More recently, people have begun to communicate directly from the keyboards of their personal computers to others who receive *electronic mail*—messages sent and received through computers. Newspapers and magazines are being produced from text stored in computer memories, and television shows are being edited with computers.

Perhaps the most controversial uses of computers occur in the workplace. Computers are rapidly changing the way we work. From the mailroom to the boardroom, corporate America is highly computerized. For example, orders for manufactured goods produced by a company are immediately entered into the company's computer system; then the computer produces reports used by a multitude of employees. The shipping department fills orders from the SHIP-TO report, and the vice president of finance uses the INVENTORY report to estimate how much money is tied up in inventory, how much demand there is for the company's products, and how long customers must wait to receive their orders. Incoming orders are relayed directly to the factory floor where computers

Computer Applications

Computers are powerful tools that are rapidly changing the way we work and play. Once they were used only by highly trained specialists in expensive data processing centers. Now they are found sitting on desks, buried inside appliances, hidden under grocery store check-out counters, and sitting on laps. This photo essay takes an in-depth look at important computer applications in several fields, ranging from home computing to publishing, mechanical engineering, and the management of merchandise and material.

1. A small girl uses her home computer to build faces on the screen. Using a computer is literally child's play if you have the right program.

HOME COMPUTERS

2. Most home computers (and many office computers) are occasionally used to play games. Because of their larger memory capacity, personal computers can play more sophisticated games than can video game machines. Many educational programs, such as Spelling Bee Games and SAT Word Attack Skills, are ''games'' with an educational theme.

3. A computer can help you set up a budget, record and track expenses, and manage investments. But some activities, such as balancing a checkbook, are so simple they may be more work to do on a computer than to do by hand.

4. Computers no larger than a briefcase can run on batteries in any location. Despite their small size, they can have memory capacities rivaling much larger computers.

6. Portable computers can provide instant price quotes for complicated sales. Financing alternatives can be compared without delay. Once an order for a sale has been taken, the portable computer can transmit the order over a normal telephone line to the corporation's main computer, and immediate confirmation of the order can be received.

5. Most transportable computers snap up into a suitcase-size unit. This computer includes a full-size detachable keyboard, a 9-inch display, a disk drive, two expansion slots that allow optional circuit boards to be plugged into the computer, a built-in printer, and 800 kilobytes of memory—all in a 25-pound package.

7. Portable computers that require an external power source and weigh 20 pounds or more are often called *transportable computers.* They can be used at both work and home.

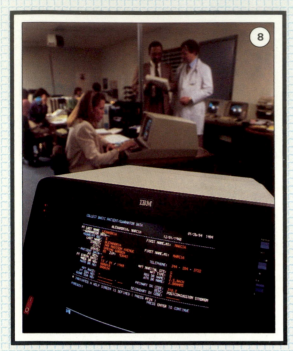

VERTICAL MARKET APPLICATIONS

Vertical software addresses the needs of people in a specific discipline or occupation, such as those of architects or farmers, who have very different information-processing needs. Software firms have created tens of thousands of programs that solve problems in specific occupations. This page illustrates software for the health-care market.

8. Shared Medical Systems (SMS) Corporation provides computer-based information systems to hospitals and physician groups. This photo shows SMS's Practice Management Services software, which allows physicians to spend more time practicing medicine, and less time worrying about administration and bill collection.

9. A constantly changing mass of federal and local regulations sets the legal requirements for record keeping in the medical field. Computerized medical systems can help hospital executives cope with these challenges.

10. The series of bars on the folder constitutes a code that can be read by a device called a *bar code reader*. This computerized coding system makes it easier to maintain accurate records regarding all aspects of a patient's stay.

EDUCATION

11. Personal computers can be an invaluable aid in preparing reports, essays, and assignments.

12. Using a computer can be thought provoking. For many activities, computers are better information processors than people.

```
Now that your program is back in
memory, why don't you change line
30 (press RETURN for a hint if you
don't remember how to change a
line).


]LIST

10 PRINT "ROSES ARE RED"
20 PRINT "VIOLETS ARE BLUE"
30 PRINT "I LOVE MY APPLE"
40 PRINT "AND PROGRAMMING, TOO!"
50 END

]30 PRINT "I'm having fun..."▓
```

13. This screen shows a tutorial program—that is, a program that guides a student through the basics of using computer programs. The best tutorial programs are highly interactive and encourage the student to experiment; the worst ones are little more than automated slide shows.

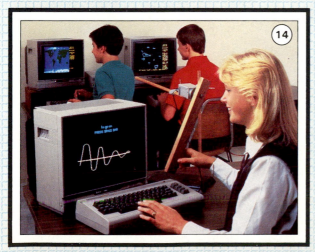

14. Education software can be fun as well as instructive. These simulation programs teach by emulating the responses of a system, such as the development of waves in an ocean.

window 1

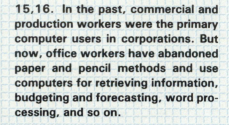

15,16. In the past, commercial and production workers were the primary computer users in corporations. But now, office workers have abandoned paper and pencil methods and use computers for retrieving information, budgeting and forecasting, word processing, and so on.

17. The "knowledge workers" in modern offices often use terminals linked by a central mainframe computer that provides electronic mail, access to collections of data called databases, a variety of application programs, and shared access to peripheral devices such as printers.

18. Instead of using a central mainframe computer, an employer might provide a personal computer for each worker. This approach can allow each employee to use excellent software for word processing, financial analysis, and other tasks.

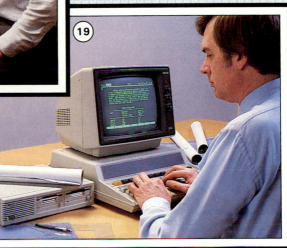

19. Most surveys of offices find that word processing is the most important computer application. Word processing software varies widely, from easy-to-use programs that are suitable for writing simple memos and reports to programs that are designed for professional typesetters.

20. Almost any computer can be used for word processing. This personal computer is used with a laser printer to produce typeset-quality documents.

21. The fields of computing and communications are merging rapidly. This computer combines a personal computer compatible with an IBM PC, a telephone, and a variety of computing and communications services in one compact unit. It offers fast, easy access to remote computers and databases, convenient one-touch dialing of telephone numbers, and the ability to execute a wide range of personal productivity software.

window 1

PUBLISHING

Computers are involved in every aspect of publishing, from the creation of text through the generation of typeset artwork for the presses.

22. Here, Atex terminals are used by reporters from the Knight-Ridder chain at the Democratic Convention in San Francisco, in July 1984.

23. News reporters are never far from computer terminals.

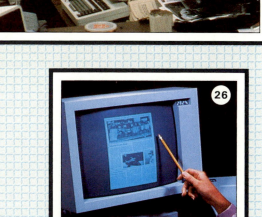

24. The abundance of terminals at the Orlando (Florida) *Sentinel* is typical of newsrooms today.

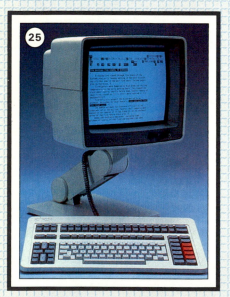

25. Reporters translate their thoughts into text with the help of high-quality word processing systems.

26. Pagination systems allow editors to preview an entire page at once, with all text in place exactly as it will appear when printed.

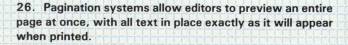

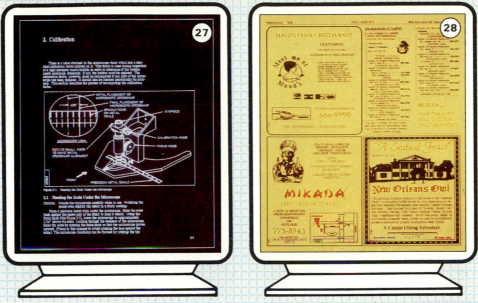

27,28. On state-of-the-art composition systems, both text and graphics can be merged on one page and previewed at a graphics workstation. These screens show pages from a maintenance manual and the Yellow Pages.

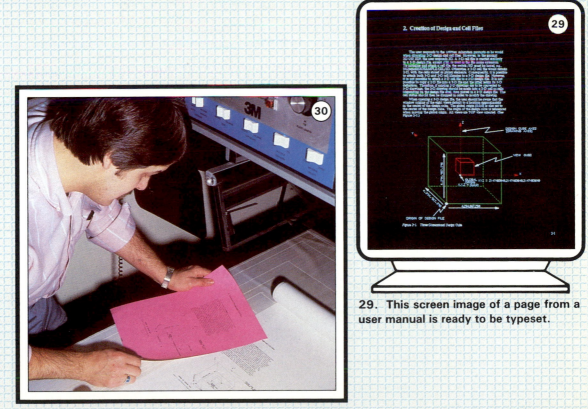

30. Here we see a scroll of typeset copy, ready for printing.

29. This screen image of a page from a user manual is ready to be typeset.

window 1

MERCHANDISE AND MATERIAL MANAGEMENT

Automated systems for the management of merchandise and material rely on having each inventory item labeled in a machine-readable manner.

31. This hand-held printer prints and dispenses gummed labels. The labels can be printed with bar codes such as UPC (Universal Product Code), as well as several human-readable fonts. Information for the labels can be entered through the keypad on the printer, or the printer can be connected to a computer.

32. Many check-out counters use laser scanning systems to read UPC codes on merchandise. These systems not only speed up the check-out process but also help the store keep an accurate inventory.

33. At Ford Motor Company's largest transmission plant in Livonia, Michigan, ScopeScan units are used to track testing on the assembly line. Each ScopeScan unit is a laser bar code reader.

34. This GERBERmover computerized manufacturing system is used in the garment and allied industries to reduce handling and track inventory. All the operator has to do is touch a button, and the hangers are automatically moved by the computer. The system monitors the time, production count, operation number, and employee identification number.

35. Each of the hangers is numbered and bar-coded, enabling individual hangers to be tracked by computer. This hanger's bar code is on the back side.

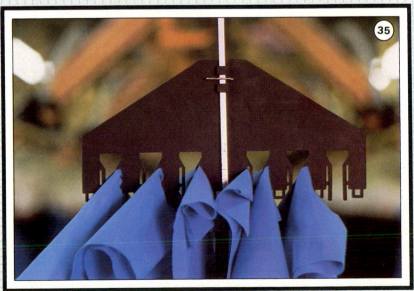

window 1

COMPUTER-AIDED MECHANICAL ENGINEERING

Computers are routinely used in mechanical engineering for a full range of design tasks: modeling in two and three dimensions, analyzing the strength of parts, drafting, computing a part's center of gravity, and so forth. Although the hardware and software required for these tasks are specialized and expensive, the expense can be justified by improved designs and shorter product development cycles.

These two pages describe just one mechanical engineering task: analyzing the structural properties of mechanical systems by using what is called finite element analysis software.

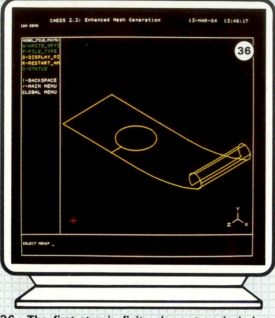

36. The first step in finite element analysis is to create an electronic model of the part or system to be analyzed. In this case the part to be studied is a spring that fits on one piece of an assembly and holds another piece in place.

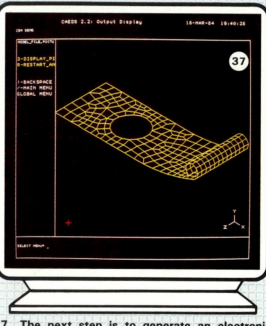

37. The next step is to generate an electronic mesh that represents the part as a large number of tiny building blocks, or "elements." These elements, together with descriptions of their strengths and interrelationships, become the basis for a simulation of how the part will perform.

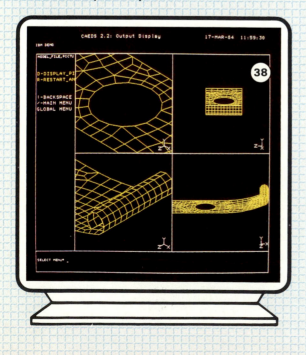

38. Once an electronic model has been created, it can be viewed from a variety of perspectives at once.

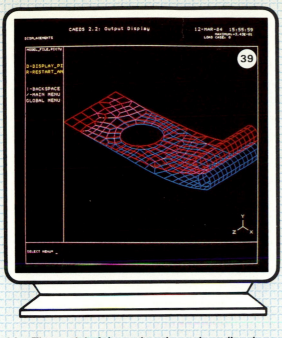

39. After the loads to be placed on the front of the spring are described, the finite element analysis software calculates how the spring will deform under stress. The blue drawing represents the undeformed shape: the deformed shape is in red.

40. The colored lines shown on this model of the spring are the stress contours. This is exactly the type of information an engineer needs to predict where, when, and how the spring will fail.

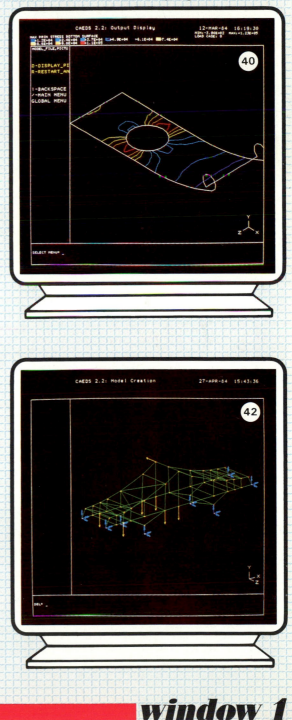

41. The model of the spring shown in earlier photographs is called a *shell model,* because in the model the spring had no thickness. Finite element analysis can also be applied to three-dimensional models, as in this model of a trip lever. The deformation of the trip lever has been exaggerated in this picture to make it visible; the actual deformation is very small.

42. A model of an entire system, such as this bridge, can also be analyzed to look for structural or vibration problems.

window 1

COMPUTER-AIDED MANUFACTURING

Numerically controlled (NC) machines can cut, stamp, and grind nearly any material. For most manufacturing operations NC machines are faster and more accurate than people, but they are less adaptable to new tasks. Although there is a tremendous variety of NC machines, this page shows only NC machines that cut.

44. This NC router cuts shoe patterns quickly and accurately. It can cut hard materials up to ¼ -inch thick.

43. Shoe designs can be scaled from one size to another quickly when the designs are stored electronically.

45. Before an NC fabric cutter is used, the layout of the patterns must be determined.

46. This NC cutting system is designed to cut limp materials for the apparel, aerospace, automotive, and related industries. It can cut through many plies of fabric at once.

47. This automated signmaking system can cut letters from adhesive-backed vinyl, draw text with ballpoint pens, and cut silk-screen masters from film. Commands can be entered on the keyboard, or the signmaker can be driven by a personal computer running graphics software.

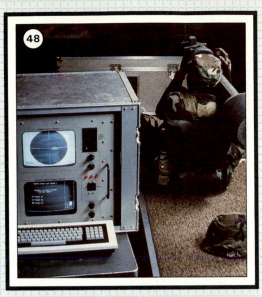

48.

MILITARY APPLICATIONS

Computers play a vital role in military command, control, and communications systems. Because military equipment is designed to be used in the hostile environment of war, military computers are frequently built to specifications that call for high standards of ruggedness, reliability, and performance.

48. Computer-based simulation systems are frequently used when actual tests are impractical or expensive. This STAGS Dragon (Simulated Tank Anti-Armor Gunnery System) is being tested at Fort Benning, Georgia. It trains students without using live ammunition.

49.

49. This stand-alone special-purpose computer uses high-speed processing to analyze telemetry data from a satellite.

50.

51.

50. This engineer is programming a path for an aircraft through a simulated battlefield on a Loral Electronic Environment Simulator.

51. Air control and tracking systems at the U.S. Navy's Virginia Capes site help controllers monitor 86,000 square miles. These systems feature exceptionally clear and large vector graphics displays.

SMALL BUSINESS APPLICATIONS

Small businesses can't afford to buy large computers or to develop software themselves. This explains why large corporations were the first to adopt computer technology. The development of personal computers and inexpensive packages of software for businesses has allowed small businesses to participate in the computer age.

52. Off-the-shelf software packages provide instant solutions to most of the data processing problems encountered by businesses. For example, accounting packages can manage the payroll, accounts receivable, accounts payable, and general ledger. Business transactions and customer lists can be recorded, stored, and reported by what are called database management systems. Word processing programs help with business correspondence. The list of business application programs goes on and on.

53. With spreadsheet programs, business relationships can be entered into "electronic worksheets." Often spreadsheet programs are used to create financial projections and then to analyze alternative business scenarios.

window 1

control the production of *numerically controlled machines*—production tools that accept numerical commands. Using these machines, computers can automate entire factories, working faster and more accurately than any person could hope to match (see Figure 1.4).

In the early 1800s English workers called Luddites destroyed automatic textile machines because they feared automation. Today, we all depend on automation and computers, large and small, to entertain, assist in our work, control other machines, and communicate with one another over great distances. Modern society cannot function without computerized control, communication, and automation.

The Power of Computers

The traditional view of a computer is that it is a "mathematical brain." Computers can carry out a million calculations per second—for example, to compute the path of a rocket to the moon, or the monthly payment on a newly purchased home. When a computer is used to do lengthy or complicated calculations, we say it is a "number cruncher." But if computers were just number crunchers, they would just be big adding machines, and computers can do far more than even the largest imaginable adding machine.

Figure 1.4 *Robots are rapidly taking over manufacturing jobs in industry. Here, an IBM robot capable of precision to 20-millionths of an inch automates the production of computers.*

Figure 1.5 *An IBM 3330 disk stores roughly a billion characters of information. The ability to "remember" a vast amount of information, and retrieve it quickly, is one of the strengths of computers.*

In fact, computers are far more useful when they are used not just to perform calculations, but to store large quantities of information for long periods of time (see Figure 1.5). They can remember, process, rearrange, calculate, display, and report new information gleaned from old information. In other words, computers have both memory and data processing power. This combination gives computers a startling ability to influence human decision making and improve people's ability to communicate.

As an example of how computers affect decision making, consider the owner of a construction company that competes against several other companies for building contracts. The owner prepares a bid for a contract by estimating the labor, materials, and time required to complete a project. The company with the lowest bid will win the contract; but if the bid is too low, the company will lose money.

The company installed a computer to do the calculations and print the reports needed to prepare a bid. The computer was like a fast adding machine, and it rarely made mistakes. But then the owner did something unusual: he started using the computer to estimate what competitors would bid on new construction projects. He did this by collecting data from past projects and past estimates by his competitors and storing this data in the computer's extensive memory. Then with its data processing capability the computer was able to identify patterns that characterized the bidding by other contractors. This information changed the contractor's way of doing business, helping him to win contracts and earn greater profits.

Besides being good at arithmetic, remembering a lot of facts, and making suggestions based on the facts, computers also help people communicate over large distances. Computer-controlled communications satellites are an obvious example of how computers help us communicate (see Figure 1.6). For a less obvious example, consider how a computer can be used in a stock brokerage firm.

An analyst for the firm can use the memory and the calculating ability of her personal computer to track the prices of stocks and bonds, but the most important function of her computer is to communicate her ideas to others. It helps her communicate in three ways. First, the analyst constructs graphs of stock and bond prices versus time in three colors on the screen of her computer. If she had to do this by hand, it would never get done. Second, she uses the computer to write a report, incorporate the graphs into the report, and then check her spelling. Finally, she sends a copy of the report to 250 clients. For some of these customers the postal service is too slow; so the analyst uses equipment such as that shown in Figure 1.7. That is, she sends the text and graphics over the telephone the same evening by using her personal computer, a telephone connection, and a program that runs her computer automatically in her absence.

These examples show that computers are more than adding machines. They are capable of storing information in various forms—for example, as numbers, text, and pictures. They not only perform calculations on the information contained in their memories but also rearrange that information in new and interesting ways, find patterns, and influence human decisions. Once the information has been processed, the computer can help disseminate it quickly to other computers and to people (see Figure 1.8).

Figure 1.6 *Earth station antennas follow satellites across the sky. Communications satellites and computers have extended the reach of global communications by many orders of magnitude.*

Figure 1.7 *Telephone systems and personal computers are rapidly being merged into integrated electronic office systems.*

The ability to recall facts, process these facts, and quickly disseminate the results to all corners of the world is the key to why computers are so important in modern society. It explains why computers have such an enormous impact on industrialized nations and their people, and why computers will help shape

Figure 1.8 *Computers can "talk" to each other and to people over the telephone line—using computers at both ends.*

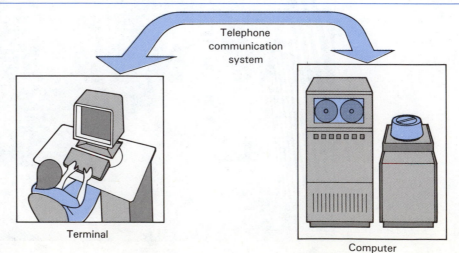

our future. It also explains why it is important to study computing. If we are to remain masters of this technology, then we must fully understand computers and what they can do.

Types of Computers

Computers come in all shapes and sizes, as Figures 1.9–1.11 illustrate. They are usually classified into three broad categories: mainframes, minicomputers, and microcomputers.

Mainframes are the largest, fastest, and most expensive computers. They are found in banks, insurance companies, large corporations, and government organizations. Very large mainframes are called *supercomputers* and are used primarily for the analysis of scientific and engineering problems. Usually mainframes serve many users and many functions; they are considered *general-purpose* machines. They are particularly good for problems requiring extensive mathematical calculations or for sharing large volumes of information among many people. Like a television network, they provide valuable and important services in bulk; but the users have little control over these services.

Minicomputers, or **minis,** are a smaller version of mainframes; they are slower and cheaper than mainframes. Often minicomputers are used in research labs, universities, and manufacturing plants. Compared with mainframes, minicomputers usually provide more specialized, well-defined

Figure 1.9 *An Amdahl mainframe computer system consisting of two central processing units and attachments for storage and communications. Many ''simultaneous'' users (not shown here) are supported by such machines.*

Figure 1.10 *A Digital Equipment Corporation VAX minicomputer. Whether used for dedicated applications or as general-purpose computer systems, minicomputers offer economy of scale in the middle of the cost/performance range.*

services; they are said to be *dedicated* to specific applications. For example, minicomputers may be used to control an assembly line in a factory, to record data in a research laboratory, to assist programmers to develop programs for other computers, or to process specific types of data for building contractors or medical doctors.

Microcomputers, or **micros,** are the smallest, least powerful computers. They are frequently **embedded** in other devices—for example, in cars, clock radios, burglar alarms, toys, microwave ovens, or space vehicles. They are also at the heart of all **personal computers**—computers that are designed to be used by one person. They are even more specialized than minicomputers. Microcomputers offer to computer users advantages and disadvantages somewhat like those provided to television watchers by a video tape recorder: although you must purchase the personal computer or video tape recorder and purchase or rent disks or tapes, you have complete control over how you use the equipment.

Actually, there is no clear line dividing one type of computer from another. All three types may be used in a similar way. For example, one or two people might use a mainframe to solve a very specialized problem in much the same

Figure 1.11 *Wang microcomputers may be used separately or clustered in an office as shown here. Word processing, communications, financial modeling, and a wide variety of office activities are performed on micros.*

way as one person might use a personal computer. Or instead of using a mainframe computer, a corporation might connect minicomputers together to handle all the record keeping for the company.

■ Anatomy of a Computer

A Computer Is a System

Whether a computer is classified as a mainframe, minicomputer, or micro-computer, it is actually a complete *system,* composed of many interacting parts. Computer systems can be divided into two distinct subsystems: hardware and software. **Hardware** consists of all the tangible parts that you can see and touch. **Software** is the intangible *control* over the hardware. Software is the total of all the programs that can be run on the computer system. A **program** is a list of instructions that the computer hardware follows. Programs tell the hardware how to behave and thus give the computer system its ''personality.''

If a computer were a component stereo system, we might imagine the music to be the software and the record player to be the hardware. In a stereo system, information is recorded on the surface of a platter, entered into the stereo through a stylus or needle, and sent to the speakers to be converted to sound. In a computer system, information is recorded on the surface of magnetic tape, magnetic disks, and other devices; it is entered through a keyboard or some other special equipment attached to the computer; and it is sent to a display screen or another device designed to accept electrical signals and convert them into human-readable form. A printer, for example, converts electrical signals into intelligible text. Figure 1.12 shows the similarity between a stereo and a computer system. Both systems receive some type of input, process it, and then produce some kind of output.

Figure 1.12 *Stereo and computer systems are somewhat analogous.*

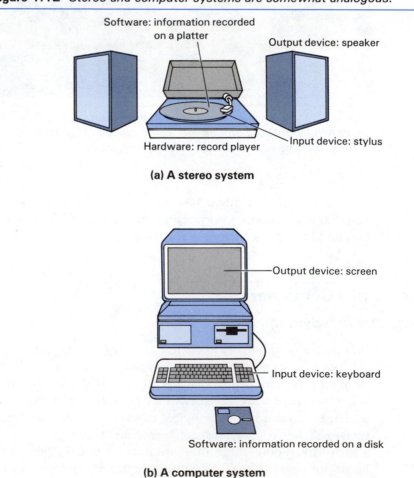

Software: information recorded on a platter

Output device: speaker

Hardware: record player

Input device: stylus

(a) A stereo system

Output device: screen

Input device: keyboard

Software: information recorded on a disk

(b) A computer system

Despite these similarities, computer systems differ in a significant way from stereos or any other kind of mechanical system. Every time a particular record is played, the stereo system repeats exactly the same tune; it can play whatever is on the record but cannot create new music. In contrast a computer system can produce different and possibly surprising results each time it is run. It is the software of a computer system that provides the ''intelligence'' for a computer system to ''play back'' a different ''tune.'' Thus software is the ''mind'' of a machine, whereas hardware is the ''body.'' Without the mind, the body does not know what to do.

Hardware Components

Every computer system performs four basic functions: input, output, processing, and storage. As Figure 1.13 illustrates, even a minimal computer has

- an *input device* such as a keyboard.
- an *output device* such as a display screen (and most likely a printer).
- a *central processing unit* (CPU) for processing data.
- short-term memory, called *main memory,* to hold programs and data temporarily while they are being used.
- long-term memory, called *external storage,* such as a disk drive, to read and write permanently stored programs and data.

An input device senses events in the computer's environment (such as pressure on a key) and converts them into electrical signals that the CPU can process. A keyboard, telephone line, and factory sensor are examples of input devices. Output devices convert electrical signals from the CPU into other forms, such as letters on paper. A display screen, printer, cruise missile, and telephone line are examples of output devices. Collectively, input and output devices are known as **I/O devices.**

The CPU contains electronic circuitry that performs arithmetic, logical comparisons (such as deciding which of two numbers is larger), and data-moving operations. In addition, the CPU must be able to temporarily hold programs and the information that is to be processed in its memory while it is working.

CPU memory is often called **main memory, primary memory,** or **RAM.** Think of it as short-term memory which holds small fragments of data and part or all of the program that controls the computer. The capacity of main memory helps determine the ''size'' of the computer. For example, a programmable calculator's main memory might store only a few hundred numbers, while a mainframe computer's main memory can store millions of numbers, letters of the alphabet, or elements of a picture.

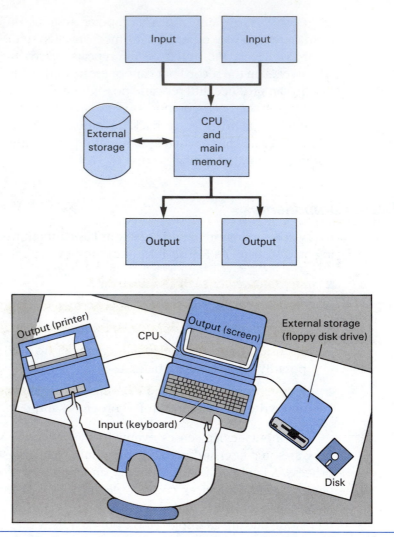

Figure 1.13 *The parts of a computer system are input/output (I/O) devices, CPU, external storage, and main memory.*

Main memory is **volatile;** that is, when the computer is turned off, the information is lost! Another form of memory is needed to provide permanent storage of programs and data. This memory is obtained by storing copies of both program and data *outside* the computer, on external magnetic media such as a tape or a disk like that shown in Figure 1.12. Magnetic media retain information even after the computer is shut off.

A **disk drive** enables the computer system to read or write information on a magnetic disk. The analogy with a video tape recorder is very close here. To play and record a television show or a movie on a video tape, you need a video tape recorder. Similarly, a disk drive is needed for the CPU of the computer to read and write programs and data on a disk.

A **peripheral** is a generic term for an auxiliary device that is attached to a computer. Thus tape and disk drives are peripherals, as are all I/O devices.

Software Components

When the CPU wants information from a magnetic disk, it must first read the information from the disk into its main memory. Only information stored in main memory is directly accessible to the CPU. But the CPU can do nothing without the intelligence of software (see Figure 1.14). If the software is not permanently stored in the main memory, then how does the computer hardware "know" how to get information when it is turned on?

This knowledge comes from two features not discussed so far. First, a small amount of nonvolatile memory is built into the computer. This is called ROM (read-only memory), and retains information even when the computer is off. Second, the program in ROM instructs the CPU to read another program from a disk, thus performing a self-helping start-up when the computer is first turned on. This process is called **booting** the computer, a reference to "pulling yourself up by your bootstraps."

Operating System Software

The notion of including software inside the computer to help run other software is basic to all computer systems. The special software that controls the running of other software is called operating system software. An **operating system** is a program that controls the operation of the computer itself. Through the CPU, the operating system programs control all I/O devices such as the keyboard, display screen, printer, disk drives, and every other device connected to the computer. In addition, the operating system makes it easy for people to operate the computer.

There are many different kinds of operating systems; some are for large mainframe computers, some for minis, and yet others are suited for personal computers. Mainframe and minicomputer systems typically use a timesharing operating system, whereas personal computer systems typically use a single-user operating system. A **timesharing** operating system controls several programs that run alongside each other. This means that several users can use the computer system simultaneously; to each user it seems as if no one else is using the computer. In contrast, a *single-user* operating system can manage only one program at a time. Hence, a single-user operating system allows only one person to use the computer system at a time.

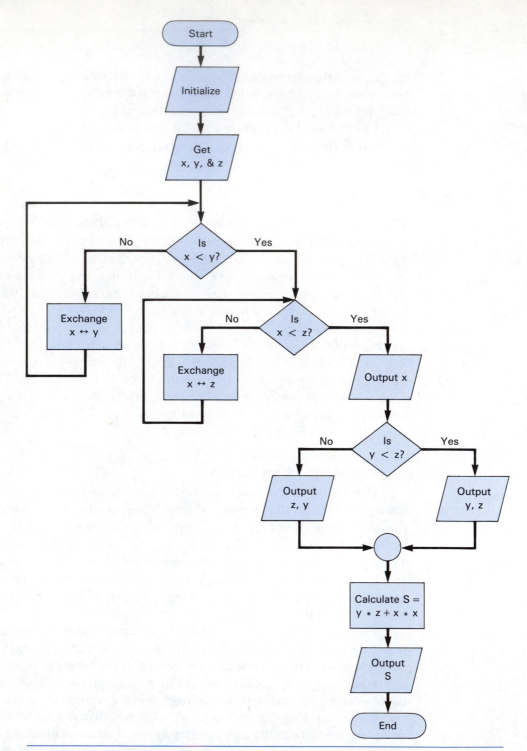

Figure 1.14 *Software controls a computer system. The diagram shown here is a blueprint from which a computer program is coded and entered into the computer's memory.*

To illustrate how timeshared mainframes and minicomputers give the illusion of simultaneous use, consider how a juggler appears to toss three balls into the air at the same time. A juggler actually holds only one ball at a time; but while one ball is in the left hand, another ball is in the air between hands, and the third ball is in the air above both hands. Each ball is given a turn to be tossed into the air. Most of the time the juggler is doing nothing!

A timesharing computer system juggles programs by keeping all but one "in the air." Only one program is ever running at any time; but because the computer is so fast, you never notice that each program spends most of its time waiting to be "tossed in the air" by the CPU. The CPU serves each program in "round robin" fashion, just as the juggler tosses each ball, one after the other, returning to the first ball to repeat the process.

The fast CPUs of mainframes and minicomputers allow many users to share access to the hardware through stations called **terminals.** A typical terminal has a keyboard, display screen, and cable that connects the terminal to the computer system. Sometimes the terminal is connected via a telephone and may be located thousands of miles away from the computer.

Personal computers may look like terminals; they have a keyboard and display screen just like a terminal. In addition, however, a personal computer has a general-purpose CPU hidden inside. As a result, personal computers are very flexible and can run virtually any type of program.

Application Software

Programs that perform specific tasks for users are called **application software.** Programs that solve mathematical equations or manage payrolls as well as programs that process words, display graphs, manage data, and play games are all examples of application software. Application software temporarily converts a general-purpose computer into a special-purpose machine that does exactly what you want done. A general-purpose microcomputer, for example, becomes a video arcade machine when it runs a game program, a serious tool for the designer when running an architectural layout program, and a tool for modern times when running a general ledger program.

We can classify application software into two broad categories: vertical software and horizontal software. **Vertical Software** is software designed to serve a narrow group of specialists. Examples include medical billing systems, project estimation systems for building contractors, and information storage for thoroughbred horsebreeders. **Horizontal software** is software designed to serve a wide group of users who, in turn, must tailor the programs to their own needs. Examples of horizontal programs are **word processors,** which are programs for preparing text such as letters, memos, reports, and even chapters in a book; **spreadsheet programs,** which display and manipulate numbers and are used for forecasting, modeling, and analysis; and programs to set up and manage **databases,** which are collections of logically related data. We will concern ourselves with horizontal programs for the most part, because of their general applicability to a wide variety of users. But you should know that horizontal software may be cumbersome and inefficient compared with vertical software specifically designed for special needs.

All application programs are supervised by the operating system program. The operating system is like an air traffic controller at a busy airport, and the application programs like airplanes. The controller determines what each airplane is allowed to do, and when it is permitted to do it. Similarly, the operating system tells when each application program is allowed to run on the CPU.

The User Interface

To use any program, you must operate it through a keyboard or some other kind of input device. To guide its users, every program employs a **user interface**—a protocol for communicating between the computer and the user. A *friendly user interface* is one that is easily understood and does not intimidate users. Since computers are sophisticated machines, nearly everyone is intimidated by a user interface at some time. But once you understand the logic and underlying model employed by the interface, using a computer can be as easy and comfortable as driving a car.

There are two main types of interfaces: text-oriented and visual. A *text-oriented interface* displays messages on the screen in words; a *visual user interface* employs pictures called **icons.** Figure 1.15 shows an example of a visual interface. In our examples in this chapter the interface is text-oriented.

Figure 1.15 *Visual user interfaces simulate a real desktop with sheets of paper, icons, and menus.*

■ A Brief Computer Session

We can illustrate the interaction between software and hardware in a computer system by walking through a typical session with a personal computer. Because using a personal computer is much like using a large timeshared computer via a terminal, this illustration can be used to introduce you to the computer you are likely to use later on. (The principal difference is that you must **log on** to a mainframe computer—identify yourself—by typing an account number and a password which identify you for purposes of billing.)

Booting the Computer

If the computer is turned off, you must first find a copy of the operating system disk and insert it into the disk drive. Then flip the power switch on to boot the operating system into the main memory. Recall that a permanent bootstrap program is read from ROM; it instructs the computer to read the operating system program from the disk into the main memory, thus bringing the computer to "life."

The first message shown on the display screen comes from the operating system. This message varies depending on the brand and model of computer. The message may ask you to supply the date and time. In reply, you type an answer to each message, pressing the [ENTER] or [RETURN] key after each entry. Here is an example, with your response shown in color.

```
Enter today's date: 10-21-86
Enter current time: 18:36:14
```

This information is used to set the internal clock of the computer.

Next, the computer's operating system provides a prompt line. In computer jargon a **prompt** is any message that tells you that the computer is waiting for you to enter an answer, supply it with needed information, or respond to an alert message. Here are some likely prompt lines:

```
Ok?
?
A>
:
```

These cryptic messages tell you that the computer is waiting for you to give it a command. A **command** is an instruction you type that tells the computer what you want it to do next.

Loading a Program

Suppose, for purposes of illustration, we want to use the computer to run a word processing program to enter and print a short letter. (For more details on word processing, see Chapter 5). Before you can run a program, you must load it into the computer. Typically, to **load** a program you enter its name as a command to the operating system. For example, suppose you respond to the prompt A> by typing the command WP.

```
A>WP
```

This command might cause a program called WP to be copied from the disk into the main memory and executed. The CPU *executes* a program by performing each instruction, one at a time.

Next, the WP program will prompt you for inputs. For example, the first WP prompt may request a name.

```
Enter the name of the document to type or edit:
```

Typing MYLETTER and pressing [RETURN] or [ENTER] causes the word processing program to fetch the text previously stored on the disk under the name MYLETTER, if it already exists, or, if no text under that name exists, to create a new document called MYLETTER.

If MYLETTER is new, the word processor clears the display screen and waits for you to type text just as if the computer were a typewriter. For example, you might enter the following letter:

```
                                 February 12, 1848

Mr. Wilkins Micawber
Care of Mr. Namby's
Coleman Street

Dear Mr. Micawber,

     I regret that I am forced to write you in the matter of a loan
you have failed to repay when due. You and I have had more than one
such business dealing.

     If the sum of 24 pounds, 7 shillings, 9 pence (principal, in-
terest and penalty) has not been received by this office before the
close of business on Monday the 20th of this month, the matter will
be turned over to my solicitors, Kenge and Carboy of Lincoln's Inn.

                                 Ralph Nickleby
```

After the letter is entered, you can store it, print it, or correct it by editing the text displayed on the screen. These operations require you to give commands to your personal computer.

Entering Commands

Terminals and personal computers have special keys on their keyboards that simplify many operations. One of the most important is the *control key*, which is labeled [CTRL] on most computer keyboards. (The Apple computer keyboard has a key marked with a small apple.) To enter many commands, you press this key and hold it down while pressing another key. For example, suppose you want to save our sample letter. *Saving* a document means to copy it from the main memory to the disk, thus making a permanent copy on the disk. The exact command for doing this varies from one word processing program to another, but with some programs you press [CTRL] and [S] simultaneously to direct the program to save a document.

The keyboard has other special keys to help you operate various programs and give commands easily. For example, a word processing program may also use keys marked [INS] (for inserting material), [DEL] (for deleting material), and [PgDn] (for paging down through the document). These keys are likely to take on other meanings when other programs are run on the computer.

Quitting

Sometimes the most difficult command to discover is the one that causes a program to stop running. Usually, if you remember just a few commands, you can ask the program to tell you what the other commands are, including the command that will stop a program and return control to the operating system. Suppose pressing [CTRL] and [L] causes a list of choices to appear on the screen such as

```
P = Set Page parameters
G = Get another document
X = Exit this program
```

Pressing [X] at this point takes you out of the word processing program. The operating system takes control of the computer, displays its prompt, and waits for you to enter a command.

If you are running a mainframe or minicomputer, you must tell the operating system that you are leaving. This is called **logging off.** Often logging off is as simple as typing

```
A>logoff
```

A personal computer, however, serves only one user at a time; so you need not log off. Simply removing the disk and turning the power off suffices.

■ Future Computing: The Dawn of an Age

Computing today is about where the automobile industry was in 1920 when a proliferation of auto makers existed: there were few interchangeable parts; the performance and efficiency of different models varied greatly; and few people were trained to use or repair the new technology or to apply it to new endeavors. The automobile industry was changing so rapidly that few people in 1920 could accurately predict the future of the automobile. Nevertheless, we will make some predictions about the future of computers. To peer into that future, we will assume that current trends will continue into the next century.

What then will the future hold? The computer will continue to influence every aspect of life. There will be increased automation, better communications, and more powerful tools in the workplace. Factory workers will operate robots and semi-intelligent machines. Executives will use sophisticated communications and control systems and think in terms of computerized mathematical models. Vast and complex simulations to study the effects of proposed changes will be performed on video displays in offices.

Entertainment will become more personalized and realistic as computer technology brings simulation into the homes of millions. The course of events in a movie will be determined by the audience and computer-controlled directing. Games will feature simulated forests, caves, deserts, and so on. Global networking will enable special-interest groups around the world to play special-purpose games or explore political, religious, or social issues through computer-controlled communication channels with automatic language translation.

Computers will continue to take over mundane, rote, and perfunctory roles. There will be greater rewards for creative thinking as computers take over jobs that require only ordinary thinking. Paramedical, paralegal, and paramanagerial robots will help people perform skilled jobs. People will be forced to ''think smarter'' rather than work harder.

The creative arts will reach new heights because the computer will enable artists to work rapidly with new materials and devices. Light, sound, metal, paint, and canvas will be simulated on a computer screen, allowing greater flexibility and artistic expression. When satisfied with the result, the artist will obtain ''hard copy'' from a computer-controlled sculpting, painting, musical scoring, or metalworking device.

Because computers will provide pervasive communications, they will have a global impact. World societies will become increasingly dependent on information managed, disseminated, and interpreted by computer systems. It will be important for nations to understand and apply computer technology to enhance the standard of living through increased productivity, increased trade, better education, a more enlightened public, and more just social systems.

As the world becomes more tightly integrated through computer networks, each society will become more dependent on others. We can only speculate on the long-term effects of this interdependence. An optimistic scenario suggests that it will bring the elimination of war, poverty, inequality, and ignorance throughout the world. A highly interdependent world can hardly afford to have regions of poverty, raging war, or instability due to social injustice.

In the near future, however, successive waves of computer and communication revolutions will have an unsettling effect. Established industries will be challenged by new ones; established institutions will be forced to change or fade away; established methods of conducting business, governing, and educating people will be affected. The old ways of doing things will be replaced by unfamiliar ways.

The computerized future can be frightening, or it can be an exciting adventure. The best way to enjoy it is to prepare for it by learning the technology. The remaining chapters of this book are dedicated to the task of preparing you for a future in an age of computer technology.

■ Summary

Our society is moving from the industrial revolution into the information age. The information age is characterized by machines that can calculate at high speed, remember tremendous numbers of facts, and communicate with other machines and people around the world. The combination of high-speed calculations and large storage capacity leads to the transformation of facts into information. Computer-generated information influences human decision making and improves people's ability to communicate. Forming such information is a fundamental activity of postindustrial society.

The combination of newly formed information and communications on a world-wide basis leads to the second major contribution of computers to modern life: better ways to disseminate information. Through computerized typesetting, newspapers, broadcasting, and electronic mail we are now able to obtain information at the speed of light. The long-term effects of these new capabilities are not known, but indications are that they will continue to profoundly change the world.

Computers come in three sizes: mainframe, mini, and micro. Each has its role in society. Mainframes are usually found in large organizations; minicomputers are used in more dedicated applications such as factory automation, and in universities and medium-sized organizations; and micros are used in dedicated applications such as personal computers or household appliances.

Regardless of their size or cost, all computers contain software. Software is classified according to its purpose. Application software is designed to solve real-world problems such as those found in the fields of accounting, engineering, or factory control. System software, on the other hand, is designed to control the computer itself and its various kinds of operating systems. Time-sharing operating systems allow many people to "simultaneously" use the same computer. Single-user operating systems are typically found in personal computers.

Key Terms

application software	logging on, logging off	prompt
booting	mainframe	RAM
command	main memory	software
database	micro, microcomputer	spreadsheet program
disk drive	mini, minicomputer	terminal
embedded computer	operating system	timesharing
hardware	peripheral	user interface
horizontal software	personal computer	vertical software
icons	primary memory	volatile
I/O device	program	word processor
load		

Discussion Questions

1. What are the two main components of a computer system? Explain how they work together.

2. What are the differences among micro, mini, and mainframe computers? How are they alike?

3. When a computer is first turned on, what causes the CPU to transfer a program from disk into main memory?

4. What are the two principal kinds of user interface? Which kind do you think is the easier to learn? To use?

5. How have computers altered the way your school conducts classes?

6. What is the difference between vertical and horizontal software? What programs might lie on the border between the two?

7. What is the relationship between application software and operating system software?

8. Suppose a movie projector, camera, and film are compared with a computer system. What is the computer's equivalent of film? Of the projector? Is this a good analogy?

9. Computers communicate with each other over the telephone. Is the telephone an I/O device?

10. What is electronic mail, and how is it different from ordinary mail?

11. Who were the Luddites, and what was their cause? Are there modern Luddites?

12. How do computers alter human decisions? Give examples of how computers have affected business, the military, and education.

13. What is the "mind" of a computer, and what is its "body"? Can computers think?

14. How does a timesharing operating system run many programs "at the same time"? What is the difference between timesharing and a single-user operating system?

Exercises

1. Is a medical billing program considered a vertical or a horizontal program? How about a tax preparation program? How about games such as PacMan?

2. Examine the keyboard of your terminal or personal computer. Which keys are used to give commands and which ones are used to enter data into the computer? Can you tell the difference?

3. Cars are vehicles for moving people; computers are vehicles for moving information. Prepare a classroom report on the kinds of information computers are capable of "moving" over communication lines.

4. Make a list of all embedded computers in your house.

5. Who makes computers? List all the computer manufacturers you can think of, then compare your list with the *Datamation 100*, a listing of the top 100 computer companies given in each June issue of *Datamation* magazine.

the CPU and storage

2

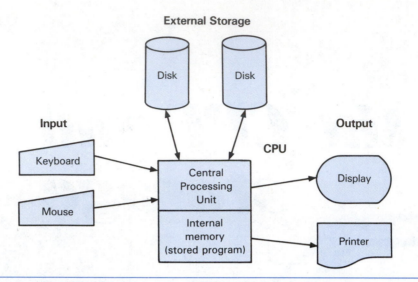

Figure 2.1 *The functional organization of a simple computer system.*

We saw in Chapter 1 that the basic organization of a computer includes input, output, external storage, and a central processor with its associated internal memory, as illustrated in Figure 2.1. This structure looks simple, even trivial, but how does it work? In this chapter we examine two basic concepts that make this simple structure very powerful: the idea of including a stored program, and a method of storing information in electrical and magnetic memories.

Once you have understood the concepts of the stored program and how information is coded and represented in the memory of a computer, we can begin examining the heart of all computers: the central processing unit (CPU) and internal storage. Close interaction between the CPU and internal storage, with its stored programs, is responsible for the "reasoning power" of computers. External memory is closely tied to the CPU; so we also examine the role of external memory in the overall computer system and the exchange of information between external and internal memory, which is called *file access*. Throughout the chapter, we will compare the power, cost, and utility of large, medium, and small computers.

■ Basic Concepts: Storing Information

We saw in Chapter 1 that computer systems are made of hardware and software. The *hardware* is the physical equipment you can see and touch, such as the disks and the display screen. The *software* is the intangible "control" that governs the computer. Software, in the form of one or more programs, tells the computer hardware what to do. In this section we will examine the relationship between the hardware and the software and how instructions and data are stored by the hardware.

Stored Programs

The most profound concept in all computing goes back to the dawn of modern science. In the mid-1800s—when Darwin was formulating the theory of evolution, electromagnetism was being discovered, and the industrial revolution was in full swing—Charles Babbage was attempting to build the first stored-program computer. A **stored-program** computer is a machine controlled by software stored within the hardware. The controlling software is called a *stored program* because the machine holds the program in its memory while the program is guiding the actions of the hardware.

One hundred years passed before Babbage's idea was rejuvenated and used in modern stored-program computer systems. (Chapter 16 gives a brief history of computing.) Today the operation of all computers depends on a memory that contains instructions in the form of a program and facts in the form of data. Stored programs are essential to modern computing because they are held within the computer machinery itself, making a computer self-contained and automatic. Thus, unlike other kinds of calculating machines such as pocket calculators, stored-program machines can operate under their own control.

Information Representation

All computer systems are limited in what they can store. The computer is a **digital** device—a device that is restricted to discrete values. In contrast, **analog** devices have *continuous* values. For example, the volume control of your TV is an analog device because it allows you to adjust the volume *continuously* in one smooth, continuous action. But the channel selector on the television set is a digital device because it restricts you to a discrete set of channels; you cannot, for example, select channel 3.14159.

Unlike your channel selector, digital computers work with just two alternatives. Like a light switch at home, a computer can "remember" an "on" or an "off," but nothing in between. To store numbers, letters of the alphabet, and graphical images, the computer must encode all information in switches that can have only one of two discrete values. For convenience, we assign a **0** or a **1** to represent whether a switch is on or off. Each 0 or 1 is one **bit** (**bi**nary dig**it**) of information. *All information in a computer is represented by a pattern of 1s and 0s.*

It takes a very large number of fast on-off switches to encode and store numbers, letters, and graphical images, so the switches of a computer are made of millions of tiny magnetic spots or very small electrical circuits which can be switched on and off very quickly. These magnetic and electrical switches use the principle that the presence of an electrical charge can be interpreted as a binary 1 and the absence of a charge as a binary 0.

A number containing only two kinds of digits—0 and 1—is called a **binary number.** (This is why modern electronic computers are often called *binary computers.*) Binary numbers are just like decimal numbers except for one important difference: they build numbers from the numerals 0 and 1 instead of the numerals 0 through 9. For example, 0100 is a binary number that is the equivalent of the decimal number 4. The appendix "How Computers Process Information" covers binary numbers in more detail.

Groups of 1s and 0s are stored in the computer's memory as binary numbers. A binary number formed from an 8-bit grouping is called a **byte**. Early personal computers worked on one byte of information at a time. Larger computers work on 16-, 32-, or 64-bit words at a time. A **word** is a fixed-length packet of bits that is handled as a unit by the computer. A computer's *word length* is determined by the size of its storage cells in memory. For example, an IBM mainframe word consists of 32 bits, or 4 bytes.

Each of the eight bits of a byte can be either "on" (1) or "off" (0). Thus, there are 256 possible patterns of on-off settings possible in a byte. (The patterns are 00000000, 00000001, . . .11111111.) These 256 patterns form the basis of a numerical code that represents the letters of the alphabet, numerals, special symbols, and any other character of information stored in a computer's memory.

Whether the information is a collection of numerical facts, alphabetic text, program instructions, or a graphical display, a computer stores it in memory as a group of encoded numbers. For example, the decimal number −5 might be represented by 11111010 (the equivalent in decimal numbers is 250). The binary pattern 01000001 (the decimal number equivalent is 65) may be an encoded representation of the letter *A,* or it may be the encoded representation of the instruction to add two numbers together. Thus the same number may have different meanings. As we will see, the interpretation of the number depends on what the CPU is expecting.

Representation of Text

We have seen that a binary code is used to represent instructions, numbers, letters of the alphabet, and graphical information. How is this possible? The secret is in *representation* and *interpretation* through binary encoding.

Representation and interpretation of text are often misunderstood, perhaps because a variety of codes are used to store text. The ASCII (American Standard for Information Interchange) code is used in small computers; other codes such as EBCDIC (Extended Binary Coded Decimal Interchange Code) are used in larger computers. The **ASCII code** establishes a 7-bit pattern for each printable character on the keyboard. Thus the letters of the alphabet, the numerals 0 through 9, and special characters such as $, &, and % are each defined by a 7-bit ASCII pattern.

For example, the upper-case alphabetic characters (*A, B, C,* and so on) are represented by 7-bit binary numbers that are the equivalent of decimal numbers 65 to 91. Lower-case alphabetic characters (*a, b, c,* and so on) range from the binary equivalents of 97 to 123. A **?** is stored as the binary equivalent of 63; even a blank space has a code: the binary number for 32.

If a computer makes a mistake and interprets a number as a character, an ASCII character as a graphical image, or one type of information as another type, the wrong results will be computed. The computer does not "know" one type of information from another. Only proper programming can prevent misinterpretation of information in a computer.

Internal Memory

Two kinds of information are needed in a computer: (1) program information that controls the actions of the hardware, and (2) factual information that is processed by the program and hardware. Both kinds of information must be stored in a memory while being used. As we saw in Chapter 1, computers have two kinds of memory to store this information: internal and external. **Internal memory** is synonymous with **primary memory, main memory, random-access memory** (RAM), or simply **memory.**

The internal memory of a computer is composed of *integrated circuits.* These high-speed electronic circuits are capable of quickly saving and retriev-

Figure 2.2 *Several 64K-bit memory chips in various stages of packaging.*

ing information. In today's technology they are printed on small chips cut from thin slices (or wafers) of large silicon crystals (see Window 8). Hence the circuits are called **memory chips.** Figure 2.2 shows several memory chips in various stages of being packaged.

Memory Capacity

Memory is divided into a large number of storage cells. We can think of them as somewhat like the safety deposit boxes on a bank vault wall, or as post office boxes, as shown in Figure 2.3. Each box or cell has its own unique electronic **address**—a number identifying its location—and each is the same size. However, unlike a post office box, locations in computer memory can hold only numbers.

It is easiest to build and use memory chips that have a round number of storage cells in binary arithmetic, which in decimal numbers means 2, 4, 8, and so on. Current memory chips tend to have between 2^{18} and 2^{20} cells; this is 262,144 to 1,048,576 bits of storage. A more convenient unit of measure for memory uses the symbol K. In the metric system K is the symbol for 1,000; but when memory is being measured, **K** is the symbol for 2^{10}, or 1,024. Thus a memory chip with 16,384 binary storage cells is called a 16K-bit chip. Similarly, **kilobit** means 1,024 bits of memory, and **kilobyte** (**KB**) means 1,024 bytes.

To designate the memory capacities of mainframe computers and hard disk drives, we need even larger units. A **megabyte** (**MB**) is 1024KB, or 2^{20} bytes, which is roughly a million characters of storage. Internal memory sizes of

Figure 2.3 *Main memory is like a collection of post office boxes: each one is numbered and stores a small amount of information. The ''boxes'' in a computer memory hold one ''character'' of information at a time. The information can be either part of a program or data.*

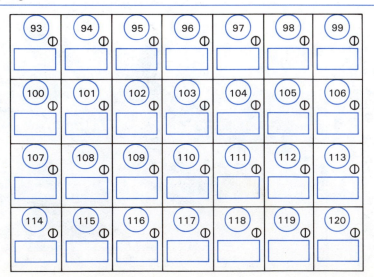

16MB are common in large computer installations, but 1 MB is considered a lot of memory in a personal computer. A **gigabyte** is 1024MB, roughly a billion characters. Large mainframe disk drives hold a few gigabytes of information, but personal computers are more likely to have hard disk drives that can hold just 10 to 40 megabytes or to use even smaller floppy disk drives.

The amount of memory the computer has is important in determining what the computer can do. A computer with less than 16KB of memory is limited to trivial applications because it can execute only tiny programs. Such a machine might be able to play video games or balance a checkbook, but it will not run a full-featured word processing program. To be useful for most professional or business applications, a computer must have at least 64KB of memory.

When you purchase software for a personal computer, it is important to match the software's requirement for main memory with the amount of memory in your computer. A 512KB program cannot run on a 256KB personal computer. Mainframe computers, however, are equipped with a **virtual memory**—a feature allowing them to accommodate programs that are larger than the main memory. In a computer with virtual memory, the hardware simulates a very large memory by automatically moving parts of a running program from internal to external (disk) memory as the program runs. Thus a 1MB memory might appear to be 100MB in size when running a very large program.

Personal computers are sometimes programmed to approximate the virtual memory of their larger cousins by use of **program overlays.** This technique partitions a large program into many shorter segments. Each segment is *swapped* from disk into main memory as it is needed, and removed from main memory when not needed. In this way a small computer can act like a big computer, but at the expense of processing speed.

Program overlays have another disadvantage. They require extra work by the programmer, who must break the program into segments and write instructions specifying when each segment is to be swapped in or out. In contrast, virtual memory is said to be **transparent** to the programmer, because it is built into the hardware and operates without requiring the programmer's attention.

Virtual memory and overlays were invented to compensate for the high cost of main memory, but over the last twenty years manufacturing techniques have lowered the cost of memory chips. A reliable rule of thumb has been that every three years the number of bits per chip quadruples, while the cost per chip stays constant. As a result, the price of memory has been dropping about 30 percent each year for nearly two decades. Perhaps the computers of the future will have sufficiently large main memories that virtual and physical memory sizes will be the same.

ROM and RAM

The two major types of internal memory are ROM and RAM. **ROM (read-only memory)** is memory that is manufactured to store permanently a fixed set of information. This book is similar to ROM because its information can be read but cannot be changed. **RAM** is the acronym for **r**andom-**a**ccess **m**emory. **Random access** implies that any piece of information can be read with an approximately equal level of difficulty and delay. In fact, the name *RAM* is misleading because both ROM and RAM are random-access memories.

The real difference between ROM and RAM is this: information that is stored in RAM can be changed. You can write new information into RAM. RAM is the computer's scratch pad. It allows the computer to store information quickly for later reference. In most computers RAM holds

- the active parts of the *operating system,* the fundamental program that controls the operation of the computer.
- the application program that is being executed (for example, a word processing program).
- part or all of the data used by the application program (for example, a letter being written with the word processing program).
- a representation of the data being shown on the video display.
- anything else that is likely to change frequently (for example, the time of day in the computer's clock, or information about the disk in external storage).

Most RAM is *volatile*—even a short interruption in the computer's power supply erases RAM, giving it a case of total amnesia. Obviously, it is not wise to store the only copy of important work in RAM. In contrast, ROM is *nonvolatile.* When you turn the computer off, the contents of ROM are not changed.

Because ROM is somewhat cheaper than RAM as well as nonvolatile, manufacturers use ROM for permanent storage of frequently used programs in the main memory of the computer. The ROM chips containing these programs are included in the computer when purchased. For example, in all personal computers ROM stores the instructions that tell the computer what to do when the power is turned on. A simple version of the BASIC programming language is usually included in a personal computer's ROM.

Portable computers can compensate for their limited (or nonexistent) external storage by using ROM to store application programs such as a word processor. The microcomputers in cars, microwave ovens, calculators, and video games are instructed to perform their special-purpose, fixed functions by a program stored in ROM.

■ The Central Processing Unit

Inside the CPU

When you start a typical personal computer by placing a disk in the disk drive and turning on the power, the CPU causes a program to be transferred from the disk into the high-speed internal memory, where the program takes control of the CPU. Acting under the program's control, the CPU shifts data back and forth between internal memory and the disk (external memory) in order to process it. Data cannot be processed directly while stored on the disk; data must be brought into internal memory to be totaled, compared, displayed, printed, and so forth. Eventually the program gives up control of the computer and ceases to operate. When this happens, you must tell the computer what to do next.

No matter what directions you give the computer, the same pattern is followed: a program is transferred into high-speed memory, where it takes over control, processes data, and finally terminates. This three-part process is called

Figure 2.4 *Main memory holds numbers; each number can be an instruction or data. The control unit fetches numbers from memory locations and interprets them as instructions. The ALU unit performs arithmetic on the numbers stored in main memory.*

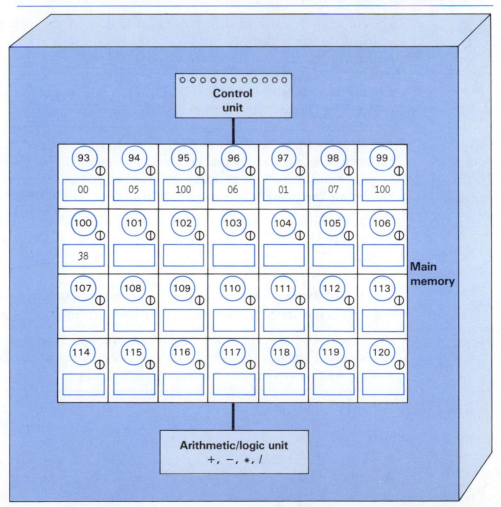

program *execution* or a program *run*. Programs are run on the CPU under control of a control unit, main memory, and an arithmetic/logic unit as shown in Figure 2.4.

The **arithmetic/logic unit** (**ALU**) does all the computing; it can add two numbers, subtract, multiply, and divide. It can compare two numbers to determine which is larger, move bits from one place to another, and keep track of time. The ALU works exclusively on encoded binary numbers. It takes its orders from binary-encoded instructions stored like any other information in main memory.

The **control unit** is the supervisor of the CPU; it fetches numbers from memory and interprets them as instructions. The control unit dissects each instruction and then directs the flow of information through the ALU, input/output devices, and main memory.

Instructions

The control unit and internal memory work in concert: the control unit fetches instructions one at a time from memory, fetches the data to be processed from main memory, and feeds the data to the ALU for processing. Each instruction is a simple operation such as adding the number in one memory location to the number in another location, moving a character from the keyboard to memory, or deciding where to find the next instruction.

Figure 2.5(a) illustrates how the control unit directs the CPU to execute a simple program to add two numbers. (We have converted the contents of memory to words and decimal numbers to make the figure easier to read, but keep in mind that all information in a computer is stored as encoded binary numbers.) The figure shows three special storage cells in the control unit.

■ The **program counter** holds the address of the next instruction to be plucked from memory. In Figure 2.5(a) the instruction from location 100 is currently executing; the program counter "points to" the next instruction in memory at location 102.

■ The **instruction register** holds the instruction being carried out.

■ An **accumulator** holds temporary results of computations inside the ALU.

Locations 100–106 in Figure 2.5 store four instructions from a program. The instruction in locations 100–101, LOAD 110, is held in the instruction register while it is being carried out. It directs the CPU to copy the contents of location 110 into the accumulator. Thus the first instruction copies 38 (the content of location 110) into the accumulator. Next the instruction from locations 102–103 is carried out. This instruction, ADD 111, adds the contents of location 111 (that is, 15) to the contents of the accumulator (38) and stores the sum back in the accumulator. Then the instruction STORE 110 copies the sum from the accumulator into the main memory at location 110. Finally, the STOP instruction in location 106 returns control of the computer to the operating system.

The Computer Itself: The Central Processor and Storage

Although a supercomputer has thousands of times the speed and storage of a personal computer, they both perform four basic functions: input, output, processing, and storage. This photo essay illustrates the processing and storage components of modern computer systems.

1. Row after row of integrated circuits are visible in this view of three circuit boards that form a high-speed graphics processor. The brown connectors on the circuit boards are used to plug the graphics processor into a DEC VAX minicomputer. The graphics processor outperforms a VAX 780 by as much as 50 times for graphics tasks such as rotating a model or changing a perspective.

AN INSIDE LOOK AT THE IBM PC/AT

The IBM AT was announced in August 1984 and quickly spawned an impressive number of "AT-compatible" computers built by competitors. Although the IBM AT includes a number of advanced technical features, it is generally compatible with earlier members of the IBM Personal Computer family. The next four pages will give you an inside view of the IBM AT.

2. Most IBM ATs are used in a business or professional environment. For a typical complete system the price ranges from less than $4,000 to more than $10,000, depending on which optional devices the consumer buys and on the dealer's markup.

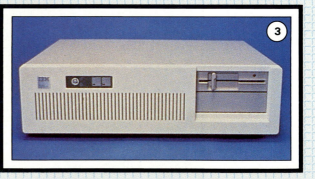

3–5. The computer is housed in a *system unit*, shown here with its cover removed. Optional components can be added to the system unit to tailor the machine to the user's needs. For example, the unit on the left is equipped with a single floppy disk drive, but the unit on the right has both a floppy disk drive and a hard disk drive.

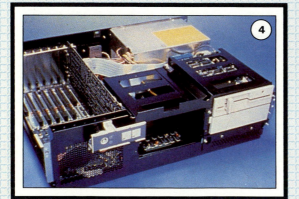

THE SYSTEM BOARD

The heart of the IBM AT is the system board. It is a large flat circuit board that lies across the bottom of the system unit.

6. The "brain" of the IBM AT is the Intel 80286 microprocessor, the large gray integrated circuit at the center of this photo. Its operations are paced at a clock speed of 6 MHz (megahertz), or 6 million cycles per second. The microprocessor receives and sends data in 2-byte chunks. Theoretically, it can manage 16 megabytes of internal memory, but few machines have anywhere near 16 megabytes of actual internal memory.

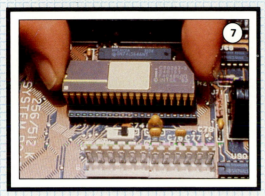

7. An optional math coprocessor can be installed in an empty socket on the system board. The math coprocessor provides high-performance processing of numbers. For programs that perform extensive mathematical operations, this can increase the processor's speed by a factor of ten or more.

8. Also on the system board is a clock/calendar. Because the clock has a battery back-up, it is not necessary to reset the date and time after turning on the machine.

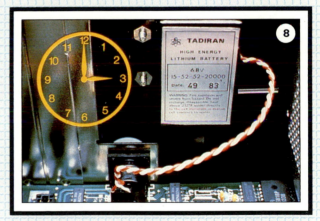

9. The system board of the IBM AT can accommodate up to 512KB (kilobytes) of internal memory. The least expensive IBM AT models come from the factory with only 256KB of installed memory, but it is easy to upgrade the computer to 512KB by pushing memory chips into empty sockets on the system board.

window 2

Long-term memory requires some form of external storage. The most common external storage devices are floppy and hard disk drives, but use of cassette tape drives to back-up hard disks is becoming increasingly popular.

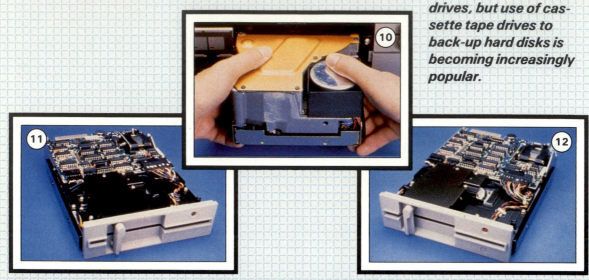

10–12. Here are three types of external storage for the IBM AT. On the top is a 20MB (megabyte) hard disk; on the bottom are 1.2MB and 360KB floppy disk drives. Both floppy disk drives look identical from the front. The system unit has enough power and space for three disk drives.

13. The disk drives are connected to the computer through blue ribbon cables that plug into a disk-controller circuit board, which in turn plugs into the system board.

14. This shows the installation of a second floppy disk drive. The 1.2MB floppy disk drives store the equivalent of about 400 pages of typed text on a single 5 1/4-inch disk.

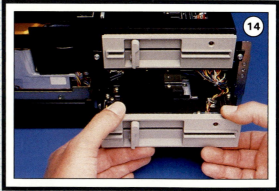

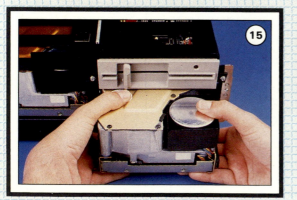

15. Instead of a second floppy disk drive, a hard disk drive can be added below the floppy disk drive. With two 20MB hard disks and a 1.2MB floppy disk drive, the IBM AT has an external storage capacity of about 13,000 pages of single-spaced typed text.

ADDING OPTIONS

The basic capabilities of the AT can be expanded by adding options such as a printer or additional circuit boards.

16. The capabilities of an IBM AT, like most computers, can be increased by shoving optional circuit boards into *expansion slots.* This photo shows the addition of a board that provides additional memory. It fits into an expansion slot on the system board.

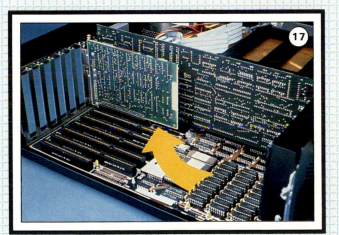

17. The yellow arrow points to a circuit board that provides two interfaces (or *ports*) for controlling peripheral devices such as printers, plotters, monitors, or mice.

18. This rear view of the IBM AT shows its eight expansion slots. This particular machine is equipped with two interface-adapter circuit boards (on the left) and one color-display adapter (in the right-most slot). Each of the interface adapters has two black connectors that can accept cables from peripheral devices. Smaller connectors are used to control devices adhering to the RS-232 serial interface standard. Larger connectors are used with devices that accept parallel data, such as many printers. The color-display adapter is used to send pictures to a color monitor.

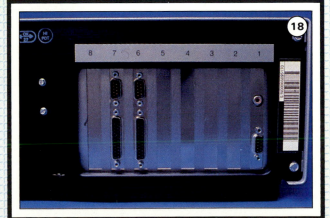

window 2

DISK STORAGE

Storage on disks provides fast and reliable access to large quantities of data.

20. Even a tiny particle of dust can scratch the surface of a spinning hard disk, so manufacturing is done in "clean rooms" to reduce the number of airborne particles.

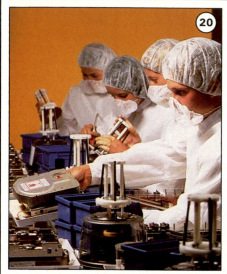

19. Hard disks store data on rapidly spinning metal platters that are coated with magnetic oxides. Each platter is polished to a mirror finish to provide a uniform surface for extremely dense storage of data.

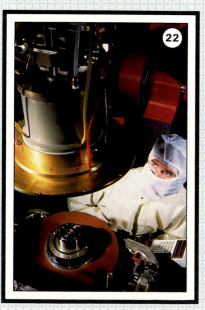

21. Large-capacity hard disks are created by stacking a number of disk platters into one disk drive assembly, called a disk pack. The read/write heads of the disk drive move in and out between the disk platters, storing data on both sides of most platters.

22. A disk drive assembly is loaded with contamination-free precision by a special-function industrial robot.

24. In this photo an IBM 3380 disk drive is being assembled in Vimercate, Italy. Model 3380 disk drives are among the most powerful of IBM's disk drives. Each 3380 disk pack can store 2.5 gigabytes (a gigabyte is roughly one billion characters) and has a data transfer rate of 3MB per second.

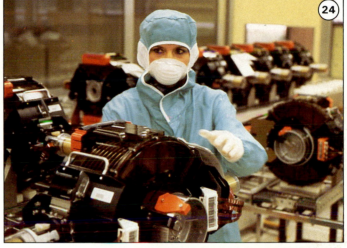

23. These 5 1/4-inch hard disk drives fit in the same space as a standard 5 1/4-inch floppy disk drive and feature from 20 to 40MB of storage, a data transfer rate that exceeds 1/2MB per second, and an average access time of 40 milliseconds (less than 1/20th of a second).

25. A disk pack is inserted in a disk drive. Removable disk drives are slightly more expensive and are more likely to be damaged by dust particles than fixed disks. In a fixed disk the disk platters are permanently sealed inside a housing at the factory. The obvious advantage of a removable disk drive is that more than one disk pack can be purchased for each drive, enabling data to be stored inexpensively on off-line disk packs.

26. Optical disks hold the promise of providing very large amounts of storage on a single disk surface. For example, this 35-cm optical disk can record up to 2.5 gigabytes per side, the equivalent of the 30-volume *Encyclopaedia Britannica.* Microscopic pits are inscribed on the disk with a diode laser, and a helium laser is used to play back the data. Most optical disks are used for permanent storage, because the pits on the disk's surface cannot be erased.

TAPE
STORAGE

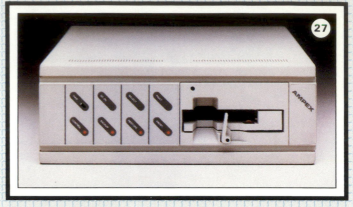

27. This small storage unit is designed for personal computer systems. It combines a 20MB fixed disk with a 25MB tape drive for backing-up the fixed disk. The tape drive accepts 1/4-inch tape cartridges and can find any file on the tape in 92 seconds.

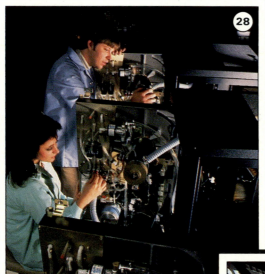

28. Large commercial tape drives use vacuum systems to start and stop loops of tape quickly without placing excessive stress on the tape. Here, data cables are being attached to tape drives made by Storage Technology Corporation.

29. Magnetic tape is an excellent medium for inexpensive, long-term data storage. Because tapes provide sequential data storage, they are rarely used when data is being processed. Instead, they are used to back-up hard disks and to store infrequently used data.

window 2

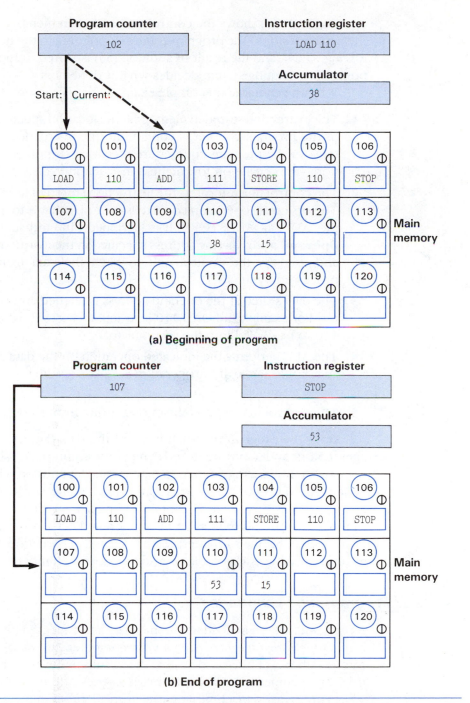

Figure 2.5*(a) The control unit fetches LOAD 110 from location 102, temporarily holds the LOAD instruction in the instruction register while it is being processed, and directs the ALU to copy 38 from location 110 into the accumulator. **(b)** After the control unit has executed each instruction one at a time, the results are stored back in memory.*

Figure 2.5(b) shows the control unit and main memory as it appears after the program stops. The program counter is pointing to the next instruction following STOP, and the result of addition (53) is stored in location 110. At this point the operating system decides what is done next.

We can generalize this simple example for all computers.

1. The instruction stored in memory at the location specified by the contents of the program counter is copied into the instruction register. The contents of the program counter are increased to point to the next instruction—in preparation for the next instruction cycle.

2. The control unit interprets the instruction stored in its instruction register. The **op-code** (operation code) tells the ALU what is to be done; for example, ADD, LOAD, STORE. It is "stripped off" and sent to the ALU. The **operand address** (the address specified in the instruction) is stripped off and used by the control unit to fetch the data from memory to be processed by the ALU.

3. The data stored at the operand address is fetched and copied into a register. For example, a LOAD 110 instruction causes the contents of location 110 to be copied into the accumulator.

4. The ALU performs the indicated operation on the data and produces a result. For example, if the operation is ADD, the sum is produced and stored in the accumulator.

5. The control unit repeats the cycle starting from step 1.

Both the program (instructions) and the data (letters, decimal numbers, ages, colors, and so on) are stored in memory as numbers. Whether the CPU interprets a number as a program step or as data depends on what it is expecting. When the ALU needs an instruction, it fetches the contents of the memory address that is supposed to contain the next instruction. It treats whatever number is at that address as an instruction and acts accordingly. If things get fouled up so that the ALU interprets a letter as an instruction, the results are just as unpredictable as if you dialed a social security number on the telephone.

Types of Programming Languages

A program that can be loaded into memory and executed immediately is called a *machine language program*. Every computer has its own **machine language**—the set of binary codes that the circuits in the ALU can execute. It is exceedingly tedious to write programs as a series of binary numbers, so no one writes programs in machine language. Instead, programmers write programs in a *programming language,* a human-oriented language for telling the computer what to do. There are hundreds of programming languages, and they differ dramatically in their grammar.

The programming language that is closest in spirit to machine language is *assembly language.* In a simple **assembly language** program, each instruction in the program corresponds to an instruction that the circuits of the computer can perform. For example, here is what the program shown in Figure 2.5 might look like as an assembly language program:

```
MOV    110,ACC      'Copy the contents of 110 into the accumulator
ADD    111,ACC      'Add the contents of location 111 to the accumulator
MOV    ACC,110      'Copy the sum in the accumulator to location 110
END                'Stop this program
```

As you can see, assembly language is a convenient way of expressing machine language. Assembly language provides instructions and addresses with names instead of using binary numbers as in machine language, and it encourages programmers to place comments in the program explaining how the program works.

Before the computer can execute an assembly language program, it must be translated into machine language. This translation is done by another program called an *assembler* that accepts an assembly language program as its input and creates an equivalent machine language program as its output. Among other things, the assembler must translate assembly language verbs, such as MOV, into their binary instruction code equivalents.

Assembly language is considered a *low-level language,* because it requires an intimate knowledge of the computer's inner workings to program in assembly language. Most programmers choose to write programs in a *high-level language,* such as BASIC, COBOL, Pascal, or FORTRAN. High-level languages are easier to understand and produce results more quickly than is possible using an assembly language.

Comparing Micros, Minis, and Mainframes

If the CPU of an Apple II could carry out the same instructions as an IBM mainframe at the same speed, IBM would lose a lot of business. Instead, the CPUs of different types of computers vary greatly in how fast they process instructions, in which instructions they can carry out, and in how many different instructions they can handle. These differences determine the "power" of a computer and determine whether a computer can execute a given program or not.

Because each instruction is extremely simple, completing a useful task takes hundreds, thousands, or even millions of primitive operations. Obviously, a CPU must work quickly to be useful. Most computers operate at speeds measured in fractions of a second. A **nanosecond** is one-billionth of a second; there are 1 million **microseconds,** or 1,000 **milliseconds,** in a second. Personal computers operate in the microsecond range whereas mini-computers and mainframes operate in the nanosecond range.

The collection of instructions that a certain computer can perform is called its **instruction set.** Large computers have large instruction sets, and small computers have smaller instruction sets. Besides the number of instructions in a computer's instruction set, the capability of each instruction is important. A mainframe computer has very powerful instructions whereas a personal computer has simple instructions. For example, a mainframe computer might have a single instruction for multiplying two 64-bit numbers, but it might take a personal computer thirty instructions to compute the same multiplication. Clearly, the power of a computer's instruction set influences how fast the computer can process data.

Figure 2.6 *A comparison of the cost, performance, and class of current computers.*

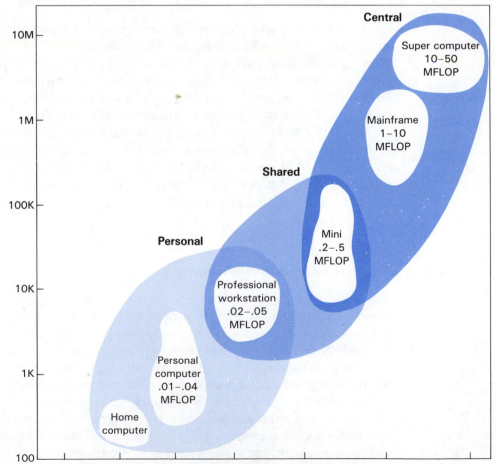

Because computers differ in both the size of the instruction set and the power of instructions, it is difficult to compare one computer with another. A general measure of performance is the **MFLOP** (million floating-point operations per second). A 1-MFLOP computer can perform 1 million floating-point operations per second. A **floating-point number** is any number with a decimal point, such as 3.1415.

If we accept the MFLOP measure of "power," then Figure 2.6 succinctly summarizes the cost versus performance of all classes of computers. At the low end, calculators cost less than $100; but their MFLOP rating is so small that it does not register on the scale shown in Figure 2.6. Personal computers operate at 0.01–0.04 MFLOP and range in cost from about $400 to over $5,000. Professional workstation computers cost more but deliver additional performance.

Figure 2.6 groups all computers into three general classes: personal, shared, and central. A *personal computer* has a single operator. A *shared computer* is timeshared; a minicomputer that supports 10 to 50 users is an example. A *central computer* is timeshared in a large organization and may support up to 1,000 users, simultaneously.

The category of central computers includes mainframes and supercomputers like the Cray X-MP. They generally cost more than a million dollars. Central computers are so expensive it is difficult to imagine anyone being able to justify one, but central computers are extremely cost-effective when speed and capacity are required. For example, a Cray X-MP supercomputer that costs $5 million delivers 6.6 floating-point operations per second per dollar, whereas a DEC VAX-11/780 minicomputer that costs $200,000 delivers only 1.65 floating-point operations per second per dollar. A $6,000 IBM PC with a floating-point coprocessor is about as cost-effective as a Cray X-MP, at 6.7 floating-point operations per second per dollar.

Microprocessors

In every personal computer the control unit and ALU are combined into a single circuit or chip. Because this component is so small, it is called a **microprocessor.**

Designing a microprocessor is an expensive proposition; so there are only a couple hundred microprocessor models. Of these models, only a few are used in personal computers. Each model has a name that sounds like the model number for a sports car. For example, the Apple II uses the Mostek 6502; the IBM PC uses the Intel 8088; and the Apple Macintosh uses the Motorola 68000. Figure 2.7 shows two views of the Motorola 68000. Programs for one microprocessor will not run on another unless they are rewritten or translated from one instruction set to the other. Depending on how a program was written, translating a program can be as much work as writing it from scratch.

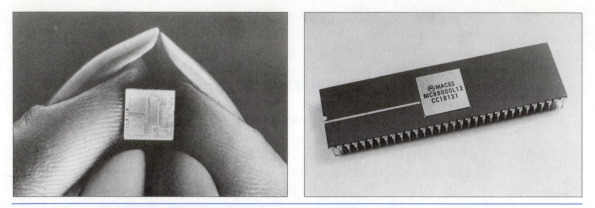

Figure 2.7 *The Motorola MC68000 microprocessor, before (left) and after (right) packaging.*

A microprocessor has a limited and simple instruction set. Four factors have a major influence on a microprocessor's power.

First, how many bits of data are processed in one operation? (An analogy is the size of the scoop on a steam shovel.) This depends on

1. the number of bits processed internally in each operation. A 6502 processes 8 bits in each operation; an 8088 processes 16 bits; and a 68000 handles 32.

2. the number of bits transferred between the microprocessor and internal memory at once—8 bits with a 6502 or 8088, but 16 bits with a 68000.

Second, how many instructions are in the instruction set and how powerful are they? (Analogy: the number of useful attachments for a tractor.)

Third, how long does it take to complete an instruction? (Analogy: the time it takes a steam shovel to dump each scoop.) This depends on

1. the **clock rate,** which paces all the operations in the CPU. Clock rates are measured in **megahertz** (**MHz**), or millions of cycles per second. For example, an IBM PC has a 4.77 MHz clock rate, which means there are 4,770,000 ticks (called **clocks**) of the CPU's clock each second.

2. the number of clocks per instruction. It takes an IBM PC 4 clocks to transfer one byte from internal memory to the microprocessor, and it can take more than 100 clocks to multiply two 16-bit numbers together.

Fourth, how much internal memory can the processor manage? Each word of internal memory needs its own unique location number or memory address; so the maximum amount of internal memory is limited by the length of each memory address. (As an analogy, consider the number of telephones that can be dialed with a 7-digit telephone number.) The 6502 uses a 16-bit memory address, which limits it to 2^{16}, or 64KB, of internal memory. The 8088 uses a 20-bit address for a maximum of 1 megabyte of memory. The 68000 uses a 24-bit address for a maximum of 16 megabytes of memory.

A microcomputer's raw processing power is not important for most applications, just as the size of a car's engine is not important for in-town driving. It is much better to have a system in which the software makes full use of a processor with rather limited capabilities than to have poor software running on a potentially powerful processor. However, some scientific problems would take years to solve with a microprocessor. When this is the case, a supercomputer is needed.

■ External Storage

External or **auxiliary storage** is the place where programs and data are stored when the power is turned off. External storage units such as tapes and disks store information as magnetic spots on magnetic oxide surfaces. A tape or disk drive reads and writes on tapes and disks by moving them past a **read/write** head (see Figure 2.8). The head reads their magnetized surfaces, converting the information into electrical impulses that it sends to the computer. On a given drive a magnetic north pole might represent a binary 1, and a magnetic south pole, a binary 0. Hence, magnetic storage devices employ a binary encoding scheme similar to that used in main memory.

Figure 2.8 *When the tape containing magnetic spots moves through an electrical field, a 1 or 0 is sensed by the read/write head. A 1 or 0 is written on the tape by energizing the electromagnetic field to induce a charge (1) or not (0).*

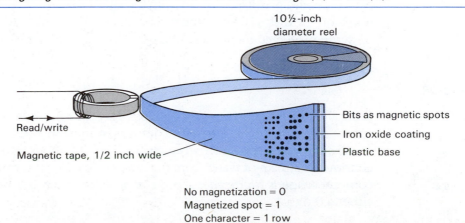

10½-inch
diameter reel

Bits as magnetic spots

Iron oxide coating

Read/write

Plastic base

Magnetic tape, 1/2 inch wide

No magnetization = 0
Magnetized spot = 1
One character = 1 row

External memory has three advantages in all computer systems.

1. Because magnetic spots do not need a constant supply of power to "refresh" themselves (as most RAM chips do), tapes and disks are *nonvolatile*. This means the tape or disk can be removed from the computer system, set aside, and then used again later. As a result, tapes and disks are used in libraries of information called *archives*. An **archival copy** of information is any information that is set aside for use later on. Word processor documents, large databases, and accumulated information are all candidates for archival storage.

2. External memory is *cheaper* per unit of storage than internal memory. A rough rule of thumb is that a tape or removable disk can store a million characters per dollar whereas internal memory can store only a thousand characters per dollar. Thus magnetic storage devices are a thousand times less expensive than electronic memories per stored character.

3. Because of the nonvolatility and low cost of magnetic media, most external storage can be *removed* and replaced by additional media. A disk can be replaced by another disk, thus extending the effective storage capacity of the computer. The fact that a disk drive can be replenished with "empty" disks is a major factor in making personal computers useful in the modern office.

Because of these advantages, external storage devices are used extensively in all computer systems.

The three most common forms of magnetic media used are magnetic tapes, floppy disks, and hard disks. All of these can be erased and recorded again and again. As new information is written, it automatically overwrites whatever was there before. To avoid accidental erasure, both tapes and floppy disks can be **write-protected.** That is, they can be marked so that you can neither write nor change any information on them. This is usually accomplished by removing a plastic ring or tab from the tape's reel or case or by covering up a notch on the disk's jacket. Tape recorders and floppy disk drives will not write on write-protected media. Most hard disks cannot be write-protected.

Tapes

Computer information is stored on tapes very similar to the tapes used to store stereo music at home, but information is stored on them differently. Your home stereo tapes probably store music as a continuous signal, much like the continuous stream of water from the kitchen tap. The information stored on a computer tape is *digitized;* each piece of information is a bit whose value is either a 0 or a 1.

Tape *density* is measured by the number of bits per inch (bpi) recorded on the tape. Mainframes typically use 1,600-bpi tapes, but some tapes store 6,250 characters per inch or more. Because typical reel-to-reel tapes are 2,400 feet long, a 1,600-bpi tape can store approximately 2,400 × 12 × 1,600 = 46 million characters of information. Most mainframe computer tapes are ½-inch wide and are 400 feet to 3,200 feet in length. Personal computer systems tend to use cartridge tapes that are ¼-inch wide.

The bits on a tape are typically arranged in 9-bit bytes across the width of the tape. The ninth bit is called a **parity bit** and is used to detect and correct single-bit errors. The bytes recorded on tape are grouped together to form **fields,** as shown in Figure 2.9. Furthermore, groups of fields are combined into **records.** For example, all fields pertaining to customer ''Jim Smyth of Portland OR 97014'' constitute a single record.

Tapes provide **sequential storage;** that is, information is recorded in sequence, one record behind another. As a result, reading and writing from tapes is slow. To read the last item on a tape, you must wind the tape past all the previous items. The time it takes to begin reading the desired information from a storage device is called the device's **access time.**

The rate at which data is read once information transfer has begun is the **data transfer rate.** Typical mainframe tapes move at speeds ranging from 25 to 200 inches per second. Thus a tape running at 200 inches per second transfers data at 200 × 1,600 = 320,000 characters per second. This may sound fast; but compared with a disk drive, tapes are slow.

Despite their slow performance, tapes have several uses. Because tape has been around since the earliest days of modern computing, almost every mainframe and minicomputer can read ½-inch reel-to-reel tapes produced by any other computer. Hence, tapes are used for exchanging and converting information.

Figure 2.9 *Tapes are sequential storage media because information is stored as a series of records. To get to any one record, the computer must read the tape from the beginning record up to the one desired.*

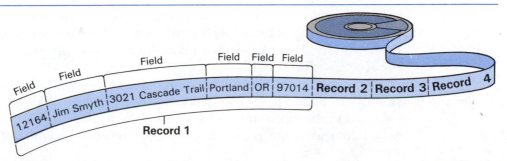

In mainframe computer centers, the low cost of tape makes it a good medium for the long-term storage of large quantities of data. For example, the social security files, income tax returns, and census data kept by the U.S. government are all stored on tape. The most frequent use of tapes is for archival storage of infrequently used data in tape libraries.

In minicomputer operations, tapes are used to transfer information from one site to another. A 40-megabyte file can be stored cheaply on a single reel of tape and sent across the country by postal delivery for a few dollars. Electronic transmission of 40 megabytes of data would take several days on a common telephone line, and cost over a thousand dollars for the phone call.

Tapes are also useful if you are using a personal computer with a hard disk drive. Small, high-speed **streaming tape drives** using ¼-inch cartridge tapes can make back-up copies of the hard disk. If the hard disk fails, thousands of records of information can be lost; so backing-up the hard disk with streamer tapes can save many days of anguish.

Disks and Disk Drives

A *disk drive* is a mechanical device for converting magnetic spots on the surface of a magnetic disk into electrical signals understandable to a computer. Magnetic fields must be in motion before they can be sensed by the drive; hence magnetic disks must rotate. The floppy disks in personal computers rotate at 300 rpm (rotations per minute); hard disks typically rotate at 3,600 rpm. Disk drives are therefore subject to wear and tear. In fact, the most common failures in computer systems occur in mechanical devices such as keyboards, printers, and disk drives.

Figure 2.10 shows how information is organized on a magnetic disk. Think of each disk as a collection of short tapes, with each tape placed in a concentric arc around the disk. In Figure 2.10 a **track** is equivalent to the imaginary short tape.

Each track is divided into pie-shaped wedges called **sectors** so that the disk drive can quickly access a piece of the track. When information is requested of the disk drive, the rotating disk first positions the requested sector under the read/write head; then the information from that sector is copied into main memory. Thus, the smallest amount of *accessible information* on a disk is the sector.

Each sector contains a fixed number of bytes—typically 256 bytes for a floppy disk, and up to 8,000 bytes for a mainframe disk. These bytes are encoded in the binary number system just as if they were in main memory. When converted into electrical signals, they represent a group of eight 0 or 1 bits.

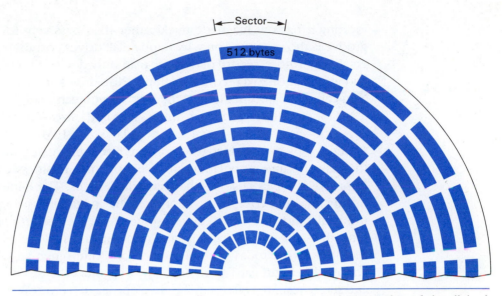

Figure 2.10 *Organization of a disk. A* track *is one complete rotation of the disk. A* sector *is a piece of a track. Each sector stores a fixed number of bytes.*

Floppy Disks

The most common external storage device for personal computers is the floppy disk drive. It reads magnetic spots from the surface of a rotating magnetic disk sealed inside of a square jacket, as shown in Figure 2.11(a). The disk is called a floppy disk because it has a flexible base, made of Mylar (plastic). This base supports the magnetic oxide recording surface. Unless a floppy disk is encased in a hard plastic protective shell, it can be bent (mildly!) without damage.

Unlike tape devices, floppy disk systems are random-access storage devices. (Recall that a *random-access device* is any storage device that can retrieve information in roughly the same amount of time no matter where that information is stored on the device.) The read/write heads of floppy disk drives can move in and out to access quickly a sector of information on any part of the disk, as shown in Figure 2.11(b). Because of this, disks are preferred over tapes even though they are more expensive.

In several ways floppy disk systems are like stereo record players. In both systems a mechanical arm rubs against the disk in order to sense the information recorded on the surface of the disk. But the analogy breaks down quickly. Floppy disks store data in concentric tracks; records store songs in spiral grooves. The pickup arm of a record player is guided by the groove in a record, but the read/write head of a floppy disk unit must be positioned over a magnetic track on a smooth recording surface. The difficulty of actively locating a narrow magnetic track rather than passively following a physical groove is the major reason why floppy disk drives cost more than record players. Furthermore, record players are read-only devices; you cannot use them to add information to a record. But floppy disk drives are true input/output units. You can write information on the disk, or you can read from it.

Floppy disks come in three standard sizes—8-inch, 5¼-inch, and 3½-inch—as well as several less popular sizes. IBM developed the original 8-inch floppy disks to load test programs into their mainframe computers. Soon the disks became popular among users of small business computers because floppy disk drives cost less than hard disk drives. The 8-inch size is still used, mainly for office computers. Improvements in manufacturing techniques led to the availability of 5¼-inch disks—sometimes called *minifloppy disks*—with almost the same storage capacity and reliability as the 8-inch disks. A majority of the disks in use today are 5¼-inch disks. Both 8-inch and 5¼-inch disks are wrapped in a stiff cardboard envelope to protect the disk from dirt, body oils, and scratches. An oval slot in the envelope leaves some of the recording surface

Figure 2.11*(a) Floppy disks are low-cost, low-density storage media for personal computers. (b) Reading and writing from a floppy disk is done by a drive. It holds the floppy in place, spins the disk inside the protective jacket, and either records or senses the magnetic spots on the surface of the disk.*

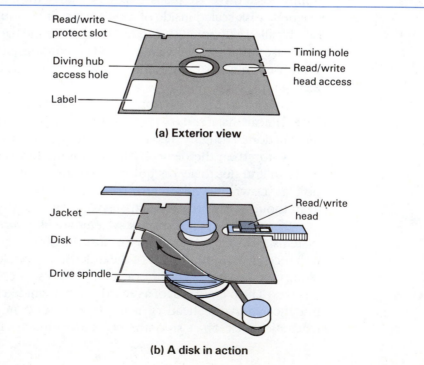

Read/write protect slot

Diving hub access hole

Label

Timing hole

Read/write head access

(a) Exterior view

Jacket

Disk

Drive spindle

Read/write head

(b) A disk in action

Figure 2.12 *A 5¼-inch minifloppy and a 3½-inch microfloppy disk.*

exposed, allowing the read/write head of the disk drive to get to the recording surface.

Figure 2.12 compares 5¼-inch floppy disks with 3½-inch disks, which are sometimes called *microfloppy disks*. Each 3½-inch disk is housed in a rigid plastic shell and can be carried safely in a shirt pocket. A sliding metal cover protects the read/write slot. The 3½-inch disks are rapidly eating into the market for minifloppy disks because they offer the same storage but are more convenient and use drive units that are only half as large.

There are few standards for recording information on floppy disks. One personal computer might store 800 kilobytes of data on a disk, while another might store only 270 kilobytes on the same disk. Of course, there is also a lack of standards for typing on paper. The number of lines of text per page, the size of the type, and whether text is typed on both sides of the page depend on the typist and the typewriter, not the paper. But whereas people can easily read text in a wide variety of formats, personal computers are less flexible. Although sometimes you can purchase special programs that will translate between formats, personal computers normally read and write disks in only one format.

Floppy disks can be removed and stored for later use. You can purchase as many floppy disks as it takes to store your information, keeping in mind that only one disk can be **on-line** (connected to the CPU) per disk drive.

Hard Disks

Hard disks use rigid aluminum platters to support a highly polished, magnetic oxide recording surface. A bent hard disk is worse than useless because it will damage the drive's read/write heads. Like a floppy disk system, a hard disk system is a random-access storage device.

Hard disks were invented before floppy disks. Since the 1960s they have been the primary external storage device for large computers. During this time their size has shrunk, their price has dropped, the density of data stored has grown, and they have become more reliable. Hard disk prices are constantly falling; in 1985 hard disks cost about one dollar for each 20,000 characters of storage. Figure 2.13 compares an obsolete hard disk platter with a modern hard disk drive.

Modern hard disks for mainframes and minicomputers store much more information than floppy disks. The hard disk units used by mainframe computers can store gigabytes; the hard disks attached to personal computers store between 5 and 100 megabytes. Hard disk systems achieve their large storage capacities in two ways.

The principal reason why hard disks can store more information than floppy disks is because they are *denser;* that is, they pack more information per square inch. They can do so because aluminum platters are less sensitive than Mylar disks to variations in temperature, humidity, and mechanical stress. This allows the hard disk drive to have more tracks per radial inch and to write more bits per inch along each track.

Another method of packing more information into a hard disk system is to employ more recording surfaces by stacking a number of platters on top of each other, as shown in Figure 2.14(a). Instead of reading from only one track at a time, a multiple platter hard disk drive can read from 1 track on each disk surface simultaneously. When multiple tracks are stacked one above the other as shown in Figure 2.14(b), we call the collection of tracks a *cylinder.* Finally, each cylinder is composed of many sectors.

Figure 2.13 *Hard disks. The obsolete hard disk platter on the left is now used as a coffee table. On the right is a modern hard disk drive, which is half the size of a standard 5¼-inch floppy disk drive. It stores 10 megabytes of information on a single removable cartridge—twice the original capacity of the obsolete platter.*

 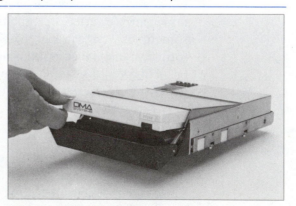

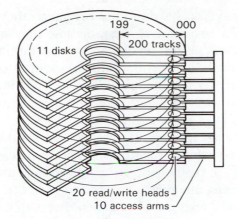

11 disks

199   000

200 tracks

20 read/write heads
10 access arms

(a) Multiple-platter disk drive

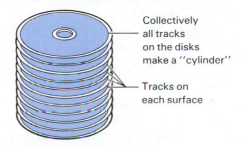

Collectively
all tracks
on the disks
make a "cylinder"

Tracks on
each surface

(b) Cylinder organization

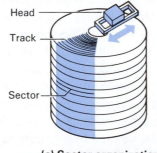

Head

Track

Sector

(c) Sector organization

Figure 2.14(a) *Hard disks contain many recording surfaces to increase recording ca-pacity. **(b)** Mainframe disk drives access entire cylinders of information at a time. **(c)** Alternatively, a stack of sectors can be accessed by moving a read/write head across all surfaces, simultaneously.*

Hard disks have another advantage: they transfer data faster than floppy disks, for two reasons. First, because they store data more compactly along each track, every revolution of the disk brings more data beneath the read/write heads. Second, hard disks spin faster than floppy disks. The standard speed for 5¼-inch floppy disks is 300 rpm. But a 5¼-inch hard disk is likely to rotate at least ten times faster, from 3,000 to 5,000 rpm. Consequently, the transfer rates are faster for a hard disk.

The fast spinning of a hard disk makes the environment inside a hard disk drive very windy. The read/write heads are carefully shaped to use the wind to float on a cushion of air a few thousandths of an inch above the disk. Maintaining this air gap is important. At 3,000 rpm (approximately 200 mph at the edge) a read/write head in contact with the disk platter soon becomes hot and scorches itself and the platter. Although this doesn't happen often, it happens often enough to have a name: **head crash.** After a head crash all data on the disk is lost forever, and the disk drive must be sent back to the factory for extensive repair.

Access times are also faster for hard disks than floppy disks. Whenever a computer is operating, its hard disk is spinning. This keeps the disk heads floating properly. It also means there is no need to wait for the disk to come up to speed. Floppy disks can't afford to turn constantly because their disk heads rub against the recording surface whenever the disk is turning. Floppy disks have roughly an 80-hour expected life of turning time. This is adequate as long as the disk is turning only while reading or writing, but it isn't long enough to allow continual rotation. It takes about half a second to bring a floppy disk to operating speed.

Some hard disk drives accept **removable disk** cartridges called *disk packs* that are similar to floppy disks. Changing hard disk cartridges takes longer than changing floppy disks because removable hard disk drives go through an air filtration cycle before beginning operation.

Other hard disks called **fixed disks** are built with the disk platter permanently mounted inside an air-tight, factory-sealed unit. Fixed disks don't need an air filtration system because there is no way for dirty air to get in. But fixed disks also have a disadvantage. Once a fixed disk becomes full of information, old data must be deleted before new data can be stored.

In short, hard disks offer several advantages over floppy disks. A small hard disk stores 10 megabytes. This is enough space to store 200 useful programs and leave enough room for the equivalent of several thousand pages of typed text. Every piece of information in the disk is available in an instant; access times are less than a tenth of a second.

Hard disks also have several disadvantages. Hard disk drives tend to be noisier than floppy disk drives because of their constant high-speed spinning. More important is the sensitivity of hard disks. Head crashes can be caused by a bent disk, dust, or cigarette smoke inside the drive, or a good thump to the side of the drive. Because hard disks operate on extremely precise mechanical tolerances, they are more sensitive to shock than floppy disks. This has retarded their use in portable computers. It is not a good idea to bounce any disk drive on a table, but the consequences can be disastrous if you are using a hard disk.

Disk Storage

The amount of information stored on a disk depends on four factors.

1. The number of tracks (concentric circles) of data from the inside to the outside edge of the disk. Generally, there are between 40 and 80 tracks on a floppy, and 200 to 500 on a hard disk.

2. The number of sectors per track. Recall that a sector is the smallest unit of information sent between the disk drive and the CPU.

3. The number of bytes stored in each sector. Generally disks for personal computers store between 128 and 512 bytes per sector; disks for large computers, up to 8,000. Double-density disks store twice as many bytes in the same-sized sector as single-density disks.

4. Whether data is written on one or both sides of the disk; that is, whether storage is *single-* or *double-sided*. As we have seen, in large systems, multiple platters are used to extend the capacity of a single drive.

For example, the Apple Macintosh records 80 tracks on a single-sided microfloppy disk. Each track has an average of 10 sectors; each sector stores 512 bytes. This gives $80 \times 10 \times 512 = 409,600$ bytes, or 400KB per disk.

Because the tracks on the outer edge of a disk are longer, the outside sectors of most disks provide the safest storage. Read errors usually occur while reading data stored on the inside tracks, where each sector is shorter. The Macintosh, however, cuts the outside tracks into more sectors than the inside tracks, making each sector approximately the same length. This allows the Macintosh to make better use of a disk's recording capability.

It is easy to get carried away with the technical details of how information is stored on disks. Just as you don't have to know much about a record to play it, you don't have to know much about a disk to store information on it. Your computer automatically handles the details of storing your information, determining which tracks and sectors to use. When the disk becomes full, the computer will not allow you to store new information until you delete some old information. You should know the storage capacity of each disk, but it is not as important to know how this figure relates to tracks and sectors. It is useful, however, to know how the information stored on a disk or tape is organized.

File Storage

The organization of information on a disk can affect how long it takes a computer to retrieve information and how much room it takes to store a file. In this section we will give a brief introduction to the terminology used to describe file structure.

A **file** is a collection of related records stored on a tape or disk. Recall from the previous discussion that a record is made up of fields; fields are composed of bytes; and bytes are composed of bits. We need not be concerned about the underlying structure of a file—only that it is composed of records. Think of a disk as a filing cabinet drawer full of manila folders (files), each of which contains records in the form of sheets of paper. Opening a file reveals its records.

A disk or tape stores many files; hence a special **directory** file is kept on each disk or tape to keep track of all other files. A directory is like a telephone book—it contains the name and number of every file on the disk. A *file name* is any string of characters assigned to the file, such as PAYROLL.DAT, WORD.HLP, or MYPROG.BAS. The name uniquely identifies each file; it is used by an application program to locate, open, read or write, and close a file. The *file number* identifies its physical location on the disk; we can let the computer take care of the number and not be concerned with it.

Most computer systems employ a **hierarchical directory,** which means that a treelike structure containing many subdirectories is used in place of a single directory. The **root directory** contains the names of files and other subdirectories, much as one file folder can be used to group other file folders together. Each **subdirectory** in turn contains the names of files or more subdirectories.

There are different types of files just as there are different kinds of information. Some files hold text, as in a word processing document, and others hold numbers, pictures, or programs. If a file contains a program, we call it a *binary file* because programs contain binary information understandable to the hardware. If a file contains pure text, we call it a *text file*.

Files can also be categorized according to how their records are accessed (see Figure 2.15). A **sequential file** contains records that can be accessed only as if they were on a tape—sequentially. The major advantage of a sequential file is that the records can be of differing lengths. A **direct-access file** contains records that can be accessed directly without reading all intervening records in the file. Direct-access files must be stored on direct-access devices such as disks. Obviously, the main advantage of a direct-access file is its access speed. However, the major disadvantage of a direct-access file is that it cannot store variable-length records.

An **indexed file** is actually two or more direct-access files. One file contains the data, and one or more other files contain indexes to the data file (see Figure 2.15). The indexes are used like an index in a book: values called *access keys* are taken from the data file and placed in the indexes in ascending order.

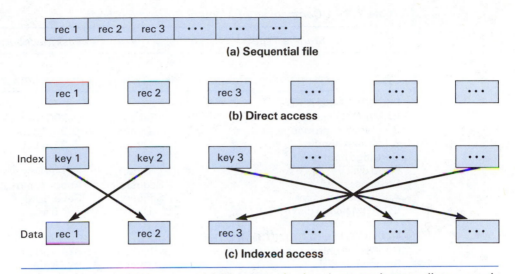

Figure 2.15 **(a)** *With a sequential file access is slow because intermediate records must be read to access a certain record.* **(b)** *Direct-access files permit fast access because intermediate records can be skipped in order to get a certain record.* **(c)** *Indexed files provide flexible access because records can be retrieved in ascending order by first looking up field values in an index file.*

Data is retrieved by first consulting the appropriate index; then the "page number" from the index is used to find the desired record in the data file.

Indexed files are flexible. Records can be retrieved in a certain order without having to sort them. New information is entered, old information deleted, and information retrieved according to its content rather than its position within the data file. In comparison with a simple direct-access file, an indexed file requires more disk space (to store the indexes) and takes more processing steps to store data.

Software developers agonize over the selection of file structure because of the tradeoffs among speed, storage overhead, and flexibility. Sequential files are good for storing text to be sent to another computer by telephone, programs to be read into memory, or text created by a word processor. Direct-access files are good for storing frequently accessed and updated information such as that found in a data management system or business application. Indexed files are used in a variety of applications ranging from database management systems to accounting applications.

Care of Magnetic Media

You need to follow some simple precautionary rules whenever you use tapes or disks. These rules stem from the fact that magnetic media are not as reliable as paper-based storage. It is difficult to erase all the writing from a piece of paper, but a magnetic disk can be erased by any strong magnetic field.

Table 2.1 *A Comparison of Memory Storage Methods*

Storage Type	Access Mechanism		
	Type	*Access Time*	*Cost Drive ($)*
MICROCOMPUTERS			
RAM/ROM chips	Random	200 ns	1,000/MB
3 1/2-inch microfloppy	Direct	0.2–.4 sec	400
5 1/4-inch floppy	Direct	0.2–.4 sec	100–500
Cartridge hard disk	Direct	50–90 ms	1,000
Fixed disk	Direct	30–90 ms	0.5K–5K
Streamer tape	Sequential	About 1 min	0.5K–2K
Audio cassette tape	Sequential	Several min	50–100
CD-ROM (video disk)	Direct	0.5 sec	400–800
MINI AND MAINFRAME COMPUTERS			
RAM/ROM chips	Random	10–150 ns	2K–15K/MB
Removable disk	Direct	25 ms	5K–35K
Fixed disk	Direct	25 ms	25K–40K
Mass storage unit	Combined	1–6 sec	500K–1M
Tape	Sequential	About 1 min	5K–20K

Notes: K = 1,000   min = minutes
M = 1,000,000   sec = seconds
KB = kilobyte   ms = millisecond (thousandth of a second)
MB = megabyte   ns = nanosecond (billionth of a second)
GB = gigabyte

The first line of defense should be to take good care of tapes and disks. Treat them as you would treat yourself. Avoid extreme temperatures and dusty or dirty environments. Don't let anything touch the recording surface, including your fingers, which deposit an oily film on everything they contact. Be very cautious near electrical devices. Tapes can lose information if they are placed above the motors in a tape drive. The ringer in a telephone can create a strong enough magnetic field to erase data from floppy disks under the phone.

But the most important rule—one that should be followed religiously—is to keep two copies of any information you don't want to lose. Then if one of the copies turns out to be unusable, you still have a duplicate, a **back-up** copy.

Backing-up a floppy disk is more convenient if you have two disk drives. You place the original disk in one drive, the back-up disk in the other, and give a COPY command, which completes the process in one step. Backing-up a floppy disk on a single drive system is more complicated. You swap the original and back-up disks in and out of the drive while the CPU copies portions of the original disk into RAM and then writes them on the back-up disk. Eventually the computer will tell you that the copy has been made, but this might be after eight or ten swaps. The number of swaps depends primarily on the relative sizes of RAM and the disks.

Backing-up a hard disk is both more important and more difficult because of its larger storage capacity. The cheapest back-up method is to copy the con-

		Media		
Capacity	Transfer Rate/Sec.	Cost of Media ($)	Volatile?	Principal Use
0.05MB–1MB	1MB–5MB	—	Yes	Main memory
0.4MB–1MB	30KB	5	No	On-line/archive
0.2MB–2MB	30KB	1	No	On-line/archive
5MB–20MB	0.4MB	90	No	On-line/archive
5MB–100MB	0.4MB–1MB	—	No	On-line
20MB–100 MB	60KB	20	No	Back-up/archive
100KB	0.5KB	1	No	Home computers
4GB	1MB	20	No	On-line ROM
1MB–64MB	4MB–64MB	—	Yes	Main memory
100MB–500MB	1MB–2MB	0.5K–1K	No	On-line/archive
0.5GB–5GB	2MB–3MB	—	No	On-line
6GB–2,000GB	3MB	10	No	On-line/archive
40MB–200MB	0.05MB–1MB	10	No	Archive

tents of the hard disk onto floppy disks. This is slow and uses up many floppy disks. For example, a 20MB hard disk holds the same amount of information as fifty 400KB floppies. One back-up method is to buy two hard disk units. Another solution is to buy a streaming tape drive, a cartridge tape system especially designed to back-up and restore the information on hard disks.

A Comparison of Memory Systems

No one would put up with the slow speed of external storage if internal memory were nonvolatile, removable, and cheap. But as Table 2.1 shows, each system has its relative merits. Most computer systems, particularly large ones, combine several storage methods in an attempt to blend the best features from each technology.

Examine Table 2.1 carefully. There is an extraordinary range of speeds and cost. Access times and transfer rates vary by many powers of ten. For example, the difference in access time between a floppy disk drive and main memory is greater than the difference in speed between a slug and a jet airplane.

Compare the cost of the access mechanisms with the cost of the removable recording media. The one-time cost of a removable hard disk drive may deter you from buying one even though each disk pack is relatively inexpensive per unit of storage. Floppy disk drives are ten times more expensive to purchase per byte of on-line storage than the disk drives used by mainframes. But a floppy drive serves the need for a low-cost, direct-access, removable media mechanism regardless of its cost-per-byte ratio.

Numerous storage methods have been developed to serve a special need or fill a niche in price and performance. For example, a **mass storage unit** combines large numbers of tape cartridges, a jukeboxlike tape-loading mechanism, a hard disk drive, and an intelligent controller into a unit that can manage many gigabytes of on-line storage. A **compact digital ROM (CD-ROM)** is similar to the digital disk players used in high-quality stereo systems that use lasers to read from an optical disk. CD-ROM is a low-cost solution to massive data storage, but its usefulness is restricted because the contents of a CD-ROM cannot be altered. Rapid changes in storage technology are expected to continue.

■ Summary

All computers—from the hand-held models to huge mainframe computers—have the same functional organization. The four functional units are: the CPU with its internal memory, external storage, input units, and output units. We have discussed the CPU, internal memory, and external storage in this chapter. The input and output units are discussed in the next chapter.

The CPU has a control unit that supervises the rest of the CPU, including an arithmetic/logic unit that does all calculations and data manipulation. Instructions from a stored program are copied from main memory into the control unit, where they guide the operations of the hardware.

For personal computers the CPU consists of a microprocessor, memory chips, and some timing and support chips, all of which are usually mounted on one circuit board. A microprocessor is a single chip containing both the control unit and the ALU. Personal computers can do the same things larger computers are capable of doing, but they are much slower and can store less information.

Although the range of costs and capacities of storage devices for mainframe computers overlaps with that of devices for minis and personal computers, generally there is a 100- to 1,000-fold difference in capacity between the two extreme forms of computing.

For fast access to large amounts of information, on-line external storage devices are needed. Direct-access storage devices, such as disk drives, provide fast access to any data they contain. Long-term storage of archival information is achieved by low-cost, permanent media such as magnetic tape.

Key Terms

access time
accumulator
address
analog
archival copy
arithmetic/logic
  unit (ALU)
ASCII code
assembly language
back-up
binary number
bit
byte
central processing
  unit (CPU)
clock rate
clocks
compact digital
  ROM (CD-ROM)
control unit
data transfer rate
digital
direct access
directory
external storage (or
  auxiliary storage)

fields
file
fixed disk
floating-point number
floppy disk
gigabyte
hard disk
head crash
hierarchical directory
indexed file
instruction register
instruction set
internal memory (main
  or primary memory)
kilobit
kilobyte (KB)
machine language
mass storage unit
megabyte (MB)
megahertz (MHz)
memory
memory chips
MFLOP
microprocessor
microsecond
millisecond

nanosecond
on-line
op-code
operand address
parity bit
program counter
program overlay
RAM
random (direct)
  access
read/write head
records
removable disk
ROM
root directory
sector
sequential storage
stored program
streaming tape drive
subdirectory
tape
track
transparent
virtual memory
word
write-protected

Discussion Questions

1. When a computer is first turned on, what causes the CPU to transfer a program from a disk into main memory?

2. Each word of a personal computer's memory is of limited size—8, 16, or 32 bits, depending on the computer. How can a computer represent very large and very small numbers in such small words?

3. How does a computer determine whether the contents of a memory word is an instruction or data, such as a number or letter?

4. Suppose a memory location contains the binary equivalent of the decimal number 66. What could the 66 represent?

5. Would it make sense to have WOM, write-only memory?

6. Why are there relatively few kinds of microprocessors?

7. What determines the speed of a CPU? When can you say that one CPU is faster than another?

8. In a truly random access memory, each word of memory can be located in exactly the same length of time. Is this true for floppy and hard disks? For internal memory?

9. Compare a disk with a book. What part of a book is analogous to the disk's directory? To the disk's files?

10. Why is a hard disk drive faster and why does it hold more information than a floppy?

11. What are the relative advantages of sequential versus direct-access file structures?

12. What is the difference (if any) between a CPU and a microprocessor?

13. What is a head crash? What causes a head crash?

Exercises

1. Look in a reference manual for a microprocessor to find the relative speeds for the various operations for arithmetic and data movement. How much faster is addition than division?

2. Look up the memory size of your personal computer (or any personal computer if you do not have one) and the memory requirements of some popular application programs.

3. A record player is a read-only device. List some other read-only or write-only devices in your home.

4. Find the number of tracks, the sector size, and the density for the floppy disks on your personal computer. How many bytes of data can be stored on each disk?

5. What is a cylinder? List the reasons why mainframe disks are faster and able to store more information than personal computer disks.

input and output

3

3

Input and output devices are the eyes, ears, arms, legs, and mouth of a computer. They allow the computer to communicate and interact with its environment. Without them, computers would be useless.

Input devices are conversion machines that translate events in the computer's environment into digital signals, a process called *digitizing*. One frequently digitized event is the movement of a key on a keyboard, but the arrival of radio waves at a satellite receiver and the vibration of air pressure at a microphone can also be digitized. In fact, anything that can be sensed electronically is a candidate for computer input. Some machines convert spoken words into electrical signals so that a computer can "hear"; other machines allow a computer to "see" by converting printed text into electrical signals. These devices are sometimes as sophisticated and cleverly designed as the computer systems they serve.

Output devices are also conversion machines, but they convert digital signals into actions. For example, printers accept digital signals and convert them into the placement of ink on paper.

Input devices include keyboards, light pens, mice, character recognition devices, voice recognition devices, and the infrared sensor in the nose of a heat-seeking missile. Output devices range from printers, plotters, display screens, telephones, and speech synthesizers to the warhead in a missile. There are literally thousands of types of input and output devices, each with its own special use and niche in the marketplace.

This chapter emphasizes the input and output devices you are most likely to use. For automobiles a steering wheel has been found to be the best "input device," but computers use a diversity of I/O devices to facilitate interaction between people and machines. It is important to choose the right I/O device for the task at hand and use it correctly. Giving you the information necessary to do this successfully is the purpose of this chapter.

■ Input Devices

Keyboards

By far the most common input device is the keyboard. It is standard equipment on virtually every personal computer and mainframe terminal. Except for specialized applications, such as drawing pictures or pointing at objects on the screen, the keyboard reigns supreme as the primary way to communicate with computers (see Figure 3.1). In the future keyboards are likely to be replaced by microphones attached to speech recognition units, enabling you to talk to computers (see Figure 3.2). But today, if you want to use a computer effectively, you must have a basic level of skill at keyboard manipulation.

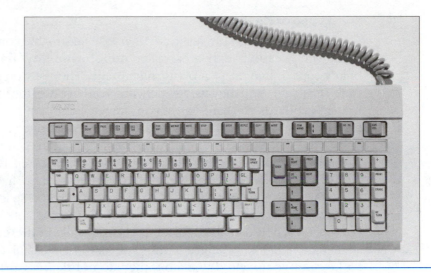

Figure 3.1 *Keyboard with separate cursor-movement and numeric keys.*

Figure 3.2 *This keyboard includes a voice recognition unit that is limited to a vocabulary with at most 160 words. The operator speaks into the microphone. A processor inside the keyboard analyzes the spoken sounds. Eventually each spoken word is converted into a keystroke or series of keystrokes.*

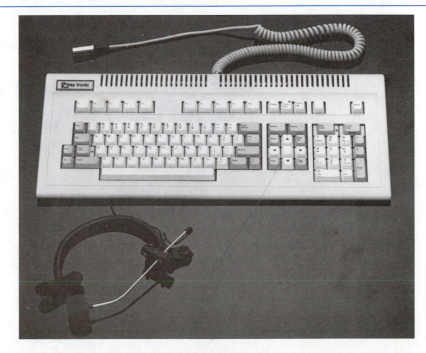

Types of Keyboards

A poor keyboard can make an otherwise reasonable computer hard to deal with. The cheapest keyboards, called **membrane keyboards,** have pictures of key-tops drawn on a flat plastic membrane. They rely on pressure to register each keystroke, and they vary widely in sensitivity. On the most sensitive membrane keyboards you cannot rest your fingers lightly on the keys; instead, your fingers must hover over the keyboard. On less sensitive models it is very difficult to tell when enough pressure has been applied to generate the keystroke. In short, membrane keyboards are not suitable for extensive typing.

Portable terminals and personal computers often have **compact keyboards;** they have less than full-size keys or reduced spacing between keys. Unless you have small hands, you may find it impossible to touch-type on a compact keyboard. The compact keyboards called **chiclet keyboards** have small rectangular keys similar to those on hand-held calculators. Although chiclet keys move up and down a bit, they do not depress as far as standard full-stroke keys. Typing quickly on a chiclet keyboard is difficult. The initial public rejection of the ill-fated IBM PCjr was largely blamed on its use of a chiclet keyboard.

Even among full-size, full-stroke keyboards there is a wide range of options and quality. Some keyboards feel mushy. They do not have a clear point at which the key seems to fall through to the bottom of the stroke. You may find it easier to type if an audible click accompanies each keystroke. But if the click is

Figure 3.3 *A numeric key pad is shaped like a familiar calculator, thus making entry of numeric information faster and more accurate.*

produced by mechanical key switches, you cannot adjust the volume. Other keyboards generate clicks through a speaker, permitting the sound to be adjusted up for work in a busy office or down for late-night typing at home. Still other computers allow you to adjust the sensitivity of the keyboard as well as the volume of the clicks.

A particularly useful feature is a *keyboard buffer;* it allows you to continue typing even though the CPU is busy doing other tasks. The buffer stores the characters you type until the CPU is ready to accept them. This feature, which is also called *type-ahead,* makes slow programs more bearable. You can begin typing a new command or text while the CPU is still working on the last operation. Keyboard buffers have room for a limited number of characters, from 2 to 20 or more. Characters in the buffer do not appear on the screen until the CPU has accepted them for processing and has echoed them to the screen. If the buffer becomes full, then the keyboard is likely to beep at you in response to further typing.

For people who must enter a lot of numerical data, it may be wise to use an auxiliary **key pad** as shown in Figure 3.3. The numeric key pad is shaped and organized like a calculator. This tends to increase both the accuracy and speed of the person entering numbers.

Keyboard Layout

The standard layout for typewriter keyboards was developed in the last century. The arrangement is known as the *QWERTY keyboard;* it is named after the order of the keys immediately above where the left hand normally rests on the keyboard. The QWERTY keyboard was deliberately designed to slow typing to prevent the hammers on early mechanical typewriters from jamming on their way to the paper. This goal quickly became irrelevant with the invention of improved mechanical typewriters. It is of no concern whatsoever with computer keyboards. But the QWERTY layout is still used on nearly all computer keyboards. Typists became accustomed to the layout and did not want to change. Even minor variations bother touch typists. For example, a common complaint about the keyboard on the IBM PC is that the location of the shift and return keys differs slightly from that on IBM Selectric typewriters.

Except for typing normal text, the most common typing operations on computers are entering numbers and moving the cursor. The **cursor** is an indicator on the screen that shows where things will happen next; usually it looks like a blinking rectangle or underline. The **cursor-movement keys** have arrows on their tops showing in what direction the key moves the cursor. There is no standard location for the cursor-movement keys, but they are easily recognized because they are marked with arrows.

Many other keys can appear on a keyboard. One of the most important is the **control key,** usually labeled [CTRL]. It operates like the shift key, but instead of a capital letter, it generates a *control-letter* that has a different character code. Control-letters rarely appear on the screen; instead they are used to give commands to programs. To type a control-letter you press [CTRL] and press a letter. Its effect will depend entirely on the program being run, but there are conventions that many programs follow. For example, a [CTRL]-[H] usually moves the cursor back one character, and pressing [CTRL]-[C] often stops execution of the current program.

Using the Keyboard

The main thing to remember when using a computer keyboard is that the keys do not have fixed meanings. On a typewriter hitting the [P] key will always print a *P* on the paper. But striking [P] on a computer keyboard might display a *P* on the screen, print a file, or pull an address out of a list of mailing labels. It all depends on how the program instructs the CPU to interpret the character.

Each keyboard has its own quirks. Most computer keyboards have **repeating keys.** This means that pressing a key longer than a second generates a constant stream of characters. Clumsy typists find repeating keys a bother because of the frequent need to delete extra characters. Some keyboards have an "intelligent" shift-lock key; when depressed, it raises all alphabetic keys to upper-case but does not affect punctuation keys or the keys on the top row of the keyboard.

Function keys are extra keys on the keyboard used to give commands, not to type text. In some programs the function keys are *user-programmable;* in other words, you can give them whatever meaning you want while using that program.

Selection Devices

Many computer operations involve pointing, selecting, or moving items already on the screen. Often you can perform these tasks more quickly with a pointing device than with the cursor keys on the keyboard. In this section we discuss several pointing devices: the touch screen, touch-tablet, pen, mouse, and puck.

Most people would say that their finger is the most natural pointing device. The touch screen shown in Figure 3.4 uses invisible sensors to tell where a finger or pencil touches the surface of the screen. Don't be surprised if the screen in Figure 3.4 looks perfectly normal; the sensors are hidden in the slanted surface surrounding the screen. The accuracy of a touch screen is limited to the nearest character or, even worse, to a group of characters. But then fingers are far too blunt to point to tiny dots on the screen anyway.

Touch screens work in a variety of ways. Perhaps the most common mechanism is the *infrared detector*. Infrared rays (heat) scan the surface of the screen. When your finger interferes with the scanning rays, the obstruction is picked up by the infrared sensors and converted into a screen location.

Figure 3.4 *A touch-sensitive screen allows you to point at and select an item on the screen.*

A **touch-tablet** is an electronic blackboard that can sense a pencil or stylus on its surface. The touch-sensitive tablet transmits the location of the stylus to the computer whenever it is touched.

Figure 3.5 shows a related pointing device, the *digitizing pen*. Digitizing pens work in a variety of ways. A **light pen** reads light from the display screen, thus allowing you to point to a spot on the screen. A **sonic pen** uses reflected or emitted sound to determine the position of the pen. If you listen closely, you can hear a sonic pen crackle.

To use either a light pen or a sonic pen, you aim it at a region of a touch-tablet or screen and then press a button on the pen. The pen reads the location of the region and sends this information to the computer. The computer uses the information to determine what was being pointed at when the pen button was pressed.

Figure 3.6 shows a **mouse,** a hand-operated pointing device. As you drag the mouse across a flat surface, it relays directional information to the computer. Most mice have one or two buttons on top that are pressed when you want the computer to take notice of the cursor's current position on the screen.

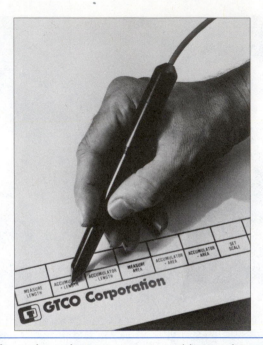

Figure 3.5 *A pen is used to point to an area on a tablet, as shown here, or directly on the display screen.*

A **puck** is a pointing device used much like a mouse, but it also has a small magnifying glass with cross-hairs. It is especially good for entering pictorial data from architectural drawings, maps, aerial photographs, blueprints, and medical images.

Figure 3.6 *A mouse is used mostly to point at and select options on the screen.*

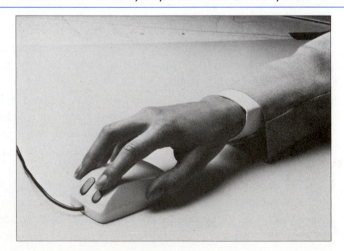

Output: Displaying and Printing

Like everyone else, you use computers to get output. Perhaps you want to look at information in a file. Or maybe you want to print a letter. Or you might need to control a blast furnace. Whatever the application, you need an output device to convert the computer's digital signals into a useful form. This photo essay will give you a better idea of how flexible output systems can be.

1. Printers and monitors vary considerably in size, quality, speed, price, and convenience. It pays to consider options carefully before making a purchase.

VIDEO DISPLAY

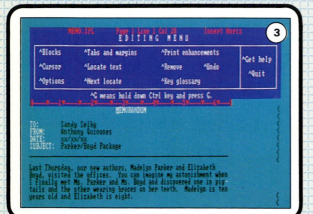

2. The Apple Macintosh uses a monochrome screen with a resolution of 512 by 342 pixels. Here the MacWrite word processing program is displaying several sizes and styles of text.

3. This picture was made with an IBM PC, a Tecmar Graphics Master color adapter card, and a 35-mm slide-maker camera system. Its resolution is 640 by 200 pixels, the same as that on a standard IBM PC color display. Because there are only 8 scan lines for each row, the characters look grainy. The memo in this screen is being edited with WordStar 2000.

4. The trend in word processing systems is toward what-you-see-is-what-you-get display. This PowerView 10 terminal, produced by Compugraphic, is used to preview work before it is typeset. PowerView processes the screen image with an Intel 80186 microprocessor supported by one megabyte of memory. The screen image can be scrolled horizontally and vertically, reduced in size, or enlarged.

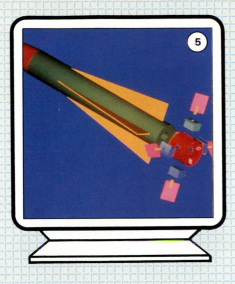

5. This image was produced by the IBM 5080 Graphics System, which is used primarily by design engineers. The screen has a viewing area 11.2 inches square and can display up to 256 colors with a resolution of 1,024 by 1,024 pixels. Today a display of this quality is too expensive for most personal computers—but in the future, who knows?

6. The 9-inch, flat-panel amber display on this portable computer has 512 by 255 pixels and an adjustable viewing angle for easy reading. Built into the top of the computer is a small ink-jet printer. The computer weighs only 25 pounds and costs less than $5,000.

7. Like most lap-top computers, the Texas Instruments ProLite uses a liquid crystal display because it consumes little power. Lighting conditions are critical for liquid crystal displays, because they depend on reflected light to produce the image.

window 3

PRINTERS

8. Most dot matrix printers can print both text and graphics. Dot matrix printers have captured an increasing share of the market as their cost has fallen and print resolution has increased.

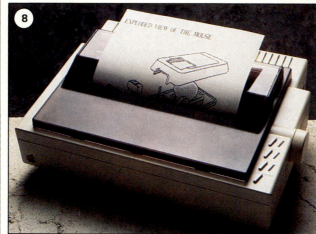

9. This color dot matrix printer has a 24-element printhead that provides 144 dot-per-inch (dpi) resolution. The suggested retail price is less than $270.

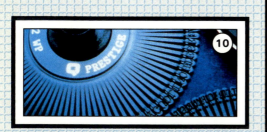

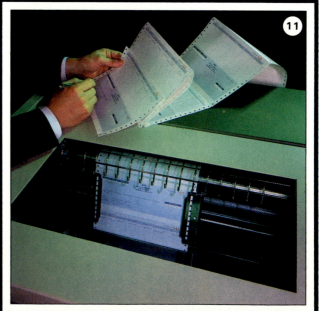

10. With daisy-wheel printers, raised images of letters are pressed into an inked ribbon and paper. They produce high-quality letters but are noisy, unable to handle graphics, and slow, printing just 10 to 80 characters per second.

11. Business documents are often created by filling in the blanks in preprinted forms.

12. Like many recently introduced laser printers, Apple's LaserWriter is based on the print engine used in Canon's personal copiers. The printer is controlled by a Motorola 68000 microprocessor supported by 2 megabytes of internal memory. It produces 300-dpi output at rates up to 8 pages per minute, and it comes with a number of built-in fonts in a range of sizes.

■ RESTAURANT ■

GRAND OPENING
COUPON
This Coupon entitles you to one free glass of wine or one slice of Chocolate Toffee Pie

Cut Here

◆
Our Newest
Watermill Restaurant
is located at 101 Savoy Ave.

The Watermill Restaurant is located between Olmstead St. and Taylor St. on Savoy Ave. Plenty of Free Parking. Open 11am-12pm Mon. thru Sun.

Savoy Ave
Olmstead St.
Taylor St.

THE WATERMILL
■ RESTAURANT ■

First Class Mail

ANNOUNCING THE OPENING OF
THE WATERMILL RESTAURANT
AT 101 SAVOY AVE.

G·R·A·N·D O·P·E·N·I·N·G

13. This sample output, which is almost typeset quality, was created using a Macintosh application program and the LaserWriter printer.

window 3

PLOTTERS

14. Pen plotters produce smoother lines than dot matrix printers, but they operate much more slowly. This inexpensive six-pen plotter prints by moving the paper back and forth while moving the pen from side to side, with 250 steps per inch. To fill in a region with color the pen must run back and forth many times, which is a slow process.

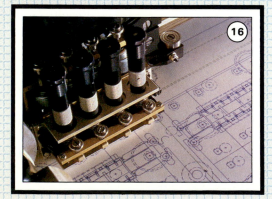

15. Engineering, architecture, and other design applications require large, high-resolution plotters. This drum plotter uses the same basic technology as the small plotter in photo 14, but it is much more accurate.

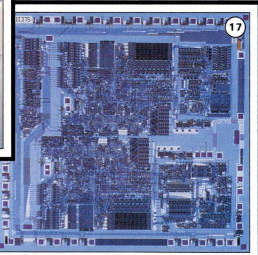

16. The pen holder of a large commercial flat-bed plotter.

17. Sample plot of an integrated circuit from an electrostatic plotter.

18. This stand-alone plotter was designed for drafters, engineers, and architects. From text entered on the keyboard, this system produces wet ink lettering for use on drawings and schematics.

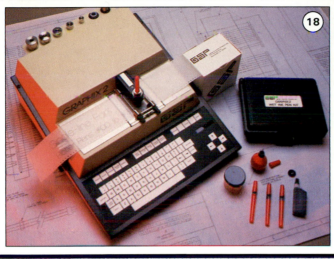

19. This laser-driven photoplotter is accurate to 0.005 of an inch, which is far smaller than can be seen by an unaided human eye.

20. A close-up view of the photoplotter's printhead.

21. High-quality photoplotters have historically been very costly—more than $60,000. This photoplotter costs $25,000. It interfaces with microcomputers, such as the IBM PC/AT shown here, with an RS-232 interface and is used to create the precision artwork for printed circuit boards.

OTHER OUTPUT DEVICES

Anything that can be controlled with electrical signals or motors can be controlled by computer. This page gives three examples of very different types of computer output.

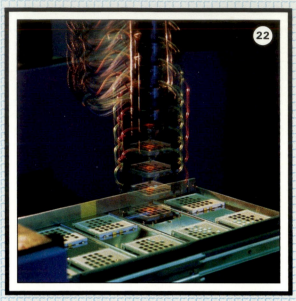

22. Computers are increasingly being called on to perform mechanical tasks. This is an automated testing system that helps ensure the quality of circuits in some of IBM's mainframe computers.

23. This fully portable, electronically controlled printer can produce labels with both bar codes and human-readable information. Because the labels are printed on thermally coated paper with a thermal printhead, no ribbons are required.

24. The electron-beam exposure system shown here etches microscopic patterns on glass plates. The system translates data on a tape into physical form by shooting an intense beam of electrons at a chemically coated glass plate. Eventually the glass plates are used as masks to fabricate integrated circuits.

Both mouse and puck can register very small movements, permitting you to point to very precise locations. It takes only a short time to become accustomed to using a puck or mouse, although most people are skeptical until they have tried one. But if your desk looks like a rat's nest, working with a mouse will be difficult because you need clear space to use it effectively.

The major advantages of a mouse over other pointing devices are its accuracy and proven efficiency. Your arm is not likely to tire as quickly when using a mouse as when you use a pen or touch screen. Furthermore, a mouse is inexpensive and rugged.

Commercial Devices

Grocery stores, banks, insurance companies, and many other organizations require specialized input devices in order to lower the cost of entering data, increase accuracy, and improve the timeliness of information. Most of these devices are connected to a minicomputer or mainframe running a timeshared operating system. The timesharing software enables the large central computer to quickly juggle hundreds of input devices "simultaneously" in order to process transactions. For example, many automated bank teller machines (as shown in Figure 3.7) are connected to a central computer. When you enter your number and select a command from the list of options, the automated teller machine sends your information as a transaction to the timeshared computer for processing. Seconds later your answer appears on the screen of the teller, or perhaps money appears.

Early commercial systems were characterized by punched paper card input from keypunch machines. A *keypunch machine* is like a typewriter except it punches holes in cards rather than printing characters on paper. Keypunch operators produced enormous stacks of cards that were read into the mainframe computer as a batch, hence the name **batch input.** The mainframe processed the entire batch of cards in one *processing cycle* before continuing on to the next processing cycle. For example, the computer might read a batch of punched cards containing all the payments and charges in a medical billing system for one day and then adjust each patient's account before moving on to the next application. Keypunch machines were eventually replaced by data entry systems that store information on magnetic media instead of cards.

Key-to-tape and *key-to-disk* systems generally link a number of workstations (each with a keyboard and screen) with a dedicated minicomputer and tape or disk storage, as shown in Figure 3.8. They collect input on tape or disk before it is entered into the mainframe system, thus relieving the mainframe computer of a substantial workload. These systems make it easier for data entry personnel to fix typing mistakes, eliminate the need to buy blank paper cards, and allow management to monitor performance automatically, through the computer. Despite these advantages, key-to-tape and key-to-disk systems are being replaced by input devices that capture information without the need for typing.

Many other batch input devices are used to collect inventory information, gather production information from workstations on the factory floor, capture shipping invoices for the day, and so forth. For example, video cameras capture graphical information such as maps, drawings, and photographs. *MICR (magnetic ink character recognition)* devices are used by banks to read the numbers written on the bottom of personal checks. MICR devices can read more than a thousand checks per minute.

An **on-line** input device is connected to the computer so data can be processed immediately by the computer. A variety of on-line input devices are used by retail stores, factories, and scientific laboratories for interactive processing. An **interactive system** is one in which the computer immediately

Figure 3.7 *Whenever you use an automatic teller machine, you are using an input device connected to a mainframe computer.*

Figure 3.8 *Key-to-disk data entry workstations.*

processes its on-line inputs. Not all on-line devices are supported by interactive processing. For example, a time clock might be on-line, but the data from the time clock might be used only once a week for payroll processing.

Most retail businesses use one or more input devices called *POS terminals* (point-of-sale terminals). Figure 3.9 shows a sales clerk using a POS terminal to verify the amount of a credit card purchase. The computer may be in the next room or thousands of miles away. When the transaction reaches the computer, the machine checks the card number to see if it is stolen, overdrawn, or currently invalid. If approved, the computer sends a validation number back to the POS terminal. By the early 1980s, a person in Australia could use a credit card on an account in New York.

Many grocery stores have converted from manual systems to the UPC systems shown in Figure 3.10. The *UPC* (Universal Product Code) is a standard way to mark groceries (and any other item in a store). The code involves two numbers: the first represents the manufacturer of the goods, and the second represents the product. The numbers are given in both human-readable and machine-readable form. The machine-readable form is called a **bar code** because it consists of variable-width bars. A bar code reader senses and converts the bar codes into numbers.

For example, suppose Dark Red Kidney Beans made by S&W Fine Foods of San Mateo, California, is assigned numbers 11194 (for S&W) and 38943 (for Red Beans). The can of beans is passed over an optical scanner that reads the bar code printed on the label of the can. A ''flying spot'' scanner reads the bar code by measuring the amount of reflected light bouncing back from the can of beans. The POS terminal deciphers the bar code, sending the numbers 11194 and 38943 to the computer. The computer uses these numbers to look up the current price of the beans, remembers the fact that the store has just sold a can of beans, and sends the price back to the cash register.

Most POS terminals work faster than a human can point or speak. The POS provides speed and accuracy, but this is not the end of the story. The information provided by a POS terminal can be used to re-order depleted inventory, measure the effects of a sale, and monitor the productivity of clerks.

Commercial input devices capture a lot of information at its source; this is often called **source data automation.** Source data automation systems require more hardware than batch systems; so their initial cost is higher. In contrast, conventional batch processing is people-intensive, slow, and inaccurate because the data must be typed by data entry operators. Because the cost of labor is increasing and the cost of hardware is decreasing, use of batch processing is likely to continue declining, while on-line interactive data entry at the source should increase.

Figure 3.9 *A retail point-of-sale terminal keeps track of buyers using credit cards. Your card number is compared with a list of invalid card numbers, and the amount of a purchase is checked against a predetermined spending limit.*

Figure 3.10 *The UPC (Universal Product Code) is used to label the package of every item sold in the grocery store with a code that specifies the manufacturer and the product.*

Other Input Devices

Input devices may be hand-held or as large as a 200-inch telescope. They may be on-line and used for interactive data entry, or they may be used to collect data in batches prior to processing. An amazing variety of input devices exists, and each provides a computer with a specific kind of tactile, visual, audible, or other input.

Some input devices go well beyond the abilities of our own senses. Magnetic resonance scanners allow computers to "see" inside our bodies. Temperature-sensing devices collect on-line data about the temperature and humidity of buildings so that a computer can adjust the climate of a warehouse, factory, or office building. Signals from video cameras in robots on an assembly line allow computers to control the actions of "seeing-eye" robots. Scientific labs use a variety of sensors to collect data from experiments; the data is entered automatically into the computer's memory for processing and graphical display. Obviously, it is wrong to assume that the sensory abilities of computer systems are inherently very limited. This prejudice only discourages the use of computers in innovative ways.

■ Output Devices

The two output devices most familiar to people who use computer systems are printers and visual display units such as screen monitors. Printers provide a permanent, printed record of information. Displays provide a quick and inexpensive way to view information.

Printers

Typewriters combine a keyboard for input and paper for output in one device. Personal computers and terminals connected to large computers separate these functions into two units, a keyboard and a printer. Anything typed on a typewriter is printed automatically because the keyboard and print mechanism are mechanically (or electrically) coupled. But a computer's keyboard is not connected directly to the printer. Instead, the keyboard and printer are each connected separately to the CPU. Characters typed on the keyboard are *not* automatically sent to the printer or display screen unless the program tells the CPU to do so.

Most printers used with personal computers today are *impact printers*. Like a typewriter, they form an image by bringing ribbon and paper into physical contact with each other. There are three major categories of printers.

1. **Letter-quality printers** create each character by striking an embossed image of a fully formed character against an inked ribbon and paper.
2. **Dot matrix printers** create each character by printing dots in a pattern.
3. **Line** and **page printers** generate characters from either dots or fully formed, raised images; but they print an entire line or page of characters almost simultaneously rather than one character at a time. These printers are not fundamentally different from letter-quality and dot matrix printers except for their higher speed and cost.

Normally, personal computers do not generate enough output to require a line or page printer, except when they are linked in a network. Figures 3.11 and 3.12 show the character printers used with most personal computers and the larger, faster, and more expensive line printers used in a mainframe or minicomputer system.

Letter-Quality Printers

A letter-quality printer can generate output that is indistinguishable from that of a good typewriter. This means that the edges of each printed character are smooth, or fully formed.

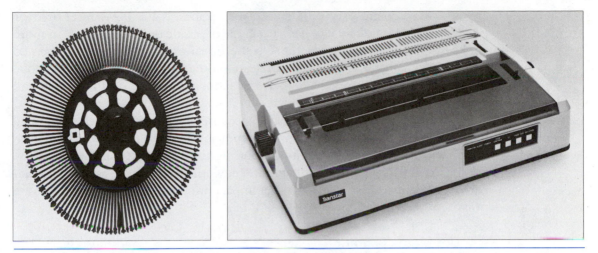

Figure 3.11 *A daisy-wheel print element (left) and a letter-quality printer (right).*

Figure 3.12 *The page printer shown on the left can merge computer-generated text with the image of a business form and print the completed form at up to 120 pages a minute. Medium-speed line printers (right) typically print 300–600 lines per minute and are used in minicomputer systems.*

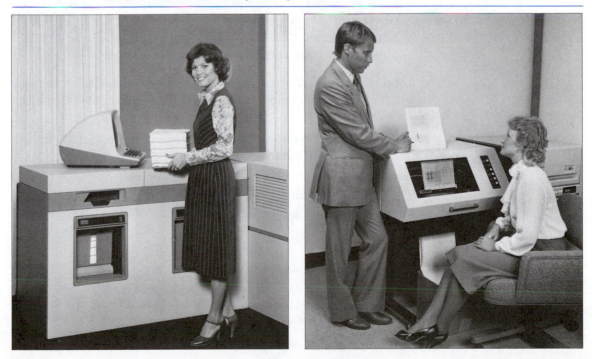

The most common type of letter-quality printer is a **daisy-wheel printer** (see Figure 3.11). A *daisy wheel* is a flat circle of plastic or metal with 96 or more spokes radiating from the center. On the tip of each spoke is an embossed image of a character. The wheel rotates continuously. As the required spoke moves in front of the print hammer, the spoke is struck onto the ribbon and paper, causing one character to be printed.

Daisy-wheel printers are reliable because they use rather few moving parts—just the print wheel, the print hammer, and the paper-advance mechanism. They generate high-quality output on normal paper, but they are slow compared with other printers. Typically they print between 15 and 70 **characters per second** (**cps**). And like other impact printers, daisy-wheel printers are noisy.

Dot Matrix Printers

Dot matrix printers obtained their name because of the way they produce each character. Instead of printing a solid letter, a dot matrix printer prints an array of dots in a pattern that only approximates the font of a typewriter.

The cheapest matrix printers generate crudely shaped characters that are clearly identifiable as computer output. Obviously, the more dense the dots are, the better the printed character looks. The density of dots is measured in **dpi,** dots per inch. The best matrix printers use many small, overlapping dots to build each character. Some manufacturers claim that the result is correspondence-quality or even letter-quality output.

If you do not need output that looks as if it were just removed from an office typewriter, then matrix printers have several attractive features.

■ Matrix printers are cheaper than letter-quality printers. They range in price from under $250 to more than $1,000, instead of from under $500 to more than $2,000.

■ Matrix printers are much faster than letter-quality printers. Slow matrix printers print 60 cps, but a rate of 200 cps or more is not unusual.

■ Most matrix printers are not limited to one size or style of character (see Figure 3.13). Because the characters are formed from dot patterns, the dots can be arranged in Greek, gothic, boldface, or italic fonts with equal ease. Some matrix printers offer many styles and sizes of type; others print in only one or two styles.

■ Matrix printers can print graphical images as well as text. If the personal computer has the proper software, a matrix printer can print bar charts, line graphs, company logos, letterheads, your personal signature, even coarse-grained photographs.

Some matrix printers are *nonimpact printers.* That is, no print hammer or similar mechanism actually strikes the paper. Examples include thermal printers and ink-jet printers.

Until now you had to make a decision,
letters, or slow printing with a daisy

Introducing the

In draft mode, the LQ-1500 del
CPS **and in the letter quality mode**
67 CPS. The LQ-1500 can **print up to**
elite, proportional, *italic*, super
control.

Figure 3.13 *A sample from the Epson LQ-1500, a matrix printer. It prints draft-quality letters at 200 cps and nearly letter-quality letters at 67 cps.*

Thermal printers burn dark spots on heat-sensitive paper. The paper is usually expensive, has a shiny surface, and tends to fade over time. On the positive side, thermal printers are inexpensive and make only a whispering, crinkly noise as they singe the paper.

Ink-jet printers work by squirting tiny droplets of liquid ink at the paper. On some systems magnetic fields deflect each drop to the proper position by acting on the drop's static electricity. The printhead shown in Figure 3.14 fires

Figure 3.14 *An ink-jet printer. On the left is an inexpensive 150-cps ink-jet printer. On the right is a close-up view of the printer's disposable printhead, which contains a rubber pouch of liquid ink.*

droplets straight at the paper from twelve microscopic nozzles arranged verti-cally along the printhead. In this system each droplet is ejected by instantly vaporizing a tiny amount of ink behind one of the nozzles, giving momentum to the ink in the nozzle.

Line and Page Printers

Mini and mainframe computers need much faster printing than provided by character printers. The required speed is achieved by *line printers,* which print an entire line at a time, or by *page printers,* which compose a page at a time. Two types of high-speed impact line printers are drum or chain printers. A common type of page printer is the laser printer.

A *drum printer* is a line printer in which the entire set of embossed charac-ters is positioned around the circumference of a cylinder or drum. As the drum rotates at high speed, a hammer pushes the paper against the ribbon at precisely the right time. The drum has 132 "rings" along its length so that a 132-column line can be printed each time the drum completes a single rotation.

A *chain printer* is a line printer in which the entire character set is embossed on a rotating chain. As the desired character passes by, a hammer presses the ribbon against the paper to make the imprint. In a typical chain printer each chain includes 5 complete character sets, and 132 hammers oper-ate in parallel to increase the speed of printing. The major advantage of chain printers over drum printers is the ease of changing fonts by changing the chain.

Drum and chain printers are fast: they print 600 to over 3,000 lines per minute. They are also expensive, costing $10,000 to $100,000. The ability to print carbon copies is a major advantage of all impact printers.

Laser printers come in micro and mainframe sizes, but they all work nearly the same way. A laser beam traces out the image on a photosensitive drum, which picks up ink particles. The paper rubs the ink particles from the drum, and the ink is "fixed" on the page by heating the page as it emerges from the printer. Because the image can be text or pictures and the resolution is excel-lent, laser printers produce typeset-quality graphics and text.

Small laser printers often use the same print engine as is used in copy ma-chines, except that the light source comes from a laser instead of being reflected off an original document. Single blank pages are fed in at one end and printed pages come out the other end. Prices range from $2,500 to more than $8,000; typical speeds are 8 pages per minute.

Large laser printers use continuous-feed paper moving at 3 to 5 pages per second through the printer (equivalent to 20,000 lines per minute). Even at this high speed the quality is exceptional. The major disadvantage of laser printers, to date, is the high cost. In the next few years this cost should decline swiftly, making laser printers the dominant printer technology where medium- to high-volume printing is required.

Table 3.1 *Some Printer Technologies*

Mechanism[1]	Quality[2]	Graphics?	Speed[3]	Reliability	Cost ($)
Impact					
Typewriter	Letter	N	15 cps	Medium	200–2,000
Daisy-wheel	Letter	N	15–70 cps	Low	500–2,000
Dot matrix	Draft/Correspond	Y	125–300 cps	Low	300–700
Chain/drum	Report	N	300–3,000 lpm	High	10K–100K
Nonimpact					
Thermal	Draft	N	30–120 cps	Low	20–200
Ink-jet	Correspond	Y	300 cps	Medium	200–2,000
Laser (micro)	Typeset (300 dpi)	Y	500–600 lpm	High	3,000
Laser (main)	Typeset (1,000 dpi)	Y	18K–21K lpm	High	50K–300K

[1]*Impact* implies noisy, multiple copies, few fonts, limited graphics. *Nonimpact* implies quiet, single-copy, many fonts, versatile graphics.
[2]Draft = draft quality
Report = report quality
Correspond = correspondence quality
Letter = letter quality
Typeset = typeset quality
dpi = dots per inch
Draft and report quality are worse than correspondence quality; next is letter quality, followed by typeset quality.
[3]cps = characters/second
lpm = lines/minute
1,500,000 cps = 20,000 lpm = 300 pages/minute

Since laser printers are nonimpact, they are limited to printing single copies. However, they are fast enough that multiple copies can be made from multiple print runs instead of from carbon copies.

Table 3.1 summarizes printer technology. Impact printers are currently the most cost effective and versatile. However, they are not the most reliable, and they are limited by the laws of physics to modest print speeds.

The future of printing is in nonimpact technologies. Ink-jet printers will perhaps take over the low-cost end of the spectrum, while laser printer technology may dominate the upper end. For all, the goal is to produce typeset-quality output quietly while increasing speed and reliability.

Displays

The cheapest **visual display unit** is a surplus television that has been pressed into service as part of a home computer system. The computer is attached to an RF modulator that also hooks up to the television's antenna leads. The **RF modulator** converts (modulates) the computer's video signal into the **r**adio **f**requency of a television channel. This arrangement works, but not well.

Television sets were not designed to display text; they cannot display 80 readable characters per line.

If price is not an overriding concern, a video monitor is used instead of a television. A **monitor** is basically a high-resolution television set that has been stripped of the speaker, channel selector, and radio-frequency receiver.

Both televisions and monitors generate images by bombarding the end of a phosphor-coated glass tube with electrons. The beam of electrons is created by an electron gun known as a *cathode;* hence monitors are often called **cathode ray tubes** or **CRTs.** Dots and lines are created by turning the electron beam on and off as it sweeps across the surface of the screen. Thus the image you see is actually a mosaic of glowing spots caused by bombarding a thin layer of phosphors with electrons. To keep a constant image on the screen, the electron beam must redraw the image on the screen 15 to 30 times a second, refreshing the quickly fading phosphors.

Raster Scan and Vector Graphics Displays

The image on a CRT screen can be generated in two radically different ways. In a **raster scan monitor** the electron beam moves horizontally back and forth across the screen, along what are called *scan lines* (see Figure 3.15). In a **vector graphics monitor** the electron beam is not limited to traveling along scan lines; instead it works by drawing straight lines from point to point.

Figure 3.16(a) illustrates the vector graphics method. A circle is constructed by drawing a polygon. Each side of the polygon is a straight line (called a **vector**). If three sides are drawn, the result is a triangle; if more straight lines are drawn, an 8-sided or 16-sided polygon is produced. If hundreds of very short straight lines are drawn, the polygon will look like a true circle.

Now look at the approximations of a circle shown in Figure 3.16(b); they illustrate the raster scan method. Each box in Figure 3.16(b) represents one position on the screen and is called a **pixel** (an abbreviation of **pic**ture **el**ement). The raster scan method approximates the circle, not by a collection of straight lines, but by filling in certain pixels. A low-resolution approximation is ob-

Figure 3.15 *Color and monochrome raster scan CRTs.*

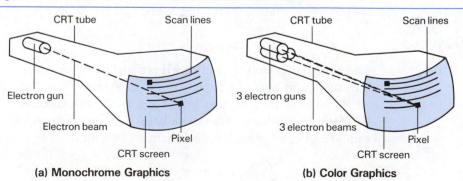

(a) Monochrome Graphics   **(b) Color Graphics**

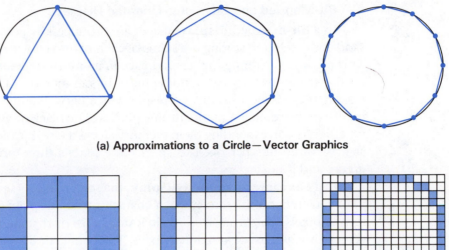

(a) Approximations to a Circle—Vector Graphics

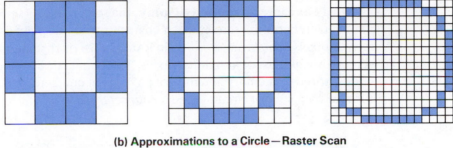

(b) Approximations to a Circle—Raster Scan

Figure 3.16 *Vector graphics and raster scan displays.*

tained by filling in a few large pixels. High-resolution images are obtained by filling in a large number of very small pixels.

The **resolution** of a picture is a measure of the accuracy of the graphical reproduction. In a raster scan monitor the resolution is determined by the number of horizontal rows and vertical columns of pixels. A 640-by-320-pixel monitor has 640 pixels along each scan line and 320 scan lines from the top to the bottom of the screen. The ratio of horizontal-to-vertical pixels is called the **aspect ratio** of the monitor and determines the shape of each pixel. If the aspect ratio is not 1, circles and diagonal lines may be distorted.

Vector graphics monitors produce extremely accurate line drawings. Because it takes more time for the electron gun to draw vectors than to scan the screen horizontally in a fixed pattern, vector graphics monitors are not good at filling in areas of the screen. As a result, an image with many dense objects will cause the screen to flicker noticeably. Vector graphics monitors are used in applications requiring a high-quality graphical display, such as computer-aided design and drafting.

Raster scan monitors are less expensive and far more common than vector graphics monitors. All television and personal computers use raster scan technology.

Before an image can be displayed on a screen, it must be stored in RAM. We will look briefly at two ways of coding and storing this image for raster scan monitors: bit-mapped and character-oriented.

Bit-Mapped and Character-Oriented Displays

In a **bit-mapped display** images are produced by coloring each of thousands of pixels and storing the status of each pixel as one or more bits in RAM. This method of storing the screen image in memory is quite simple; each pixel on the screen has a corresponding bit or bits in memory. For a monochrome display there is a one-to-one correspondence between bits in the bit-map and pixels on the screen. A monochrome pixel will be black or white depending on whether its corresponding bit in memory stores a 0 or 1. Color displays require at least three bits per pixel to specify the pixel's three primary colors: red, green, and blue.

In a **character-oriented display,** the screen image is produced by drawing characters on the screen. Each character to be displayed is assigned a pattern of pixels. The image is stored in RAM as a list of characters to appear on the screen, not as a list of individual pixels. The conversion between the character codes stored in memory and the dot patterns of characters on the screen is performed by a special circuit called a *character generator.*

Table 3.2 *The IBM Personal Computer Character Set*

DECIMAL VALUE → / ↓ HEXADECIMAL VALUE	0 / 0	16 / 1	32 / 2	48 / 3	64 / 4	80 / 5	96 / 6	112 / 7	128 / 8	144 / 9	160 / A	176 / B	192 / D	208 / C	224 / E	240 / F
0 / 0	BLANK (NULL)	►	BLANK (SPACE)	0	@	P	`	p	Ç	É	á	¼ Dots On	⌐	⊥	∝	≡
1 / 1	☺	◄	!	1	A	Q	a	q	ü	Æ	í	½ Dots On	├	┤	β	±
2 / 2	☻	↕	"	2	B	R	b	r	é	FE	ó	¾ Dots On	┬		γ	≥
3 / 3	♥	‼	#	3	C	S	c	s	â	ô	ú		┴		π	≤
4 / 4	♦	¶	$	4	D	T	d	t	ä	ö	ñ		┘		Σ	∫
5 / 5	♣	§	%	5	E	U	e	u	à	ò	Ñ		┤		σ	∫
6 / 6	♠	▬	&	6	F	V	f	v	å	û	ª		├		µ	÷
7 / 7	•	↨	'	7	G	W	g	w	ç	ù	º		┤		τ	≈
8 / 8	◘	↑	(	8	H	X	h	x	ê	ÿ	¿		┤		Φ	°
9 / 9	○	↓	)	9	I	Y	i	y	ë	Ö	⌐		┤		Θ	•
10 / A	◙	→	*	:	J	Z	j	z	è	Ü	¬		┴		Ω	·
11 / B	♂	←	+	;	K	[	k	{	ï	¢	½		(black)		δ	√
12 / C	♀	∟	,	<	L	\	l	|	î	£	¼		(black)		∞	η
13 / D	♪	↔	–	=	M	]	m	}	ì	¥	¡				∅	²
14 / E	♫	▲	.	>	N	^	n	~	Ä	Pts	«				∈	■
15 / F	☼	▼	/	?	O	_	o	△	Å	ƒ	»		(black)		∩	BLANK 'FF'

Reprinted from the IBM Technical Reference Manual, courtesy IBM Corporation.

A character-oriented display is nowhere near as flexible as a bit-mapped display, for two reasons. First, only a limited set of characters can be displayed, usually less than 256 (see Table 3.2). So there is not likely to be, for example, a character that looks like the mirror image of a question mark. Second, each character must appear in a fixed position on the screen. With a character-oriented display you cannot shift a letter half of a column position left or right.

The difference between these two coding schemes has important implications for the amount of memory that is required to store a screen image. In most character-oriented systems, each character takes two bytes to store: one byte specifies which symbol should appear in each character position and the other determines the character's display attributes, such as its color or whether it should blink on and off. Thus a 25-line-by-80-column screen requires $25 \times 80 \times 2 = 4{,}000$ bytes of storage space. In contrast, a 640-by-320 pixel color display requires $640 \times 320 \times 3 = 614{,}400$ pixels or 76,800 bytes to store an entire screen. In short, character-oriented displays require far less memory than bit-mapped displays.

Some computers can generate either a bit-mapped or a character-oriented display. This allows them to store images in the bit-mapped format of graphics programs and to save memory space by storing images in a character-oriented format for text-based programs.

Most character-oriented terminals store their character patterns in ROM, so you cannot change the font or size of text unless you modify the hardware. For this reason, many personal computers allow the character patterns to be stored in RAM where they can be changed by a running program. The Macintosh, for example, has its character generator take its character patterns from RAM, so it can change fonts and character sets in midstream.

Liquid Crystal Displays

Briefcase-sized computers that run on batteries cannot afford the size or power required for a CRT display. Instead, like digital watches, they often use a liquid crystal display (see Figure 3.17). A **liquid crystal display (LCD)** is a flat panel rather than a bulky tube—an excellent shape for portable or light-weight computers.

An LCD does not generate any light itself; rather it depends on reflected light. It has a liquid crystal material and a grid of wires sandwiched between two sheets of polarizing glass. When current is passed between crossing wires, the crystals shift position, rendering the liquid opaque. The pattern of dark-and-light produces the image of a character. This works well in some light conditions and poorly in others.

Qualities of a Good Display

A good-quality monitor is very important. No one wants to spend hours peering into a screen filled with blurry characters. Many factors influence a monitor's readability, including

Figure 3.17 *This notebook-sized computer has an 8-line by 40-column liquid crystal display (240 by 64 pixels).*

■ the monitor's color. The phosphors in a **monochrome monitor** glow in only one color. The two most popular colors for monochrome monitors are light green, followed by amber. Endless debates occur over which color is best. The Apple Corporation broke with tradition by choosing a black and white monitor for their Macintosh computer. **Color monitors** break each pixel into three dots: red, green, and blue. Color monitors create excellent graphics, but their characters are not quite as readable as those on monochrome monitors because the extra dots per pixel make each pixel fuzzier.

■ the resolution of the screen. Resolution is measured horizontally and vertically. The number of scan lines determines the vertical resolution; the number of pixels along each scan line sets the horizontal resolution.

■ the reflective properties of the screen. Glare from a light bulb is very annoying. Etched faceplates, mesh screens, or even a simple cardboard shade can be used to reduce unwanted reflections.

Plotters

A **plotter** is a printerlike output device that prints pictures rather than alphanumeric information. Most plotters use a stylus or pen to draw an image on paper (see Figure 3.18). A plotter is used instead of a graphical printer when high-resolution drawings are needed. For example, commercial *flat-bed plotters* can move 10,000 steps per inch. Such a machine is indispensable for drawing electronic circuits or making precise mechanical drawings.

Pen plotters are not well suited for filling areas in a drawing because they fill an image by drawing many lines side by side—a time-consuming process. *Photoplotters* do not have this problem because they use a light source (often a laser) to draw high-resolution images on photosensitive paper. A special-purpose photoplotter (called a *typesetter*) was used to typeset this book.

Other Output Devices

The most familiar output devices—printers, visual display units, and plotters—use the media of paper or monitors to produce some type of image as their output. If you wish to use some other media, chances are there is an output device that will do the job. For example, a **COM** (**c**omputer **o**utput **m**icrofilm) device records computer output on microfilm instead of paper. Vast amounts of information can be compactly stored on microfilm. If you need presentation-quality slides, special cameras and slide makers are available that connect to the display screen of a personal computer or take pictorial information directly from memory and produce developable film. Making presentation-quality slides with these devices is as easy as taking a picture with your Polaroid.

In theory at least, just about anything—even entire factories—can be hooked up to a computer and become an output device. For example, most paper products such as paper plates, tissue paper, cups, and paper towels are

Figure 3.18 *A plotter converts graphical information into hard copy.*

made automatically by computer-controlled machines. The computer senses temperature, moisture, and other characteristics of the pulp and directs the machinery during the paper-making process.

■ Interfaces

Every input, output, and external storage device in a computer system must have its own electrical circuitry, or **interface,** linking it to the CPU. The interface may conform to the specifications for a standard interface, or it may be a custom interface like the one required to support a special-purpose device such as a video disk player (see Figure 3.19).

A standard interface, which is often called an **I/O Port,** makes it easy and reliable to connect pieces of equipment that adhere to the standard (see Figure 3.20). The best-known standard interface is the **RS-232 serial port.** This standard defines the timing and other electrical properties of an interface used to connect computers to telephones, mice, printers, and other serial devices. A *serial device* is any I/O device that communicates by sending or receiving a string of bits one after the other through one data line. A *parallel device,* in contrast, sends or receives information in packets all at once over many (usually eight) data lines. The industry standard for parallel interfaces is the **Centronix parallel interface** developed by the Centronix Corporation and used by many

Figure 3.19 *Video disk players combined with personal computers are being used increasingly in education and training.*

Figure 3.20 *Devices can be connected to standard I/O ports by plugging cables into the back of your personal computer.*

other manufacturers. Parallel interfaces can send and receive data faster than serial interfaces because they send more bits in each time segment, but both the RS-232 and the Centronix interface will work faster than character printers or typical modems.

Because large computer systems require much higher performance than personal computers, they use channels instead of standard interfaces to connect I/O devices to the CPU. A **channel** is actually a special-purpose computer that handles I/O for the general-purpose mainframe. Many devices can be attached to a channel, including printers, plotters, and terminals. A *daisy-chain* channel is one in which many devices are connected like pearls in a necklace. Information is sent along the daisy chain to be picked off by the destination device.

The equivalent of a channel in a personal computer is the slot, as shown in Figure 3.21. A **slot** is a connector inside your computer where a custom interface or adapter card can be plugged into your system. An **adapter card** is a circuit board that contains special I/O interface circuits; for example, a color graphics adapter. A **combination card** integrates many functions on a single card. For example, one combination card might include extra RAM, serial and parallel ports, and a system clock; another might include a hard disk adapter or color graphics adapter along with extra RAM. Slots are also used to extend the hardware by adding extra main memory, more disk drives, modems, and so forth.

Reliable, universal interfaces take a long time to develop, and the personal computer field is still quite young. Although it is safe to assume that any shaver or mixer will work with your home's electrical system, it is best to be cautious when buying or using computer peripherals. Before you make a purchase, be sure that the devices have compatible connectors, interfaces, and transmission speeds.

Figure 3.21 *Adapter cards are plugged into slots inside your personal computer. These cards provide standard and nonstandard connections to your computer.*

■ Summary

We have surveyed only a few of the major input and output devices available; there are many more. The keyboard is the most common input unit, although voice recognition devices should become practical in the near future. Printers and visual display units are the most common output units. Most of the input and output devices for personal computers are smaller versions of those found on mainframe computers.

To use a computer you do not need a detailed understanding of its parts, just as you don't need to know how the parts of a car work before learning to drive. But you do need a basic understanding of how the functional units fit together and what they do. Carefully choosing the right I/O device is just as important as selecting the right computer. So keep in mind ease of use, speed, cost, versatility, quality, and reliability when you select I/O devices.

Key Terms

adapter card	cathode ray tube (CRT)
aspect ratio	Centronix parallel interface
bar code	channel
batch input	character-oriented display
bit-mapped display	characters per second (cps)

chiclet keyboard
combination card
compact keyboards
control key
cursor
cursor-movement keys
daisy-wheel printer
dot matrix printer
dots per inch (dpi)
function keys
interactive system
interface
I/O port
letter-quality printer
light pen
line printer
liquid crystal display (LCD)
membrane keyboard

monitor: monochrome, color
mouse
on-line, off-line
page printer
pixel
plotter
puck
repeating keys
resolution
RF modulator
RS-232 serial port
slot
sonic pen
source data automation
touch screen
touch-tablet
visual display unit

Discussion Questions

1. Can information be sent directly from an input device such as a keyboard to an output device such as a printer?

2. Which peripheral devices are strictly for output? Which are strictly for input? Which perform both input and output functions?

3. Other than speed, what characteristics would you use in comparing printers? Rank these in importance. Is speed the most important?

4. Suppose that speech recognition devices are perfected for personal computers and are quite inexpensive. What effect would this have on the use of personal computers in business, education, or elsewhere? Would the impact be different if the devices were expensive?

5. Personal computers offer great potential for handicapped persons. For various handicaps, such as blindness, describe the special input and output devices that would enable a person with the handicap to use a personal computer.

6. How does the QWERTY keyboard slow a typist down? Does this suggest another type of keyboard? How should this new keyboard be introduced?

7. What is meant by the term *letter-quality printing?* Can a dot matrix printer produce letter-quality printing? If so, how small would each dot have to be?

8. A touch screen has limited accuracy. What devices would allow you to point to an individual pixel, such as the dot in the letter *i*?

9. A plotter can draw much as you might draw on a pad of paper. Considering that most printers cannot back up to a previously printed line, discuss how a plotter might operate differently from a printer.

10. An RS-232 interface is used for serial communication whereas a Centronix interface is used for parallel communication. Which does your computer use to communicate with your printer?

11. An impact printer can be used with multiple carbon-copy paper to make several copies of the same report. Can an ink-jet printer make multiple copies using carbon-copy paper? Why not?

12. If a computer could fully understand spoken commands, why would it still be necessary to have bar code readers, POS terminals, and other types of input devices?

13. What are some of the things a mouse might be used to point at on the screen of a personal computer?

14. What is a computer interface? Why would you need to know what kind of interface your computer uses?

15. Why would anyone use a plotter if they also had a graphics printer?

16. Why are there so many different ways to enter information into a computer?

Exercises

1. Determine how long it would take to print a 15-page report on a letter-quality printer at 30 cps and on a dot matrix printer at 150 cps.

2. If a 9"-by-9" touch screen can only resolve the end of a 1/4"-by-1/4" finger, how many "points" can be located on the screen with a standard finger?

3. Printers are rated according to their speed. If a typical printer for a personal computer can print 120 characters per second, how long will it take to print the contents of a page containing 66 lines of 80 characters each? Assume the speed rating does not include the time for a carriage return. What effect does this have on the actual time it takes to print the page?

4. A notebook-sized computer usually has a small liquid crystal screen. Figure 3.17 shows a 240-by-64-pixel screen. If this screen displays 8 lines, each with up to 40 characters per line, what is the size of the dot matrix for each character? Keep in mind that at least one dot is needed to separate a line or a character.

using
software

4

The best way to learn about computing is to use a computer. In this chapter we describe what you need to know about software in order to begin computing. Later chapters delve into specific applications. What is important now is to get an overall idea of how the programs in a computer system work together and to learn how to perform essential tasks such as running programs and managing files. If you use a personal computer, you should also know how to perform maintenance operations such as formatting and backing-up disks. To use a mini or mainframe computer you must know how to log on and off the computer.

In the first section of the chapter we describe how the parts of the operating system work together to control the computer system. This part describes how the operating system schedules the tasks to be done, controls interactions with peripheral devices, manages main memory and the storage of files, and provides other useful services. In the next two sections we explain how you accomplish the most frequently performed tasks by giving commands either by typing on the keyboard or by using a pointing device, such as a mouse. Even though you might use just one of these systems, you should study both. The contrast helps illustrate the difference between form and function in computer programs. In the last section we discuss application software—the programs that direct a computer to perform specific activities such as writing a letter, playing Space Invaders, or printing paychecks.

■ Operating Systems

An *operating system* is a set of control programs that govern the operation of a computer. Whenever the computer is running, the operating system is present and provides the computer with the ability to manage automatically the use of its memory, interact with peripheral devices, and execute application programs.

In our discussion of operating systems we will give examples from two specific systems: the Macintosh operating system and **PC-DOS** (**P**ersonal **C**omputer-**D**isk **O**perating **S**ystem). The Macintosh operating system is a proprietary operating system developed by Apple and is available only for the Macintosh and its predecessor, the Lisa computer. PC-DOS is IBM's name for its single-user operating system for the IBM PC family of personal computers. Actually, PC-DOS is a slightly modified version of MS-DOS, an operating system owned and licensed by Microsoft to scores of personal computer manufacturers, including IBM. Together, PC-DOS and MS-DOS are the dominant operating systems for 16-bit microcomputers.

The Macintosh operating system and PC-DOS have fundamentally different user interfaces. PC-DOS is a **command-line operating system;** commands are given by typing a line, such as TYPE LETTER.JIM. Command-line operating systems are by far the most common type of operating systems for all types of computers—micro, mini, and mainframe. Whereas command-line systems accept commands from the keyboard, the **visual operating system** used by the Macintosh accepts commands from a mouse. The commands are given by moving or selecting pictures (called *icons*) and items from menus. Thus a visual operating system is said to use a **visual interface** between the computer and the user. In contrast, command-line systems use a **textual interface.**

Operating System Compatibility

Like most actively supported software, PC-DOS is revised about once a year on an entirely unpredictable schedule. Each revision adds new features or removes old **bugs**—program errors or design flaws. For each revision the operating system is given a new version number. The number indicates how extensive each revision is. For example, relatively minor changes were made from PC-DOS 1.0 to PC-DOS 1.1. But PC-DOS 2.0 had many new features, including hierarchical file directories and support for a hard disk.

All of the versions of PC-DOS are **upward compatible;** in other words, you can upgrade your operating system to the newest version and still use most of the application software written for the older versions. Without upward compatibility, using the new version of the operating system would require buying a whole new set of application software.

For large data processing centers the cost of modifying their software to use a new, upwardly incompatible operating system can be enormous. More than a trillion dollars have been spent developing programs to run on the IBM 360 series of mainframe computers and its successors. The desire to avoid converting their software locks established data processing organizations into one brand of computers.

Operating systems vary widely in their size and complexity. Early 8-bit personal computers such as the Apple II were limited to 64KB of memory. Every extra byte in the operating system meant there was less room for the application program and data; so operating systems for these microcomputers provided only the bare essentials for controlling the computer. Because memory is less constrained in 16- and 32-bit machines, their operating systems provide a wider range of functions and more convenience. Still, the operating systems for most personal computers are quite crude by the standards of mainframe computers, which use operating systems that occupy megabytes of memory and generally have very sophisticated support for executing concurrent programs, allocating memory, and managing large databases.

Major Components

Although the parts of an operating system vary, all operating systems have components functioning as a (1) supervisor, (2) input/output manager, (3) file manager, and (4) command processor. You don't have to know how these parts work to use a computer, just as you don't have to know how an engine works to drive a car. But learning what these four basic parts of the operating system do will give you the background necessary to use it with more authority and less confusion.

Supervisor

At the heart of all operating systems is the **supervisor,** or *kernel;* it schedules and coordinates the activities of other programs. Think of the supervisor as a traffic cop who signals when each activity is permitted to take place. Whenever a computer is running, its supervisor is loaded in internal memory, directing and controlling.

The supervisor in a mainframe computer's operating system is much more complex than in a single-user system. Because mainframe computers can have more than a thousand concurrent users, their supervisors must allocate brief time slices to each user, a process known as *timesharing.* The supervisor in a multiuser computer must also record who is using which computer resources so that users can be billed accurately for services. Finally, the supervisor must ensure that one user's programs cannot affect another user's programs or data.

Input/Output (I/O) Manager

In general, all data transferred to and from peripheral devices is filtered through the **I/O manager.** It insulates the rest of the programs in the computer system from the peculiarities of the peripheral devices. For example, on a personal computer the I/O manager might translate the keyboard's character codes into the coding system used by the rest of the computer. On a mainframe computer the I/O manager might translate the ASCII character codes (described in Chapter 2) that are generated by many terminals into the EBCDIC character codes used for internal processing.

With a good operating system, it is possible to add a hard disk or a faster printer to the computer system just by modifying the I/O manager—without making any changes to other software. This characteristic is called **device independence.** The software that tells the I/O manager how the new hardware functions is called a **device driver** and is usually provided free by the vendor of the add-on device as a way to promote sales.

An even stronger form of hardware independence, called **machine independence,** allows application software to be moved from one member of a family of computers to another without programming changes. This can make it possible to replace a small mainframe computer with a larger one overnight so long as both computers use the same operating system. For example, most IBM mainframe computers can be interchanged in this way.

File Manager

Everything on disk is stored in a file. Each file has its own name and stores one type of information—for example, a program or data. A data file might contain text for a last will and testament, a recipe for banana bread, or a digitized picture. A program file might be a BASIC program, a utility for copying a disk, or a word processor.

Whatever the contents of a file, the **file manager** is responsible for saving, deleting, copying, loading, naming, and renaming files. The file manager also provides in effect a translation between our *logical* view of the file—the file name and the type of data it stores—and the *physical* arrangement of data on disk. As we saw in Chapter 2, data on a disk is grouped into sectors, with each sector forming part of a track. The file manager provides this translation from file names to storage locations by maintaining a directory in a special file on the outside edge of each disk. Recall that the *directory* (also called a **file allocation table**) is an index giving the name and storage locations of each file. Many file managers allow files to be grouped together in a hierarchical manner by setting up subdirectories. A *root directory* provides an index listing the names of files and other subdirectories.

Suppose the file manager is asked to copy 2,400 bytes from main memory to create a new file named BASEBALL.BAT on a disk with 512 bytes in each sector. Although the exact procedure for storing a file varies somewhat from one operating system to another, in general the file manager must

- examine the disk's directory files to find five unused sectors.
- modify the appropriate directory file to include an entry for the new file and list the sectors it occupies.
- tell the I/O manager to copy the data file from main memory onto the five previously unused disk sectors.

Command Processor

The **command processor** (also called a **shell**) communicates between the user and the rest of the operating system. It accepts commands from the user, makes sure they are valid, and then takes the appropriate action. For example, if you ask the computer to copy BASEBALL.BAT and call the new file GOLF.TEE, the shell will translate the command and relay the request to the file manager. If the disk doesn't have enough room to store GOLF.TEE, then the file manager sends a coded error message, which the shell might translate to read: INSUFFICIENT FREE SPACE ON DISK—COMMAND ABORTED.

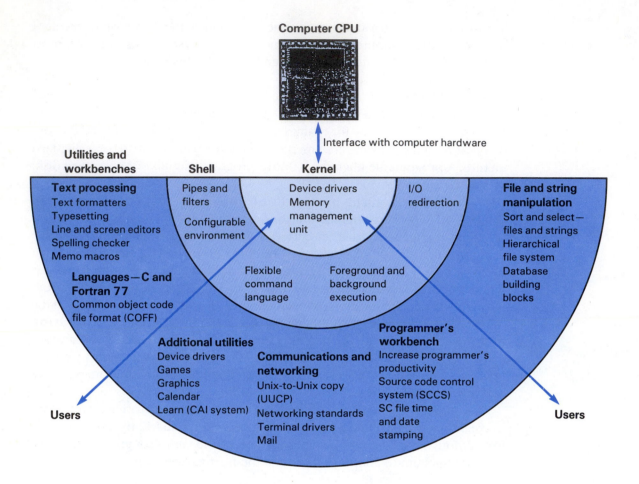

Computer CPU

Interface with computer hardware

Utilities and workbenches	Shell	Kernel	

Text processing
Text formatters
Typesetting
Line and screen editors
Spelling checker
Memo macros

Pipes and filters

Configurable environment

Device drivers
Memory management unit

I/O redirection

File and string manipulation
Sort and select—
files and strings
Hierarchical
file system
Database
building
blocks

Languages—C and Fortran 77
Common object code
file format (COFF)

Flexible command language

Foreground and background execution

Programmer's workbench
Increase programmer's productivity
Source code control system (SCCS)
SC file time and date stamping

Additional utilities
Device drivers
Games
Graphics
Calendar
Learn (CAI system)

Communications and networking
Unix-to-Unix copy (UUCP)
Networking standards
Terminal drivers
Mail

Users

Users

The multiuser, multitasking Unix operating system from Bell Labs is a layered system. The *kernel* interfaces directly to the computer's central processing unit (a microprocessor chip, in the case of supermicros) and is modified to run on different CPUs and to alter hardware-related operations such as memory management. Because Unix is written in C, a high-level language, it is less hardware-dependent than operating systems written in lower-level machine language. This trait makes Unix easy to transport from one system to another. Surrounding the kernel is the *shell,* which serves as a programming language and as a command language interpreter, reading lines typed by the user and interpreting them as requests to execute certain programs. Around the shell are various *utilities* and *workbenches* such as text processing and support for the C and Fortran 77 languages. Some parts of Unix, such as the *programmer's workbench,* which helps software developers, aren't required by all users and are sometimes dropped in Unix-derived systems sold by companies that license the operating system. These firms also modify parts of Unix to meet different requirements. The kernel might be changed to run on different chips, for instance, or menus might be added to help novice users interact with Unix.

—Reprinted with permission, *High Technology* magazine, December 1983. Copyright © 1983 by High Technology Publishing Company, 38 Commercial Wharf, Boston, Mass. 02110.

Figure 4.1 *The Unix operating system.*

Figure 4.1 gives a rather technical description of how the Unix operating system shell acts as an intermediary between users and the kernel or command processor of the operating system. The Unix operating system was developed by Bell Laboratories and is available on a wide variety of micros, minis, and mainframes.

Many operating systems have more than one shell available for different types of users. For example, programmers might prefer to use a shell with a command-line interface, whereas casual users might choose to use a shell with a visual interface. From a technical viewpoint, building a shell for an existing operating system is nowhere near as difficult as building a new operating system from scratch.

Sometime during a computer session you are bound to say to yourself, "I have typed this series of operating system commands over and over again." Perhaps you must make a back-up copy of a file with one command before you start word processing with another. This repetition can be avoided if your operating system's shell allows you to establish batch files. A **batch file** is simply a file that contains a series (or batch) of operating system commands. For example, you might build a batch file containing one command to back-up the file and another to start word processing. Then you can accomplish the work of two commands with a single command that tells the shell to begin executing the batch file. The shell will take commands one at a time from the batch file and execute them.

Mainframe operating systems generally provide extensive features for building complicated batch files. Collectively these features are known as a **job control language (JCL).** Programmers use job control languages to link application programs to run one after another. A full-featured job control language can make an otherwise unfriendly operating system seem reasonable to casual users because the obnoxious commands can all be hidden inside batch files.

Memory Management

In some portable computers the entire operating system is permanently stored in ROM; but on most computers the operating system is too large to fit into main memory at once. Instead, the operating system is broken into two parts, the resident portion and a set of transient utility programs.

The **resident** part of the operating system is loaded into memory as soon as the computer is turned on, a process called *booting* the computer. The resident part always contains the essential routines for controlling the computer and its peripherals and may contain some frills as well. The essentials are the operating system supervisor, the I/O manager, and at least some of the file manager.

The **transient utility programs** remain on disk until one of the programs is requested. Then the requested program is transferred into memory.

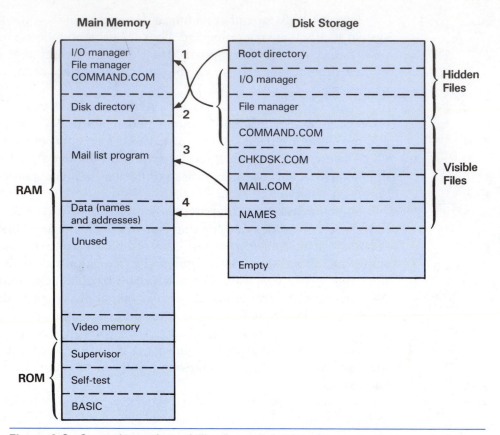

Main Memory   **Disk Storage**

RAM

ROM

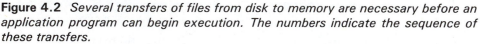

Figure 4.2 *Several transfers of files from disk to memory are necessary before an application program can begin execution. The numbers indicate the sequence of these transfers.*

Commands that are resident in one operating system may be transient utilities in another; the choice is made by the operating system designer, not by the user. If a command for a transient utility is given when the computer cannot find that utility program on the disk, an error message is displayed, or, on a personal computer, a request for the system disk is made.

The way an operating system manages memory is best illustrated with a specific example. We will describe how PC-DOS manages a computer session in which a program for a mailing list prints names and addresses onto mailing labels. Figure 4.2 shows how main memory and the disk files might be laid out for this application. On the disk

- the three hidden files contain the disk's root directory and the file and I/O managers of the operating system. A *hidden file* is the same as any other file except that its name doesn't appear in directory listings of file names.

- COMMAND.COM contains the operating system command processor.

- CHKDSK.COM contains the transient utility program that implements the CHKDSK command.
- MAIL.COM contains the mailing list application program.
- NAMES contains the data file of names and addresses to be printed.

Before the machine is turned on, main memory is blank except for programs stored in ROM. In an IBM PC, ROM contains the operating system supervisor, some self-test programs, and a truncated version of Microsoft BASIC. When the computer is turned on, it immediately looks for a **system disk** (a disk containing the operating system). If the system disk is not found, generally the computer responds with an error message and waits. Programs must be in memory before they can be executed. Thus, four transfers from disk to memory are necessary before the mailing list program can print the mailing labels (see Figure 4.2).

1. Loading the I/O manager, the file manager, and the command processor (COMMAND.COM) into memory. This is done by switching on the computer, which activates instructions in ROM that load the resident portion of the operating system from the disk.

2. Loading a copy of the disk's directory into memory. This allows the computer to read files from the disk faster. At this point the operating system displays a prompt, signifying it is ready for a command.

3. Loading the mailing list program into memory. You do this by typing MAIL NAMES. This command not only tells the operating system to load MAIL.COM into memory but also tells the mailing list program to use the data file NAMES.

4. Transferring names and addresses from NAMES to memory. MAIL.COM carries out this process, formats the names and addresses to look good on mailing labels, and sends them to the printer.

In this example you had to give only one command to begin running the application program because the disk had been conveniently configured to store all the programs and data necessary for the application. The movements of data between disk and memory are vastly more complicated in a timeshared operating system with virtual memory. (Recall that a virtual memory operating system automatically moves parts of a program from external to main memory and makes the computer look as if it had an unlimited amount of main memory.) Fortunately the increased complexity in memory management is well concealed from the user.

■ Using a Command-Line Operating System

When you begin using a computer, you will find that the tasks you perform most frequently are

- running an application program.
- copying and deleting files, and other file operations.
- formatting new disks, backing-up disks, setting the system clock, logging on and off, and other maintenance tasks.

In this section we will explain how to perform these operations on a computer that has a command-line operating system. Although specific commands vary from one command-line operating system to the next, the general approach is fairly standardized.

Command-line interfaces are not easy for beginners to use, because the user must remember commands and type them exactly. The computer prompts a command by displaying a character like ? or A > . Each command is typed on a new line. It begins with a **keyword,** which is usually a verb such as TYPE, MOVE, or KILL. Normally a keyword is followed by one or more **parameters** (also called **arguments**) telling the keyword what to do. A parameter can be a file name, but it might be a number specifying how fast to send characters to the printer. A keyword and its parameters must be separated by a **delimiter,** generally a space or comma, to indicate where one part of the command ends and the next part begins. For example, in the command COPY DATA.OLD DATA.NEW, the keyword is COPY, the two delimiters are the blank spaces, and the parameters are the file names DATA.OLD and DATA.NEW. The number and type of parameters varies depending on the keyword and the action desired.

Running a Program

Becoming proficient with PC-DOS takes time and practice. Each command begins either with the name of a program file or with a keyword. If it begins with a program file name, then the operating system loads the program file into memory and begins executing the program. For example, to execute a word processing program stored on disk as the file WORD.COM, you type WORD and enter the command by pressing the carriage-return key, marked [↵].

If the command begins with a keyword, then the operating system executes the command. For example, if you type TYPE LETTER.JIM, the file named LETTER.JIM is displayed on the screen. After completing the command, the operating system shows that it is ready for the next command by displaying a *prompt,* such as B > or A > . Incorrectly typed commands elicit the error message BAD COMMAND OR FILENAME, followed by another prompt.

Besides acknowledging that the computer is ready for the next command, the prompt designates the default drive. The **default** drive is the drive that PC-DOS searches to find a file if it is not told explicitly where the file is stored. If the prompt is A > , for example, then PC-DOS will search drive A to find the file named BASEBALL.BAT; but it will search drive B to find the file

Input:
Entering, Editing, and Sensing

To get useful results from a computer, you must first enter data into it. You might want to enter text, edit a computerized drawing, or have the computer automatically record data from a scientific experiment. Regardless of the task at hand, you will need an input device. If you have the right input device, the task will go smoothly or even effortlessly. The wrong device will make the entire computer system seem unfriendly. This photo essay illustrates how computers can collect data.

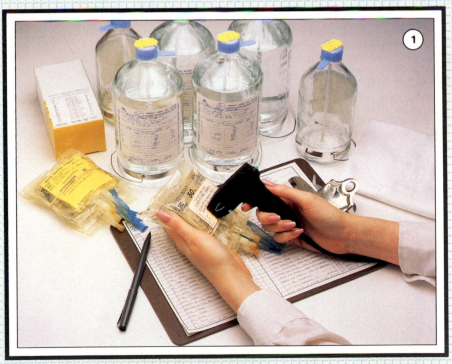

1. Inventory records of medical supplies need accurate and timely maintenance. This optical character reader makes the task as easy as passing a wand over a pre-printed label.

KEYBOARDS

2–5. Anywhere you find a computer—dorm room, classroom, computer center, or automobile service center—you are likely to find a keyboard. The keyboard is undoubtedly the most common input device. Because of the importance of computers in our society, touch-typing has become a very useful skill.

6. Even small portable computers have full-size keys to make touch-typing possible. Because the keyboard must be small on a portable computer, the number of keys is limited.

7. The IBM Personal Computer AT keyboard has two columns of function keys on the left. On the right is a numeric key pad that can also serve as a cursor-movement key pad.

8. The operator is entering data from checks with the help of a cash receipts program. The white text on the screen represents a computerized business form; only the green fields can be modified by the operator. Notice that the operator has entered the word *EASTON* in the customer number field, causing the computer to change the field's color to orange and display an error message on the bottom of the screen.

9. A typical data entry workstation. In the background is a Modular Composition System 8400 phototypesetter, the brand of typesetting machine that created the text you are reading.

window 4

SELECTION AND POINTING DEVICES

Steering wheels are standard equipment on cars; so you don't see cars with steering levers or joysticks. The computer industry has fewer standards than the automobile industry; so you can choose how you want to enter data into computers. You can use devices such as a joystick, trackball, light pen, touch screen, mouse, and graphics tablet to select and point.

10. This touch screen uses infrared emitters and sensors to determine where a finger or pencil is touching the screen. Here you see a screen image of a card file. Individual cards can be examined by pointing at their tags.

11. Although touch screens appear convenient, they have limitations. Fingers are blunt instruments that leave an oily film on the screen. You cannot see through your finger, and after a while, your arm is likely to complain about using a touch screen.

12. A mouse is a pointing device that relays directional information to the computer as it is dragged across a flat surface. It takes little practice to become a proficient mouse user. Generally, you move the mouse to point or draw; you click a button to select or initiate actions.

13. An enthusiastic mouse user.

GRAPHICAL DATA ENTRY

Graphics design requires specialized input devices that are capable of digitizing — or tracing — points that indicate the shape of the design.

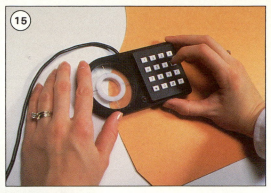

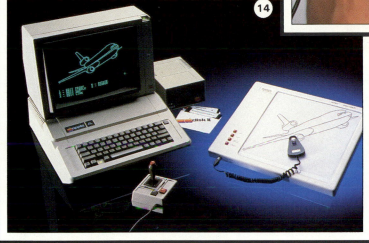

15. Designs can be digitized by placing the design on a graphics tablet and tracing it with the puck. The key pad on the puck is used to enter specific points and to issue commands.

14. A graphics design workstation. This system includes a joystick for positioning the cursor on the screen and a tablet with a hand-held puck for entering the outline of drawings.

16. A light pen can accurately sense where it touches a CRT screen. The upper and right edges of this screen represent an electronic key pad of commands. With a light pen you can quickly choose commands and draw on the body of the screen.

window 4

COMMERCIAL INPUT DEVICES

The market for commercial input devices is characterized by an extreme diversity of data collection equipment.

17. An automatic teller machine (ATM) dispenses cash and conducts banking transactions. Banks have been putting ATM units where the customers are—high-volume retail outlets, airports, and hotels.

18. A fully programmable, portable data collection terminal. With up to 256 kilobytes of memory for data storage, this battery-powered terminal is able to collect extensive amounts of data with its keyboard and optical wand reader. Through a built-in modem, the terminal can send and receive data over ordinary phone lines to a host computer. It is designed for uses such as auditing shelf prices or keeping records of a delivery route—applications that require sophisticated data management by a hand-held unit.

19. Laser-powered bar code readers are able to automatically scan bar codes from as close as three inches, or as far away as three feet.

20. Wherever the movement of products must be recorded quickly and accurately, hand-held optical character readers are useful. These devices help with inventory control in stores, libraries, and assembly lines.

21. This compact OCR makes short work of entering data from utility bills.

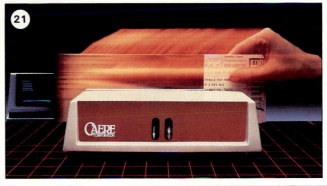

22. Membrane keyboards are inexpensive to manufacture and virtually indestructible. They perform well in harsh environments, such as restaurants where liquids might be spilled on them.

OTHER INPUT DEVICES

Anything that can be sensed electronically can become input to a computer.

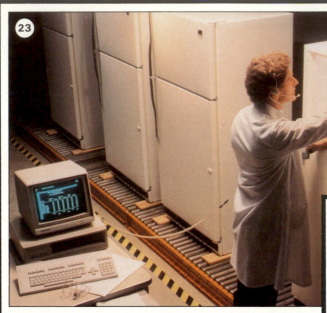

23. Voice input systems are frequently used in applications where the operator's hands are occupied with tasks other than data entry. These systems allow the computer to "listen" to a limited vocabulary of spoken words.

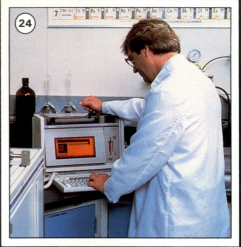

24. With the appropriate interface card, personal computers can accept data from laboratory instruments. The data can be stored for later analysis, allowing experiments to run unattended.

25. In the foreground is an optical character recognition reader. Because it can read the text on normal typed pages, it eliminates the need to enter documents manually into the computer system.

B:BASEBALL.BAT. You change the default drive by typing the letter of the new default drive followed by a colon. For example, if the original prompt is B > , then you type A: in order to change the default drive. As a result, the prompt is also changed to A > .

Most computer programs rely heavily on default values to reduce the amount of information that must be requested from the user. For example, the disk-formatting utility will, by default, make double-sided disks unless you specifically request single-sided disks.

File Names

In PC-DOS you must follow some rigid rules when you name a file. A file name contains two main parts: a *primary file name* containing one to eight characters and an optional *extension* with one, two, or three characters. For example, you might name three files JIM, INVENT.RPT, and FORMAT.COM. These files might contain a memo to Jim Martin, an inventory report, and the transient operating system utility that formats new disks.

One drawback of magnetic media is that people cannot sense magnetic signals directly and must rely on the computer system to report what a disk or tape contains. The short file names of PC-DOS don't help matters much: a file name like INVENT.RPT may not jog your memory about what is in the file six months after you created the file. This problem is exacerbated if you use a hard disk, because it can contain well over a thousand files.

Fortunately there are some standard conventions for naming files that make it easier to determine what is stored in each file. For example, one convention is that any file ending with the extension .COM is a machine language program. Some other conventions are

- .BAS contains a BASIC language program.
- .BAT is a batch file containing operating system commands.
- .DOC contains documentation—instructions about how to run or use a program.
- .EXE contains an executable program and is similar to a .COM file.
- .PAS contains a Pascal language program.
- .PIC contains a picture or graphics file.
- .SYS contains system parameters used to initialize a program.
- .TXT contains a text file.
- .WKS contains a worksheet created with the Lotus 1-2-3 program.

A complete file name includes two other parts that describe where the file is located. The first part of a complete file name is the name of the drive storing the file. Thus the file A:ELMER.GLU is stored on drive A. Disk drives arc named by single letters. On a two-drive floppy disk system the left-hand (or upper) drive is usually named A, and the right-hand (or lower) drive is named B.

The middle part of a complete file name identifies the subdirectories (if any) in which the file is located. Remember, a subdirectory is an index file that contains the names and locations of other files. For example, the file name C: \ LETTERS \ 1985 \ BIRTHDAY.MOM states that the BIRTHDAY.MOM file is stored inside the subdirectory named 1985, which in turn is located inside the subdirectory named LETTERS, all of which reside on drive C. In this example the C: \ LETTERS \ 1985 part of the file name is called a **path,** because it describes the route that must be followed to find the file. Subdirectories are particularly important on hard disk systems, because without them the root directory would contain all of the entries for the disk's files. Imagine trying to find a file in a root directory with over a thousand file names in it.

File Management

The most important file management operations are

- examining a root directory or subdirectory to see what files are in it.
- erasing files.
- copying files.

We will give examples of each of these operations.

Directory Information

Probably the most frequently used command is DIR. It extracts a list of file names, file sizes in bytes, and the times when files were created from a disk's default directory. Then it formats the list as a report and sends the report to the screen (see Figure 4.3). In all the PC-DOS examples in this chapter, characters typed by the user are **shown in color;** output generated by the computer is shown in black.

CHKDSK (check disk) is a nonresident PC-DOS disk-management utility command. It produces a report about the contents of a disk and the status of the memory. In Figure 4.4, the report shows that one of the authors' hard disk drives is about two-thirds full.

Deleting

Erasing files is straightforward. The command ERASE B:DRAWINGS.FEB deletes the file DRAWINGS.FEB from drive B. Actually, only the file name is deleted from the directories on the disk; the file's content is not affected until a subsequent operation causes another file to occupy its space. But because PC-DOS doesn't provide an UNERASE utility to cancel the deletion, the practical effect is the same as if the file were instantly and permanently erased.

```
C>DIR C:\

Volume in drive C is DISK-C
Directory of  C:\
COMMAND  COM    22042   8-14-84   8:00a
CONFIG   SYS       97  10-26-85   6:46p
AUTOEXEC BAT      128   1-23-85  11:09p
PROGRAMS      <DIR>      9-29-85   2:19p
SYMPHONY      <DIR>      9-29-85   3:35p
MSTOOLS       <DIR>      9-29-85   3:51p
TOPVIEW       <DIR>      9-29-85   3:54p
BACKUP        <DIR>     10-10-85   3:01p
        8 File(s)   7903232 bytes free

C>
```

← DIR is short for "directory."

← Volume means "disk" in PC-DOS.

← This reports the names and sizes of individual files.

← This reports the names of subdirectory files—that is, files that contain other files.

Figure 4.3 *DIR (directory). This example shows how to request a listing of the files in the root directory of disk drive C.*

Wild card characters are used to specify a category of items. For example, with the asterisk (*) you can indicate several files with just one specification. Thus, the command ERASE LETTERS.* erases every file on the default drive that has the primary file name LETTERS, regardless of the file extension (LETTERS.JIM, LETTERS.SUE, and so on).

Figure 4.4 *CHKDSK (check disk). This utility produces a short report about the contents of a disk (in this case a 22MB hard disk) and the amount of memory in the machine.*

```
C>CHKDSK
Volume DISK-C     created Mar 2, 1985  8:01p

22177792 bytes total disk space
  423936 bytes in 15 hidden files
   69632 bytes in 26 directories
13780992 bytes in 1030 user files
 7903232 bytes available on disk

  589824 bytes total memory
  393888 bytes free

C>
```

← CHKDSK is short for "check disk."

← The disk's name and when it was formatted.

← This reports on the types of disk files and their collective sizes.

← This indicates the amount of main memory (RAM) in the machine.

Copying

The COPY command makes copies of specific files. For example, the command COPY A:BASEBALL.BAT B:GOLF.TEE copies A:BASEBALL.BAT to drive B forming the file GOLF.TEE. Or, instead of copying one file at a time, you can copy many files with one COPY command by using a wild card character. For example, the command COPY B:*.DOC will take all the files on drive B that have the extension .DOC and copy them on the disk in the default drive.

Maintenance Tasks

The maintenance tasks you perform will depend on the type of computer system you use. On personal computers you must know how to format new disks and back-up used disks. On mainframe computers the operators are responsible for periodically backing-up disk files; so these operations don't concern most users. For mini and mainframe users it is essential to know how to log in and log off, but these operations have no counterpart on a single-user system. All of these tasks are important enough to warrant specific examples.

Formatting Disks

Formatting a disk (also called **initializing** a disk) involves erasing the disk and giving it an empty root-directory file. Disks come from the manufacturer in a blank, or unformatted, condition; files cannot be stored on an unformatted disk. Formatting should be approached with caution. A disk cannot be used until it has been formatted, but formatting a disk by mistake erases its contents completely. Formatting a hard disk by accident can be a major disaster if adequate back-up procedures have not been followed.

Figure 4.5 shows the dialog between the user and PC-DOS for disk formatting. The command line begins with the keyword FORMAT followed by

Figure 4.5 *Dialog of a sample formatting operation.*

```
B>FORMAT A:/S
Insert new diskette for drive A:
and strike any key when ready

Formatting...Format complete


    362496 bytes total disk space
     40960 bytes used by system
    321536 bytes available on disk

Format another (Y/N)?N
```

← PC-DOS prompts the user to make sure the correct disk is formatted.

← It takes about 40 seconds to format a disk.

← A standard PC-DOS double-sided disk has 40 tracks/side, 9 sectors/track, and 512 bytes/sector, or $2 \times 40 \times 9 \times 512 = 362,496$ bytes.

the argument A:/S. The A: specifies that the disk to be formatted will be in drive A. The /S is an option switch that tells the format program to initialize the new disk with a copy of the operating system, making it a system disk. **Option switches** are used to override default values. Other option switches for the FORMAT command are /1, to create a single-sided disk, and /V, to write an electronic name on the disk.

Backing-up Disks

It is an excellent idea to copy periodically disks that store letters, reports, spreadsheets, and other data files. Then, if a file is destroyed—either by accidental erasure or by mechanical failure—you will have a copy of the information on another disk. For very important information, such as business records, you should follow a regular schedule of making back-up disks. At least one set of back-up disks should be stored away from the computer.

Disks are copied with the DISKCOPY command, a nonresident utility. For example, the command DISKCOPY B: A: causes the operating system to ask for the disk that is being copied to be put in drive B and the target disk to be put in drive A. After receiving a confirmation from the keyboard that the correct disks are in the drives, a copy of the disk in drive B is written on the disk in drive A.

Many vendors of software for personal computers have decided to copy-protect the disks they sell in an attempt to prevent users from making unauthorized copies. A **copy-protected** disk is manufactured with an intentional defect that prevents a normal COPY or DISKCOPY utility from making copies of selected files. As a general rule, only program files are copy-protected. So even if you use copy-protected programs, you should make back-up copies of the data files you create.

Logging On and Logging Off

Before you begin working on a mini or mainframe computer, you must give a command to log on to the computer. **Logging on** identifies you as a valid user, assigns a job number to your computer session, and starts billing your account. Generally the log-on command requires a user name (or a user number), a password that corresponds to the user name, and possibly an account number. You should avoid showing or telling your password to others, because it is your private key that provides access to your account. The following example shows a typical log-on sequence for a Digital Equipment Corporation TOPS-20 operating system:

```
Carnegie-Mellon University TOPS-B, TOPS-20 Monitor 4(3352)-2
@LOGIN (USER) LEWIS
Password:                         ←LEWIS types in his
 Job 34 on TTY112 14-Jul-85 10:14:11      password here.
@
```

Although LEWIS types his password into the computer, it isn't displayed on the screen. This makes it hard for others to read LEWIS's password and log on with it later.

Once you have logged on, you can run programs and compute in the same basic way as on a personal computer. When you have finished your computer session, you need to log off to stop the computer from billing your account. Logging off is usually a simple one-word command like BYE or LOGOFF. For example,

```
@LOGOUT
Killed Job 34, User LEWIS, TTY 112,
  at 14-Jul-85 11:34:52 Used 0:01:34 in 1:20:41
```

In this example, LEWIS was logged on for an elapsed time of one hour and twenty minutes, but used only one minute and thirty-four seconds of CPU time.

■ Using a Visual Operating System

Even before games such as Pong and PacMan popularized visual interfaces, computer scientists at Xerox's Palo Alto Research Center were developing a visual interface as the basis of an operating system. They decided to model the interface on a desktop, making the computer screen look like a desk on which papers could be piled on top of each other or placed in in-baskets, outbaskets, file folders, and trash cans. Pictures on the screen represented these objects, as well as printers and pads of blank paper. In 1981 Xerox announced the first commercial computer featuring a visual interface (see Figure 4.6). Immediately recognized by computer professionals as a technical masterpiece, the Xerox Star Information System received little attention from the general public because a typical workstation cost $30,000. The Apple Lisa, introduced in 1983, used a similar visual system at an introductory price of $10,000. There still were few buyers. Then, in 1984, the introduction of the Apple Macintosh brought the price of a visual operating system to less than $2,500. Finally the cost of visual interfaces had become competitive with that of textual ones.

To illustrate how a visual operating system works, we will use the Macintosh as an example. All commands to the Macintosh operating system can be made with the mouse or the keyboard. We will explain only the mouse commands. You need to type only when you want to name a new file, rename an old one, or enter information to be stored. The mouse controls an arrow that is used to point at objects on the screen. By moving the mouse along a surface, you move the arrow on the screen.

Figure 4.6 *The Xerox 8010 Star Information System. The display has a very high resolution for its visual interface.*

Running Programs

The first step to run an application program is to switch on the power and slip a disk containing the application program into the drive. The appearance of the screen depends on what disk is inserted. Figure 4.7 shows one example. The gray area of the screen represents the desktop. The two icons represent a disk and a trash can sitting on the desk.

The next task is to open the disk to see its contents. The quickest way to do this is to move the mouse until the arrow on the screen points at the disk icon and then click the button on the mouse twice (called **double-clicking**). This opens a **window,** a rectangular viewing area covering part of the screen, such as the box labeled Update Disk in Figure 4.8.

The icons in the Update Disk window tell you what files are on the disk. Those in Figure 4.8 have the following meanings:

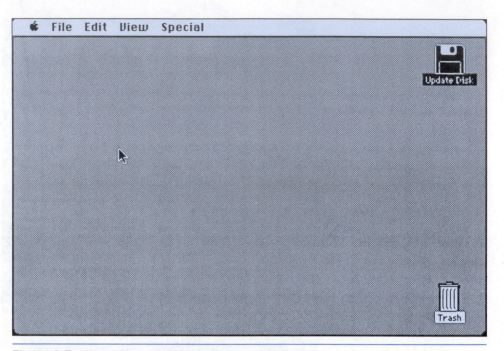

Figure 4.7 *A nearly empty Macintosh screen display.*

Figure 4.8 *Window showing the contents of Update Disk.*

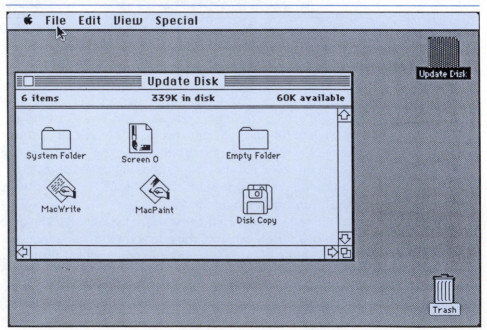

- System Folder is a subdirectory containing files that in turn contain most of the operating system. (64KB of the operating system is stored in ROM.)

- Screen 0 is a data file created by a command that copies the image on the screen into a disk file. Screen 0 can be modified and edited by the MacPaint drawing program.

- Empty Folder acts as a supply of blank file folders. You can organize the information on a disk by putting files inside folders—the Macintosh's equivalent of a subdirectory. Using file folders is important if the disk includes many files because it is difficult to find a specific file if all the files are kept in one large unorganized mess.

- MacWrite is a word processing program.

- MacPaint is a drawing program.

- Disk Copy is a transient operating system utility for copying disks.

To run an application program (such as MacPaint or MacWrite), you just move the mouse on the surface of your desk until the arrow on the screen points at the program's icon and then double-click the mouse. Within a few seconds the screen changes and you can begin word processing or drawing.

Figure 4.9 *Second-level menus. These "pull down" from the menu bar.*

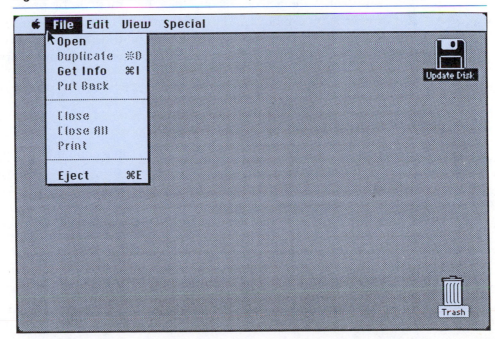

There is also a slower method of giving commands that is worth describing because it illustrates Macintosh's two-level menu system. Look again at Figure 4.7. The text at the top of the screen forms part of a **menu bar;** each word on the bar is one item that can be selected. Pointing at a word on the menu bar and then pressing and holding down the mouse button causes a **pull-down menu** to appear on the screen (see Figure 4.9); that is, a list of options appears below the word. You *select* one of these options by moving the mouse until the arrow points at the desired item on the menu and then releasing the button. Thus you can also open Update Disk by selecting the File option from the menu bar and then selecting the Open option from the pull-down menu.

Notice that some items on the menu in Figure 4.9 are not available for selection at this time. For example, if nothing has been opened yet, the Close option is written in gray. The available items appear black. If you select Open, the pull-down menu vanishes, leaving the screen as it appeared in Figure 4.8. Although this procedure sounds complicated, with only a few minutes of practice it becomes surprisingly natural.

File Operations

You can also give commands on the Macintosh by pointing at and moving icons with the mouse. For example, look again at Figure 4.8. To delete Screen 0 from the Update Disk, you move its icon to the top of the trash can icon. To do this you point at the Screen 0 icon, "pick up" the icon by pressing and holding down the mouse button, drag the icon across the screen to the trash can by moving the mouse, and then release the button. When the button is released, the icon for Screen 0 disappears. This sequence takes many words to describe, but it takes only a second or two to do.

Window Operations

There are several ways to handle windows in a computer system. The Macintosh uses the most common method, free-form windowing. Figure 4.10 looks like a typical, cluttered desktop; its free-form windows look like objects stacked on top of one another. A **free-form window** can be opened and closed, moved, resized, and scrolled.

- *Opened and closed.* Once a window is opened, it remains open until you close it by clicking the close box, a tiny rectangle in the window's upper left-hand margin or by selecting the Close option from the File menu.

- *Moved.* A window can be moved about on the screen. Pointing at part of a window buried in the pile and clicking the button brings that window to

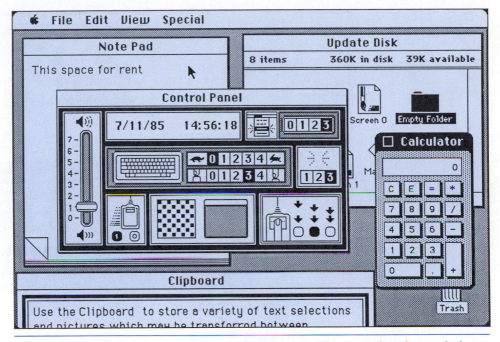

Figure 4.10 *Windows stacked on top of each other. These are free-form windows.*

the top (or foreground) so you can see it and work on its contents. On the Macintosh, windows in the background are deactivated—or frozen in place—until they are activated again. The active window can be moved or dragged by pointing to its upper edge, pressing the mouse button, and dragging it across the screen.

■ *Resized.* You make a window larger or smaller by moving its lower-right corner.

■ *Scrolling.* Because a window may not be large enough to display the entire data file, you may have to resort to *scrolling,* which means moving the contents of a window up, down, left, or right. To scroll, you select one of the arrows in the bars on the side and bottom of the window (see Figure 4.8) or you drag the small box in the bar.

A **tiled window** technique is often employed on systems where memory is limited. In a tile system the windows cannot overlap (see Figure 4.11). Instead, the viewing screen is divided into nonoverlapping regions called **tiles.** Since the tiles do not overlap, the entire rectangular area of each window is visible at all times. Tiled windows can be opened and closed and resized, but in a different way from the methods used with free-form windows.

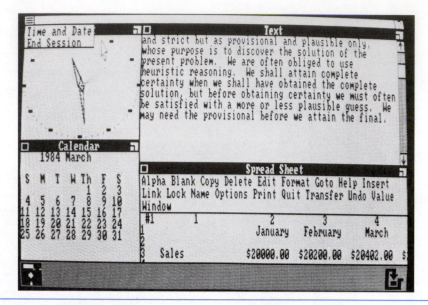

Figure 4.11 *Microsoft Windows creates tiled windows.*

- *Opened and closed.* To open another window you must cut an existing window in two. Closing a window causes its "buddy" to fill in the void.

- *Resized.* An existing window is resized, but not moved, if you move the boundary between two windows.

Windowing requires powerful processors, and using tiled instead of free-form windows conserves processor speed and storage because the computer does not need to save and then restore a hidden, overlapped part of each deactivated window. Consequently, switching from one window to the other is fast and memory-efficient.

Desk Accessories

The windows in Figure 4.10 illustrate some of the convenient utilities (called **desk accessories**) in the Macintosh operating system.

- *Note Pad* has eight pages on which text notes can be stored. You flip the pages up and down by clicking the upturned corner on the bottom of the pad.

- *Control Panel* adjusts characteristics of the hardware, such as the volume of the speaker and the repeat rate of the keys.

- *Calculator* works like a regular four-function pocket calculator.
- *Clipboard* is not technically a desk accessory, but it is present in most application programs. The clipboard transfers information between programs. For example, if you place a drawing on the clipboard while using MacPaint, you can retrieve it and put it into a letter while using MacWrite.

■ Application Software

The major categories of software are application software and system software. As we saw in Chapter 1, *application software* performs a specific task for computer users, such as word processing. **System software** includes all programs designed to help programmers or to control the computer system. Examples include operating systems as well as the tools programmers use to write new programs—*interpreters, compilers, assemblers, debuggers,* and *editors.* We won't be concerned with system software again until Chapter 15 on Programming.

Several layers of software normally insulate a user from a computer's hardware characteristics, as Figure 4.12 illustrates. The innermost layers are occupied by the operating system. The outer layer consists of the programs you use directly. By definition, application software resides on the outer layer of Figure 4.12.

There are some interesting similarities between application software in a computer and the driver of a taxicab. Just as the parts of a taxi (headlights, motor, wheels, and so on) cannot act on their own, so computer hardware (CPU, printer, keyboard, and so on) is inactive without software. As a passenger in a taxi, you don't need to know how the taxi works or even how to drive; you just tell the driver where you want to go. The driver is responsible for getting the cab to the destination. So too, few computer users know how the computer works or how to program. Instead, they give directions, and the application software translates the directions into instructions for the hardware. Thus application software adapts the computer to the task you want done.

Commercial Application Packages

Thousands of application programs have been written and are available for sale. Each is designed for a particular type of activity. If you cannot find a satisfactory prewritten application program, then you can have a program written to your specifications. For example, a control program for a one-of-a-kind piece of

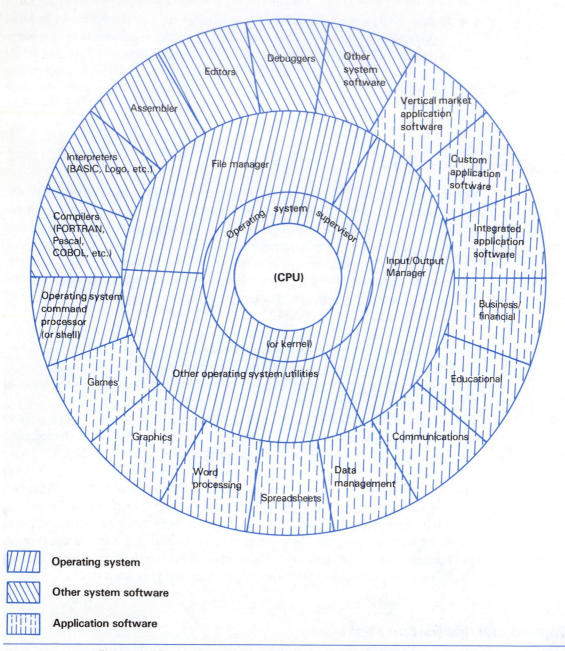

Operating system

Other system software

Application software

Figure 4.12 *The layers of software in a computer system.*

machinery would need to be written from scratch. Although custom programs perform exactly as needed for a specific application, they require expensive and lengthy development. The trend in the computer industry has been away from custom programs and toward commercial application packages that can be purchased and used immediately with little or no modification. This is particularly true in the personal computer field, where the cost of developing a substantial custom program is likely to exceed the cost of all of the hardware in the personal computer system.

Using the right application package for a job is just as important as using the right tools to build a house. Many problems experienced by beginners can be traced to using the wrong program. For example, you could write and print a letter with a spreadsheet program, but doing that makes as much sense as cutting a two-by-four in half with a hammer. Choosing the right application program and learning to use it effectively are so important that the bulk of this book is about just that.

Commercial application packages normally include all the materials needed to use the program—instructions, program disks (or tapes), and so

Figure 4.13 *Lotus 1-2-3®, a commercial application package.*

forth. For example, Figure 4.13 shows Lotus 1-2-3, a program that combines excellent spreadsheet processing with the ability to produce graphs and manipulate limited amounts of textual data. The package contains

- a notebook of program documentation. **Documentation** is printed material describing what a program does, how to use the program, what error messages a program generates, and so forth.
- two copy-protected system disks (original and back-up).
- two auxiliary disks filled with less frequently used programs.
- a tutorial disk that teaches how to use the package.
- a plastic keyboard overlay with definitions for the function keys.

Most programs must be *installed* before you can use them the first time. Commercial programs generally come with "cookbook" installation instructions and special installation programs. You must follow these instructions carefully to copy system tracks onto the application disk correctly, configure the program for your particular monitor (color or monochrome), install your printer, and so on. The installation of computer programs for mainframe computers is normally performed by employees of the computer center, thus relieving computer users of this responsibility.

New users tend to get confused about which mode is active. A **mode** is a state in which only a restricted set of operations can be performed. For example, if a word processor is in the text entry mode, then any text that is typed on the keyboard is added to the document being created. But if the word processor is in a command mode, then the same keystrokes may be interpreted as commands to erase, move, or reformat text in the document.

Good programs use a number of techniques to help the user switch quickly between modes, recognize which mode is active, and operate effectively within each mode. Some of these techniques are to

- provide a **help system**—a display of explanatory information—at the touch of the [HELP] key.
- display menu on the screen to prompt the user with choices of available commands.
- assign commonly used functions to the keyboard's function keys.
- design the program to operate in a manner similar to systems that most people are already familiar with. For example, a file management program might mimic the operations of a Rolodex card file, an integrated package might simulate a clipboard in the way data is transferred among its component programs, and so forth.
- use windows to display several types of information on the screen at once and to make it easy to switch from one mode to another.

■ use special selection devices, such as a mouse or touch screen, to enter commands, allowing the keyboard to be reserved for entering data.

Integrated Applications

An **integrated program** is a collection of related programs combined into a unified package that provides a means of transferring data among the components. Integrated programs make sense when the programs perform related functions or similar tasks or when they use the same data. For example, an integrated accounting program may combine programs that take care of all of the basic accounting systems maintained by a business—accounts payable, accounts receivable, inventory management, the payroll, and the general ledger. A recent trend in personal computer software is to integrate the functions of word processing, spreadsheet processing, graphics, and data management into an integrated package. As computer systems have increased in capability, we have seen steady increases in the integration of programs.

Programs are often integrated into one package in order to unify the *user interface*—the communication between the computer and the user. When each program has a common user interface, learning how to operate one part of the package makes learning all the other parts easy because they share a common mode of operation. Other reasons for software integration include

■ providing a means for switching easily, without delay, from one task to another—for example, from entering orders to tracking inventory and back again.

■ providing a common data format for operations that transfer data from one component to another, such as from a spreadsheet to a word processing document.

Integration tends to make software more powerful, versatile, and complex. Increased power and versatility are certainly commendable, but increasing complexity may make software difficult to use. As software becomes more powerful, it usually requires computers with larger memories and faster disk drives—and users with greater sophistication.

Comparing User Interfaces

Not only is there great versatility in computer applications, there also are a wide variety of user interfaces. New users often find this disconcerting because there are few hard and fast rules to rely on when operating a computer. A command that works in one program is not likely to work in other programs. The meaning of keyboard keys also changes from one program to the next. For example, in one program pressing [S] may display an *S* on the screen, and in other programs it might shoot a missile or store a file. Even the on-off switch can have different meanings. On some computers it immediately disconnects the computer from all power; on others it is merely a request for the computer to stop executing application programs, save all work in progress on disk, and then turn off the power.

Which interface a program uses has a major influence on how long it takes a beginner to learn to use the program and how long it takes an expert to get tasks done. To a certain extent there is an inverse relationship: the easiest method to learn may be the slowest method to use. Some programs try to sidestep this conflict by offering a combination of methods. For example, common commands may be assigned to function keys, less frequently used commands might require menus.

It takes little time to become comfortable with visual interfaces like that on the Macintosh, but they can be limiting because visual interfaces usually do not allow you to take short cuts. Command-line interfaces are easy for programmers to create and require little computer memory or processing. They provide the software designer with unlimited flexibility because any word can be assigned a meaning and built into the command interpreter. Using a program with a command-line interface is similar to doing traditional computer programming. The major difference is that with computer programming the commands are accumulated in a file for later processing rather than being executed as soon as they are typed.

Menu-based interfaces are helpful for the novice because all available choices are shown on the screen. Full-screen menus fill the entire screen with options. These menus not only show what options are available but also describe briefly what each option means. They are often used in complicated but infrequently run programs, such as end-of-the-month accounting programs. Menu bars occupy one or two lines to display the available options. Choosing an option from a menu bar often leads to a subsidiary menu, prompting another choice. Subsidiary pull-down menus, like those on the Macintosh, don't obscure the view of the screen until they are needed. This makes them convenient for the user, but they are harder than other menu systems for programmers to create.

Software developers consume much of their time and energy debating the best user interface for programs. Some argue that a mouse or windows should be used to achieve a consistent interface. Others argue that technological devices are merely gadgets, that the easiest programs to use employ extensive menu systems. Still others argue that making an interface easy to use is less important than creating a responsive system that requires few keystrokes to issue commands. In this book we show examples of how all of these systems work.

■ Summary

This chapter has presented the information about software that you need to know to begin computing. We have seen that several layers of software lie between the user and the hardware of a personal computer system.

We described the parts of an operating system and how the operating system controls the computer. Through the command processor of the operating system, you have access to the file manager for manipulating files (copying, deleting, renaming, formatting, and so on) and to the operating system supervisor for loading and executing application programs. Knowing how the operating system manages the computer's resources will help you to understand the progress of any computer session, whether you are involved in word processing, data management, communications, or just playing games.

Every computer program has its own set of commands that must be learned before the program can be used effectively. We have seen several ways of giving those commands: by typing command lines, by choosing options from menu bars and pull-down menus, and by manipulating icons.

Key Terms

argument	integrated program
batch file	job control language
bug	keyword
command processor	log on
command-line operating system	machine independence
copy-protected	menu bar
default	mode
delimiter	option switch
desk accessory	parameter
device drivers	PC-DOS
device independence	pull-down menu
documentation	resident
double-clicking	shell
file allocation table	supervisor
file manager	system disk
formatting	system software
free-form window	textual interface
help system	tiled window
initialize	tiles
I/O manager	transient utility

upward compatible
visual interface
visual operating system

wild card characters
window

Discussion Questions

1. What is the difference between application software and system software? What kinds of programs might be in a gray area between the two?

2. Why are floppy disks sold blank rather than formatted?

3. What is a file? What conventions for naming files are used on your computer?

4. Why are wild card characters convenient? Think of some tasks that would be easier to perform with wild card characters than without them.

5. What happens if you make a typing mistake in a command-line system? If you make a typing mistake when giving a command, is the result likely to be a valid command?

6. What is the difference between device and machine independence?

7. How much on-line help should be provided by an operating system? An applications program?

8. What is the significance of upward compatibility? Is downward compatibility as important as upward compatibility?

9. Describe the features of an ''ideal,'' easy-to-use interface for an airlines reservation system. How might this interface differ from the ideal interface for a game? For a word processor?

10. In a command-line operating system, a batch file stores textual commands. How might a visual operating system store commands in a batch file?

11. Suppose the directory of your diskette contains the following file names:
    TICTAC.EXE   README.DOC
    ALGEBRA.DAT   DEFAULT.TXT
    STARTUP.BAT
    What do you suppose each file contains? Comment on the importance of choosing meaningful file names.

Exercises

1. Prepare a list of the operating system commands for your computer. Rank the commands according to how often you are likely to use them.

2. Determine which commands in your computer's operating system are resident and which are transient.

3. List the advantages of an integrated program over a collection of individual programs that perform the same tasks. List the disadvantages.

PART TWO

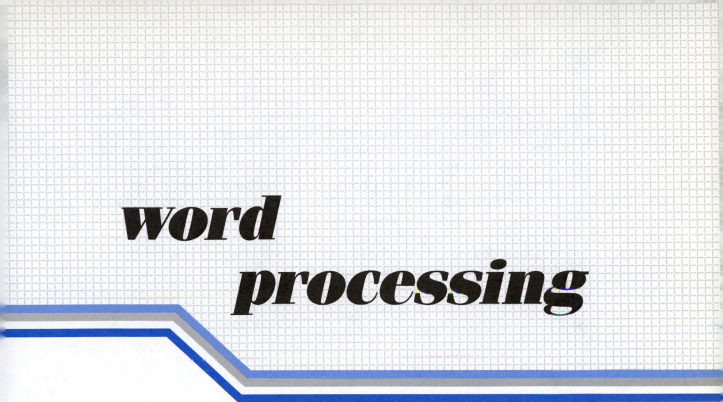

word processing

Every word processing program is designed to do the same thing: to help the person behind the keyboard create a good-looking written document. For our purposes, word processing means using a computer to enter, edit, format, and print text.

There is nothing magical or complicated about word processing. First, the word processing program is loaded into memory and takes control of the computer. Then, the text of the document is typed, and editing commands are used to revise it. Additional commands allow you to control how the text will look on paper when it is printed. The document can be saved on a disk to be recalled later. When all editing is completed, the document is sent to the printer.

It is a safe bet that word processing sells more personal computers than any other application. Writers come to love their word processing systems because they eliminate most of the drudgery associated with traditional, paper-based methods of translating thoughts into printed documents. Moving characters around on a monitor to alter your words before committing them to paper is easy. It is possible to delete text, move paragraphs, or lengthen all of the lines on a page with at most a few commands.

Word processing is particularly useful for documents that must be revised several times before they are printed in final form. To revise a document on a typewriter, you must retype the entire document. Not only is this retyping wasted effort, but it is likely to introduce new typographical errors.

Part II teaches you about word processing in two chapters. Chapter 5 provides detailed examples to explain the basic concepts you need to understand in order to create a simple memo or letter. It also describes the functions that form the heart of a word processor, such as moving paragraphs, laying out the page design, and formatting paragraphs. Chapter 6 compares the features provided by various word processors and describes some of the ''bells and whistles'' of sophisticated word processing. These advanced features include changing the appearance of characters (boldface, italics, and so on), checking the spelling of words electronically, designing and printing form letters, and assembling large documents.

word processing basics

5

- ■ **Understanding the Screen Display**
  On-screen Text Formatting
  Off-screen Print Formatting

- ■ **Editing**
  Cursor Control
  Scrolling
  Inserting, Replacing, and Deleting
  Block Operations
  Search and Replace

- ■ **Text Formatting**
  Page Design
  Paragraph Layout

- ■ **Memory Management**
  Disk-based Versus Memory-based Word Processors
  Back-up

Word processing beginners need to know what functions are commonly available and how to use them. That is what this chapter covers. It contains detailed examples of common word processing features: moving the cursor, scrolling, simple editing, moving blocks of text, and formatting the text to look good. The chapter concludes with a discussion of how a word processor manages the computer's memory, describing where the characters generated by your keystrokes are moved and stored in every stage of word processing.

After you've read this chapter, you will be ready to use a word processing program. Sit down with the appropriate manufacturer's manual, or better yet, experiment with word processing at a keyboard.

■ Understanding the Screen Display

Figure 5.1 shows a typical screen display while a letter is being entered and edited. Notice that the screen is broken into two areas. The bottom part shows the text that is being edited. The upper part gives the status of the program, such as where the cursor is located, and *help information,* such as how to give commands.

Figure 5.1 *Typical screen display of an on-screen formatting word processor while editing a letter.*

```
Cursor: PAGE 1 LINE 10 COL 5   Editing: A:LETTER        } Program
COMMAND:  Copy    Delete  Format  Help     Insert          status/help
          Move    Print   Quit    Save     Undo            information
L----!----!----!----!----!----!----!----!----R
John Doe
123 Main St.
Anytown, USA


Dear John,

    Thank  you for your interest in my record            Text in the
collection.  I am tempted to sell my 1948 Gene            document
Autry  album,  but my cat cannot live  without            being edited
it.
                     Yours  truly,


                     Mary Smith
```

Nearly all word processors reserve part of the screen to display status and help information. Understanding this portion of the screen is a good first step toward mastering any application program. In Figure 5.1 the status/help information gives

- the current location of the cursor (page 1, line 10, column 5).

- the name of the text file being edited (LETTER) and its location (disk drive A).

- a list of commands. This list includes commands that allow you to *move* text from one place in the document to another, to *print* the document on a printer, to *quit* word processing and begin another task, and to *save* a copy of the document on a disk.

- the location of the left and right margins (indicated by "L" and "R" on line 4 of the screen).

- the positions of the tab stops (indicated by "!" on line 4 of the screen).

The amount and the kind of status and help information provided vary widely from one word processor to another. Many word processors use a large part of the screen to help you remember what commands are available. Obviously, as more status and help information is displayed on the screen, less room is left to show the text being edited. New users tend to want all the status and help information they can get. Experienced users usually want an uncluttered display showing as much of their text as possible. This conflict is often resolved by allowing the user to choose how much of the screen will be devoted to each function.

On-screen Text Formatting

Figure 5.2 shows the result of printing the letter in Figure 5.1. Notice that the text in the two figures looks identical except for the top and left-hand margins, which are appropriately larger in the printed document. This what-you-see-is-what-you-get method of word processing is called **on-screen text formatting** or **screen-oriented word processing.**

In theory, on-screen formatting allows you to edit and adjust the appearance of text on the screen until it looks just the way you want it printed. In reality, an on-screen formatter may not provide an exact copy of what the text will look like on paper. For example, the display may not be capable of showing all of the different types of characters (boldface, italic, and so on) that the printer can generate. The accuracy with which text is represented on the screen is one of many features to look for in evaluating word processing systems.

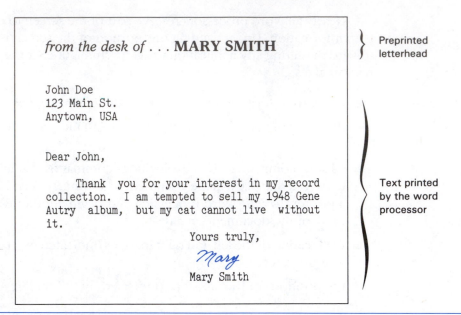

from the desk of . . . **MARY SMITH**   } Preprinted
                                                             letterhead

```
John Doe
123 Main St.
Anytown, USA

Dear John,

     Thank  you for your interest in my record
collection.  I am tempted to sell my 1948 Gene
Autry  album,  but my cat cannot live  without
it.
                       Yours truly,

                       Mary
                       Mary Smith
```

} Text printed
  by the word
  processor

Figure 5.2 *The result of printing the letter shown in Figure 5.1.*

Off-screen Print Formatting

A different method of word processing, called **off-screen print formatting**, relies on a two-step process for creating the printed product. In the first step you enter the text and special print-formatting commands are embedded in the text to describe how the document should look when printed. But the display on the screen shows both the text and the print-formatting commands; it does not look like the document will look on paper.

Usually these commands must be preceded by a special character—such as an at-sign (@), a period (.), or a backslash (＼)—to enable the print formatter to distinguish them from regular text. Often the commands must begin in the first column of a line and may appear by themselves on a line. Each off-screen formatter has its own set of embedded commands. For example, Figure 5.3 shows a screen display that contains both embedded print-formatting commands and text. The first line contains three of these commands.

- ■ @LM sets the left-hand margin of the printed document to column 10.
- ■ @RM sets the right-hand margin to column 55.
- ■ @FLUSHLEFT specifies that the following lines are to be printed flush with the left-hand margin.

In the second step a **print-formatting program** uses the embedded commands to control the printer. These commands are not printed. They are used only to control the appearance of the printed product. When the text in

Figure 5.3 is run through a print formatter, the printed result will look just like the letter in Figure 5.2.

The obvious drawback of off-screen print formatting is that it is difficult to visualize how the text will look when it is printed. At times this can lead to disastrous results. For example, imagine that you decide to go to lunch while the print formatter sends a 120-page document to the printer. When you return, you discover that you made just one misspelling—but it was in the @NO-UNDERLINE command on the fourth page. The result is that the last 116 pages are underlined by mistake! Fortunately, this kind of error can often be caught before printing if the off-screen formatter has a **print-preview** feature, which allows you to preview on the screen what the document will look like when printed.

The trend in word processing is clearly toward screen-oriented formatting. It is helpful, especially for a beginner, to see what the document looks like without printing it or using a separate print-preview operation. But building a word processor that is 100 percent screen-oriented is a difficult technical challenge. It takes a high-resolution monitor, a capable processor, and elegant software to display a document as it would appear when printed while simultaneously letting the user edit it. Most word processors attempt to organize the screen like the printed page but reserve some formatting operations for the printing stage. For example, the lines on the screen may have the same number of characters as they will have when printed, but the spacing between words may be more uniform on paper than on screen.

Figure 5.3 *Typical screen display of an off-screen print formatter.*

```
    Cursor: PAGE 1 LINE 3 COL 11    Editing: A:LETTER
-----------------------------------------------------
@LM 10  @RM 55  @FLUSHLEFT
John Doe
123 Main St.
Anytown, USA
@BLANKLINES 2
Dear John,
@PARAGRAPH  @JUSTIFY  @BLANKLINES 1
Thank you for your interest in my
record collection.  I am tempted to sell my 1948
Gene Autry
album, but my cat cannot live without it.
@TAB 25 Yours truly,
@BLANKLINES 2
@TAB 25 Mary Smith
```

Program status/help information

User text and print-formatting commands all run together

Many of the examples of text formatting in this chapter are from PFS:WRITE and WordStar. Both are widely used on a variety of computers. They illustrate very different approaches to word processing.

PFS:WRITE is a menu-driven word processor that is designed to satisfy the needs of casual users by providing a limited—but very easy to use—set of program features. Except for the status information on the screen, the PFS:WRITE display looks like a portion of the page to be printed. The program even draws lines on the screen that indicate the edges of the paper. These advantages come at a cost: PFS:WRITE has quite limited formatting and printing abilities.

WordStar is a full-featured word processor that is designed for intensive use by writers or secretaries. Although it is billed as a ''screen-oriented word processing system specifically designed for ease of use,'' many of its formatting options require the use of **dot commands.** These are cryptic, embedded print-formatting commands that begin with a period in the first column of a line. You need a little experience and imagination in order to predict from the screen display exactly what a WordStar document will look like, but WordStar is certainly better in this respect than a true off-screen print formatter.

■ Editing

Editing is the fun part of word processing. It allows you to express your thoughts—by typing them into the computer—so that they can be seen on the screen. If you don't like what you see, then you can use editing operations to quickly insert or delete words or sentences.

Before you can begin editing, you must begin running the word processing program. On a personal computer this might involve turning on the computer, loading the operating system, typing the name of the word processing program, and waiting until the word processing program is loaded into memory and takes control of the computer. On a mainframe computer it is necessary to log in first. If you want to edit an existing document, tell the word processor the name of the file that contains the document. This causes some (or all) of the file to be transferred from the disk into main memory. Alternatively, you can edit an empty file—in other words, create a new file.

To enter and edit a simple document such as a letter, you need to learn only four editing operations.

1. Moving the cursor to where you want to make changes
2. Scrolling text on the screen so that you can view other parts of the document
3. Adding new characters of text, by inserting or replacing characters
4. Deleting characters

After we have discussed these essential operations, we will describe two intermediate techniques that make it much easier to revise a document: block operations and search-and-replace operations. *Block operations* manipulate entire groups of characters at once, such as moving a paragraph. *Search-and-replace operations* allow you to locate numerous occurrences of a group of characters (such as "Smith"), and if you wish, to replace them (for example, with "Smyth").

Cursor Control

The *cursor* is the indicator on the screen that shows where things will happen next. In order to make a change in the text, you must move the cursor to where the change is to be made. Thus it is important to be able to move the cursor around the screen in an efficient manner.

Most keyboards have cursor-movement keys (also called *arrow keys*): the [←] key moves the cursor one position to the left; the [→] key, to the right; the [↑] key, up; and the [↓] key, down. For example, if you press [→] four times and then press [↓] once, the cursor moves over four columns and down one line, as Figure 5.4 illustrates. To move the cursor all the way to the end of a line, hold down [→]. The cursor will float across the line. When it reaches the last character on the line, it will jump to the beginning of the next line and begin floating across it. You can use the [←] key in the same way to move right to left across a line. When the cursor reaches the first character on the line, it will jump to the last character on the previous line.

Figure 5.4 *Effect of pushing the right-arrow key four times and the down-arrow key once.*

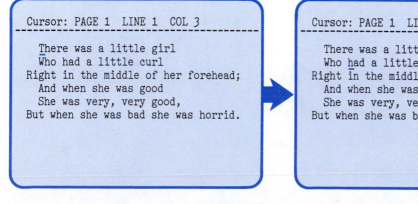

```
Cursor: PAGE 1  LINE 1  COL 3
-----------------------------------
    There was a little girl
    Who had a little curl
Right in the middle of her forehead;
    And when she was good
    She was very, very good,
But when she was bad she was horrid.
```

```
Cursor: PAGE 1  LINE 2  COL 7
-----------------------------------
    There was a little girl
    Who had a little curl
Right in the middle of her forehead;
    And when she was good
    She was very, very good,
But when she was bad she was horrid.
```

Scrolling

Scrolling moves lines of text up or down on the screen, allowing new parts of the text to be seen. As text is scrolled, all of the central lines of text move down (or up) the screen; lines disappear off the bottom (or top) of the screen; and new lines of text appear at the top (or bottom) of the screen. Thus you can view all of the text even though there is too much text to fit on the screen at once.

It may be useful to think of scrolling as a process similar to the one shown in Figure 5.5. That is, a document is displayed as if the image were being transmitted by a stationary television camera pointed at a scroll that contains the document being edited. The scroll's handles (which are outside the viewing area of the camera) wind the text up and down in front of the camera. As the scroll is wound up, lines of text disappear off the top of the viewing area and new lines show up on the bottom.

Figure 5.5 *Scrolling.*

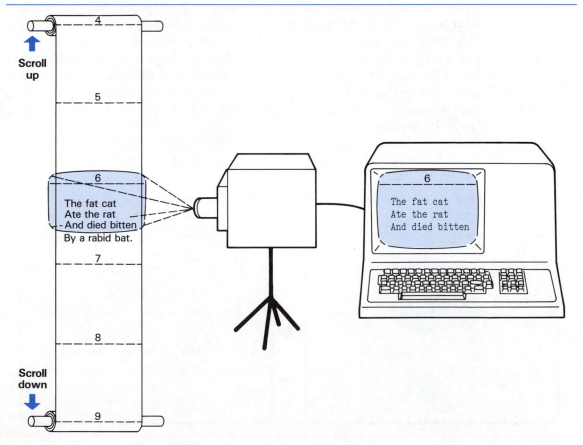

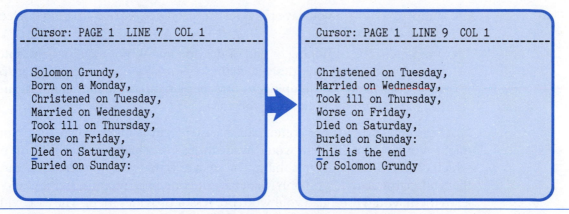

Figure 5.6 *Scrolling two lines by pushing the down-arrow key twice.*

Holding down the down-arrow key moves the *cursor* line by line down the screen until it nears the bottom; then the *text* on the screen begins to jump up one line at a time. Most word processors begin scrolling the text before the cursor has reached the bottom line (see Figure 5.6). This guarantees that you can see at least one line of text below the line marked with the cursor (unless, of course, the screen is displaying the end of the document), which helps you understand the context of the area being edited. Naturally, only the text scrolls on the screen; any status or help information stays put.

You can use the cursor keys to scroll one line at a time to the bottom of a document; but if the document is long, this procedure is time-consuming and boring. Full-featured word processing programs offer an alternative: they provide various commands that move the cursor quickly from one part of the text to another. Commonly available cursor-control commands allow you to

- move one character at a time—up, down, left, or right.
- move one word at a time, forward or backward.
- jump to the beginning or end of the current line.
- jump to the upper left-hand corner of the screen, which is called the **home** position.
- jump to the bottom of the screen.

Even more powerful than these simple cursor-control commands are commands that involve

- scrolling up or down one line at a time.
- scrolling up or down one screen of text at a time, which is called **paging** through the document. Many keyboards have keys labeled [PgUp] and [PgDn] that allow you to page through a document.

■ jumping to where you have previously put a *place marker*—a kind of electronic bookmark.

■ jumping to the beginning or end of the document. For example, the software designer may have designated the keystroke sequence [CTRL]-[PgUp] as a command for jumping to the beginning of the document and [CTRL]-[PgDn] for jumping to the end.

Learning to use these commands is easier than it might seem. Still, you might wonder why anyone would want to learn so many commands, all of which do essentially the same thing. The answer is that you don't have to learn them all, particularly if you only want to write one-page memos. But if you do learn them, you will be glad your word processor provides them. The ease with which you learned to use the program soon becomes less important than the number and power of a word processor's commands. It is surprising how quickly a person who buys a simple, easy-to-use program stops saying, "Gee, this is easy," and starts complaining, "Boy, it takes a long time to get anything done with this product."

Inserting, Replacing, and Deleting

You will spend more time using the basic, one-character-at-a-time editing operations than you spend using all other word processing commands put together. For this reason, you must have a good understanding of how to insert, replace, and delete characters in a document.

Insert Versus Replacement Mode

There are two general ways to enter new characters into a document.

■ They can be *inserted,* meaning they are added between existing characters.

■ They can *replace* existing characters, meaning they "type over" existing characters.

Usually the status portion of the screen indicates which of these methods the program is using, as shown in the upper-right corners of the screens in Figure 5.7. When the program is in the **insert mode,** new characters are added to the text as they are typed. When the program is in the **replacement mode,** new characters take the place of characters already in the text. Most programs begin in the insert mode because it is used more frequently.

The choice between insert and replacement modes is often made with a toggle switch. Each time a **toggle switch** is thrown from one setting to the other, the new value is maintained until the switch is thrown again. Common

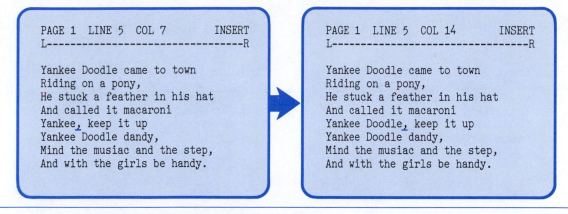

Figure 5.7 *Inserting "Doodle" in line 5.*

household light switches operate this way. If you throw a switch to turn a light on, it stays on until you throw the switch again. Similarly, if you use a toggle switch to give a command to the computer, that command remains in effect until you throw the toggle switch again. Generally, the same command is used to toggle the switch from one value to another. Toggle switches are used for many commands in word processing programs.

The actual command used to toggle between insert and replacement modes varies widely from program to program. With WordStar on an IBM PC you simply push the [INS] key. With WordJuggler on an Apple III you press [7] on the numeric key pad to enter the insert mode, and you type [SHIFT]-[7] to enter the replacement mode.

Inserting characters is the most common editing operation; it is how text is entered or added to a document. With most word processors it is also the simplest operation. You merely move the cursor to where you want to add text and then type it in. But some word processing programs require that you type a command before you begin inserting text.

Each character you type causes three things to occur.

- It pushes the rest of the characters on the line to the right.
- It inserts the character in the document at the current cursor position.
- It moves the cursor to the next column position.

A space is treated the same as any other character. It is inserted and deleted from text in the same manner as a visible character, and it takes up the same amount of memory in the computer. Thus, in order to insert "Doodle" in Figure 5.7, you must move the cursor to the comma on line 5, hit the space bar once, and type "Doodle."

```
PAGE 1  LINE 4  COL 18     REPLACE          PAGE 1  LINE 4  COL 23     REPLACE
L--------------------------------R          L--------------------------------R

Yankee Doodle came to town                  Yankee Doodle came to town
Riding on a pony,                           Riding on a pony,
He stuck a feather in his hat               He stuck a feather in his hat
And called it macraone                      And called it macaroni_
Yankee Doodle, keep it up                   Yankee Doodle, keep it up
Yankee Doodle dandy,                        Yankee Doodle dandy,
Mind the musiac and the step,               Mind the musiac and the step,
And with the girls be handy.                And with the girls be handy.
```

Figure 5.8 *Correcting the spelling of* macaroni *by replacing "raone" with "aroni."*

For some tasks, such as fixing typing errors, it is quicker to replace characters than to first give a command to delete the erroneous characters and then to insert the correct ones. Figure 5.8 shows an example. In general, the replacement mode is convenient when a change does not increase the number of characters in the document. Thus the replacement mode is more efficient than the insert mode if you are rearranging transposed letters, such as changing *recieve* to *receive,* or correcting a column of numbers, as in changing

$$
\begin{array}{ccc}
\$ \ 198.43 & & \$ \ 298.43 \\
26.21 & \text{to} & 62.21 \\
7.01 & & 7.11
\end{array}
$$

Word Wrap

A typewriter's bell rings as the carriage nears the end of a line. If the typist doesn't return the carriage, the typing soon stops with the carriage stuck against the right margin.

With a word processor there is no listening for the typewriter bell or peeking to see if the next word will fit on the line. If a word is too long to fit at the end of a line, it is automatically moved to the next line (see Figure 5.9). The [RETURN] key is used only to end paragraphs. This feature is called **word wrap.** By eliminating the need to determine where to stop each line, word wrap increases the rate at which you can enter text.

Deleting Characters

A single character is erased by moving the cursor to the character to be deleted and typing a **character-delete command.** Although the exact

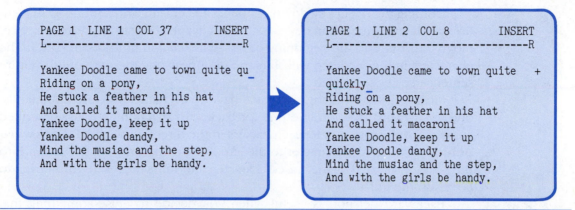

```
PAGE 1  LINE 1  COL 37        INSERT          PAGE 1  LINE 2  COL 8         INSERT
L--------------------------------R            L--------------------------------R

Yankee Doodle came to town quite qu_          Yankee Doodle came to town quite   +
Riding on a pony,                             quickly_
He stuck a feather in his hat                 Riding on a pony,
And called it macaroni                        He stuck a feather in his hat
Yankee Doodle, keep it up                      And called it macaroni
Yankee Doodle dandy,                          Yankee Doodle, keep it up
Mind the musiac and the step,                 Yankee Doodle dandy,
And with the girls be handy.                  Mind the musiac and the step,
                                              And with the girls be handy.
```

Figure 5.9 *Word wrap moves "qui" to the next line when the* i *in* quickly *is typed.*

command for this operation will vary from program to program, the command
will always be simple. In this discussion, we assume that your keyboard has a
key labeled [DEL], which is used to delete the character immediately under the
cursor.

When you use an eraser or correction fluid to remove characters from
paper, blank spaces remain. But notice in Figure 5.10 that when the character *a*
is erased from *musiac,* the rest of the line is shifted one place to the left to fill
the void. For most purposes, this is much nicer than having a blank space remain after a character is erased.

Figure 5.10 *Pressing [DEL] to delete the* a *in* musiac.

```
PAGE 1  LINE 7  COL 14       REPLACE          PAGE 1  LINE 7  COL 14       REPLACE
L--------------------------------R            L--------------------------------R

Yankee Doodle came to town                    Yankee Doodle came to town
Riding on a pony,                             Riding on a pony,
He stuck a feather in his hat                 He stuck a feather in his hat
And called it macaroni                        And called it macaroni
Yankee Doodle, keep it up                     Yankee Doodle, keep it up
Yankee Doodle dandy,                          Yankee Doodle dandy,
Mind the musiac and the step,                 Mind the music and the step,
And with the girls be handy.                  And with the girls be handy.
```

Holding the [DEL] key down continues the erasing and shifting so that entire words and phrases can be deleted. If you want to delete an entire sentence, move the cursor to the beginning of the sentence and hold down [DEL]. The characters in the sentence will shift and disappear one by one until the entire sentence has been deleted.

Most word processing programs have two character-delete commands, one for forward deletion and one for backward deletion. We just described **forward deletion;** it deletes characters in the direction we read. **Backward deletion** deletes the character to the left of the cursor, moves the cursor into the position vacated by the erased character, and shifts the rest of the line left to cover up the hole.

Backward deletion is useful when you decide to erase something that you've just typed because you can do so without moving the cursor to the beginning of what you want to delete. Backward deletion is used often to remove typographical errors immediately after they are made. Usually forward deletion is used when you need to go back and edit the document for meaning or style.

Besides deleting individual characters, most word processors have specific commands for deleting the current word, deleting to the end of the line, and deleting an entire block of text. Unless the product you are using has an UNDO command that allows you to cancel the last command, it pays to be careful about how you use these more powerful deletion commands. Otherwise you may find yourself retyping a lot of text.

Block Operations

If you want to move or delete a large number of characters, one-character-at-a-time operations are inefficient. Instead, **block operations** are used to manipulate many characters simultaneously. These usually involve two separate operations: first you mark off the block of characters; then you give a command to manipulate the block.

To mark a block of characters you must identify the beginning and end of the block. Normally, this involves four steps: (1) move the cursor to the first character of the block, (2) issue a command to mark the beginning of the block, (3) move the cursor to the last character of the block, and (4) issue a command to mark the end of the block. However, the exact procedure for marking a block varies from one word processing program to another. With some programs you can move the markers for the beginning and the end of a block independently; with others you must perform all four steps as a unit in a specified order. Some word processors provide short cuts; they offer one-step commands for marking the current word, sentence, or paragraph. And still others allow you to select a block of text by pointing with a mouse.

Generally, once the block is marked off, it is displayed differently from the rest of the text. Some programs present the block in **inverse video,** reversing the screen colors in the marked area; others use a different intensity for the characters in the block, which is called **highlighting.**

Deleting Blocks

Once you have marked a block, it should take only one command to delete all of the characters in the block. There are two possibilities for what happens to the deleted characters. First, the block may be thrown away permanently. Because a block may contain many pages of text, this method will not seem very "friendly" if you make a mistake. Second, the word processor may move the block into a separate area of memory called a **buffer** (or a *clipboard*). You can retrieve a block from the buffer later, but moving something new into a buffer throws away the buffer's previous contents.

Figure 5.11 illustrates the use of a buffer. In the left-hand screen line 7 and line 8 (which is a blank line) have been marked as a block and are shown in color on the screen. In addition to the cursor's location, the status information area of the screen shows what is stored in the buffer by displaying the first and the last five characters between curly brackets. Evidently the buffer is empty in the left-hand screen because there are no characters between the brackets. The right-hand screen shows that the block has been moved to the buffer by displaying "Sydne...1845 " between the brackets.

Not all word processing programs use buffers. And some programs that use a buffer do not display any of its contents. A few programs allow many different buffers to be established so that several blocks can be stored in memory at once. Most word processors have a limited buffer size. If the block size exceeds this limit, then the operation must be done in parts.

Figure 5.11 *Deleting a block of text. The colored line and the blank line following it are removed from the document and placed in the buffer.*

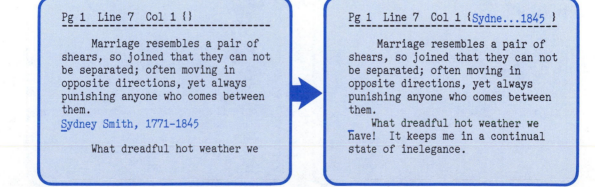

Cut and Paste

Throughout most of this century newspaper editors have cut articles into pieces so that they can be pasted together in a different order. No more. Today, word processors provide editors with the ability to "cut and paste" electronically. Electronic cutting and pasting is faster and neater than using scissors and glue.

Besides deletion of a block, the usual cut-and-paste operations are

- *block-move,* which moves the entire block from one location to another.
- *block-copy,* duplicating the block in a new location.
- *block-save,* which saves the block as a new file on a disk.
- *block-read,* merging a file on a disk into the document.

As in deleting a block, the first step in any cut-and-paste job is to mark the block to be manipulated. There are two common ways to move or copy a block.

1. In the simpler method you place the cursor where the block is to be moved and then give the command to move or to copy the block. The command to move the block transfers it from its original position to where the cursor is. The command to copy the block leaves the block in its original position and places a copy in the document right after the cursor.

2. The second method follows the cut-and-paste analogy more closely. In the "cut" part, you give a command to move or to copy the block into the buffer. For the "paste" part, you place the cursor where the block is to be inserted and give a command to restore the block, which copies the buffer's contents back into the document. In Figure 5.12 the block that was placed in the buffer in Figure 5.11 has been pasted into the document.

Figure 5.12 *Pasting a copy of the buffer into the document.*

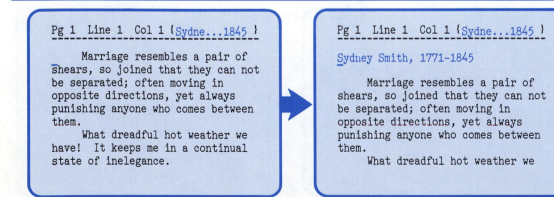

Search and Replace

Any good word processing program will search a document to find a word or phrase (called the **search phrase**). We will use PFS:WRITE (as implemented on the IBM PC) as an example because its search-and-replace operations are easy to understand, although they are not particularly flexible.

Pressing the function key [F7] begins the search by displaying the colored prompts shown in the bottom of Figure 5.13. Suppose you are searching for *June*. This is done by typing "June" in response to the SEARCH FOR: prompt, and then pressing [ENTER]. Then PFS:WRITE searches the document, beginning at the cursor's location, to find the first occurrence of *June*. Because PFS:WRITE ignores the difference between upper- and lower-case letters in search operations, the first match it finds might be "JUNE" (or "june"). When a match is found, the program returns to the normal edit mode with the cursor at the beginning of the phrase it found.

Replacing one word or phrase with another is also a simple operation. Suppose that the easiest way to write a July sales report is to make a copy of the June report and modify it. Rather than searching for *June,* this situation calls for replacing every *June* with *July.* This is done by

Figure 5.13 *Prompts for a search-and-replace operation.*

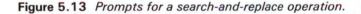

```
June 6, 1984


Mr. and Mrs. William Anthony
2119 Dixon Drive So.
Renton, WA 98055

Dear Mr. and Mrs. Anthony:

Enclosed are your tickets for your charter flight to Maui the
second week of July. You will find vouchers for your
condominium and car rental in the folder with the airplane
tickets.

I am also enclosing a brochure and price list for tours,
excursions, and sports instruction available on Maui itself.
Please let me know, either before or after you arrive, if you

Search for: June
Replace with:
Manual or Automatic (M/A):  M
```

- pressing [F7] to display the prompts shown in Figure 5.13.
- typing ''June'' after the SEARCH FOR: prompt.
- pressing [TAB] to tab down to the REPLACE WITH: prompt.
- typing ''July'' after the REPLACE WITH: prompt.
- and pressing [ENTER] to complete the command.

When [ENTER] is pressed, PFS:WRITE looks for the first occurrence of *June*. If a match is found, it asks whether the replacement should be made. If you type ''Y,'' the replacement is made; if you type ''N,'' the phrase is left alone. Either way, PFS:WRITE continues searching the document until a match with the search phrase cannot be found or you type ''Q'' in response to the replacement prompt.

Automatic search and replace changes every occurrence of the search phrase with the replacement phrase without stopping to ask for permission. This feature is handy, but it can lead to serious problems if the search phrase is more common than expected. For example, if you replace all occurrences of *too* with *to,* ''tool'' and ''took'' become ''tol'' and ''tok.''

Many times, searching for a word or phrase is more convenient than using cursor-movement commands, especially if you are not sure which page you want. If you choose a phrase that occurs only in the desired section or part, the search command will quickly move the cursor to it.

An obvious use of search and replace is for correcting a consistently misspelled word. Search and replace can also relieve some of the tedium of typing a document that contains many repetitions of a phrase such as ''the Constitution of the United States of America.'' Typing ''CUSA'' instead of ''the Constitution of the United States of America'' saves 43 keystrokes. Later, the phrases can be expanded in one **global search-and-replace** operation that performs an automatic search and replace on the entire document. The abbreviation must be unique. If you choose ''us'' instead of ''CUSA,'' then the replacement occurs in any word containing *us—use, customer, rust, versus,* and so on.

The left-hand screen in Figure 5.14 shows the nursery rhyme ''Peter Piper'' as it would appear if ''ppp'' had been typed instead of ''peck of pickled peppers.'' After an automatic search-and-replace operation changes ''ppp'' to ''peck of pickled peppers,'' the lines in the right-hand screen of Figure 5.14 no longer fit on the screen. As a result, the characters that extend past the screen's edge are indicated by a '' + '' in the last column position. You can view the end of these lines by attempting to move the cursor off the right edge of the screen, which causes the text to scroll horizontally. *Horizontal scrolling* is particularly useful for documents that are wider than standard 8 1/2-by-11-inch paper.

Some word processors do not support horizontal scrolling. For example, PFS:WRITE has a maximum line length of 78 characters and does not allow

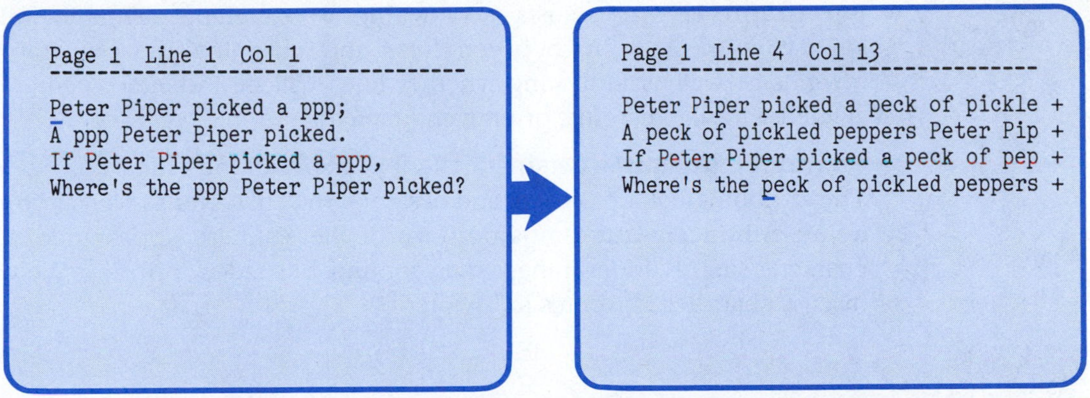

```
Page 1  Line 1  Col 1                      Page 1  Line 4  Col 13
-----------------------------              ------------------------------
Peter Piper picked a ppp;                  Peter Piper picked a peck of pickle +
A ppp Peter Piper picked.                  A peck of pickled peppers Peter Pip +
If Peter Piper picked a ppp,               If Peter Piper picked a peck of pep +
Where's the ppp Peter Piper picked?        Where's the peck of pickled peppers +
```

Figure 5.14 *Replacing "ppp" with "peck of pickled peppers."*

lines to extend off the edge of the screen as shown in Figure 5.14. Instead, a line that would extend off the screen is reformed automatically into shorter lines.

Powerful word processors offer many search-and-replace options. Rather than always searching forward through the document, you can specify a backward search from the cursor. Or it might be possible to request a global search without first moving the cursor to the beginning of the file. You might be able to choose from among several definitions of what constitutes a match. For example, the optional criteria might be

- literal (must match exactly; so "june" would not match "June").
- whole words only (so "jump" would not match "jumps").
- words in specific positions (only matches words at the beginning or end of a line).
- words containing wild card characters (so "pre*" would match "predict," "prefer," and so on).

■ Text Formatting

Most of what you have learned so far about word processing has been about editing—the process of entering, deleting, and reordering characters. This section deals with **text formatting**—controlling the appearance of the document so it looks good on paper. Formatting activities fall into three categories.

- **Page design** determines the general boundaries of where text will be placed on the page. This includes establishing the top, bottom, left, and right margins; providing the text (if any) to appear at the tops and bottoms of pages; and requesting page breaks.

- **Paragraph layout** adjusts text within a paragraph. This includes specifying the spacing between lines and changing the paragraph's margins as well as indicating whether lines will be indented, centered, aligned with the margins, or uneven in length.

- **Character attributes** determine the appearance of individual characters. The attributes include the size and design of the character as well as **character enhancements**—modifications of the standard appearance of a character such as underlining, superscripting, or shadow printing. We will discuss character attributes in Chapter 6.

Page Design

For a word processor to print correctly, it must know how big each piece of paper is and how large to make the margins. Figure 5.15 illustrates the terms used in page design. Some of the terms need further explanation.

- Page length is generally given in terms of the number of lines per page. It can be set for standard 8 1/2-by-11-inch paper or for envelopes, mailing labels, odd-size pages, or extra-long sheets of paper. The most common setting is 66 lines, which allows 6 lines per inch on 11-inch paper.

- **Headings** and **footings** are the text at the tops and bottoms of pages. They are typed into the file only once; the word processor places them on each page automatically.

- Top and bottom **margins** are the spaces between the horizontal edges of the paper and the *regular* text. Headings and footings are printed inside the top and bottom margins and are not considered part of the body of the page.

The page width, left margin, line length, and right margin are all related to each other. Some word processors calculate the line length from the page width and the left and right margins; others require that you specify settings for the left margin and the line length.

Sample Layout Commands

Figure 5.16 shows the page layout menu used by PFS:WRITE to set the margins and headings shown in Figure 5.15. The colored areas of the screen are prompts; after each prompt PFS:WRITE provides a default value for that item. An item's default value is changed by first pressing [TAB] to move the cursor from item to item until the desired item is selected, and then typing a new value. When all the items are set correctly, press [ENTER]; then the values are accepted.

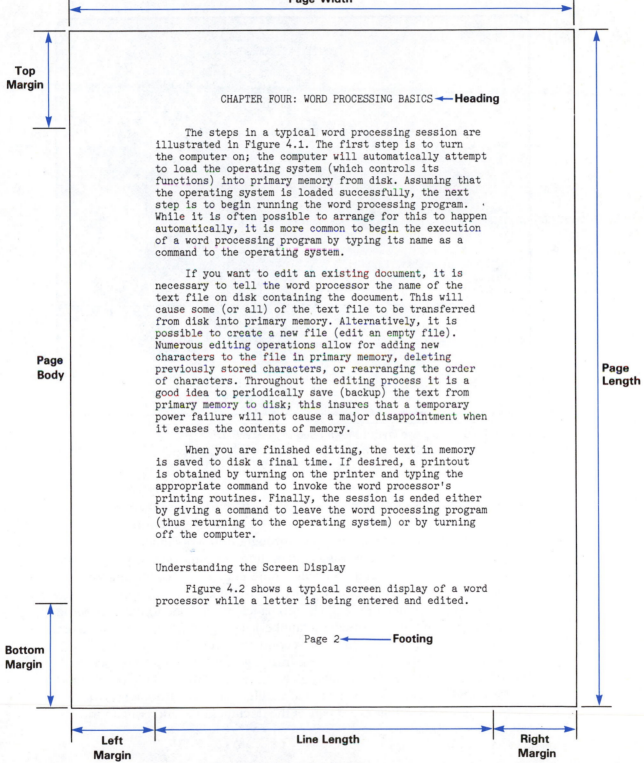

Page Width

Top Margin

CHAPTER FOUR: WORD PROCESSING BASICS ◀── **Heading**

    The steps in a typical word processing session are
illustrated in Figure 4.1. The first step is to turn
the computer on; the computer will automatically attempt
to load the operating system (which controls its
functions) into primary memory from disk. Assuming that
the operating system is loaded successfully, the next
step is to begin running the word processing program.
While it is often possible to arrange for this to happen
automatically, it is more common to begin the execution
of a word processing program by typing its name as a
command to the operating system.

    If you want to edit an existing document, it is
necessary to tell the word processor the name of the
text file on disk containing the document. This will
cause some (or all) of the text file to be transferred
from disk into primary memory. Alternatively, it is
possible to create a new file (edit an empty file).
Numerous editing operations allow for adding new
characters to the file in primary memory, deleting
previously stored characters, or rearranging the order
of characters. Throughout the editing process it is a
good idea to periodically save (backup) the text from
primary memory to disk; this insures that a temporary
power failure will not cause a major disappointment when
it erases the contents of memory.

    When you are finished editing, the text in memory
is saved to disk a final time. If desired, a printout
is obtained by turning on the printer and typing the
appropriate command to invoke the word processor's
printing routines. Finally, the session is ended either
by giving a command to leave the word processing program
(thus returning to the operating system) or by turning
off the computer.

Understanding the Screen Display

    Figure 4.2 shows a typical screen display of a word
processor while a letter is being entered and edited.

                    Page 2 ◀── **Footing**

Page Body

Page Length

Bottom Margin

Left Margin   **Line Length**   **Right Margin**

Figure 5.15 *Page design terms.*

```
                    DEFINE PAGE MENU

                    Left margin: 15

                    Right margin: 70

                    Top margin: 8

                    Bottom margin: 8

                    Lines per page: 66

Heading (Left/Center/Right): C
Line 1: CHAPTER FOUR: WORD PROCESSING BASICS
Line 2:

Footing (Left/Center/Right): C
Line 1: Page 1
Line 2:
-----------------------------------------------------------------------


F1-Help                    Esc-Main Menu                    Continue
```

Figure 5.16 *The page layout menu used in PFS:WRITE.*

This method is easily learned but very restrictive because there is only one page layout menu for the entire document. For example, the top and bottom margins must be the same on all pages throughout the document.

PFS:WRITE makes the headings and footings the same on every page in the document. This means that if you want a different heading or footing for various parts of a document, then those parts must be kept in different files. For each new page it prints, PFS:WRITE automatically adds one to the number in the footing (if the footing contains a number). Thus, the footing line in Figure 5.15 reads "Page 2" because it is the second page in the file.

Figure 5.17 illustrates how the margins and headings are set with WordStar. The top line of the display gives the name of the file being edited and the location of the cursor. The next line is called the **ruler line;** it sets the line length. The next seven lines are part of the document file and contain the following dot commands:

.MT 8 (*margin top*) and .MB 8 (*margin bottom*) set the top and bottom margins to 8 lines.

.HM 4 (*heading margin*) and .FM 4 (*footing margin*) place the heading and footing 4 lines above and below the body of the text.

.PO 14 (*page offset*) shifts the printed page (not the text on the screen) 14 spaces to the right, establishing the page's left margin at column 15.

.HE CHAPTER FOUR: WORD PROCESSING BASICS provides the text and the placement of the heading. The heading is not automatically centered. You can change the heading on any page by inserting another .HE command at the appropriate place in the text.

.FO Page # sets the footing line. If the footing contains a # character, the page number is printed in place of #.

Figure 5.17 *WordStar screen display to print the page shown in Figure 5.15.*

```
         C:SAMPLE.WS  PAGE 1 LINE 1 COL  06
L----!----!----!----!----!----!----!----!----!----!----R
.MT 8_                                                            <
.MB 8                                                             <
.HM 4                                                             <
.FM 4                                                             <
.PO 14                                                            <
.HE            CHAPTER FOUR:  WORD PROCESSING BASICS              <
.FO                          Page #                               <
     The steps in a typical word processing session are
illustrated in Figure 4.1.  The first step is to turn
the computer on; the computer will automatically attempt
to load the operating system (which controls its
functions) into primary memory from disk.  Assuming that
the operating system is loaded successfully, the next
step is to begin running the word processing program.
While it is often possible to arrange for this to happen
automatically, it is more common to begin the execution
of a word processing program by typing its name as a
command to the operating system.                                 <
                                                                 <

     If you want to edit an existing document, it is
necessary to tell the word processor the name of the
text file on disk containing the document.  This will
cause some (or all) of the text file to be transferred
```

For books or other large manuscripts, it is nice to have the headings and footings appear on the side of the page farther from the binding. With WordStar you can do this (by placing a [CTRL]-[K] in the headings and footings). In many books the headings are different on odd- and even-numbered pages (for example, "Chapter 2" might appear on the odd-numbered pages and "Introduction to Chemistry" on the even pages). But neither WordStar nor PFS:WRITE allows you to do this.

Page Breaks

A **page break** occurs when one page ends and another begins. Page breaks occur automatically when all the lines between the top and bottom margins are filled. Normally, screen-oriented word processors show the page breaks on the screen. But an off-screen print formatter provides no clue during editing about where page breaks will fall.

There are times, such as at the end of a section or chapter, when you want to start a new page rather than fill the rest of the current page. The WordStar command to force a page break is .PA. After this command is given, WordStar displays a line of hyphens on the next screen line; this signals the end of the page. The PFS:WRITE command to force a page break is *NEW PAGE*. But PFS:WRITE does not consider the *NEW PAGE* command until printing; so all the page breaks after a *NEW PAGE* command are displayed incorrectly on the screen.

Paragraph Layout

Words, lines, and paragraphs have different meanings in word processing than in everyday life. In word processing a **word** is a string of letters or numerals. Words are separated one from another by spaces, punctuation marks (commas, periods, question marks, and so on), and carriage returns. To a word processor, *R2D2* is as valid a word as any other.

A **line** is one row of text on the screen or on paper. At the end of each line is a carriage return, which can be either hard or soft. A **hard carriage return** is a return generated by pressing [ENTER] (or on some keyboards, [RETURN] or [↵]). **Soft carriage returns** are generated automatically by the word wrap feature. When a word extends beyond the maximum line length, word wrap moves the last word on the line to the next line and places a soft carriage return at the end of the old line.

A **paragraph** is a string of characters ended by a hard carriage return. Paragraphs can be quite short, and they don't necessarily form a complete thought. For example, if you type "Bananas" and press [ENTER], then type "Apples" and press [ENTER], and then type "Oranges" and press [ENTER], you will place three one-word paragraphs in the document.

Paragraph Reforming

Insertion, deletion, and other editing operations will shorten some lines and lengthen others. On a typewriter the changed paragraphs would need to be retyped. But this is where a word processor shines. **Paragraph reforming** will shift words up to fill the shortened lines or move words down to trim the long ones.

To reform a paragraph, the word processor first removes the soft carriage returns (and any other "soft" characters previously added by the word processor, such as **soft spaces,** which spread out the line to end squarely with the right margin). Then it determines which words fit on each new line. Finally it adds soft carriage returns at the ends of the new lines (and possibly other "soft" characters). The word processor may reform paragraphs automatically or only when the user requests reforming.

In PFS:WRITE a paragraph is reformed whenever a change is made in it. As characters are inserted into a paragraph, words are moved off the end of the current line, which makes the rest of the paragraph ripple with action as the effect of the insertion trickles down. Some people find this **dynamic paragraph reforming** disconcerting because of the constant movement on the screen.

WordStar doesn't reform a paragraph unless you ask it to do so by typing [CTRL]-[B]. Then the paragraph containing the cursor is shaped to fit within the current margins of the ruler line, as illustrated in Figure 5.18. In the figure the end of each paragraph is indicated on the screen by a "<" in the right-most column of every paragraph's last line. WordStar reforms only one paragraph for each [CTRL]-[B] that is typed. If the cursor is in the middle of a paragraph, then a [CTRL]-[B] reforms only the bottom part of the paragraph. Most people find this type of reforming—**manual paragraph reforming**—inferior to dynamic paragraph reforming because it requires more work.

Figure 5.18 *Reforming a paragraph in WordStar by typing [CTRL]-[B].*

```
Pg 1  Line 1  Col 1
L--------------------------R


_    Marriage resembles a pair of
shears, so joined that they can not
be separated; often moving in
opposite directions, yet always
punishing anyone who comes between
them.                              <
     What dreadful hot weather we
have!  It keeps me in a continual
state of inelegance.               <
```

```
Pg 1  Line 7  Col 1
L--------------------------R


     Marriage resembles a pair
of shears, so joined that they
can not be separated; often
moving in opposite directions,
yet always punishing anyone who
comes between them.            <
_    What dreadful hot weather we
have!  It keeps me in a continual
state of inelegance.           <
```

Reforming a paragraph can cause hyphenation problems. A long word that falls in the middle of a line before reforming might not quite fit after reforming. If the word is moved to the next line, the current line must have either a large blank space at the end or big gaps between the words. WordStar can solve this problem. When it is operating in a mode called **hyphen-help,** it pauses during paragraph reformation whenever moving a word to the next line would leave the current line very short. It suggests a place to hyphenate the word and then asks whether the word should be hyphenated. You can turn WordStar's hyphen-help on and off with a toggle switch. Usually the hyphen-help mode is not needed for normal-width lines; but for narrow lines it helps avoid ugly gaps between words.

A hyphen inserted using hyphen-help is called a **soft hyphen, ghost hyphen,** or **nonrequired hyphen**—the terms all mean the same thing. In contrast, a **hard hyphen** is part of a word, as in *one-upmanship.* Soft hyphens are printed only if they happen to fall at the end of a line; hard hyphens are printed regardless of their location. If editing moves words around again, you do not have to delete the soft hyphens; they are not printed unless they fall at the end of a line.

Some word processing programs have a third type of hyphen called **nonbreaking hyphens;** these hyphens cannot be used at the end of a line. For example, you might want a nonbreaking hyphen in the phrase "24-line display" to ensure that "24-" does not appear at the end of one line, with "line display" on the next.

Line Spacing

On most programs you can change the distance between lines from one paragraph to the next. Thus, a page might be doubled-spaced except for a single-spaced paragraph in the middle. WordStar, for example, can be set to place none, one, or even eight or nine blank lines between each line of text. Whenever a paragraph is reformed, the current line-spacing value is used.

In contrast, PFS:WRITE treats line spacing as a global characteristic; it cannot be varied within a document. The line spacing is set to single-space or double-space as part of the PRINT command.

Paragraph Margins

Suppose you want to distinguish long quotations from the rest of a document by using narrower margins for the quotation. To do this and similar tasks efficiently, it is important to be able to vary the margins of a paragraph independently from the margins of the page. On WordStar you can do this by temporarily changing the left and right margins of the ruler line and then reforming the paragraph. For example, suppose that when you entered the document the ruler line was

```
L----!----!----!----!----!----!----!----!----!----!-------R
```

Now if you want one paragraph to have narrower margins, before reforming that paragraph you might adjust the ruler line to look like

```
L----!----!----!----!----!----!----!----!----!--R
```

The left and right margins can be set at any time during the program.

Many other methods of controlling indentation and spacing are possible. For example, Multimate allows you to establish multiple ruler lines so that it is easier to set up a document with several columns. In addition most word processors allow tab stops to be set and removed; the tab stops make it easy to move across the screen quickly.

Centered, Ragged, and Justified Text

Almost every word processor has a simple, convenient command for centering a line between the left and right margins (see Figure 5.19). Centering makes titles stand out from the rest of the text.

Handwritten and typed documents have **ragged right** margins. In other words, the right-hand edge is ragged; the ends of lines look uneven. On most word processors a ragged right margin is the default value.

Occasionally, ragged left lines are necessary; for example, some letter formats call for the date to be aligned with the right margin—that is, ragged left. Neither PFS:WRITE nor WordStar has a specific command to create a ragged left margin, but you can make individual lines ragged left by inserting spaces at the beginning of the line until the end of the line is flush with the right margin.

Figure 5.19 *Samples of ragged-right, centered, and ragged-left text.*

```
L--------------R           L--------------R           L--------------R
The text in this           The text in this           The text in this
screen is flush            screen is centered         screen is flush
with the left-hand              between the           with the right-hand
margin.                    left- and right-hand               margin.
                               margins.
```

To **justify** text is to align it within boundaries. **Left-justified** text is placed flush against the left margin. Numbers are usually **right-justified** so that their decimal points fall in the same column. The printing in newspapers and books is both left- and right-justified. Because ''left- and right-justified'' is a mouthful, text with straight left and right margins is simply said to be **justified.** Justified documents look professional, but studies have shown that documents with ragged right margins are easier to read.

Text is justified by padding short lines with spaces. Most monitors display characters in fixed positions on the screen. On these systems it is either impossible or extremely slow to shift a character left or right less than a full column position. Consequently, these systems generally justify text on the screen by inserting full column-width spaces between words. Even if the spaces are spread out as evenly as possible, they are noticeable, especially on narrow lines.

Justified text often looks better on the printed page than on the screen. For example, most daisy-wheel printers can position the printhead in 1/120-inch increments. If the word processing software and the printer communicate correctly, these printers can insert very tiny spaces between letters and words to give a professional appearance (see Figure 5.20). This is called **microspacing.** The printer spreads enough of the 1/120-inch spaces between the letters and spaces to equal the number of whole spaces needed to fill the line.

Both PFS:WRITE and WordStar have a toggle that turns justification on and off. WordStar uses full-width spaces to justify lines on the screen; but if the printer is capable of microspacing, then it uses variable-width spaces to justify printed text. PFS:WRITE makes no attempt to justify text on the screen and does not use microspacing regardless of the printer's capabilities.

Microspacing does not produce printed text identical to typeset text. Professional typesetters use **proportional spacing** to achieve perfect spacing (see Figure 5.21). In proportional spacing, letters are placed in fields with different widths; for instance, an *M* is given more room than an *a*. This keeps the space

Figure 5.20 *Text justified with fixed-width spaces and microspacing.*

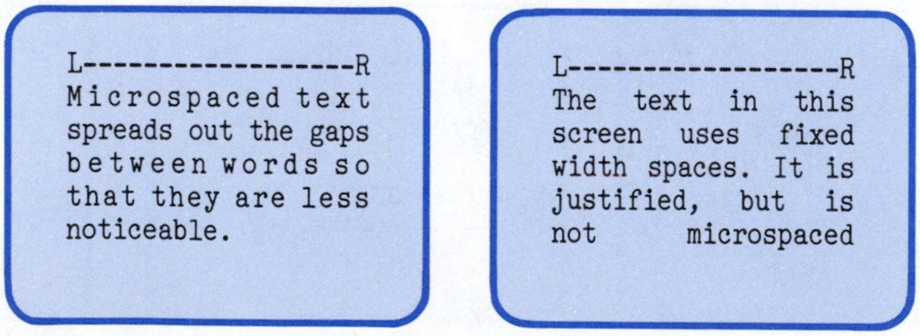

```
L-----------------R        L-----------------R
Microspaced text           The   text   in   this
spreads out the gaps       screen  uses   fixed
between words so           width spaces. It is
that they are less         justified,  but   is
noticeable.                not        microspaced
```

```
Prestige Pica

Prestige Pica is a taller, bolder
and more formal version of Pica.
It is frequently used in legal
typing.

10 pitch
```

```
Boldface

Boldface is a classic style, originally
designed for newspaper use.  It
is striking and formal in appearance.

Proportional space
```

Figure 5.21 *Sample output from a fixed-width and a proportionally spaced print wheel.*

between each letter the same, permitting more text to fit on each page without reducing the document's readability. Neither PFS:WRITE nor WordStar can create proportionally spaced documents.

■ Memory Management

Most word processors automatically manage the computer's memory so that they never have to give a message like

```
FATAL ERROR:  MEMORY FULL; PLEASE RE-BOOT.
```

It is nice to know that the system will not "crash" because you attempt to enter more text than will fit into memory. Still, this does not mean that you can afford to be ignorant about where your text is being stored. Understanding how your word processor manages memory is important if you want to write a long document—or if you want to recover the last five pages of a document that have been accidentally deleted.

Disk-based Versus Memory-based Word Processors

All word processors load the entire contents of short documents into memory. This allows short response times even when you move from one end of the document to the other, because it is not necessary to access the disk. How a long document is handled by the computer depends on whether the word processor is a memory-based or a disk-based system.

Memory-based word processors *require* that the entire document fit into memory while it is being edited. If a document is large enough to fill the available memory, it must be broken into pieces before more text can be added. Each piece is saved as a separate file on a disk. For example, in an IBM PC with 128KB of main memory, PFS:WRITE limits each file in a multifile document to 16 pages of single-spaced text. If the main memory is larger than 128KB, each file can also be larger. Other examples of memory-based word processors are AppleWriter II and WordJuggler.

Editing a long document on a memory-based word processor can be a real chore, particularly if it is necessary to move text frequently from one of the document's files to another. **Disk-based word processors** are more convenient; they can edit files that are too long to fit into memory at once. Figure 5.22 shows how a disk-based word processor loads the text that is being edited into

Figure 5.22 *Disk-based document editing.*

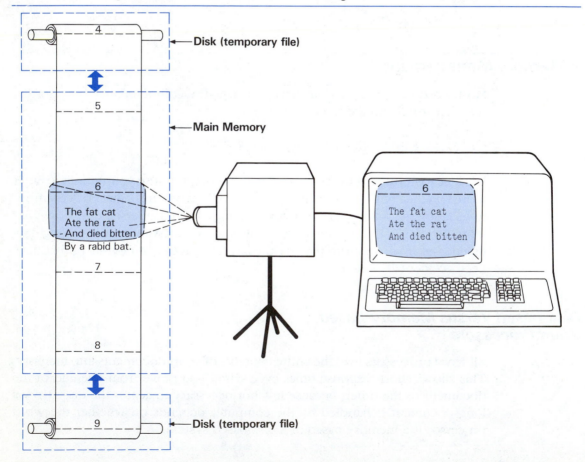

memory while the rest of the document is stored in temporary disk files. As a result, the size of a document is limited only by the storage capacity of the disk, which typically is between 200 and 1,200 kilobytes for floppy disks and 10 to 100 megabytes for personal computer hard disks. Examples of disk-based word processors are WordStar, Multimate, Microsoft Word, and WordPerfect.

Scrolling through a large document with a disk-based word processor is occasionally interrupted while some of the text in memory is moved to the disk and replaced by new text. As with program overlays (discussed in Chapter 2), the data transfers happen automatically and are noticeable only because of the noise of the drives and the delay. Sometimes the delay can be substantial. On many systems the command to jump to the bottom of a 100-page document takes over a minute to execute.

Back-up

The best defense against a serious loss of data is to have extra back-up copies of the file stored on disk. That way when something happens to the master copy, a back-up copy can take its place.

Almost all word processors provide some back-up automatically. They alter the contents of memory or temporary disk files to reflect changes made during an editing session; the changes do not affect the master copy (if any) that is on the disk. If something really drastic occurs, it is possible to abandon (*quit*) the current editing session without transferring (*saving*) anything to the disk, leaving the master file unmodified. Abandoning an editing session can be a mixed blessing. You are not likely to be enthusiastic about losing the results of two hours of editing just because you deleted a paragraph by accident.

Sometimes the word processor will abandon the current editing session without asking for your approval. A loss of electricity for a second or more causes this reaction. Less frequently, a bug in the word processing program sends the machine into never-never land until it is rebooted. The way to protect against these problems is to save periodically a copy of the edited text. A few word processors, such as WordPerfect, can be set up to transfer edited text automatically to the disk after a specified length of time (or a specified number of keystrokes), but typically the operator must request that text be saved.

Many word processors retain the original master file as a back-up file whenever the document being edited is saved. For example, assume that you begin by editing a file named A:LETTER, causing a copy of the LETTER file to be transferred from disk drive A to memory. Now assume that after editing the text in memory you request the revised text to be transferred to the disk. Many word processors implement this command by first giving a new name to the old master file A:LETTER (perhaps calling it A:LETTER.BAK), and then saving the new, edited text as the file named A:LETTER. Some systems even allow you to specify how many generations of a file should be retained by assigning generation numbers to back-up files. For example, if the system is set to retain two back-up generations and you ask to save a new version of the file A:LETTER, then the previous version of A:LETTER would be renamed A:LETTER.1, the previous version of A:LETTER.1 would become A:LETTER.2, and the previous version of A:LETTER.2 would be thrown away.

We would be remiss if we didn't emphasize again that disks are not as reliable a storage medium as paper. Crumpling up a piece of paper, or even spilling coffee on it, is not likely to make its contents unreadable. Not so with disks. Important files should always be stored on two disks and the disks should be stored separately.

■ Summary

This chapter has covered a lot of ground, and perhaps you are beginning to feel that learning to use a word processor is difficult. That impression would be misleading. Some things—like brushing your teeth, riding a bicycle, or using a word processor—are harder to describe than they are to do.

Most of the time spent working with a word processor is spent on the four fundamental operations of entering and editing: (1) moving the cursor, (2) viewing the text by scrolling, (3) entering new characters of text (using either the insert or the replacement mode), and (4) deleting characters. You can become comfortable with these four operations with only an hour or so of practice.

The usual steps in creating a letter, memo, or other document are quite simple.

- Begin running the word processing program.
- Give a name to the file that will contain the document.
- Type the document in the insert mode. Use the operations for deleting, inserting, and replacing characters to correct simple typing mistakes.
- Scroll to view the document during proofreading and editing. For each correction move the cursor to the appropriate location and make the change using the character-delete, insert, or replace operations.
- Save the document on a disk periodically and immediately before quitting.
- Print the document by turning the printer on and typing the PRINT command.
- Quit the word processing program.

There are two methods for specifying how to format the characters to be printed. Some word processors use on-screen text formatting (what-you-see-is-what-you-get). Off-screen print formatting ignores the appearance of text on the screen and uses special print-formatting commands embedded in the text to control the appearance of the printed document.

Word processors have a wide variety of convenient editing, formatting, and printing features. Whole blocks of text can be deleted, copied, and moved anywhere. Phrases can be located and replaced throughout the document. Options for page design include headings, footings, page numbers, and forced page breaks. Word wrap automatically returns the carriage at the end of a line. In most products the margin and tab settings can be viewed on the screen and the settings changed if needed.

Electrical storage in main memory is less reliable than magnetic storage on disk. Both are less reliable than storing information on paper. Making copies of your work on a disk (and on paper) is like buying an insurance policy: usually you don't need it; but when you do, it pays off handsomely.

Key Terms

automatic search and replace	justified
backward deletion	left-justified
block operations	line
buffer	manual paragraph reforming
character attributes	margins
character-delete command	memory-based word processing
character enhancements	microspacing
deletion (backward and forward)	nonbreaking hyphen
disk-based word processing	nonrequired hyphen
dot command	off-screen print formatting
dynamic paragraph reforming	on-screen text formatting
footing	page break
forward deletion	page design
ghost hyphen	paging
global search and replace	paragraph
hard carriage return	paragraph layout
hard hyphen	paragraph reforming
heading	print-formatting program
highlighting	print-preview
home	proportional spacing
horizontal scrolling	ragged right margin
hyphen-help	replacement mode
insert mode	right-justified
inverse video	ruler line

screen-oriented word processing
scrolling (down and up)
search phrase
soft carriage return
soft hyphen

soft spaces
text formatting
toggle switch
word
word wrap

Discussion Questions

1. Compare the capabilities of typewriters with those of word processors. What types of tasks would be easier with a typewriter? When would you prefer a word processor?

2. Can you give a general rule about when it is more efficient (needing fewer keystrokes) to correct an error by using the insert mode rather then the replacement mode?

3. When are you likely to use forward deletion? Backward deletion? Which are you more likely to use?

4. Would you prefer to use a full-featured off-screen print formatter or a simple on-screen formatter? Why?

5. Describe the steps necessary to change the address in a letter stored on a disk.

6. What happens if you accidentally turn off the computer while using your word processor? Is everything lost?

7. When is it more efficient to use block operations rather than one-character-at-a-time operations? How many keystrokes must you make to move a block on your word processor?

8. Suppose a word processor can perform block operations only on a character, word, sentence, paragraph, or page. Is this a serious limitation?

9. Suppose the words *bright* and *night* were misspelled as "brite" and "nite" throughout a document. Could one global search-and-replace operation be used to correct the misspellings of these words?

10. What is the difference between hard and soft characters?

11. Which type of paragraph reforming would you prefer—dynamic or manual? Why?

12. What is the difference between microspacing and proportional spacing? What types of documents require proportional spacing?

Exercises

1. Determine what status and help information is displayed by your word processor while editing. Be sure you understand what all of the characters on the screen mean.

2. Consult the manual for your word processor to find the keys to press for the following commands:
   a. Load the word processing program.
   b. Name the file containing the document.
   c. Move the cursor up, down, right, or left.
   d. Scroll up and down.
   e. Move the cursor to the beginning or the end of the document.
   f. Delete a single character at the cursor or to the left of the cursor.
   g. Toggle between the insert and the replacement modes.
   h. Save the document in a file.
   i. Print a document.
   j. Exit from the word processing program.
   k. Quit an editing session without saving the changes made during the session.

3. Would you use character-delete and insert or character-replace to correct the errors below?
   a. `I think I mispelled a word.`
   b. `In 1942 Columbus sailed the ocean blue.`
   c. `$ 2,345.23`
      `  32,679.21`
      `$35,674.46`
   d. KNOCK! NOCKK! WHOSE THERE?
   e. I think that that I shall never see,
      A poem as tree.

4. Consult the manual for your word processor to find all of the ways to move the cursor other than up, down, left, and right a single line or character.

5. Determine what happens to the previous copy of the document when you save a modified version on a disk with your word processor.

6. Use your word processor to write a letter requesting an annual report from General Electric Corporation. Request an annual report from Westinghouse. How much less time did you spend preparing the second letter?

7. Experiment with the word wrap feature of your word processor. How does it define a word? What effect do characters such as numerals or dashes have? What is the maximum word length?

8. Determine the maximum block size (if any) that your word processor can handle.

9. Consult the manual for your word processor to find all of the criteria for a match that can be used in a search.

10. Can you exit from your word processor without saving the document? Do you think a word processor should give you a message if you attempt to do this?

advanced word processing

6

6

In Chapter 5 we described the mechanics of writing, editing, and formatting with a word processor. This chapter covers the intermediate features provided by most word processors and the "bells and whistles" of sophisticated word processing. Along the way you will gain perspective on the differences among word processing programs and acquire a sense of how important it is to choose your word processing program wisely.

The timesavers and writing aids described in this chapter are not mandatory for most writing projects, but they can be very convenient. Any serious writer should master them. The features can help you create better-looking documents with much less effort. They make it possible to

- get information about how to use the word processor.
- edit several files at the same time and transfer information among them conveniently.
- undo commands given in error, erasing their effect as if they had never happened.
- change the size and style of characters.
- prevent the last line of a paragraph from being printed on the top of a new page.
- reserve room for a table or figure that doesn't fit at the bottom of a page.
- avoid the need to shift text before or after footnotes by hand by arranging for footnotes to be printed appropriately at the bottom of the page.
- proofread a document for spelling errors at 10,000 characters per minute.
- look up the synonyms of a word at the touch of a button.
- merge names and addresses from one file with a standardized letter in another to print hundreds of "individualized" letters.
- number all the pages in a large document correctly, even if parts of the document are stored in many files.
- assemble a personalized letter in a couple of minutes from prewritten paragraphs.
- create an index or a table of contents, complete with accurate page numbers, as a by-product of writing the document.

■ Comparing Word Processors

The mistakes people make in selecting a word processor are amazing. Any bare-bones word processor can handle a one-page letter or memo. But a bare-bones word processor is the wrong product to use if you are sending out hundreds of personalized letters; a word processor that can produce form letters is much more efficient. Similarly, a casual user who plans to write short memos does not want a word processor designed for professional typesetters.

Table 6.1 *A Comparison Chart for Four Word Processors*

Feature	PFS:WRITE	WordStar	WordStar 2000	Microsoft Word 2.0
Cursor Movement				
by character/word/line/paragraph	Y/Y/Y/N	Y/Y/Y/N	Y/Y/Y/N	Y/N/N/N
horizontal scrolling	No	Yes	Yes	Yes
supports editing with a mouse	No	No	No	Yes
Deletion				
by character/word/line	Yes	Yes	Yes	Y/N/N
recover deletions (UNDO commands)	No	No	Yes	Yes
by marked block	Yes	Yes	Yes	Yes
Display				
separate windows into different files	No	No	Up to 3	Up to 8
bold/underline/italics displayed on screen	Y/N/N	No	Y/Y/N	Y/Y/Y
paragraph reforming	Dynamic	Manual	Dynamic	Dynamic
Block operations				
copy/move block within file	Yes	Yes	Yes	Yes
move columns (rectangles) of text	No	Yes	Yes	No
save/load block to or from disk	No	Yes	Yes	Yes
Page design				
print multiple columns (galleys) on a page	No	No	No	Yes
widows and orphans avoided automatically	No	No	No	Yes
floating figures/tables/footnotes	No	Y/Y/N	Y/Y/N	Yes
Page headings and footings				
single line/multiple line	Y/Y	Y/N	Y/Y	Y/Y
odd/even page distinctions	No	Some	Yes	Yes
Help				
number of screens available	8	About 20	About 100	About 100
context-sensitive	Yes	No	Yes	Yes
Spelling correction	Optional	Optional	Yes	Yes
Document assembly				
chaining files together	Yes	Optional	Yes	Yes
glossary of boilerplate paragraphs	No	No	No	Yes
automatic index, table of contents	No	Optional	Optional	No
form letters with address insertion	Optional	Optional	Optional	Yes
Printer control				
microspace justification	No	Yes	Yes	Yes
proportional spacing	No	No	Yes	Yes
multiple copies printed automatically	Yes	No	Yes	Yes
print spooling (editing while printing)	No	Yes	Slowly	Yes
Hard disk support	Yes	Yes	Yes	Yes
Copy-protected disk	Yes	No	No	Yes
Minimum memory requirement	128KB	64KB	256KB	256KB

The first step in choosing a word processor is to define your writing needs. How often will you use it? How important is ease of use versus long-run convenience and advanced features? What type of documents will you create? Do you have any unusual writing needs, such as the need to print scientific equations containing Greek letters? What type of printer will you use?

After you have answered these questions, you need to know what types of features you can expect to find. One source to check is the reviews printed in magazines like *InfoWorld* and *Personal Computing.* The comparison charts at the end of these articles often go on for page after page with concise but cryptic labels for each feature. Table 6.1 is an abbreviated chart that compares the features of four word processors available for IBM PCs: PFS:WRITE, WordStar, WordStar 2000, and Microsoft Word.

- *PFS:WRITE* is designed for easy use by casual users. Most of its commands are prompted by full-screen menus. As a result, even someone unfamiliar with computers can begin using it productively after just an hour or two of practice.

- *WordStar* was one of the first word processing programs for personal computers that was designed for professional use. Some of its commands require a combination of keystrokes, such as pressing [CTRL]-[K] and then [B] to mark the beginning of a block. Other features are implemented by inserting dot commands in the text to control how a document is printed. It takes many days of practice to become comfortable with the full range of WordStar's commands; but once the commands have been learned, they are far less intrusive than the frequent appearance of full-screen menus.

- *WordStar 2000* is an extensive revision of the original WordStar program. It has so many new features that it takes eight double-sided disks to store all of the programs, the help messages, the dictionary, and the tutorial. Clearly, WordStar 2000 was designed to be used on a hard disk system. New features include true proportional spacing of printed output, better screen display of bold and underlined characters, the ability to divide the screen into windows, and a built-in spelling checker.

- *Microsoft Word* is a state-of-the-art program with many innovative features for creating professional quality-documents quickly. It allows the user to create typeset documents, to print footnotes easily, to create format files (known as *style sheets*) containing instructions on how to format a particular type of document, and to use a mouse to speed up editing.

Among other things, Table 6.1 illustrates that word processors are definitely not the same. Which one is "best" depends on the type of writing to be done; a word processor should be selected with care. A complete list of the features available in commercial word processors would fill an encyclopedia; in this chapter we describe a sample of important features.

■ Convenience Features

A car equipped with power steering, air conditioning, and power locks for the doors is easier to operate and more comfortable than a stripped-down model. A word processor equipped with convenient features has similar advantages—and it may cost no more than a bare-bones package. Today's word processors are full of short cuts, writing aids, formatting tricks, and other helpful features. Some make life easier for beginners; others are essential for specific tasks; and still others sound better in advertisements than they work in practice. This section describes three useful features: on-line help, windows, and UNDO commands.

On-line Help

At its best, on-line help is like a reference manual that consistently falls open to the right page. A **context-sensitive help system** silently observes which function is being used and stands ready to present information about that function and what can be done next—all at the touch of the [HELP] key (see Figure 6.1). If the initial display is not helpful, most systems have menus from which you can select the topic for the next screen of information.

Figure 6.1 *When asked for help about its Define Page Menu (shown in Figure 5.16), PFS:WRITE provides this display.*

```
Define Page
Options          What to enter

LEFT MARGIN      Column number of the left edge of the document.

RIGHT MARGIN     Column number of the right edge of the document.

TOP MARGIN       Number of lines for the top margin.

BOTTOM MARGIN    Number of lines for the bottom margin.

LINES PER PAGE   Number of lines on each page. An 8-1/2 by 11 inch
                 page is typically 66 lines long.

HEADING AND      Whatever you type in the heading or footing item, WRITE
FOOTING          will print on each page of the document. You are
                 allowed two lines for each. To position the heading
                 and footing between the margins, type L (Left margin),
                 R (Right margin) or C (Center). To have WRITE
                 print page numbers, type the number of the first page
                 (usually 1) in the footing. Type 0 in the footing if
                 you want the page number omitted from a cover page.

                 Esc-Main Menu                        Continue
```

Windows

Suppose you are writing a paper and are trying to coordinate the introduction of a topic on page 2 with the main exposition on page 20. On many word processors the best way to do this is to put *place markers* on both pages and use a command to jump back and forth between the pages. But some word processors offer a more convenient method: both areas of text can be displayed simultaneously in different windows on the screen.

In word processing a *window* is a region of the screen that works as if it had its own TV camera pointed at a scroll of text (see Figure 6.2). Most word processors use tiled windows (described in Chapter 4); they cannot overlap as free-form windows do. For example, WordStar 2000 can split the screen horizontally into three windows of identical size, as shown in Figure 6.3. Microsoft Word is more flexible. It allows up to eight windows to be established by splitting existing windows horizontally or vertically (see Figure 6.4).

Figure 6.2 *Windows on a screen split horizontally.*

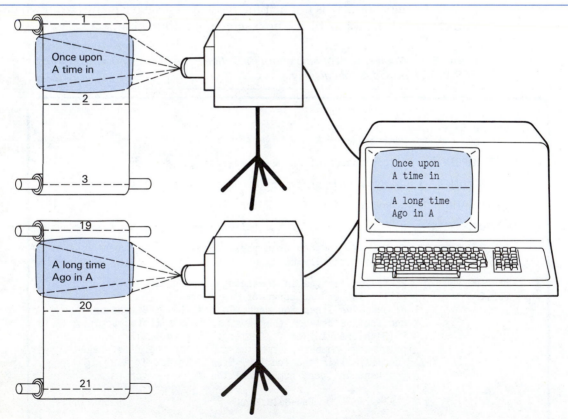

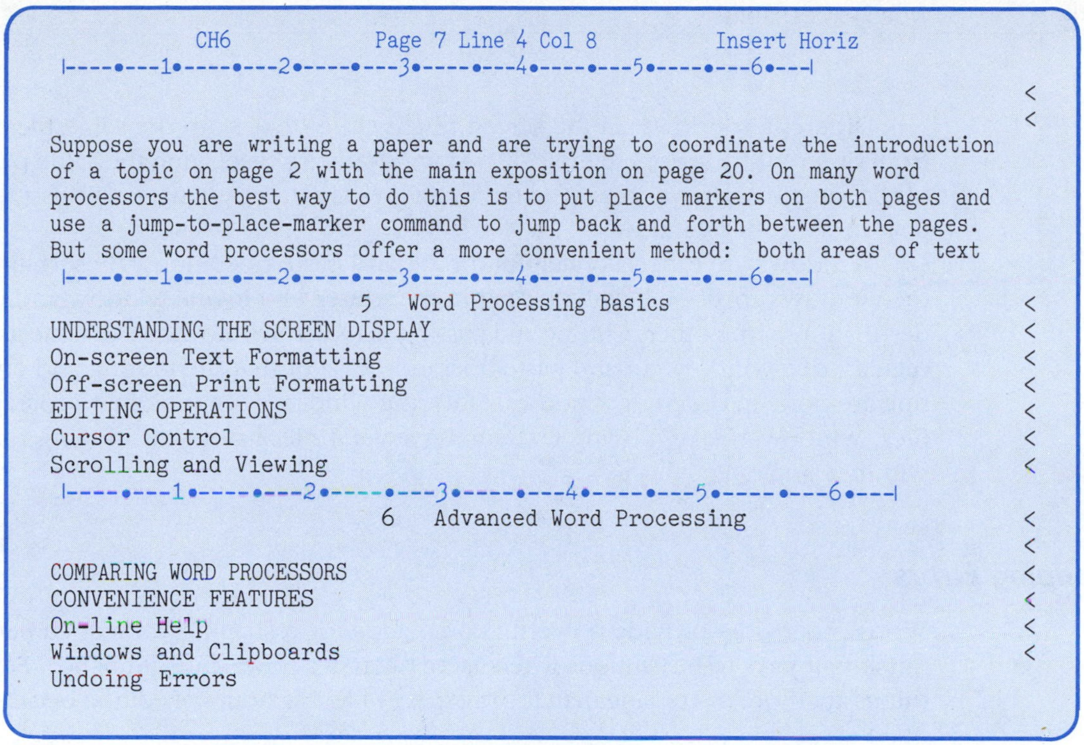

```
|----•----1•----•----2•----•----3•----•----4•----•----5•----•----6•----|
                                                                          <
                                                                          <
Suppose you are writing a paper and are trying to coordinate the introduction
of a topic on page 2 with the main exposition on page 20. On many word
processors the best way to do this is to put place markers on both pages and
use a jump-to-place-marker command to jump back and forth between the pages.
But some word processors offer a more convenient method:  both areas of text
|----•----1•----•----2•----•----3•----•----4•----•----5•----•----6•----|
                        5   Word Processing Basics                        <
UNDERSTANDING THE SCREEN DISPLAY                                          <
On-screen Text Formatting                                                <
Off-screen Print Formatting                                              <
EDITING OPERATIONS                                                       <
Cursor Control                                                           <
Scrolling and Viewing                                                    <
|----•----1•----•----2•----•----3•----•----4•----•----5•----•----6•----|
                        6   Advanced Word Processing                      <
                                                                          <
COMPARING WORD PROCESSORS                                                <
CONVENIENCE FEATURES                                                     <
On-line Help                                                             <
Windows and Clipboards                                                   <
Undoing Errors                                                           <
```

Figure 6.3 *WordStar 2000 splits the screen horizontally into at most three windows.*

Figure 6.4 *Microsoft Word can split the screen into eight separate window tiles.*

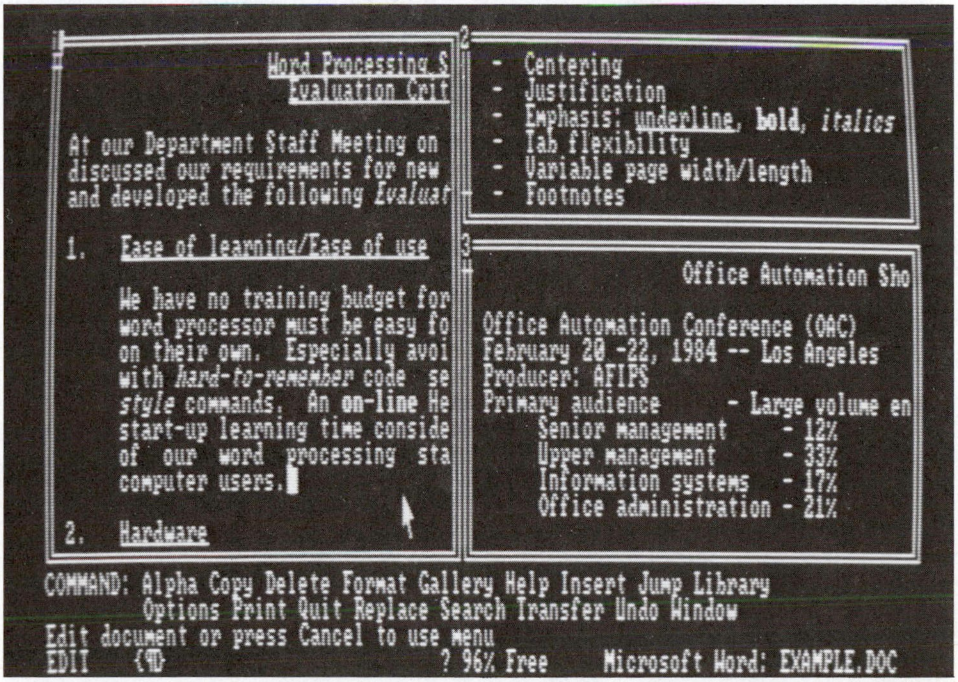

Different windows on the screen might show text from the same file or from different files. For example, if two windows are displaying the same part of the same file, then as text is edited in one window, the changes will also appear in the other window.

Windows are especially helpful for cut-and-paste operations. By scrolling the windows appropriately, you can put the source text in one window and its destination in the other. Cutting and pasting between windows is the same as a regular, one-window cut-and-paste operation except that the pasting and cutting are done in different windows. Since the windows can look into separate files, windows make moving text among several files as easy as moving text within a single file.

Undoing Errors

Word processors provide powerful commands for reshaping your document quickly. It pays to be cautious when using the more powerful commands. Few things are more distressing than the prospect of losing hours of editing because of an error.

The simplest defense against making serious errors is to be careful. For most operations, once a command is given, execution is immediate. But some operations are so destructive that the word processor requires a confirmation. For example, if you gave a command that would delete the entire document, the word processor might respond with the statement

```
DELETING ENTIRE DOCUMENT--TYPE "Y" TO CONFIRM
```

Some word processors offer another safety device: an **UNDO** command, which reverses the effect of the previous command. Pretend for the moment that instead of moving ten pages of text from one spot in memory to another, you have deleted all ten pages. The UNDO command would allow the ten pages to be restored to memory.

In practice, the UNDO command is not as helpful as it sounds. It is difficult to implement an UNDO command on a word processor—so many don't. Even word processors with an UNDO command generally undo only the effect of the very last command. Typing a second UNDO command cancels the effect of the first one; it does not allow you to work your way back to correct a mistake made several commands ago. Being limited to reversing the effect of the last command is more serious than it sounds at first. For example, Microsoft Word interprets insertion or deletion of a single character as a command. As a result, you cannot undo a command that deleted ten pages if you bump the space bar while considering what to do.

■ Character Attributes

The appearance of documents produced by a word processing system depends on the combined capabilities of the printer and the software. Buying an expensive, versatile printer is a mistake if the software you plan to use doesn't have commands for simple character attributes like boldface or underlining. Similarly, there is no sense in acquiring a state-of-the-art word processing package designed for typesetting if you use a thermal dot matrix printer. And there is another pitfall to avoid in choosing a printer and software: even if the documentation for both the printer and the software claim they accommodate a particular printing feature, they might use different coding systems to describe the feature. Because the character codes for ordinary letters and numbers are standardized, getting a printer to work like a simple typewriter is not difficult. But advanced features, such as shifting from plain text to italic, have not been standardized.

Sizes and Styles

With appropriate software and the right printer, a personal computer can produce typeset documents. This book, for example, was written on three IBM PCs and two Macintoshes. Drafts of chapters were printed on various dot matrix printers, a letter-quality NEC Spinwriter, and two nearly-typeset-quality laser printers built by Hewlett-Packard and Apple. After chapters were edited for content and style, command codes describing the page layout, type styles (called **fonts**), type sizes, vertical line spacing, and so on were added to the document files. Finally, a Compugraphic 8600 phototypesetter produced the text you are reading.

Most printers can print characters in only one size at a time; so we will not discuss typesetting in detail. Many dot matrix printers can be placed in a *graphics mode,* in which they accept commands specifying which dots to print rather than which characters to print. The Apple Macintosh builds printed characters out of a large number of individually specified dots. As a result, it can print characters in many sizes and styles (see Figure 6.5). In a similar manner, a Macintosh in conjunction with Apple's LaserWriter printer can print text and graphics with a 300 dot-per-inch resolution—nearly typeset quality.

Enhancements

Character enhancements include boldface, underline, subscript, superscript, strikeout, italics, compressed, and double-width. Figure 3.13 showed some character enhancements for dot matrix printers; Figure 6.6 does the same for letter-quality printers.

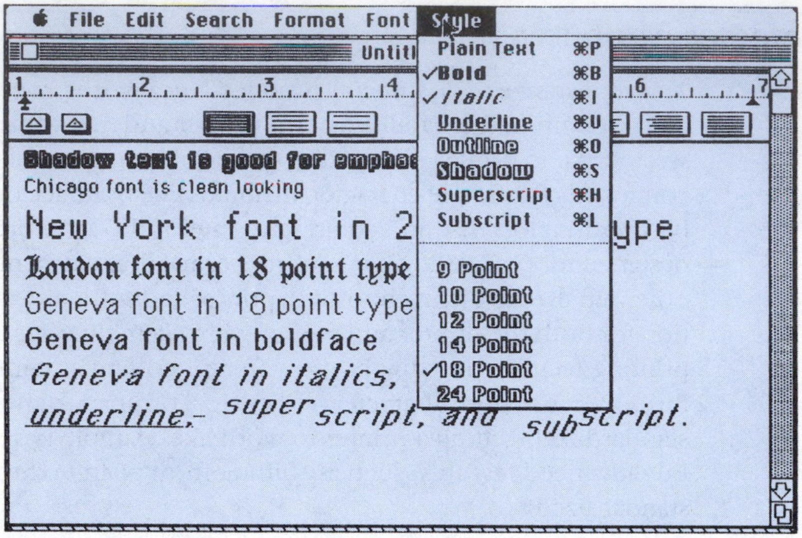

Figure 6.5 *Samples of the fonts provided by MacWrite.*

The procedure for enhancing a character depends on the program.

- In PFS:WRITE you enhance each character individually by repeatedly pressing a function key. The only enhancements available are bold and underlined characters.

- In both WordStar and WordStar 2000 you place print-control characters before and after the text to be enhanced. For example, in WordStar typing [CTRL]-[S] turns on underlining; the next [CTRL]-[S] turns it off again.

Figure 6.6 *Character enhancements available from a letter-quality printer.*

Bold letters are printed twice, shifted slightly for the second printing.

Super scripts and sub scripts require the paper to be advanced and retracted.

Double-striking is not visible with a quality ribbon, but works with faded cloth ribbons.

Underlining text is used more than ~~striking out passages~~.

Overprinting prints two characters in the same position, as in Ø.

Changing the **pitch** (the number of characters printed per inch) c a n s t r e t c h a l i n e o u t or squeeze it together.

■ In Microsoft Word you mark a block of text and then select the enhancements for the block.

Whether character enhancements are visible on the screen depends on the capabilities of the display and on the software. For example, if you use an IBM PC with a color monitor, Microsoft Word displays not only underlining but also double-underlining. But on the same monitor, none of the other programs displays underlined text correctly. Instead of underlining a character, PFS:WRITE and WordStar 2000 change the character's color. The original WordStar does the worst job of all: it displays both the text in the file and the print-control characters that it uses as print-formatting commands. So when the sequence ^STHIS TEXT IS UNDERLINED^S is printed, it would look like this: <u>THIS TEXT IS UNDERLINED.</u>

■ Page Breaks Revisited

Putting page breaks in the right spot can be difficult, especially when a document includes not only paragraphs but also footnotes, tables, figures, or section headings. At times there is no good way to break a page short of rewriting the text. In this section we describe the problems in creating page breaks as well as the partial solutions offered by some word processors.

Widows and Orphans

Sometimes an automatic page break places the first line of a paragraph at the bottom of a page, forming an **orphan line;** or it may place the last line at the top of a page, forming a **widow line.** It is generally agreed that widows and orphans are ugly, but there is no entirely satisfactory way to get rid of them without editing the text. Most word processors ignore widows and orphans, and it is a good idea to scroll through the document just before printing to eliminate them. You can get rid of orphans by adding a blank line before each one. To remove widows, edit the paragraph, jam the last line of the paragraph into the bottom margin of the page, or give the command to insert a page break before the next-to-last line in the paragraph.

Neither WordStar nor PFS:WRITE automatically avoids widows and orphans, but both have commands you can use to insert a page break. Microsoft Word avoids widows and orphans by refusing to put a page break after the first or before the last line of a paragraph. Instead, it shifts lines to the next page. Consequently, Microsoft Word never puts a page break in a three-line paragraph. If the paragraph doesn't fit entirely on the current page, it is printed on the next page. Microsoft Word does not provide a way to turn off this automatic treatment of widows and orphans.

Figures and Tables

Blank space can be placed in a document by inserting blank lines. But if you are reserving blank space for a figure or table that is to be physically pasted in later, then the blank lines must all be kept on the same page. WordStar and Microsoft Word use different methods to set up **floating figures,** that is, figures that are printed as a unit on the next page if they don't fit completely on the current page.

In WordStar you can reserve continuous blank space by using the command for a conditional page break. You type .CP and the number of lines that must stay together. For example, the command .CP 20 will force an immediate page break if fewer than 20 lines remain on the page; otherwise the command is ignored.

In Microsoft Word each paragraph has a set of attributes that define how the paragraph is to be formatted and printed. These attributes are selected from a menu that offers choices for line spacing, margins, alignment (left, centered, right, and justified), and so forth. One of the attributes is the *keep* attribute; it "keeps" the paragraph together in one piece, moving it as a unit to the next page if necessary.

Both of these methods of reserving continuous space can result in wasted blank space at the bottom of a page. Neither WordStar nor Microsoft Word has an option that floats a figure or table to the next page *after first filling the current page with text.*

Footnotes

Footnotes create their own special problems. They can appear at the bottom of the page or in a group at the end of the document. Whenever a new footnote is added to a document, all subsequent footnotes must be renumbered (unless the footnotes are referenced alphabetically, such as by the authors' names). The rules of style for footnotes are full of exceptions, and a majority of word processors do not provide special features for handling them. In word processors that do offer special help with footnotes, two features predominate: automatic numbering and bottom-of-page placement.

If a word processor provides automatic numbering, no matter how many footnotes are added or deleted, the footnotes are numbered correctly when printed. Some word processors offer automatic numbering for elements other than footnotes and page numbers, such as chapters, sections, theorems, figures, and tables.

Bottom-of-page placement floats the footnote down until it is printed after the regular text on the page.[1] The procedure for implementing this feature

---

[1] This footnote illustrates bottom-of-page placement.

varies. On some word processors you identify footnotes by marking them specially in the text, as in

```
@Footnote(¹This footnote illustrates bottom-of-page placement.)
```

In contrast, Microsoft Word stores the text for footnotes in a special section at the end of the document. Footnotes can be entered and edited in this section by opening up and using a *footnote window* on the screen. Each footnote in the section is associated with a footnote *reference mark* in the body of the document. There are commands for inserting reference marks in the body of the document and for editing the footnote section. During printing, the reference marks are replaced by the footnote numbers, and the footnote text appears either at the bottom of the pages with footnote numbers or at the end of the document depending upon what the user has selected.

■ Dictionary Aids

Near every typewriter there is likely to be a pocket dictionary, and within arm's reach of many writers is a thesaurus. For the most part, these books are used mechanically: a word is looked up to verify its spelling or discover its synonyms. Mechanical tasks are what computers excel at; so it shouldn't be surprising that there are **electronic dictionaries**—often called **spelling checkers**—and **electronic thesauruses.** Of the two products, electronic dictionaries are the more important, because they remove most of the drudgery associated with proofreading for typographical errors.

Electronic Dictionaries

A dictionary program performs the most time-consuming part of manual spelling correction: it identifies which words cannot be found in a dictionary. Checking and, if necessary, correcting words that are not in the dictionary still requires human intervention and is the most time-consuming part of computerized spelling correction.

A dictionary program works by checking to see if the words in a document file are in a list of correctly spelled words. Any word that does not match one of the words in the list is displayed as a **suspect word.** Some dictionary lists have more than 100,000 words. Most include between 20,000 and 80,000 words; so validly spelled words have a good chance of being in the dictionary. For example, in CorrectStar (a portion of WordStar 2000) the main dictionary contains 65,000 words drawn from the *American Heritage Dictionary* and occupies 304KB of disk space—not particularly compact. Because the program requires a minimum of 256KB of memory, it cannot be used on 8-bit computers.

Standard dictionaries do not include many of the words in your written vocabulary, such as the proper nouns you use frequently: your last name, the name of the street you live on, and so forth. Unless the electronic dictionary can be modified, these words will be displayed as suspect words over and over again. **Dictionary maintenance** utilities adapt the dictionary program to your vocabulary over time either by adding words to the main dictionary or by placing them in an auxiliary dictionary. Some dictionary programs offer special-purpose auxiliary dictionaries filled with medical or legal terms.

The performance of a dictionary program depends on how it looks up words in the dictionary. Many dictionary programs make two passes through the document file. On the first pass they begin by building a sorted list of all the different words in the file—without regard to whether the words are in the dictionary. Then the sorted list is compared against the dictionary to determine suspect words. On the second pass these programs either correct or flag the suspect words. In programs that flag suspect words, one letter of each suspect word is changed to a special symbol (such as [) that can be found later by search-and-replace operations.

Unlike these two-pass programs, CorrectStar proceeds by checking each word in the document file until it finds a suspect word; it then suggests a replacement word from its dictionary list and pauses for an instruction. Thus it is a one-pass, interactive dictionary program. CorrectStar and other one-pass dictionary programs store at least part of the dictionary in main memory. In CorrectStar this internal dictionary contains 9,000 of the most common English words and occupies 22.5KB of main memory. According to the documentation, 89 percent of the words in an average document are found in the internal dictionary, without recourse to the rest of the dictionary on the disk.

We can also classify dictionary programs by the type of word list they maintain; the two types are root word dictionaries and literal dictionaries. **Root word dictionaries** save storage space by stripping the prefixes and suffixes from words before checking them against the dictionary. For example, they do not store *tool* and *tools* as separate words. The disadvantage of a root word dictionary is that some invalid words like *gooses* (GOOSE + S) and *fastly* (FAST + LY) might be accepted as correct. Fortunately, people don't make this type of error very often. **Literal dictionaries** accept only exact matches; any word that does not match a word in the dictionary exactly becomes a suspect word. Even though they usually include more words than root word dictionaries, literal dictionaries are more likely to question the spelling of words with several prefixes and suffixes, such as *microcomputers* or *repeatedly*.

What do you do when a dictionary program has found a suspect word? The options available for handling suspect words vary from program to program. As Figure 6.7 shows, you can tell CorrectStar to do any of the following:

```
         SPELL.SPL        Page 1 Line 1 Col 34          Insert Horiz

 ┌─────────────────────────────────────────────────────┬──────────┐
 │ Add to dictionary        Correct all occurrences     │ Get help │
 │ Ignore                   Next suggestion             │          │
 │ Type correction          Previous suggestion         │ Escape   │
 └─────────────────────────────────────────────────────┴──────────┘
                    Press Return to correct as suggested.
     Suspect word:   chaufer
      Suggestion:    chauffeur

 |----•---1•----•---2•----•---3•----•---4•----•---5•----•---6•---|
 I have a rather garrulous chaufer  While he rarely leaves me
 lacking for conversation, he occasionally leaves me speechless.     <
                                                                     <
 The other day my garrulus friend managed to run a red light which
 had the misfortune, quite by accident, to occur in the middle of
 a sentence. We were immediately pulled over by an afishl repre-
 sentative of the law. The officer inquired why my chaufer did
 not akseed to the stop light in the first place. My friend
 replied that he thought it an odd place for a stop sign, and
 hadn't seen it.                                                      <
                                                                     <
 My chaufer noticed the officer's accent and inquired if they
 might both be from Brooklyn. When it turned out that they were,
```

Figure 6.7 *CorrectStar, an interactive dictionary program.*

- *Add to dictionary.* This option places the suspect word in an auxiliary dictionary—called a **personal dictionary**—so that the word will never again be classified as a suspect word, in this or any future session. The personal dictionary is stored on the disk.

- *Ignore.* When this option is selected, the suspect word is added to the dictionary for the duration of the spelling correction session, and CorrectStar continues checking words in the file.

- *Type correction.* The program replaces the suspect word with whatever is typed on the keyboard (after verifying that this replacement is in the dictionary).

- *Correct all occurrences.* If this option is chosen, CorrectStar automatically replaces every occurrence of the suspect word in the document with the suggested replacement. This is handy for those pesky words that are consistently misspelled.

- *Next suggestion* and *Previous suggestion*. These options allow all of CorrectStar's suggested replacements to be examined (or re-examined) one at a time. CorrectStar begins by showing the suggestion it considers most likely. Some words are sufficiently different from the words in CorrectStar's dictionary that it has no suggestions; it rarely has more than four or five suggestions.

Programming a computer to make reasonable suggestions for a misspelled word is not easy. Most programs help with spelling correction by providing a **dictionary look-up** function that allows you to examine portions of the dictionary list, as shown in Figure 6.8. Some dictionary programs avoid the task completely by simply flagging the suspect words. The easiest mistakes to catch are straightforward typographical errors: transposed letters, a missing letter, or an extra letter. All of the possible combinations of these errors can be compared with the dictionary; because English is a sparse language, only a few (if any) suggestions will be found. It is very difficult for dictionary programs to suggest reasonable corrections for phonetic errors, such as the use of *chaufer* instead of *chauffeur* or *fonetic* instead of *phonetic*. CorrectStar is one of the few products that usually suggests the right word to correct phonetic errors.

Dictionary programs are not proofreaders; they cannot tell when correctly spelled words are used incorrectly. They will not notice "that too errors are inn this quotation." After the dictionary program has caught the misspellings, it is best to read the document carefully for sense.

Figure 6.8 *The dictionary look-up function of The RANDOM HOUSE Proofreader.*

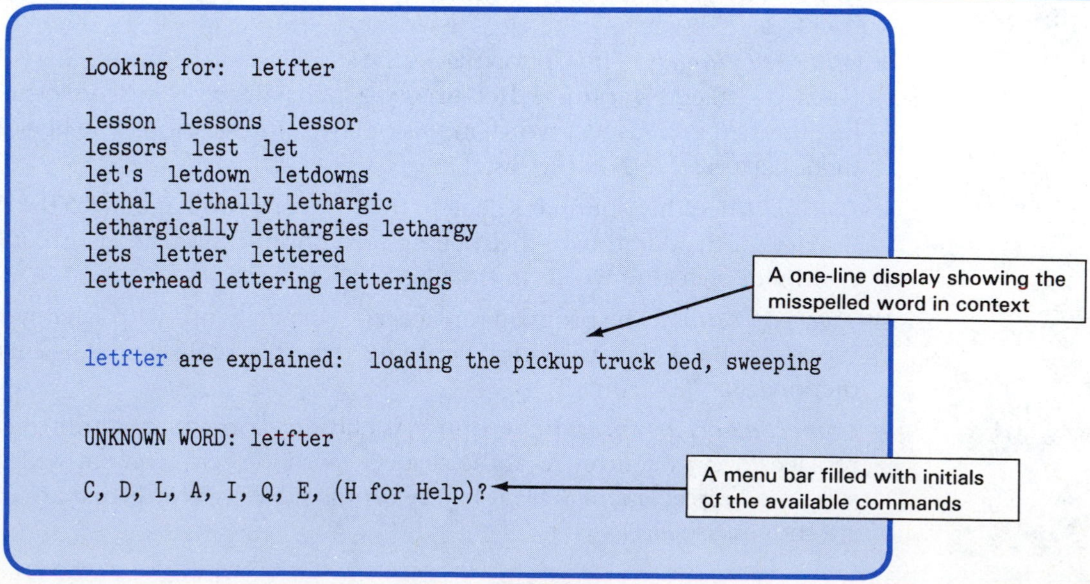

```
Looking for:  letfter

lesson  lessons  lessor
lessors  lest  let
let's  letdown  letdowns
lethal  lethally  lethargic
lethargically lethargies lethargy
lets  letter  lettered
letterhead lettering letterings


letfter are explained:  loading the pickup truck bed, sweeping


UNKNOWN WORD: letfter

C, D, L, A, I, Q, E, (H for Help)?
```

A one-line display showing the misspelled word in context

A menu bar filled with initials of the available commands

Electronic Thesauruses

Electronic dictionary programs differ from traditional paper-based dictionaries because they do not provide definitions. True dictionaries on disk will not be common until disk capacities increase, but a useful intermediate product is an *electronic thesaurus* on disk.

Because it is very easy to use, The Random House Electronic Thesaurus will serve as an example. This thesaurus is sold as part of a system that also includes a word processor, a spelling checker, a spreadsheet program, and a list manager. During word processing you can request the synonyms of any word on the screen by moving the cursor to the first letter of a word, which is called the **target word,** and pressing function key [F10]. If the target word is not one of the 4,400 key words in the thesaurus, the program displays a message that gives the entries immediately before and after the target word, as in

```
LINCOLN not in thesaurus. Found LIMPID and LINE.
```

If the target word is in the thesaurus, then the bottom part of the screen is covered by a pop-up display that gives the synonyms, as in

```
[appreciate]- (v.) be thankful for, esteem, value, be aware of,
rise or increase in value.
```

■ Form Letters

Form letters eliminate most of the work associated with printing standard business replies, and the ability to print them is invaluable for producing "personalized" mass mailings. If properly prepared, a computerized form letter is indistinguishable from a manually produced business letter, except possibly by its lack of errors.

A **form letter** is printed by merging data into a **master letter,** which is sometimes called a **matrix letter;** it contains all the text that doesn't change from one letter to the next. Figure 6.9 provides an example. A master letter has only one unusual characteristic: special **fields** receive the text that varies with each copy of the letter. Most often, fields are used to insert names and addresses; but they can contain any information, such as payments received, winning lottery numbers, or dates. Fields are given **variable names** to keep track of which pieces of information go where. For example, in Figure 6.9, the variable names are FIRST, LAST, STREET, CITY, and STATE. The information to fill in the fields can come from the keyboard, a data file, or a combination of the two. Because keyboard data entry is simplest, we will discuss it first.

```
L----!----!----!----!----!----!----!----!----!---R
<<FIRST>> <<LAST>>
<<STREET>>
<<CITY>>, <<STATE>>


Dear <<FIRST>>,

     Thank you, <<FIRST>>, for your kind donation
to my campaign fund.

     I have been trying to schedule a trip to
<<CITY>> for the last two weeks to talk about
<<CITY>>'s problems, but so far the timing hasn't
worked out right.


Sincerely,


Senator Wilson T. Krebbs
```

Figure 6.9 *The master file for a typical form letter.*

Keyboard Data Entry

If the information for the fields comes from the keyboard, then for each variable name in the master letter, the word processor displays a prompt and waits for an entry. For example, the dialog for the master letter shown in Figure 6.9 might proceed as follows (the characters in color are typed by the user):

```
Enter data for FIRST: Jim
Enter data for LAST: Bassett
Enter data for STREET: 1045 Lone Pine Road
Enter data for CITY: Stayton
Enter data for STATE: Oregon 97383
Please wait for printing to complete . . .
Enter data for FIRST: STOP
```

The finished form letter would look like the top letter in Figure 6.10.

The exact procedure for entering data varies from program to program. Some programs have handy features for customizing the prompts or for setting fields (such as the date field) to a fixed value for all copies.

Using a Data File

Information to fill in the fields of a form letter can also come from a data file. Building a data file is easier with the help of a file management program, as described in Chapter 9. But in a pinch, most word processors can create an adequate data file.

To print form letters, the word processor needs to know the data file's name and which fields in the data file correspond with which variable names in the master letter. There are many ways of giving the word processor this information. For example, we will assume that the name of the data file might be placed in the first line of the master letter with the command ⟨⟨USE B:DONOR.DAT⟩⟩ and the names of the data file's fields might be placed in the first line of the data file. Thus, the data file B:DONOR.DAT might contain

```
STREET, CITY, STATE, FIRST, LAST
1045 Lone Pine Road, Stayton, Oregon 97345, Jim, Bassett
312 High Plains Drive, Bend, Oregon 97509, Lora, Faucet
980 Friendly Oaks Manor, Roseburg, Oregon 97821, Steve, Miller
```

Figure 6.10 *The finished form letters.*

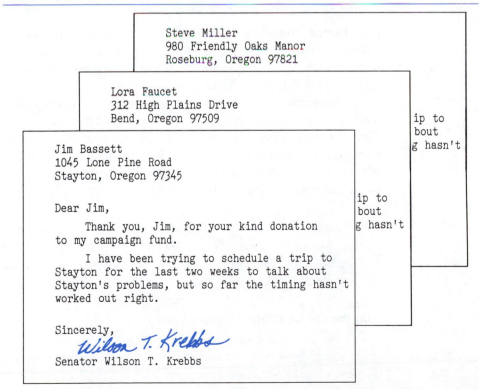

```
Steve Miller
980 Friendly Oaks Manor
Roseburg, Oregon 97821


Lora Faucet
312 High Plains Drive
Bend, Oregon 97509


Jim Bassett
1045 Lone Pine Road
Stayton, Oregon 97345

Dear Jim,

     Thank you, Jim, for your kind donation
to my campaign fund.

     I have been trying to schedule a trip to
Stayton for the last two weeks to talk about
Stayton's problems, but so far the timing hasn't
worked out right.

Sincerely,

Senator Wilson T. Krebbs
```

In this example, fields in the data file are separated by commas and are not in the same order as the variable names in the master letter. Each of the three lines in this data file would supply the data for one form letter, as shown in Figure 6.10.

■ Large Documents

Large documents are much harder to create than letters or short papers. The problem is not just that big documents have more pages but also that coordinating all the parts is more of a chore. As the document grows, its file size increases until it won't fit conveniently in one file. As soon as it is split into separate files, tasks like moving paragraphs cease to be simple operations. Instead, they require reading and writing in various files, changing disks, and the like. Even more bothersome are the chores of coordinating the page numbers among all the parts and creating an accurate table of contents and index. Managing a large document is simplified if you have a word processor that supports document chaining and can collect page references automatically.

Document Chaining

Document chaining allows information in several files to be merged and printed sequentially as if everything were in one big file. This way each file is kept to a manageable size; yet the whole document is printed at once with the pages numbered properly from start to finish.

Document files are chained together by placing in a **master file** a print-formatting command that suspends printing of the master file, prints a second file, and then continues printing the master file. Think of the master file as a form to be completed that receives its information from other files. For example, in PFS:WRITE the document-chaining command is *JOIN followed by the file name and *. Suppose the master file contains

```
Tom appeared on the sidewalk with a bucket of whitewash and a
long-handled brush. *JOIN SAWYER.TOM* Thirty yards of board
fence nine feet high. Life to him seemed hollow, and
existence but a burden.
```

And the file SAWYER.TOM contains

```
He surveyed the fence, and all gladness left him and a deep
melancholy settled down upon his spirit.
```

Then printing the master file produces

```
Tom appeared on the sidewalk with a bucket of whitewash and a
long-handled brush. He surveyed the fence, and all gladness
left him and a deep
melancholy settled down upon his spirit.
Thirty yards of board
fence nine feet high.
Life to him seemed hollow, and
existence but a burden.
```

Besides illustrating how document chaining works, this example shows that PFS:WRITE doesn't correctly reform paragraphs that contain a JOIN command. This is not a major flaw because most often document chaining is used to merge whole paragraphs or even larger units—not just sentences—with the master file. For example, a master file might include JOIN commands for each part of the document, as in

```
*JOIN B:TITLE.PG*    *NEW PAGE*
*JOIN A:CHAPTER.1*   *NEW PAGE*
*JOIN A:CHAPTER.2*   *NEW PAGE*
        .
        .
        .
*JOIN A:CHAPTER.9*   *NEW PAGE*
```

One use for document chaining is to customize letters by inserting **boilerplate** paragraphs—prewritten passages. For instance, a politician might insert a standardized paragraph about his support for social security in letters to the elderly (with a *JOIN SECURITY.OLD* command) and a paragraph about his support for more jobs in letters to teen-agers (with a *JOIN MORE.JOB* command). Lawyers often use boilerplate paragraphs in writing contracts, wills, and other legal documents. Because it is inconvenient to store each paragraph in a separate file, some word processors allow the boilerplate passages to be stored in a **glossary,** a data file designed to facilitate access to commonly used passages of text.

Nested chaining permits several levels of document chaining, such as organizing sections into chapters and then consolidating the chapters into a single document. For example, with nested chaining the master file might contain a *JOIN BEAM.JIM* command, and the BEAM.JIM file might contain a *JOIN CROW.OLD* command.

Page References

No matter how late in a document's development a table of contents and index are created, something inevitably comes up that changes the page references. Few tasks are more disheartening than reworking these aids because a couple of pages have been added or deleted from the beginning of a report—nearly every page reference must be changed. But if you have the right word processing products, a table of contents, list of figures, list of tables, bibliography, and index can be produced with relatively little extra effort as a by-product of preparing the document for printing. For example, as the printing routines send the main text to the printer, a program might keep track of the chapter titles and section headings and the page references for these. It might also automatically format this information and place it in a file that can be edited or printed. Not only does this feature eliminate the need to renumber all the page references manually when the document changes, it also results in fewer mistakes.

None of these reference aids are created by magic. Each item must be marked in a way the word processor recognizes. For example, StarIndex, an optional companion product for WordStar, recognizes two kinds of index entries.

Figure 6.11 *StarIndex extracts index entries, such as those marked in the screen, to provide the data to create indexes automatically.*

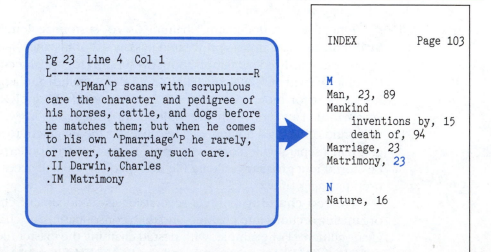

- **Embedded entries** create index items out of regular text in the document. An embedded entry is entered by placing a [CTRL]-[P] before and after text in the document.

- **Supplied entries** create index items by inserting a dot command in the document followed by the word or phrase to appear in the index. Dot commands beginning with .IM form major entries (with bold page numbers) in the index; those beginning with .II form regular entries (see Figure 6.11).

WordStar ignores these markings when it prints the document. But when StarIndex is asked to process the document, it scans from top to bottom, extracting the index entries along with their page numbers. Then it sorts the information alphabetically, formats it, and puts the finished index in a file on the disk. A sample screen display that includes index entries and a portion of the index StarIndex would create are shown in Figure 6.11.

■ Summary

Word processing is such a big improvement over pencils and typewriters that even a poor word processor can impress a new user. Few people have the time or opportunity to test numerous word processing programs; so most people choose their word processing program because it came with their computer system or was recommended by friends. As a result, the world is filled with people who happily use an inferior word processing program or one that is inappropriate for their needs.

In this chapter we described a number of useful word processing features to help you determine the types of features you would find useful. Even more important, we compared the features of four word processing programs to show that all word processing programs are not the same.

Key Terms

boilerplate	document chaining
context-sensitive help	electronic dictionary
dictionary look-up	electronic thesaurus
dictionary maintenance	embedded entry

field	orphan line
floating figures	personal dictionary
fonts	root word dictionary
form letter	spelling checker
glossary	supplied entry
literal dictionary	suspect word
master file	target word
master letter	UNDO
matrix letter	variable name
nested chaining	widow line

Discussion Questions

1. Should a word processor produce the same on-line help for beginners, intermediates, and experts?

2. Why would it be difficult to implement an UNDO command that could undo the effects of the last five commands?

3. What would be an ideal method of handling the placement of orphans, widows, footnotes, tables, and figures?

4. How could a spelling checker be designed to minimize the time and effort devoted to correcting suspect words?

5. What are the advantages and disadvantages of root word and literal dictionaries?

6. What factors determine how a large document such as a book should be broken into separate files?

7. How would you design the specifications for an automatic index-generating program?

Exercises

1. Determine the on-line help available on your word processor.

2. Determine the types and styles of characters that your printer can produce. Can your word processor use them?

3. List possible options for handling suspect words.

4. Describe the limitations of spelling correctors.

5. Design a user interface for an on-line dictionary system that includes definitions, synonyms, and antonyms.

6. Describe a window-based user interface for generating form letters.

7. Investigate what features would be required in a word processor for a language such as German, French, or Russian.

PART THREE

electronic spreadsheets

Our present ability to understand the world in terms of numbers is the result of a series of advances affecting how numbers are represented and processed. Even in prehistorical times people needed help remembering and manipulating numbers; the scratch marks on cave walls remain as evidence of our ancestors' limited memory. The introduction of clay tablets and paper made numerical records more portable and erasable. The abacus increased the speed and accuracy with which numbers could be added and subtracted; it became the first mechanical processing aid. The invention of a symbol for zero and the Hindu decimal system made arithmetic easier and led to many advances in higher mathematics. Logarithm tables and slide rules eliminated most of the work of multiplying and dividing. The early part of this century saw the widespread use of mechanical and electromechanical adding machines; these have been replaced in the last two decades by electronic desktop and hand-held calculators. The last major step in this progression occurred with the introduction of the first spreadsheet program, Visicalc, in 1979.

The first version of Visicalc used only 16KB of memory and stored data on tape cassettes. Despite its initial limitations, Visicalc did something no program had done before: it made a computer's numerical processing abilities available to people who did not have previous computer experience. Since Visicalc's introduction, literally hundreds of competitive spreadsheet programs have been written, and spreadsheet processing has become one of the most popular applications for personal computers.

A spreadsheet program does for numerical work what a word processor does for writing: it provides flexibility, convenience, and power. Spreadsheet programs include many functions that help users enter, move, label, and display numbers. But the real advantage of spreadsheet programs is their ability to store not only numbers but also formulas for calculating numbers. When critical numbers are changed, the entire model is recalculated, updating other numbers as necessary to keep everything self-consistent and in balance. In a sales forecast, for example, as soon as one month's sales estimate is changed, the full-year's estimate is automatically adjusted.

This ability to do instantaneous "what-if" recalculations allows people to experiment with the relationships among numbers in a manner that was previously impractical. For example, if the sales estimate in a typical five-year financial plan is changed, adjustments must be made in manufacturing costs, overhead costs, warranty returns, and many other items. A spreadsheet program makes these changes automatically, but in the past it could take an accountant hours of error-prone, tedious figuring on paper to predict the implications of changes in a forecast's basic assumptions. Such arduous work discouraged experimentation and limited how many assumptions about the future were explored.

Part III teaches you about spreadsheet processing in two stages. The first stage is to learn the concepts necessary for simple models; Chapter 7 contains detailed examples of these common features and concepts. Chapter 8 describes the second stage, which is to understand the advanced features that allow spreadsheet programs to construct professional and sophisticated applications.

spreadsheet basics 7

7

A **spreadsheet** program transforms the computer into a "number-crunching" tool capable of solving problems once tackled with a pencil, scratch pad, and calculator. It is especially useful for time-consuming tasks such as performing the same calculations with different starting assumptions or choosing among several alternatives.

Like any other powerful tool, spreadsheets have their own terminology and basic operations that must be mastered before sophisticated applications can be undertaken. In this chapter we explain the concepts necessary for typical spreadsheet applications and describe features that all spreadsheet programs provide in one form or another. We explain each step in a simple session and describe the basic operations: how to view the worksheet, edit and enter cells, rearrange portions of the worksheet, and give simple commands.

■ Understanding the Worksheet

Figure 7.1 illustrates how a spreadsheet program stores and displays data. Data is stored and edited in an enormous sheet built out of small rectangular storage bins called **cells.** We will call this sheet the **worksheet.** (Others may call it a *spreadsheet, matrix,* or *template.* We use the term *spreadsheet* to refer to the program and *worksheet* to refer to the model that the program allows you to create.) Because the display is much smaller than the worksheet, only a tiny rectangular portion of the worksheet shows in the display's window. Using the cursor keys, a mouse, or another pointing method, you can scroll the window horizontally and vertically to view any portion of the worksheet.

Data in a worksheet cell passes through several layers of processing before it appears in the display window. These layers can be thought of as processing filters that calculate the cell's value and convert the value into the desired format for display. Each cell stores a **value rule** that tells the spreadsheet how to calculate the cell's value. The value rule might simply be the value itself, such as the number 689.5539 or the label "Sales"; or it might be a *formula,* which is an expression stating how the value is to be calculated. Each cell also has one or more **format rules** that tell the spreadsheet how to display the value. For example, a format rule might cause the value 689.5539 to appear on·the display as $689.55.

The size of the worksheet depends on the program. A common size is 64 columns wide by 256 rows deep, although some worksheets have hundreds of columns and thousands of rows. Although Figure 7.1 labels both the rows and the columns with numbers, most programs label the columns with letters. But if there are 64 or more columns, they cannot all be designated with just the 26 letters of the alphabet; it's necessary to use two letters to designate the later columns. This means that the first 26 columns are labeled A to Z and the later

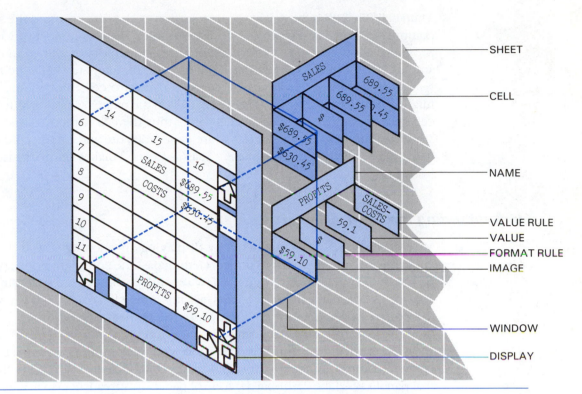

Figure 7.1 *A worksheet is an aggregate of cells that can get values from one anoth-er. You can think of each cell as having several layers in front of the sheet that com-pute the value of the cell and determine the format of the presentation. For example, each cell has a value rule, which can be the value itself or a way to compute it, as well as a format rule, which converts the value into a form suitable for display. A cell's image is the formatted value as displayed in the rectangular part of the sheet appearing in the window.* Adapted from ''Computer Software,'' by Alan Kay. Copy-right © 1984 by Scientific American, Inc. All rights reserved.)

columns AA, AB, . . . AZ, BA, BB, and so on until the end of the worksheet. In most programs the name of a cell is the cell's column letter(s) followed by its row number, as in R2, D2, Z80, AD1986, or A1.

Some programs label both the rows and the columns with numbers; these products need a way to indicate whether a number refers to a row or a column. One way to do this is to precede row numbers with an *R* and column numbers with a *C*. Thus, instead of referring to the upper left-hand cell of the worksheet as cell A1, you would call it cell R1C1. An advantage of this convention is that it can be adapted to three-dimensional worksheets. For example, if a spreadsheet allows information to be stored on more than one worksheet at a time—like a pad of paper—the third dimension might be preceded with a *P* for ''page.''

Then cell R5C2P8 is the cell at the intersection of the fifth row and the second column of the eighth page in the worksheet tablet. However, most spreadsheet programs allow only one worksheet (or page) in memory at a time. In our examples we use letters to designate columns and numbers to designate rows.

Most spreadsheets allow you to assign names to cells. For example, you might give cell C5 the name "Sales" and cell C6 the name "Costs." Notice that a cell's name is different from a cell's value; thus the cell named "Sales" might store the number 689.55. Formulas are easier to write and understand if cells have been given logical names; "Sales – Costs" makes more sense than "C5 – C6."

Understanding the Control Panel

Most spreadsheet programs begin by displaying an opening screen that contains the program's copyright notice. Getting past the copyright notice (usually by pressing any key or by waiting a few seconds) produces a display similar to Figure 7.2. It is made up of two parts: a status and help area, which we will call the **control panel,** and the window into the worksheet.

The control panel performs the same function as a car's dashboard: it shows you what the product is doing, tells you what options are available, and lets you control the activity. It is important to understand everything the control panel says. Like dashboards, control panels in spreadsheets vary from one product to the next, but there are common features. Nearly all spreadsheets have one or more lines devoted to each of three functions.

Figure 7.2   *A typical (reduced-size) spreadsheet screen display.*

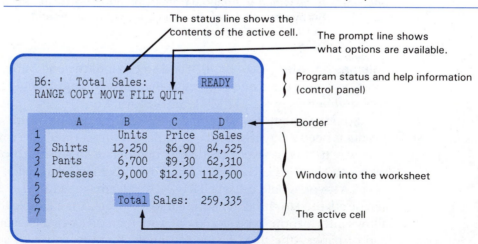

■ The **status line** tells you the coordinates of the cell that is available for immediate use and displays this cell's value and format rules.

■ The **prompt line** shows you what options are available while you are giving a command. It does this by displaying a menu bar or asking questions.

■ The **entry line** allows you to communicate with the program by displaying the information you have typed since the last time you completed a command or entered data into a cell. The entry line operates like a scratch pad because it allows you to edit commands and data before they are completed or entered. In some programs the status line functions as the entry line whenever data is being entered.

Moving, Scrolling, Paging, and Jumping

The **active cell** (also called the **current cell**) is the cell available for immediate use or modification. It is marked on the screen by highlighting, underlining, or reversing the color (inverse video) of the cell's contents. We use highlighting in the examples in this chapter.

Whenever you begin editing an empty worksheet, cell A1 is the active cell. You can mark any cell in the window as the active cell by using the cursor-movement keys. Whereas in most programs the cursor-movement keys move the cursor, in spreadsheet processing they change which cell is the active cell by one column or row at a time (see Figure 7.3).

If you try to move the active cell off the edge of the window, the window scrolls to a different part of the worksheet, as shown in Figure 7.4. Notice that scrolling does more than shift the contents of the window: the window's borders are also relabeled, and the coordinates of the active cell identified in the status line are adjusted.

Figure 7.3 *Changing the active cell by pushing the down-arrow key [↓].*

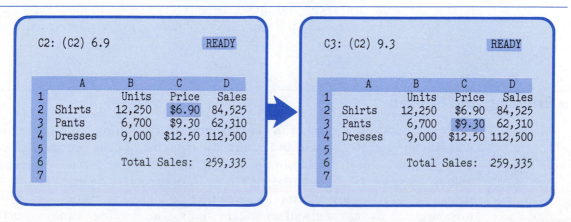

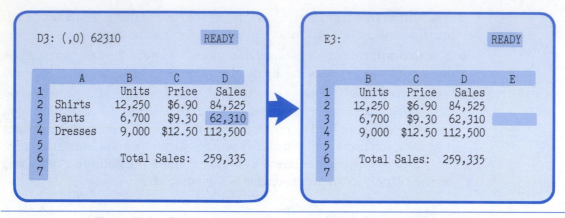

Figure 7.4   *Scrolling one column by pressing the right-arrow key [→].*

Given enough time, you can use the cursor keys to scroll the window to show any part of the worksheet. On most keyboards if you hold down the cursor keys, the repeat-key feature is invoked, and scrolling continues until the window runs up against an edge of the worksheet; then the scrolling stops. Most spreadsheets beep if you try to scroll past the edge of the worksheet—in effect saying, ''You can't go there.''

Scrolling between distant parts of the worksheet with cursor keys is tedious; fortunately, there are other, quicker methods. Most spreadsheets have special commands for **paging** through the worksheet one full screen (about twenty lines or seventy columns) at a time. For example, paging up and down is often done by using [PgUp] and [PgDn] keys. For moving long distances in the worksheet, the fastest method is to jump between points. The usual procedure is to type a special symbol (often > or =), indicating, ''I want to jump to another part of the worksheet.'' In response, a prompt in the control panel displays a message similar to ENTER CELL TO JUMP TO. You complete the command by typing the name of the cell and pressing the [ENTER] key. Immediately, the window displays a region of the worksheet containing the requested cell.

■ Entering and Editing

Moving around the worksheet soon becomes second nature. Your attention will quickly shift to entering and editing the contents of cells because that is how you get to see the results of calculations. But before we give examples of editing cells, we should describe the modes of operation encountered during spreadsheet processing and the methods used to shift between modes. It is disconcerting to get caught in an unexpected mode, because without much warning the keys have different meanings.

Ready, Enter, and Command Modes

Every spreadsheet has three modes of operation, which we call the *ready mode, entry mode,* and *command mode.* The program begins in the **ready mode,** which is used to move around the worksheet. The spreadsheet shifts instantly from the ready mode to one of the other modes whenever a letter, number, or one of a set of special symbols is typed.

Typing a slash (/) is the normal way of entering the **command mode.** A menu bar then appears in the control panel, and you select a command from the menu bar. But a few commands are so important that most spreadsheets give them their own command keys. Jumping is one such command; you invoke the command just by pressing a specified key, without first typing a slash. We will discuss commands and how they are given later in this chapter.

Typing any letter (*A* to *Z*), number (0 to 9), or one of a few special symbols (such as a quotation mark, plus, minus, at-sign, or left parenthesis) shifts the program into the entry mode. **Entry mode** is used to enter new information into the active cell. The characters of the new entry appear on the entry line in the control panel as they are typed (see Figure 7.5). While in the entry mode you cannot scroll the screen or do anything other than type and edit a new entry for the active cell. You can use the left- and right-arrow keys to move the cursor back and forth across the entry to insert or delete characters.

The normal way to exit from the entry mode is to press the [ENTER] key, which discards the old contents (if any) of the active cell, stores the new entry in the active cell, and returns the program to the ready mode. Once [ENTER] is pressed, the old entry is gone and cannot be recovered. But if you have not pressed [ENTER], you can escape from the entry mode without affecting the contents of the current cell, usually by pressing the escape key [ESC].

Figure 7.5   *The left-hand screen shows an entry being typed. The right-hand screen shows the entry's effect after the [ENTER] key has been pressed.*

The entry line shows the new entry while it is being typed in and edited.

A3: 'Pants			LABEL
Slacks_			

	A	B	C	D
1		Units	Price	Sales
2	Shirts	12,250	$6.90	84,525
3	Pants	6,700	$9.30	62,310
4	Dresses	9,000	$12.50	112,500
5				
6			Total Sales:	259,335
7				

A3: 'Slacks			READY

	A	B	C	D
1		Units	Price	Sales
2	Shirts	12,250	$6.90	84,525
3	Slacks	6,700	$9.30	62,310
4	Dresses	9,000	$12.50	112,500
5				
6			Total Sales:	259,335
7				

Labels Versus Numbers and Formulas

The value rule in each cell can store one of three types of information: a label, a number, or a formula. A **label** is a string of normal text characters, such as "Smith," "Dresses," "123 Main Street," and "Pro-Forma Income Statement." Labels help identify the items in the worksheet. A **number** might be the integer 4 or the floating-point number 3.14159. A **formula** is generally an instruction to calculate a number. (In some spreadsheets formulas can also be used to process text.) For example, 5 + 4 is a valid formula. This trivial formula reads "five plus four" and results in the number 9. Formulas may be quite complex and are the most powerful part of spreadsheet processing.

Cells that store numerical data can be used in mathematical formulas; cells storing labels cannot. For example, a formula can add the values of a group of cells storing numbers. But it makes no sense to add labels, such as "Pants" and "Dresses," or "apples" and "oranges."

As soon as you type the first character of an entry, most spreadsheets decide whether the entry will store text (a label) or numerical data (a number or a formula). If the first character is a letter, the entry is assumed to be a label, as shown in Figure 7.6. If it begins with a number or an arithmetic symbol (such as a plus, minus, or left parenthesis), the entry is assumed to be numerical data or a formula.

Because most entries beginning with a letter are labels, and most other entries are numbers or formulas, it saves time to have the spreadsheet program guess which type of entry is being made. But for some entries the guess is incorrect. For example, although "123 Main Street" and the social security number "543-64-9856" do not begin with letters, they need to be stored as labels. The "123" of "123 Main Street" should be stored as the character 1, followed by

Figure 7.6   *Default assumption. When you begin to enter "Shirts" by typing an* S, *the program signals that it assumes the entry is a label by changing the status line to say "Label".*

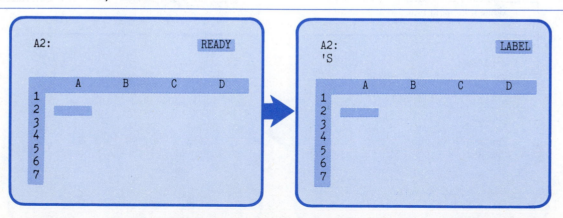

the character 2, followed by the character 3. This string of three characters is not a number; it is merely three characters in a row. (If you are curious about how the keystroke [7] could be stored as a number or as a label, read the Appendix, "How Computers Process Information.")

These examples indicate the need for a way to override the default assumption that all labels begin with letters. The usual procedure is to begin this kind of label by typing a quotation mark ("). The spreadsheet interprets the quotation mark as a command to begin the entry mode and enter a label regardless of the first character in the entry.

Entering Labels and Numbers

In order to make our discussion as concrete as possible, let's suppose you want to build a worksheet like the one in Figure 7.3 to forecast sales for a clothing manufacturer. Your first step is to turn on the computer, load the operating system and the spreadsheet in memory, and begin editing an empty worksheet. You type the labels and numbers in the sales forecast into the worksheet one at a time by repeatedly

- marking a particular cell as the active cell with the cursor-movement keys.
- typing an entry.
- pressing the [ENTER] key.

Figure 7.6 shows the very beginning of this process. When all the labels and numbers have been entered, the window showing the worksheet would look like the window in the left-hand screen in Figure 7.7. The sales figures and the total have not been entered because they will be calculated by formulas.

Notice that the information in Figure 7.7 is poorly formatted in comparison with the same information in Figure 7.3. The column headings are not

Figure 7.7 *Entering a formula into the worksheet.*

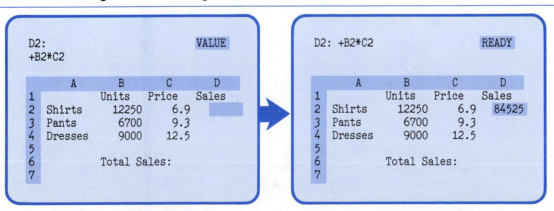

aligned with the numbers beneath them, and the numbers do not have commas, dollar signs, or even the correct number of digits after the decimal point. Obviously, the spreadsheet has made some assumptions about how the entries should look that are inappropriate for this forecast, such as left-justifying all the labels and right-justifying all the numbers. Later in this chapter we discuss using format rules to change the appearance of entries. For now it is sufficient to know that entering data and formatting the data to look good are often separate steps.

Entering Formulas

If a spreadsheet could only record labels and numbers in a grid of cells, it wouldn't have much practical use—a simple text editor would be more convenient and just as powerful. A spreadsheet is useful because it can store formulas—instructions for calculations—inside the cells.

As an example, look again at Figure 7.7. Suppose you want cell D2 to show the result of multiplying the units of shirts in cell B2 (12,250) times the price per shirt in cell C2 ($6.90). In spreadsheet arithmetic an asterisk means ''multiply''; a slash means ''divide''; and a plus and minus mean ''add'' and ''subtract.'' Therefore you might type the formula 12,250*6.9 into cell D2. But the numbers in cells B2 and C2 have already been entered into the worksheet once; there is no need to enter them again for the formula in cell D2. Instead of telling the spreadsheet which numbers to multiply, you can tell it which cells contain the numbers. Typing the formula +B2*C2 into cell D2 causes the spreadsheet to find the value of cell B2, multiply it by the value of cell C2, and display the result in cell D2, as shown in the right-hand screen in Figure 7.7.

The plus sign in the formula +B2*C2 is very important. Let's suppose that it had been omitted and B2*C2 had been typed into cell D2 instead of +B2*C2. Since the first character of the entry is now a letter, the entry would be stored as a label, not as a formula. Labels are treated as text and are not processed to see if they make mathematical sense; so the window would now display B2*C2 for cell D2.

Some spreadsheet programs carry out operations from left to right across a formula. With these programs the formula 2 + 2/4 equals 1 because the addition is done first. Other spreadsheets respect the normal order of operations assumed in algebra or computer programming: multiplication and division are done before addition and subtraction. These programs evaluate 2 + 2/4 as equal to 2.5.

For many formulas the order in which the operations are performed is critical. One way to avoid problems is to take a few seconds to type 2 + 2/4 into a cell to determine which way your spreadsheet evaluates expressions; another is to use parentheses. Whatever is enclosed in parentheses is done first. For example, any program will find that (2 + 2)/4 equals 1 and that 2 + (2/4) equals 2.5. If appropriate, parentheses can be nested, as in ((5/8) + (13/7))/2. When there are nested sets of parentheses, the operations in the innermost set of parentheses are done first.

Note that the spreadsheet *stores the formula,* but it *displays the result* of computing the formula. The difference is important. You can check to see what is stored in a cell by making it the active cell and looking at the status line of the control panel. However, when you look at a cell in the worksheet window, you do not see the cell's contents as they appear on the status line or in memory. Instead, you see a processed version. The processed version of a formula is the value that results from evaluating the formula. The processed version of a label might vary from the stored version by being right-justified or centered in the cell or by being truncated.

Specifying Ranges of Cells

Notice that our sample worksheet in Figure 7.7 also calls for the total sales to be given. To obtain this figure you might put the formula +D2 + D3 + D4 in cell D6. But clearly, this approach would be cumbersome if the sales forecast had forty or fifty sales items. A more reliable method is to specify a range of cells to be added. A **range of cells** is a rectangular group of cells that are treated as a unit for some operation.

A range can be as small as a single cell, or it can be part of a column, part of a row, an entire row or column, or even a large rectangular region of cells. The exact syntax for specifying a range varies from program to program. Some programs allow you to use a mouse for marking ranges of cells on the screen; others let you use the cursor-movement keys. But the usual procedure is to type the name of the upper-left cell in the range, a delimiter (generally a series of periods or a colon), and the name of the lower-right cell. For example, the range that includes cells D2, D3, and D4 might be specified as D2..D4. A range of cells within one row has the same row number for both end points of the range, as in the range A20..Q20. One specification can encompass an entire worksheet, as in A1..JQ2048.

For most commands and functions used in spreadsheets you must indicate the range of cells to be processed. For example, you can

- ■ save a range of cells on a disk as a file.
- ■ print a range of cells on the printer.
- ■ use a function to add, average, or find the largest value in a range of cells.
- ■ use a command to copy, move, or delete a range of cells.

Entering Functions

Spreadsheet formulas can process ranges of cells as well as individual cells, but the standard arithmetic operators (+, −, /, and *) do not work on ranges. For example, you cannot divide the values in one range by the values in another with a formula like D2..D4/E2..E4. Instead, you must use a built-in function designed to manipulate ranges.

Built-in functions are tools provided by the spreadsheet that perform a specific type of processing such as adding a column of numbers or computing the average of a range of values. Figure 7.8 shows how the SUM function adds the values of all the cells in a range to produce a total. A function is used by typing its name into a cell and then giving the function's arguments (if any) inside parentheses. With some spreadsheets a function must begin with an identifying character. For example, in Figure 7.8 the SUM function is preceded by an at-sign (@) to identify it as a function; the range stating which cells to add is enclosed in parentheses. Other spreadsheets allow functions to run in with the rest of the formula, as in 8 + AVERAGE(2,4,6) + 10, which is equal to 22.

A formula can consist of a single function, or it can contain many of them, or built-in functions and arithmetic operations can be mixed in the same formula. In general, you can put a function in a formula wherever a number would be valid. For example, assume that the sum of the numbers in cells D9..F9 is 20. Then 2 + (@SUM(D9..F9)/10) is equal to 4. Even nested functions are acceptable in a formula. For example, @COS(@SUM(A1..A5)) takes the cosine of the sum of the values in cells A1 through A5.

There are many ways to obtain the same mathematical result with spreadsheets. For example, the following two formulas will both find the average value of all the nonblank cells in the range from cell B4 to cell B152:

```
@AVERAGE(B4..B152)
@SUM(B4..B152)/@COUNT(B4..B152)
```

Figure 7.8   *Using the SUM function to add three cells.*

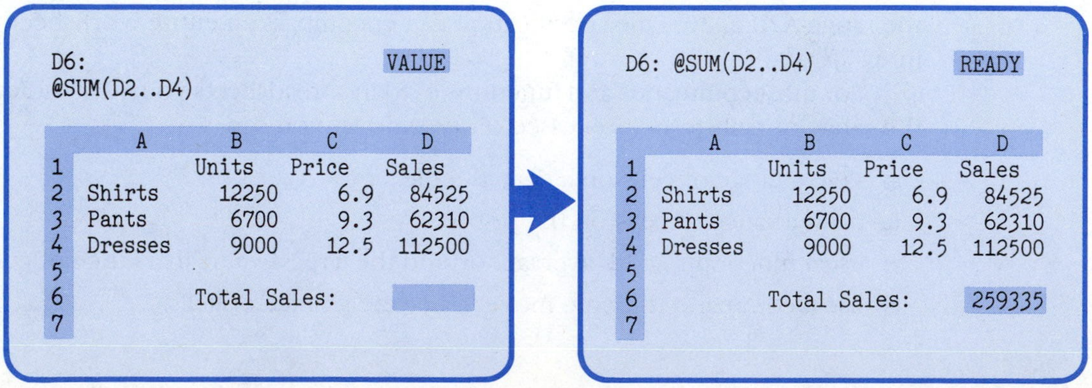

The first formula assumes the existence of a built-in function that finds the average of a range of cells directly; nearly all spreadsheets have such a function. The second formula goes the roundabout route of totaling the range of values, then counting the number of nonblank cells, and finally dividing the two numbers to obtain the average.

Automatic Recalculation

The advantage of using cell references rather than absolute numbers in formulas becomes apparent when a worksheet is modified. Consider Figure 7.8 again. If the formula in cell D2 is 12250*6.9, then no matter what changes are made to cells B2 and C2, the display for cell D2 stays the same. Thus, if the number of shirts sold (the value of cell B2) is changed from 12,250 to 6,000, the value of the sales displayed in cell D2 is not changed accordingly. Of course, you could edit the formula in cell D2 to reflect the change, but you can avoid this unnecessary work by writing formulas with cell references instead of absolute numbers. Then, whenever the value in a cell is entered or modified, every formula in the worksheet is automatically recalculated.

We will talk in Chapter 8 about how the automatic recalculation feature can be turned off to speed data entry. For now, it is reasonable to assume that the feature is always turned on. If a formula refers to a cell that was changed, either directly or indirectly, then the formula is recalculated and its new value is displayed in the worksheet. Figure 7.9 shows how the sales for shirts (cell D2) and the total sales (D6) are recalculated when the number of shirts (B2) is changed. Spreadsheets encourage people to experiment with different assumptions—known as "what-if" analysis—because it is fun to see the effects of a change ripple across the numbers in the window.

Figure 7.9   *"What-if" analysis. Changing the number in cell B2 shows what will happen to sales if fewer shirts are sold.*

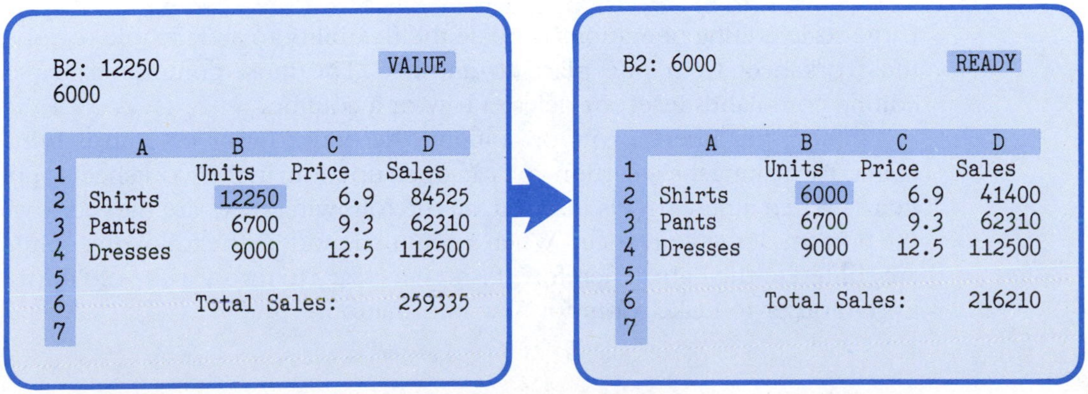

```
B2: 12250                    VALUE
6000

        A       B       C       D
1             Units   Price   Sales
2  Shirts    12250     6.9   84525
3  Pants      6700     9.3   62310
4  Dresses    9000    12.5  112500
5
6          Total Sales:      259335
7
```

```
B2: 6000                     READY

        A       B       C       D
1             Units   Price   Sales
2  Shirts     6000     6.9   41400
3  Pants      6700     9.3   62310
4  Dresses    9000    12.5  112500
5
6          Total Sales:      216210
7
```

■ Revising and Rearranging

When you first enter data into a worksheet, the cycle of repeatedly marking the active cell and typing an entry works well enough; but revising data or rearranging information already in the worksheet requires more efficient methods. That is why spreadsheet programs have numerous commands for editing cells, inserting and deleting rows and columns, and copying and moving ranges of cells.

Editing and Erasing Cells

Suppose you place a label in a cell, and then you notice that the label is misspelled. Or imagine that you enter a formula and the result displayed is obviously incorrect because a set of parentheses is missing. Either of these mistakes could be corrected by starting from scratch and typing the correct entry. But there is an easier way: the contents of any cell can be edited.

The usual procedure is to mark the cell you wish to edit as the active cell and then give the EDIT command (generally by typing /E). This puts the spreadsheet in the entry mode—but instead of starting with an empty entry, the entry begins with the active cell's contents. Once in the entry mode you can use the cursor-movement keys to position the cursor where the change should be made and add or delete characters from the entry until it is correct.

An existing entry can always be replaced by giving the cell a new entry, but the new entry must have some content. You can't erase an entry by simply pressing the [ENTER] key. To erase a cell, you must use the ERASE command. (It is often called something like BLANK, CLEAR, or ZAP to avoid first-letter conflicts with the EDIT command.) Generally, you can delete more than one cell with the ERASE command by giving a range of cells as its argument. Since a whole region of the worksheet can be thrown away, the ERASE command should be used with caution.

Inserting and Deleting Rows and Columns

Large-scale editing operations provide the flexibility to shift whole regions of the worksheet from one place to another. The most common large-scale editing commands insert or delete a row or a column.

When you insert a row or column, the new row or column is initially blank. By making the insertion you can open up room in the worksheet for new items. When a new row is inserted, all the following rows are moved toward the bottom of the worksheet. When a column is added, the following columns are shifted to the right. Therefore it isn't necessary to throw away old information in order to make room for new information.

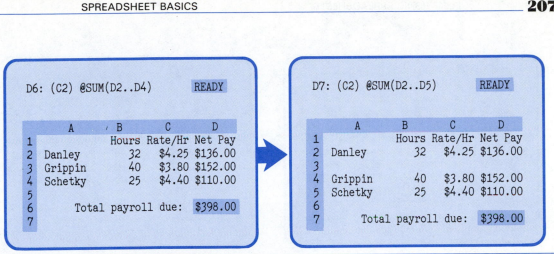

Figure 7.10 *Inserting a new row 3.*

Inserting a row or column has another very important effect: all the formulas in the worksheet are automatically adjusted to refer to the correct entries *even though the entries may now be in new cell locations.* Study Figure 7.10 to see the effect of inserting a new row 3. You can see in the status line that when the entry in cell D6 is moved to cell D7, its formula is adjusted from @SUM(D2..D4) to @SUM(D2..D5). (The (C2) in the status line before the formulas for cells D6 and D7 is a format rule causing these entries to be displayed as dollars-and-cents numbers.) The reference to cell D2 has not been changed because inserting the new row did not affect row 2. But the reference to D4 has been modified because that entry is now in a new location, D5.

Similarly, whenever a row or column is deleted, the spreadsheet attempts to adjust the remaining formulas to refer to the correct entries. For example, if column F is deleted, then the formula @AVERAGE(A12..S12) will be changed to @AVERAGE(A12..R12).

Deleting a row or a column removes unwanted material from the worksheet, but deletion commands can be quite dangerous because of unexpected side effects. For example, suppose a worksheet filled with financial information has an income statement in the area bounded by cells A1 and F50 and a balance sheet in the range H1..Z50. Deleting a row removes the *entire* row from the worksheet. This means that the seemingly innocent operation of deleting a line from the income statement will also remove material from the balance sheet.

Deleting a row or column also has a negative side effect if formulas elsewhere in the worksheet contain references to the deleted entries. Such a formula is rendered invalid because it refers to an entry that no longer exists. For example, in Figure 7.11 the formula that calculates the total payroll due is rendered invalid when one of the rows on which the formula is based is

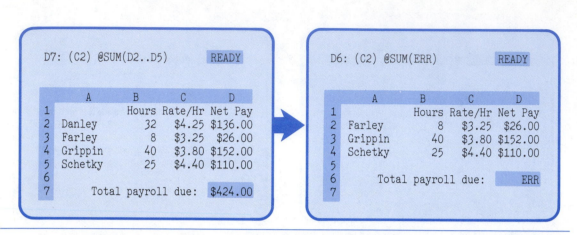

```
D7: (C2) @SUM(D2..D5)          READY              D6: (C2) @SUM(ERR)             READY

        A       B     C      D                          A       B     C      D
1             Hours Rate/Hr Net Pay            1             Hours Rate/Hr Net Pay
2 Danley       32   $4.25 $136.00              2 Farley        8   $3.25  $26.00
3 Farley        8   $3.25  $26.00              3 Grippin      40   $3.80 $152.00
4 Grippin      40   $3.80 $152.00              4 Schetky      25   $4.40 $110.00
5 Schetky      25   $4.40 $110.00              5
6                                              6     Total payroll due:        ERR
7     Total payroll due:  $424.00              7
```

Figure 7.11 *When row 2 is deleted from the worksheet, the formula for the total payroll becomes invalid because the formula referred to row 2.*

deleted. When a formula is invalid, the worksheet window displays a terse error message, such as ERR, @ERROR, or #REF, as you can see in the status line in Figure 7.11.

Exchanging, Cutting, and Pasting

Every spreadsheet has commands for moving entries from one location to another. These commands make it possible to redesign the layout of the worksheet by changing the order in which entries appear. Within limits, this allows you to divide the construction of a worksheet into two phases. In the first phase you concentrate on entering data and building formulas until the computations have been completed. In the second phase you rearrange everything until the visual layout is appropriate for a report.

Spreadsheets use two fundamentally different ways of moving information: (1) exchanging the order of rows or of columns, and (2) cutting and pasting areas of the worksheet. Both methods have pitfalls you need to avoid; so it is essential to understand them clearly and to use them correctly.

Nearly all spreadsheets allow you to rearrange the worksheet by exchanging the order of entire rows or columns. For example, Figure 7.12 shows the effect of moving row 2 to row 6. Notice how the original rows 3 through 6 are shoved up to become rows 2 through 5, making room for the original row 2 to become row 6. Formulas are revised automatically so that cell references point to the new worksheet locations. For Figure 7.12 this means that formulas which originally referred to row 2 now refer to row 6; references to the original row 3 now refer to row 2; and so on. Thus the formula in cell D7 changed from @SUM(D2..D5) to @SUM(D6..D4). For most situations this method of revising formulas preserves the functional relationships in the worksheet despite the new location of cell entries. But it does not seem to work well in Figure 7.12: the evaluation of cell D7 has decreased from $424.00 to $246.00 and no longer provides an accurate total.

As long as the worksheet is fairly simple, the strategy of rearranging the worksheet by exchanging rows or columns is workable but tedious. But if a worksheet has several "pages" of information in different areas, you cannot use these commands to reorganize one area without disturbing the other areas. Multiplan, Lotus 1-2-3, and most recently developed spreadsheets provide another way of rearranging entries: they allow a region to be cut from the worksheet and pasted in somewhere else. With this strategy you can avoid moving an entire row or column when you need to move only a localized region.

In the "cut" part of a cut-and-paste procedure you specify the range of cells to be moved, usually by designating the upper-left and lower-right cells of a rectangle. This step works as if all the entries in the range of cells are removed from the worksheet and placed on a clipboard. Some programs leave a blank area in the worksheet corresponding to the cells that were moved, but Multiplan shifts cells to fill in the region. It does this by asking whether cells beneath the region should shift up or whether cells to the right of the region should shift left.

In the "paste" operation you tell the spreadsheet where to place the entries obtained in the cut operation. Lotus 1-2-3 throws away the previous contents of the region where new entries are pasted. For example, in Figure 7.13 eight cells are cut from the worksheet and pasted in two rows down from their previous location into row 5. The paste operation destroys the payroll information for Schetky and invalidates the formula for total pay due by erasing the previous entry of cell D5. It is important to paste entries into blank areas of the worksheet if you use a product like Lotus 1-2-3, because it gives no warning before it tosses out the previous contents of the region.

Figure 7.12 *Exchanging rows by moving row 2 to be the new row 6.*

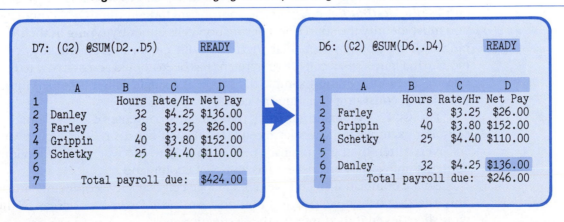

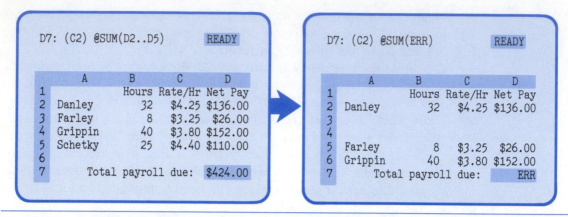

Figure 7.13 *Moving the entries in cells A3..D4 to cells A5..D6.*

Copying

The COPY command fills out a worksheet by taking existing cell entries and replicating them in other cells. Careful use of the COPY command can reduce the number of keystrokes needed to complete most worksheets by at least half. The command is especially useful if you are making projections because once a relationship has been entered for one time period, it can be copied across rows or columns to see the effect over time. Similarly, if you have developed an expense budget for one month, you can use the COPY command to extend the budgeting formulas across another eleven rows or columns to create a full-year budget. Or if one line has been entered in a conversion table (such as a table that converts from degrees to radians, or from centigrade to Kelvin temperature), you can complete the remaining lines easily by using the COPY command to replicate the formulas in the first line.

To copy labels or numbers the spreadsheet must know which cells contain the entries to be copied (the *source cells*) and which cells are to receive new entries (the *destination cells*). At the appropriate time in the COPY command you must identify the source and destination cells either by typing in their cell ranges or by pointing out their locations with cursor-movement keys or a mouse. In Figure 7.14 a cell full of hyphens has been copied across a row to emphasize a heading. In this example the source is a single cell; it is copied into a destination consisting of a range of cells.

The COPY command destroys the previous contents of the destination cells. For example, the asterisks in cell D2 of the left-hand screen of Figure 7.14 are overwritten by the hyphens. There is no way to recover a cell's previous contents unless the spreadsheet has an UNDO command.

Unlike commands that move or exchange cells, a COPY command affects only the destination cells. It has no effect on formulas in other areas of the worksheet, even if they refer to the destination cells.

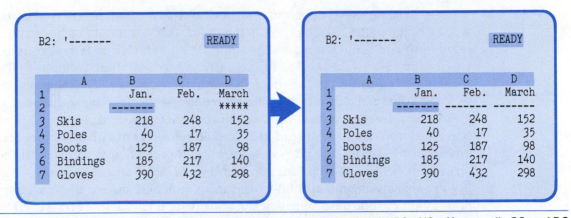

Figure 7.14 *Copying a label from cell B2 to the cells B2..N2 affects cells C2 and D2 on the screen and cells D2..N2 off the screen's edge.*

Copying formulas is more complicated than copying labels and numbers because you rarely want the spreadsheet to perform *exactly* the same calculation in two different places of the worksheet. Instead, you normally want a set of similar computations to be done—with appropriate adjustments in the formulas to reflect their new locations. For example, many worksheets have a total column that adds the numbers in earlier columns, as in Figure 7.15. If the formula in row 3 of the total column is @SUM(B3..M3), then it doesn't make sense to copy this formula unchanged into row 4 or row 5 of the total column. Instead, in row 4 you want the formula @SUM(B4..M4), so that the formula in row 4 totals the numbers in row 4. Similar changes must be made to the formula as it is copied into succeeding cells down the total column.

Figure 7.15 *Copying a formula from cell N2 to the cells N3..N85 using relative cell references.*

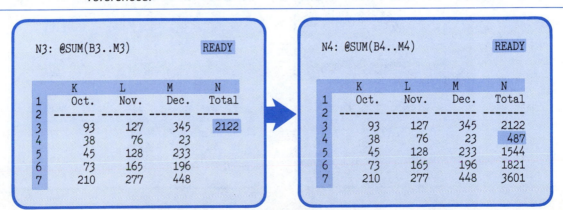

To make these changes in the new formulas, you need to tell the spreadsheet that the cell references in the source formula should be interpreted *relative* to the formula's current position. With **relative cell references,** when a formula is copied into a cell two rows down and three columns to the right of its original location, all row numbers in the formula will be increased by two and column letters will be shifted three letters through the alphabet.

Some references should not be adjusted when a formula is copied from one location to another; instead, they should remain as **absolute cell references.** For example, a good way to organize a projection is to place all the projection's critical assumptions in cells in a well-labeled area of the worksheet. If you are analyzing the cash flow from an apartment complex, these assumptions might include the occupancy rate, the inflation rate, and several tax rates. When formulas are copied in this worksheet, references to the cells containing these assumptions should not be adjusted.

Figure 7.16 illustrates the need for both kinds of cell references. With a single COPY command you can copy a range of formulas (C5..D5) into another range (C6..D88), filling an entire region of the worksheet in one operation. But when you copy the formula in cell C5, you want the reference to cell C1 to be an absolute reference because the cell contains the sales markup rate for the entire worksheet; when the formula is copied, this reference should not be changed. In contrast, the reference to cell B5 should be relative because it contains the cost of an item for a specific row; this reference should therefore be changed when the formula is copied.

Different spreadsheets distinguish absolute from relative references in different ways. Lotus 1-2-3 and Multiplan allow you to label a cell as absolute or relative when you enter a formula. With Lotus 1-2-3 cell references are relative by default, but it is easy to override the default by putting dollar signs before

Figure 7.16 *Copying the formulas in C5..D5 to C6..D88 using both relative and absolute cell references.*

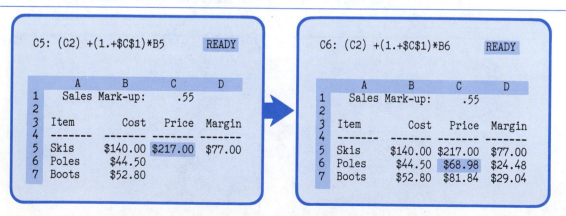

the row number and column letter of a cell. For example, the reference to cell C1 in the status line in Figure 7.16 is written C1 to indicate that it is an absolute cell reference. Similarly, the formula @SUM(B1..D1) will add the contents of cells B1, C1, and D1 regardless of where the formula is copied.

Two dollar signs are needed to specify an absolute cell reference because Lotus 1-2-3 also lets you create **mixed cell references,** which are half-absolute and half-relative. For example, the formula @SUM($B1..$D1) will be copied without changes if it is copied across a column, but it will read @SUM($B2..$D2) if it is copied into the cell immediately below its original location. Mixed cell references are useful if you have a row full of assumptions for a single type of item, such as the inflation rate from 1980 to 1990. In this situation any reference to the row number should be absolute, but a reference to the column letter should be relative.

Visicalc and SuperCalc do not allow the parts of a formula to be permanently identified as relative or absolute. Instead, they wait until the final step in the COPY command to ask you to choose—reference by reference—whether the parts of the formula should be treated as relative or absolute.

■ Giving Commands

In every spreadsheet session you need to give commands. For example, to end a session you must give the QUIT command, generally by typing /Q. We have already mentioned some basic commands, including the commands that allow you to copy data from one spot in the worksheet to another, erase the contents of a cell or range of cells, and insert or delete rows and columns. In this section we will describe how you select a command and discuss the commands that allow you to format the way information is presented inside the worksheet window, load information from a disk into the worksheet, print all or some of the worksheet as a report, and save all or part of the current worksheet on a disk.

Menu Bars

Most IBM PC spreadsheets use a combination of menu bars and function keys to let the user select commands. In contrast, all of the popular Macintosh spreadsheets, such as Jazz and Excel, use pull-down menus similar to those shown in Figure 4.8. We will describe using menu bars in detail, but most of what is said applies equally well to pull-down menu systems.

Spreadsheets use menu bars because they require such a small part of the screen—just one or two lines in the control panel—leaving most of the space available for the worksheet window. But because spreadsheets have many commands with many options (two hundred or more is not unusual), the main menu is only a listing of *categories* of commands. Subsidiary menus are needed to choose a specific command. As a result, choosing the right category from the main menu can be difficult. For example, beginners might suspect that the correct choice from the main Multiplan menu to delete a file on disk is Blank or Delete, when it is actually Transfer.

The two major types of menu bars are keyword menu bars and one-letter menu bars. **Keyword menu bars** usually require two screen lines. For example, the menu bar used in the IBM PC version of Multiplan looks like

```
COMMAND: Alpha Blank Copy Delete Edit Format Goto Help Insert Lock Move
         Name Options Print Quit Sort Transfer Value Window Xternal
```

In comparison, the **one-letter menu bars** are more cryptic but take less screen space because they display only the initial letter of each command keyword (see Figure 7.17). Menu bars encourage software developers to invent new command keywords as a way of avoiding first-letter conflicts. If there is an EDIT command, then the ERASE command is likely to be called ZAP. It doesn't take many keywords like ZAP before it becomes difficult to remember what the letters on a one-letter menu bar mean—not that it is especially easy to remember what they mean anyway.

Whether a spreadsheet uses a menu bar with letters or keywords, the procedure for giving a command is the same. First you activate the menu bar by typing a slash (/). Then you make a selection by typing the first letter of the keyword. Choosing a letter from the main menu bar usually leads to subsidiary menu bars that prompt yet more choices. This process continues through as many subsidiary menus as necessary to specify all the options and parameters for the command, at which time the command is completed. For example, if

Figure 7.17 *SuperCalc's menu bar, which is filled with initials.*

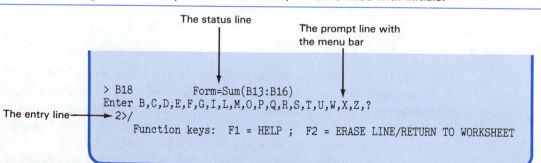

you press the [F] key for FORMAT from the main SuperCalc menu bar, the original menu bar is replaced with one having the following options:

```
Enter Level: G(lobal), C(olumn), R(ow), or E(ntry)
```

Selecting an item from this subsidiary menu bar determines whether the whole worksheet, one column, one row, or a single cell will be affected by the command. This menu is followed by yet another menu asking how the selected portion of the worksheet should be formatted when it is displayed in the window: whether text should be right- or left-justified; whether numbers should be displayed in integer, exponential, or dollar-sign format; and so forth. Only after choices have been made from three menus is the FORMAT command completed. Normally the program returns to the ready mode automatically once the command is completed. You can abort a command at any time before the command is completed, generally by pressing the escape key [ESC].

Formatting

The largest category of commands in spreadsheets is made up of commands that create format rules controlling how the contents of cells will be displayed. The emphasis is appropriate because reports are generated by printing an area of the worksheet as it would appear on the screen. This makes it necessary to adjust the cells until they look good enough for a printed report.

Early spreadsheets had very crude formatting abilities, but each succeeding generation of spreadsheets has had more formatting options. For example, in Lotus 1-2-3 numbers can have commas in the appropriate places, leading dollar signs or trailing percent signs, and a user-specified number of digits after the decimal point. Lotus 1-2-3 is a second-generation spreadsheet that provides most of the examples in this chapter.

A spreadsheet knows how to display labels and numbers because it stores a format rule inside each cell along with the cell's value rule. The format rule for the active cell is visible on the status line of the control panel just before the cell's label, number, or formula. For example, if you flip back to Figure 7.3, you will notice that the status line shows the contents of cell C3 as (C2) 9.3, but the display shows $9.30. The (C2) instructs the spreadsheet to display the number 9.3 in **currency format** with two digits after the decimal point. If you use Lotus 1-2-3 and call for the currency format, numbers will be displayed with a leading dollar sign, commas between thousands, and negative numbers in parentheses.

Let's see how to tell Lotus 1-2-3 to right-justify column headings so that they line up correctly with numbers. In Lotus 1-2-3 labels are aligned in cells based on their *label-prefix,* the first character in the label itself. If the first

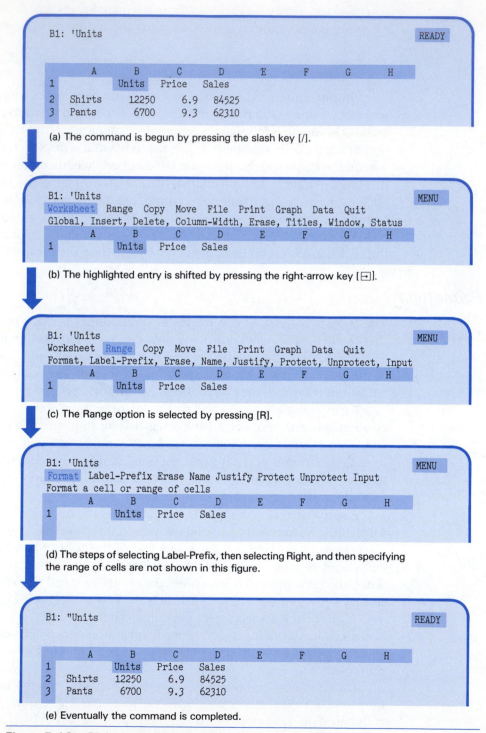

```
B1: 'Units                                                    READY

          A        B       C       D       E      F      G      H
1              Units   Price   Sales
2    Shirts     12250     6.9   84525
3    Pants       6700     9.3   62310
```

(a) The command is begun by pressing the slash key [/].

```
B1: 'Units                                                     MENU
Worksheet  Range  Copy  Move  File  Print  Graph  Data  Quit
Global, Insert, Delete, Column-Width, Erase, Titles, Window, Status
          A        B       C       D       E      F      G      H
1              Units   Price   Sales
```

(b) The highlighted entry is shifted by pressing the right-arrow key [→].

```
B1: 'Units                                                     MENU
Worksheet  Range  Copy  Move  File  Print  Graph  Data  Quit
Format, Label-Prefix, Erase, Name, Justify, Protect, Unprotect, Input
          A        B       C       D       E      F      G      H
1              Units   Price   Sales
```

(c) The Range option is selected by pressing [R].

```
B1: 'Units                                                     MENU
Format  Label-Prefix  Erase  Name  Justify  Protect  Unprotect  Input
Format a cell or range of cells
          A        B       C       D       E      F      G      H
1              Units   Price   Sales
```

(d) The steps of selecting Label-Prefix, then selecting Right, and then specifying the range of cells are not shown in this figure.

```
B1: "Units                                                    READY

          A        B       C       D       E      F      G      H
1              Units   Price   Sales
2    Shirts     12250     6.9   84525
3    Pants       6700     9.3   62310
```

(e) Eventually the command is completed.

Figure 7.18 *Right-justifying an entry with Lotus 1-2-3.*

character is an apostrophe, the label will be left-justified, as shown in Figure 7.18(a). To realign all the labels in a range, we take the following steps:

1. Press [/], which shifts the program into the command mode, as indicated by the MENU prompt on the status line in Figure 7.18(b). Two menu bars appear in the control panel. Immediately below the main menu bar is a subsidiary menu bar that displays what the next set of options will be if the highlighted option on the main menu is chosen. You can use the cursor-movement keys to highlight different options on the main menu so that the subsidiary choices for each can be examined.

2. Press [R] to select the Range option from the main menu. The subsidiary menu advances up the screen one line to become the new main menu.

3. Select Label-Prefix from the current main menu.

4. Then select Right (for right-justify) from another menu.

5. Finally, select the range of cells.

When the command is completed, the screen looks like Figure 7.18(e). The selection process sounds more complicated than it is. You can give the entire command in ten keystrokes: /RLRB1.D1 [ENTER].

Printing

You can print a report at any time during a spreadsheet session. The report's appearance depends greatly on your answers to two questions.

1. Which cells are to be printed? You specify the range of cells to be printed by giving the upper-left and lower-right corners of the range.

2. Should the cells be printed as they appear in the display or as they are stored in memory? Both types of report are shown in Figure 7.19. Printing the cells as they are stored in memory allows the formulas to be audited for accuracy, but normally reports are printed to show cells as they appear in the worksheet window.

The quality of the reports that a spreadsheet can generate depends on the printing options the spreadsheet supports. Some examples of useful capabilities for report formatting are

- splitting the region of the worksheet to be printed into smaller units, each of which fits on a single page. This is called **pagination.** To paginate, the spreadsheet must know the length and width of the paper and the margin settings of each page.

- allowing the user to establish headings or footings for each page.

```
B1: "Units
C1: "Price
D1: "Sales
A2: 'Shirts
B2: (,0) 12250
C2: (C2) 6.9
D2: (C0) + B2*C2
A3: 'Pants
B3: (,0) 6700
C3: (C2) 9.3
D3: (C0) + B3*C3
A4: 'Dresses
B4: (,0) 9000
C4: (C2) 12.5
D4: (C0) + B4*C4
B6: '    Total Sales:
D6: (C0) @SUM(D2..D4)
```

```
              Units    Price    Sales
Shirts       12,250   $6.90   $84,525
Pants         6,700   $9.30   $62,310
Dresses       9,000  $12.50  $112,500

             Total Sales: $259,335
```

(a) The worksheet printed as it is stored in memory   **(b) The worksheet printed as it looks on the screen**

Figure 7.19 *Two ways to print a worksheet.*

- sending a string of control characters to set up the printer. For example, these characters might cause the report to be printed with compressed characters, allowing a 132-column report to fit on an 8 ½ -inch wide piece of paper.

- allowing the report to be printed with or without the borders identifying the rows and columns of the worksheet.

- storing the specifications for a report (headings, footings, printer-setup string, and so on) so that they don't need to be entered each time a report is printed.

- printing the worksheet "sideways" on a page (rotated 90 degrees) so that wide reports can be printed without page breaks between columns.

- "printing" the worksheet to a disk rather than on paper so that the disk file can be used as input to other programs.

Loading, Saving, and Quitting

The first command in most spreadsheet sessions loads an existing worksheet from a disk. You can edit more than one worksheet in a session, but few spreadsheets allow more than one worksheet to be active at the same time. This means that as a new worksheet is loaded into memory, the contents of the previous worksheet are either erased or merged with the contents of the new worksheet.

Most spreadsheet programs store the active worksheet in memory. Keep in mind that memory is volatile. It is extremely discouraging to lose several hours' worth of work because of a power outage. Periodically save a copy of the worksheet on a disk if you are making useful modifications or additions to it.

If you have made changes in the worksheet that have not been saved on a disk, the spreadsheet generally will give you a final opportunity to save the worksheet before it returns control of the computer to the operating system. Thus the last two commands in a session are likely to save the revised worksheet on a disk and end the session.

■ Summary

Spreadsheets manipulate information by storing it in a large grid of cells. Most of the time spent working with a spreadsheet is spent moving the active-cell marker around the screen, entering data to be stored in a cell, and giving commands to change the formatting information stored in cells. While you are working with a spreadsheet, the screen will display a control panel, which helps you use the program and allows you to see entries as they are stored in memory, and a worksheet window, which shows you a processed version of the worksheet's contents.

Each cell of the worksheet stores a number, a label, or a formula; many also store some formatting information. The formulas can perform arithmetic operations on three types of data: absolute numbers, cell references, and built-in functions, which are special tools that perform a specific type of processing, such as adding a column of numbers or computing the standard deviation of a range of values.

In most spreadsheet programs commands are given by typing a slash (/) and then making selections from menu bars and responding to questions. Some spreadsheet programs use pull-down menus to issue commands. Regardless of whether menu bars or pull-down menus are used, several selections are necessary to complete most commands. Spreadsheets have numerous commands that can help you edit cells and rearrange the worksheet. These commands allow you to redesign the worksheet without entering information into the worksheet a second time.

You can increase the power of both functions and commands by specifying a range of cells to be processed. This allows one operation to affect an entire region of the worksheet.

Spreadsheets vary widely in their ability to format and print reports. The crudest systems do little more than dump the contents of the screen to the printer; the best systems generate good-looking reports with page breaks and page headers.

You do not need prior experience with a computer to use a spreadsheet, but some training and study are required. A general rule of thumb is that it takes forty hours of reading, practice, experimentation, and mistakes before a beginner feels proficient with most of the advanced features of a spreadsheet, though it shouldn't take more than an hour or two to begin building simple models. The rule of thumb may not hold for you. Some spreadsheets are easier to master than others, either because they have fewer features or are designed better. Some people are more comfortable with math and numerical models than others. Regardless of your situation, now that you've read this chapter you are ready to begin using a spreadsheet. Start by skimming the appropriate manufacturer's manual or pocket guide; then experiment with some of this chapter's examples at a keyboard.

Key Terms

absolute cell reference	mixed cell reference
active cell	number
built-in functions	one-letter menu bar
cell	pagination
command mode	paging
control panel	prompt line
currency format	range of cells
current cell	ready mode
entry line	relative cell reference
entry mode	spreadsheet
format rules	status line
formula	value rule
keyword menu bar	worksheet
label	

Discussion Questions

1. Is using a spreadsheet more like programming the computer or like using a word processor?

2. What types of tasks would a manufacturing accountant use a spreadsheet for? A personnel manager? A civil engineer? Would their needs for computational support differ?

3. How should the cells in a worksheet be labeled? Why?

4. What information would be useful in the control panel? Would the time of day be useful? The number of entries made in a session?

5. Why do spreadsheets have several modes of operation? Would spreadsheets be easier to use with more modes? What might the additional modes be?

6. This chapter gave examples of several types of menu bars. Which would be easiest for a beginner? Which would be quickest for the expert?

7. What could a three-dimensional worksheet do that a two-dimensional worksheet could not do conveniently?

8. What would be the easiest way to erase a group of cells if the spreadsheet's ERASE command erases only a single cell?

9. Suppose you are working with information in three separate areas of a worksheet. How should these areas be positioned in the worksheet so that inserting or deleting rows or columns in any one of the areas will not disturb the other two areas?

10. Why is the formula in Figure 7.11 made invalid by the deletion of row 2?

11. In a spreadsheet that allows only entire rows or columns to be moved, how can you move a rectangular group of cells from one location in the worksheet to another?

12. How could you print and assemble a worksheet that is longer and wider than a page?

Exercises

1. Refer to the SuperCalc illustration in photo 3 of Window 7. Identify which cells contain labels, numbers, and formulas. Write the formulas necessary to complete the worksheet. Then try entering the worksheet to see if your solution works.

2. Determine the maximum number of rows and columns in your spreadsheet program. How much memory would it take to fill each cell with the word *overflow?*

3. Give formulas for each of the following:
   a. Add cells A1, B2, C3, and D4.
   b. Multiply the sum of the first twenty columns of row 6 by the sum of the first ninety rows in column 6.
   c. Add the average of columns 3, 4, 7, and 9. Assume the first 120 rows of each column contain useful information.

4. Suppose the formula in cell A4 is 13 + B2 and in cell D5 is 6*B2. If the value in cell B2 is 3, what are the values of cells A4 and D5? Find the new values if the formula in cell D5 is 6*A4.

5. You are a stockbroker, and the following table presents the portfolio of one of your clients:

Stock	No. of Shares	Purchase Price (per share)	Market Price (per share)
Control Datum	200	$53.50	$40.00
Dow James	350	$8.75	$12.125
Gen. Tire	100	$98.00	$59.25
XYZ	2000	$5.25	$4.375

a. Use a spreadsheet to generate a report that shows the information in this table. Provide columns for the market value for each stock and the percentage of gain or loss for each stock. Include a line that shows the total market value of the portfolio and the total gain or loss for the portfolio.

b. Experiment with the model to find out what market price of Dow James makes the current market value of the entire portfolio equal to its purchase price.

6. Discover what happens in a MOVE or COPY command when the source is larger than the destination and when the source is smaller than the destination.

7. Assume your worksheet contains the names of fifty states in cells B2 to B51, their populations in cells C2 to C51, and their areas in cells E2 to E51. Give the commands and formulas to place each state's percentage of the total population in cells D2 to D51 and each state's percentage of the total area in cells F2 to F51.

advanced spreadsheet processing

8

- **Designing Templates**
  Protecting Cells
  Hiding Cells
  Creating Forms
- **Changing the Appearance of the Worksheet**
  Changing Column Widths
  Titles and Window Panes
  Types of Format Rules
  Formatting Limitations
- **Recalculating Formulas**
  Automatic Versus Manual Recalculation
  Order of Recalculation
  Circular References

- **Transferring Information**
  Copying Worksheets
  Merging Worksheets
  Linking Worksheets
  Moving Data Among Applications
- **Advanced Functions**
  Statistical and Mathematical Functions
  Financial Functions
  String Functions
  Date Functions
  Logical Functions
  Look-up Tables
- **Keyboard Macros**

8

In Chapter 7 we described the mechanics of solving common mathematical problems with a spreadsheet. This chapter covers the advanced features that are necessary to implement more sophisticated applications. For simple projections or one-shot calculations you can get by without the features described in this chapter, but they are essential for complex worksheets or applications that require many people to interact with the worksheet. With the features described in this chapter you can

- protect some cells from being accidentally modified.
- hide parts of the worksheet from view and require that a password be given before they can be seen or modified.
- use part of the worksheet as a form that guides the user through the process of entering data.
- adjust the width of columns to fit the data they store.
- keep title lines or columns frozen in one place on the screen when the rest of the worksheet is scrolled.
- divide the display window into panes that look into separate areas of the worksheet.
- turn off automatic recalculation to speed up data entry.
- alter the order in which the spreadsheet recalculates formulas.
- consolidate information from several worksheets.
- transfer data between the spreadsheet and other applications, such as word processing or graphics.
- have the current date loaded into a cell each time the worksheet is recalculated or perform calculations on dates stored in cells.
- build tables of information into the worksheet and include formulas that "look up" the appropriate entry in the table.
- store commands so that a long series of commands can be implemented by a single keystroke.

These features are essential for serious spreadsheet applications. Learning about them is a necessary prerequisite to becoming adept at solving problems with a spreadsheet.

■ Designing Templates

So far we have assumed that the same person (1) creates the worksheet by entering formulas and headings, and (2) enters data in the worksheet. Because one person can often perform both tasks, spreadsheets help break down the separation between computer users (clerks, accountants, and so forth) and computer professionals (programmers, system analysts, and so on); spreadsheets reduce the need for computer professionals because even people who do not understand programming languages can develop spreadsheet

224

applications. Still, there is often a reason for having a professional design the worksheet: one knowledgeable professional can design a high-quality solution for many users. Here are some examples.

- A financial manager might design a worksheet to be used by the managers of a firm's departments. The worksheet could help each manager complete a detailed budget that is consistent with the firm's budget policies.

- An industrial engineer might design a worksheet that predicts for other engineers the size of motor required to accelerate a given mass through a specified distance in a fixed time while being affected by friction and inertia.

- A tax accountant might design a worksheet to help customers predict the effects of alternative tax strategies.

- A construction expert might design a worksheet to help clerks prepare estimates of construction costs based on the amount of materials required for a job.

In each of these examples the application is developed by one person who is knowledgeable about both the spreadsheet and the task to be done and who tries to make the worksheet useful to people who know little about either the spreadsheet or the necessary calculations. This is done by creating a worksheet that contains both the labels that identify the items in the application and the formulas that perform the calculations—but has blank cells where the data for the application will go. Such a half-completed worksheet is called a **template** because it contains rules that guide how the data is to be processed but does not contain the data.

Figure 8.1 illustrates the difference between a template and a completed worksheet. The template in the left screen contains the labels and formulas necessary to calculate the monthly payments, year-end balances, and interest on a

Figure 8.1 *On the left is an empty template; on the right the template has been completed by filling in the values for cells C1 through C3.*

	A	B	C	D
C2: (C0) '				READY
1	Interest Rate:			
2	Principal:			
3	Number Years:			
4		Monthly	Ending	Interest
5	Year	Payment	Balance	Paid
6	1	ERR	ERR	ERR
7	2	ERR	ERR	ERR
8	3	ERR	ERR	ERR

	A	B	C	D
C2: (C0) 4000				READY
1	Interest Rate:		15.0%	
2	Principal:		$4,000	
3	Number Years:		3	
4		Monthly	Ending	Interest
5	Year	Payment	Balance	Paid
6	1	$138.66	$2,860	$524
7	2	$138.66	$1,536	$340
8	3	$138.66	$0	$128

loan. All of the calculated cells in the template display the error message ERR, because the template does not include data for the interest rate, the principal, or the number of years the loan will run. In the right screen the template has been completed by typing these numbers in cells C1 through C3. A loan officer in a bank could use a more detailed version of this template to generate a customized loan report for each new client.

A good template guides the user through the process of entering data and prevents the user from modifying the template's formulas. It is *bullet-proof,* impervious to the numerous errors made by beginners. Bullet-proof templates are constructed by protecting some of the worksheet's cells from modification, by hiding the worksheet's calculations from view, and by creating forms that help guide data entry.

Protecting Cells

Most spreadsheets have some form of a PROTECT command that gives protected status to a range of cells. A **protected cell** cannot be edited, deleted, or moved unless the cell's protected status is first removed with an UNPROTECT command. In effect, protecting a cell is the same as locking the cell's contents from further modification. The UNPROTECT command acts as a key that unlocks cells.

Figure 8.2 demonstrates how cell protection can prevent the formulas in a loan analysis from being accidentally modified. Three cells are unprotected and are shown in color; these cells are used to enter the interest rate, the principal, and the length of the loan. Any attempt to modify other cells in the worksheet produces an error message, as shown in the right-hand screen.

To make the development process smoother, many spreadsheets have a two-level protection system—one level for each cell plus a *global protection*

Figure 8.2 *Only the three cells in color are unprotected. Thus an attempt to enter the number 420 in cell D7 produces an error message.*

```
D7: (C0) 12*B7-(C6-C7)      VALUE
420

           A       B       C       D
1      Interest Rate:   15.0%
2         Principal: $4,000
3      Number Years:      3
4            Monthly  Ending Interest
5      Year Payment  Balance    Paid
6         1 $138.66  $2,860     $524
7         2 $138.66  $1,536     $340
8         3 $138.66      $0     $128
```

```
D7: (C0) 12*B7-(C6-C7)      ERROR
420
Protected Cell--Press [ESC] key
           A       B       C       D
1      Interest Rate:   15.0%
2         Principal: $4,000
3      Number Years:      3
4            Monthly  Ending Interest
5      Year Payment  Balance    Paid
6         1 $138.66  $2,860     $524
7         2 $138.66  $1,536     $340
8         3 $138.66      $0     $128
```

system. A two-level system gives each cell its own protected or unprotected status and also allows the entire protection system to be enabled or disabled. While the worksheet is being developed and tested, the protection system is left disabled. During this time the status of individual cells is adjusted so that all the cells are protected except those that the user will employ to enter data or will need to modify. When the worksheet works as desired, the global protection system is activated so that only the unprotected cells can be modified.

Some spreadsheet programs permit an additional level of protection: they allow a password to be established. If a password is established when the global protection system is turned on, then the spreadsheet will not turn off the protection system without asking for and receiving the password again. Obviously, it would be a serious mistake for the worksheet's developer to forget the password, because then there would be no way to modify the protected cells.

Hiding Cells

Another useful way to protect cells from unwanted modification is to hide them from view. Some worksheets provide a straightforward method of hiding columns: set the column width to zero. A column whose width is zero doesn't show in the display or on printed reports. But its cell entries are stored in memory, and calculations in the hidden entries can affect the cells that are displayed.

You can also hide entries by placing them in a remote, unused portion of the worksheet. Because the area available in most worksheets is enormous, this can be an effective strategy for hiding entries. A possible problem is that many spreadsheet programs require a few bytes of memory for every cell in the active area of the worksheet, even for cells that appear to be empty. Generally, the worksheet's **active area** is the rectangular region that extends from cell A1 in the upper-left corner, to the nonblank cell farthest to the worksheet's right, down to the nonblank cell farthest toward the bottom. As a result, placing an entry in a remote cell can create a very large active area and therefore require most of the computer's main memory; it can even produce a memory-full error message. With these spreadsheets it is important to pack all the cell entries into as small a rectangle as possible in the upper-left corner of the worksheet.

Creating Forms

Almost all businesses use standard forms to record transactions. A form speeds up the process of entering data by providing blanks for each data item. It also increases the accuracy with which data is entered by clearly labeling each blank and by ensuring that every data item is entered. Computerized forms have another advantage: as soon as an entry is placed in one blank, the cursor jumps to the next blank. Since the blanks in a form are not necessarily on adjacent lines or in adjacent cells, this can eliminate many cursor-movement keystrokes.

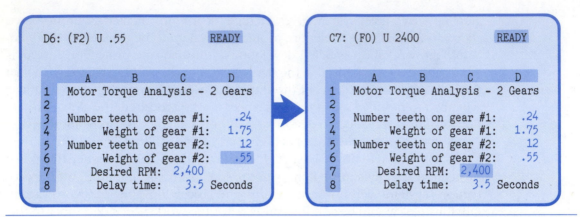

Figure 8.3 *Pressing the down-arrow key [↓] while entering data into a form moves the active-cell marker to the next unprotected cell—in this case, cell C7.*

Generally, spreadsheets construct forms by giving protected status to all cells except those which are blanks in the form. When data items are entered in the form, the active-cell marker jumps directly from one unprotected cell to the next. This is shown in Figure 8.3, where pushing the down-arrow key [↓] moves the active-cell marker from cell D6 to the next unprotected cell, C7.

Forms are used extensively by most data management systems; so it is not surprising that the spreadsheets that do the best job managing forms are part of

Figure 8.4 *On-screen business forms are used to add, view, and modify records in lists.*

integrated programs combining spreadsheet and data management functions. For example, Figure 8.4 was prepared with Jazz, a Macintosh program that combines word processing, record management, and spreadsheet components with telecommunications and graphics modules. Figure 8.4 shows a form that can be used to add, view, or modify records in a customer list. Once data is in the list, it can be analyzed with formulas to answer such questions as, What is the average age of my customers?

■ Changing the Appearance of the Worksheet

Format rules change the appearance of the worksheet without actually modifying the worksheet itself. In Chapter 7 we discussed format rules that affect only one cell at a time, such as right-justifying text. This section describes format rules that affect many cells at once; for example, rules that change the width of a column or divide the window into window panes.

Changing Column Widths

Columns naturally need different widths because they are used for different types of information. In most worksheets the left-most column identifies the contents of the rows with labels such as names, items for sale, or months of the year. These labels nearly always require more room than the numbers in the following columns. For example, a list of names requires a column approximately 20 characters wide, but the scores from a midterm exam fit in a column only 4 characters wide.

The number of characters that a single cell can contain varies from one spreadsheet to the next, but a typical number is around 250—many more characters than the usual column width. Thus you can type a long label into any cell without regard to the cell's column width. But keep in mind that what a spreadsheet displays as a cell's contents and what is stored in memory may differ. Some spreadsheets truncate labels in the display, showing only the portion that fits inside the cells in the worksheet window.

Entering a name or a report with a spreadsheet that truncates labels in the display requires careful attention to detail. The text must be broken into parts, and the parts must be entered as separate labels into adjacent cells. Once a worksheet has been filled out in this manner, changing the width of columns destroys the appearance of the worksheet. Figure 8.5 demonstrates the disastrous effect of changing the width of all the columns from six to eight characters with this type of spreadsheet. Notice that in the left screen the entry in cell A5 was truncated to read ''Dan La''; ''tham'' was therefore entered in cell B5. But in the right screen the column width has been increased, allowing more of cell A5 to be displayed. As a result, cells A5 and B5 together now read as ''Dan Laththam'' instead of the correct name, Dan Latham.

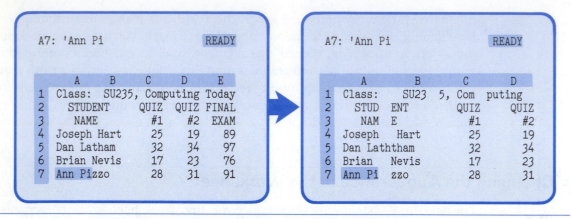

Figure 8.5 *The effect of expanding the width of all columns from six to eight characters if labels are truncated at the end of their respective cells.*

Many spreadsheets allow a long label to extend past the right edge of its cell, if the cell to the right is empty. This means that you don't need to chop headings and other lengthy items of text into cell-width units before entering them into the worksheet. Instead, you can type the text into one cell and leave the cells to its right empty. A label will not extend into a neighboring cell that appears empty but actually contains some blank spaces. As Figure 8.6 illustrates, this labeling system adapts to changes in the width of columns more gracefully than the labeling system shown in Figure 8.5. All of the cells in column B of Figure 8.6 are assumed to be empty; the text that appears in column B of the worksheet window is stored in the cells in column A.

Figure 8.6 *The effect of expanding the width of all columns from six to eight characters if labels can expand into adjacent cells.*

```
A7: 'Ann Pizzo              READY          A7: 'Ann Pizzo              READY

       A      B      C      D      E              A      B      C      D
1  Class:  SU235, Computing Today     1  Class:  SU235, Computing Today
2    STUDENT    QUIZ   QUIZ  FINAL     2    STUDENT        QUIZ   QUIZ
3    NAME        #1     #2    EXAM     3    NAME            #1     #2
4  Joseph Hart   25     19     89      4  Joseph Hart      25     19
5  Dan Latham    32     34     97      5  Dan Latham       32     34
6  Brian Nevis   17     23     76      6  Brian Nevis      17     23
7  Ann Pizzo     28     31     91      7  Ann Pizzo        28     31
```

Changing the column width can also affect numbers. The high-order digits of a number are not truncated in order to make a number fit in its cell. But depending on the format rules in effect, the digits past the decimal point might be rounded (causing 4.55 to become 5), or a long number might be converted into scientific notation (causing 12,000,000,000 to become 1.2 E +10). Otherwise, if a number is too long to fit, the cell on the screen is filled with a warning character, such as !!!!!!, *******, or ######. If you widen the column, the number will appear.

Most spreadsheets store numbers internally with the equivalent of eleven to fifteen decimal digits. Thus, if you type the number 1.234567890123456789 into a cell, the spreadsheet might store the number as 1.23456789012. The full number is used in any calculation regardless of how the number is displayed on the screen.

Titles and Window Panes

The maximum size of a worksheet depends on the spreadsheet program and on the amount of memory in the computer, but worksheets can store a lot of information. Exploring a worksheet filled with long lists of data is easier when the row or column titles are kept frozen on the screen while you scroll the rest of the window (see Figure 8.7). The TITLE command allows you to do just that. It keeps a portion of the worksheet fixed in place regardless of how the rest of the worksheet is moved.

You might think of the TITLE command as a way to expand the border along the top or side of the screen so that it includes several rows or columns of the window. For example, suppose you use the TITLE command to expand the border in a monthly budget to include column A. Then when you scroll to see

Figure 8.7 *Scrolling the window when the first four rows are locked in place as a title.*

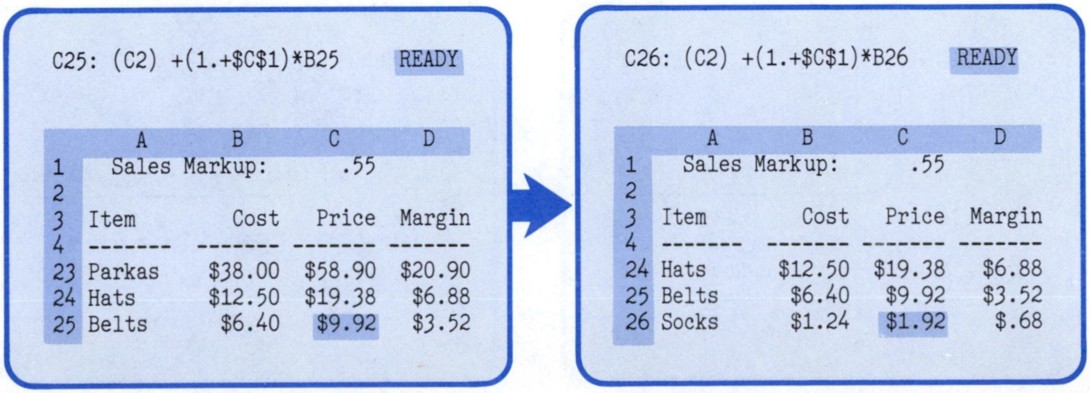

column K of the budget, column A, which gives the labels for the expense categories, will remain on the left edge of the window.

Suppose you need to compare the numbers in an income statement in one part of a worksheet with a balance sheet in another. Jumping back and forth from one statement to the other is inconvenient. A better solution is to give a command that splits the window into **window panes** that "look" into different portions of the worksheet (see Figure 8.8).

Most spreadsheets display a maximum of two panes at a time. You can choose whether the split runs horizontally or vertically across the screen. On a typical 24-line screen, the window is 20 rows high (3 lines are devoted to the control panel, and 1 line is occupied by the window's border). The window can be split into panes of unequal sizes; so the top pane might have 5 rows, leaving the bottom pane 14 rows (1 line goes to a border separating the panes). Or the window might be split vertically so that the left pane has 30 column positions and the right pane has 40.

Almost all spreadsheets require that both window panes look into the same worksheet, but many spreadsheets allow each pane to have its own formatting rules. Thus if the same cell appeared in both panes, it might not look the same. For example, one pane might be set to display formulas as they are stored in memory; the other might display formulas as they are evaluated by the spreadsheet. This arrangement would be useful if you are checking whether the formulas work as expected.

Several commands must be mastered to use window panes successfully, and they vary from one spreadsheet to the next. It is important to know the command that jumps the active cell from one pane to the other. The cursor-movement keys will not move the active cell out of the current pane; instead, when the active cell is moved against the edge of the pane, the pane begins to scroll. If the panes are **synchronized,** then scrolling one pane causes the other

Figure 8.8 *Scrolling the bottom pane of the window.*

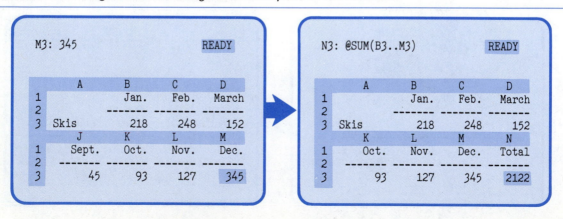

Productivity Software: A Professional's Tools

White-collar workers are rapidly abandoning conventional office products in favor of more powerful tools. Typewriters are being replaced by word processors. Pencils, multicolumn paper, and calculators are giving way to electronic spreadsheets. Information in filing cabinets is being moved to hard disks controlled by data management programs. Letters are traveling through electronic mail systems. Graph paper remains unused as graphics programs transform lists of numbers into instant charts and graphs. All of these new tools have been given a collective name: personal productivity software. This photo essay will give you a clearer view of the capabilities of these new software products.

1. In this screen each of six programs is given its own window in which to display information. Windowing makes it easy to switch quickly between different tasks.

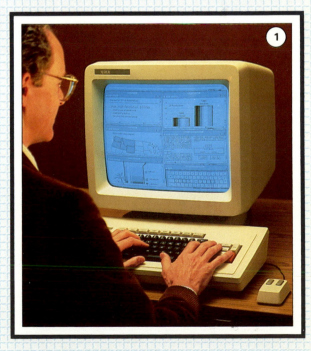

ELECTRONIC SPREADSHEETS

Electronic spreadsheet programs automate the process of editing and manipulating worksheets containing numbers. Spreadsheets have evolved through several generations since Visicalc, the first spreadsheet program, was introduced in 1979.

2. Visicalc was so important to the early success of the Apple II computer that some people called it the Visicalc machine. By today's standards Visicalc had very crude features. For example, it displayed numbers without commas and had no on-line help system. Despite Visicalc's shortcomings, it ushered in an entirely new way to manipulate numbers.

3. Visicalc soon had scores of copycat competitors, known as "Visi-clones." Most of these products offered better features, a lower price, or both. This screen shows SuperCalc, one of Visicalc's strongest competitors in 1981. SuperCalc introduced an excellent help system and can be displayed in color.

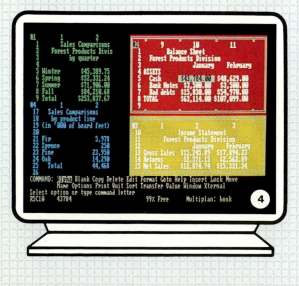

4. Multiplan won *InfoWorld* magazine's 1982 Software Product of the Year award. Multiplan provided a host of improvements including complete words in its menu, the ability to establish up to eight windows on the screen, and a way to link numbers between worksheets so that changes in one worksheet would automatically affect other worksheets.

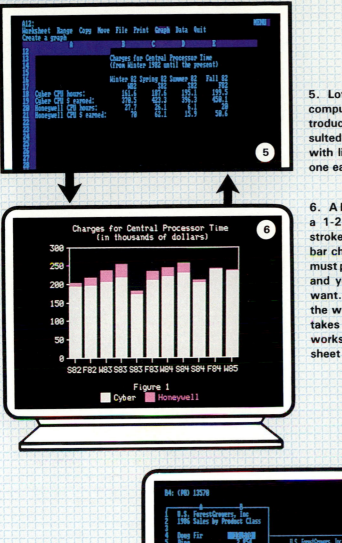

5. Lotus 1-2-3 became the best-selling personal computer program within a few months of its introduction in late 1982. Its instant success resulted from combining an excellent spreadsheet with limited graphics and data management in one easy-to-use package.

6. A Lotus 1-2-3 bar chart. Once numbers are in a 1-2-3 worksheet, it takes only a few keystrokes to convert them into a simple pie chart, bar chart, or line graph. To create a graph, you must point out which numbers are to be graphed, and you need to select the type of graph you want. Although 1-2-3 can't display a graph and the worksheet simultaneously on one screen, it takes only five keystrokes to switch from the worksheet to the graph and back to the worksheet again.

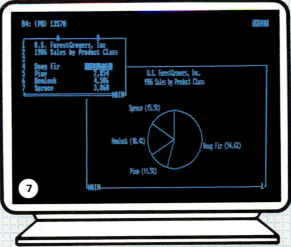

7. In mid-1984 Lotus Symphony combined Multiplan's windowing abilities with an improved version of 1-2-3's spreadsheet. Also included in the package are simple graphics, record management, word processing, and telecommunications. This screen shows a small spreadsheet window and a larger graph window. If a number in the spreadsheet window is changed, the graph is immediately redrawn to reflect the change.

window 5

WORD PROCESSING

8. More people have probably learned to use word processing than any other computer application. Word processing frees writers from the tyranny of paper when making revisions.

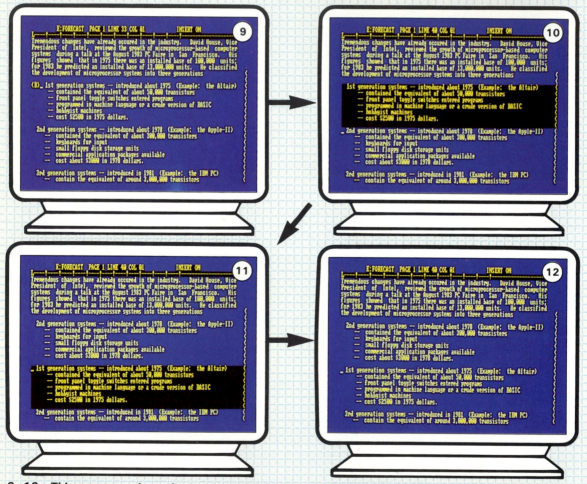

9–12. This sequence shows how a paragraph is moved with WordStar, a popular word processing program. The first step (photo 9) is to move the cursor to the beginning of the paragraph and to insert a marker in the document. At this point the marker is <B>. In photo 10 the cursor has been moved to the end of the paragraph and another marker has been inserted, causing the paragraph to turn yellow on the screen and the first marker to disappear. In photo 11 the paragraph has been transferred to its new location. Finally, in photo 12 the markers are removed.

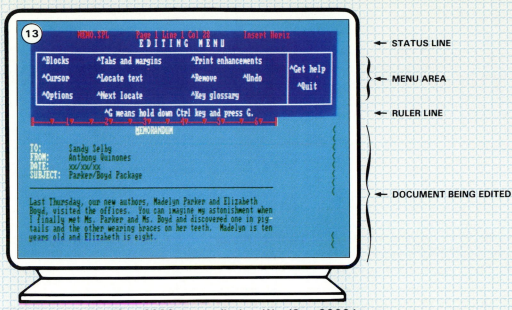

← STATUS LINE

← MENU AREA

← RULER LINE

← DOCUMENT BEING EDITED

13. A typical WordStar 2000 screen display. WordStar 2000 is an enhanced version of the original WordStar program and is primarily designed for use on personal computers with hard disks. It attempts to make the document look on the screen exactly as it will look on paper, but this is not always possible. For example, this color monitor cannot display bold characters (characters with a fatter than average outline), so they appear in white instead.

14. A spelling checker looks up each word in the document in its own dictionary. Words not in the dictionary are highlighted as suspect words. In this screen the spelling checker can't find the word *Trans* in its dictionary, so it suggests the word *Trap*.

DATA MANAGEMENT SOFTWARE

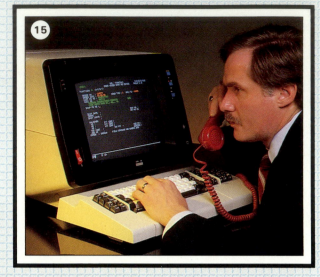

15. Businesses rely heavily on data management systems to do their record keeping. Most data management systems allow business forms to be displayed on the screen, making it easy to enter, revise, or query data about a particular transaction.

16. Lotus Symphony provides record management but not database management. This means Symphony can manipulate information in one file conveniently but cannot extract or process information from several files at once. Record management systems are well suited for such everyday tasks as keeping a calendar of appointments, maintaining a Christmas card mailing list, or recording the names, addresses, and phone numbers of clients.

17. Cullinet's Goldengate is an integrated program for personal computers that contain spreadsheet, graphics, word processing, and electronic mail systems as well as the relational database management system illustrated here. A relational database management system can create tables of information, join tables together, select subsets of a table, and answer questions like, How many departments have a travel budget greater than $5,000?

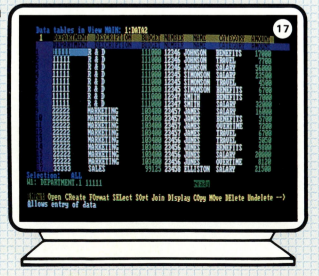

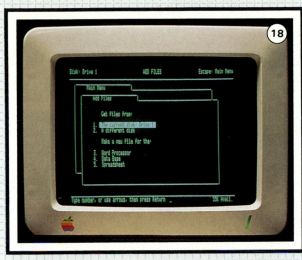

INTEGRATED PROGRAMS

An integrated program is a collection of related programs combined into a unified package. Bundling related programs into an integrated program simplifies communication between the computer and the user and makes it easy to switch from one task to another.

18. With Apple Corporation's AppleWorks program, you follow the same procedure to create a new file whether you are using the program's word processor, data manager, or spreadsheet.

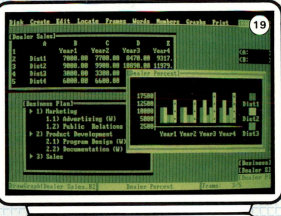

19. Switching from one task to another in an integrated program is quite simple if each task is given its own window on the screen. This screen, which is from Ashton-Tate's Frameworks, shows a graph, a spreadsheet, and an outline in different windows.

20. Two types of windows are in common use: tiled and free-form. This display shows tiled windows; the viewing area is broken up into nonoverlapping regions called tiles. Free-form windows appear to sit on the screen in the same way pieces of paper can pile up on a desktop.

window 5

HELP SYSTEMS

Help systems dispense a full screen of explanatory information at the touch of the [HELP] key. Most systems are quite helpful; a few are a waste of time. The best help systems are said to be context-sensitive, meaning they pay attention to what you are doing in the program when help is requested and display information relevant to that task.

```
                HELP - EDITING MENU - 1 of 5
             Press G now to change the menu display level.

DOCUMENT.EXT    Page 1  Line 1        ← Status Line shows information
                   E D I T I                         about document.

┌────────┬──────────────────┐
│ ^Blocks      ^Tabs and margin│    ← Menu Area lists choices of action.
│ ^Cursor      ^Locate text    │
│ ^Options     ^Next locate    │
│              ^C means hold dow│
├──┴──┴──┴──┴──┴──┴──┴──┴──┴──┴─┤   ← Ruler Line shows tabs and margins.
│  When I recall my manual typewrit
│ tedious hours spent retyping manuscr
│ dark coffee stains that ruined my wo  ← Window shows typing and editing.
│ literally ironing the creases out of
│ able to print a fresh copy is a bles
│ threw my typewriter away!
└──────────────────────────────┘

          Press Spacebar for more help or Escape to leave help.
```

21. WordStar 2000 provides context-sensitive help; so it often seems to work like a user manual that automatically falls open to the right page.

```
E3:                                                        HELP

Working in a SHEET Window                                    97

In a SHEET window you can enter data into cells. The cells can contain:

    Numbers: stored with 15 digits of precision, displayed in format you
    define (no commas or spaces allowed in numbers, unless you change the
    Punctuation setting on the International settings sheet)

    Labels: text

    Formulas: instructions to calculate a number or to concatenate strings

    @Functions: special formulas "built into" Symphony for manipulating
    both numbers and strings (labels)

For a menu of SHEET commands, press [MENU].

SHEET Commands        Punctuation Setting    Formulas       Strings
Labels                Numeric Display Formats @Functions     Help Index
```

22. Lotus Symphony has one of the best help systems on the market today. Because it is context-sensitive, it will provide spreadsheet information if you are working on a spreadsheet, graphing information if you are constructing a graph, and so on. But Symphony's help system goes one step further; it provides a list of related topics on the bottom of each help screen. You can view the help screen for a related topic by first moving the highlighted cursor box onto the name of the topic and then pressing [RETURN].

pane to scroll in the same direction. Generally, there is a command that toggles from synchronized to independent scrolling and back again. Figure 8.8 shows the effect of scrolling the bottom pane of the window when the panes are not synchronized.

Types of Format Rules

We have discussed several format rules that affect how values are displayed in the window: the width of columns, left- or right-justified labels, and so forth. Most format rules can be given in two ways: a **global format rule** affects the entire worksheet; an **individual format rule** applies to a single cell or column.

Because global format rules affect the entire worksheet, changing the global column-width setting adjusts the width of all columns simultaneously, just like the examples in Figures 8.5 and 8.6. An individual format rule overrides a global format rule. Thus, changing the global column-width setting will not affect a column that has been given its own individual format rule with a previous command. If a worksheet has many narrow columns for numbers and a few wider columns for labels, the quickest way to set up the worksheet is to use a global command to make all the columns narrow, and then widen the label columns with individual column-width commands.

Some spreadsheets have a three-level hierarchy for format settings. For example, you might use the integer format (123) as the global setting for numbers, the currency format ($123.45) as the setting for column D, and the general format (123.45) as the setting for cell D4. Individual cell settings override column or row settings, which in turn override the global setting.

Formatting Limitations

Spreadsheets have more commands for formatting than for any other process, but even so, they have definite formatting limitations. Occasionally, you will not be able to adjust the worksheet to look exactly as you want. Perhaps a number should appear centered in its cell, but the spreadsheet's manual doesn't list an option for centering numbers. You might try entering the number into the worksheet as a label—but then you can't refer to it in formulas. Or suppose you want the columns in a report to be staggered on the page. Although manuals rarely mention this limitation, in all spreadsheets a column must have the same width from the top to the bottom of the worksheet.

Often it is best to live with the formatting limitations and accept a report that isn't laid out character for character the way you would design it by hand. If every character must be in exactly the right spot, it may be necessary to transfer the information to a word processor so that editing can proceed without the limitations inherent in a cellular worksheet.

■ Recalculating Formulas

Automatic Versus Manual Recalculation

How are the values in a worksheet revised when a new value is entered? Most spreadsheets evaluate every formula in the worksheet whenever any entry is changed; this is called **automatic recalculation.**

A worksheet can have hundreds or thousands of formulas. Evaluating all the formulas takes time, especially if some of the formulas involve heavy-duty calculations, such as logarithms or statistical functions. If the worksheet is large and complicated, it can take five or ten minutes to complete the job. Obviously, this is too long to wait between making entries. Setting the spreadsheet to manual recalculation avoids these delays. With **manual recalculation** formulas are evaluated only when you give the command to recalculate. On most spreadsheets this command is given by typing an exclamation point (**!**) in the ready mode.

Order of Recalculation

When a critical assumption in the worksheet is modified, you can sometimes see the changes ripple across the window in a specific order. The traditional recalculation order is to evaluate the active cell, then evaluate the formulas in column A by working down the column one cell at a time, then evaluate column B, column C, and so forth. This is known as **column-oriented recalculation.**

You cannot assume that all the numbers on the screen represent stable values just because the worksheet has been recalculated. For example, suppose you type the formula +1+A1 into cell A1. This formula turns cell A1 into a counter that displays how many times the worksheet has been recalculated. Every time the worksheet is recalculated, the number in cell A1 is increased by 1, and a new number is displayed. This formula will not converge to a stable value; instead, it will continue counting.

Some worksheets require several recalculations before the numbers they display become stable. For example, the worksheet in Figure 8.9 must be recalculated twice before a change in the sales markup (cell C1) is reflected in the total margin displayed in cell C7. On the first recalculation the formula in cell C7 is evaluated before the numbers in column D have been adjusted to reflect the new sales markup. After the second recalculation everything is self-consistent again.

One way to avoid the need for two recalculations would be to move the formula for the total margin from cell C7 to cell D7. That way the margin for each item would be calculated before the total margin. Another solution is to use row-oriented recalculation. **Row-oriented recalculation** evaluates formulas in the worksheet from left to right across each row, starting with the top

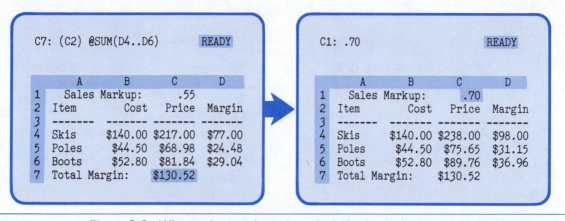

Figure 8.9 *When column-oriented recalculation is used, changing cell C1 (the sales markup) leaves the total margin in cell C7 inconsistent with the rest of the worksheet—unless the worksheet is recalculated twice.*

row in the worksheet. Row-oriented recalculation works well for the example in Figure 8.9 because the "Margin" numbers are in earlier rows than the "Total Margin" number. Some spreadsheets have a command that allows you to choose whether row- or column-oriented recalculation should be used.

Multiplan, Lotus 1-2-3, Symphony, and most recently developed spreadsheets do not blindly follow a fixed recalculation order. Instead, they postpone calculating a formula until all the cells it depends on have been evaluated. Thus, if the formula in cell B4 depends on the values in cells C8 and F9, the contents of cells C8 and F9 are processed before cell B4. This is called a **natural recalculation order** because it respects the natural relationships among cells.

Circular References

If cells depend on each other in a circular manner, there is no natural recalculation order. The simplest example of a **circular reference** is a cell whose formula refers to the cell's own value.

Figure 8.10 provides more complicated examples of circular references. It shows the income statement of a profit-sharing company that gives employees a bonus based on net profit. This worksheet contains two circular references: the formula for the employee bonus in cell D6 is calculated as 30 percent of net profit (+.30*D7), and the formula for net profit in cell D7 is calculated as the prebonus profit minus the bonus (+D5 – D6). Thus cell D6 depends on cell D7, but cell D7 depends on cell D6. When the worksheet in the left screen in Figure 8.10 is recalculated, the bonus becomes 1,800 (calculated as +.30*6,000), and the net profit becomes 4,200 (calculated as 6,000 – 1,800). After another

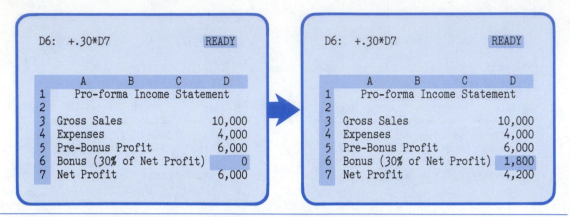

Figure 8.10 *A circular reference. The bonus depends on the net profit and the net profit depends on the bonus.*

recalculation the numbers for bonus and net profit become 1,260 and 4,740, respectively. It takes eight more calculations for the numbers to stabilize at their final values of $1,384.62 and $4,615.38. Some circular references converge to a stable set of values; others never produce a set of self-consistent numbers.

■ Transferring Information

Nearly all spreadsheets employ a two-dimensional worksheet format, but many applications are best solved with a three-dimensional format for reports. For example, consider the task of creating expense budgets for a firm with fifty cost centers. Let's assume that the budget for each cost center has twelve months of expenses for thirty expense categories. The budget for a single cost center will have a variety of identifying labels and about four hundred numbers (thirty expense categories times twelve months, plus various total figures). The final budget report for the firm will require over fifty pages—one page for each cost center and at least one summary page for the firm's aggregate expense budget.

The three dimensions in this report are months, expense categories, and cost centers. You could make the report fit on one two-dimensional worksheet by placing each cost center's budget in a different area of the worksheet, but this is an inconvenient solution. The worksheet would include 20,000 numerical entries (50 cost centers times 400 numbers per cost center). It would be hard to coordinate the entry of so many numbers into one giant worksheet, and few personal computers can create a worksheet with 20,000 numerical entries.

At this point we should mention that probably the best way to handle this budget is to use a data management program (discussed in Chapters 9 and 10). Budgeting is characterized by a large amount of data and by limited arithmetic computations—just the type of problem that data management programs solve best. Still, you can handle this budget with a spreadsheet program if you place each cost center's budget in its own worksheet and then consolidate these worksheets into other worksheets to obtain total budget figures. We will review the three most common methods of consolidating information from several worksheets: (1) copying information from one worksheet to another, (2) merging worksheets by adding their values together, and (3) linking worksheets so that changes in one worksheet affect the contents of another.

Copying Worksheets

Almost all spreadsheets allow information to be copied from one worksheet to another, but the procedure varies from one spreadsheet to the next. For example, on the Macintosh version of Multiplan you cut (or copy) a region of the *source worksheet* onto the clipboard, then load the *target worksheet* into memory, and finally paste the clipboard's information into the target worksheet. (Recall that a *clipboard* is a temporary storage region, sometimes called a *buffer,* that holds a single clipping. If you cut a second clipping, the contents of the clipboard are replaced by the second clipping.) Text and numbers come through the copying process without change, but only the results of formulas are copied—not the formulas themselves. Format rules are not copied; so the information may look different in the target worksheet.

In contrast, Lotus 1-2-3 allows information to be read directly into the current worksheet from a worksheet stored on a disk. First you move the active cell to the upper-left corner of the region to receive the new information. Then you give the /FILE-COMBINE-COPY command. Either an entire worksheet or just a portion can be copied from the disk into the current worksheet. Cells that are copied into the current worksheet replace any previous entries. This makes it important to position the active cell carefully before giving the COPY command; a careless command can destroy an entire worksheet.

Merging Worksheets

Information is not aggregated when you copy it from one worksheet to another; it is merely transferred. That is why some spreadsheets provide a command that merges the contents of two worksheets by adding the numbers in them together.

For example, Lotus 1-2-3 aggregates worksheets with a /FILE-COMBINE-ADD command. The only difference between this command and the /FILE-COMBINE-COPY command is in how the incoming cells from the worksheet on a disk are merged with the current worksheet in memory. The /FILE-COMBINE-ADD command does not transfer labels and empty cells from the worksheet on disk; it takes only values (numbers and the results of formulas).

The rules for merging an incoming value into the current worksheet depend on the type of cell it is merged with.

■ Number cells have their value added to the incoming value, so that the sum of the two values is displayed.

■ Empty cells acquire the value of the incoming value.

■ Label and formula cells are not affected by the incoming value; they retain their original contents.

Suppose you want to use the /FILE-COMBINE-ADD command to summarize cost-center budgets into a department budget. The first step is to create a template for the department budget that has empty cells (or zeros) where the expense values belong. The next steps are to use /FILE-COMBINE-ADD commands to add the values in the cost-center worksheets stored on disks to the

Figure 8.11 *The effect of a /FILE-COMBINE-ADD command, which merges the numbers from a worksheet on disk with the worksheet in memory.*

Worksheet in Memory

A1: 'Metals Department   READY

	A	B	C	D
1	Metals Department			
2				
3	Item	Jan.	Feb.	Mar.
4	Salaries	$2,300	$2,300	$2,340
5	Supplies	$940	$800	$780
6	Travel	$0	$0	$0
7	Electric	$450	$500	$490

Worksheet on Disk

	A	B	C	D
1	Cost Center: 12, Metal Stamping			
2				
3	Item	Jan.	Feb.	Mar.
4	Salaries	$5,000	$5,050	$5,100
5	Supplies	$300	$540	$420
6	Travel	$0	$0	$2,000
7	Electric	$95	$95	$95

A1: 'Metals Department   READY

	A	B	C	D
1	Metals Department			
2				
3	Item	Jan.	Feb.	Mar.
4	Salaries	$7,300	$7,350	$7,440
5	Supplies	$1,240	$1,340	$1,200
6	Travel	$0	$0	$2,000
7	Electric	$545	$595	$585

Revised Worksheet

template for the department budget. Figure 8.11 illustrates the result of using the command. With a similar procedure you could aggregate the department budgets into a budget for the entire firm.

Linking Worksheets

A target worksheet into which information is copied or merged is not affected by subsequent changes to the source worksheets. Anyone who has been through a budgeting process knows how serious this limitation can be; budgets inevitably go through numerous revisions before everyone is satisfied. This disadvantage can be removed by permanently linking the worksheets.

For example, the Macintosh version of Multiplan links information between worksheets as easily as it copies information. Instead of using the PASTE command, you use the PASTE-AND-LINK command. It copies information into the target worksheet, but the transferred information is linked to its original location. This means two things. First, the linked cells in the target worksheet are locked; they cannot be changed or copied unless you use an UNLINK command. Second, whenever the target worksheet is loaded into memory, its linked cells receive their entries directly from the source worksheet.

Figure 8.12 shows two cost-center budget worksheets that are linked to their department's worksheet. The information in the department worksheet comes from rows 5–11 in each of the cost-center worksheets. Suppose that the number in cell R5C2 (row 5, column 2) of the worksheet for Cost Center 12 is changed from 5,000 to 3,000. Because cell R1C1 of the Metals Department worksheet is linked to cell R5C2 of Cost Center 12's worksheet, the next time that the Metals Department worksheet is loaded into memory the value for cell R1C1 will change from 5,000 to 3,000.

The procedure for creating the links between the worksheets in Figure 8.12 is straightforward but lengthy.

- A region is selected from the Cost Center 12 worksheet, causing the region to appear in inverse video (white on black).
- The region is copied to the clipboard.
- The Metals Department worksheet is loaded into memory, and the contents of the clipboard are pasted and linked into it, beginning with cell R1C1.
- The Metals Department worksheet is saved, and the worksheet for Cost Center 13 is loaded into memory.
- The cycle of selecting a region, copying it to the clipboard, loading the Metals Department worksheet, and pasting and linking is repeated.

Obviously, pasting and linking the cost-center expenses into the department worksheet has not created a total department budget. To do that you must

Link

(a) The Budget Worksheet for Cost Center 12

(b) The Budget Worksheet for Cost Center 13

Link

(c) The Metals Department Worksheet

Figure 8.12 *Linking worksheets. The expense numbers on the worksheets for Cost Centers 12 and 13 are linked to the budget worksheet for the Metals Department.*

place formulas in the department worksheet that add the expenses of the cost centers.

Worksheets can be linked in intricate patterns if necessary. For example, cost-center worksheets could be linked to department worksheets, which in turn could be linked to the worksheet for the entire firm. Because linked information is updated only when a target worksheet is loaded into memory, the order in which worksheets are revised and saved is critical. For example, a change in a cost center's worksheet will not affect the worksheet for the total firm unless the appropriate department worksheet has been loaded into memory and saved in the meantime.

Moving Data Among Applications

Moving data between stand-alone programs is often time consuming and bothersome. For example, to move part of a Lotus 1-2-3 worksheet into a WordStar document you must

- load Lotus 1-2-3 and the worksheet into memory.
- ''print'' the portion of the worksheet you want to transfer. Instead of printing to a printer, you must request the print operation to send its output to a disk as a data file.
- load WordStar and the document into memory.
- merge (also called *import*) the data file into the document with a BLOCK-READ command.

These four steps are necessary because WordStar cannot directly read Lotus 1-2-3 worksheet files, but it can read files that Lotus 1-2-3 has ''printed'' to a disk. This type of rigmarole is common when moving data between stand-alone programs because they usually store data in their own specialized formats on disk.

If your computer work involves several application areas—for example, if you are writing a letter (word processing) that contains a graph (graphics) illustrating a relationship you discovered with a numerical model (spreadsheet analysis), then an integrated program may work better for you than an assortment of stand-alone programs. An *integrated program* consists of a tightly bundled set of specialized programs for activities like word processing, spreadsheet calculations, database management, graphics, project control, scheduling, communications, and so forth. These specialized programs are called **components.** In almost all integrated programs one component is central, the basis for all the others in two ways.

First, one component is usually the center of communications, the center of data transfers. For example, Figure 8.13 shows two integrated programs, each of which includes spreadsheet, graphics, database management, word

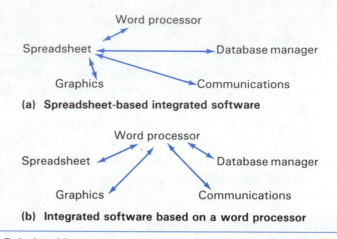

(a) **Spreadsheet-based integrated software**

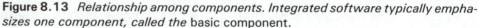

(b) **Integrated software based on a word processor**

Figure 8.13 *Relationship among components. Integrated software typically emphasizes one component, called the* basic component.

processing, and data communications components. An arrow points to a component if data can be transferred to it from another component. In Figure 8.13(a) data can be transferred from the spreadsheet to any other component, and from any component to the spreadsheet; but data cannot be transferred directly between the other components. Thus in this case the spreadsheet is the central component; this is a *spreadsheet-based integrated program.*

Second, the central component may determine the form of the data in all other components and thus exert a strong influence on the other components. For example, if the spreadsheet is the central component, then all other components may operate with rows and columns. The word processor may store text by expanding a spreadsheet column until it is as wide as the printed page, and the fields in the database manager may be equated to cells in the spreadsheet.

A major advantage of integrated programs is the ease with which data can be transferred from one component to another. Data can be taken from one program and entered into another by a simple cut-and-paste operation. Most integrated programs use a special file—a clipboard—to hold data while it is being moved from one component to another.

Another advantage of having a unified collection of components is the speed with which you can move from one processing activity to another. For example, you may begin a session by preparing a sales forecast with a spreadsheet, as shown in Figure 8.14(a); then use the graphics component to construct a bar graph showing your forecast; and then insert the graph into a memo in the word processing component, as shown in Figure 8.14(b).

When one component of an integrated program is actively in use, you are in a certain corresponding mode, or context. The most common method of **context switching** (moving from one component to another) is **windowing.**

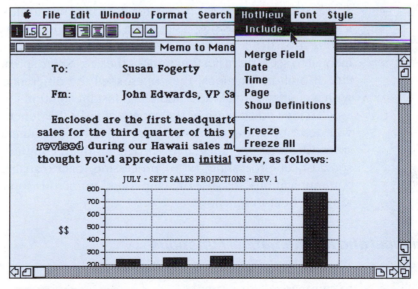

(a) Worksheet

(b) Word Processing

Figure 8.14 *Using an integrated program to transfer information from a worksheet to a memo. Sales data in the spreadsheet window (a) is first transferred to a graph window, where it is transformed into a bar graph. Then the bar graph is copied and linked to a memo in a word processing window.*

Recall that a window is a region on the screen where a single component is displayed. Windowing is used to display several components, using multiple windows, at the same time.

A clipboard file used in conjunction with windowing can provide several powerful methods of merging components into a unified whole. Cutting and pasting removes the data from the source window. For this reason, programs usually provide a *copy-and-paste* operation that does not destroy the original data. Copy-and-paste operations make static (dead) copies of the original data. If the original version of the data is modified after the copy has been made, the copy remains unchanged. A few of the newest integrated programs support *copy-and-link* operations that create "live" linkages between components. For example, a portion of the spreadsheet window in Figure 8.14(a) is copied and linked to a graph window to construct a bar chart, which in turn is linked to the memo shown in the word processing window in Figure 8.14(b). Later, if you change the numbers in the spreadsheet, both the bar chart in the graph window and the copy of the bar chart in the word processing window will automatically reflect those changes.

■ Advanced Functions

Spreadsheets provide short cuts for common financial, statistical, mathematical, and other processing tasks through built-in functions. Whenever you are having a particularly difficult time constructing a formula, check a reference manual to see if there is a function for the task. Some spreadsheets provide dozens of built-in functions; they often spell the difference between struggling with a clumsy formula and finding an instant solution.

To give you a sense of the variety of tasks that functions can perform, we will describe a few of Lotus Symphony's built-in functions. Symphony is a spreadsheet-based integrated program that combines components for spreadsheet processing, word processing, data management, graphics, and communications. Because of Symphony's numerous applications, it has a wide range of built-in functions.

Statistical and Mathematical Functions

Statistical functions provide summary statistics; thus they accept a list of items to summarize. For example,

- @AVG(*list*) averages the values of the items in the list.
- @MAX(*list*) finds the maximum value of all the items.
- @STD(*list*) computes the standard deviation of the items.

```
        A      B       C        D
 1   Test   Test            Column B's
 2   Data   Results         Test Formulas
 3   ----   -------         -------------
 4      4        4   <-----  @AVG(2,4,6)
 5      9       15   <-----  @MAX(A4..A8)
 6     15  5.26877   <-----  @STD(A4..A8)
 7      0       -1   <-----  @COS(3.14159)
 8      3  403.428   <-----  @EXP(6)
 9               4   <-----  @INT(4.9)
10         0.18087   <-----  @RAND
```

Figure 8.15 *Examples of statistical and mathematical functions.*

In contrast, *mathematical functions* accept a single number, perform a mathematical transformation on it, and return a single number. Figure 8.15 shows examples of both statistical functions and the following mathematical functions:

- @COS(*value*) computes the cosine of the value.
- @EXP(*value*) finds the exponential of the value.
- @INT(*value*) returns the integer part of the value.
- @RAND generates a random number between 0 and 1. This function doesn't require an argument.

Financial Functions

Spreadsheets also provide *financial functions,* which calculate the effect of interest rates on sums of money over time.

- @IRR(*guess, range*) calculates the interest rate that makes the cash flows given in the range equal to zero. IRR stands for "internal rate of return." IRRs are calculated by trial and error; *guess* is an arbitrary starting point.
- @NPV(*interest rate, range*) finds the net present value of the series of cash flows given in the range discounted at a constant interest rate.
- @PMT(*principal, interest rate, #-of-periods*) yields the payment that will pay off the principal of a loan borrowed at the specified interest rate after the specified number of payments have been made.

For example, suppose cells A1 through D1 of a spreadsheet hold the numbers −2000, 1000, 1000, and 1000. Then the formula @IRR(15%,A1..D1) is equal to 23.375 percent, and the formula @NPV(20%,A1..D1) is equal to $88.73. The formula that calculates the monthly payment in cell B6 of Figure 8.1 is @PMT(C2,C1/12,C3*12).

String Functions

Symphony provides an unusually large number of *string functions,* which perform operations on text. Figure 8.16 illustrates some of these.

- @CODE(*string*) returns the ASCII code number of the first character in the string.

- @LEFT(*string, value*) truncates the string after the number of characters given by *value.*

- @LENGTH(*string*) calculates the number of characters in the string.

- @LOWER(*string*) converts all the characters in the string to lower-case letters.

- @REPEAT(*string, value*) produces a label made up of the number of repetitions of the string specified by *value.*

- @VALUE(*string*) converts the string from label format into value format. In other words, it converts a series of characters that look like a number into a number the spreadsheet can use in calculations.

Figure 8.16 *Examples of string functions.*

```
                         A               B         C
  1  Test Data
  2  ------------------------------
  3  Beware the Jabberwock, my son!
  4                                             Column A's
  5  Test Results                               Test Formulas
  6  ------------------------------             -------------
  7                             66 <--- @CODE(A3)
  8  Beware                        <--- @LEFT(A3,6)
  9                             30 <--- @LENGTH(A3)
 10  beware the jabberwock, my son! <--- @LOWER(A3)
 11  -=-=-=-=-=-=-=-=-=-=        <--- @REPEAT("-=",10)
                              450 <--- @VALUE("4.5E2")
```

Date Functions

Symphony allows you to calculate with dates and times as easily as with any other numbers. To help Symphony do its math, dates are assigned consecutive integers, starting with January 1, 1900, as the number 1. Times are assigned fractional numbers, starting with midnight as the number 0.0 and with noon as 0.5. Thus, April 27, 1985, at 3:09 A.M. is stored as 31164.1318171296. Fortunately, Symphony provides format rules that instruct the spreadsheet to display dates and times in a variety of traditional formats, such as 27-Apr-85 or 03:09:49 AM.

You might use Symphony's date functions to print the current date automatically in reports. This can be done with the @NOW function, which retrieves the current time from the computer's clock whenever the worksheet is recalculated. The @NOW function might display 04/24/85 or 3:09 AM; the result depends on the current time in the computer's clock and the format rule assigned to the cell containing the function. Date functions might also be used to search a list of insurance policies for policies that have expired.

Logical Functions

Symphony also provides *logical functions,* which are used to test the condition of cells or to choose between two values for a cell. Most logical functions test whether a condition is true or false. Symphony assigns the value 1 to conditions that are true and the value 0 to conditions that are false. For example, in Figure 8.17 the condition A4 < A5 is false (and hence equal to 0), because the number

Figure 8.17 *Examples of logical functions.*

```
          A      B       C        D
    1    Test   Test            Column B's
    2    Data  Results          Test Formulas
    3    ----  -------          -------------
    4      4        4 <----- @IF(A4<A5,A5,A4)
    5      0       12 <----- @IF(A6>10,A7,A8)
    6     15     3.75 <----- @IF(A4<>0,A6/A4,0)
    7     12        0 <----- @IF(A5<>0,A6/A5,0)
    8               0 <----- @ISNUMBER(A1)
    9               1 <----- @ISNUMBER(A4)
```

in A4 is not less than the number in A5. The two logical functions illustrated in Figure 8.17 are

- @IF(*condition, value1, value2*), which returns *value1* if the condition is true; otherwise it returns *value2*.

- @ISNUMBER(*cell-reference*), which returns 1 (true) if the specified cell has a numeric value or is empty; otherwise it returns 0 (false).

Look-up Tables

A *look-up function* allows you to retrieve an entry from a table. This is useful for retrieving taxes from a tax table or for assigning letter grades to students based on the points they have earned in class. Symphony's look-up functions are quite versatile. The function that searches a typical vertical table filled with numbers is @VLOOKUP(*value, column-range, offset*). It compares the specified value with the numbers in the column range and returns an entry from the *offset* column.

For example, assume a professor wanted to assign grades to students based on the following point scheme:

Points	Letter Grade
0 to 149	F
150 to 199	D
200 to 249	C
250 to 299	B
300 or more	A

The first step would be to build a look-up table in the worksheet with the point cutoffs in one column and the letter grades in another, as in

	A	B	C	D	E	F
1	Grade Lookup Table			Student	Points	Grade
2	Points	Grades		Name	Earned	Assigned
3	0	F		Andros	215	C
4	150	D		Beck	250	B
5	200	C		Decker	307	A
6	250	B		Gillis	29	F
7	300	A		Poole	265	B
8				Zoller	312	A

The formula to calculate Andros's grade in cell F3 is @VLOOKUP(E3,A3..A7,1). It searches down column A looking for the pair of cells that bracket the value in cell E3, 215. The smaller of the two bracketing values is used (200); so in this case the entry to be returned is selected from row 5. The *offset* of 1 indicates that the entry should be returned from one column to the right of the *column-range,* in this case column B, resulting in a grade of C.

■ Keyboard Macros

Spreadsheet applications often involve repetitive commands. Perhaps you must type the same phrase in many cells. Or maybe you must give the commands to print an earnings projection repeatedly, interrupted only by making quick changes to the model's assumptions. Because computers are best at repetitive activities, it is reasonable to expect them to do these tasks for you.

Some spreadsheets allow you to write a script of commands describing a sequence of tasks. This script is then associated with a single key on the keyboard and is played back at the touch of that key. The script of commands is called a **macro** or a **keyboard macro.** It associates a sequence of keystrokes with a single key on the keyboard. When the macro's key is pressed, the keystrokes are automatically typed one at a time; the spreadsheet interprets them just as if you had typed them yourself.

The simplest keyboard macro types a word or phrase whenever the macro is invoked. For example, a macro might type the 57-keystroke phrase

```
Computing Today: Microcomputer Concepts and Applications
```

whenever [ALT]-[C] is pressed. More complicated macros associate a series of commands with a single key. For example,

- ■ [ALT]-[F] might display a business form on the screen and prompt the user through the process of entering a business transaction.

- ■ [ALT]-[M] might invoke a macro that merges portions of several worksheets on a disk into the current worksheet.

- ■ [ALT]-[P] might establish the line length, margins, heading, and footing for a report and send the report to the printer.

- ■ [ALT]-[S] might save a copy of the current worksheet on disk and move the active cell to cell A1.

The procedure for using a macro varies widely depending on the program, but it usually requires three basic steps.

1. Store the macro. Generally, you do this by storing the keystrokes that make up the macro as entries in cells. For example, you might type ''Computing Today˜'' in cell Z8 of the worksheet. (The character ˜ in this macro represents a carriage return.)

2. Associate the macro with a key. Generally, you do this by giving a special name to the cells that store the macro. For example, cell Z8 might be given the name \ C. In Lotus 1-2-3 this would "attach" the keystrokes stored in cell Z8 to the [ALT]-[C] key.

3. Invoke the macro. Usually this is done by typing the key associated with the macro. For example, pressing [ALT]-[C] would cause Lotus 1-2-3 to type "Computing Today" followed by a carriage return into the active cell.

There is both an easy and a hard way to create keyboard macros. Lotus Symphony illustrates the easy way; it has a *learn mode* that you can use to teach Symphony exactly what the macro is to do. You begin the learn mode by pressing a function key labeled LEARN. While in the learn mode you type the procedure just as you normally would; then you stop Symphony from recording your keystrokes by pressing [LEARN] again. In addition to executing your commands as you type them, Symphony silently records your keystrokes in an area of the worksheet called the *learn range.* Once the procedure is recorded, it can be edited, given a name, and used like any other macro.

In contrast, Lotus 1-2-3 illustrates the hard way to create macros: you must type the macro directly into the worksheet's cells. Although this would not be too difficult for our simple example, it is hard to remember the exact sequence of keystrokes necessary for a complicated procedure. Most people find they must work through the procedure once at the keyboard, carefully writing down each keystroke. Then they type the keystrokes into cells where they are given a name and made into a macro.

Most spreadsheet macros are created for one of two reasons. First, a macro can relieve the tedium of entering the same lengthy set of commands over and over again. Second, for commands that are given infrequently—such as commands to print reports or consolidate data—a macro "remembers" the commands better than people do.

If you are developing sophisticated templates, there is a third reason to create macros: they can allow the spreadsheet to make decisions. If it includes a few programming commands, the spreadsheet program can create *programmable macros;* it can upgrade the macro facility into a full-blown programming language. For example, Symphony supplies special programming commands that can be embedded inside a macro to allow it to make IF . . THEN . . tests, GOTO jumps, and SUBROUTINE calls (these are control structures familiar to any programmer). By placing an IF . . THEN . . command inside a macro, for instance, you can write a macro that erases a range of cells if the value in cell B5 is equal to 0 and does something else if the value is not equal to 0. Other macro programming commands allow a macro to display messages on the prompt line of the screen, pause for inputs from the keyboard, and store the inputs in specified cells.

Programmable macros provide the ultimate in power and versatility for spreadsheet applications, but they are not for the novice or the faint-hearted. In the hands of a motivated professional, programmable macros can create interactive templates that help walk the user through the steps to complete the application.

■ Summary

This chapter described some of the advanced features that allow spreadsheets to be used for sophisticated applications. Many spreadsheet features were not discussed. We have omitted some features, such as a global search-and-replace feature or an ability to give names to areas of a worksheet. Other features are covered in more detail elsewhere in the book, such as advanced forms management, sorting, and limited data management commands (Chapter 9) and graphing abilities (Chapter 12).

Most of the time spent interacting with a spreadsheet is not spent constructing formulas; it is spent entering data to obtain the results of calculations. Frequently, one person constructs a template that contains the formulas, and other people use the template. A substantial amount of knowledge can be built into a template. If a template is constructed carefully with protected cells, input via forms and menus, and helpful keyboard macros, then the user needs very little understanding of how the spreadsheet program or the template works to obtain impressive results.

Global format settings have a major effect on how information is presented on the screen. Chief among these settings is the width of columns. With most spreadsheets you can also give each column its own width setting. Other settings determine how many window panes are in the window, whether some rows or columns are frozen as titles on the window, and how numbers and text are formatted.

Each recalculation of a large worksheet takes a long time. By turning off the automatic recalculation feature, you can enter data without waiting for a recalculation between each entry. Three ways of recalculating the worksheet are to evaluate formulas (1) column by column, (2) row by row, or (3) in a natural order that postpones evaluating a formula until the cells it depends on have been processed. Circular references set up a mathematical paradox in the worksheet; the paradox may or may not resolve itself with repeated recalculations.

Worksheets can be consolidated to transfer information or to summarize data. The consolidation can occur by copying information from one worksheet to another, by adding the values in two worksheets with a merge operation, or by permanently linking worksheets. Data can be transferred between a stand-alone spreadsheet and another application program, but it is generally easier to transfer data among the components of an integrated program than it is to transfer data between stand-alone programs.

Built-in functions make it much easier to construct formulas for statistical, mathematical, and financial calculations. In addition, they can make it possible to process text inside a formula, to perform calculations on dates and times, and to look up values in a table.

Macros not only save keystrokes for the expert user; they can also make a template much easier for a beginner to use. Simple macros are fairly easy to construct; they eliminate repetitive typing. Advanced macros can turn a spreadsheet into a programming language. This provides the tools a professional needs to build powerful and easy-to-use applications, but these tools are not for a novice.

Key Terms

active area
automatic recalculation   manual recalculation
circular reference   natural recalculation order
column-oriented recalculation   protected cell
component   row-oriented recalculation
context switching   synchronized
global format rule   template
individual format rule   windowing
keyboard macro   window panes
macro

Discussion Questions

1. What might be some design and style rules for constructing templates to be used by clerical personnel?

2. What is the difference between protecting and hiding cells?

3. Who should decide who should know the password for a set of protected cells? Who should be able to change the password?

4. Besides protecting and hiding cells, what are some other methods of preventing modification of cells?

5. Which is better: to select an initial column format as wide as the expected largest value and then decrease its width when finished or to select a narrow column format and then increase its width?

6. How can you locate all of the forward references in a worksheet?

7. Can you have a column with zero width? How might it be useful?

8. Can you suggest a scheme that would prevent a user from accidentally destroying information when copying or merging worksheets?

9. Suppose a worksheet is linked to several other worksheets and each time it is loaded, the calculations take five minutes. This is rather awkward if no changes have been made to the other worksheets. What are some ways to avoid this problem?

10. Should an integrated program be based on one basic component such as a spreadsheet or a database, or should its basis be independent of the components? Why?

11. Besides convenience, what are some other advantages of spreadsheet functions?

12. Where should macros be placed on a spreadsheet? Why?

Exercises

1. Find formulas that give circular references to two cells and do not converge to a set of stable values.

2. Draw the worksheet that results if you decrease the width of all columns in Figure 8.5 from six characters to four.

3. Design a template for the grade book of a professor.

4. Design a template for a state or federal short-form tax return.

5. Design a template for a state or federal long-form tax return that links the various schedules to the main form.

6. Design a template for a monthly appointment calendar.

7. Compare the cell-protection features of three spreadsheet programs.

8. Describe how to merge a portion of a worksheet with another worksheet if the portion to be merged is not a rectangular-shaped group of cells.

9. Design a worksheet to record the frame-by-frame bowling scores for a five-person team bowling a three-game series. Display each person's scores for the three games, each person's total score, and the total team score.

PART FOUR

data management

In the early days of computing (circa 1950) computers were used exclusively to compute formulas. Then in 1957 the hard disk drive was invented and rapidly installed in computer systems. A hard disk could store more information than the computer's main memory, and it was much faster than magnetic tape. The invention of high-speed disk drives with modestly large capacity made it possible both to store large amounts of information within a computer system and to retrieve the information in a timely fashion. This led to a shift in how computers were used—away from numerical calculations and toward transaction processing and information retrieval.

As the use of computers grew, so did the number of data files stored by organizations. By the late 1960s a typical data processing department maintained thousands of data files. The task of keeping track of them was becoming unmanageable. The most obvious problem was the substantial effort required to keep track of all the file names and catalog the types of data stored in each file. Another problem involved redundant data. For example, some of the data in a payroll file might be the same as that in a personnel file—a clear waste of storage capacity. A more subtle problem resulted from the direct linkage between programs and the data files they used: each time the layout of a data file was changed—to add a new field or expand the width of an existing field, for example—all the programs that used the data file had to be modified to reflect the new structure. As a result, data processing departments spent most of their programming time modifying old programs (called program maintenance) instead of developing new ones.

These problems led to the development and use of database management systems (DBMS)—software for controlling, reading, and updating the information in a collection of files. A DBMS acts as a buffer between programs and data; it helps keep track of where data is stored. More importantly, a DBMS solves many of the problems associated with redundant data and program maintenance by separating the physical storage of data from the logical structure of data as seen by programmers—a division that is at the root of database management software and is explained thoroughly in Chapter 10.

The first database management systems were designed to handle the needs of data processing departments and were very difficult to use. Full-time professionals called database administrators were necessary to lay out the structure of databases and to contend with the complexities of the DBMS software. To circumvent the need for programmers and database administrators, software developers invented a whole new genre of software called record management software. A record management system is a collection of programs for managing data stored in a single file. Record management systems emerged in the 1970s to make it easy to set up a data file, enter and edit the data in the file, and print reports from the file.

In the 1980s low-cost personal computers became widely available with relatively large disk drives. These computers could easily manage large lists when equipped with data management software, but they aggravated the earlier problems of the 1970s: either they required programming expertise to be used effectively or they were limited to single-file applications.

Today, most popular database management programs for personal computers are miniature duplicates of mainframe systems. For example, Rbase 5000 was derived from RIM (Relational Information Management System), a database management system for large computers, and dBase III evolved from mainframe computers at the Jet Propulsion Laboratory. These programs handle multiple files and include various methods for processing the data stored in these files. Because they are essentially scaled-down mainframe programs, an experienced database management person is needed to utilize their features fully. Recent versions of these programs are much easier to use than their earlier counterparts, and it may eventually be as easy to use a full-featured database management system as a simple record management system.

Part IV introduces you to data management software in two steps: Chapter 9 describes record management systems and Chapter 10 describes database management systems. Record managers are used to keep any large list that must be quickly retrieved and displayed. A database management system can do all the things that a record management system can do, but it can do these things to two or more files simultaneously. In addition, as we describe in Chapter 10, a DBMS usually incorporates many features above and beyond those found in a record management system.

record management basics

9

A **record management system** is a collection of programs for processing a single file of information, and it is the simplest form of database management. The main purpose of the system is to extract information in the form of a printed report, a document containing data from your computer files. Although it can handle only one file of information, a record management system remains one of the best ways to organize and process a large volume of data. You can easily enter, look up, modify, and selectively delete information that is stored in a record management system. The system provides a cushion between you and the computer's storage devices. You do not have to be concerned with how data is stored in files, how the information is arranged internally, or how the programs process the data stored on disk. Record managers insulate you from the details of information storage and retrieval.

Nearly every manager, educator, or professional person keeps some kind of list by hand. For example, a teacher keeps a grade book; a salesperson keeps a list of sales leads. We begin this chapter with an example of list management by hand. Then we will show how the list is put into a computer and follow the evolution of the list through a typical data processing cycle. We will illustrate how to instruct the record management system to generate reports, and we will examine one of the most powerful concepts found in record management software—that of a form. Forms make it much easier to understand your data, and in some record management systems they allow on-screen calculations. Along the way you will learn principles of file organization, sorting, and indexing and the processing techniques used by most file management programs.

Steps In Record Management

The User Interface

The first step in understanding how to use a record management system is to understand the underlying model assumed by the people who designed your software. The underlying model is visible as the user interface—the prompts, menus, and other screen displays that appear when the program is run. Record management systems use various models.

Figure 9.1 *A simple list is scrolled on the display screen.*

```
Adams     123 Main      86501    10.00
Baker     7070 Yakima   65001     0.00
James     335 Maple     99123     6.00
Jones     380 Oak       10755    20.50
King      950 Edison    39588     9.50
Smith     555 Park      55143     0.00
Thomas    10  Downing   43210    10.00
```

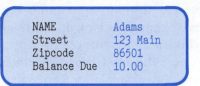

```
NAME          Adams
Street        123 Main
Zipcode       86501
Balance Due   10.00
```

Figure 9.2 *Rolodex-style screen display.*

Perhaps the simplest model is that of a piece of paper containing a written list. In the case of a record management system, the "piece of paper" is the display screen, and the list is scrolled onto the screen, as illustrated in Figure 9.1. Record management systems that use a list as their model are simple to understand, easy to use, but not particularly powerful.

The Rolodex card file provides the model for many record management systems. A Rolodex card file is a collection of cards that can be rotated around a drum so that you can locate a particular name, phone number, or address. Some record management programs actually display a simulated Rolodex card on the screen and electronically "flip through" the cards for you. Figure 9.2 illustrates how the first row of data in Figure 9.1 might appear on the screen of a Rolodex-style system.

Using a Rolodex card file as a paradigm for a computerized filing system is a way to make the software easy to use. If you are familiar with the Rolodex, then you will be able to understand the record management system by analogy. Similarly, if you are familiar with business forms, you should find it easy to understand systems that use forms as their model.

Forms are templates or models that can be used in record management systems to capture input data, display data in a recognizable format, and facilitate printed outputs. Figure 9.3 shows how the information in Figure 9.2 might appear in a simulated business form.

Lists and simulated Rolodex files not only provide a logical way to look at your data but also establish boundaries on what you can do with the system.

Figure 9.3 *A business form containing one entry in a list.*

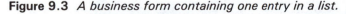

```
Adams                                    10.00
---------------------------        -------------
       Last name                   $ Balance Due


123 Main                           86501
---------------------------        -----
       Street                      Zipcode
```

For example, a Rolodex system is typically limited to doing what a manual Rolodex system does: look up information, print mailing labels, and so forth. A system built around the model of a business form is more flexible and might be able to check the input data to guarantee that it is within certain bounds (greater than zero, for example) or verify that all the blanks in the form have been completed before it accepts the form for storage.

Input-Process-Output Cycles

The next step in understanding how record management systems work is to understand the information flow assumed by the software. Most systems use one or more business processing cycles as a model of the flow. For example, in a billing system the information flow might consist of the phases shown in Figure 9.4. The customer list is stored as a file on disk, and the record management software is used throughout a monthly cycle consisting of the following phases:

1. New charges and payments are entered into the customer list.
2. Customer inquiries are satisfied by retrieving certain customer's billing information upon request.
3. The difference between payments and charges accumulated for the month is added to the current balance to arrive at a new (next month's) balance.
4. The bills and perhaps mailing labels are printed.

Figure 9.4 *Monthly billing cycle.*

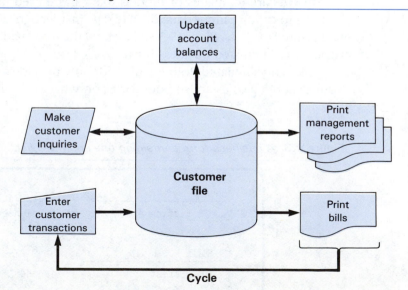

5. Reports are printed telling management how much is owed in receivables; who is 60, 90, and 120 days overdue; how much money was taken in during the month; and so on.

Each month the cycle is repeated. New information is entered and bills are printed for mailing; the reports provided by the system allow management to keep tabs on bills owed and paid; customer inquiries are satisfied. A record management system designed to support this kind of processing cycle would probably be able to sort the customer list into alphabetical order, extract only the customers who are behind with their payments, and perform simple addition and subtraction on the numbers stored in each customer record.

The billing cycle is only one of many models assumed by typical record managers. Other processing models are also valid; for example, the cycle assumed in a bibliographic system. The processing phases in a literature-search system might consist of the following:

1. Enter abstracts of new articles.

2. Automatically extract meaningful keywords from abstracts.

3. Search for abstracts using keywords.

4. Print the top ten abstracts found.

5. Delete abstracts that have not been referenced for two years.

In a bibliographic record management system, monthly cycles may be meaningless. Instead, the cycle might be repeated only when a certain number of new abstracts have accumulated.

In place of the low-level details of bits, bytes, records, and files, a record manager imposes a superficial model or paradigm between you and the computer. Before you can operate the record management system software, you must understand the paradigm. Most of the time the paradigm is simple; so the amount of training is minimal. However, a good record management system is more complex than a manual Rolodex file. For this reason you must become familiar with general concepts of record management systems ranging from basic operations on lists, on-screen forms management, to report generation.

Report Generation

Report generation is such an important part of record management that it is worthwhile to elaborate on it. A **report generator** (also known as a *report writer*) is a program for producing reports from lists stored in one or more files. Record management systems vary greatly in the flexibility and capability of their report writers.

The simplest report generator prints a single list in columnar format; each field of the record is printed in a column of each page. A more sophisticated report generator can print column-oriented reports (for management); print row-oriented reports (for mailing labels); perform arithmetic operations such as computing percentages, totals, and formulas; and print headings, the date and time, and labels for columns.

Even more sophisticated report generators can selectively retrieve and print portions of a list. For example, you might want to print only the names and departments of employees who have worked for the company for more than 20 years or who earn more than $50,000 per year. To carry out these tasks, the report generator must understand "queries" that look like mathematical problems, such as

```
PRINT NAMES, DEPARTMENTS
    WHERE 1985 - DATE_OF_HIRE >= 20
    OR ANNUAL_SALARY >= 50000
```

A good report writer will let you select where each column will appear on the printed page, what the column heading says, which columns of numbers are to be totaled, averaged, or printed as a percentage, and whether the report is to be printed on continuous forms or on cut sheets of paper. Once you have specified how a report should be laid out, it should be possible to save the specification for later use. After a number of report specifications have been created and stored, it should then be a simple matter to request any report—whether you want to print a report of past-due accounts, a report in mailing-label format, or a report listing recent subscribers.

■ List Management by Hand

A successful magazine must keep track of who its subscribers are, whether they have paid their subscription fee, and perhaps names for mailing notices, bills, and so on. Suppose the subscription list contains the last name, street address, zip code, and balance due for each subscriber. Part of the list might contain the following data:

Name	Address	Zip	Balance
Adams	123 Main	86501	10.00
Smith	555 Park	55143	0.00
Jones	380 Oak	10755	20.50
James	335 Maple	99123	6.00
Thomas	10 Downing	43210	10.00
King	950 Edison	39588	9.50
Baker	707 Yakima	65001	0.00

If this list is handled manually, it is probably recorded on cards, with each row of data on a single card. The card file is stored in a file cabinet and retrieved whenever the circulation manager needs to look at it.

Operations

The subscription list is of little value to the magazine if it simply stays in the cabinet. Instead, it is retrieved many times each month (see Figure 9.5). New names are added and old names removed. Addresses are changed whenever a subscriber moves. And the list is used whenever magazines are sent to all subscribers.

For each use of the subscription list there is an associated operation. Here are some of these operations.

- **Data entry.** When the magazine began its business, the subscription list was empty, and a batch of names was entered. Recall that this is called **batch data entry** because the batch of names was entered all at once.
- **Insert.** Over time the names of new subscribers might be inserted at the end of the list, at the beginning, or in the middle, making it necessary to move half of the cards to make room for the new entry. Insertion is a more specific operation than data entry because insertion implies a preference for where the new name is placed in the list.

Figure 9.5 *File cabinet showing operations on the card file.*

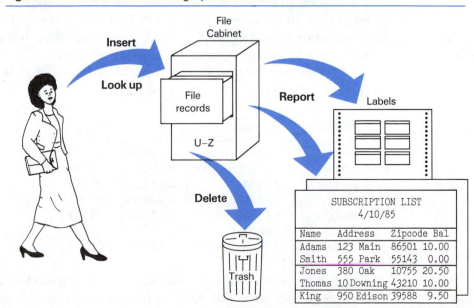

- **Look-up.** Once the list contains names, names and information associated with them might be retrieved in a look-up operation. Once the appropriate card is found, the name, address, zip code, and balance can be read.

- **Modify.** After a look-up operation it might be necessary to change some data in the list. Suppose Jones pays $20.50, leaving a balance of $0.00. A modify operation would change the balance from $20.50 to zero.

- **Delete.** After a look-up operation the name can be removed from the list by discarding the card.

In each of these operations we used the subscriber's last name as a key for retrieving the desired information. A **key** is any piece of information used to *uniquely* identify an item in a list. The key in our example was the subscriber's last name, but it could have been the street address, zip code, or a combination of these. For example, the balance and the zip code could have been used together to locate all the subscribers with a balance of $0.00 and the zip code of 65001. When a key is made up of several pieces of information, it is called a **compound key** or **composite key.** Composite keys are useful for answering questions like: How many subscribers live in the area with zip code 99123 and have a balance equal to zero? A look-up operation always uses a key to locate an entry in a list.

Sorting Lists

One way to reduce the time and effort needed to look up a name in a list is to put the names in alphabetical order, as in a telephone book. Then you do not need to read all names in the list just to find one of them. We say a list is in **ascending order** if it is in alphabetical or numeric order. It is in **descending order** if it is in reverse alphabetical or numeric order.

A list can be put in alphabetical order by sorting it. Suppose the subscription list is to be kept in ascending order, as follows:

@Name	Address	Zip	Balance
Adams	123 Main	86501	10.00
Baker	7070 Yakima	65001	0.00
James	335 Maple	99123	6.00
Jones	380 Oak	10755	20.50
King	950 Edison	39588	9.50
Smith	555 Park	55143	0.00
Thomas	10 Downing	43210	10.00

The @ before "Name" indicates that names are being used as the key. To sort the list as shown, the cards must be physically rearranged into alphabetical order by name.

Look-ups take considerable time and effort when lists become long, and so sorting is used to reduce the work. Yet sorting is itself a tedious job. Computers can easily sort a list for you, performing what is called a **sort operation.** In fact, the speed of a computerized record management system and its ability to sort lists are two good reasons to use a computer to keep lists. A great number of sorting algorithms—that is, procedures for swapping records until the list is in order—have been developed for computerized sorting; their differences are a topic worthy of technical discussion, but we will leave this investigation to the reader. As a user, you do not need to know which sorting algorithm a record management system uses, because all the algorithms end up accomplishing the same task.

Indexing Lists

Sorting is one way to keep a list in order, but it is not always the best way. Consider again our magazine subscription list. The U.S. Postal Service offers lower postage rates to customers who sort their mail into ascending order by zip code and bundle the envelopes into groups of two hundred each. To take advantage of these lower mailing rates, the magazine must sort its subscription list by zip code. Thus the subscriber's name is no longer the key, and the list becomes

@Zip	Name	Address	Balance
10755	Jones	380 Oak	20.50
39588	King	950 Edison	9.50
43210	Thomas	10 Downing	10.00
55143	Smith	555 Park	0.00
65001	Baker	707 Yakima	0.00
86501	Adams	123 Main	10.00
99123	James	335 Maple	6.00

Obviously, a single list cannot simultaneously be in order by name and by zip code. Of course, it is possible to keep two lists: one by name, the other by zip code. But if this is done, the two lists will contain much of the same information. How can we have both orderings without creating two redundant lists?

The answer is to use an **indexing operation** to establish an index for the file. Every good book has an index containing key words and their location (page number) in the book. Similarly, we can keep a list in order by indexing instead of sorting. An **index** maintains ascending or descending order among the entries of the list.

Indexing has several advantages over sorting. Most important, with indexing you can keep the list in order by more than one key. This is accomplished by maintaining separate indexes, one for each desired order. For our subscription example, this method requires two additional index cards for each subscription list, but the amount of redundant data is kept to a minimum. Here is how it works.

First, numbers are assigned to the entries in the original list.

MASTER LIST

#	Name	Address	Zip	Balance
1.	Adams	123 Main	86501	10.00
2.	Smith	555 Park	55143	0.00
3.	Jones	380 Oak	10755	20.50
4.	James	335 Maple	99123	6.00
5.	Thomas	10 Downing	43210	10.00
6.	King	950 Edison	39588	9.50
7.	Baker	707 Yakima	65001	0.00

Call this the **master list** because it contains all information in the original subscription list. Notice that the master list is in no particular order. In fact, it is in the same sequence as the initial data entry list. Furthermore, it has no keys as the previous version of the list did. The keys are kept in separate index lists, which hold only the keys and references to entry numbers in the master list, as follows:

@NAME INDEX		**@ZIP INDEX**	
Key	Entry # in Master	Key	Entry # in Master
Adams	1.	10755	3.
Baker	7.	39588	6.
James	4.	43210	5.
Jones	3.	55143	2.
King	6.	65001	7.
Smith	2.	86501	1.
Thomas	5.	99123	4.

The indexes no longer hold redundant data. They consist merely of a list of keys in order plus a pointer to the master list. To look up a name, you use the name index; to retrieve the cards by zip code, you use the zip index. Thus to take advantage of the lower mailing rates, you would use the zip index to retrieve cards from the master list in the appropriate sequence. When the list in the zip index is exhausted, all subscribers will have been retrieved from the master list.

Indexes help to keep both name and zip code orders. But now three lists must be managed: the master list containing all the subscribers and two index lists that contain keys and pointers. If you change an entry in the master list, you must update the corresponding information in the two index lists. This is a complicated mess when done by hand, but it is easy for a computer to do.

■ File Management by Machine

Files as Lists

The magazine subscription list illustrates the complexity of the simplest application of list management in business. It is easy to see how useful a machine would be for sorting and indexing the subscription list. The list can be stored as a data file. Each entry in the list becomes a record, and each record might have four fields. (Recall that a *record* is a collection of related data items, and a *field* is a part of a record reserved for a particular item or type of data.) In our example the NAME, ADDRESS, and ZIP fields hold text; the BALANCE field holds a number.

In general, a file can hold any list, and the records can contain any combination of text and numbers. You must tell the system the *width* (number of characters or bytes) and the *type* of information (numeric or text) in each field. It is a simple matter to lay out a file as follows:

1. Identify the records in your list. These become the records in your file. Choose logical, meaningful groupings such as name, address, and balance.

2. Identify the name, type, and width of the fields of each record. Some record management systems allow fields to have variable lengths, but most require a fixed field width. So if the contents of a field will vary in length, select the longest or most likely maximum width for that field.

3. Think ahead and decide which fields will be used as sort or index keys (for look-up, printed reports, and so on). This is important to know not only when laying out a file but also when selecting record management software.

File Setup

There are many methods of file layout, but the most common one is called the mnemonic method of field placement. The **mnemonic method** uses the field names as you would. For example, the fields for a mailing list are called NAME, ADDRESS, ZIP, and BALANCE. You simply enter these names into the program, and the record management system takes care of placement within the record. For each field of the record you enter the field name, width, and type. For example, the subscription list is laid out as follows:

```
        File: SUBSCRIBE

    Field         Width        Type
    _____

    NAME            30         Text
    ADDRESS         25         Text
    ZIP CODE         6         Text
    BALANCE        6.2         Numeric
```

The entry for the type of the BALANCE field indicates that this field is a number. The entry for the width of the BALANCE field—6.2—indicates that the number has a total width of 6 characters including the decimal point and that there are 2 digits. For example, BALANCE could be − 10.95 or 5.00, but it could not be 1295.30.

Data Entry

Once the file layout has been determined, you are ready to enter data into the file. In a simple record management system you can enter data simply by typing values into the computer. You may be expected to separate each field with a comma, as shown in Figure 9.6. Or you may be prompted for each field value, as shown in Figure 9.7. (In all the screen displays in this chapter, characters shown in color are typed by the user; characters in black are generated by the computer.)

The record management system usually allows you to edit the values before they are recorded on disk. Thus you may correct a spelling error or change a value before it is recorded. As you enter the records, they are added to the end of the growing file; each additional entry is appended to the existing ones.

File Processing

Data files can be processed in a number of ways. For example, the magazine subscription list might be used to do the following on a day-by-day basis:

- Find out if Jones has paid the annual subscription fee, or if not, how much is due.
- Find out if Johnson is a subscriber.
- Change the address of every subscriber who has moved in the past month.
- Modify the balance due for everyone who has made a payment.
- Add a new record for every new subscriber.
- Remove a record whenever a subscription is terminated.

Each of these tasks involves one or more primitive operations common to all record management systems. These are

- *Look-up*. Find and display on the screen a record whose key is specified. For example, find the record for Jones.
- *Insert*. Add another record to the file. For example, add a new subscriber to the list.
- *Delete*. Remove a record from the file. For example, remove Jones from the file when Jones's subscription terminates.
- *Modify*. Look up and change one or more fields in the record. For example, retrieve the record for Jones and change the ADDRESS and ZIP fields because Jones has moved.

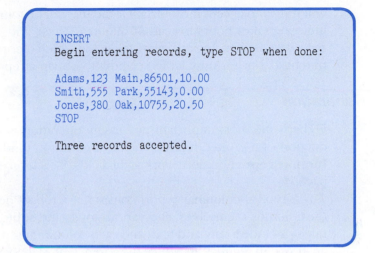

```
INSERT
Begin entering records, type STOP when done:

Adams,123 Main,86501,10.00
Smith,555 Park,55143,0.00
Jones,380 Oak,10755,20.50
STOP

Three records accepted.
```

Figure 9.6 *Data entry without prompts.*

These operations seem simple enough, but they can pose major problems. For example, suppose the subscription list was kept in order by ascending zip code. If a new record is inserted into the list, what happens to the zip code order? In a record management system that uses the sort operation to keep records in order, an insert operation renders the list out of order again.

The subscription list continues to grow with each new record inserted. Sooner or later the disk will become full, and the record management system

Figure 9.7 *Data entry with prompts.*

```
NAME:      Adams
ADDRESS:   123 Main
ZIP:       86501
BALANCE:   10.00

NAME:      Smith
ADDRESS:   555 Park
ZIP:       55143
BALANCE:   0.00


NAME:      Jones
ADDRESS:   380 Oak
ZIP:       10755
BALANCE:   20.50
```

will refuse to accept more data. Or the file will become so large that sorting or indexing takes hours instead of minutes. These and other problems must be considered when you are trying to decide which record management system to purchase, but for now let us see how to obtain a report.

Report Generation

Perhaps the most important processing operation is *report generation*—production of a printed report. The most common kind of report is called a **columnar report** because it prints the fields of each record in columns across the page.

A typical columnar report consists of a report heading, column heading, the columns themselves, and various totals and subtotals. The report heading might include a date and text, and each column might also be given a heading, as shown in Figure 9.8. Notice the absence of ADDRESS in the report. A report generator allows you to select the information you want to print. In the case of Figure 9.8, the subscription file was printed with the following field assignments:

Column 1:   NAME
Column 2:   ZIP CODE
Column 3:   BALANCE

Totals and Subtotals

In addition to printing certain fields in columns, most report generators can provide totals and subtotals. For example, the balances could be totaled and printed at the bottom of the BALANCE column. Subtotals could also be printed for groups of records; this is done in reports that contain breaks. A **report break** is a position within a report where a prespecified field changes value from one record to the next. A **break subtotal** is a subtotal that is printed whenever a break occurs in a report.

Figure 9.8 *A sample columnar report.*

```
        MAGAZINE SUBSCRIPTIONS    5/30/85
                ABC CORP.


        Subscriber      Zip code     Balance Due

          Adams          86501         10.00
          Smith          55143          0.00
          Jones          10755         20.50
          James          99123          6.00
          Thomas         43210         10.00
          King           39588          9.50
          Baker          65001          0.00
```

```
                    SALARIES BY JOB TITLE
                           6/30/85

   Employee    Title           Salary    Subtotal    Grand Total

    Airth      Analyst         $17,000
    Rogers     Analyst         $23,250
    Thayer     Analyst         $25,700
                                         ─────────
                                          $65,950

    Edling     Asst. Programmer $12,500
    Moran      Asst. Programmer $14,200
                                         ─────────
                                          $26,700



                        .
                        .
                        .

    Lagier     Zoologist       $32,440
                                         ─────────
                                          $32,440
                                                     ──────────
                                                     $3,248,945
```

Figure 9.9 *A report with subtotals.*

Figure 9.9 illustrates a report that includes breaks and subtotals. Here an employee file is printed in ascending order by job title. If the value in the JOB TITLE field changes, a break subtotal for the records with the same job title is printed, and a new subtotal is started. At the end of the report, the total salary balance is printed in the last column.

In more complicated reports there may be more than one level of subtotals, causing breaks within breaks. Furthermore, the numeric values may be obtained by detailed calculations in addition to simple summation. Figure 9.10 illustrates a report with these two additional features. It contains columns for CUST-ID, PART-NO, QTY, COST, and BILLED. The report has two break levels. First, it breaks when there is a change in CUST-ID and prints a total for each customer. Second, for each value of CUST-ID it breaks for a change in PART-NO and prints the total for a given part number within a given CUST-ID. In addition, the report uses a calculation to obtain the values for the column BILLED. These values are computed from the formula BILLED = QTY * COST; that is, the unit cost is multiplied by the quantity ordered to obtain the billed amount.

Report generators that employ columnar totals, breaks, subtotals, and calculations are quite versatile. Most business reports needed can be generated from a file management system that has these features.

```
                    ORDERS FOR MONTH    3/85

      CUST-ID         PART-NO.     QTY.      COST      BILLED

       C9513           Y65           3        2.50       7.50
                                     1        1.75       1.75
                       ***TOTAL FOR THIS PART-NO. =       9.25

                       Z32           2        3.95       7.90
                       ***TOTAL FOR THIS PART-NO =        7.90
            *******************TOTAL FOR THIS CUST-ID =  17.15

       MO125           B55           1        3.50       3.50
                                     4        3.50      14.00
                       ***TOTAL FOR THIS PART-NO =       17.50
            *******************TOTAL FOR THIS CUST-ID =  17.50


       ************************TOTAL FOR ENTIRE REPORT =  34.65
```

Figure 9.10 *A report with two levels of subtotals and a calculated field. The report shows that two customers ordered $34.65 worth of parts.*

Sort Versus Index Methods

Report generators may use either the sort/report or the index/report method. If you use a *sort/report generator,* it is necessary to sort the file before printing or displaying the report. This involves selecting the primary and secondary sort keys. A **primary sort key** is any field within the file that is sorted first. The **secondary sort key** resolves how records with the same primary key values should be ordered.

The mailing list associated with the subscription file provides a good example of primary and secondary sort keys. If you want the mailing labels to be printed in ascending zip code order, you select the ZIP field as the primary sort key. Most likely, the zip codes will not be unique because many subscribers live in the same neighborhood. Therefore, you would want a second-level sort to be performed on the names with identical zip codes. For example, if the primary sort key is ZIP, and the secondary sort key is NAME, we might get

Primary key	Secondary key
10001	Adams
10001	Jones
10001	Wilson
10210	Baker
10210	Smith
10210	Watson
10210	Zeno
10355	Hamm
10355	Myer

In the *index/report method* it is not necessary to do a sort before generating the report if the proper indexes were specified when the file was set up. However, if you need an index that was not specified when the file was set up, then the index must be constructed before a report can be printed.

The principal differences between sort/report and index/report generators are convenience, speed, and the required storage space for files. The sort/report method is slower than the index/report method and requires a new sort every time the ordering is changed. The index/report method is faster and usually requires less disk space, but it may be inconvenient to specify the indexes before the file is constructed.

Forms Management Systems

When you visit your family doctor, register for school, apply for a job, pay your income taxes, or apply for a bank loan, you must fill out a form. In fact, a business form is one of the most familiar kinds of document. Most record management software allows you to use forms to give meaning to your data and help you enter data, format output, select a record, and provide access control. An **on-screen form** appears on the computer monitor during data entry. A **report form** is used during report generation to format data. When the ability to manage forms is combined with file management, even simple record management systems can be extremely powerful.

On-screen Forms

A form is a template or overlay used to ''see'' the data stored in a record. For example, the form in Figure 9.11 could be used to enter values for the NAME, ADDRESS, ZIPCODE, and BALANCE fields in the subscription file. Notice that

Figure 9.11 *A simple on-screen form.*

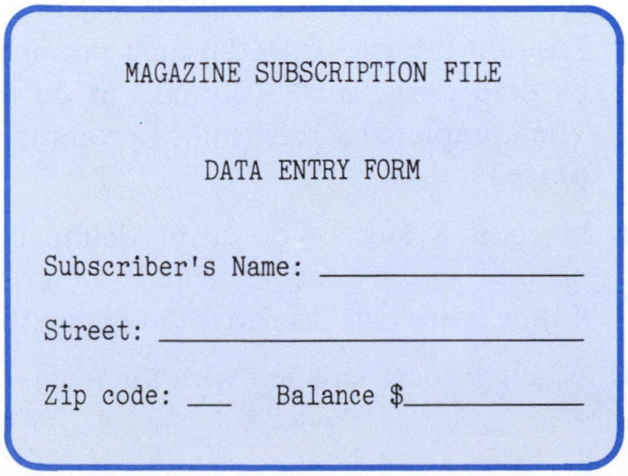

```
        MAGAZINE SUBSCRIPTION FILE


            DATA ENTRY FORM


Subscriber's Name: _____

Street: _____

Zip code: ___    Balance $_____
```

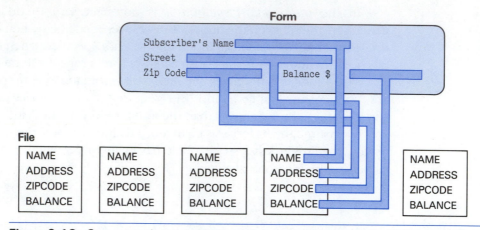

Figure 9.12 *Correspondence between a data entry form and the fields of a file record.*

the form defines not only where data is placed on the screen but also the width of each field. The correspondence between each on-screen field and each file field is shown in Figure 9.12.

You can design a form to appear any way you want. You design the data entry form by "drawing" it on your screen when the file is initially set up. For example, with many commercially available file managers you could construct the subscription file form as follows:

1. Use the arrow keys (or equivalent) to position the cursor where you want to enter the prompt. (In Figure 9.11 the prompts are "Subscriber's Name," "Street," and so on.)

2. Enter the prompt followed by the **field designator,** which defines the width of the field. We have used underscores as the field designator; but in your program the field designator may be a colon, space, or some other special character.

3. Position the cursor to the next prompt, and enter the prompt including its field designator. Continue to do this for all prompts in the form. The completed screen full of prompts is called the **form mask** or **template.**

4. In most systems you must define the correspondence between the prompts and the record fields by entering the field names into the form as if they were data, as shown in Figure 9.13.

5. When you are satisfied with the form, save it on the disk.

```
Subscriber's Name NAME___________________

Street ADDRESS_____________________________

Zip code ZIP__   Balance $ BALANCE__
```

Figure 9.13 *Creating an on-screen form.*

In many systems the operations for file definition and forms definition are identical. That is, defining the form also defines the contents of the file.

Data Entry and Editing with Forms

Once the form is defined and you are ready to enter data into the file, the form is displayed on the screen, and the computer waits for you to fill in the blanks. You terminate each entry by pressing [ENTER], and the cursor moves automatically from field designator to field designator as you enter values from the keyboard. After you have entered a name and address, for example, the form in Figure 9.13 would appear on the screen as shown in Figure 9.14.

As soon as the form is completed, the computer asks if everything is correct before saving the values to the disk. If you are satisfied with the values entered in each blank, the values (not the form itself) are recorded in the file as a single record of data. If you are not satisfied, then you can modify any field. To make a correction, move the cursor back to the field you want to modify and type the correction. For example, if you corrected the street address given in Figure 9.14 and added the zip code and balance, then the form and its contents might appear as shown in Figure 9.15.

Figure 9.14 *A partially filled-in form during data entry.*

```
Subscriber's Name Jefferson__________

Street 5199 Hall St.________________

Zip code____   Balance $____________
```

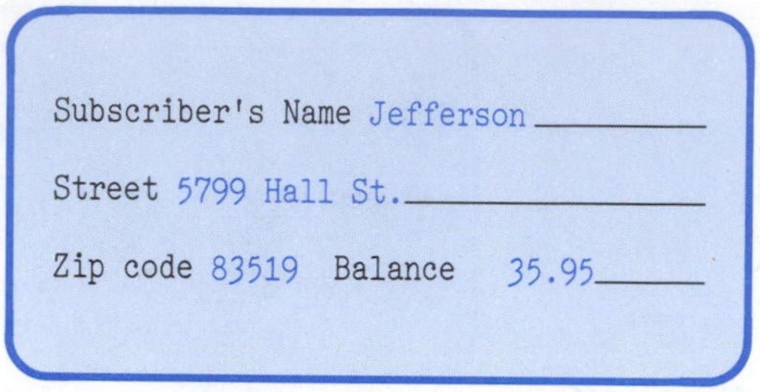

```
Subscriber's Name Jefferson _____

Street 5799 Hall St._____

Zip code 83519  Balance    35.95_____
```

Figure 9.15 *The completely filled-in form during data entry.*

Keep in mind that only the contents of the form are written to the data file. The form itself is merely a template that helps you enter the data. It is not written to the data file; instead, it is stored on the disk in a separate file.

Selective Look-up

When you perform a look-up operation using a form, the form is again displayed on the screen. This time, however, you supply *search values*. The record management system searches the file to retrieve a record with fields that match the search values you enter into the form. For example, to look up "Jones" in the magazine subscription file, you enter "Jones" as the search value for the NAME field when the form is displayed, as the search template in Figure 9.16 illustrates. A blank field in the search template means you do not care what the field's value is. The matching record found by the file management program might look like the right-hand screen in Figure 9.16.

Many systems allow you to specify other matching values besides equality. For example, you might want to retrieve the next record with a balance greater than zero. For this look-up operation the "greater than" symbol is used, as shown in Figure 9.17.

Figure 9.16 *A selective look-up operation.*

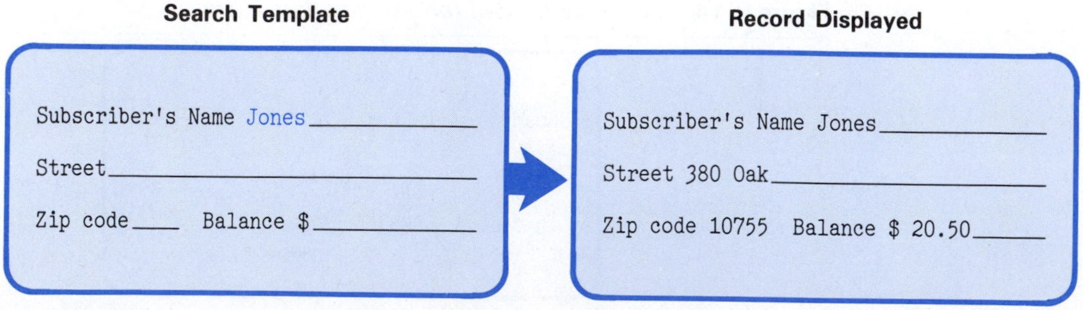

Search Template

```
Subscriber's Name Jones_____

Street_____

Zip code_____  Balance $_____
```

Record Displayed

```
Subscriber's Name Jones_____

Street 380 Oak_____

Zip code 10755  Balance $ 20.50_____
```

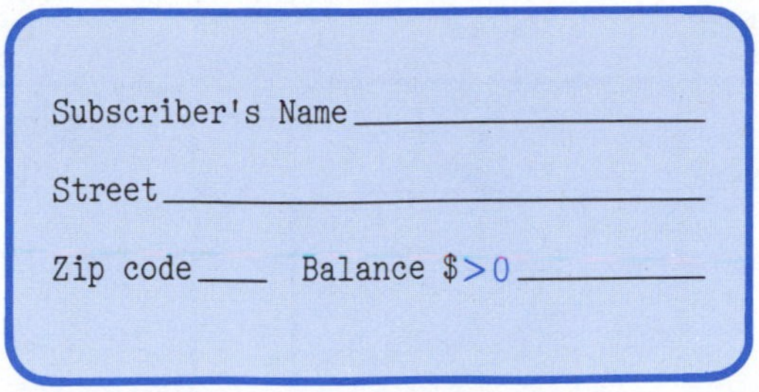

Subscriber's Name _____

Street _____

Zip code ____   Balance $>0 _____

Figure 9.17 *A search template to retrieve all records with a positive balance.*

Modify and Delete

Forms are also used to modify and delete records. Both modify and delete operations require an initial look-up operation. Once the retrieved record is on the screen, you can edit the values in the same way as during data entry.

Editing a record in a form is equivalent to modifying it, and blanking out all of the form's fields is equivalent to deleting it. Insertion and data entry are also equivalent operations. Thus forms make a file management system easier to use.

Printing via Forms

You can also use a form to format printed output. The form may be identical to the data entry form, or it may be a separate form designed specifically for printed output. For example, a mailing-label form is a specially designed output form that differs from its input counterpart.

Usually, only part of a file is printed. This can be done easily by using search values within a form. Suppose a special mailing is to be sent to only those subscribers who live in regions with a zip code greater than 50,000 and less than 90,000 and who have positive account balances. To obtain a printed list of these subscribers, you need to use two screen forms, as shown in Figure 9.18. These forms contain search values that specify the following:

```
(50,000 < ZIP < 90,000) and (BALANCE > 0)
```

Thus the report will contain all records with ZIP values 50001 through 89999 and a BALANCE greater than zero.

If these search values are applied to our original list of subscribers, the printed report will contain only one matching entry, as shown in Figure 9.19. If more than one record had matched these conditions, they too would have been printed along with the form.

Lower-limit Search Values

Subscriber's Name _____

Street _____

Zip code >50000   Balance $ >0_____

Upper-limit Search Values

Subscriber's Name _____

Street _____

Zip code <90000   Balance $ >0_____

Figure 9.18 *Search templates for printing a specified part of a subscription list.*

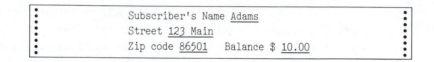

Subscriber's Name <u>Adams</u>
Street <u>123 Main</u>
Zip code <u>86501</u>   Balance $ <u>10.00</u>

Figure 9.19 *The subscription report generated by Figure 9.14.*

Printing formatted records is not the same as printing columnar reports. In Figure 9.19 the output is not arranged in columns; instead, it is formatted by the screen form. This is why many forms management-oriented systems also provide a report generator for laying out and printing forms.

On-screen Calculations

One of the most powerful features of screen forms is the ability to embed calculations within the form. The calculations are stored with the form and not the data. This means the record management system can retrieve a record from a file, perform the calculations specified by the form, and then display the record, the results of the calculations, and the screen form.

Suppose the magazine has a finance charge for late payments. If the late-payment charge is 5 percent of the balance due, 1.05 times the balance is charged to the subscriber if the balance is not paid within a certain time (say, 60 days). If you embed the calculation in the form (as shown in Figure 9.20), then whenever a record is retrieved and displayed on the screen (or printed) using this form, the late charge is also displayed. Figure 9.21 illustrates this feature.

```
Subscriber's Name N A M E _ _ _ _ _

Street A D D R E S S _ _ _ _ _ _

Zip Z I P _ _ Account Balance $ B A L A N C E

Late C H A R G E = 1.05 * BALANCE
```

Figure 9.20 *A form setting up a file with a calculated late charge.*

```
Subscriber's Name A d a m s _

Street 1 2 3 M a i n _ _ _ _

Zip 8 6 5 0 1   Account Balance $ 1 0 . 0 0

Late 1 0 . 5 0
```

Figure 9.21 *A report showing the late-payment charge.*

Embedded calculations can speed data entry. Suppose during the initial data entry all the BALANCE fields should be 0. Instead of entering 0 for every record in the file, you can specify the calculation BALANCE = 0.00 in the data entry form. There are times when the embedded calculations are helpful, and other times when they should be turned off. This can be done easily with a multiple-form file management system.

Multiple-Form Systems

A **multiple-form** file management system lets you define one form for data entry, other forms for printing, and yet other forms for look-up, inserting, and sorting or indexing operations. In addition, any form can shield information from view by preventing certain fields from being displayed. When some fields are to be kept confidential, the form can control access by enforcing password protection.

Suppose the BALANCE field in the subscription file is to be viewed by some users of the file system but not modified. To do this, you might create a look-up form with an associated read-only password (see Figure 9.22). A **read-**

```
                    READ-ONLY LOOKUP

Password_____
Name_____
Balance_____
```

Figure 9.22 *A form limiting access with a password.*

only password is one or more characters that must be entered correctly before the program will let you view any data stored in the file. When a look-up is requested, the read-only password and NAME must be given. If the password is correct, the value of BALANCE is displayed. Otherwise, access is denied.

You can also use a form to specify which fields are to be kept in order via indexes. It is possible simultaneously to maintain order on two or more fields using an index form, as shown in Figure 9.23. The @ symbol designates an index field. The form in Figure 9.23 specifies two indexes: one on NAME and another on ZIP. When this form is used to look up a record in the file, either the @NAME or @ZIP index is used to retrieve records in order by name and zip code.

A multiple-form system for the subscription file is illustrated in Figure 9.24. Each form performs a specific function within the monthly processing cycle of the file.

■ The INPUT form is used to enter new records into the file. It contains all of the fields, as shown earlier.

Figure 9.23 *A form with two indexes.*

```
                    INDEXED FORM

Password _____
Name @ N A M E
Street A D D R E S S
Zip @ Z I P    Balance $ B A L A N C E
```

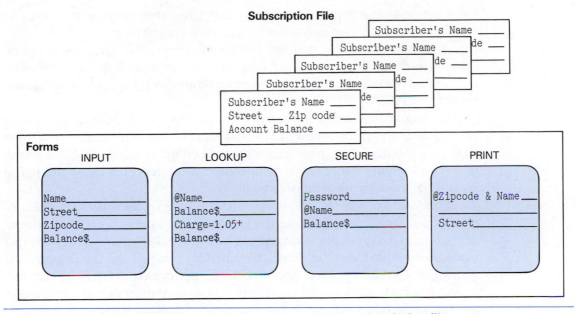

Figure 9.24 *A multiple-form system for the subscription file.*

- The LOOKUP form is used to retrieve records, using NAME as a key, and then calculate the late charge. CHARGE is computed and displayed on the screen along with the other fields in the record, but CHARGE is not part of the file.

- The SECURE form includes a password field. The password must be given before access is allowed. This form also retrieves records in order by using NAME as a key.

- The PRINT form is used to print labels. It retrieves records in order, using the composite index containing ZIP and NAME as primary and secondary sort keys.

■ Summary

Lists are used in a wide variety of businesses to keep track of subscriptions, sales leads, inventory, client names, and so on. No matter what the application is, all lists are processed by performing operations: data entry, look-up, modify, delete, insert, and report generation. Most lists are kept in some kind of order to speed information retrieval. The order can be obtained by sorting the list or by constructing one or more indexes. Lists can be kept manually, but a computer file is generally the best way to manage lists when they become very long or when processing becomes complicated or time consuming.

A file management system simplifies rudimentary data processing operations. These include file setup and data entry as well as look-up, insert, delete, and modify operations and additional processing such as sorting, indexing, and report generation.

Columnar reports are printed outputs in which each field of a record is printed in a separate column. A report generator lets you design your own headings, footings, date, page numbers, and column headings. Typical report generators require a sort or index operation if the report is to be printed in ascending order by one or more key fields.

Forms add power to a file management system by increasing access control, extending the ability of the file management system to perform calculations, and making the file management software easier to use. A system that manages multiple forms can do much more than a single-form file system. One form is designated for each operation to be performed throughout the file-processing cycle. For example, one form may be used to enter data and another to print records.

Records can be retrieved easily when search values are entered into a form. Matching conditions such as equal, greater than, and not equal are commonly employed in file management software. In an indexed system one or more indexes can be embedded in a form. The index specifies an ordering of the file such that a look-up or print run will retrieve the records in ascending order. Even composite indexes can be embedded and used to control access to the file.

Key Terms

ascending order	form mask
batch data entry	index
break subtotal	index operation
columnar report	insert operation
composite key	key
compound key	look-up operation
data entry	master list
delete operation	mnemonic method
descending order	modify operation
field designator	multiple-form
form	on-screen form

primary sort key report generator
read-only password secondary sort key
record management system sort operation
report break template
report form

Discussion Questions

1. What is the difference between on-screen forms and report forms?

2. Is there any difference between the data entry and insertion operations?

3. How large must a list be before it is easier and faster to use a computer instead of handling it manually?

4. What information is needed before determining the fields in a record?

5. Why is indexing important? How does indexing compare with sorting?

6. What is the most common file-processing operation?

7. Why are screen forms convenient?

8. How does a user specify the records to be retrieved?

9. What kind of user interface and processing cycle does your record management software assume?

10. How would you obtain a columnar report with a system that uses forms to format the printed output?

Exercises

1. List the operations in a record management system.

2. Describe a record format for a record management system for a newspaper if subscribers have the following options:
   a. Newspaper: morning, evening, Sunday
   b. Billing: weekly, monthly, every six months, annual
   c. Delivery: carrier or mail

3. Define the steps to add two fields to the magazine subscription file—one for a billing date and one for payment received.

4. List the advantages and disadvantages of a sort/report generator.

5. Design an on-screen form for a registration system for a college class.

6. Design an on-screen, multiple-form file management system for a billing system for a health club. Assume the membership classes and monthly dues are: family, $45; single adult, $25; and junior, $20. The club initiation fee is $500 for a family, $300 for a single adult, and $150 for a junior. The initiation fee may be paid either in a lump sum (minus a 10 percent discount) when joining or monthly over a three-year period.

7. In a sorting system (versus an index system), how long would it take to sort a list containing 1,024 records if the sorting technique required N $*$ Log N seconds to sort N records (assume Log is base 2)?

database management 10

10

A **database management system** (**DBMS**) is a collection of programs that provide convenient access to data stored in a database. A **database** is merely a grouping of one or more data files. The primary difference between a DBMS and a record management system is that a DBMS allows simultaneous access to multiple files, but a DBMS is also likely to have better features for restructuring and maintaining files and for automatic file processing. A DBMS can do more than a record management system.

This chapter explains by example how most DBMS programs work. These examples show how to set up a database, use it to retrieve specified data, and process the information in one file to obtain new information stored in another file. For example, you can direct the DBMS to compute a total from a field in one file and then add the total to a balance in a master file.

The management information systems (MIS) departments in major corporations use mainframe computers with full-scale DBMS systems, which are more complex and comprehensive than the DBMS software found on most personal computers. In many instances, a personal computer DBMS is a scaled-down version of a mainframe DBMS. Rbase 5000, dBase II/III, Revelation, Informatix, and other popular DBMS systems for personal computers originated on large computers. The major difference between DBMSs for mainframes and personal computers is the size and sophistication of application-development tools.

A complete DBMS includes facilities for printing reports from multiple files, making back-up copies of existing files, and converting data from one format into another format. These and other features are important to understand when attempting to select a DBMS. We will devote an entire section of this chapter to the necessary and desirable features of a DBMS.

■ Basic Concepts

Overall Structure of a DBMS

A computer-based DBMS system in some ways resembles a public library where people can share documents such as books, magazines, films, and newspapers. Access to the thousands of documents is possible because the books are catalogued in a logical way, such as with the Dewey Decimal system or the Library of Congress system. It's easier to retrieve a document by using a catalog than by simply browsing through the entire library, because card catalogs provide a standard way of accessing information. If we use the terminology of database management systems to describe a public library, we would call the entire collection of documents the *database* and the dictionary and card catalog the *logical schema.*[1]

In a computer, a **logical schema** is a standard way of organizing information into accessible parts, just as the card catalog of a library is a standard way of organizing documents. Schemas contain machine-processable descriptions of the contents of the database so that users can easily browse and retrieve data from the database. The logical schema is separate from the **physical schema,** which describes how data is actually stored on disk. The data may reside in thousands of files spread across many disks or tapes; but because the logical schema insulates you from the physical schema, physical data access is handled by the DBMS and is not apparent.

There is another similarity between a DBMS and a library. Most people use only a small portion of the card catalog or library, and they have different ways of viewing the library. An artist probably thinks of the library as a place to find copies of rare and beautiful paintings; an engineer views the library as a source of technical data such as mathematical tables and engineering journals; and a business executive might use the library to read stock market reports. These different views may result in different ways of retrieving books, newspapers, and magazines; yet the underlying information is stored in the same way for all users of the library. Using the terminology of database management systems, we would call each individual view of the library a **subschema.** The forms we discussed in Chapter 9 are primitive examples of subschemas because they provide a "window" into a file.

Figure 10.1 shows the overall relationships among people, machines, and processes in a large DBMS as they might appear in a major corporation, but even a DBMS for personal computers incorporates the fundamental ideas of the figure. This chart is best understood by reading it from left to right and from top to bottom, like a page of a book. The top row shows the people and programs that feed data into and receive information from the database management system, as well as examples of the technology they might use to collect and analyze that information. A large DBMS can interact with many users at the same time, and the users can be people sitting at a terminal or application programs running in a multitasking computer system. Thus at a certain time the DBMS might be in the process of sending payroll information to an accounting program, receiving sales transactions from clerks, and printing management reports. Financial projections, marketing models, statistical analysis, engineering

---

[1]The *American Heritage Dictionary* defines *schema* as "a summarized or diagrammatic representation of something; an outline." Furthermore, according to this dictionary, *schemata* is the plural form of *schema.* Computer terminology has historically abused the English language, and this is no exception—most DBMS experts use the word *schemas* when discussing more than one schema. We will adopt this common spelling.

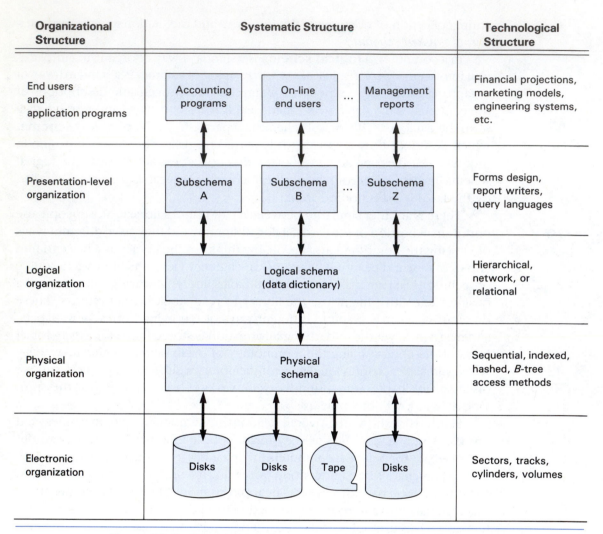

Organizational Structure	Systematic Structure			Technological Structure
End users and application programs	Accounting programs	On-line end users ...	Management reports	Financial projections, marketing models, engineering systems, etc.
Presentation-level organization	Subschema A	Subschema B ...	Subschema Z	Forms design, report writers, query languages
Logical organization	Logical schema (data dictionary)			Hierarchical, network, or relational
Physical organization	Physical schema			Sequential, indexed, hashed, B-tree access methods
Electronic organization	Disks	Disks	Tape	Disks	Sectors, tracks, cylinders, volumes

Figure 10.1 *Organizational, systematic, and technological structures in a large database management system.*

calculations, or other technology may be incorporated into an application program or employed by an end user to collect and analyze information. In the following sections we will examine the other structures depicted in Figure 10.1.

Subschemas

The second row of Figure 10.1 indicates that the data in a database is filtered, formatted, and rearranged as appropriate for a particular set of users. In a large DBMS, each user can "see" only a small part of the entire database; most of the data is shielded from view. The descriptions of how the database should look from a particular user's perspective are stored in each subschema. The subschemas include information used by form designers, report writers, and query-language processors. Because many DBMSs for personal computers are designed to be used by a single user, some do not support the creation of subschemas.

As an illustration of the role of subschemas in a DBMS, consider a simple database for a small company. Assume the database contains the following information about employees:

Fields in database	*A sample employee's information*
NAME	Steve Johnson
ADDRESS	1755 NW Arthur Circle, Corvallis, OR 97330
PHONE	(503) 753-1143
HIRING DATE	8/15/81
BIRTH DATE	12/17/51
SALARY	$43,000
SOC-SEC-NUM	543-64-6466

The logical schema for this database would include the names of each field (NAME, ADDRESS, and so on), the type of data stored in each field (text, date, integer, and so on), and other information necessary to complete the logical description of the data. The database might be used by many programs and people in the corporation. For example, the payroll programs need salary information to print pay checks, and the personnel department needs to know when employees are eligible for retirement. To accommodate these different needs, two subschemas might be established, as follows:

Payroll subschema	*Personnel subschema*
Display format:	Display format:
STANDARD	SCREEN FORM
Fields:	Fields:
NAME	NAME
SOC-SEC-NUM	HIRING DATE
SALARY	AGE
Password:	SOC-SEC-NUM
ALPHA12	Calculations:
	AGE = TODAY'S DATE − BIRTH DATE

The syntax in this example is merely representative of how the subschemas might be laid out; database management systems vary greatly in how schemas and subschemas are constructed. The important point here is that each subschema tells the DBMS how to receive data from and present information to a particular set of users or application programs. Thus, when a payroll program uses the payroll subschema to ask the DBMS for information about Johnson and provides the necessary password, the DBMS would respond with:

```
Steve Johnson
543-64-6466
43000
```

Alternatively, if in May of 1986 a clerk uses the personnel subschema to request information about Johnson, the DBMS would display

```
NAME: Steve Johnson    HIRING DATE: 8/15/81
AGE: 34                SOC-SEC-NUM: 543-64-6466
```

Notice how the DBMS calculates the employee's AGE from the employee's BIRTH DATE and TODAY'S DATE (the date in the computer system's clock).

This example illustrates some fundamental characteristics of how a DBMS shares information among users. Subschemas can be used to create very different, personalized views of the same data. Information might be arranged in a different order and presented in different formats. A subschema can be used to hide sensitive information (such as salaries) from view simply by omitting fields from the subschema's description. It can also be used to create new information from the physical information in the database by performing calculations.

Also notice how effectively a subschema shields its users from the details of how data is organized in files or is stored on disk. The payroll program will work equally well if the database stores the information it needs in one large file, in two smaller files, or in some other manner. Because the payroll subschema describes how data is to be passed to the payroll program, it doesn't matter to the payroll program how data is actually stored.

This illustrates one of the most important consequences of the DBMS approach to managing information: **transparency.** The physical structure of the database is opaque to users and application programs; they do not "see" it at all. This means that application programs can be written in different programming languages, can view the data differently, or can be modified without destroying other users' access. For example, the payroll program's view of data in the database can be changed without affecting the personnel program *even though they may both access the same information.*

Logical Structure

The third row of Figure 10.1 shows the logical organization within a DBMS. The way that the logical schema is constructed influences the behavior of the entire DBMS, because it controls what data is stored in the database and how the data may be accessed. Here are some typical goals for the design of the logical schema.

■ Data should not be stored redundantly in the database. For example, if employee names are paired with social security numbers in one part of the database, they should not be stored a second time in another part. Redundant data storage wastes storage space and opens the possibility of data inconsistencies. For example, if Steve Johnson's social security number is stored twice in the database, once as 543-64-6466 and once as 432-53-5355, that is a **data inconsistency.**

■ The methods of organizing data should be understandable. You should not need an advanced degree in software engineering to construct queries to determine, say, how many employees work in the Los Angeles sales office.

■ The methods of accessing data should be efficient. The DBMS should quickly dispense with routine processing, such as posting a day's sales transactions to an accounts-receivable master file.

■ The logical schema itself should be flexible and expandable. It should adapt gracefully as your needs for data storage and retrieval change.

These design goals often conflict. For example, the most efficient structure for processing may be the least flexible. Balancing these goals successfully can be tricky and is one reason large database systems are generally developed by data processing professionals called **database administrators.**

There are three dominant technologies used to construct logical views of a database: hierarchical, network, and relational. These all accomplish the same basic task of cataloging the data in the database, but they use very different models to describe the data.

Hierarchical Schema

A **hierarchical model** establishes a top-to-bottom relationship among the items in a database, much like the relationships among members of a family on a family tree. Each member of the tree has a unique parent or owner; to reach a member you must pass through the owner. Figure 10.2 shows how a database for a class list might appear in a hierarchical schema. This structure seems quite natural because all students for a given class are grouped under that class.

The student records shown in Figure 10.2 are grouped into sets. A **set** is a collection of records under one branch of the treelike DBMS structure and is the fundamental unit of aggregate information in a hierarchical DBMS. All the students under class CS211 are said to belong to one set.

When a hierarchical model is used, the relationship among items in the database is established when the schema is constructed. This means the hierarchy is static and cannot be changed easily once the database is set up. This fixed structure makes some tasks far easier than others. For example, it is a trivial matter to read from Figure 10.2 the names of the students in class CS212, but

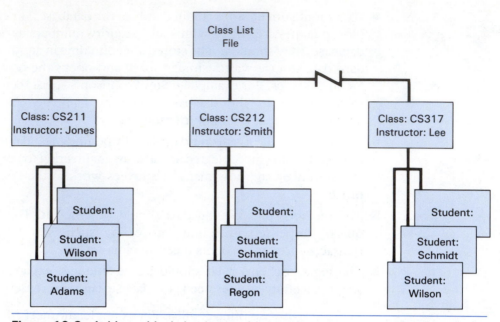

Figure 10.2 *A hierarchical database with a one-to-many access path between classes and students.*

the entire class list must be searched to determine the classes being taken by Schmidt.

Most business data naturally has a hierarchical structure: transactions belong to specific accounts; clients belong to sales regions; and so forth. For these cases the restrictive structure of a hierarchical model may be acceptable. The first mainframe database management systems were hierarchical; and largely because of the difficulties associated with converting from one database model to another, most large corporations still use hierarchical databases.

Network Schema

The network schema is very similar to the hierarchical schema—with one important difference, as shown in Figure 10.3. Instead of restricting the structure to a one-to-many relationship between owner and members, the **network schema** permits many-to-many relationships. For example, as Figure 10.3 illustrates, many students may be enrolled in many classes, and many instructors may teach many students, and a network schema can reflect these relationships.

A network schema establishes an **owner-coupled set** made up of owner records and member records. Once established, the owner-coupled set is static and cannot be changed easily.

Many network DBMSs have been implemented on mainframe computers. In fact, use of the network schema has been recommended by CODASYL

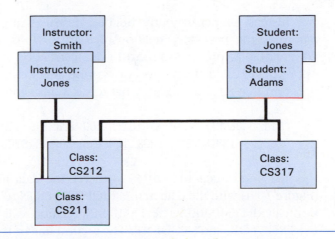

Figure 10.3 *A network database consisting of a many-to-many access path between students and classes and between instructors and classes.*

(Conference on Data Systems Languages), and network databases are sometimes called CODASYL databases. They are more flexible than hierarchical databases, but because the owner-coupled sets are fixed when the database is designed, their importance has decreased.

Relational Schema

A **relational schema** stores data in tables, as shown in Figure 10.4. Each table is called a **relation;** each row of a relation is called a **tuple;** and each tuple is divided into fields called **domains.** Thus, a relation follows the model of a file containing records and fields.

Unlike the hierarchical and network models, a relational database imposes very little structure on the data when it is stored. For example, it is not immediately apparent from the REGISTRATION relation in Figure 10.4 what classes Schmidt is taking; nor is it obvious what students are in class CS212. The tuples in the REGISTRATION relation are not automatically linked either by classes (as in a class list) or by students (as in a student schedule).

Figure 10.4 *A relational database stores data in tables called relations.*

SCHEDULE Relation			REGISTRATION Relation	
CLASS	INSTRUCTOR		CLASS	STUDENT
CS211	Jones		CS212	Adams
CS215	Franklin		CS317	Schmidt
CS317	Lee		CS211	Wilson
CS201	Feldstein		CS212	Schmidt
.	.		.	.
.	.		.	.
.	.		.	.

Instead of permanently building linkages among items in a relational database, the necessary relationships are established temporarily by query commands. A **query command** is an instruction given to the DBMS to look up, retrieve, calculate, move, copy, print, and so forth. A **query** is a miniature program that tells the DBMS what to do. For example, in the query

```
JOIN SCHEDULE WITH REGISTRATION FORMING TEMP-REL
DISPLAY INSTRUCTOR FROM TEMP-REL WHERE STUDENT = "Joe Schmidt"
```

the first line directs the DBMS to merge the data in the SCHEDULE relation (Figure 10.4) with the data in the REGISTRATION relation, creating a new relation called TEMP-REL. The TEMP-REL relation will have three fields: CLASS, INSTRUCTOR, and STUDENT. The second line of the query tells the DBMS to display the name in the INSTRUCTOR field for all the tuples in the TEMP-REL relation whose STUDENT name is Joe Schmidt. The effect of these two commands is to display the names of Joe Schmidt's instructors.

A **query language** is a special-purpose programming language for searching and manipulating data. Query languages differ from one relational DBMS to another. They can be menu-driven or command-driven; they can be simple or complex. The queries may be stored in a program to be executed later, or they may be executed as soon as they are typed in at a terminal. The query languages of most relational DBMSs are more sophisticated than our example, but even this simple example shows how powerful a simple query can be. For the examples in this chapter we use a query language similar to those used by many relational DBMSs for personal computers.

In the last ten years relational database management systems have become very popular, particularly among users of personal computers. Relational systems provide more flexibility in manipulating data than either hierarchical or network systems, because they offer powerful query languages that aren't limited by a fixed set of relationships among data items. The chief complaint about relational database systems has been their poor processing efficiency. This complaint has become less valid as their speed has improved and as the cost of computing has declined.

Physical Structure

The last two rows of Figure 10.1 show the physical organization and electronic structure of a database system. Normally the DBMS hides the details about where and how data is stored in the computer system, so that users can concentrate on their application rather than on the details of the physical storage and retrieval of files.

Common physical structures for files in a DBMS include hashed, sequential, indexed, and _B_-tree files. Each file structure has definite advantages and disadvantages that depend on the storage device's characteristics, the importance of fast access versus compact storage, the types of queries the file must answer, and a host of other factors. Despite these important technical issues, you should remember that even if the DBMS (or in some cases the database administrator) chooses an inappropriate file structure for your files, the only effects noticeable to you should be slower response times or larger storage requirements. To emphasize the difference between a logical view and a physical view of the data, we will discuss one type of physical structure: hashed files.

Hashing is a way of assigning the records in a direct-access file to specific tracks and sectors of a disk in a manner that allows each record's location to be determined quickly. In a hashed file the location of a record is determined by a **hashing function,** a mathematical formula that transforms a file key into a record location. An example of a simple hashing function is the so-called **shift-fold function;** it adds part of a key together to come up with the record number. For example, a social security number might be a key that is transformed into the location of a hospital patient's medical record by hashing the social security number. The shift-fold function partitions the social security number into 3-digit numbers, the numbers are totaled, and the least significant 3 digits are taken as the location of the medical record.

> Social security number: 542-22-4455
> Shift-fold hash: 542 + 224 + 455 = 1,221
> Record location: 221 (retain only the three least significant digits)

This hashing function transforms social security numbers into record locations ranging from 0 to 999. If 1,000 disk tracks are assigned to store the medical record file, then the output of the hashing function can be used directly to point to a single track location for both storage and retrieval.

In order to use hashed files, the DBMS must also establish overflow storage areas and must be able to restructure the hashed file. Overflow storage areas are necessary because several different social security numbers might hash into the same record location, creating the need to store some of these records on overflow tracks. As the number of records in the file grows, the number of overflow tracks will grow until the file must be completely restructured. Restructuring normally involves modifying the hashing function, allocating more storage area to the file, and copying all the records from the old file structure to the new file structure.

■ Relational DBMS Programs: Concepts and Examples

Relational DBMS programs for personal computers continue to grow in number and sophistication. For this reason, and because they reflect a well-developed theory, in this section we examine examples of these programs and the concepts they employ.

Creating the Data Dictionary

A **data dictionary** is a special file containing the names, data types, and widths of all fields in all files maintained by the DBMS; it is a major component of the database's logical schema. You create a new file by adding a new entry into the data dictionary. Most DBMSs use the mnemonic method (discussed in Chapter 9), as shown in the following example.

Assume that you want to create an accounts-receivable file to keep track of the names and account balances of customers. You give the CREATE command and then respond to the resulting prompts. (Words printed in black are prompts from the DBMS program; all other words are entered by the user to tell the DBMS what to do.)

```
CREATE
ENTER FILE NAME: MASTER
ENTER TABLE STRUCTURE: ACCOUNT_NUM,N,5
                       NAME,C,25
                       BALANCE,N,10,2
```

The CREATE command enters the new file called MASTER into the data dictionary. The response to the ENTER TABLE STRUCTURE prompt indicates that MASTER contains records (tuples) with three fields. The response ACCOUNT_NUM,N,5 specifies that the ACCOUNT_NUM field is numeric (N) and is 5 columns wide. Similarly, NAME is a character field (C) and is 25 characters wide. BALANCE is a numeric field 10 columns wide of which 2 columns hold decimal digits.

Entering Data

To enter data into the MASTER file, use the APPEND command (or its equivalent). For example,

```
APPEND MASTER

ACCOUNT_NUM:      544
NAME:             M. Watson
BALANCE:          0.


ACCOUNT_NUM:      STOP
ONE RECORD ADDED TO MASTER
```

As each new record is entered, it is appended to the end of the file.

You can view the contents of the file by using the DISPLAY command. For example, to see only the records with a BALANCE equal to zero, the command and response are

```
DISPLAY MASTER WHERE BALANCE = 0.

1. 387   M. Smith   0.00
2. 544   M. Watson  0.00
3. 865   V. Baker   0.00
```

Printing a Report

Before printing a report you might want to sort the file into ascending order by ACCOUNT_NUM. To do so you will need a second file to hold the ordered list. Suppose you call the new file SMASTER. It is created by the following dialog:

```
CREATE
ENTER FILE NAME: SMASTER
ENTER TABLE STRUCTURE:      SACCOUNT_NUM,N,5
                            SNAM,C,25
                            SBAL,N,10,2
```

Now you can sort on key ACCOUNT_NUM. First select the file you want to sort and then enter the SORT command.

```
USE MASTER
SORT ON ACCOUNT_NUM TO SMASTER
SORT COMPLETE
```

You must wait while the sort is done. When it is finished, the response SORT COMPLETE alerts you to the fact that the SMASTER file now contains the entire MASTER file in order by ACCOUNT_NUM.

Now you can print a columnar report containing two columns with the subheadings ACCOUNT_NUM and BALANCE DUE. To do so you go through the following dialog:

```
USE SMASTER
REPORT
ENTER REPORT NAME: MREPORT
PAGE HEADINGS? (Y/N)      YES
ENTER PAGE HEADING:      MASTER FILE REPORT
ENTER COL, WIDTH, CONTENTS:   1,10,SACCOUNT_NUM
ENTER COL HEADING:  ACCOUNT
ENTER COL, WIDTH, CONTENTS:   2,20,SBAL
ENTER COL HEADING:  BALANCE DUE
ARE TOTALS REQUIRED? (Y/N)      YES
TOTAL WHICH COLUMNS:  SBAL
SUBTOTALS IN REPORT? (Y/N)      NO
```

This dialog tells the DBMS to print a report named MREPORT. The report has a heading: MASTER FILE REPORT. Two columns are defined: SACCOUNT_NUM and SBAL. Each column has a column heading, and the SBAL column is given a total.

Queries

Relational DBMS programs use queries to get quick answers to questions like How many? Queries often employ **aggregate functions;** these are functions that scan the entire file to compute an answer. Examples include the functions SUM, COUNT, MAX, and AVG.

For example, suppose you want to know how many customers in the MASTER file owe you money. You could use the COUNT aggregate function to find out. You type

```
COUNT MASTER WHERE BALANCE > 0.00
```

The DBMS scans the entire file looking for records matching the condition that BALANCE is greater than 0.00 and then displays the answer. Other English questions and typical queries to obtain the answers are

English question	Relational query
What is the total amount owed in MASTER?	SUM BALANCE FROM MASTER FOR BALANCE > 0.
What is the highest balance due?	MAX BALANCE FROM MASTER

Restructuring Files

One of the most powerful features of a relational DBMS is the ease with which files can be manipulated. Three important file manipulation commands are

- **SELECT,** which extracts some of the records from a file.
- **PROJECT,** which extracts some of the columns from a file.
- **JOIN,** which merges two files.

Taken together, the SELECT, PROJECT, and JOIN commands constitute a **relational query language** for processing multiple files. Most commercial relational DBMS programs use these commands in one form or another.

SELECTing Records from a Table

The SELECT command works much like the DISPLAY command except that SELECT produces an output file. SELECT constructs a new table by extracting records from an existing table according to some search condition.

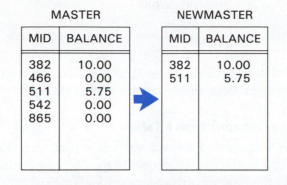

MASTER

MID	BALANCE
382	10.00
466	0.00
511	5.75
542	0.00
865	0.00

NEWMASTER

MID	BALANCE
382	10.00
511	5.75

(a) SELECT MASTER WHERE BALANCE > 0. FORMING NEWMASTER

TRANSACTION

TID	AMOUNT	DATE
382	0.00	1/11/85
466	5.00	1/15/85
511	12.50	2/10/85
542	10.00	12/2/84
542	6.50	12/15/84
542	10.00	11/6/84

NEWTRANS

TID	AMOUNT
382	0.00
466	5.00
511	12.50
542	10.00
542	6.50

(b) PROJECT TID, AMOUNT FROM TRANSACTION FORMING NEWTRANS

MASTER

ID	BALANCE
387	0.00
410	10.00
466	25.95
542	23.50

TRANSACTION

ID	AMOUNT
387	3.50
387	10.75
466	−12.20
542	13.95
542	6.38

BOTH

ID	BALANCE	AMOUNT
387	0.00	3.50
387	0.00	10.75
466	25.95	−12.20
542	23.50	13.95
542	23.50	6.38

(c) JOIN MASTER WITH TRANSACTION FORMING BOTH

Figure 10.5 *Forming new files with SELECT, PROJECT, and JOIN commands.*

For example, if you give the commands

```
SELECT MASTER WHERE BALANCE > 0. FORMING NEWMASTER
```

a table called NEWMASTER is created with all records from MASTER that have a BALANCE field greater than zero, as Figure 10.5(a) shows.

PROJECTing Columns from a Table

The PROJECT command forms a vertical subset of an existing table by extracting specified fields from all records in the file, eliminating duplicate records, and writing the new records to a new file. For example, the commands

```
PROJECT TID, AMOUNT FROM TRANSACTION FORMING NEWTRANS
```

create a table NEWTRANS that includes only the TID and AMOUNT fields, as Figure 10.5(b) shows. Notice that the last row of the TRANSACTION table was dropped because it is a duplicate.

JOINing Two Tables into One

If two files have a field in common, they may be joined into a third table. The JOIN command constructs a new, wider table by appending one record in one table with another record in the other table when both have the same value in the common field. All records that fail to have the same value in the common field are ignored and left out of the new table. For example, you could create a new file called BOTH by giving the commands

```
JOIN MASTER WITH TRANSACTION FORMING BOTH
```

The new file BOTH contains ID, BALANCE, and AMOUNT, as shown in Figure 10.5(c). Notice that the ID value of 410, which occurs in the MASTER table, does not occur in the TRANSACTION table; therefore, this record is left out of the new file BOTH.

■ Features of a DBMS

Now that you have had a brief introduction to what a DBMS can do and how to set up a DBMS, we will look more closely at several features that every DBMS should provide—including a data dictionary, query facility, report generator, data interchange facility, data integrity facility, and file restructuring facility. Understanding these features will help you recognize them immediately in the DBMS you choose to use.

Data Dictionary

Every DBMS has a data dictionary, which tells the DBMS what files are in the database, what these files contain, and what attributes are possessed by the data. For each file in the database the data dictionary always includes

- the name (or number) of the data field.
- the type of data stored in each field, such as TEXT, NUMERIC, DATE, or DOLLARS.
- the width of each field.

In addition, a DBMS may make data entry easier and more reliable with the help of **editing attributes;** that is, rules that govern the way data is entered into the database. Here is a list of some attributes commonly found in DBMS programs for personal computers.

- *Upper and lower limits on numeric data.* This ensures that only values falling within certain limits are permitted during data entry.
- *Password security levels.* A password is often kept for the entire file to prohibit unauthorized access to the file. Additionally, the data dictionary may contain many passwords: one for read-only access, another for data entry, and still another for updating the file.
- *Forms control.* One or more screen forms may be stored in the data dictionary, as described in Chapter 9.
- *Validation fields in other files.* A field in another file may be searched for a certain value before data is allowed to be entered. For example, entries into a transaction file might be checked to guarantee that the customer number being entered has a corresponding record in a customer account file.

Figure 10.6 *A compressed mailing-list file and its associated secondary file.*

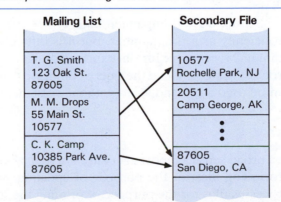

- *Compressed information.* In some DBMS programs data compression is used to save disk space. For example, a mailing list can be compressed by eliminating the CITY and STATE fields from all records, as shown in Figure 10.6. Because the zip code uniquely identifies which city and state are intended, the data dictionary need only reference the city and state in a second file.

- *Data integrity control.* The date and time of last access, the date and time of last back-up, and the date and time of the most recent modification to the file may be kept in the data dictionary. This information is useful for maintaining control over your information and becomes extremely helpful if there is a system failure.

Query Facility

The *query facility* is the method the DBMS provides to request data. A good query facility allows nonprogrammers to process and update information stored in the database. This facility is especially important in a relational DBMS because relationships among fields are established by query commands.

Not all DBMS programs require you to learn a query language like the one we used in our examples. With some programs you can use near-English commands such as

```
For each part supplied, find PNO and the names of all LOCATIONS
supplying the part.
```

```
Find SNO and STATUS for suppliers in London.
```

Natural-language inquiries such as "Find," "How many," and "What" are common in many relational DBMS programs, but natural-language processing of general file updates is difficult. For this reason, query facilities that use pictures and diagrams are one of the most prevalent methods of giving commands to a DBMS.

Setting up and implementing a typical query command may not require proficiency as a programmer, but it is difficult to accomplish without some training. Most people hire an expert to design, set up, and implement the DBMS processing steps. Once the query commands are entered into the DBMS, they can be used again and again without assistance from an expert.

Report Generator

In a broad sense a report generator is a special kind of query facility. Instead of processing files for the purpose of updating another file, a *report generator* processes files for the purpose of printing the results on paper. A good report generator lets you select one or more fields from one or more files.

ORDER File

ODISTRICT	OTROOP	OUNITS	COST
North	1	200	1.50
North	2	175	1.50
North	3	800	1.50
North	4	50	1.50
South	1	350	1.50
South	2	100	1.50
South	3	125	1.50

SALES File

SDISTRICT	STROOP	SUNITS	PRICE
North	1	125	2.95
North	2	175	2.95
North	3	651	2.95
North	4	50	2.95
South	1	330	2.95
South	2	15	2.95
South	3	119	2.95

Figure 10.7 *The Girl Scout Cookie database showing boxes of cookies ordered and sold.*

Figures 10.7 and 10.8 illustrate typical output for a hypothetical report on sales of Girl Scout cookies. The troops are divided into two districts: the North district has four troops, and the South district has three troops. The ORDER file

Figure 10.8 *A report generated from the ORDER and SALES files shown in Figure 10.7.*

```
                    Girl Scout Cookie Sales Report              Page 1
                               By District
                                6/30/85

 District Troop#  #Ordered  $Cost/box   $Cost #Sold $Price/box   Gross      Net

 North      1       200       1.50     300.00   125    2.95     368.75    68.75
 North      2       175       1.50     262.50   175    2.95     516.25   253.75
 North      3       800       1.50    1200.00   651    2.95    1920.45   720.45
 North      4        50       1.50      75.00    50    2.95     147.50    72.50
                   _____              _____ _____           _____  _____

 DISTRICT TOTALS   1225              1837.50  1001            2952.95  1115.45

 District Troop#  #Ordered  $Cost/box   $Cost #Sold $Price/box   Gross      Net

 South      1       350       1.50     525.00   330    2.95     973.50   448.50
 South      2       100       1.50     150.00   151    2.95      44.25  -105.75
 South      3       125       1.50     187.50   119    2.95     351.05   163.55
                   _____              _____ _____           _____  _____

 DISTRICT TOTALS    575               862.50   464            1368.80   506.30

 GRAND TOTALS      1800              2700.00  1465            4321.75  1621.75
```

keeps track of the number of boxes of cookies purchased by each troop at $1.50; the SALES file keeps track of the number of boxes sold by each troop at $2.95. These two files can be joined to produce a report similar to the one shown in Figure 10.8. However, there are several fields in the desired report that do not exist in the database. These additional fields can be calculated during the report as shown in the following example.

Suppose you set up a report from the COMBINED file shown in Figure 10.9. A typical dialog with a relational DBMS report generator might appear as

```
FILE NAME:  COMBINED
PAGE NUMBERS (Y/N)?  YES
DATE OF REPORT (Y/N)?  YES
HEADING, LINE 1:  Girl Scout Cookie Sales Report
HEADING, LINE 2:  By District
```

At this point you have completed the setup for the report date, heading, and pagination.

The next phase establishes which fields are to be included in the report columns. Notice the column numbers and the calculations that must be defined.

```
Enter Column Number:  1
     Field Name:     DISTRICT
     Field Width:    9
     Field Heading:  District

Enter Column Number:  2
     Field Name:     TROOP
     Field Width:    8
     Field Heading:  Troop#
          .
          .
          .
Enter Column Number:  4
     Field Name:     Total_Cost = OUNITS * COST
     Field Width:    11
     Field Heading:  $Cost/box
          .
          .
Enter Column Number:  8
     Field Name:     Gross_Sales = SUNITS * PRICE
     Field Width:    10
     Field Heading:  $Price/box
```

COMBINED File

DISTRICT	TROOP	OUNITS	COST	SUNITS	PRICE
North	1	200	1.50	125	2.95
North	2	175	1.50	175	2.95
North	3	800	1.50	651	2.95
North	4	50	1.50	50	2.95
South	1	350	1.50	330	2.95
South	2	100	1.50	15	2.95
South	3	125	1.50	119	2.95

Figure 10.9 *The file resulting from the following relational JOIN operation: JOIN ORDER USING ODISTRICT & OTROOP WITH SALES USING SDISTRICT & STROOP FORMING COMBINED.*

Once you have entered all the information about the columns, you must tell the report generator where you want breaks and totals. Figure 10.8 shows a one-level break on DISTRICT and a grand total on five fields.

```
Break Field Name:   DISTRICT
Field Name to Total:   OUNITS
Field Name to Total:   COST
Field Name to Total:   SUNITS
Field Name to Total:   Gross_Sales
Field Name to Total:   Net_Sales
Field Name to Total:
```

A similar dialog is carried out for GRAND TOTAL field names, completing the setup phase.

For the next phase the file must be sorted or the appropriate index used so that the file prints in the order shown. In either case, the primary key is DISTRICT and the secondary key is TROOP. Finally, the file COMBINED can be printed to obtain the report shown in Figure 10.8.

A programmer using a language such as COBOL may require from several days to two weeks to write a program to print a report, but you can obtain a report from a DBMS in two to three hours using its report generator. Yet two to three hours seems like a long time when you are not trained to set up and print a report. For this reason it may be desirable to have a DBMS expert set up your reports and save the setup information for you to use.

Compatibility with Other Programs

A good DBMS provides ways to move data between the DBMS files and other programs. The most typical interchange is a transfer of information between the DBMS and spreadsheet, word processing, and graphics programs. For example, you may use a spreadsheet to perform calculations in a financial model and then cut these calculations out of your spreadsheet and paste them into a DBMS file. Or you may want to select a record from your DBMS file and move it into a portion of a spreadsheet. Depending on the conversion programs being used, transferring data can be as easy as posting and removing a piece of paper from a clipboard, or it can be quite difficult. Data in a DBMS file is normally made available to other programs through the *data interchange facility* of the DBMS.

File Formats

Every program that produces output to a disk file uses a format that may or may not be compatible with the output files of other programs. The simplest format is a sequential file containing ASCII text. The records of such a file vary in width depending on the length of each line of text stored.

A worksheet file produced with Lotus 1-2-3 is written in the WKS format; Multiplan worksheets are written in SYLK format; and documents from Multimate, MacWrite, and other word processor programs include printer-control and character font codes. These files must be preprocessed to remove the special printer codes or to rearrange the data so that it matches the arrangement expected by the DBMS.

Spreadsheet Files

Spreadsheet data is generally stored on disk in an ASCII text format that includes all the information needed to reconstruct the spreadsheet. Consider the following two-by-two spreadsheet:

```
        A           B
1    Rent        175.00
2    Bills       325.00
```

This spreadsheet may be stored as the following text (check your spreadsheet manual for the format used by your program):

```
>B2:/F$325.00
>A2:/"Bills
>B1:/F$175.00
>A1:/"Rent
```

The first cell designation specifies cell B2. The symbol /F$ says that cell B2 contains a number formatted as a dollars-and-cents value. The value in cell B2 is

325.00. Cell A2 contains text; cell B1 contains 175.00; and cell A1 contains text. Thus the file contains everything needed to reconstruct the spreadsheet.

Now suppose the spreadsheet information is to be converted and stored in a DBMS file. To do the conversion you must tell the data interchange program in the DBMS which spreadsheet cell corresponds to what field in the file. For example, if the data dictionary entry in the DBMS specifies four fields (EXPENSE, AMOUNT, DEPARTMENT, and MONTH), then the correspondence between DBMS fields and spreadsheet cells might be

```
EXPENSE:      A1
AMOUNT:       B1
DEPARTMENT:   C1
MONTH:        D1

EXPENSE:      A2
AMOUNT:       B2
DEPARTMENT:   C2
MONTH:        D2
```

This example would move the contents of eight cells into the database file, forming two new records.

Word Processing Files

Most word processing documents are stored as regular text files. Thus you need only convert your records into text in order to transfer information from a DBMS file to a word processor. However, some word processing programs encode text files in their own internal format. In this case, to transfer data from a DBMS file to the word processor, you must convert the DBMS file into a regular text file and then read the text file into the word processor's internal format with a utility provided as part of the word processing package.

Suppose you want to export a list of customers and their account balances to a word processing file. You can specify either columnar or comma format. Your choice depends on whether you want each record to appear in your word processing document as several lines or as a single line. If you want the record to appear on several lines, use a columnar format to list the fields to be extracted. For example, the fields might be

```
NAME
ADDRESS
ZIPCODE
BALANCE
```

If you prefer the comma format, then you might give the following list of fields to be extracted:

NAME, ADDRESS, ZIPCODE, BALANCE

Similarly, suppose you want to import data from a word processor to your DBMS file. If you specify a columnar format, the DBMS will expect one field value to appear on each line. If you specify a comma format, the DBMS will expect the field values to appear on one line with commas separating the values. The following two examples illustrate the difference in these formats:

Columnar format	Comma format
Adams	Adams, 123 Main, 86501, 10.00
123 Main	Smith, 555 Park, 55143, 0.00
86501	
10.0	
Smith	
555 Park	
55143	
0.00	

Restructure Ability

If you owned a gasoline service station in 1979, you would appreciate the importance of being able to restructure database files. In 1979 the price of gasoline went over $1.00 per gallon. Many databases had to be changed because the price field was not wide enough to accommodate the additional digit. But if you tried to rectify the problem by simply modifying the entry in the data dictionary, it would no longer be compatible with the actual data stored in the corresponding file. The only answer was to restructure the file so that it could hold the larger value.

In most DBMS programs you must copy all of the data from the original file into a new file in order to restructure it. The new file might be created with more fields than the original file; the fields might be in a different order; or some of the fields might be wider or narrower. After the data has been copied into the new file, the original file can be deleted, and the name of the new file can be changed to that of the original file.

Data Integrity

One of the most overlooked features of a good DBMS is the *data integrity facility*. It consists of back-up and restore routines for file maintenance, control for files that are shared with other users, and other programs to guarantee the safety of your data.

Back-up Copies

There are a number of reasons for periodically making back-up copies of your files. The most obvious reason is to protect your valuable investment of time and effort. A single disk can hold thousands of records, and in an instant lose those records. A back-up copy is your best protection against complete loss. In addition, back-ups provide some not-so-obvious benefits. A file back-up can restore previously deleted records to an active state and provide information for an audit trail.

Recovery of Lost Information.   A **secure DBMS** performs a special kind of delete operation. Whenever you delete a record, it marks the record with a deletion flag rather than actually erasing the record from the disk. The record is still recorded in the file; but because it is flagged, it is skipped whenever a look-up, modify, or print operation is performed. A sophisticated back-up program can copy the active and "deleted" records to another file, making the deleted records active again. This kind of recovery of information is called *back-up with restore*.

Audit Trails.   In most business applications you must guarantee the validity of information stored in a file. Various methods can provide such guarantees—for example, crosschecking, balancing debits and credits, and so forth. One of the simplest methods is to produce an audit trail. An **audit trail** is the recorded history of insertions, deletions, modifications, and restorations performed on a file. A complete audit trail is maintained if the DBMS stores the date and time of every modification made to every record in the file. But because keeping such a trail is impractical, most systems maintain a less-than-perfect trail instead.

One way of obtaining a satisfactory audit trail is to produce periodically a dated report containing all records in the file and to print all modifications to the file as they are made. The report and the printed transactions together constitute a reasonable audit trail. A back-up copy can also be part of an audit trail because it provides a dated copy of all records at a certain point in the life of the file. A history of the file can then be reconstructed from the periodic back-up reports and the record of modifications.

Multiple-User DBMS

Whenever two or more users share access to a file, certain problems may arise. In particular, the DBMS may be susceptible to a **race condition;** that is, a condition where two concurrent activities interact to cause a processing error. For example, suppose one user of the file is modifying a record when a second user attempts to look up the same record. Does the second user obtain the new version of the record, or the record as it was prior to the modification? This outcome for the second user is uncertain.

Now consider what happens if the first user retrieves a record just before a second user modifies one of the fields in the record. The first user may decide whether to modify the record on the basis of values that were changed by the second user—without knowing that the second user has modified the record. Again, a race condition occurs because the outcome is uncertain.

These are only two of the problems associated with multiple access to a shared file. To overcome these problems the DBMS must be able to lock the file whenever modifications are performed. A file is **locked** if only one user is allowed access to it. The shared file must be locked before any user can modify, delete, or insert a record into the file. Some systems use a *record lock* so that simultaneous modifications can occur elsewhere in the file, but not to the locked record.

■ Evaluating DBMS Programs

Most DBMS programs accomplish the same basic functions, but they differ in a myriad of ways once you consider the frills. We have covered the basic properties of a DBMS without dealing with the "extras." Table 10.1 presents an excellent list of items to consider if you are selecting a DBMS for a personal computer. In addition, the following extra features go beyond what we have discussed but can greatly enhance your ability to get work done:

■ *Multiple files.* A relational DBMS allows you to combine files into a single, wider file by the JOIN command, but this is not the quickest or easiest way to handle a multiple-file problem. A multiple-file DBMS that allows simultaneous access to several files can make life much easier.

■ *Screen forms.* As we saw in Chapter 9, most record management systems use one or more screen forms. A good DBMS will allow you to design multiple forms for each file to help with input, editing, and viewing.

■ *Password security.* Passwords can control who can read from a file and who can write on it. Some DBMS programs provide a password for each field in each file or require a password to access the database through a given subschema. Carefully consider the importance of passwords when selecting a DBMS.

■ *Multiple-user capability.* Is it important to permit one person to enter data into a file while another person retrieves data from the same file? If so, then your DBMS must support multiuser access to files. This capability will grow in importance as networks of personal computers proliferate.

Table 10.1 *A Typical Checklist for Selecting a DBMS*

A. General Information
Program name:_____
Data base type:_____

B. User Support
☐ None: Company shows only P.O. box or refuses to talk to users.
☐ Weak: Company will respond to problems if submitted in writing.
☐ Moderate: Company will respond to calls during business hours.
☐ Strong: Company maintains a 24-hour telephone hot line.

C. Requirements and Compatibility
Minimum central memory:_____K
Maximum usable central memory:_____K
Printers supported:_____
Operating system(s) supported:_____

Hard disk compatibility:
☐ None ☐IBM PC XT
☐ IBM PC with expansion chassis

Hard disk support:
☐ Complete program and data may reside on hard disk.
☐ Program and data may reside on hard disk, but floppy must be in machine.
☐ Only data may exist on hard disk.
☐ Neither program nor data may reside on hard disk.

Electronic disk support:
☐ Complete program and data may reside on electronic disk.
☐ Program and data may reside on electronic disk, but floppy must be in machine.
☐ Only data may exist on electronic disk.
☐ Neither program nor data may reside on electronic disk.
☐ Program creates and uses its own electronic disk.

D. User Interface
☐ Menu driven
☐ Command driven
☐ Choice between menu and command operation
☐ Driven by a programming language
☐ Macro definition capability
☐ Password protection
☐ "Turnkey" systems

E. Communication with Other Programs

Reading:
☐ ASCII (serial string format)
☐ ASCII (two-dimensional format)
☐ 1-2-3 .WKS
☐ VisiCalc .VC
☐ VisiCalc .DIF
☐ Multiplan SYLK
☐ dBASE II

Writing:
☐ ASCII (serial string format)
☐ ASCII (two-dimensional format)
☐ 1-2-3 .WKS
☐ VisiCalc .VC
☐ VisiCalc .DIF
☐ Multiplan SYLK
☐ dBASE II

☐ Modern transfer required for communication with other programs

F. Searching and Sorting
Maximum simultaneous search criteria:_____
Maximum simultaneous sort criteria:_____
☐ Ad hoc queries possible.
Available search logic:

	Date	Dollar	Floating point	Integer	String	Yes/No
AND	☐	☐	☐	☐	☐	☐
OR	☐	☐	☐	☐	☐	☐
NOT	☐	☐	☐	☐	☐	☐
IF . . . THEN	☐	☐	☐	☐	☐	☐
IF . . . THEN . . . ELSE	☐	☐	☐	☐	☐	☐

Search types:
☐ Wild card
☐ Soundex (phonetic)
☐ Search & replace

Case independence:
☐ Searches are case independent.
☐ Sorts are case independent.
☐ Case independent searching is a user option.

Indexing:
☐ Indexing is possible.
(Number of keys allowed:_____)
☐ Index keys must be defined when the data base is created.
☐ Any field (indexed or not) may be defined as a key when search or sort is initiated.
☐ Any relevant command can be used with indexed variables.

G. Reports
Maximum report width:_____characters.
☐ Page breaks are supported.
☐ Control breaks are supported.
☐ Titles on each page are supported.
☐ All fields for a record must be printed on a single line.
☐ Any field may be placed anywhere on a page.

H. Forms
☐ Program has forms design capacity.
(Up to_____separate screens may be defined.)
☐ Data checking is permitted.
☐ For data type ☐ For data range
☐ Color is permitted.
☐ Sound is permitted.
☐ Program has its own input routine that cannot be easily altered.

I. Program Capacities
Maximum number of records:_____
Maximum record length:_____
Maximum number of fields per record:_____
Maximum field length:_____
Maximum file size:_____
Maximum number of variables:_____
☐ A data base can span more than one floppy disk.
☐ Guidelines are supplied for estimating storage requirements.

Source: *PC World* (July 1984), vol. 2, no. 7. p. 239.

In addition, remember to consider other features, including

- flexibility of the report generator.
- capability of data interchange facility to import and export files.
- ease of use.
- effectiveness of error handling and recovery.
- quality of documentation.
- clarity, simplicity, and power of the query language.
- power and number of screen forms.
- file access time.
- processing speed.
- price.

■ Summary

Two goals of a DBMS are to eliminate the need for a programmer and to provide an easy-to-understand model of data. Menus, commands, and query languages are used to eliminate programming; a DBMS schema makes the DBMS general yet easy to understand. But neither of the two goals is fully achieved by today's DBMS programs. Some programs are easier to use but less powerful than others. Powerful programs tend to be complex and difficult to understand. At the root of the difficulty is the likelihood that an application is intrinsically complex because of the complex nature of the task.

DBMS software maintains separate subschemas so that independent users and programs can access and interpret the data in their own way; maintains a comprehensive logical schema so that a uniform, consistent, and correct structure is guaranteed at all times; maintains a physical schema so that the location of specific data items can be determined; and provides a variety of functions to users such as report generation, file conversion, query processing, and password protection.

A hierarchical DBMS imposes a one-to-many relationship on data items when they are stored and works on sets of data. These programs easily model hierarchical structures such as corporations or governmental organizations. For this reason, hierarchical DBMS programs appear natural to use. A network DBMS imposes a many-to-many relationship on data items when they are stored. In practice, hierarchical and network models are more complex and difficult to use than relational models, in which the relationships among data are established only after data are stored. A relational DBMS uses tables as the schema for data. Tables, rows, and columns of fields are processed by giving commands to the DBMS. These commands establish the relationships among files, records, and fields.

In addition, every DBMS must have a data dictionary to hold the database's structural information. Some systems include additional editing features in their data dictionary such as upper and lower bounds on numeric input and forms.

Every DBMS must provide some way to process, update, and retrieve information. Typically, a query language provides the directions for processing files. In addition, a querylike language can be used to generate reports on the screen. A report generator produces printed output, however, rather than updating a file.

A good DBMS also provides ways to share information with other software. This might consist of an ability to work in conjunction with a standard programming language like COBOL. Another way to share information is through a data interchange program that is used to transfer a database file to a spreadsheet, word processor, or telecommunications file. Furthermore, a DBMS should be able to transfer data from one file format to another format within the DBMS itself, allowing files to be restructured without resorting to manual re-entry of data.

Finally, a DBMS must allow you to protect the database from damage in the event of a power outage or other failure leading to loss of information. A variety of methods for backing-up files and rebuilding the file structure are part of any good DBMS.

Key Terms

aggregate function	lock
audit trail	logical schema
database	network schema
database administrators	owner-coupled set
database management system (DBMS)	physical schema
data dictionary	PROJECT command
data inconsistency	query
domains	query command
editing attribute	query language
hashing	race condition
hashing function	relation
hierarchical model	relational query language
JOIN command	relational schema

secure DBMS   subschema
SELECT command   transparency
sets   tuple
shift-fold function

Discussion Questions

1. How can you tell the difference between a record management system and a database management system? Is there a gray area between them?

2. What are the differences between a hierarchical and a relational DBMS?

3. Why is English not a good query language?

4. What would be the most important features in the check list of DBMS features for a church that uses volunteers to keep track of its books? For the payroll department of a 1,000-person corporation?

5. Why is the ability to exchange information between DBMS and non-DBMS files a desirable feature?

Exercises

1. List advantages and disadvantages of hierarchical, network, and relational database management systems.

2. For your DBMS find the maximum
   a. number of files.
   b. number of records per file.
   c. number of fields per record.
   d. number of characters per field.
   Also determine the types of data allowed.

3. Describe the information in a data dictionary.

4. List the steps in adding a new record to a DBMS file.

5. Give some safeguards for preventing loss or accidental change of information in a DBMS.

6. Investigate the data interchange capabilities of your DBMS.

7. Diagram a relational database containing three files: PARTS, SHIPMENTS, and SUPPLIERS. The PARTS file has fields for PART_NUM, PART_NAME, COLOR, QUANTITY, and WEIGHT. The SHIPMENTS file has fields for PART_NUM, DATE, SHIP_QTY, SUPPLY_NUM, and PRICE. The SUPPLIERS file has fields for SUPPLY_NUM, SUPPLY_NAME, and ADDRESS. Diagram how the database might look in a hierarchical model. Repeat the exercise for a network database. How do the hierarchical, network, and relational databases differ?

8. Give some examples of the applications and subschemas that might be used to design a management system for student registration and transcript information.

PART FIVE

application areas

In 1915 Lee De Forest and his associates stood trial for mail fraud after attempting to sell stock in a manufacturing company. De Forest claimed that he had invented a device that would make transatlantic telephone conversations possible. De Forest narrowly escaped prison, but his associates were convicted when the prosecutor persuaded the judge that transatlantic telephony was impossible. Two years later De Forest successfully applied the audion tube (the first vacuum tube) to transatlantic broadcasting. Since those days the audion tube has made possible modern radio, radar, television, first-generation computers, and ultimately Silicon Valley.

Nowadays few people are skeptical of advances in computer technology. In fact, we rather expect constant, exciting innovations. Hardware advances such as speech synthesis, voice recognition, seeing-eye cameras, and touch-sensitive screens are being developed with increasing rapidity. Larger memories and faster processors are opening the door to advances in software such as picture programming, natural-language inquiry, and expert systems that give advice on a variety of topics. These capabilities will soon be expected of the lowliest personal computer.

Part V extends your knowledge of hardware and software into the frontiers of graphics, communications, and miscellaneous programs for accounting, education, entertainment, and so forth. These are among the most dynamic areas of computing because no dominant software or standard hardware has emerged. Chapter 11 examines how communications hardware and software are weaving a network of computers into a world-encompassing web the like of which has never before been seen. In Chapter 12 we describe computer graphics—an area that until recently was stunted by the high cost of internal memory and color displays. Today the software for creating graphics is becoming more powerful and easier to use. In Chapter 13 we survey the thousands of useful programs that we have not discussed elsewhere. Many of these programs provide tailor-made solutions for specialized applications.

11

communications and computing

11

In the past ten years three trends have combined to create a turbulent and dynamic environment in computer communications. First, the quantity of information stored in computers has more than quadrupled, a change that in turn has expanded the need to share information among computers. Second, the entire field of communications—from telephones and television to music recording—has begun switching from analog to digital storage and transmission methods. This switch is causing the fields of computing and communications to merge. Third, a shift in the relative costs of computing equipment has erased the historical cost advantage of centralized mainframes and is encouraging the use of decentralized personal computers.

Computer communications is a field not only of turmoil and rapid growth but also of many market niches, specialized pieces of equipment, and weak standards for hardware and software. It is an exciting environment that leaves communications specialists divided about what the future will bring and how to prepare for it.

In the first half of this chapter we introduce computer communications by explaining how a personal computer or terminal can be linked by telephone to any of thousands of other computers. This introduction explains the technology involved in sending data over telephones, the software used to link personal computers to other computers, and the types of tasks that can be accomplished with a personal computer and a telephone.

The second half of the chapter generalizes the concepts in the first half to the entire field of computer communications. Here we discuss communications media (wires, cables, airwaves, and so forth), how the media are used efficiently, and how computers can be linked in various types of networks.

■ Telecommunications

Telecommunications is a very general term. It refers to any transmission of information over long distances using an electromagnetic signal similar to that used in telephones or radios. When the term is used in discussions of personal computers, it usually refers to something much more specific: attaching a personal computer to the telephone system to move data from computer to computer.

With telecommunications and a personal computer you can

- read the day's headline stories or search the last few months of news for articles on a particular topic.
- send letters to be printed and delivered by the post office.
- receive mail that was deposited instantly in your "electronic mailbox" by correspondents living across town, across the continent, or abroad.

- order books, cameras, and other items at a substantial discount.
- match wits with aliens in a game of Star Trek.
- search vast libraries of bibliographic references for citations that match your query.
- "download" free public domain programs to be used later or swap files with out-of-town friends.
- use a mainframe or supercomputer to run programs and solve problems beyond the capability of your personal computer.
- send a list of today's sales to your firm's head office or order inventory to be delivered for tomorrow's sales.
- request financial or stock market information for a specific company.
- post and read messages on a free computer bulletin board.

To begin telecomputing you need to solve three problems. First, your personal computer must be physically attached to the telephone lines. This requires a hardware interface that allows the personal computer to "talk" on the phone lines. The connection to the other computer is made by dialing the appropriate telephone number. Second, you need communications software to control the personal computer while it is sending and receiving data. Third, the communications software on your personal computer must be set to use the protocol used by the other computer. The **protocol** controls how messages are passed between machines. It establishes such important parameters as how fast characters are sent and whether characters are sent one at a time or in groups called *packets*.

Telecommunications Hardware

To understand how a computer transmits information through the telephone system, it is necessary to learn something about the methods used to encode data into electrical signals. All of the parts in a computer (disk drives, CPU, printer, and so on) talk to each other by sending digital signals, as shown in Figure 11.1(a). **Digital signals** change from one voltage to another in discrete, choppy jumps. Generally, the presence of a positive voltage at a specific time represents the binary digit 1; the absence of a voltage represents the binary digit 0. In contrast, **analog signals** represent information as variations in a continuous, smoothly varying signal wave. Analog transmission methods dominated every aspect of the communications field prior to the invention of the transistor.

Digital signals have two major advantages over analog signals.

1. Digital signaling allows faster transmission of computer-generated data. Electrical circuits can encode and decipher bits as digital pulses more quickly than they can represent bits in a signal wave.

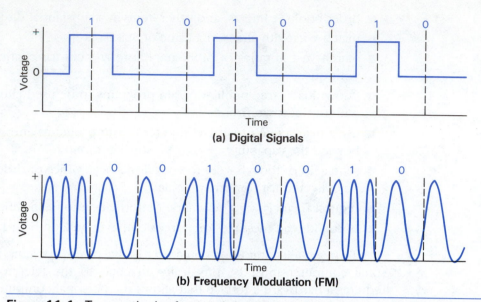

Figure 11.1 *Two methods of transmitting information through wires. In digital signaling each bit is represented by the presence or absence of a voltage at a specific time. In frequency modulation each bit of data is represented by a tone during a period of time.*

2. Digital signaling is more accurate because transmission errors can be detected and corrected. For example, assume that the digital signal for a binary 1 is to be encoded as +5 volts, and that a binary 0 is to be encoded as 0 volts. Now assume that a signal is sent out at +5 volts but is received at +4.5 volts because of transmission errors. In this case the receiving circuit will correctly interpret the incoming signal as a binary 1 because +4.5 volts is closer to +5 volts than to 0 volts. Analog transmissions do not have a comparable method of correcting errors.

For these reasons, telephone systems are rapidly converting from analog to digital transmission methods. Unfortunately, very few residential telephone exchanges allow home phones lines to use digital signals. This means that the digital signals of a personal computer must be translated into analog signals before they can be sent through most telephone systems.

Frequency modulation (FM), which is illustrated in Figure 11.1(b), is one of several methods of analog signaling. It is the transmission method used in FM radio. It also forms the basis for the relatively slow, but very common, Bell System 103 method of transmitting computer data over phone lines. When frequency modulation is used to transmit binary data, a high-pitched tone during a given unit of time represents the digit 1, and a lower-pitched tone represents the digit 0.

For computers to send and receive messages over analog telephone systems, they must be able to convert digital signals to analog signals and vice versa. The process of converting digital to analog signals is called **modulation.** **Demodulation** does the reverse. **Modem** is short for **mo**dulate and **dem**odulate, and a modem is a device that can perform both functions. Modems modulate data transmissions at fairly high frequencies so that they can send and receive data as quickly as possible. Knowledgeable people avoid eavesdropping on telephone conversations between computers because they make a continuous, high-pitched shriek.

The appearance of modems varies substantially, as Figure 11.2 illustrates. Many portable computers come from the factory with built-in modems. Most desktop personal computers have expansion slots in which an optional circuit board containing the modem can be inserted. Alternatively, it is almost always possible to connect an external modem to a personal computer through a serial interface (an RS-232 port) on the computer. External modems—which are also called *stand-alone* or *free-standing modems*—have the advantage of working with a wide variety of personal computers; but they require their own electrical power plug, often cost more than built-in modems, and make the computer system less portable.

Modems come in two major categories: direct-connect and acoustically coupled. **Direct-connect modems** plug directly into telephone jacks (see Figure 11.3); they make a very reliable electrical connection to the telephone system. An acoustically coupled modem (or **acoustic coupler** for short) is attached to the telephone system by jamming the phone's handset into two flexible receptacles in the coupler. Then a speaker in the coupler talks into the mouthpiece in the handset, and a microphone in the coupler listens to the earphone in the handset. Having all these microphones and speakers talking to each other across air gaps makes acoustic couplers slow and unreliable.

Modems range in price from well under $100 to over $2,000 for commercial-grade, high-speed modems. The cheapest modems are compatible with the Bell 103 standard—meaning they follow a widely accepted standard for frequency modulation that is limited to transmitting 300 bits per second (bps). It normally takes 10 bits to transmit 1 character. Thus a 300 bit-per-second modem will transmit about 30 characters per second (cps), taking more than a minute to fill a 24-line-by-80-column screen. Most people read faster than 30 cps.

Modems operating at 1,200 bps (120 cps) transmit text as fast as most people read. They have been dropping rapidly in price recently, from over $2,000 a few years ago to less than $300 in late 1985. At the same time, their popularity has increased dramatically. In 1985 several 2,400-bps modems selling for less than $800 were introduced. If current trends continue, within ten years there will be more 2,400-bps modems in operation than 1,200- and 300-bps modems.

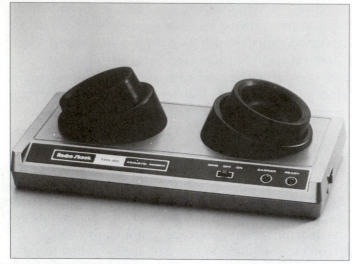

(a) Acoustical Coupler

(b) External Modem

(c) Internal Modem

Figure 11.2 *Comparison of an acoustical coupler, an external modem, and an internal modem, which is shown with its communications software and user manual.*

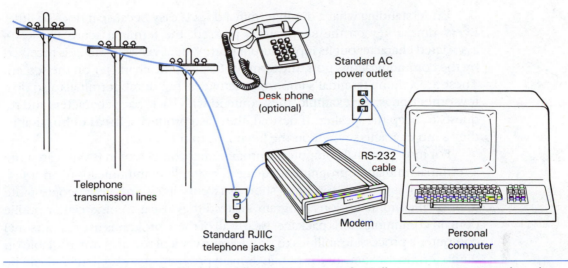

Figure 11.3 *Typical cabling arrangements for a direct-connect external modem.*

Very few personal computers are attached to modems that transmit faster than 2,400 bps, primarily because high-speed modems can cost as much as the personal computer itself. Also, the maximum reliable transmission rate of an average voice-grade telephone connection is around 2,400 bps. If faster transmission is necessary, it is possible to lease special lines from the telephone company that transmit up to 9,600 bps.

Communications speeds are often given in terms of a baud rate. The **baud rate** is the number of data signals the communications line transmits each second. Technical purists point out that the baud rate and bits per second are not the same, because some elegant coding schemes pack two or more bits into each signal. But most people use the terms *baud rate* and *bits per second* interchangeably.

Communications Software

Terminal Emulation

The simplest type of communications software makes a personal computer pretend it is a computer terminal. This is called **terminal emulation.** Although there are many types of computer terminals, the most common type is called an *ASCII terminal* (a reference to the character code used by the terminal), a *Teletype* (historically the most common type of electromechanical terminals), or simply a **dumb terminal.** *Dumb terminal* is a well-accepted term for an ASCII terminal that has no processing abilities on its own.

Understanding what a dumb terminal does is easy because it does so little. Every time a key on the keyboard is pressed, the terminal sends the key's associated character out its input/output port. Whenever a character is received by the communications port, the terminal displays the character on the screen. These are a dumb terminal's important activities, but dumb terminals also do a few other things. For example, they contend with backspace characters and requests to beep the speaker. If desired, they also produce a **local echo;** that is, they send characters typed on the keyboard to the screen.

For most personal computers a programmer competent in BASIC can write a terminal-emulation program adequate for simple communications in a few hours. Such a program can be as short as twenty lines. Still, few people write their own communications program. Instead they use a commercial or public domain communications package. Nearly all of these programs use the personal computer's processing abilities to provide convenient features not available on dumb terminals. Some of the public domain programs are excellent and can be acquired from computer-user groups for a nominal copying fee. The commercial programs tend to come with better documentation and marketing support; their prices range from around $20 to more than $200. Often a communications program is sold with a modem as a package.

Transferring Files

The most important feature to look for in a communications package is the ability to upload and download files. Sending a file from your personal computer's primary memory or disk to another computer is called **uploading.** Retrieving information and storing it on a disk as a file is called **downloading.**

The ability to transfer files is important for several reasons. For some applications, such as exchanging computer programs, it is the reason for communicating in the first place. Other activities, such as sending and receiving electronic mail, are completed faster when information is transferred as a file. Completing tasks quickly can save money. Most forms of telecomputing involve charges based on the length of the phone call.

Frills for Convenience

Communications programs also offer frills, features that are nice to have. One such feature is the ability to do limited editing, copying, or deleting of files without leaving the communications program.

A very popular feature is **auto-dialing,** which allows you to dial telephone numbers by typing them on the keyboard. Auto-dialing isn't possible unless you have a **smart modem**—a modem capable of accepting commands such as dialing instructions from your computer.

Another useful feature requiring a smart modem is the ability to create and use **dialing directories,** which store the telephone numbers and communications parameters of remote computers in a file and make it easy to log on to remote computers. Recall that *logging on* is the process of identifying yourself to a computer; often it involves typing a user identification number (user id) and a password. Good dialing directories store and issue your user id, password, and the entire log-on sequence. If you want to log on to a remote computer, you just select the computer's name from a list. Then the software-smart modem combination takes over—dialing the number, listening for the carrier signal, and issuing whatever commands are necessary in order to log on.

The **auto-answer** feature allows a personal computer to answer incoming calls without human assistance. This feature is necessary for unattended operations such as storing and forwarding messages.

Communications Protocols

Human communication follows an informal set of rules, which could be called a *communications protocol.* For example, while you're talking to a group of people, it is best to look at them, not at the sky or the ground. When meeting someone new, it is common to shake hands. Interrupting someone in midsentence is generally impolite.

Computers also use communications protocols, but their protocols are more formal than those people use. Furthermore, computers using different protocols cannot speak directly to each other. One of the most fundamental levels of a communications protocol for computers regulates when each computer is allowed to transmit.

Half-Duplex or Full-Duplex

Human beings communicate best when only one person talks at a time. In the computer field this is called **half-duplex** transmission. Half-duplex transmission limits communication to one direction at a time. If the computer on one end of the line is transmitting, the computer on the other end cannot respond until the entire message is sent. More often, personal computers use **full-duplex** connections, which allow simultaneous two-way transmission. Each end of the line is assigned a different frequency for speaking so that the ''voices'' don't interfere with each other.

Long distance telephone connections are often poor, and static on the line can garble characters. A process called **remote echoing** provides a simple way to double-check the accuracy of the transmission. The remote computer echoes every character as it is received. Then each letter you type travels to the remote computer, is echoed back, and eventually appears on your screen. If the letter you receive back is not the one you typed, you can backspace and type it again. Depending on the workload of the remote computer, the round-trip transit time can be quite noticeable. (Be warned that very often—though it is technically incorrect—the term *half-duplex* is used for local echo and *full-duplex* for remote echo.)

Occasionally, you may log on to a computer that doesn't echo your characters. This can be very disconcerting. All your typing will seem to vanish into a black hole and will not appear on the screen. On the other hand, you may get both local and remote echoes. In this case, everything you type shows up on the screen twice, as in "HHEELLLLOO." To correct these problems you need to be able to switch the local-echo feature on and off.

Asynchronous or Synchronous

Perhaps the most important distinction in transmission mode is between synchronous or asynchronous. Asynchronous transmission is slower, simpler, and cheaper. **Asynchronous protocols** transmit characters one at a time. The transfer of data is coordinated by preceding each character with a *start bit*—a signal that transmission of a character has begun—and ending it with one or more *stop bits*. The ritual of preceding and following data with start bits, stop bits, and other control data is called **handshaking.** In addition, remote echoing is very frequently used in asynchronous communication.

Synchronous protocols send and receive characters at agreed-upon times at a fixed rate. They normally send packets of characters instead of just one character at a time. Synchronous communication is faster and more complex than asynchronous methods. Personal computers rarely use synchronous communication except to interface with IBM host computers or local area networks.

Error Correction

Even the best modems and telephone lines occasionally garble characters, producing errors in the information received. As long as this happens rarely—say, for one in ten thousand characters—the errors probably will not bother the average user of electronic mail. However, garbled characters are intolerable when program files—as opposed to data files—are transmitted. If even one bit in a 20,000-byte program file is received incorrectly, the program is likely to be useless.

Transmission errors can be avoided if both computers use **error detection and correction** software. To detect errors the transmitting computer sends characters in packets with a *check figure* at the end of each packet; this figure is a mathematical function of the characters in the packet. The receiving computer calculates the same mathematical function on the packet it receives. If the result matches the check figure sent by the transmitting computer, the receiving computer acknowledges successful receipt of the packet. Otherwise, the packet is retransmitted. In short, error detection is accomplished by sending characters in packets with a check figure; error correction is accomplished by retransmitting packets that contained errors.

For error correction and detection to work, both computers must be using the same error-checking protocol. For personal computers the most popular

Communications: Transporting Data

The development of microprocessors brought machine intelligence to previously dumb products. Terminals became personal computers, cash registers became point-of-sale terminals, wrist watches became digital alarm chronometers, and, unfortunately, some household appliances learned to talk, saying things like, ''Beep, your coffee's done.'' The first intelligent products had little or no ability to communicate, but that has changed. Today intelligent office products are linked into integrated office systems. Satellites, microwave links, and telephone transmission systems provide widely dispersed equipment with access to databases managed by large host computers. This photo essay gives you a glimpse into the consolidation of two fields: communications and computing.

1. New telephone systems encode and transmit voice messages as digital signals rather than analog signals. As a result, both voice and data can be transmitted conveniently by one communications systems.

SATELLITES

Satellites provide high-speed digital communications among widely dispersed locations. They allow large amounts of computer-generated data to be transmitted quickly between data processing centers.

2. Large antennas allow RCA Americom's Satellite Operations Control Center to monitor and control up to eight communications spacecraft in orbit. Without frequent earth-based supervision, communications satellites would soon wander out of position and become useless. Two small microwave relay antennas are visible near the skyline.

3. The control console inside the RCA Satellite Control Center.

4. A satellite earth station located in Dallas, Texas, forms a major hub in the EDS Corporation's nationwide communications network.

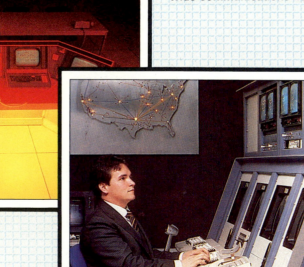

5. The EDS communications control center.

FIBER OPTICS

Optical fibers transmit data as pulses of laser light, not as electrical signals. They are extremely fast, compact, insensitive to electrical disturbances, and secure from eavesdropping. Despite these advantages, conventional twised-pair wire and coaxial cable are used more often than optical fibers because of their lower cost.

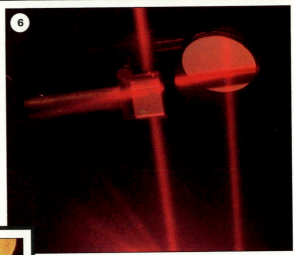

6. A helium neon laser is used to test a glass preform before it is drawn into optical fiber.

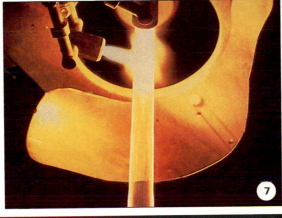

7. In one step in the production of glass fiber, an oxygen-hydrogen flame travels the length of a quartz tube, causing chemical reactions at the point of heat.

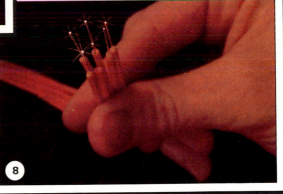

8. Although the finished glass fibers are tiny, they can transmit hundreds of telephone conversations at once.

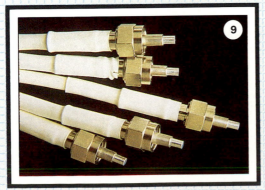

9. Tandem uses five fiber-optic strands in each FOX system link between its computers. The fibers are connected to the system with screw terminations for easy installation.

Business information is a precious commodity. It can be stored and shared effectively by centralized data processing centers in conjunction with telecommunications networks.

10. Row upon row of hard disk drives are a common sight in large computer centers. This view shows one of three "supercenters" maintained by GE Information Services, the world's largest commercially available teleprocessing network.

11. Although a commercial hard disk drive stores from 100 megabytes to more than 5 gigabytes (100 million to 5 billion characters), large installations require many drives. Hard disk drives provide fast data retrieval; access times are measured in milliseconds (thousandths of a second).

12. Telex's MIS (management information systems) Center in Tulsa expedites communication between corporate headquarters and other Telex operations.

13. Tapes are used to store infrequently used data and to back-up data stored on disk drives in case of disk failure. Only one reel of tape can be mounted at a time on each tape drive.

14. Most magnetic tapes are *off-line,* meaning they cannot be read by the computer unless they are mounted on a tape drive by a computer operator. Storing data on tape is inexpensive; a 2,400-foot tape costs about $20 and can store over 100 megabytes.

15,16. Law enforcement and health-care workers need quick answers from large databases. Usually these requirements are met by connecting desktop terminals to a central host computer. The connection can be made with a dedicated wire running directly between the two, with a permanently leased telephone line, or with dial-up telephone service. Often the terminal and the host computer are linked by a number of intermediary communications devices such as concentrators, modems, and local area networks.

LOCAL AREA NETWORKS

Local area networks allow devices in a limited area to be connected so that any device on the network can communicate with any other device.

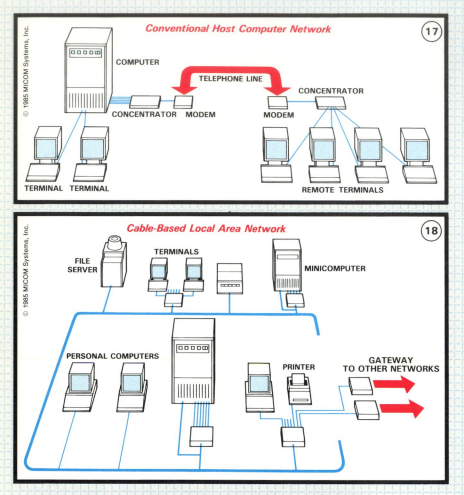

Conventional Host Computer Network (17)

© 1985 MICOM Systems, Inc.

COMPUTER

TELEPHONE LINE

CONCENTRATOR

CONCENTRATOR   MODEM   MODEM

TERMINAL   TERMINAL

REMOTE TERMINALS

Cable-Based Local Area Network (18)

© 1985 MICOM Systems, Inc.

FILE SERVER

TERMINALS

MINICOMPUTER

PERSONAL COMPUTERS

PRINTER

GATEWAY TO OTHER NETWORKS

17. In a conventional computer network, all peripheral devices are connected to the host computer. If you want one terminal to talk to another, the message must pass through the host computer first. To use the telephone lines efficiently, concentrators and other communications devices splice messages from several terminals onto one telephone line.

18. In a cable-based local area network, all devices are connected to one cable. Often the cable is similar to the coaxial cable used in cable TV systems. Local area networks use a number of methods to prevent the electronic ''voices'' of the devices from colliding. Local area networks are very reliable; unless the cable is cut or damaged, the entire network cannot fail.

(19)

19. With a local area network, an office work group using personal computers can share a hard disk drive and printer. Networks also allow users to send and receive electronic mail.

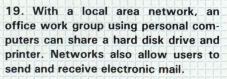

TELEPHONE TERMINALS

Nowhere is the consolidation of communications and computing more evident than in the development of telephone terminals.

20. This personal communications terminal combines a powerful terminal and a full-featured telephone in one unit. The phone features a built-in speakerphone for hands-free calls, the ability to enter and revise a phone list with 200 entries using the retractable keyboard, and a built-in calculator. The unit can also emulate a DEC VT100 terminal or an IBM 3270 terminal.

21. This telephone unit has all the capabilities of the terminal shown in photo 20, but it also contains a personal computer compatible with an IBM PC. Mostly hidden by the man's arm are two floppy disk drives. Inside the unit are a microprocessor that can run IBM PC software for business applications and 512KB of memory.

22. A sales clerk telephones the National Data Corporation (NDC) to obtain credit card authorization for a customer. NDC's network links the consumer, the bank, and the merchant for fast and efficient credit service.

23. A waitress in a Tokyo restaurant uses CATNET, a nationwide credit verification system introduced by IBM in Japan.

OTHER TERMINALS

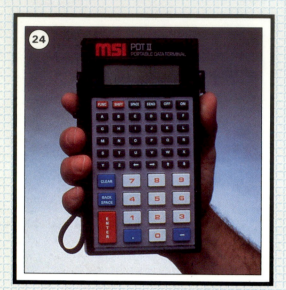

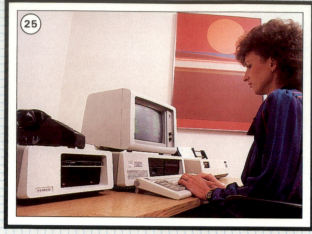

25. You can temporarily convert virtually any personal computer into an intelligent computer terminal by adding a modem and a communications program. This allows the personal computer to be connected to a host computer to run applications such as order entry, electronic mail, or electronic funds transfer.

24. This hand-held portable data terminal can be connected directly to telephone lines with a standard RJ11 snap connector for data transmissions with a host computer. Its clock can "wake up" the terminal and automatically dial a telephone number at a preset time, allowing transmissions to occur unattended late at night, when long distance rates are low. Data can be entered through the keyboard or with a variety of bar code readers. The terminal operates for up to a hundred hours on four AA alkaline batteries. It provides up to 16KB of data storage.

26. Researchers at RCA Labs are testing teletext systems. These systems can be used to display news and weather information, present stock market quotations, or advertise shopping specials. A teletext system transmits data to television sets by encoding it in the vertical blanking interval (the black bar visible when vertical hold isn't working) of a video frame. Then a teletext decoder in the television decodes the data into text and graphics to be displayed on the screen.

protocol for error detection is XMODEM. It was developed and placed in the public domain by a Chicagoan named Ward Christianson—a fact that says something about the grassroots spirit of the early days of personal computer communications. Most standards in the computer world are set by large corporations or international committees.

Making the Connection

Dialing the telephone number of a computer is the easy part of establishing communications between computers. The hard part is setting your communications software to use the same protocol characteristics as the remote computer. Generally, this is done by making selections from a menu for such items as

- the baud rate. This depends primarily on the capability of the modems. Typical baud rates are 110, 300, 1,200, and 2,400.

- the number of start and stop bits. Most asynchronous links use one start bit and two stop bits per character.

- the parity setting. A **parity bit** is a redundant bit of information that allows the receiving computer to determine whether a character has been garbled in transmission. For example, if the parity setting is *even,* then the sum of all of the character's bits plus the parity bit should be equal to an even number. The possible parity settings are even, odd, and no parity.

Once all the necessary settings have been determined, they can be stored in a dialing directory. Re-establishing communications is then much easier than making the initial connection.

Whom to Talk To?

There is a bewildering diversity of computers and most of them—particularly the larger systems—can be reached by telephone. It would be impossible to describe all the applications of telecomputing, but we will touch on the major ones related to personal computing.

Public Access Message Systems

A relative newcomer to the telecommunications world is the **public access message system (PAMS),** which is often called a **bulletin board system.** Almost anyone who uses a personal computer can set up and operate a bulletin board system. All you need is a personal computer, a telephone line, a smart modem with auto-answer capabilities, and one of the many public domain PAMS programs. Very little marketing is necessary. Just place messages on the other PAMS in your area. Then load the program in your computer and let it answer the incoming calls.

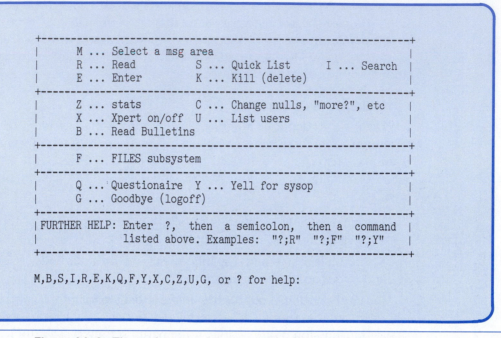

```
+-------------------------------------------------------------+
|      M ... Select a msg area                                |
|      R ... Read         S ... Quick List      I ... Search  |
|      E ... Enter        K ... Kill (delete)                 |
+-------------------------------------------------------------+
|      Z ... stats        C ... Change nulls, "more?", etc    |
|      X ... Xpert on/off U ... List users                    |
|      B ... Read Bulletins                                   |
+-------------------------------------------------------------+
|      F ... FILES subsystem                                  |
+-------------------------------------------------------------+
|      Q ...'Questionaire Y ... Yell for sysop                |
|      G ... Goodbye (logoff)                                 |
+-------------------------------------------------------------+
| FURTHER HELP: Enter  ?,  then  a semicolon,  then a command |
|              listed above. Examples:  "?;R"  "?;F"  "?;Y"   |
+-------------------------------------------------------------+

M,B,S,I,R,E,K,Q,F,Y,X,C,Z,U,G, or ? for help:
```

Figure 11.4 *The main menu from a public access message system.*

A PAMS responds to an incoming call by sending a "welcome" message and instructions about how to use the system. The instructions are usually easy to follow, though often they are quite condensed in order to save time for experienced users. It helps to have an adventurous spirit. Typically you choose an option from a menu of possible commands listed on the screen (see Figure 11.4). For example, typing "M" might allow you to leave a message on the bulletin board; "R" to read messages; and "D" to download a program. If you get confused, most systems display help information if you type "?" or "H."

Public messages can be read by anyone who wants to browse through them. Some systems allow private messages to be routed to specific recipients. Typically, as soon as you've logged on, a system informs you of private messages with a statement such as YOU HAVE 3 PIECES OF IN-COMING MAIL.

There are more than fifteen hundred PAMS in the United States. No one knows exactly how many there are because they can come and go at the flick of a switch. Don't be surprised if your first few calls to a bulletin board result in busy signals. The systems are popular, and most can communicate with only one user at a time.

All PAMS are not the same. Some cater to the users of particular types of machines, especially Apple IIs, Radio Shack computers, CP/M machines, and IBM PCs. Others are operated by manufacturers or vendors to promote their products. A few specialize in religious or sexual messages (DIAL-YOUR-MATCH). But because there is no charge for using a PAMS—except for the cost of the phone call if it is long distance—most systems are used by a wide range of people.

A main use of PAMS is to leave messages for people to read later instead of talking in "real-time." Some people use PAMS to jot graffiti; others, to discuss technical developments in computers. Most messages are heavily sprinkled with jargon related to computers.

Public access systems are used for more than just sending and receiving messages. Some systems allow you to play games. Many can upload and download programs. Still others allow you to order products or services from the system operator.

Other Personal Computers

Contrary to what the ads for the overnight delivery services say, the fastest way to move documents across the country is not to stuff them into an expensive air-delivered pouch. Instead, they can be transmitted quickly over ordinary phone lines between two personal computers. Each end needs a personal computer, a modem, and software that supports file uploading and downloading. At 300 bps a double-spaced ten-page report can be sent in slightly less than ten minutes. At 2,400 bps it should take about one minute.

Personal computers don't have to be the same model or brand to communicate over the phone. Characters traveling along a telephone line are represented in standardized codes and are interpreted by the receiving computer without regard to the brand name of the transmitting computer. Thus telephone links between computers can be used to sidestep the compatibility problems associated with floppy disks. A majority of today's personal computers use the same type of floppy disks (5 1/4-inch), but many different recording formats are used. As a result, disks filled with information frequently cannot be used to exchange information between different personal computers. For example, without a special program neither an Apple II nor an IBM PC can read files written by the other, even though they both accept the same blank disks. Although it may seem strange to have an Apple II phone an IBM PC sitting on the other side of an office, it might be the most convenient way to transfer information between the two.

A word of caution is in order. Just because it is possible to exchange files between different machines does not mean the files will be useful after they have been transferred. Most programs that execute on an IBM PC will not execute on an Apple II, and vice versa. It makes more sense to transfer data files such as a spreadsheet template or a word processing document.

General-Purpose Mainframes

A personal computer's ability to emulate a terminal allows you to tap the storage and computation resources of mainframe computers. Perhaps you need to analyze census data stored on magnetic tape. This requires access to a tape drive and good statistical programs. Chances are very good your personal computer doesn't have either. But with the right software it can emulate a terminal to use a mainframe. Many universities have mainframes with tape drives, excellent statistical programs, and the ability to crunch away on large data sets in short order, solving statistical problems in minutes that would take your personal computer days or weeks to solve—if it could solve them at all.

Linking personal computers with mainframes can transform communications in companies that have many branch offices. For example, a personal computer in each sales outlet can be programmed to phone the company's mainframe at predetermined times in the night, when long distance rates are low. Each personal computer might upload the last day's sales activity. After a minute of processing, the mainframe could download a list of replacement parts being shipped and a list of back-ordered parts. Then both computers could hang up, ready for the coming sales day.

Information Utilities

Companies that sell time on their timeshared mainframe computers have developed innovative services to attract customers. These companies, called **information utilities,** now offer services ranging from electronic mail to news stories, investment services, biorhythms, and travel guides. Three of the largest information utilities are The Source, operated by the Source Telecomputing Corporation; CompuServe, an H&R Block Company; and the Dow Jones News/Retrieval Service, operated by Dow Jones & Company, publishers of the *Wall Street Journal*.

Rates for using the services of information utilities are based mostly on **connect time,** the time you are logged on to the utility. The charges go from a low of $6 an hour to well over $100 an hour. Rates are higher during "prime time," which usually coincides with normal business hours. Normally you are billed at a higher rate if you use a 1,200-baud instead of a 300-baud modem. But a 1,200-baud modem can sometimes pay for itself if you can accomplish your work faster. Other fees can include one-time registration fees, monthly minimum usage fees, data storage charges (based on the number of bytes stored, if any), added charges for reading newsletters or searching databases, and charges for mailing letters and telegrams.

Here is a list of a few of the services offered by The Source.

- *Communications.* Allows sending electronic mail to the computer mailboxes of other subscribers, "chatting" with another subscriber through a keyboard-to-keyboard conversation, participating in on-line computer conferences, posting and reading messages on public bulletin boards, sending Western Union Mailgram messages, and mailing first-class letters.

- *Business and investment.* Includes instant stock and bond quotations, portfolio analysis, employment services, and an electronic version of the *Washington Post*.

■ *News and sports.* News stories from a variety of wire services including United Press International are stored for seven days. You can search for the news you want by using keywords.

■ *Consumer services.* Offers electronic catalog shopping for everything from air conditioners to Zenith utility software. Includes movie reviews.

■ *Travel services.* Includes complete airline schedules for all domestic and most international flights as well as the Mobil Restaurant and Hotel Guides.

One unique service provided by information utilities is the ability to search quickly through large volumes of information and find all items that match criteria you specify. Information utilities that specialize in storing and searching information are often called *encyclopedic databases, bibliographic databases,* or *on-line databases.* There are over a thousand on-line databases. Most cater to specific types of information—legal, medical, business, and so on.

Figure 11.5 *A sample search of KNOWLEDGE INDEX℠, a bibliographic database, offered by Dialog Information Services, Inc.*

```
?  BEGIN COMPUTERS AND ELECTRONICS ◄───────       I want to search COMPUTERS AND
Now in COMPUTERS AND ELECTRONICS                  ELECTRONICS, the index to computer
(INSPEC copr. IEE)                                and electronics magazines
Search No. 7482945

?  FIND PERSONAL COMPUTER AND ENERGY CONSERVATION ◄──   Find citations that discuss both personal
                                                         computers and energy conservation

    440  PERSONAL COMPUTER
    699  ENERGY CONSERVATION                            There are 440 citations on personal
S1    2  PERSONAL COMPUTER AND ENERGY CONSERVATION      computers, 699 citations on energy
                                                         conservation, and two articles that
                                                         discuss both topics

?  DISPLAY S1 ◄───────────────────────────────         Show me the first citation

    ENERGY CONSERVATION WITH A MICROCOMPUTER ◄          Article title
    JACKSON, D.R.; CALLAHAN, J.M.
    UNIV. OF CONNECTICUT ENERGY CENTER, STORRS, CT, USA
    BYTE (USA)  VOL. 6  NO. 7  178-208  JULY 1981 ◄      Name of periodical
    Document Type:   JOURNAL PAPER                       Date
    (4 Refs)                                             Abstract or Summary
    PRESENTS SEVERAL TOOLS THAT CAN BE USED IN CONJUNCTION WITH A PERSONAL COMPUTER
    —TOOLS THAT WILL ALLOW ONE TO UNDERSTAND ENERGYUSE PATTERNS AND CHANGE THESE
    PATTERNS WITH SOUND TECHNICAL AND ECONOMIC DECISIONS. TH    Here is all the information you need to
    PROVIDING A BACKGROUND ON HEAT TRANSFER AND HOW IT GOVERNS  obtain the article—the authors, title,
    IN A BUILDING. THEY OUTLINE AN EXAMPLE THAT DEMONSTRATES THE magazine, issue date and page number,
    MUST PERFORM TO DETERMINE THE YEARLY ENERGY REQUIREMENTS FC plus an abstract summarizing the content
    INCLUDED IN THIS EXAMPLE IS A PROGRAM THAT CAN BE USED TO SIMPLII THESE CALCULATIONS.
    THEY ALSO DISCUSS ENERGY CONSERVATION OPTIONS AVAILABLE AND HOW TO DETERMINE THE
    ECONOMIC PAYBACK TO IMPLEMENT THESE MEASURES.
    Keywords:  HEAT  TRANSFER;  PERSONAL  COMPUTING;  COMPLETE  COMPUTER  PROGRAMS;
    MICROCOMPUTER; PERSONAL COMPUTER; ENERGY-USE PATTERNS; HEAT TRANSFER; ENERGY
    REQUIREMENTS; PROGRAM
                                                         Keywords—These terms can be used
                                                         to find more articles on these concepts.

?  LOGOFF ◄──────────────────────────────────          I have enough information for now;
Leaving COMPUTERS AND ELECTRONICS                        please end this session
6/29/82   11:38:17 EST
0.031 Hours   $0.74   User U99999
```

Figure 11.5 illustrates how powerful this type of service can be. It shows the result of a search of KNOWLEDGE INDEX, a bibliographic database operated by DIALOG Information Services. In less than two minutes KNOWLEDGE INDEX searched more than a half-million citations from 2,300 journals and magazines to find the two articles discussing both personal computers and energy conservation.

Searching an on-line database is not as easy as Figure 11.5 might lead you to believe. Asking the proper queries takes a knowledge of the database's command structure and experience with what requests are likely to produce useful results. Beginners tend to ask questions that yield either no matches with their criteria or hundreds of matches. Neither result is particularly useful. Costs can accumulate quickly when you are paying from $20 to $100 an hour to do the searches. Some searches are best left to trained professionals, such as librarians or consultants. However, some on-line databases offer not only manuals but also excellent training courses on how to use their system. Figure 11.6 illustrates another approach: use a communications package tailored to the specific database being used.

Figure 11.6 *Texas Instruments' NaturalLink communications package. This package makes it easy to query the Dow Jones News/Retrieval service. The NaturalLink screen is divided into windows, each containing a list of words or phrases that will make up a portion of the command. The user simply selects one of the options and hits the [RETURN] key to make a selection. Based on what the user has chosen, the next set of options is displayed. Each element selected builds a portion of the English question used to obtain information from the Dow Jones News/Retrieval database.*

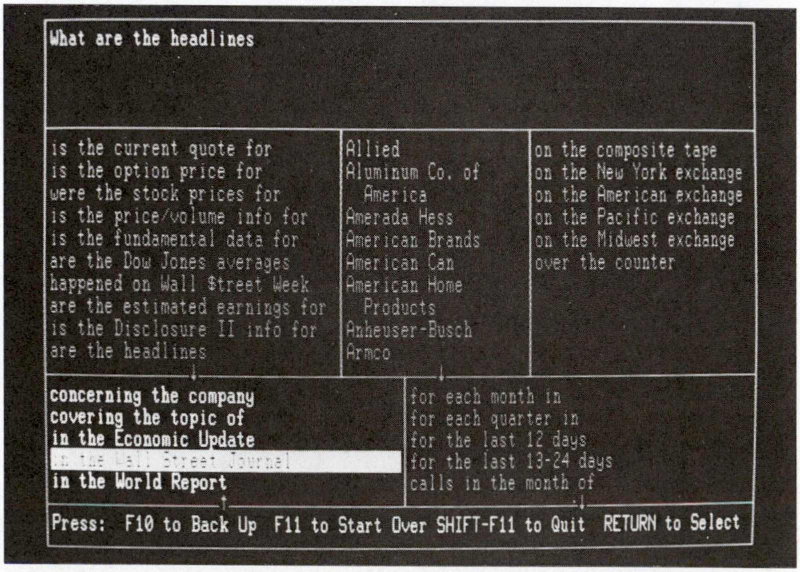

■ Computer Networks

So far our discussion of computer communications has been limited to simple point-to-point transmissions. A point-to-point communications link is like a conversation between two people. In contrast, a computer network links computers together in a web that allows transmissions among many devices, like a discussion among a roomful of people. A computer **network** is a collection of communicating computers and the communications media connecting them.

For example, computers can be connected to a local area network that bridges the gap between numerous personal computers, minis, mainframes, printers, and large-capacity storage disks. Like telecommunications, a **local area network (LAN)** provides a way of connecting computers, but a local area network links computers with other computing equipment within a limited area—for instance, in one building or industrial plant. Some local area networks are established to allow many personal computers to share an expensive peripheral device, such as a large hard disk or a high-quality printer. Other networks are established so that information can be shared conveniently, as in an interoffice electronic mail system.

A network is characterized by the media it uses to carry messages (wires, cables, microwaves, and so forth), the way in which the network links devices together (in a star, ring, or other pattern), and the expansiveness of the network—whether it is limited to one building or spans a continent. In addition, the network's communications protocols determine how and when devices can communicate. We explore all of these issues, but first we describe a basic shift in the costs of communicating and computing that encouraged the development of networks.

The New Economics of Computing

From the 1950s until the 1970s it was substantially less expensive to buy one large computer than to purchase two smaller computers that, combined, had the same processing power. To get the most from their computing dollars, organizations consolidated their purchases by centralizing data processing operations. Large host computers were timeshared among many users. Early systems hooked all equipment to the central computer, which was responsible for controlling all communications. In this way, early corporate users spread the cost of expensive mainframes over many users who shared access to the same equipment and information.

Most large computer systems still follow this pattern, but the cost of the links needed by centralized computing centers has not been falling as rapidly as the cost of computing, as shown in Figure 11.7. As a result, the cost of providing each user with a personal computer is about the same today as the cost of connecting an equivalent number of terminals to a timeshared mainframe.

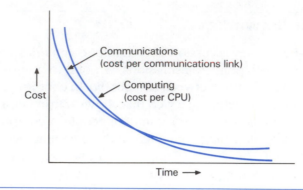

Figure 11.7 *The relative costs of communications and computing.*

The rush to buy personal computers in place of terminals has created a major shift from centralized to decentralized or distributed computing. In a **distributed computing** environment, geographically separate computers are connected in a network to work on a common task. This shift toward personal computers wasn't caused exclusively by economics; personal computers have many advantages over timeshared computing. They offer greater control to the user, "friendlier" operation, and a faster response for most tasks.

But decentralized personal computers have a major disadvantage: they are harder to link together to share information and peripheral devices. As the cost of the actual computer has plunged, the cost of peripheral devices has grown as a percentage of the total system. Expensive laser printers, high-precision graphical devices such as plotters, digitizers, and color displays, and the (relatively) high cost of storage devices have contributed to the need for interconnected workstations rather than separate personal computers. The economics of computing has dictated a new way to think about computing: share the peripherals and data, but disperse the processors to the people who need processing time and instantaneous response.

Communications Media

Many characteristics of a computer network—its speed, cost, and physical range—are largely determined by the media it uses to transmit messages.

Most telephone systems use **twisted-pair wire** to connect phones to the central switching station. Twisted-pair wire is inexpensive and is easy to run through walls in an office building. Its major disadvantage is its relatively low **bandwidth;** that is, its low capacity for carrying information. Twisted-pair wire is used in low-speed LANs (1 megabit per second or less).

A **coaxial cable** is a round cable in which one wire is a sleeve that shields the other, like cable TV wire. Coaxial cable offers much greater speed (up to

100 megabits per second) and is impervious to external electrical signals. It is used in high-speed networks where the cost of the cable is not an overriding concern.

A **fiber-optic cable** is a bundle of strands of glass that conduct laser light. Fiber-optic cables are rapidly replacing metal cables because they are lighter, cheaper, and capable of extremely high transmission speeds. A standard coaxial cable can transmit 5,000 voice conversations, whereas a fiber-optic cable can transmit ten times as many.

Wires and cables are suitable for connecting computers and devices when they are in the same room or building, but what about geographically distributed computer networks? Telephones and modems provide a low-speed method of connecting remote computers, but large corporations utilize other methods as well.

A **dedicated** or **leased line** is a special telephone line that connects a pair of computers. The advantage of a dedicated line is increased speed and continual availability. No dialing is required nor is a busy signal possible. A dedicated, point-to-point line is useful when large amounts of information are to be transmitted on a continual basis.

Microwave relay stations are used to transmit data and voice from one city to the next. Microwaves are extremely short radio waves that have a high bandwidth, but they cannot bend around the earth's curvature. A series of relay stations can connect corporate headquarters with dozens of branch offices. Renting time on microwave relay stations may be cheaper than renting a dedicated line.

A **ground station** may be used to send and receive information from satellites. Computers are excellent users of communications satellites because of their fast and constant transmission rates.

Mainframes communicate around the world through communications satellite **transducers,** which are similar to radio antennas. Because each communications satellite has many transducers, it is possible to rent one just as a company might rent a dedicated telephone line.

Transmission Efficiency

Most high-speed transmission methods, such as microwave relays or satellites, cost the same amount of money regardless of whether the entire transmission capacity is used. For example, it is not possible to install half of a satellite ground station. This has led to the development of clever ways to use the transmission capacity of high-speed communications links.

A **multiplexer** is a communications device that spreads the cost of a high-speed line over many users. A multiplexer timeshares the communications line by merging data from many users into the same line. There are two types of multiplexers: time-division and frequency-division.

A **time-division multiplexer** combines many low-speed channels into one high-speed transmission by interweaving them in time slots. Channel one is allocated time slot one; channel two time slot two, and so forth. The time slots are strung together like beads in a necklace and sent as one high-speed signal. When the signal is received, the low-speed signals are split out again and sent to their destination.

A **frequency-division multiplexer** divides the high-speed signal into frequency bands, like the frequencies used by FM radio stations. Each channel is assigned a certain band and the composite signal sent. At the receiving end the different channels are split out from their frequency bands and sent to their destinations.

Broadband transmission uses frequency-division multiplexing to transmit simultaneously text, data, and video or audio signals. This allows computers to handle a two-way video conference with a dispersed group of people who want to display computer-generated graphics as well as hear each other talk. In contrast, in **baseband** transmission the entire communications spectrum is dedicated to one form of information.

A **concentrator** is an ''intelligent'' multiplexer; it can perform preliminary operations on the data before it is multiplexed and sent to another computer. Thus it is an I/O device that unburdens the mainframe computer by taking care of many details of message transmission.

A **front-end computer** is a step beyond a concentrator in ''intelligence.'' A front-end computer handles all of the communications chores of the mainframe. This way, a mainframe computer is not constantly interrupted to acknowledge receipt of a message, to do multiplexing and demultiplexing, and to check for transmission errors. Some front-end computers perform rudimentary processing similar to word processing.

Network Topology

The efficiency, reliability, and cost of a computer network are also affected by its topology. A **network topology** is a kind of connection pattern. For example, a simple point-to-point topology connects a pair of computers together with a cable.

A more flexible point-to-point topology is obtained by linking computing equipment with a t-switch and cables (see Figure 11.8). With a **T-switch** you can rearrange the connections between computing equipment by turning a dial on the t-switch instead of unplugging and plugging cables. T-switches are inexpensive, ranging in cost from $50 to over $300. Their most common application is to allow several personal computers or terminals to share a peripheral device such as a printer or plotter. Printers are frequently shared in this way because they are used intermittently. It is often possible for several people in an office to share one letter-quality printer with little inconvenience.

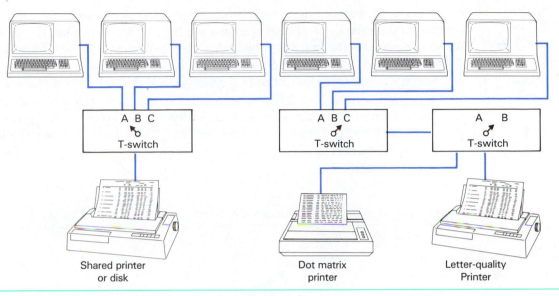

Figure 11.8 *Two t-switched networks.*

T-switched networks require human intervention to route signals to their destination. For this reason most people do not refer to them as computer networks, reserving the term for collections of computers and cables that can route messages automatically among devices.

A **star network** consists of a central computer surrounded by one or more satellite computers (see Figure 11.9). The central computer is called the *hub* because all requests for data must go through the central computer, which is called the *central server*. Star networks are simple but not very reliable—if the central server breaks down, the entire network is disabled in the same way that the failure of a timeshared computer system disables all users. Star networks are the dominant topology for mainframe computers and their peripherals, as well as for telephone systems.

A **ring network** consists of a cluster of computers connected by a ring (see Figure 11.10). In a ring network, failure of one computer does not prevent the other computers from interacting with the remaining computers. Rings are sometimes used along with a *token-passing protocol* to coordinate access to the network. A **token** is a control signal that determines which computer is allowed to transmit information. The token is passed from one computer to another computer, thus enabling each computer to use the network. Because only one token exists in the network, only one computer can use the ring at a time.

A **bus network** contains a single, bidirectional cable connecting one or more computers (see Figure 11.11). Information is passed between any two computers, one pair at a time, by seizing control of the common wire, or *bus,* transmitting a message, and then releasing the bus. Buses do not use the transmission media as efficiently as other network topologies because of the way traffic congestion can delay the use of the bus.

Bus networks often use a **CSMA** (carrier-sensed multiple-access) protocol to direct traffic on the bus. A CSMA protocol is similar to a party line in a rural telephone system. On a party-line phone, everyone is allowed to pick up the phone and talk if no one else is using the line. In a CSMA network, each device has access to the network when the network isn't busy.

Figure 11.9 *A star network. A central network server controls the network.*

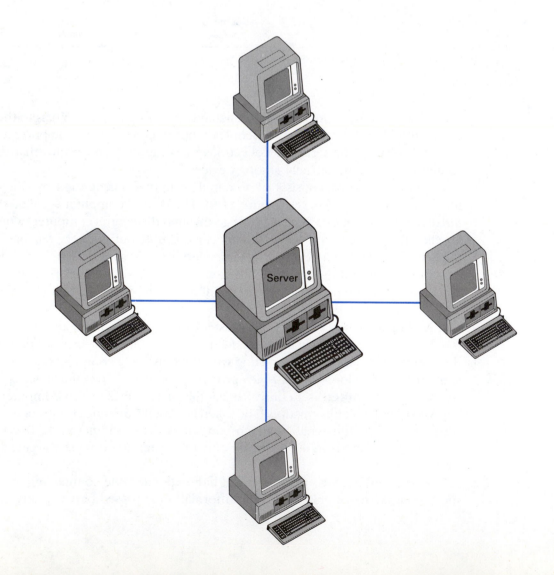

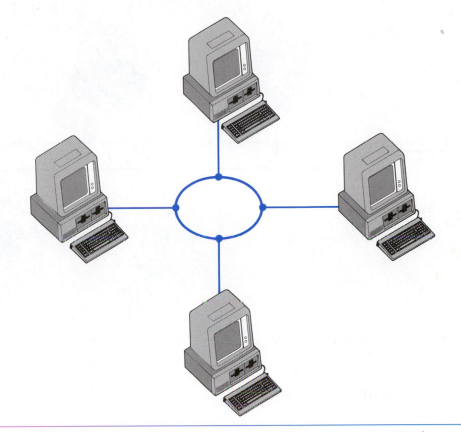

Figure 11.10 *A ring network. Messages are passed from one computer to the next along a ring.*

Two methods are commonly used to prevent devices from transmitting messages at the same time. With a CSMA/CA protocol (the *CA* means "collision avoidance") special circuitry in the LAN guarantees that only one device can transmit at a time. In contrast, with a CSMA/CD protocol (the *CD* means "collision detection") devices can begin transmitting any time the network isn't busy. Occasionally two or more devices might begin to transmit messages at the same time, causing the messages to be garbled. If this happens, each device stops transmitting and generates a random number specifying how long it must wait before it can try transmitting again. The difference between these two protocols is a subtle one, but a CSMA/CA protocol becomes more efficient as greater demands are placed on the LAN.

Bus networks offer more flexibility in how devices are wired together than star or ring networks. The simplicity of CSMA protocols (such as the Ether-net standard developed by Xerox) has made the bus topology very popular for small networks.

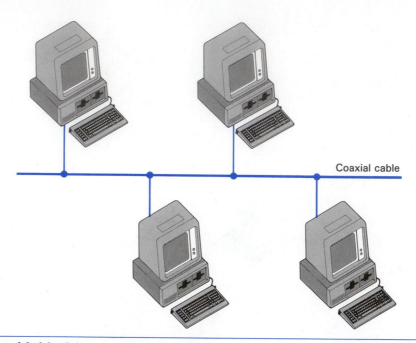

Figure 11.11 *A bus network. Messages vie for time on the shared bus.*

Coaxial cable

Packet-Switching Networks

Telecomputing can be expensive, especially if you make long distance calls during the day when rates are high. Instead, hobbyists do nearly all their telecomputing locally or in the evenings and on weekends. But there is another way of reducing telephone charges: you can use a **packet-switching network** such as GTE's Telenet or Tymshare's Tymnet.

Using a packet-switching network is just like dialing a remote computer directly—except that the response time is slightly slower, the log-on procedure is more complicated, and the cost is usually lower. In major cities (and some smaller ones) firms such as GTE and Tymshare have local numbers that you can dial to connect your computer to their network. If you don't live in an area served by a packet-switching network, you will have to make a toll call to the nearest city. Once connected to the network, you type the identifier of the remote computer you want. Then the packet-switching network takes over and routes information through the network between your personal computer or terminal and the remote computer.

Packet-switching networks are not free, but using one is almost always cheaper than making a long distance call of the same length. The networks can charge less than the regular long distance rates because they use the telephone system more efficiently than ordinary telephone calls. Most of a conventional call is spent waiting while the operator is thinking, reading, or typing at a slow rate. Packet-switching networks overcome this handicap by sharing the same communications channel among more than one user. Information is sent through the network in packets that include the packet's source and destination. Routing decisions are made by concentrators that send packets to each other over semipermanent telephone connections based on the addresses contained in the packet.

Using a packet-switching network in conjunction with the major information utilities is particularly convenient. Because these utilities have prior agreements with the packet-switching networks, you do not need a contractual arrangement with the network; the utility does the billing. Most utilities bundle the cost of using the network into their basic rate; others charge for it as a separate item on your monthly bill.

Local Area Networks (LANs)

A LAN is used to share peripherals and data among computers in close proximity. The LAN automatically routes messages among the devices on the network. A unique address is given to each device attached to the network. When one computer sends a message to another computer, the message is formatted into one or more packets in a manner roughly similar to that used by packet-switching networks. The packet contains both source and destination addresses so the LAN will know where to send the message.

Figure 11.12 *A local area network based on coupling devices to a common bus.*

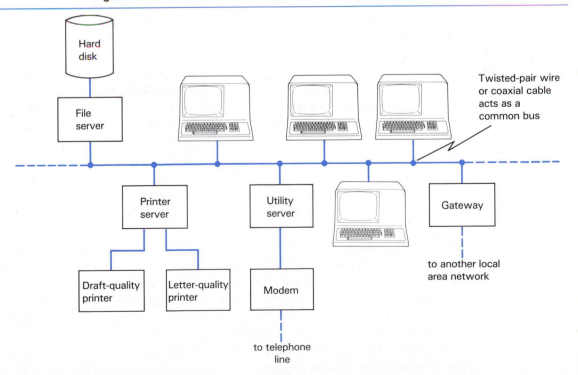

Figure 11.12 shows one configuration for a local area network: all of the network's devices, or **nodes,** are coupled to a common bus. The AppleTalk network shown in Figure 11.13 is an example of such a network. The network in Figure 11.12 includes the following:

- **File server.** A file server controls a hard disk and connects it to the network (see Figure 11.14). The file server is likely to establish a private storage space on the disk for each user as well as an area for public files. It may also keep track of passwords for files.
- **Utility server.** A utility server allows everyone on the network to use several peripheral devices, such as a modem or a plotter.
- **Printer server.** A printer server shares the access to the network's printers among all users. It is likely to include a memory buffer so that files can be accepted faster than the printer can print them.
- **Gateway.** A gateway allows devices on one network to communicate with devices on another network.

Because local area networks use digital transmission and cover a limited physical range (usually less than several miles), they can provide fast transmission rates. Less expensive, lower-speed networks use twisted-pair wiring. Even these networks transmit from 50 kilobits to 1 megabit per second—which is much faster than the usual speed of telecommunications over public telephone lines. Faster networks employ the same coaxial cable used in cable TV to provide transmission rates from 1 to 100 megabits per second. At 10 million bits per second the text in this book could be transmitted in 1 second. Such ultrafast transmission rates are important if many devices must send or receive data at about the same time.

To increase the speed of the network some LANs use a **cache,** a special memory buffer. The cache stores copies of the most recently retrieved records—hoping to save a transmission and disk-read. It is common for software to use file records more than once during a file-update cycle. If the desired record is in the cache of the computer that wants it, the overhead associated with message transmission and file retrieval is avoided.

Print spooling is a software feature of networks that helps to save time. Normally, when two or more computers want to use the same printer, one must wait while the other uses the printer. But with **print spooling,** the second computer is allowed to continue as if it also had the printer by *spooling* its output into a disk file. Then, when the first computer finishes with the printer, the spooled print file is copied to the printer. In the meantime, the second computer can continue without waiting.

Table 11.1 compares local area networks available for IBM PCs. The chart shows that local area networks differ greatly in price and capability. Notice that all of the LANs listed have a bus topology. But if a LAN requires a dedicated network server, it will run like a star network even though it has the physical pattern of a bus network. All requests for access to the disk and printer will be

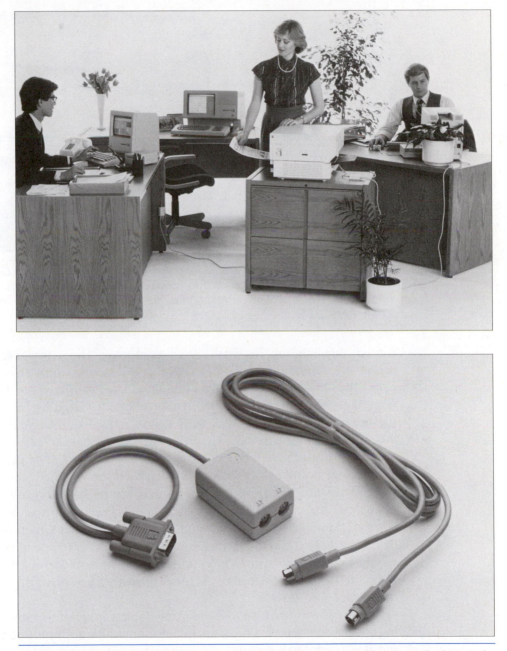

Figure 11.13 *The AppleTalk Personal Network allows up to thirty-two devices to be connected to a CSMA/CA local area network limited to 230 kilobits per second. On the top are several Macintosh computers sharing access to a LaserWriter printer. All that is needed to connect a Macintosh to the network is the $50 cable and connector box (shown on the bottom).*

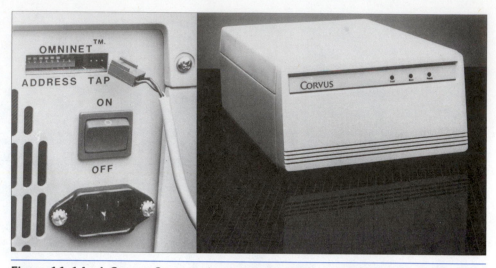

Figure 11.14 *A Corvus Systems hard disk attached to the Corvus Omninet, a network that supports up to sixty-four devices with a data transmission rate of 1 megabit per second. The connection is made with a simple plug on the end of a twisted-pair wire.*

routed through the network-server computer, thus decreasing the LANs usefulness. On the other hand, a LAN that does not require a dedicated server may have difficulty coordinating multiple access to a shared file. If two or more computers attempt to update the data stored in a shared file, a *race condition* (described in Chapter 10) may occur. Most networks use *file locks* or *record locks* to prevent the loss of data from race conditions.

From a user's viewpoint, the complexity of the LAN's communications protocol and cabling methods are hidden by layers of software. The LAN software makes the "other" disks and printers on the LAN appear as if they were connected directly to your computer. For example, suppose your computer has two floppy disks (labeled A and B) and the LAN has a hard disk file server (labeled disk F). Then to copy a file from the file server to one of your disks, you would use the same basic COPY command as you would to copy a file from one floppy to the other. Instead of copying from drive A to drive B, you might copy from drive F to drive B.

Special software for LANs can turn your computer into a mailbox for sending and receiving memos or a calendar for scheduling appointments. For example, if you want to schedule a meeting with three other people, you might run a special program on your computer that copies their appointment files to your computer, searches all four files (yours and the three others) for a mutually agreeable time, and then updates the files with the meeting's time and place.

LANs are so powerful that they threaten to take over the conventional functions of timeshared mainframes within large organizations. Because each computer in a LAN has its own memory and processor, a LAN that connects thirty personal computers can provide more computing power than a

TABLE 11.1 *Local area networks*

Vendor	Product	Speed (Mbps)	Protocol	Topology	Requires dedicated server	Supports multiple operating system	Caching	File locking	Record locking	Includes software	Print spooling	Cable type	Max. stations	Max. cable length (feet)	Gateway?	Price
Autocontrol Inc.	Soft/Net	1	CSMA	Bus	No	Yes	No	Yes	Yes	Yes	Yes	Coaxial	255	7,000	No	$1,195
Complexx Systems	XLAN	1	CSMA	Bus	XT	Yes	No	No	No	No	No	Twisted-pair	192	10,000	Yes	$1,450
Concord Data Systems	Token/Net	5 per 6 channels	Token passing	Bus	No	No	No	No	No	No	No	Coaxial	1,000 per Channel	20 miles	No	$3,485
Corvus Systems	Omninet	1	CSMA/CA	Bus	Recommended	Yes	No	Yes	Yes	Yes	Yes	Twisted-pair	64	4,000	No	$2,970
Davong Systems	MultiLink	2.5	Token Passing	Bus	No	Yes	Yes	Nop	Yes	Yes	Yes	Coaxial	255	20,000	No	$3,000
The Destek Group	Desnet	2	CSMA/CA	Bus	No	Yes	No	Yes	Yes	No	Yes	Coaxial	350	6,500	No	$2,800
Digital Micro-systems	HiNet	.5	SDLC	Bus	Proprietary	Yes	Yes	Yes	Yes	Yes	Yes	Twisted-pair or ribbon for short distances	63	5,000	Yes	$13,280
DY-4 Systems	Dynasty	1	CSMA/CD	Bus	Proprietary	Yes	Yes	Yes	Yes	Yes	Yes	Twisted-pair	64	4,000	Yes	$10,260
Fox Research Inc.	10-Net	1	Ethernet	Bus	No	No	No	Yes	Yes	Yes	Yes	Twisted-pair	32	2,000	No	$2,780
Gateway Communi-Cations	G-Net	1	CSMA/CD/ CA	Bus	XT	Yes	Yes	No	Yes	Yes	No	Coaxial	255	7,000	Yes	$1,995

Reprinted from *PC WEEK*, June 19, 1984, p. 48. Copyright © 1984 Ziff-Davis Company.

minicomputer. But the limitations of LANs should be remembered also. A LAN is restricted in size, and LANs can become bogged down just as mainframes do if there is too much activity on the network.

Network Layers

Networking is a rapidly changing area of computer and communications technology. This has led to a wide variety of nonstandard parts, diverse approaches, and general confusion. For this reason, the International Standards Organization proposed the ISO Reference Model for Open System Connection, or simply **ISO layers,** as a standard for describing and categorizing network components. The ISO layers are seven levels found in all networks.

Physical
Link
Network
Transport
Session
Presentation
Application

The *physical layer* defines the electrical characteristics of signals passed between the computer and communications devices such as a modem or a network interface adapter. The voltage levels, baud rate, and so forth are determined at the physical level.

The *link layer* controls error detection and correction, transmission over a single data line between computers, and the nature of the interconnection, such as whether it is synchronous or asynchronous.

The *network layer* constructs packets of data, sends them across the network, and "de-packetizes" the message at the receiving end. The *transport level* transfers control from one computer to the next across the network.

The first three layers (physical, link, and network) are wrapped together when the telephone and a modem are used. The network layer is the collection of telephone lines and switching equipment maintained by the telephone company. The link and physical layers are embedded in the modem and telephone sets at either end of the telephone connection.

The *session layer* establishes, maintains, and terminates logical connections called *virtual circuits* for data transfer. A **virtual circuit** links two devices in the network together temporarily in a manner analogous to the way a telephone call links two telephones. The session layer also enciphers data for security purposes (if necessary) and establishes the necessary handshaking such as full-duplex and message formatting.

The *presentation layer* defines the user's port into the network in terms of control codes, how data should be formatted, and other attributes specific to the message being transmitted. For example, the presentation layer defines what is a control code to "clear the screen." It may also define how data is to be formatted to conform to the format expected by the receiving computer's software.

Finally, the *application layer* consists of software being run on the computer connected to the network. The operating system software of a personal computer falls into the "application layer" as far as the network is concerned. Thus, copying a file from one computer to another computer on the same network is an application-layer operation.

As an example of how these layers interact, consider the problem of reading a record from a file on a remote computer's disk. Suppose the request to read the file comes from a database management program on a personal computer; thus it originates at the application level. The read request is passed to presentation-level software on the personal computer and is converted into the format defined by the presentation layer of the particular network being used. The formatted read request is passed on to the session-layer control program, which translates the logical name of the remote computer (such as drive F) into a physical name (such as device number 12,539), selects the protocol to be used (full- or half-duplex), and passes the message on to the transport layer. The transport and network layers work together to form one or more packets out of the message. The packet is guided through the network by the transport and network control programs. When the transport layer guides the packet containing the read request to the remote computer, it uses the link and physical layers. The link layer simply establishes an error-free connection from the sender to the receiver. Link control on a CSMA network would involve collision detection or avoidance, error detection, and retransmission of messages received in error. The read-request packet is passed through physical circuitry that obeys physical laws of electronics—transmission rates, coding conventions, and protocol. Once the packet reaches the remote computer, the transport and network software running on the remote computer de-packetize the message and pass it on to the session layer. The message works its way through the presentation layer to the application layer of the remote computer, where the read operation is done. Finally, the process is reversed to return the file record to the requesting computer.

All future computer networks are likely to follow the ISO layers we have described. This should make it easier to connect equipment from different manufacturers to the same network and for messages to be transferred from one type of network to another. But the techniques, performance, and cost of each new network will vary depending on the cleverness of the implementation.

■ Summary

The goal of telecommunications is to exchange information among machines. Through telecommunications a personal computer can be connected to virtually any other computer.

Data is transmitted through wires using digital and analog signals. Digital signals are used within computers, in most local area networks, and in some parts of the phone system. Generally, analog signals are used for computer transmissions over ordinary phone lines. Personal computers are attached to public telephone systems with a modem, which converts signals back and forth between digital and analog.

Communications software instructs a personal computer to behave like a computer terminal. After the ability to emulate a dumb terminal, the most important capability of communications software is the ability to upload and download files.

The purpose of a communications protocol is to establish a set of rules for computing equipment to follow while transmitting and receiving data. The protocol determines whether data are transmitted synchronously or asynchronously, with or without error detection and correction, in packets or one character at a time, with full- or half-duplex operation, and with local echoing or remote echoing.

Computers in a limited physical area can be coupled with other electronic equipment in a local area network. These networks provide faster data transfer than public telephone systems and allow many computers to share peripheral devices and information.

Key Terms

acoustic coupler	direct-connect modem
analog signals	distributed computing
asynchronous protocols	downloading
auto-answer	dumb terminal
auto-dialing	error detection and correction
bandwidth	fiber-optic cable
baseband	file server
baud rate	frequency-division multiplexer
broadband	frequency modulation (FM)
bulletin board system	front-end computer
bus network	full-duplex
cache	gateway
coaxial cable	ground station
concentrator	half-duplex
connect time	handshaking
CSMA	information utility
dedicated line	ISO layers
demodulation	leased line
dialing directory	local area network (LAN)
digital signals	local echo

microwave relay station
modem
modulation
multiplexer
network
network topology
nodes
packet-switching network
parity bit
printer server
print spooling
protocol
public access message system (PAMS)
remote echoing

ring network
smart modem
star network
synchronous protocols
telecommunications
terminal emulation
time-division multiplexer
token
transducer
t-switch
twisted-pair wire
uploading
utility server
virtual circuit

Discussion Questions

1. How does digital communication differ from analog communication?

2. What transmission methods are used by low-speed and by high-speed modems?

3. What are the relative merits of acoustic couplers versus direct-connect modems?

4. What are some situations in which uploading or downloading capabilities would be important?

5. How does a protocol control the exchange of information between computers? What protocols are used by personal computers?

6. What type of remote computer would you telephone if you wanted to
   a. try out telecommunications at the least cost?
   b. determine the price of gold on December 13, 1984?
   c. run a 10,000-line simulation program written in FORTRAN?
   d. send a first-class letter to your grandmother in Alaska so it will arrive within two days?
   e. exchange computer programs with another personal computer user?
   f. find out the final score of a basketball game that ended about an hour ago?

7. Why can a packet-switching network charge rates lower than those for normal long distance calls?

8. What are the major reasons for establishing a local area network?

9. What is the difference between a concentrator and a multiplexer?

10. How does a CSMA/CA protocol compare with a party-line telephone connection?

Exercises

1. Find out what public access message systems are available in your local area and the types of services they provide.

2. Use the listings in the Bibliography to ask some information utilities for information on their services and rates. (The utilities all have toll-free numbers.) Compare the services they offer and their rate schedules.

3. Examine the manual provided with a communications package. List the package's features and rank them according to which features you feel would be most useful.

4. Ask three companies that sell local area networks for information about their networks. Write a report comparing their strengths and weaknesses.

5. If a LAN transmits at 1 megabit per second, and ten computers are using it at the same time, what is the worst possible delay in copying a file across the network? Assume each of the ten computers is attempting to do the same thing: copy a 50,000-character file from one computer to another on the same network.

6. What is the difference between file and record locking? Is it possible to lock permanently an entire LAN so that nobody can use it by accidentally locking a series of files? (Consider the possibility that two computers may try to alternately lock a file and then print it.)

7. Frequency-division multiplexing can be used to combine slow transmissions to form a high-speed transmission. How might a two-channel broadband network be used to transmit simultaneously voice and computer data? How might this be useful for two people at distant locations who want to discuss a computer graphics display?

8. Light travels at 186,000 miles per second. Suppose a satellite averages 24,500 miles from the surface of the earth.
   a. If two computers next to one another transmit through a satellite directly overhead, how long does it take for one computer to receive one 8-bit byte of asynchronous data from the other computer? Assume transmission speeds of 9,600 bits per second. Because the transmission is asynchronous, each byte must be accompanied by 2 bits—a start and a stop bit.
   b. Now, assume that each byte must be acknowledged by the satellite, leading to a two-way handshake between the sender and the satellite, and another two-way handshake between the satellite and the receiver. Assume that a single bit is transmitted in each acknowledgment. How long does it take to copy 10,000 bytes from one computer to the other?

graphics

12

In 1962 Ivan E. Sutherland built a computer system that enabled a person to draw on a televisionlike screen. His device was expensive, slow, and not very sophisticated; but it was the beginning of modern computer-generated graphics. During the 1970s techniques for drawing on an electronic screen improved while the cost of computer hardware declined. Then in the 1980s low-cost RAM chips appeared that made it possible to store and quickly access a vast amount of information in a very small box at a very low cost. These chips gave graphics its biggest boost. Low-cost memory is ideal for graphical computing because "a picture is worth a thousand words" of storage.

We discussed one use of computer graphics earlier: to provide a *visual operating environment,* so that the computer uses pictures instead of text to communicate with you. In this chapter we describe other uses of computer graphics. We will see how you can display information as a graph or chart and how you can draw pictures, print them, save them in a disk file, and retrieve them for use later. Specifically, we will examine presentation graphics, graphics editors, and entertainment graphics. We will discuss both the technology and the usefulness of computer graphics. Before you continue reading this chapter, you should examine Window 7 on graphics.

■ Basic Concepts

The world of computer graphics can be broadly categorized according to the ways of generating the graphics and the types of uses. There are two ways of generating graphics—bit-mapped and vector graphics. Recall from Chapter 3 that a *bit-mapped* picture is one made of thousands of small pieces called pixels, and a *vector* picture is made of straight-line segments joined to form curves, circles, polygons, and so forth. The difference between these technologies is narrowing, but it still affects what you can do and how you can do it. A monitor is designed to generate either bit-mapped or vector graphics.

As Figure 12.1 illustrates, there are three main uses of graphics: entertainment, presentation graphics, and computer-aided design. The entertainment category is a catch-all category that includes numerous applications in art, education, animation, and games.

Presentation graphics is the term used to describe high-quality graphs, charts, and diagrams produced in order to present facts, trends, and comparisons in a report, meeting, or convention. Presentation graphics turn numbers into pictures so that they can be easily understood.

Often the ability to produce presentation graphics is built into spreadsheets, database, and word processing programs to aid you in analyzing trends, cycles, and other relationships in the data they store. For example, you might plot numbers from two rows of a spreadsheet in order to see the relation-

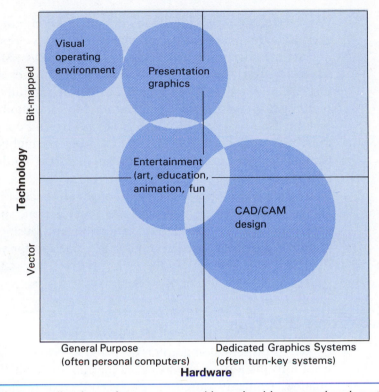

Figure 12.1 *Applications of computer graphics using bit-mapped and vector graphics technology.*

ship between two sets of data, or you might plot the numbers from one field of a database file against another to reveal the relationship between the two fields. In either case, you might then move the resulting graph to a word processor document for inclusion in a report. Some people consider this type of presentation graphics a separate category and call it **analytic graphics** because the resulting charts are used to analyze data and are less sophisticated than those produced by stand-alone programs.

A third use of graphics is for computer-aided design. For this type of computer graphics you need a **graphics editor.** It is like a word processor except that it helps you edit pictures instead of text. A graphics editor is used to create drawings on the screen with electronic tools such as a simulated paintbrush, eraser, pencil, and so forth. With a graphics editor you can then edit the sketch by moving, rotating, enlarging, and so on. Once you have obtained the desired design, the sketch can be printed. MacPaint and MacDraw are examples of graphics editors for the Apple Macintosh; PC Paintbrush and 4-Point Graphics from International Microcomputer Software are two examples of graphics editors for the IBM PC.

CAD/CAM (**c**omputer-**a**ided **d**esign and **c**omputer-**a**ided **m**anufacturing) programs are special-purpose graphics editors developed especially for designing and manufacturing new products. Many CAD/CAM programs perform **solids modeling**—producing three-dimensional images and cross sections of solids. A CAD/CAM system can aid in drafting, architecture, engineering, and building manufacturing tools for automobiles and similar industrial products. It may be used to design clothing, make advertising copy, or create props for a theatrical production. One CAD/CAM program might be used to design electronic circuit boards, another to design high-rise buildings, and yet another to design airplanes.

Graphics editors are also used along with special programs to create graphics for entertainment, computer-aided instruction, special effects in movies, and applications in the medical, scientific, and business worlds. The motion picture industry has used computer-aided design for years.

■ Presentation Graphics

Usually, a presentation graph is prepared for viewing by decision makers who want information in a compact but meaningful form. The information may be obtained from any source and can be entered from the keyboard. In a personal computer the most likely electronic sources are spreadsheet, database, or word processor files. To use most presentation graphics programs you must also own a graphics display device. In addition, a graphics printer or plotter is needed to obtain hard copy of the chart. A few programs, such as ChartStar from MicroPro, work without a graphics display; but if you do not have one, you cannot preview the graph on the screen before printing it.

Presentation graphs include line graphs, bar charts, pie charts, scatter diagrams (points "scattered" on an *x-y* grid), and a variety of other types of pictorial displays. Table 12.1 summarizes the kinds of charts typically available in each of a variety of programs. In the following sections we will describe these various types of charts; then we will discuss some of the features that simplify the creation of a graph or enhance its appearance.

Line Graphs

Simple *line graphs* are used to show the relationship between two or more variables. For example, you might use a line graph to depict the volume of integrated circuits sold versus time from 1964 to 1974, as shown in Figure 12.2. The volume is one variable and time is another variable; the line graph shows the relationship between them. Notice that Figure 12.2 also depicts the relation-

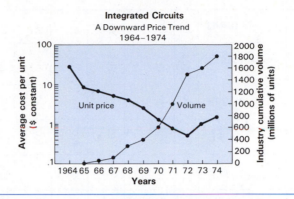

Figure 12.2 *Line graph with two vertical axes.*

ship between unit price and time. Thus it is actually two line graphs superimposed on the same time axis. As a result, the volume-time relationship can be studied in the context of the relationship between unit price and time.

Line graphs contain a heading, horizontal and vertical axes, scaling factors, and sometimes additional information such as a legend that explains the symbols used in the graph. The *heading* is simply a title placed at the top, bottom, or center of the graph. The vertical and horizontal *axes* are straight lines that have been labeled with numbers. Each axis is *scaled* so that the smallest and largest numbers fit on the axis.

When using a presentation graphics program to draw a line graph, you must specify the horizontal and vertical axes, scaling factors, and the variables to be plotted on the graph. Headings and legends can be added manually or automatically to the finished graph. For example, ChartStar from MicroPro requires that you

- select a linear or logarithmic scale for the *x*- and *y*-axes.
- give minimum and maximum values for both *x*- and *y*-axes.
- choose the color to be used by each line drawing.
- select the number of lines to be plotted on the graph.
- decide whether you want legends displayed.
- choose the symbols to be used in the line drawing, and the type of line.
- select the labels on the *x*- and *y*-axes.
- decide whether you want grid lines on the graph.
- determine the size of the units to be marked on the axes.
- enter any optional footnotes in the graph.

TABLE 12.1 *Presentation Graphics Programs and their Capabilities*

Vendor	Product	Types of Charts Available												
		Bar	Line	Pie	Text	Regression	Stacked Bar	Bar-Line Combination	Exploding Pie	3-D	Gantt	Bubble	Organization	Drafting
Analytical Software	Boardroom Graphics	Yes	Yes	Yes	Yes	Yes	No	Yes	No	Yes	No	No	Yes	No
Business and Professional Software Inc.	BPS Business Graphics	Yes	Yes	Yes	Yes	Yes	Yes	Yes	Yes	No	No	No	No	No
Data Business Visions Inc.	GDSS	Yes	Yes	Yes	Yes	Yes	Yes	Yes	Yes	Yes	Yes	Yes	Yes	Yes
Decision Resources Inc.	Chart-Master	Yes	Yes	Yes	Yes	Yes	Yes	No	Yes	No	No	No	No	No
Desktop Computer Software	Graph'n Calc	Yes	Yes	Yes	Yes	Yes	Yes	No	Yes	No	No	No	No	No
Digital Research Corp.	DR Graph	Yes	Yes	Yes	Yes	No	Yes	Yes	Yes	No	No	No	No	No
Duncan Atwell Computerized Technologies Inc.	LENIPREZ	Yes	Yes	Yes	Yes	No	Yes	Yes	Yes	Yes	Yes	Yes	Yes	Yes
Enertronics Research Inc.	Energraphics	Yes	Yes	Yes	Yes	Yes	Yes	Yes	Yes	Yes	Yes	Yes	Yes	Yes
Fox and Geller Inc.	Grafox	Yes	Yes	Yes	Yes	No	Yes	No	Yes	No	No	No	No	No
Ganesa Group International Inc.	Statmap (1)	No	No	No	No	No	No	No	No	No	No	No	No	No
Ganesa Group International Inc.	P.B.G.	Yes	Yes	Yes	Yes	No	Yes	No	Yes	Yes	No	No	No	No

Company	Product														
Graphic Communications Inc.	*Graphwriter*	Yes	Yes	Yes	Yes	Yes	Yes	Yes	Yes	Yes	Yes	Yes	Yes	Yes	No
Idea Ware	*The Grafix Idea*	No	No	Yes	No	No	No	No	No	No	No	No	No	Yes	Yes
Innovative Software Inc.	*Fastgraphs*	Yes	Yes	Yes	Yes	Yes	Yes	Yes	Yes	Yes	No	Yes	Yes	Yes	Yes
International Software Alliance	*Caligraph with Image*	Yes	No	Yes	No	No	Yes	Yes	No	No	No	No	No	No	No
Micrografx	*PC Draw*	drawing only													
Miracle Computing	*Graphit*	Yes	Yes	Yes	Yes	Yes	Yes	Yes	Yes	Yes	Yes	Yes	Yes	Yes	No
Mosaic Software Inc.	*Super ChartMan II ChartMan IV*	Yes	Yes	Yes	Yes	Yes	Yes	Yes	Yes	No	No	Yes	Yes	Yes	No
Omicron Software	*Plotrax*	Yes	Yes	Yes	No	Yes	Yes	No	No	No	No	No	No	No	No
Peachtree Software	*Business Graphics*	Yes	Yes	Yes	Yes	Yes	Yes	No	No	No	No	No	No	No	No
Plantronics/Frederick Electronics Corp.	*Draftsman for ColorPlus*	Yes	Yes	Yes	No	No	Yes	Yes	No	No	No	No	No	Yes	Yes
Prentice-Hall Inc.	*VCN Execuvision*	Yes	Yes	Yes	Yes	Yes	Yes	Yes	No	No	No	No	No	Yes	Yes
PC Software	*Executive Picture Show*	Yes	Yes	Yes	Yes	Yes	Yes	Yes	No	No	No	No	No	Yes	Yes
Redding Group Inc.	*GrafTalk*	Yes	Yes	Yes	Yes	Yes	Yes	Yes	No	No	No	No	No	No	No
Pixel Applications	*Pixel Visuals*	No	No	Yes	No	No	No	No	No	No	No	No	No	Yes	Yes
Softel Inc.	*Videogram*	drawing only													
Software Publishing Corp.	*pfs:GRAPH*	Yes	Yes	Yes	No	Yes	Yes	Yes	No	No	No	No	No	No	No
Software Solutions Inc.	*Graphease*	Yes	Yes	Yes	No	Yes	Yes	Yes	No	No	No	Yes	Yes	Yes	No
Willy Verbestel Inc.	*Micrograph by 2Y's*	Yes	Yes	No	Yes	Yes	Yes	Yes	No	No	No	No	No	No	No

Area-Fill Chart

Area-fill charts, like simple line graphs, are used to show the relationship between variables. But an *area-fill chart* includes some texture in the area under the line graph to increase the effectiveness of the presentation. For example, Figure 12.3 is an area-fill chart showing the ups and downs in the stock market.

Curve-Fitting Chart

A *curve-fitting graph* is a line graph in which the line is obtained by fitting a mathematical curve to the data. These curves are constructed with a mathematical technique called **regression analysis.** Most presentation graphics programs provide only a limited number of mathematical functions. Usually one function results in a closer fit to the data than the others. The idea is to find a mathematical relationship among the variables—if such a relationship exists—and to use the resulting curve to make predictions. For example,

- *Linear functions* draw a straight line through the raw data.
- *Weighted average functions* smooth out variations in the data by computing a weighted average of the last *N* data points.
- *Exponential functions* draw exponentially increasing (or decreasing) curves through the data.
- *Logarithmic functions* allow one or both axes to be compressed according to a logarithmic rule.
- *Power curve functions* draw a curve through the data by using the mathematical formula $\log y = b \log x + \log a$.

Often these curves are combined with other kinds of charts to show both the raw data and an approximate fit to a mathematical curve. For example, Figure 12.4 shows a bar graph of raw data along with a line obtained by fitting the data to a mathematical curve.

Figure 12.3 *Area-fill chart.*

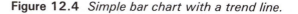

Figure 12.4 *Simple bar chart with a trend line.*

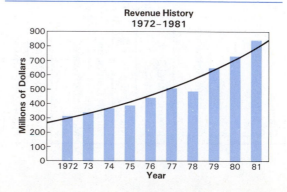

Computer Graphics: From Art to Computer-Aided Design

Most people think of a computer as a text and number processor, not as an image processor. This stereotype is changing quickly. Because manipulating images requires healthy amounts of storage and processing, the earliest users of computer graphics were draftsmen, cartographers, design engineers, and other professionals who could afford the expense. Only in the 1980s have low-cost memories and capable microprocessors brought computer graphics into wide use. Continued improvements in hardware will undoubtedly lead to even wider use of computer graphics. This photo essay provides a glimpse into the ''state of the art'' of computer graphics.

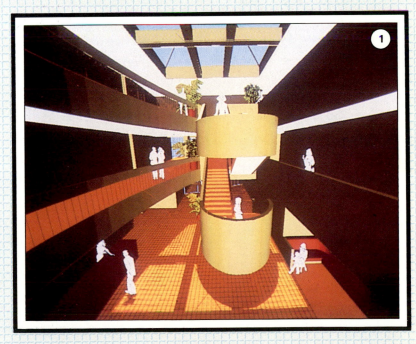

1. The architectural firm, Davis and Marks of Boston, Massachusetts, created this three-dimensional model of a lobby on an Intergraph color workstation for the Liberty Mutual Insurance Company. It shows several advanced features, including shadows and nonfaceted shading of curved surfaces.

DRAWING PROGRAMS

Drawing programs allow you to paint on an electronic canvas (the screen) with electronic brushes, pencils, spray-paint cans, rollers, and erasers. You create a drawing by selecting tools one at a time and then using them to draw. For example, to spray part of the screen with paint, you first pick up the spray-paint can from a toolkit shown on the screen. Then you move the can to the screen's drawing area and hold down the mouse's button. Picking up tools and using them is normally done by pointing with a mouse and clicking the mouse's button, but many programs also accept keyboard commands. When the drawing is finished, a printer or plotter is used to transfer the screen image to paper.

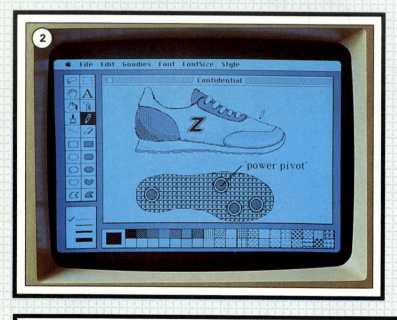

2. The MacPaint program from Apple has been a major reason for the popularity of the Apple Macintosh. MacPaint is fun to use and can produce extremely professional drawings.

3. This employment form was created using MacDraw and printed on the Apple LaserWriter printer.

The Watermill Restaurants, Inc.

125 West Broadway
Personnel, Suite 300
Cambridge, Ma. 02142

PERSONNEL REQUISITION

REQUISITION NO.

EMPLOYMENT SPECIALIST

JOB TITLE	DATE NEEDED

DEPARTMENT NAME/NUMBER	JOB LOCATION

SHIFT ☐ DAYS ☐ SWING ☐ GRAVEYARD	SALARY RANGE	☐ EXEMPT ☐ NON-EXEMPT

☐ PERMANENT ☐ TEMPORARY (DURATION)	PAY GRADE

☐ ADDITION TO HEAD COUNT ☐ REPLACEMENT (NO ADDITION TO HEAD COUNT)	NAME OF EMPLOYEE REPLACED

CAUSE OF REPLACEMENT

TO WHOM WILL EMPLOYEE REPORT?	WHO WILL CONDUCT INTERVIEW

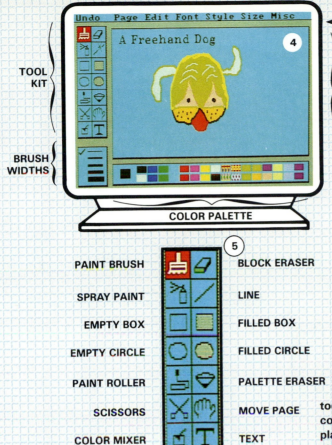

TOOL KIT

BRUSH WIDTHS

PULL-DOWN MENU BAR

DRAWING AREA

COLOR PALETTE

4. MacPaint's success has spawned many imitators. This drawing was created in a few minutes using PC Paintbrush, a color drawing program that runs on computers compatible with the IBM PC.

PAINT BRUSH — BLOCK ERASER

SPRAY PAINT — LINE

EMPTY BOX — FILLED BOX

EMPTY CIRCLE — FILLED CIRCLE

PAINT ROLLER — PALETTE ERASER

SCISSORS — MOVE PAGE

COLOR MIXER — TEXT

5. The PC Paintbrush toolkit. Electronic tools often perform better than their physical counterparts. For example, brightly checkered, plaid, or paisley paint can be sprayed from an electronic spray can.

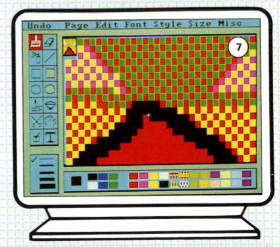

6. MacPaint and its imitators use pull-down menus to give access to the program's commands. For example, if you choose Brush Shapes from this menu, you can change the shape of the paintbrush's tip.

7. In this screen the drawing has been greatly enlarged so that the dog's red tongue fills the bottom of the drawing area. This enlarged display is created when you choose the option labeled FATBITS; it allows you to make tiny editing changes conveniently.

window 7

BUSINESS GRAPHICS

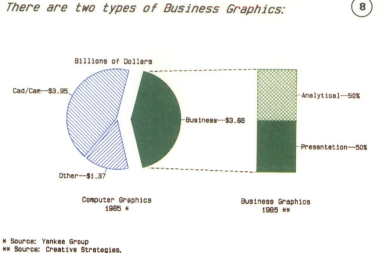

8. Graphs can help a business manager in two ways. First, a quickly generated *analysis graph* helps a manager find patterns and trends in otherwise meaningless tables of numbers. Second, a well-labeled *presentation graph* helps communicate a message to other people. This graph was sent to a plotter by Graphwriter, a graphics package for microcomputers that is designed expressly for preparing high-quality presentation graphics.

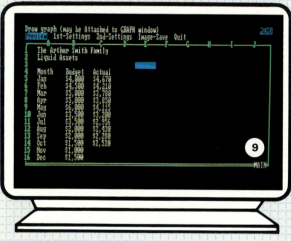

9. Many spreadsheet programs come with the ability to produce analysis graphs. This screen shows two columns of numbers stored in a spreadsheet created by Lotus Symphony. Symphony is a spreadsheet-based program that can produce line graphs, bar charts, pie charts, and stock market graphs.

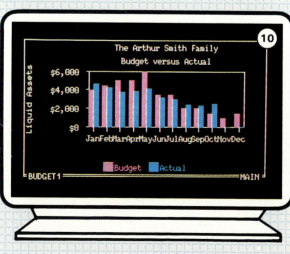

10. In this screen the Symphony program has converted the numbers from the spreadsheet into a bar graph. If the necessary raw data is already in the spreadsheet, it takes only a minute to create a graph of this complexity.

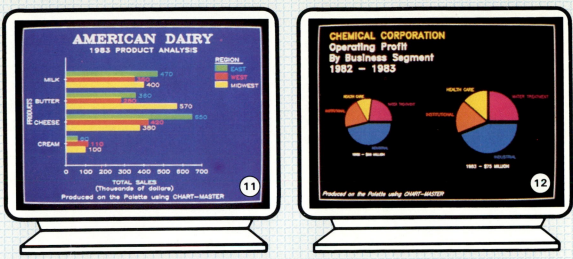

11,12. These presentation-quality graphs show better labels than most graphics packages can produce. Designing and entering high-quality presentation graphs require some skill and patience.

13. Text charts are useful for presenting lecture outlines, but surprisingly, many graphics packages can't create good-looking text charts.

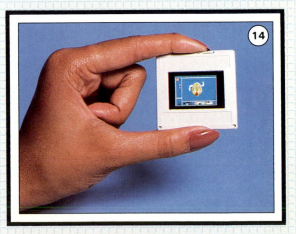

14. Once a graph looks OK on the screen, it can be reproduced on a variety of media. For example, the graph might be printed on paper, plotted on an overhead transparency, or photographed on a 35-mm slide.

window 7

ARCHITECTURE

Graphics and architecture have always been inseparable, but it has taken recent improvements in graphics hardware and software to bring computer-based methods into all phases of architectural design.

15. A CalComp computer-aided design system. Shown on the display, and on the pen plotter, is a drawing of a checkpoint for airport security.

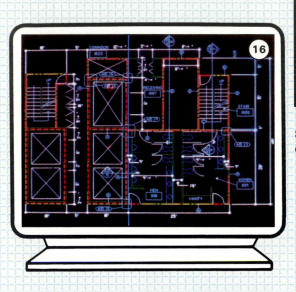

16. Complete floor plans can be displayed and modified before they are committed to paper.

17. Solids-modeling software can provide a three-dimensional view of a proposed design.

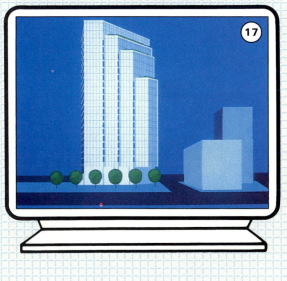

18. Three-dimensional views of the construction of a processing plant make it easy to see how pipes, equipment, and steel fit together.

CARTOGRAPHY:
THE ART OF MAKING MAPS

Digital mapping starts by capturing large geographical data sets in a map database. Then map analysts identify and correct errors and convert the data sets into useful maps.

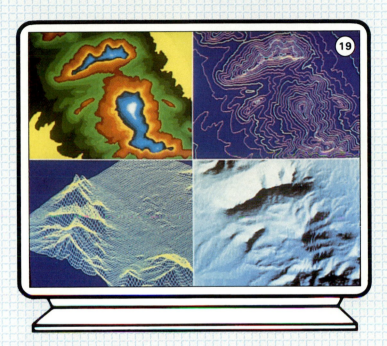

19. Once inside the computer, geographical data can be displayed in many ways. Here terrain is depicted by using (clockwise from upper left) color-coded elevations, contour lines, shaded relief, and rotated profiles.

20. This is a color-coded, shaded relief view showing features of the terrain as if they were illuminated from a light source above the screen. Shaded relief perspectives can even be displayed in stereo for viewing with 3-D glasses.

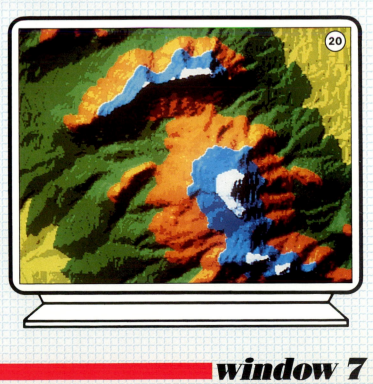

COMPUTER-AIDED MANUFACTURING

Numerically controlled machines and robots can execute very long sequences of movement commands precisely and quickly. But developing accurate sequences of commands is not an easy task. The process is accomplished more quickly and more reliably if the sequences can be simulated on a computer screen before they are tried on the actual machines.

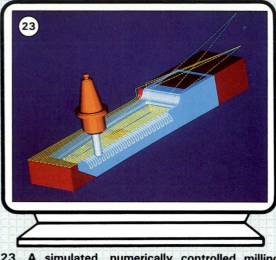

21. A simulated spot-welding operation.

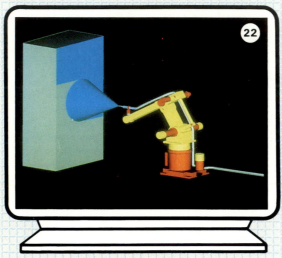

22. A simulated painting operation.

24. This crankshaft is modeled with Intergraph Sculptured Surfaces software.

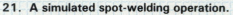

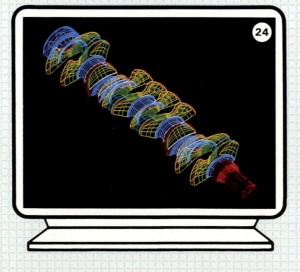

23. A simulated, numerically controlled milling sequence.

25. A die-forged crankshaft for a diesel engine.

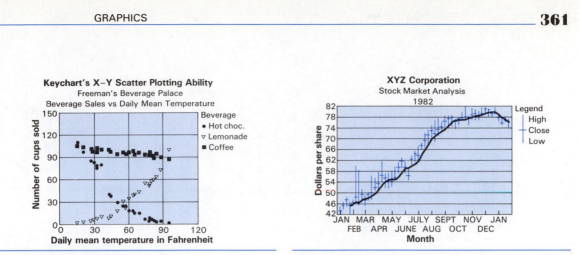

Figure 12.5 *Scatter diagram.*

Figure 12.6 *High-close-low chart.*

Scatter Charts

Scatter charts and diagrams are used to show the distribution of data values. You might use a scatter chart to show how different types of consumers buy different types of products, or how one kind of data is clustered around certain regions of the graph, as shown in Figure 12.5.

A special type of scatter chart, a *high-close-low chart,* is used in stock market analysis and statistical analysis to show the spread of values in certain data. Figure 12.6 shows a high-close-low chart for stock prices, but a similar scatter chart could be used to show the average value, plus or minus the standard deviation value, of SAT test scores among high school seniors over the past 20 years.

Bar Charts

A *simple bar chart* shows the variations in one set of values; a *multiple bar chart* illustrates the relationship between variations in several sets of values. For example, bar charts are commonly used to display changes in corporate revenues, expenses, and profits over a period of time.

Depending on the visual effect you desire, you might choose a simple bar chart, a chart with clustered or stacked bars, or a chart with bars displayed in a three-dimensional perspective. Figure 12.7 shows a simple bar chart with the different kinds of hatch patterns available in KeyChart, produced by SoftKey Software Products. A *hatch pattern* is a graphical texture used to distinguish one set of data from another set. Figure 12.8 shows a clustered bar chart in which four sets of data are compared by clustering four bars next to one another at each coordinate on the *x*-axis (that is, for each year). Clustered bar charts make it easy for you to contrast sets of values. Another way to compare sets of values is to use a stacked bar chart, as shown in Figure 12.9. Bars are stacked on top of one another at each coordinate on the *x*-axis, and different hatch

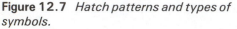
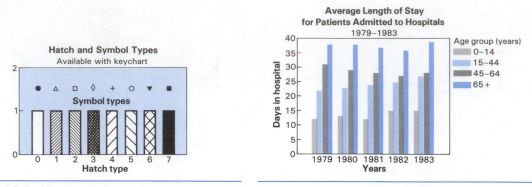

Figure 12.7 *Hatch patterns and types of symbols.*

Figure 12.8 *Cluster bar chart.*

patterns are used to distinguish each set of values. Such a chart might be useful to show how much each sales district contributed to the total sales of a national corporation in each of six months. Figure 12.10 shows a variation called the plus-minus bar chart. The vertical axis spans plus and minus values; hence the bars may extend below the *x*-axis as well as above it. The legend defines the meaning of each hatch pattern. Figure 12.11 shows another variation in bar charts: the horizontal bar chart. Turning the chart on its side may make it easier to understand, or it may simply be the best way to print the chart. A three-dimensional bar chart is like a clustered bar chart except that the bars in each cluster group are projected onto a three-dimensional cube. Your printed output will give the impression of depth: the clustered bars are placed one behind the other rather than next to each other.

To create a bar graph you not only select the type of bar chart but also enter into the drawing program

- the chart title.
- the number of bars per clustered group (if it is a clustered bar chart).

Figure 12.9 *Stacked bar chart.*

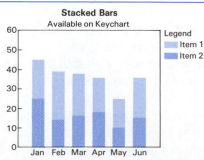

Figure 12.10 *Plus-minus bar chart with hatch patterns.*

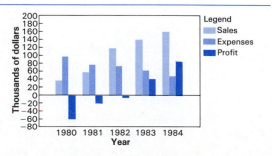

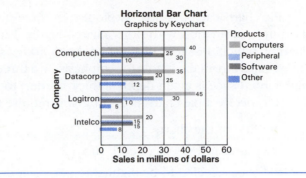

Figure 12.11 *Horizontal bar chart.*

- legends and hatch patterns.
- *x*- and *y*-axis labels.
- *x*- and *y*-axis minimum and maximum values.
- *x*- and *y*-axis scaling information.
- whether to display values at the top of each bar.
- whether to overlay a curve fit line.
- footnotes, such as the source of the data, date, and so on.
- other information such as the size and type of lettering.

Pie Charts

Pie charts are used to show parts (the slices) as a fraction of the whole (the pie), and to compare the sizes of the slices to each other and to the whole. For example, you might use a pie chart to show the proportion of dollars spent on various item in a budget, as illustrated in Figure 12.12.

Figure 12.12 *Pie chart.*

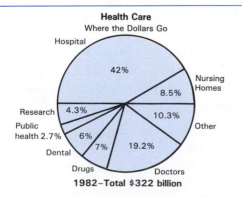

Figure 12.13 *Exploded pie chart.*

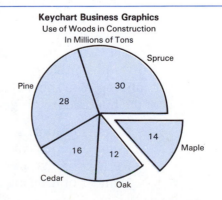

Pie charts can be simple, exploded, or three-dimensional, and they can be used in combination with other charts. Figure 12.13 shows an exploded pie chart on which the slices are hatched. An *exploded slice* is slightly disconnected and set apart from the whole for emphasis. In a three-dimensional pie chart, the highlighted slice is given depth (a thick border) to set it apart.

To specify a pie chart most programs require that you enter

- the title of the chart.
- the name and values of each slice.
- the slice selected to be highlighted or exploded (if any).
- whether the slices are to be displayed as a percentage of the whole or as actual values.
- the color, texture, and hatching patterns of the slices.
- other information such as footnotes.

Keep in mind that unlike a line or bar chart, a pie chart displays proportions rather than absolute values. A column of numbers is first totaled to obtain the whole, and then each number is divided by the total to obtain a percentage. The percentage determines the size of each slice in the pie.

A Summary of Features

A graphics package should allow you to enhance a graph by emphasizing certain phrases or headings through the use of different sizes and styles of characters. In addition, a good presentation graphics program can fit lines or curves to the points plotted in a graph. This feature is especially important if you want to make projections.

Some graphics programs are especially good for making overhead slide transparencies. A typical program lets you print or display part or all of a picture—sometimes in color—so you can copy it onto a transparency. Plotters will plot directly on an overhead transparency with the use of special pens. Additionally, a *slide show facility* allows you to play back a series of pictures directly from the computer's screen. The slide show facility lets you determine the delay between the presentation of each slide or overlay.

The extent and versatility of presentation graphics programs continue to grow, thus making the process of selecting the most suitable program confusing. You should consider the following features before purchasing one of the hundreds of programs now available:

Number of fonts	Transparency facility
Number of pen colors	Slide show facility
Number of text sizes	Data interchange
Number of hatching patterns	Math functions

Underlining?	Title lines
Italics?	Footnotes
Justify (left, right, center)	Chart types:
Help facility	clustered bar
Regression lines:	stacked bar
linear	line
exponential	scatter
logarithmic	pie
parabolic	area
Printer support?	combinations
Font styles:	On-screen preview?
bold	Memory required?
roman	Interface with graphic designs:
script	mouse
gothic	tablet
Helvetica	puck
	light pen

For example, version 1.3 of EnerGraphics from Enertronics Research Inc. sells for $350 and requires an IBM PC with 128K, a graphics adapter, and either a plotter or graphics printer. It has the following characteristics:

- Graphic formats are predefined, including screen formats, so you can use "standard" formats.

- Output is adjustable for paper, overhead transparencies, and film.

- Graphs can be produced with hatching, color, legends, headers, four fonts, unlimited font sizes, axis scaling, grid display, and automatic tic precision.

- The program accepts keyboard input and converts input from spreadsheet formats.

- Bar, line, curve-fit, pie, text, project-scheduling, organization, bubble, high-close-low, and three-dimensional surface charts can be constructed.

Most word processors, spreadsheets, and database managers can be used in conjunction with stand-alone graphics programs. For example, the MacWrite word processing program for Macintosh computers can import MacPaint and other chart-drawing program files into a document. Some spreadsheet and database management programs such as Lotus 1-2-3 and Jazz have their own chart-drawing capability; as a result, you can quickly convert numbers into graphs. In fact, this type of integrated graphics is becoming the most common form of presentation graphics. As a general rule, however, stand-alone graphics programs can create more sophisticated graphs and require far more effort than the graphics routines contained in integrated programs.

■ Integrated Graphics for Analysis

Integrated programs frequently offer graphing routines that allow data to be converted into simple on-screen graphs with a minimum of effort. In this section we will discuss how data is converted into a graph by the graphics routines of spreadsheets, word processors, and database management systems.

Spreadsheet Graphics

Suppose you are using a spreadsheet that can produce graphics. The spreadsheet contains a list of sales for each quarter of each of three years (see Figure 12.14). You can make a bar chart of a row or column from the data in the spreadsheet. For example, to draw a bar chart showing sales in each quarter of 1983, you ask for the graphics option of the program and then select the type of display to be used. The dialogs that follow show your response in color and typical computer prompts in black.

```
Graphics
Type: Bar
```

Then the program prompts you for the range of cells that provide the labels for the horizontal axis, as in

```
Horizontal: B2...E2
```

The horizontal axis is labeled with the contents of cells B2 through E2 (Qtr 1, Qtr 2, Qtr 3, and Qtr 4), as shown in Figure 12.15(a). Similarly, the dialog

```
Vertical: B3...E3
```

indicates that the vertical axis is to be made up of the numerical values in cells B3 through E3 (13,768; 19,850; 24,385; and 8,190). Notice that a horizontal row from the spreadsheet in Figure 12.14 is plotted vertically in the bar chart in Figure 12.15(a).

Figure 12.14 *Spreadsheet model of sales by quarter.*

	A	B	C	D	E	F
1			Quarterly Sales (× $1,000)			
2	Year	Qtr 1	Qtr 2	Qtr 3	Qtr 4	Annual
3	1983	13,768	19,850	24,385	8,190	66,193
4	1984	10,540	12,510	16,150	12,300	51,500
5	1985	14,100	9,360	11,325	15,612	50,397
6						

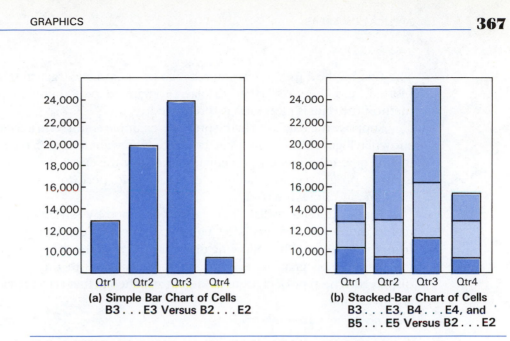

(a) Simple Bar Chart of Cells B3 . . . E3 Versus B2 . . . E2

(b) Stacked-Bar Chart of Cells B3 . . . E3, B4 . . . E4, and B5 . . . E5 Versus B2 . . . E2

Figure 12.15 *Typical bar graphs obtained from a spreadsheet.*

Now suppose you want to compare the sales in each of the three years. To do this you must select three vertical sets of data and plot them all on the same bar chart. You could use a stacked bar chart and stack one set on top of the other, or you could use three-dimensional or side-by-side clustered bar charts.

Suppose you want to obtain a comparison by drawing a bar chart with three vertical components: A, B, and C. The following dialog causes three vertical bars to be drawn for each quarter, as shown in Figure 12.15(b):

```
Vertical For A: B3...E3
Vertical For B: B4...E4
Vertical For C: B5...E5
```

The bars are stacked on top of each other and would appear in different colors on a color display or with different hatch patterns when printed.

Spreadsheet graphics allows you to plot any row or column of data against any other row or column of data. You can choose types of displays such as bar, line, or pie, as well as various combinations such as stacked bar or line bar. You can also save the graphical representation of the data in a disk file and retrieve it as you would retrieve a word processing document.

Database Graphics

You can construct a graph from the values stored in a database file either by extracting all the values at once and then using a plotting program to draw the graph, or by directly retrieving the data and plotting each value one by one.

The first method uses a data interchange program to extract the values to be plotted, and then a separate display program to plot them. In the second method the data is plotted as it is retrieved.

Suppose the data used in the previous example is stored in a database file as shown in Figure 12.16. This time, however, you want to draw a pie chart showing the quarterly sales as a percentage of sales for the entire year. To do this, the graphics program must total the sales in each field, perform division to obtain a fraction, and draw the pie chart.

Figure 12.17(a) displays percentages obtained by retrieving, totaling, and manipulating the raw data (sales figures), rather than displaying them directly from the database. The following dialog is typical of the way you would direct the graphics program to extract and total data before the percentages are displayed. The type of chart to be drawn and the file that is to provide the data are given first.

```
Graphics
Type: Pie
File: Quarterly
Fields: Qtr1
       Qtr2
       Qtr3
       Qtr4
```

The fields must be specified; then each record is retrieved, and the data from these fields are totaled. Because you do not want all records to be read, you must specify a search condition. In this example the search condition is that you want records only for the year 1983.

```
Match: YEAR = 1983
```

This causes the fields of only one record to be extracted and plotted, as shown in Figure 12.17(a).

Figure 12.16 *Database file containing quarterly sales.*

	Quarterly Sales File				
Year	Qtr 1	Qtr 2	Qtr 3	Qtr 4	Annual
1983	13,768	19,850	24,385	8,190	66,193
1984	10,540	12,510	16,150	12,300	51,500
1985	14,100	9,360	11,325	15,612	50,397

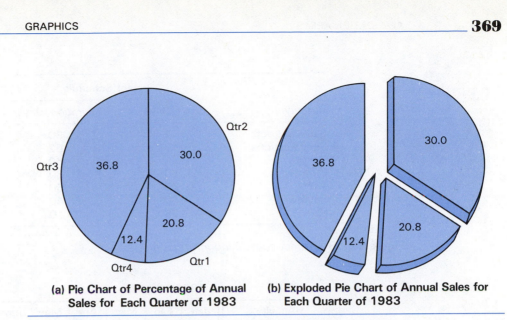

(a) Pie Chart of Percentage of Annual Sales for Each Quarter of 1983

(b) Exploded Pie Chart of Annual Sales for Each Quarter of 1983

Figure 12.17 *Pie charts plotted from a database file.*

The pie chart shown in Figure 12.17(b) contains the same results, but in exploded form. Exploded pie charts are easier to read than normal pie charts. When done in color, they add easy-to-understand meaning to numerical information.

Database graphs can be produced as bar, pie, line, and combination graphs in a variety of ways. Typically, you select one or more fields of each record to be plotted. These fields may be totaled to get a percentage, or the raw values may be used. Horizontal and vertical axes are selected when plotting a bar, line, or scatter diagram.

Word Processor Graphics

Once in a while you may want to take numbers from a document and turn them into graphs, but more often you'll want to cut a list of numbers from some other application and paste them into your word processing document as a graph. In either case the list of numbers is transformed into a diagram in much the same way as spreadsheet or database information is plotted.

Some word processing programs permit both text and graphics to coexist in a document at the same time. The Macintosh MacWrite word processor, for example, will accept graphics from the desktop clipboard, insert the graphics into a document, and both display and print the text and graphics. Most word processors require that you leave space for graphs within the text of the document, prepare the graphs with a separate program, and then manually paste them into the printed document. The details vary greatly from one program to another.

	Project Schedule	
Activity	*Start (Day)*	*Duration (Days)*
Sign contracts	1	30
Specifications	18	62
Design	50	60
Prototype	70	60
Test	125	50
Review	150	40
Final	175	10

Figure 12.18 *Project-scheduling information.*

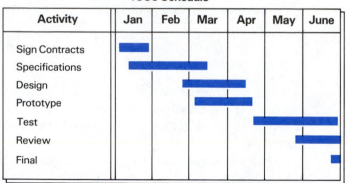

Figure 12.19 *Typical Gantt chart for project scheduling.*

Gantt charts are generally used in conjunction with a word processor. A **Gantt chart** plots activity on a project against time to provide a visual representation of a project schedule. For example, a Gantt chart can be constructed from a word processing file containing the text shown in Figure 12.18. This text gives the starting day and number of days required to complete each activity throughout the project. You simply tell the Gantt graphics program what date you want for Day 1 and where the three columns of data are stored. The program does the rest automatically, producing a Gantt chart like that in Figure 12.19.

■ Graphics Editors

A graphics editor is a program that draws graphical images by interpreting commands entered from a keyboard, mouse, touch-tablet, or light pen. There are two fundamentally different types of graphics editors: bit-mapped and vector graphics.

Bit-mapped editors store the screen image in memory as a grid of memory cells representing individual pixels. The screen image is constructed and modified by changing the values stored in the bit map. When you use a bit-mapped editor, drawing on the screen is similar to drawing on paper. In contrast, **vector graphics editors** build a mathematical model in memory of the objects to appear on the screen. The model consists of interconnected objects such as lines, circles, cylinders, boxes, and arcs. The screen image provides a view of how the mathematical model looks. Using a vector graphics editor is similar to constructing a model out of building blocks or the objects in a Tinker Toy set.

Bit-mapped editors excel in artistic applications, but they are not suitable for analytical applications such as finding the center of gravity of an object, rotating a three-dimensional model to view it from the side, or calculating the strength of a bridge. Thus, "paint" programs usually take a bit-mapped approach to graphics, whereas "analytic" programs take a vector graphics approach. These differing approaches show up in the way each editor operates.

A "Paint" Graphics Editor

In this section we describe a simple, general-purpose graphics editor using several examples. The details differ from one graphics editor to the next, but the general techniques remain the same. The example adopts a "paint" or bit-mapped approach similar to that used by MacPaint or PC Paintbrush.

Because a graphics editor processes pictures instead of text, it may seem unusual at first. Most graphics editors are driven by a menu of icons (called *tools*) or descriptive words that show what commands the editor can perform (see Figure 12.20). You tell the editor what to do by selecting an item from the menu—for example, by pointing with a mouse. The following list describes a few such commands:

- LASSO. Select an object on the screen for the purpose of moving, duplicating, or erasing it.
- SELECT. Select a region of the screen for the purpose of moving, duplicating, or erasing it. The difference between LASSO and SELECT is that by using LASSO you can select an object within a region without selecting the background surrounding the object (even though the background is within the region selected).
- PAN. Move your viewpoint around the drawing area. Since the drawing area may be too large to fit within the screen, PAN allows you to roam around a larger area than you can see on your screen at any one time.
- TEXT. Enter characters, numbers, or whatever from the keyboard.
- FILL. Add color, shade, or hatch patterns to an enclosed region by filling it with a pattern or color.

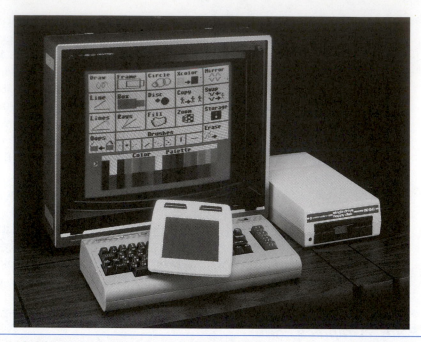

Figure 12.20 *An icon menu. Each command is represented on the screen by a picture of a tool.*

- SPRAY. Spray a mist or pattern on the screen.
- PAINT. Draw a line or brush stroke on the screen.
- RUBBER BAND. Draw a straight line from point A to point B. The line stretches from point A, like a rubber band, as you move its end point to point B.
- RECTANGLE. Draw a rectangle by selecting its upper-left corner and then rubber banding to its lower-right corner.
- POLYGON. Draw a polygon by pointing at and selecting its vertices.
- CIRCLE. Draw a circle by defining its center and radius.
- ERASE. Remove or erase everything from a certain region on the screen.
- CUT. Remove a portion of the drawing from a region of the screen and save it in the "scratch pad."
- PASTE. Copy the drawing from the "scratch pad" to a certain region of the screen.
- ROTATE. Rotate a region of the screen.
- ZOOM. Magnify or shrink a portion of the screen.
- MIRROR. Draw symmetrical patterns about one, two, or more axes.

- DRAG. Move a region or object across the screen.

- STRETCH. Distort an object or region by compressing or stretching it along the horizontal or vertical axis.

- GRID. Show a horizontal and vertical grid overlaid with the drawing.

A good way to see how a graphics editor works is to use it to draw a very simple picture. All pictures, no matter how simple or complex, are made up of many trivial graphical components. For example, the house shown in Figure 12.21(e) is actually made up of three rectangles, a triangle, and a freehand drawing.

The house was drawn by first selecting RECTANGLE from the menu. (This option might be called BOX or FRAME, as it is in Figure 12.20, or some other equivalent name in another graphics editor program.) If you are using a mouse, you select RECTANGLE by pointing at its icon and clicking the mouse button once. If you do not have a mouse, use the cursor-movement keys.

Next, move the pointer to where you want the upper-left corner of the rectangle to appear and hold the mouse button down while you drag the mouse toward the lower-right corner of the rectangle. When the lower-right corner has been reached, release the mouse button; the rectangle stays in place. If you are using a tablet, point by touching the surface of the tablet.

Figure 12.21 *Building a simple house using a graphics editor.*

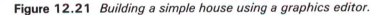

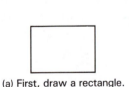

(a) First, draw a rectangle.   (b) Next, draw a polygon.   (c) Then a square.

(d) Fill the rectangular door
with a hatch pattern.

(e) Draw a freehand sidewalk.

To put the roof on the house as in Figure 12.21(b), select POLYGON from the menu. Next, move the cursor to where you want the top of the roof and click the mouse button once; then move to the lower-left vertex of the triangle and click a second time. Notice how the edge of the polygon follows the cursor—this is called *rubber banding,* for obvious reasons. At each vertex a click of the mouse causes the vertex to stay put and the next edge to stretch following the movement of the mouse. Finally, when the triangle is closed at the top vertex (you have gone all the way around the triangle), click the mouse button twice to indicate that you are done.

To construct a window, draw a second rectangle (a square) inside the first rectangle, as shown in Figure 12.21(c). The rectangular door shown in Figure 12.21(d) requires an additional touch. After you draw it, select FILL from the menu. FILL usually gives you a choice of patterns to use when filling in an enclosed polygonal area. Select a hatch pattern like the one shown in Figure 12.21(d), move the cursor to any point inside the rectangular door, and click the mouse button once. The entire door area will be filled with the hatch pattern.

To draw the sidewalk shown in Figure 12.21(e) select PAINT. When you use this command, shape and design depend on a steady hand. Hold the mouse button down while moving the mouse to draw the outline of the sidewalk. Your drawing may not be very smooth because the shape of the sidewalk follows the path of the moving mouse.

If you make a mistake or want to re-enter an object, select the UNDO command (OOPS in Figure 12.20); the last action you performed will be undone. Alternatively, you can remove portions of the picture by selecting ERASE. Most graphics editors offer numerous other options that we have not illustrated, such as aids for drawing straight lines, French curves, shading, texture, and so on.

A Vector Graphics Editor

In most of this chapter we discuss bit-mapped graphics because it is the most common technology in the personal computer world, but vector graphics editors are most commonly used for professional design and drafting on larger computers. Recall that a *vector* is defined by coordinates such as the locations of the end points of a straight line. This feature makes it possible for a computer to calculate mathematical properties of the objects on the screen, present different views or perspectives of the objects, and store drawings in much less memory space and perform operations that require greater precision and accuracy than is possible with bit-mapped graphics editors.

Vector-oriented editors can display their models on either raster scan or vector graphics monitors (see Chapter 3 for a description of these monitors). Graphical objects such as straight lines, circles, rectangles, and arcs are stored

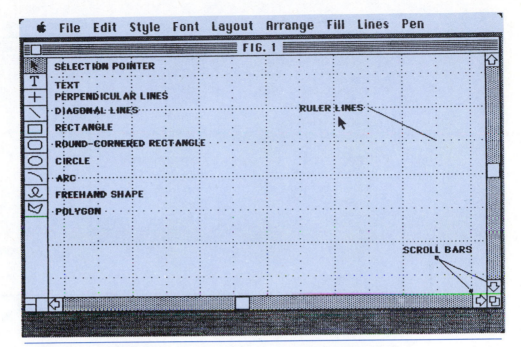

Figure 12.22 *MacDraw tools and drawing board showing rule lines.*

internally as vectors, but they can be displayed as bit-mapped regions on a raster scan monitor. Macintosh's MacDraw is a popular example of a vector-oriented editor that runs on a raster scan computer system.

The tools provided by a vector-oriented graphics editor are very similar to the tools of a "paint" graphics editor, but they behave differently. Figure 12.22 shows the tools provided by MacDraw; text, lines, rectangles, circles, and polygons are all represented by small icons at the left of the drawing area. To draw an object, first click a tool with the mouse, and then place the object on the drawing board.

Vector-oriented editors are used to obtain very precise drawings (for architectural, engineering, and design work). For this reason the MacDraw drawing board is calibrated in 1/2-inch horizontal and vertical ruler lines. This grid is very precise, allowing you to place an object within 0.05 inch of where you want it. In fact, MacDraw has a grid mode that automatically displays the horizontal and vertical coordinates as you move an object around the drawing board.

Figure 12.23 shows one of the menus. Selecting the Drawing Size option allows you to set the size of the drawing board in 8-by-10-inch pages. Figure 12.24 shows how to select the number of pages used in your electronic drawing board.

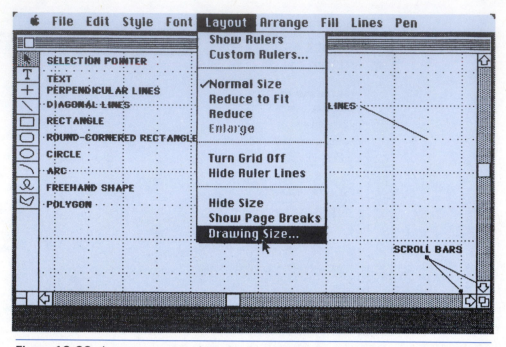

Figure 12.23 *Layout menu and a selection—to set the size of the drawing board.*

Figure 12.24 *Your drawing board can be up to 12 pages wide by 5 pages long. Each page is 8 inches wide by 10 inches long, thus permitting accurate drawings up to 100 inches wide by 50 inches long.*

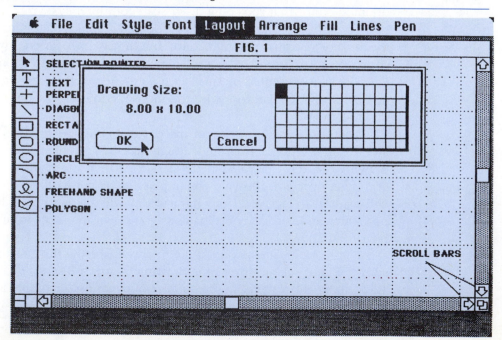

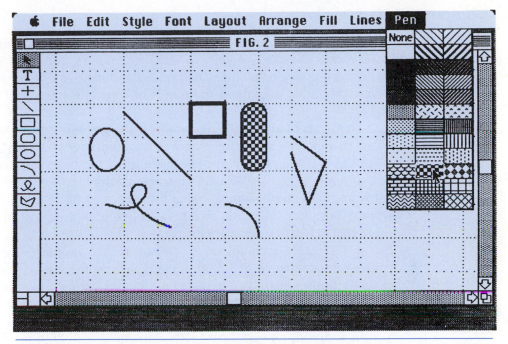

Figure 12.25 *Some vector objects obtained by using the tools shown at the left of the drawing board.*

Each tool produces a graphical object that is described by one or more vectors. In Figure 12.25 the circle tool was used to draw the circle, the diagonal-line tool draws the diagonal line, and so forth. The circle is defined by a center point and its radius; the diagonal line by the locations of its end points; and the triangular-shaped polygon by the locations of its corners. Even though these objects are displayed on a bit-mapped screen, they are manipulated as vectors.

You cannot erase part of a vector, move part of it, or merge it with another vector object. Instead, the entire vector is moved, overlapped with other objects "behind" it, and erased as a complete entity. The inner region of a vector can be filled, as shown by the checkerboard pattern in Figure 12.25. The texture of lines can be changed, even after the object has been drawn, by selecting the object and then choosing a pen texture.

Vector objects can be measured, rotated, overlapped, printed, and mathematically "smoothed." When stored, they take up less space than bit-mapped images. For example the examples shown in Figure 12.25 require less than 2KB of disk space when MacDraw is used, but they occupy 6KB when converted to a MacPaint bit-mapped image.

Because vectors are mathematical objects, meaningful mathematical calculations can be performed on them. For example, vector graphics editors are used to prepare the models of physical objects that are submitted to finite element analysis programs to determine the object's strength, flexibility, or other properties (see Window 1, Computer Applications).

Computer-Aided Design

CAD/CAM systems are used to design and manufacture cars, boats, tools, high-fashion dresses, shoes, jewelry, pottery, computers, computer software, special effects in motion pictures, newspaper and magazine advertisements, consumer products, maps, and thousands of other products and services used daily.

The heart of all CAD/CAM systems is the graphics editor, which lets you enter, manipulate, and store images in the computer system. However, most CAD/CAM graphics editors use special-purpose hardware and software as part of a turn-key system. A *turn-key system* is a complete system of hardware and software purchased together so that the user need only "turn the key" to get started. Turn-key CAD/CAM systems are not cheap; they cost from $10,000 to more than $100,000 per workstation.

A CAD/CAM graphics editor uses a mouse or puck the way a word processor uses a keyboard. Both input devices control what goes in the computer. A mouse can be used to draw lines, circles, boxes, and so forth, much as a keyboard is used to enter characters and numbers into a computer. Figure 12.26 shows a designer using a puck to digitize graphical data.

In addition, powerful computers equipped with high-resolution displays are needed in solids modeling as shown in Figure 12.27. A solids-modeling graphics editor is capable of showing three-dimensional images and cross-sections of images in solid form. Notice the contrast and texture that can be

Figure 12.26 *A designer using a puck to enter very precise graphical data into a CAD/CAM editor.*

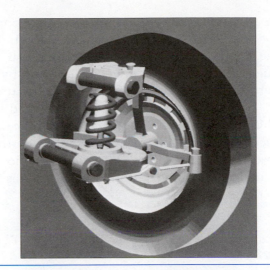

Figure 12.27 *Display from a solids-modeling editor.*

produced by using a solids-modeling graphics editor. Figure 12.28 shows a nonsolid display of a three-dimensional drawing. The computational requirements of the editor used to create Figure 12.28 are much less demanding than that required by the editor that created the image in Figure 12.27.

Figure 12.28 *Arcad's interactive design system provides a library of 2,000 standard symbols to use in architectural drawings.*

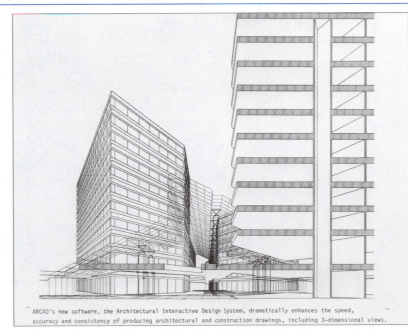

ARCAD's new software, the Architectural Interactive Design System, dramatically enhances the speed, accuracy and consistency of producing architectural and construction drawings, including 3-dimensional views.

The ultimate in CAD/CAM is the CAM portion—computer-aided manufacturing—which is the portion that produces the manufactured goods. For example, after a designer perfects a circuit board, the CAM system is supposed to guide the production of the circuit boards by controlling machinery, creating parts lists, and generating the production artwork masters.

CAD/CAM systems are often integrated with numerically controlled machines. The CAD/CAM system might produce a punched tape containing the directions for an automatic lathe or a list of instructions for a welding robot. The instructions are loaded into the machine tool or robot. Parts are then manufactured, tested, and adjustments made until the production line is perfected.

Art and Animation

Both computer art and animated graphics have exploded onto the technological scene since the invention of low-cost personal computers. High-resolution graphics systems have replaced canvas, brush, and paint with the electronic stylus and color monitor. The computer has given the artist an extremely fast and versatile tool.

Figure 12.29 *Still-frames of a flying bird.*

Animation is just one of the many possible uses of computer-aided design, but it is perhaps the most intriguing aspect of computer art. Cartoonists in the motion picture industry have produced animations for more than half a century. An image of a person appears to move if a series of still-frames is shown in rapid succession. The same idea is used in producing animation in a computer. A picture is *animated* by moving one or more objects across the screen. Actually, an object can be rotated, translated (moved to a new location), or both rotated and translated simultaneously.

If the motion takes place fast enough to simulate life, we say the animation is done in **real-time.** A real-time animation usually involves more complex motion than simple rotation and translation. For example, a picture of a person walking across the screen requires movement of the whole object (person), movement of parts of the object (legs), and a fluid coordination of the moving parts (coordination between legs and body).

Suppose you want to animate a flying bird, as shown in the still-frames of Figure 12.29. The still-frames are made by reproducing the bird's body and changing the position of the wings. The frames (e)–(g) are identical to frames (a), (b), (c). But in frames (a)–(d) the wings move down; in frames (e)–(g) the wings move up. The bird will appear to fly when the still-frames are rapidly displayed, erased, moved, and subsequently displayed on the screen. The animation is controlled by a sequence of commands similar to

```
DRAW FRAME (a)
ERASE
MOVE
DRAW FRAME (b)
ERASE
MOVE
DRAW FRAME (c)
ERASE
MOVE
```

You can repeat the sequence for as long as you want. You would have to draw more complex sequences to achieve more realistic animation, but the concept is the same.

A number of sophisticated animation programs are designed to aid in the production of games and educational software. One of the most promising and interesting uses of animation is in the creation of interactive stories. In an **interactive story** the outcome is not known beforehand. In fact, each time the story is played back, a different ending may be possible. The story changes according to the interaction between the computer and the human. The script may produce one result when a person answers yes to the question, Should the hero go into the cave?, but another result when a person answers no to the same question. Because of this interaction, interactive stories are more complex than a movie or play.

Digitized Images

One of the fastest-growing areas of computer graphics and bit-mapped graphical editing is the field of **digitizing** images; that is, converting a photograph, landscape, or other visual image into a bit-mapped image using a camera or special light-detector. The camera or light-detector converts various shades of gray into pixels and feeds the pixels into the computer's memory.

Figure 12.30 shows the result obtained by digitizing a black-and-white drawing using the Macintosh and a light-detector called Thunderscan. Thunderscan replaces the ribbon in the Apple Imagewriter printer—thus making the Imagewriter *read* from the paper, rather than print on it. This extremely clever digitizer is simple: a light is cast onto the paper and the reflected light is registered by a light-sensitive detector. The detected light is converted into various shades of gray, sent to the computer, and displayed on the computer's screen.

Figure 12.31 shows what the Macintosh screen looks like while Thunderscan is digitizing the image inserted into the Imagewriter printer. You can

Figure 12.30 *Digitizing images.*

(a) Original drawing to be digitized

(b) Digitized image from Thunderscan

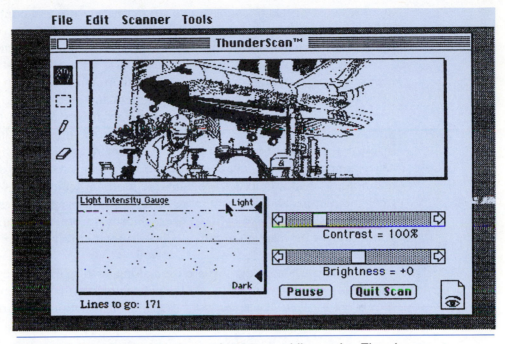

Figure 12.31 *Viewing window as it appears while running Thunderscan.*

adjust the contrast and brightness levels of the digitizer to suit the original image. After the image has been entered, you can modify it to change shading, cut and paste parts of the original, and copy the image to MacPaint.

Digitizers provide a quick way to enter images into a computer. Then you can use an editor to modify, enhance, or erase portions of the image. On a personal computer the image looks rough because the resolution is low. On a larger computer the resolution might be high enough that you would have difficulty differentiating between a computer image and a regular television image. In fact, many special effects on television and in motion pictures are nothing more than enhanced computer-generated images.

■ Summary

There are three general categories of graphics programs: (1) presentation graphics for drawing bar charts, graphs, and business diagrams; (2) graphics editors for doing CAD/CAM and generalized drawing; and (3) educational and entertainment graphics.

Presentation graphics programs are frequently used in conjunction with spreadsheets, word processors, and database managers. They produce specialized graphs and charts for the purpose of communication and analysis.

Most graphics editors work in conjunction with programs for designing new products, tools, or parts. They work with input devices such as a mouse or puck and with output devices such as plotters and graphical printers.

The simplest graphics editors simulate an artist's tools in the way they draw on the screen. These "paint" programs store the screen image as a bit-map in memory. The most sophisticated CAD/CAM graphics editors store the object being drawn as a mathematical model in memory using vector graphics technology. Vector graphics programs are more difficult to use when drawing freehand pictures, but they are more accurate for lines and other well-behaved mathematical shapes like cylinders and ellipses. Another advantage of vector graphics over bit-mapped graphics editors is their ability to store compact images on disk.

Special-purpose programs are used along with graphics editors to create entertainment graphics, such as animated sequences that are played back as if they were movies. These are used in games, instruction, and artistic applications that require special effects.

Key Terms

analytic graphics
bit-mapped editor
CAD/CAM
digitizing
Gantt chart
graphics editor
interactive story
presentation graphics
real-time
regression analysis
solids modeling
vector graphics editor

Discussion Questions

1. Vector graphics is a much older technology than bit-mapped graphics. Explain why advances in RAM technology have made bit-mapped graphics dominant in personal computers. What are the advantages and disadvantages of each?

2. Presentation graphics can be created from the graphics option of a word processor, spreadsheet, or database manager or from a stand-alone presentation graphics program. Discuss when you might prefer to use each of these programs to create a bar chart.

3. How might rubber banding work with RECTANGLE, CIRCLE, and POLYGON commands?

4. What is PAN and ZOOM? What is the difference between FILL and SPRAY?

Exercises

1. Become familiar with a bit-mapped graphics editor. What is the difference between the PAINT and DRAW commands?

2. Use a graphics program to duplicate the spreadsheet graph shown in Figure 12.15(b). Count the number of keystrokes needed to modify a single cell of the spreadsheet and then to redraw the graph.

3. Show how a stick figure is animated by drawing a six-frame sequence of still-frames. Use a graphics editor to draw the six frames.

4. How much memory would it take to store a 780-by-520-pixel bit-mapped display, assuming 8-bit bytes? Suppose each pixel can take on 16 colors and assume that the 16 colors are encoded in 4 bits. How many bytes of memory would be required? How many 640-by-320-pixel images would fit on a 360KB disk?

5. Suggest how a word processor could be designed to handle both text and graphs within the same document. What problems with disk space do you suppose would be encountered for the word processing files?

6. Use a database manager to create a file containing the following information:

Year	Barrels
1978	1,051,345
1979	1,967,002
1980	835,981
1981	955,300
1982	1,000,382
1983	1,499,999
1984	2,044,678
1985	2,894,053

Construct a bar chart plotting barrels versus year and then a pie chart in which each slice of the pie shows the percentage of the total number of barrels in a year.

7. Dot matrix printers use a form of printer graphics to print characters. Compare the character patterns of a bit-mapped display with the character patterns of a dot matrix printer.

software review

13

- **Utilities**
  File Recovery and Conversion
  Sorting Programs
  RAM Disks and Desk Accessories
- **Business Applications**
  Home Finance
  Business Accounting Systems
- **Vertical Market Applications**
- **Education**
  Drill and Practice
  Training
- **Entertainment**
  Video Arcade Games
  Adventure Games
  Simulation

13

The software in a computer system adapts a general-purpose computer to a specific task. Because computers are normally purchased to solve specific problems rather than to provide raw processing capabilities, software has fueled the sales of computers. For the same reason, it's a good idea to choose the software you want to use before you decide which computer to purchase. For example, a dietician may purchase a particular computer because it runs a program that offers special features for producing diets customized to the needs of individual patients. Or a company may purchase a computer because it runs a particularly good set of accounting programs. These decisions eventually make some computers a success and others a failure, depending on the software available for them.

Throughout this book we have examined the features of productivity software. These general-purpose application programs—for word processing, spreadsheets, data management, graphics, and communications—are useful to just about everyone and illustrate concepts relevant to all computer programs. But it is important to remember that productivity software is only a small portion of the software for computers.

Software developers have produced a program for virtually every conceivable application. There are literally tens of thousands of programs aimed at small markets for special purposes, such as analyzing the strength of I-beams, controlling laboratory equipment, or copy-protecting disks. Often, using a special-purpose program will provide a much better solution than adapting a general-purpose application program.

For convenience, software is grouped into categories by function and by application area. In this chapter we try to give you a feel for the range and diversity of programs in a few categories. Specific programs will be highlighted as examples of typical products in the various categories. The chapter is not comprehensive; many application areas are not even mentioned. The purpose of the chapter is to increase your awareness of special-purpose programs, so that you will look for appropriate programs whenever you are faced with a special or unusual problem.

Utilities

Utilities are programs that help you use the operating system more effectively. A variety of utility programs come with the computer's operating system; for example, most people would consider the program that formats a disk to be a utility program. Other utilities can be purchased to supplement and fill gaps in the operating system. Here are a few of the hundreds of types of utility programs.

- *Sorting utilities* order the items in data files.

- *Editors* create, save, and edit programs and data files.

- *Copy-protection* utilities make disks that cannot be copied by standard disk-copy routines.

- *Copy-cracking* utilities make copies of copy-protected disks.

- *Keyboard-enhancement* utilities allow a number of keystrokes to be assigned to a single key.

- *Screen-display design* utilities assist in creating and changing screen displays.

- *Security and access control* programs ensure that access to data and program files is limited to authorized users.

- *Resource optimization* utilities monitor the performance of the system, optimize the organization of data on direct-access storage devices, maintain utilization statistics, and so forth.

Because utility programs are system programs, they are frequently geared to the technical needs of programmers and may not be easy to use.

File Recovery and Conversion

More often than users would like, a file is deleted accidentally. The file is still on the disk, but it is no longer listed on the disk's directory. If you write another file on the disk, it may take the space occupied by the erased file; but as long as the erased file is still on the disk, it can be recovered. A **file recovery** utility guides you through the steps of recovering an erased or damaged file.

The procedure for recovering files depends on the operating system and on the file recovery utility. Often the process is easier if you remember the size of the erased file or its relative position in the disk's directory. If you don't remember this information, the recovery program will scan the directory for entries that look valid and attempt to recover them. If this effort is not successful, it may read the entire disk, looking for areas that resemble files and asking if any of the files it has found is the desired one.

File conversion utilities help you cope with the frustrating problem of incompatible file formats. You may locate a much-needed file or program but discover that it is in the format for a different type of disk, a different operating system, or an application program that uses a unique storage format. Conversion utilities allow one computer to read and copy disk files from another computer, to convert files between operating systems, and to convert application program files. For example, you might use a conversion utility to read a Kaypro II disk on an IBM PC or to convert WordStar document files into standard DOS files.

Sorting Programs

Ordering information is one of the most common tasks performed on computers. With a **sorting program** you can choose to sort information with one or more sort keys—such as name, age, social security number, or zip code. Efficiency is crucial because sorting a large set of records can take a long time. Hence almost all sorting programs are written in assembly language.

Important differences among sorting programs include the types of keys allowed, the maximum key size, and the maximum number of sorting keys. Another important feature is the ability to be used conveniently with a wide variety of data file formats.

RAM Disks and Desk Accessories

To be compatible with small personal computers, many programs are designed to use only a certain amount of main memory—say, 64KB or 256KB. Even if a computer has additional memory, these programs will not use it. But if you have a RAM disk or a desk accessories program, you can make good use of this "extra" memory.

A **RAM disk** (also called an *electronic disk*) is a program that makes part of memory appear to other programs as if it were a high-speed disk drive. Because the access time for main memory is much less than for mechanical disk drives, RAM disks can make programs run substantially faster, especially programs that must access the disk many times. However, if you want the RAM disk files to be permanent, you must remember to save them on a magnetic disk.

A **desk accessories** program provides an instantly available kit of tools such as an electronic calendar, calculator, and note pad. The desk accessories program is loaded into memory before any application programs are run and stays in this reserved area of memory even when other programs are executed. Normally the desk accessories program is inactive, allowing other programs to function without interruption. You activate the desk accessories by giving a special keystroke combination such as pressing the [CTRL] and [ALT] keys at the same time. Once activated, the program suspends the current application program and presents itself through windows on the screen.

Figure 13.1 provides an example. It illustrates Sidekick (Borland International, Scotts Valley, California), which won *InfoWorld* magazine's Software

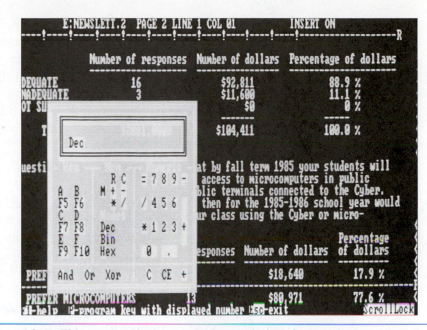

Figure 13.1 *This screen shows a calculator window from a desk accessories program that is superimposed on a memo being edited with WordStar. The desk accessories program has suspended WordStar while the calculator is being used.*

Product of the Year award in 1984. The screen shows a WordStar word processing session in which the user has activated a Sidekick calculator window to do some quick arithmetic calculations. The calculator is superimposed on top of the WordStar display. Other Sidekick desk accessories include a monthly calendar for all months from the year 1901 through 2099; a phone directory for storing names, addresses, and phone numbers; an autodialer for placing phone calls (a modem is required to use this function); and a note pad for jotting down notes and editing files. Pressing [ESC] deactivates Sidekick, causing its windows to disappear and the application program to continue from wherever you were when you activated the desk accessories.

■ Business Applications

Business applications are the most common use of mainframe computers and one of the most common uses of desktop personal computers. A few types of business programs include the following:

■ *Tax planning and preparation* programs compare alternative tax strategies and help prepare tax returns. Tax planning programs allow you to perform "what-if" calculations to explore the effects of various tax shelters, changes in income, depreciation methods, individual retirement accounts, estate plans, and the like. Tax preparation programs help you fill out the tax return itself. Often they can print directly on the IRS forms and schedules.

■ *Stock and bond analysis* programs are tools for screening, evaluating, and selecting investments. Some of these programs focus on *technical analysis,* an analysis of the security's market price and volume statistics. Other programs stick to analyzing *fundamentals;* that is, facts from past financial statements, expected earnings, or subjective evaluations of the company's management and products. Both types of programs allow you to establish a database of information on a list of securities to be tracked. Information can be entered into the database by hand, but most programs can also extract the necessary information automatically from an information utility such as the Dow Jones News/Retrieval Service. Once the information is in the database, the program can identify securities having specified characteristics, print reports, or display graphs.

■ *Real estate analysis* programs can provide guidance on transactions that would take hours to calculate by hand. Typically these programs can perform many types of investment comparisons, such as comparing the costs of purchasing and renting, calculating a loan amortization schedule, projecting a cash flow, calculating the annual return from owning a property, or determining if it is possible to qualify a buyer for a particular property.

■ *Inventory management* programs assist with the planning, purchasing, and distribution of inventory. For example, a *requirements planning* program combines a manufacturer's production schedule with information in the firm's bills of materials (which is a list of the parts that go into a product) to arrive at a schedule of when parts should be ordered. A *vehicle scheduling and loading* program determines an efficient way to transport materials to numerous locations, taking into account the physical constraints of the available vehicles.

■ *Time management and billing* programs keep track of the time a professional spends on a client and generate the appropriate bills.

■ *Project management* programs schedule tasks, allocate resources, and monitor the progress of a project.

■ *Accounting* programs record and summarize the effects of business transactions. Because this is an essential activity of every business, accounting software is the most common type of business software. Most *home finance* programs are simply accounting programs designed for the limited needs of a family instead of a business. Because of their importance, we will examine some of the characteristics of accounting programs for both home and business uses.

Home Finance

A home finance program helps record, summarize, print, and graph financial transactions. Basically it is a miniature accounting system designed to be used by a family.

Home finance programs almost always use full-screen menu prompts to guide the user through the process of making selections (see Figure 13.2). This means that you don't have to memorize cryptic commands before beginning to use the program.

Figure 13.2 *The main menu of the Dow Jones Home Budget program.*

```
                                MAIN MENU

    ACCOUNT/CODE NAMES

    BALANCES
                                              ENTER FIRST
    DESKTOP CALCULATOR                        LETTER OF A
                                              COMMAND:
    ENTER TRANSACTION
                                                 OR
    HARDCOPY TOGGLE
                                          * TO TERMINATE SESSION
    MONTHLY SUMMARY

    POST AUTOMATIC TRANSACTIONS

    RECTIFY TRANSACTIONS

    START NEW MONTH
                                          409 transactions entered
    TRANSACTIONS LISTING                      12-25-1986
                                                 00:27:46
    UTILITIES

    2 ND LEVEL MENU
```

```
          Ken White's Personal Finance System          Page 1
                     CHART OF ACCOUNTS
                      as of 12-25-86


Account                      Short  Type of   Beginning   Current
Number   Account Name        Name   Account   Balance     Balance
-------  -------------------- ------ --------  ----------  --------------
  10     Gasoline            Gas    Expense        0.00           43.12
  20     Entertainment       Fun    Expense        0.00           17.00
  30     Credit Union        CU     Asset     24,633.50       25,580.12
  40     Savings Account #1  Sav1   Asset        417.97          620.80
```

Figure 13.3 *The first page of Ken White's chart of accounts.*

Like all accounting systems, a home finance program operates with the help of a chart of accounts. You must tell the program what accounts you want when you set up the system, but it should also be possible to modify the chart of accounts later. For example, with the program shown in Figure 13.2 you would type an *A* to add or change entries in the chart of accounts. Figure 13.3 illustrates the beginning of a chart of accounts.

Once the chart of accounts has been established, you can begin entering transactions. On many home budgeting programs it is possible to correct a transaction that has been entered in error. For example, with the system shown in Figure 13.2 you would begin correcting a transaction by typing an *R* for RECTIFY TRANSACTIONS from the main menu. In contrast, many business accounting systems do not allow erroneous transactions to be corrected directly; instead you must enter a new transaction to adjust for the erroneous one. This restriction makes unauthorized tinkering with the accounting records more difficult.

You can write transactions down on paper more quickly than a home finance program can record and enter them, but this type of system pays off when you want to generate reports. You should be able to display or print a cash-flow statement, a personal net worth statement, and various types of transactions listings. In addition, most systems allow you to graph the activity in each account or account category. These graphs can show trends in your spending that you hadn't noticed before.

A home finance program will not help if the only accounting activity you do each month is to balance your checkbook—that can be done more quickly by hand. But if you are already recording your expenses, a home finance program can make the process more reliable and improve the quality of information received from your efforts.

Business Accounting Systems

Figure 13.4 gives an overall view of the accounting system of a small business, with a dashed line around each component. A business may purchase a stand-alone program for each component or an integrated accounting system that links all the components. Stand-alone components are fine for businesses that are gradually converting to the computer, but they may make it inconvenient to transfer or receive information from other components. An **integrated accounting system** is designed so that individual components can function either independently or together.

Just as in a manual accounting system, the general ledger is the heart of a computerized accounting system. Information from the other components is

Figure 13.4 *Overview of an accounting system for a small business.*

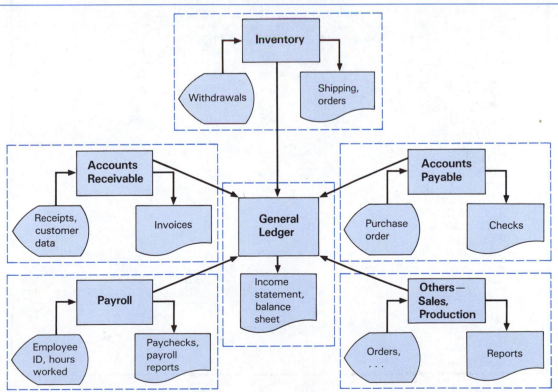

fed into the general ledger as well as the balance sheet, income statement, and other reports generated from the general ledger. For example, Peachtree Business Accounting Software is a menu-driven integrated accounting system. It includes modules for the general ledger, accounts receivable, accounts payable, inventory control, payroll, fixed assets, job cost, and sales invoicing. Figures 13.5 and 13.6 are from the payroll module. Figure 13.5 is the screen display for changing personal information about an employee. The editing commands are described in the lower right portion of the screen. Square brackets surround the field to be changed; you can move these brackets from field to field with the tab key. Figure 13.6 shows a page from a payroll summary report.

Figure 13.7 is taken from *Honeywell Source: A Software Magazine*. The figure shows how programs are listed in the magazine's directory of software and describes an on-line payroll and human resource management system designed for large businesses. The description of the program is worth reading

Figure 13.5 *One of the input forms for modifying information in the payroll file in the PeachPay payroll program.*

```
EF   M2.20            Maintain Employee File

DEPARTMENT..: 2    EMPLOYEE CODE..: DDD    TITLE..: PERSONAL INFORMATION
                                           PROCESSING STATUS...: PC


NAME............: DONALD D. DARLINGTON
ADDRESS.........: 4567 SPRINGWOOD DRIVE SE
ADDRESS.........:
CITY,STATE......: [HUNTSVILLE, ALABAMA]
ZIP CODE........: 35803
SOC. SEC. NO....: 284-41-4567
PHONE...........: 205-298-2514
COMMENT.........: SE DISTRICT TECH REP
STATUS (A/I)....: A
DATE EMPLOYED...: 07/10/77
DATE TERMINATED.: 01/01/00
LAST CHECK DATE.: 04/23/82
LAST CHECK NO...:  2208
LAST CHECK AMOUNT:    344.07

                         'TAB' TO APPROPRIATE FIELD, MAKE CHANGE.
                         'RETURN' WHEN ALL CHANGES COMPLETE.
                         'ESC' TO EXIT WITH NO CHANGES MADE.
```

```
RUN DATE 04/30/84          T. L. James Enterprises          PAGE 12
                              PAYROLL SUMMARY

DEPARTMENT 02

02DDD    DONALD D. DARLINGTON           284-41-4567

                          QUARTER-TO-DATE           YEAR-TO-DATE
EARNINGS - REGULAR    :        1333.28                  5666.44
           OVERTIME 1 :         400.00                  1700.00
           OVERTIME 2 :         166.68                   708.39
           COMMISSIONS :          0.00                     0.00
                          ---------------            -----------
           GROSS PAY  :        1899.96                  8074.83

DEDUCTIONS-FICA       :         127.28                   540.94
           FEDERAL WH. :         327.48                  1391.79
           ALABAMA WH. :          55.56                   236.13
           TAX #2     :           0.00                     0.00
           INSUR. DED. :          11.52                    48.96
           COFFEE DED. :           1.84                     7.82
                          ---------------            -----------
           TOTAL DED. :         523.68                  2225.64

HOURS    -REGULAR     :         160.00                   680.00
          OVERTIME 1  :          32.00                   136.00
          OVERTIME 2  :          10.00                    42.50
                          ---------------            -----------
          TOTAL HOURS :         202.00                   858.50

WEEKS WORKED          :           4.00                    17.00
```

Figure 13.6 *The payroll summary report generated by the PeachPay payroll program.*

carefully; it mentions many of the features that distinguish an inexpensive payroll system for small businesses from a comprehensive system for major corporations.

■ Vertical Market Applications

Vertical market applications is a catchall category for job-specific software. Programs in this category are diverse, as the following list illustrates:

■ *Facilities scheduling* programs handle reservations for racquetball, tennis, golf, and so on.

Sample Product Profile

Product Name: Title of the Program

System Type Supported: The specific Honeywell central processing unit(s) on which the product has been installed.

Operating System: Operating system(s) required for this product to function.

Languages: Specific programming languages(s) in which the product is written.

Program Summary: Highlights the features, functions, and capabilities of the product. Includes software prerequisites and documentation available. For a more comprehensive listing of documentation, see the Honeywell Publications Catalog, order number AB81.

Number of Installations: The number of locations at which the product is installed.

Hardware Requirements: Hardware requirements such as memory, tape, disk, peripheral or other system requirements for the product to operate.

Mode of Operation: Method used when processing data.

Support Services Available: Services available from the vendor to support the product.

Contact Data: The vendor's name, company, address and phone to contact for further information on the software product.

Marketing ID: Number to identify and order Honeywell products.

CYBORG SYSTEM, THE
System(s) Type supported: Level 64, DPS 7, Level 66, DPS 8

Operating Systems: GCOS 64, GCOS III
Languages: COBOL-68, COBOL-74
Product Summary: The Cyborg System is an integrated online payroll and human resource management system that utilizes a consolidated employee data base. The Cyborg System includes a new English language report writer. Payroll and personnel professionals may create their own reports and online screens with no previous technical training. Users may create, test, and load new reports, screens, and online calculations with no compiles or interim steps through Cyborg's On-Line facility. The Payroll System offers up to 500 unique earnings and 500 unique deductions. The system includes a Tax Service which informs the user of all federal, state, and local tax changes. Tax changes are transactional and do not require recompilation of the Cyborg program. There is a Labor Distribution feature which offers 98 automatic labor splits and unlimited labor splits through time documents. The system offers direct deposits, allowing each employee to have multiple deposits to multiple accounts and banks. Other standard features include Automatic Check Reconciliation, Unlimited History, and General Ledger Interface. The Cyborg Human Resource Information System is designed to be personnel-event oriented. Online screens and data are organized to give you all of the information necessary to process a human resource event, without searching through a series of unrelated transactions. The system comprises nine online modules: Basic Human Resource Record-Keeping, Benefits Administration, EEO/Affirmative Action, Applicant Tracking, Employee Health and Safety, Employee/Labor Relations, Manpower Planning, Position Control, and Time Attendance.
Number of Installations: 425
Hardware Requirements: Tape drives, printer
Mode of Operation: Online or Batch
Support Services Available: Training/Education, Telephone Assistance
Contact Data
Marketing Department
Cyborg Systems, Inc.
2 N. Riverside Plaza
Chicago, IL 60606
Tele. 312-454-1865
Marketing ID: N/A

Figure 13.7 *A sample product profile for an integrated payroll and human resource management system. Reprinted with permission of* Honeywell Source Magazine, *copyright 1985.*

- *Structural analysis* programs help compute the strength of walls, bridges, and other physical objects.

- *Process-control* programs monitor and regulate the equipment in factories, laboratories, and buildings.

- *Operations research* programs solve mathematical problems in which many variables are interrelated; for example, you might use an operations research program to find the shortest, quickest, safest, or most scenic route for a traveling salesperson.

- *Farm management* programs compute and record the yields of test plots for farmers.

- *Architectural* programs create preliminary architectural drawings, remodeling plans, and furniture rearrangements for homeowners and builders.

Vertical market applications are the most difficult programs to find. Computer stores are not likely to stock them because the volume of sales is low and specialized knowledge and training are needed to sell them effectively. The best sources of information about these programs are professional magazines and software catalogs. The prices for the programs range about as wide as their applications—from less than $100 to more than $100,000.

Expert systems are one type of vertical market software. These systems are an application of research on **artificial intelligence,** which seeks to develop computer systems that simulate human reasoning and intelligence. An **expert system** simulates the reasoning of a human expert in a particular subject. In medicine, for example, a physician diagnoses a disease from a set of symptoms and laboratory results. The diagnosis is based on the training, knowledge, and experience of the physician. However, there may be many possible diagnoses, some of which are more probable than others. Expert systems have been designed to aid in the diagnosis of a disease from a set of symptoms.

The Internist (N-Squared Computing, Silverton, Oregon) is an example. The menu-driven program allows the user to enter and edit a set of symptoms, perform a diagnosis by analyzing the set of symptoms, and query the disease database for all of the symptoms of a disease. Symptoms are entered by selecting items from two menus. The first menu lists parts, functions, and products of the human body (see Figure 13.8); the second lists particular common symptoms (Figure 13.9). The Internist program allows the user to perform two types of analysis to arrive at a diagnosis: one lists the diseases associated with all of the observed symptoms (see Figure 13.10); the other ranks diseases according to the number of symptoms they have in common with the selected symptoms.

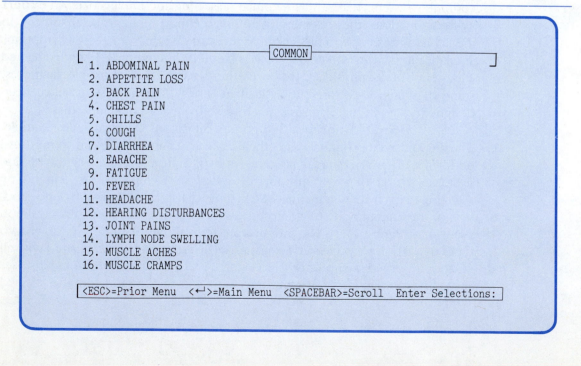

```
┌──────────┤ >>  BODY PART/FUNCTION/PRODUCT MENU  << ├──────────┐
│                                                               │
│   <1> ABDOMINAL/EATING   <12> EARS/HEARING    <23> LIPS       │
│   <2> ANAL               <13> EYES/VISION     <24> LYMPH NODE │
│   <3> ARMS               <14> FACIAL          <25> MALE GU    │
│   <4> BACK               <15> FEET            <26> MOUTH      │
│   <5> BLOOD/BLEEDING     <16> FEMALE GU       <27> NECK       │
│   <6> BONE               <17> HAIR-BODY       <28> NEUROLOGICAL│
│   <7> BOWEL MOVEMENT     <18> HANDS           <29> NOSE/SMELL │
│   <8> BREASTS            <19> HEAD            <30> PULSE      │
│   <9> BREATH ODOR        <20> HEART           <31> RESPIRATION│
│  <10> CHEST              <21> JOINTS          <32> SKIN       │
│  <11> COMMON             <22> LEGS            <33> SPEECH     │
│                                               <34> THROAT     │
│                                                               │
├───────────────────────────────────────────────────────────────┤
│ <ESC>=Prior Menu   <↵>=Main Menu │ Enter number of desired selection: │
└───────────────────────────────────────────────────────────────┘
```

Figure 13.8 *The menu from Internist for selecting those parts, areas, processes, or products of the human body associated with the symptoms of the disease.*

Figure 13.9 *The menu from Internist for selecting the symptoms of the disease.*

```
┌────────────────────────┤ COMMON ├────────────────────────┐
│  1. ABDOMINAL PAIN                                        │
│  2. APPETITE LOSS                                         │
│  3. BACK PAIN                                             │
│  4. CHEST PAIN                                            │
│  5. CHILLS                                                │
│  6. COUGH                                                 │
│  7. DIARRHEA                                              │
│  8. EARACHE                                               │
│  9. FATIGUE                                               │
│ 10. FEVER                                                 │
│ 11. HEADACHE                                             │
│ 12. HEARING DISTURBANCES                                 │
│ 13. JOINT PAINS                                          │
│ 14. LYMPH NODE SWELLING                                  │
│ 15. MUSCLE ACHES                                         │
│ 16. MUSCLE CRAMPS                                        │
├──────────────────────────────────────────────────────────┤
│ <ESC>=Prior Menu  <↵>=Main Menu  <SPACEBAR>=Scroll  Enter Selections: │
└──────────────────────────────────────────────────────────┘
```

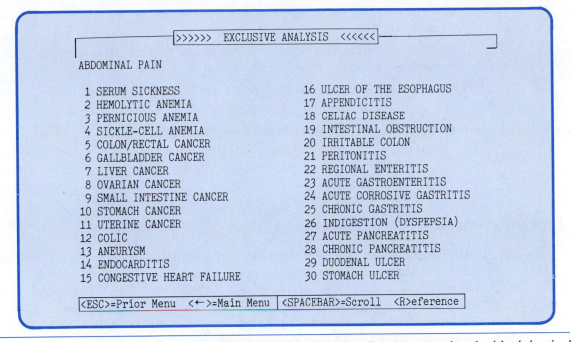

Figure 13.10 *The screen display showing the diseases associated with abdominal pain.*

■ Education

The use of computers in education originated in the early 1960s with mainframe computers. However, computers and terminals with graphics abilities were expensive, and developing good educational software required enormous time and manpower. Today, many educational programs reflect their mainframe origins; but most of the newer software takes advantage of the graphics, sound, and other features of the personal computer. According to a recent Gallup poll, nearly one-half of all personal computer owners use their computers for education.

Use of the computer as an educational tool is called *computer-assisted instruction (CAI)*. In CAI the computer presents information, works with the student, and tests for mastery of the material—sometimes replacing a human teacher. Through its interaction with the student, the computer can match the presentation to the student's needs and responses. Computers perform some tasks well, such as drills, but do others poorly. CAI is an area with great, but as yet unfulfilled, promise. Here are some examples of educational software.

■ A *drill-and-practice* program teaches facts, such as arithmetic operations, spelling, or state capitals.

- An *authoring language* assists educators in the development of CAI materials.
- A *tutorial* program guides novices through the basics of using other computer programs.
- An *arcade-based training* program teaches basic typing skills.
- A *drawing* program allows children to create animated figures.
- A *simulation* program teaches by emulating the responses of the system being studied. For example, a simulation program might teach basic economics by having the student make economic decisions and then showing the effects of the decisions.

Drill and Practice

Drill-and-practice programs emphasize the learning of facts through repetition. Most drill-and-practice programs soon become boring for the student, although the computer never gets tired or bored. Software developers have made drill-and-practice games that automatically adjust the pace or the skill level to performance. Some programs allow the teacher to customize the materials by altering or adding lessons. Although these programs are available for many subjects, by far the most popular cover arithmetic, spelling, and reading.

Training

Manuals for computer software and hardware are notorious for being poorly written and aimed at experienced programmers. This explains the surprising number of training programs designed to teach beginners about computers, operating systems, programming language commands, and popular application programs. Many application programs come with a tutorial training disk. Some companies distribute tutorial disks for their programs for a nominal charge to promote sales.

There are also a variety of training programs that combine learning and fun. MasterType (Scarborough Systems Inc., Tarrytown, New York) uses an arcade game to teach typing. Enemy "words" come in waves from the four corners of the screen and attempt to destroy a player's space ship; typing the word destroys the enemy word. The speed goal set by the player determines the rate at which the enemy words "attack." MasterType is menu-driven and has eighteen lessons. Among the options in the main menu are beginner mode (in which the "words" are single letters), a demonstration of the program, and lesson mode (in which the player can select a new lesson, view words in a lesson, create a new lesson, or delete a lesson). The more difficult lessons use eight- and nine-letter words, numbers, shifted symbols, and punctuation marks. After each wave of words a player's speed and score are given.

■ Entertainment

According to most surveys, the most frequent reason for purchasing a home computer, especially an inexpensive one, is for entertainment. Software developers have exhibited remarkable creativity in designing challenging and entertaining games. Many programs offer several options; for example, you can choose whether the opponent will be the computer or another person, and you can select the level of play (beginner, average, expert). Usually the program keeps statistics as the game progresses, displays a summary that rates performance, and keeps track of the highest score. Three of the most popular types of game programs are video arcade games, adventure games, and simulation games.

Video Arcade Games

Video arcade games have long been popular. In Pong, the first electronic game introduced in 1974, players control paddles in a game that resembles table tennis. Space Invaders, Asteroids, PacMan, Centipede, Frogger, and Donkey Kong are familiar titles. Many of the arcade games for personal computers are variations and improvements of these commercial games. In most you maneuver an object (space ship, frog, and so forth) to evade or destroy enemy objects before they destroy you. Most personal computer games work with either the keyboard or joysticks. Although still not up to the standards of commercial arcades, new games are taking advantage of the improved graphics and sound capabilities of personal computers.

Adventure Games

One of the first games developed for mainframe computers appeared in 1975. It was called *Adventure,* and it quickly achieved cult status and led to the development of a host of similar role-playing games. The object of these games is to solve a puzzle or find a treasure. The games have been set in a variety of worlds—ancient times, future times, caves, insane asylums, planets, castles. A puppet or narrator brings the player into the unknown world, describing the scene and obeying commands typed by the player. To win, the player must solve puzzles, explore mazes, and overcome obstacles using whatever clues and objects are discovered.

Adventure games are complicated, challenging, and engrossing. Maps, clues, and other aids are available for the faint-hearted. Most adventure games have a large vocabulary of words that they accept as commands. An essential part of adventure games is to determine what these words are by guessing them and observing the result. The Zork trilogy (Infocom Inc., Cambridge,

Massachusetts) is considered one of the best and most challenging. A sample Zork II dialogue is given in Figure 13.11. Lines beginning with ">" are commands given by the player.

Simulation

Simulation programs involve the player in decision making. The player might be in charge of running a large corporation, playing the stock market, flying an airplane, performing in the track-and-field decathlon, commanding forces in a war, or controlling the outbreak of a very contagious disease. Simulation programs overlap both the entertainment and the education categories.

One of the most famous simulation programs is Flight Simulator (Microsoft Corporation, Bellevue, Washington). It is a realistic, three-dimensional simulation of a Cessna 182 single-engine plane (see Figure 13.12). The upper portion of the screen shows the view out the windshield. The lower portion displays the instrument panel and radio stack with thirty-two readings (airspeed, altimeter, turn indicator, heading indicator, fuel gauge, and so forth). It has all the instruments and equipment required by the government for day and night flight. Both the instrument panel and the view are updated several times a second.

Figure 13.11 *Sample dialog from Zork II, an adventure game.*

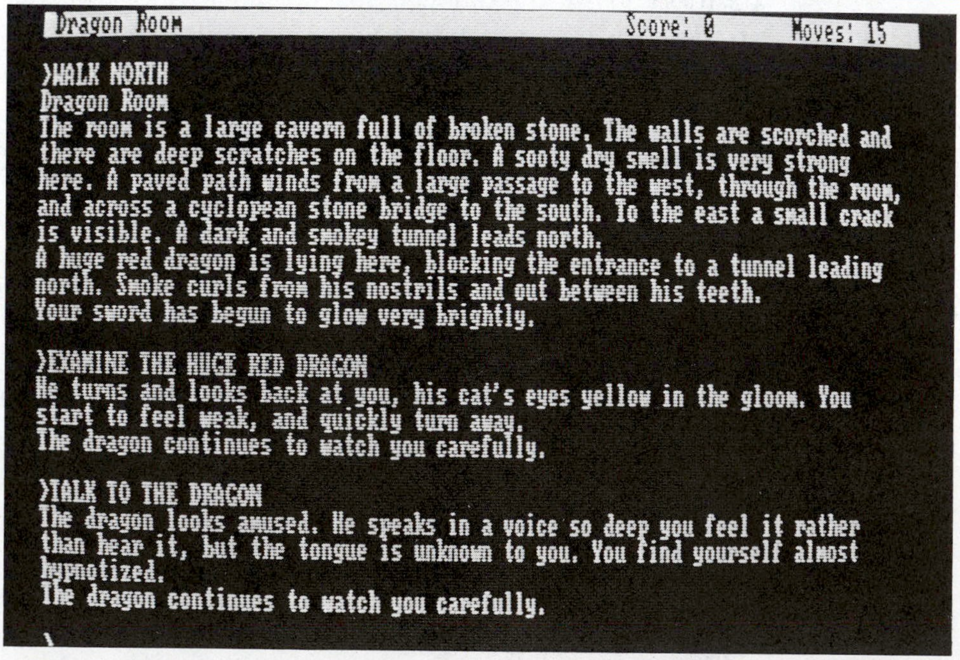

Figure 13.12 *A simulated view from a Cessna-182 provided by Microsoft's Flight Simulator.*

From the keyboard you can control the throttle, aileron, rudder, elevator trim, and flap controls. Takeoffs and landings are possible at twenty-two airports. You can choose the time of day and season of the year, and select from a variety of weather conditions including types of clouds, surface winds, winds aloft, and turbulence. It takes a certain amount of knowledge and skill to land the plane without crashing. Adventurous players can test their flying skills against World War I German biplanes.

■ Summary

This chapter has presented a glimpse into the variety of software available for computers. The chapter included specific examples of programs from several categories in order to illustrate the diversity of special-purpose programs. No attempt was made to present a comprehensive view of software; entire software categories—such as engineering, governmental, and scientific—were not covered at all. Our goal has been to emphasize the importance of choosing software appropriate for the task to be done. Often this involves using a special-purpose program rather than adapting a general-purpose program or developing a program from scratch.

Throughout the history of the modern digital computer, software development has lagged behind hardware development. New types of software will evolve as developers discover more uses for computers and as the features and capabilities of computer hardware improves.

Key Terms

artificial intelligence	integrated accounting systems
desk accessories	RAM disk
expert system	sorting program
file conversion	utilities
file recovery	vertical market applications

Discussion Questions

1. Many computing problems can be solved with general-purpose software or with a vertical market program. What general rules or guidelines can you suggest for determining which type of software should be used?

2. What types of differences would you expect among educational programs, games, and vertical market software that are all simulation programs?

3. Why are almost all utility programs written in assembly language or machine language?

4. What are some advantages and disadvantages of integrated accounting systems?

5. Should a programmer or software company that develops an expert system be liable for any injury or damage resulting from use of the system?

Exercises

1. During the early 1960s a newspaper misquoted a computer developer as predicting that the computer would become the world chess champion. Read about chess-playing programs. How good is the best chess-playing program?

2. Find the thirty top-selling application programs. Put them into the categories used in this chapter. What is the most popular category? Do the same thing for one year ago. Are there any differences?

3. Select a specific category of system utilities and find all of the programs available for your personal computer in that area. Do the same for vertical market applications.

PART SIX

developing
new systems

The complexity of a large information system can be mind boggling; systems can consist of hundreds of very involved and highly interrelated programs. For example, a typical airline reservation system may be used by thousands of people and contain several million lines of programming code supported by tons of documentation.

With all of this power comes a new set of problems. Even if everyone agrees that changes in a system are necessary, there may be little consensus about how the new system should work or how the conversion to the new system should proceed. As the size and complexity of these systems continue to grow, our ability to cope with them declines. For these reasons, the development and modification of large or complicated computer systems are handled by specialists called system analysts. A system analyst uses a technique called system analysis to deal with the complexity and size of modern computer systems.

System analysis is the computer-age equivalent of the scientific method. In system analysis, the problem is defined and analyzed and solutions are recommended to management. This process has been formalized and called the system analysis method. In Chapter 14 we describe each phase of system analysis.

One job of a system analyst is to specify exactly what a new system will accomplish and how it will operate. These specifications act as a blueprint that guides construction of the system. Programmers use some form of *programming language to translate these specifications into instructions a computer can execute.*

Before the system analysis method was used, an alarming increase in the time and effort required to develop software led to a search for the causes of failures and cost overruns. In the 1970s it was discovered that early detection of incomplete or incorrect designs prevented most cost and schedule overruns. The idea of early detection of potential problems spread to programming, and it soon became apparent that even seemingly simple programs are incredibly complex when carefully analyzed—difficult enough to require years of testing by the fastest computers! The impracticality of exhaustive testing of complex programs prompted the second major event in developing new systems: simplification of programming by adopting a programming style called structured programming. *Structured programming has produced significant improvements in software technology in just the past fifteen years.*

Programming is just one phase in the development of a computer system, but with the continual declines in the cost of hardware, it has become an increasingly costly portion of the system-building process. Because programming is costly and so important to the success of a new system, we have devoted an entire chapter to it. In Chapter 15 we discuss two broad aspects of programming: programming languages and programming techniques—in particular, the techniques of structured programming. Like the formal methods of system analysis examined in Chapter 14, the strict rules of structured programming described in Chapter 15 establish ground rules for how to solve problems efficiently.

The introduction of inexpensive personal computers with a wide range of preprogrammed application packages has decreased the importance of formal system analysis and design in the selection of small computer systems. Although the principles of system analysis are appropriate to consider when buying a personal computer, they are rarely applied rigorously to personal computer acquisitions. To emphasize the contrast between large and small computer systems, in Chapter 16 we discuss issues related specifically to the purchase of personal computer systems—including the need to obtain current information about what personal computers can do, to choose hardware and software that are compatible, and to plan for future expansion.

system analysis

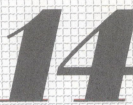

14

- ■ **What Is System Analysis?**
  What Is a System?
  The Systems Approach
  The System Life Cycle

- ■ **System Investigation**
  Reasons for Change
  Needs Analysis
  The Feasibility Study

- ■ **System Analysis**
  Data Gathering and Analysis
  Data Flow Diagrams
  The Requirements Report

- ■ **System Design**
  *From Data Flow Diagram to
  Hierarchy Diagrams*
  Walkthroughs and Prototypes
  The Design Report

- ■ **System Development**
  *Purchasing Hardware and
  Software*
  Software Development
  Documentation

- ■ **Installation, Maintenance,
  and Retirement**

14

Information systems are the central nervous system of large and small corporations, governmental organizations, and educational institutions. Devising and helping to implement these systems is the job of the system analyst. It is one of the most challenging jobs in the information age.

In the early days of computer systems little was known about how to conceive, design, and implement information systems. Now the process is understood as an application of general systems theory. Even though many questions remain unanswered, general systems theory has provided a solid basis for a methodology used to analyze and design information systems, a methodology called the *systems approach*. Using this approach, system analysts consider an information system as a complex, evolving collection of hardware, software, people, and processes. In this chapter we define what a system is, describe how information systems fit into general systems theory, and then explain each phase of the system's life cycle.

■ What Is System Analysis?

What Is a System?

There are many definitions of *system* that we might apply to computer-based information systems. According to the IEEE Standard Glossary of Software Engineering Terminology a **system** can be defined three ways.[1]

1. A collection of people, machines, and methods organized to accomplish a set of specific functions.

2. An integrated whole that is composed of diverse, interacting, specialized structures and subfunctions.

3. A group of subsystems united by some interaction or interdependence, performing many duties but functioning as a single unit.

A computer-based information system fits all three definitions. It involves people, machines, and methods; it behaves as an integrated whole; and most information systems are composed of a group of subsystems.

General systems theory provides another way of defining a system—as a collection of inputs, outputs, and processor activities with feedback, a boundary, and an environment. As you can see in Figure 14.1, *inputs* enter the system

[1]The ANSI/IEEE Standard 729-1983 can be obtained from IEEE, Inc., East 47th Street, New York, NY 10017.

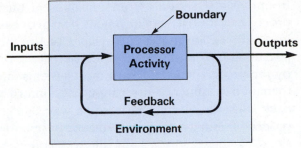

(a) General system structure

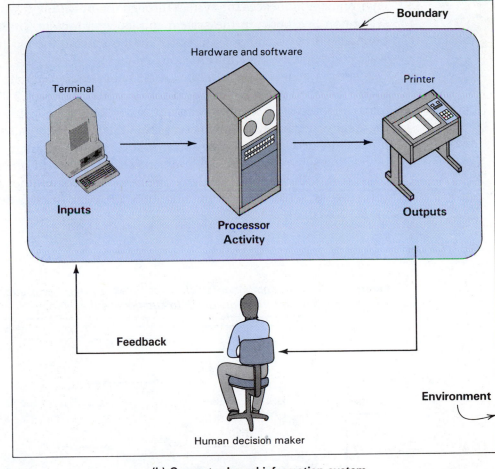

(b) Computer-based information system

Figure 14.1 *System theory as it applies to a computer-based information system.*

from outside—typically from human users, but also from other machines and processes within the environment. The **processor activity** transforms inputs into outputs. For example, in Figure 14.1(b) the processor may produce a report as output, given certain input data. Hence *outputs* are the results produced by the processor activities. In most systems information about the outputs is then used to influence future inputs; this information is called **feedback.** Feedback is used to correct or in some way alter the next wave of inputs to the processor activity. In an information system, feedback consists of new decisions, payments, charges, updates to accounts, and any input that is a result of previous outputs.

The **environment** is the world immediately surrounding the system. The environment influences the system through the **boundary,** which provides a separation line between the system and its environment. In Figure 14.1 the boundary is between human users of the system and the hardware and software components of the information system.

Most systems are too complex to be understood as a whole; so they are subdivided into components called **subsystems.** Figure 14.2 illustrates a system composed of three subsystems: inventory, billing, and accounting. Each of these subsystems may be rather complex in itself; hence the subsystems may in turn be divided into subsystems, and so forth. When a system is divided into interacting subsystems, the environment and boundary of one subsystem become part of the processor activity or environment of another subsystem. An **interface** is a channel for communication across a boundary between two or more subsystems.

Figure 14.2 *The components of a complex system are subsystems. Each subsystem may be further divided into additional subsystems.*

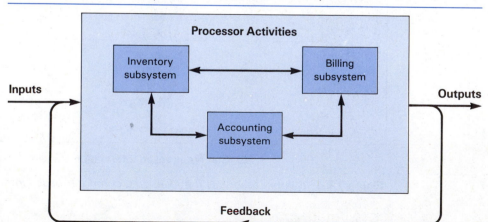

The Systems Approach

Large organizations must process information about everything from billing, inventory, accounting, and payroll to automated manufacturing, production control, and personnel services. Because their information-processing needs are so vast and demanding, many people, machines, and methods must be used to control massive amounts of data, collect facts, make decisions, and disseminate information to a variety of places within the organization. In short, large organizations have evolved complex information-processing systems.

A **system analyst** is a person trained in the analysis of complex business systems, which typically involve a computer system. System analysts evaluate proposals, recommend changes, and assist management in bringing about change. They analyze the existing systems, propose ways of implementing changes, design new systems, and guide the implementation of the new system.

To carry out these tasks, system analysts use the systems approach. The ideas from general systems theory that we have described form the basis of this approach. According to the **systems approach,** an existing or new information system can be analyzed as a system of components called subsystems.

One of the most important functions of a system analyst is to identify properly the subsystems and the interfaces among subsystems. This is not always easy because the components of some systems are so bound together that they cannot be cleanly separated.[2] For example, the problem of hunger in a country may be the result of an uneducated populace, a corrupt political system, and an undeveloped economic system. It may not be possible to decompose this system into subsystems that can be tackled in isolation. Attempts to improve the educational system, for example, may fail because it is hard to educate a starving population governed by insecure political leaders.

Fortunately, few business systems are as "messy" as this example. Most business systems can be characterized by flows of information from place to place. System analysts frequently represent these flows in a data flow diagram, a graphical method of describing subsystems and their interfaces. Figure 14.3 shows a simplified data flow diagram for a system containing subsystems.

The System Life Cycle

Another tenet of the systems approach is that how a system should be managed varies from phase to phase in the system life cycle. The term **system life cycle** is used to describe the steps or phases a system goes through from the time it is

[2]"A mess is a system of problems. A system is a whole that cannot be decomposed into independent parts. From this it can be shown that a system always has properties that none of its parts have and that these are its *essential* parts" (Russell Ackoff, "The Art and Science of Mess Management," *Interfaces,* 11 [February, 1981], 20–26).

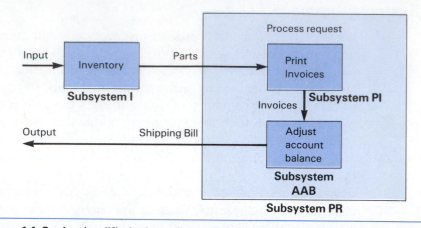

Figure 14.3 *A simplified data flow diagram showing the interfaces among subsystems. Subsystems I and PR communicate through "parts." Subsystem PR is composed of subsystems PI and AAB, which communicate through "invoices."*

conceived until it is phased out of existence. The names and number of phases in a system life cycle vary with different industries, organizations within industries, and system analysts. For our purposes, we divide the system life cycle into the following seven phases:

Life-Cycle Phase	*Activities*
Investigation	Identify needs; determine feasibility
Analysis	Understand current system; identify new requirements
Design	Propose alternatives; design the new system
Development	Develop and test the new system
Installation	Replace the old system with the new one
Maintenance	Evaluate, repair, and enhance the system
Retirement	Phase out the system and terminate it

Identifying these phases provides a framework for controlling, estimating, and observing the evolution of a system, as Figure 14.4 illustrates. Each phase produces **documentation,** which is written or pictorial information that describes the system, and this documentation forms the basis of a management review that determines whether the project should proceed to the next phase. Thus a system life-cycle model provides management with definite, verifiable checkpoints during the project's development. A Gantt chart similar to Figure 14.5 is typically used to schedule and estimate the duration of each phase.

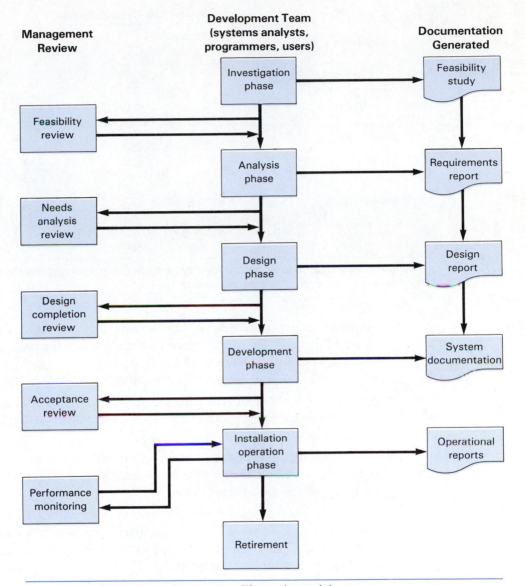

Figure 14.4 *The phases in a system life-cycle model.*

▪ System Investigation

Reasons for Change

Most organizations are swamped with requests to change their information systems. The following are some of the reasons for these requests:

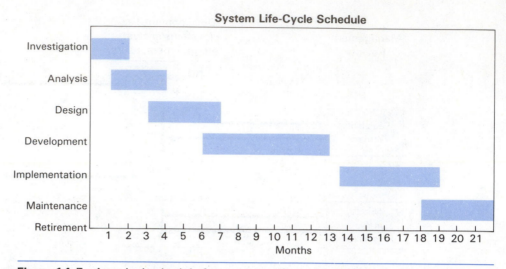

Figure 14.5 *A typical schedule for a system life cycle showing the duration of each phase and the expected starting dates.*

- *Problems in an existing system* are perhaps the most common reason to change a system. The sales department may be unhappy with the system because sales leads arrive too late, or the engineering department may want to improve the accuracy of calculations.

- *New requirements* that result from corporate reorganization, growth, or the marketing of a new product may force the company to expand or modify its current systems.

- *New technology* may be required in order to obtain maintenance and spare parts, or it may be cheaper to convert to new, better technology than to continue to use the existing system.

- *Governmental regulations* such as new tax laws, payroll deductions, and paperwork requirements can force changes in software. For example, the company may be required to change its accounting procedures before it can bid on government contracts.

- *Broad improvements* in performance may be possible (by making changes in procedures or machines or by training people), or they may be necessary because the existing system is overloaded.

Needs Analysis

The backlog of proposed changes must be evaluated to determine which ones are feasible and to provide a basis for comparing proposals. Thus the first task for a system analyst is to investigate the proposed change, a task that includes three steps.

1. Define the problem in terms of a need. This step is called *needs analysis*. It produces a statement of the needed change.

2. Suggest several solutions to the problem defined in step 1.

3. Evaluate the feasibility of each alternative and recommend the "best" solution.

The first step, defining the problem, may not be as easy as it sounds. Complaints and reports about problems often hide the real problem. For example, a national marketing manager who suggests that a faster computer be obtained to speed printing of a daily sales report may not understand that the data used in the report is entered late in the day, thus causing the report to be late. This problem may in turn be traced to a shortage of data entry clerks or to the fact that the data is generated by the West Coast branch, which is in a different time zone.

To identify the real problem to be solved, the system analyst conducts interviews, surveys users, and studies the current system. The system analyst finds answers to what, who, where, when, and why the problem exists.

The purpose of the second step, finding alternative solutions, is to ensure that all alternatives have been fairly evaluated. The temptation is to pursue the first solution that comes to mind, but doing so may mean overlooking a better solution.

Finally, the system analyst attempts to decide which of the alternatives is the best solution and to estimate the cost of implementing it. At this point it is also good to examine other issues, including the following:

■ *Economic feasibility.* This includes not only what the cost is but also, When will the change pay for itself? How much will it save in the long run?

■ *Technical feasibility.* Can the change be made? Is the technology available to implement the improvement?

■ *Operational feasibility.* What effect will the change have on methods and procedures, on people, and on the way the company is run?

The Feasibility Study

The main purpose of the system investigation phase is to create a feasibility study. This report is prepared in a consistent format so that it may be compared with the feasibility studies for other proposals—not all will be implemented. According to industry surveys, the average data processing department has a two- to three-year backlog of projects with completed feasibility studies.

The feasibility study must briefly and clearly describe the problem and the alternatives considered, and make a recommendation. The length and completeness of the report will vary with the importance and size of the problem being studied. A typical report contains

- a brief description of the present system.
- a statement of the problems, both real and apparent.
- a list of the alternative solutions considered.

Feasibility Study: 12-342   Analyst: J. Sundy
Date Prepared: 2/14/86

PRESENT SYSTEM

The present system consists of two subsystems: order-entry-and-inventory, and purchase-backordered-parts-from-suppliers. The order-entry-and-inventory subsystem is run by one order entry clerk and one inventory clerk. The purchase-backordered-parts-from-suppliers subsystem is run by one shipping clerk and the inventory clerk who also works on the order-entry-and-inventory subsystem.

NEEDS ANALYSIS

The current system is unreliable because when backordered parts arrive from suppliers they are not always entered into the inventory file. This means some parts are "lost" in the warehouse because they are not recorded in the inventory file maintained by the computer system.

The two subsystems need to be coordinated so that the supplier parts are properly posted into the inventory file. This will guarantee that the backorders are added to the inventory.

ALTERNATIVE SOLUTIONS

Two alternatives were considered:

1. Hire an additional clerk to update the inventory file each day, after daily shipments from suppliers have arrived at the shipping and receiving dock.
2. Modify the software of the computer system to automatically update the inventory file when backorders are received and filled.

- a feasibility analysis for each alternative solution.
- a discussion of the recommended alternatives pointing out any hidden problems, side effects, or related information that might be useful to management.
- a brief financial analysis and an estimated development schedule.

```
Solution #2 is recommended because it is reliable and in the long
run more cost effective.

                    FEASIBILITY OF SOLUTION #2

The costs and benefits of the proposed solution are based on the
following assumptions:

Cost of "lost" inventory / year ......... $ 100,000.00
Expected life of new system (years) .......        10

The following estimates are based on current dollars and have not
been adjusted for inflation:

COST:
     Estimated cost of software development .. $  150,000.00
     Estimated cost to train personnel     ..      25,000.00
     TOTAL COST TO IMPLEMENT #2            ....... $  175,000.00

BENEFIT:
     Estimated cost of "lost" inventory (10 yrs) $1,000,000.00

BREAK-EVEN ANALYSIS:     1987      1988      1989
   Cost                 175,000    -0-       -0-
   Benefit               -0-      100,000   100,000
----------------------------------------------------------------
   Net                 -175,000  +100,000  +100,000
   Cumulative          -175,000  - 75,000  + 25,000

The new system pays for itself in the third year. In ten years the
new system will realize an $825,000 savings.
```

The report is given to management. If it is approved, the next phase begins.

As an example, consider the feasibility study on pages 420 and 421 that describes a problem in a distributorship company. The company takes orders from dealers, fills these orders from parts stored in a warehouse, and sends the parts to the dealers or, if the warehouse does not have them, backorders the parts.

■ System Analysis

During the system investigation the analyst defined what the problem is; in the second phase—system analysis—the analyst decides what needs to be done to solve the problem. Whereas the system investigation is preliminary, systems analysis is more detailed. The succeeding phases—design and development—are even more detailed. Thus the systems approach illustrates **top-down analysis and design** because each succeeding phase is more detailed than the phase before it.

The purpose of the system analysis phase is to formulate what needs to be done as a list of requirements. There are three basic steps in this phase.

1. Gather and analyze data about the current system.

2. Describe the current and the proposed systems in terms that everyone can understand.

3. Document the requirements of the proposed system in a report that is given to management for consideration.

Data Gathering and Analysis

To achieve the level of detailed understanding required by the analysis phase, the analyst must study documents that describe manual and automated procedures; conduct interviews with people currently doing the work; perform surveys using questionnaires designed to uncover hidden problems, needs, and desires; and observe the operation of the company from an objective point of view.

Data Flow Diagrams

During the second step of the analysis phase the analyst must describe the existing and proposed systems. The diversity of large organizations complicates this task. Each person in a large organization is familiar with the terminology and methods unique to his or her skill. For example, financial experts understand ledgers and journals; engineers understand equations and blueprints; and software developers are familiar with flowcharts, programming languages, and operating systems. How can the analyst describe the existing and proposed systems in a form that everyone can understand?

One commonly employed method of describing an existing or proposed system is the data flow diagram. A **data flow diagram** is a graphic representation of an information system showing data sources, data destinations, data storage, the processes performed by subsystems, and the logical flow of information between the subsystems.

In a data flow diagram inputs, outputs, interfaces, and feedback loops are all called **datagrams.** Processor activities, methods, and procedures are collectively called **actigrams** because they represent activities. Figure 14.6 shows the symbols used to represent datagrams and actigrams.

A data storage symbol (also called a *pictogram*) represents files and lists. Thus it shows data "at rest" whereas a datagram symbol indicates data "in motion." The name of the storage file is inscribed in the data storage symbol, as shown in Figure 14.7. The small "stick people" in Figure 14.7 indicate that information is being transmitted by people rather than by computer.

Recall that the purpose of system analysis is to specify requirements for a new system. How does the data flow diagram relate to the requirements? Each actigram defines a function to be performed by the system; therefore all functional requirements are given by the actigrams. The data storage symbols define what information must be held in the system; therefore all storage requirements are given by the list of storage entities in the system. Finally, the datagrams are used to show connections between subsystems and the information

Figure 14.6 *The symbols used in a data flow diagram to describe a system.*

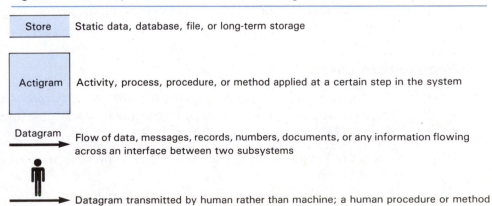

Store — Static data, database, file, or long-term storage

Actigram — Activity, process, procedure, or method applied at a certain step in the system

Datagram — Flow of data, messages, records, numbers, documents, or any information flowing across an interface between two subsystems

Datagram transmitted by human rather than machine; a human procedure or method

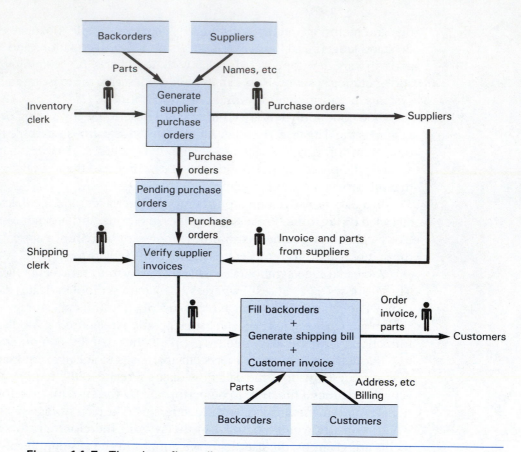

Figure 14.7 *The data flow diagram for the ''purchase parts from suppliers'' subsystem of a wholesale distributor.*

that flows across interfaces between subsystems. Thus the datagrams which connect actigrams and storage symbols indicate the system interface requirements.

The Requirements Report

The requirements report describes the findings of the system analysis, lists the requirements of the new system, and gives the new schedule for system development. Generally, the requirements report contains

- a brief restatement of the problem and the objectives of the proposed solution.
- a data flow diagram describing the present system.

- a data flow diagram describing the proposed new system and a list of requirements (for storage, functions, and interfaces in terms of methods, procedures, and documents).
- a revised Gantt chart showing the system development schedule.
- a formal request to start the next phase.

The heart of this report is the proposed system shown as a data flow diagram. Figure 14.8 provides an example. It gives one possible solution to the "lost" inventory problem in our sample feasibility study; the double-lined datagrams and stick people in the figure indicate the proposed changes. Central to these changes is the actigram that defines the function to "fill

Figure 14.8 *The complete proposed system showing how to integrate the "order entry and inventory" subsystem with the "purchase parts from suppliers" subsystem. The double-lined datagrams and actigram indicate the proposed changes.*

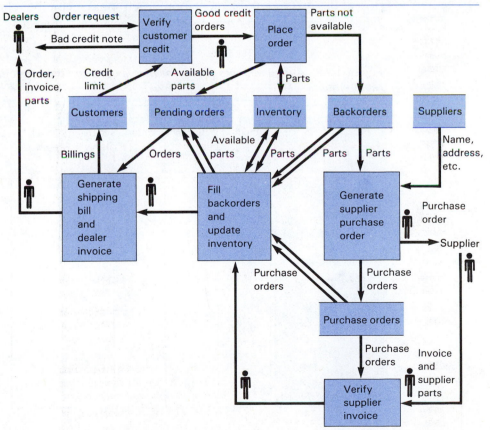

backorders + update inventory.'' This function integrates the previously separate functions of filling orders and updating the inventory file.

The requirements report should be specific about the requirements since this is the main function of the report, and the completed system will be compared against these requirements to determine if they were met. Therefore, it is common practice to include various check lists in the requirements report to emphasize features of the data flow diagram.

A requirements check list for the ''lost'' inventory example is shown in Figure 14.9. Compare it with the data flow diagram in Figure 14.8. The required functions are listed down the page in Figure 14.9 and the actigrams (functions performed by the system) are listed across the page. Notice that some required functions overlap or seem redundant. This occurs because the functions are listed from the perspective of different people. One clerk may ''clear backorders'' while another one may ''fill backorders.'' Actually they are the same thing, but viewed from different perspectives.

The last column of the check list is reserved for verification of the requirements after the system has been developed. This is one of the advantages of top-down design and implementation: each phase can be checked against requirements stated in previous phases to ensure a ''correct'' system.

Figure 14.9 *A requirements check list that is used to verify function requirements.*

Required Function \ Actigram	Verify credit	Verify supplier invoice	Place order	Generate shipping bill	Fill back-orders	Generate supplier P.O.	Requirement Achieved
Verify customer credit	✔						
Bill customers				✔			
Ship orders to dealer				✔			
Take in orders	✔		✔				
Backorder parts			✔			✔	
Clear backorders				✔	✔		
Parts inventory					✔		
Inventory update					✔		
Fill backorders				✔	✔		
Verify supplier invoice		✔					

Total _____

Additional check lists are included to state clearly the system's storage requirements, processing speed, and user convenience. Together the data flow diagram and check lists clearly and precisely define the system and proposed changes.

■ System Design

Once the requirements report is approved by management, the third phase of the system life cycle—system design—can begin. Whereas system analysis defines *what* is to be done, system design tells *how* it is to be done. The purpose of system design is to translate the data flow diagram (or equivalent analysis documents) into documentation that states how the new system should work, how the requirements are to be met, and how the major components of the system should be implemented. Think of system design as a blueprint or road map of the system to be implemented.

A "good" design is compatible with the current software and hardware, flexible enough to be modified when needed, easy for people to use, and technically and economically feasible. These are obvious virtues, but how are they achieved?

Contemporary designers believe that top-down designs provide the answer. **Top-down software design** is the process of designing a program by first identifying its major components, which are called **modules;** then decomposing them into lower-level components, a process known as stepwise refinement or **hierarchical decomposition** or **modular decomposition,** because the resulting system is structured as a hierarchy of modules; and repeating this process until the desired level of detail is achieved.

Applying top-down design to an entire information system is one popular method used by analysts to obtain good hardware and software systems. The technique has been widely adopted as part of the **structured design methodology:** a disciplined approach to design that adheres to a specific set of rules based on principles such as top-down design, stepwise refinement, and data flow analysis.

From Data Flow Diagram to Hierarchy Diagrams

Suppose we follow the transformation of the "lost" inventory example shown in Figure 14.8 into a structured design. The first step in structured design is to translate the data flow diagram into a hierarchical collection of modules, such as the one shown in Figure 14.10(a). The module at the top of the hierarchy corresponds to the entire system, but through successive refinement, modules are broken into other modules, and so forth until the smallest modules are obtained.

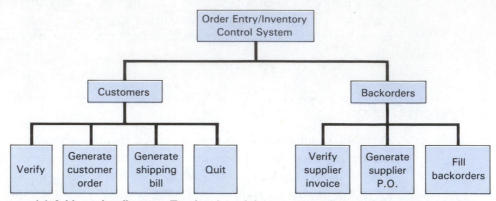

(a) A hierarchy diagram: Top-level modules corresponding to the user interface

Menu Titles

Menu Bar:	Customers		Backorders
Pull-down Items	Verify customer credit Generate customer order Generate shipping bill and invoice Quit		Verify supplier invoice Generate supplier P.O. Fill backorders

(b) User interface: Pull-down menus corresponding to modules

Figure 14.10 *Transforming a data flow diagram into a structured design and user interface. In (a) the top-level modules are shown in a hierarchy diagram. The user interface, shown in (b), consists of pull-down menus corresponding to program modules.*

There are two popular ways to go about the partitioning into subsystems: functional decomposition and data decomposition. In **functional decomposition** the designer attempts to partition the diagram according to the logical "closeness" of the actigrams. For example, in Figure 14.11, because placing orders, generating shipping bills, and verifying dealer credit are three related functions, they are put into one subsystem while all others are put in another subsystem.

In **data decomposition** the data flow diagram is partitioned according to the "closeness" of the datagrams and data storage items. For example, customers and pending orders might be closely related, whereas inventory, backorders, suppliers, and purchase orders might be considered another logical collection. Notice that either method of partitioning can lead to identical results as shown in Figure 14.11. On large systems it is likely that two designers using the same method of partitioning will create different partitions. For example, data storage items might be partitioned into the subsystems as follows: (1) suppliers and backorders, (2) inventory and purchase orders, and (3) customers and pending orders.

In most modern computer systems the user interface is also considered when the data flow diagram is transformed into a hierarchy of modules. Suppose, for example, that the system is to be written with a pull-down menu interface. Each pull-down menu is given a title, and the titles are listed on a menu bar at the top of the screen as shown in Figure 14.10(b). When a title is selected from the menu bar (with either the keyboard or a mouse), its menu pulls down so that you can select one of its items.

The hierarchy diagram in Figure 14.10(a) corresponds closely to the user interface in Figure 14.10(b). Nouns in a menu are usually associated with

Figure 14.11 *Partitioning the data flow diagram into subsystems.*

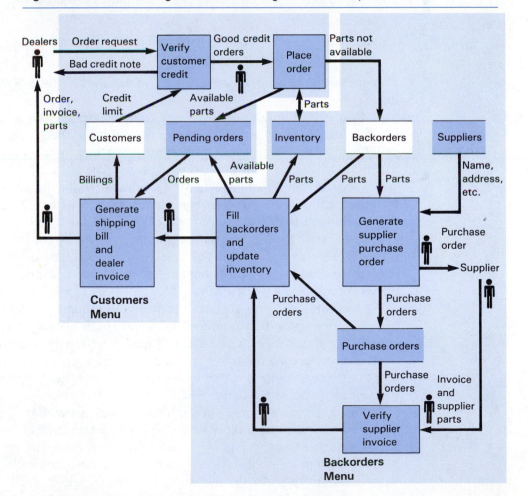

storage devices and data; verbs are associated with actigrams. Because data decomposition was used in Figure 14.10(a), the titles on the menu bar are nouns and the items are verbs describing the actions performed by the modules.

Walkthroughs and Prototypes

Regardless of how careful the designer is, the resulting design may be incomplete, incorrect, or difficult to use. For this reason the system analyst often tests a proposed design using several techniques.

The most frequently used technique is the **design walkthrough.** In a design walkthrough the system analyst prepares an overview of the design and presents it to users, programmers, and consultants to answer the following questions:

1. Is it complete—does it do everything we want it to?
2. Is it correct—does it satisfy the requirements specified by the requirements report?
3. Is it feasible—can it be implemented quickly and cheaply in a way that is compatible with existing systems?

Managers do not attend the walkthrough so that the criticisms will be penetrating.

If the walkthrough finds weaknesses in the design, the analyst must go back to the drawing board and come up with another design, repeat the walkthrough, and eventually get the approval of the group. Once approved by the group, the design is presented to management.

A second method of proving the "goodness" of the design is an emerging technique called *rapid prototyping*. A **prototype** is a program that simulates the real thing: it accepts user inputs, produces predefined reports, and in general gives the same appearance as the completed program in order to let users try the system before it is constructed. The designer also constructs sample output reports to show to users, programmers, and consultants and obtains their reactions through detailed discussions.

A prototype is constructed quickly by combining predefined modules from a library of standard modules for common parts of every program. For example, the menu system shown in Figure 14.10(b) is quickly and easily generated using a "menu-maker" program. The user can then use the menu system to identify problems with the user interface, and possibly with the deeper parts of the proposed system.

Prototyping is very effective at finding problems with the completeness, correctness, and compatibility of a proposed system. In fact, prototyping is perhaps the best way to find operational problems in the design. When users actually attempt to use the system, they become aware of bottlenecks, inconveniences, and gaps in the system's capabilities. These are difficult to discover prior to building the complete system by any other means. Suppose, for example, after a day of using the prototype it is discovered that all information in the inventory file can be accidentally destroyed by a novice user. Before the system is actually used—and information lost—the system can be redesigned or critical checks added to ward off such accidents.

The Design Report

The design report documents the design so that a correct, complete, and easy-to-use system will be developed according to the design. This report will be used constantly during the development phase. It will be changed to reflect improvements in the system when a design flaw is discovered. And it will be used to maintain, enhance, and modify the system after it is put into use.

The design report should include

- data flow diagrams of all systems and subsystems.
- a hierarchy chart showing the top-level modules.
- requirements check lists for all functions, data, and performance criteria (speed, capacity of files, and so on).
- Gantt charts for the entire project.
- revisions as they are made during the life of the system.

We have given a very simplified explanation of the design phase in order to explain concepts rather than the details of the process. To give you some idea of the complexity of design, consider the following issues that must be addressed by the designer:

- Will the system meet the user's needs?
- Are the right reports produced?
- Do they contain the right information?
- Are they formatted the way users expect?
- Does the user interface clearly explain how to operate the system?
- Do users feel comfortable with the displays?
- What happens when the user commits an error?
- Is the system protected from accidental use? Abusive use?
- How should inputs be checked and validated?
- Are procedures clearly documented and accessible?
- Will it be easy to train users?
- Will the system be easy to modify?
- Are procedures for back-up, audit trail, and error recovery adequate?
- Have all requirements been met?
- Is the approach the best one?

■ System Development

The purpose of the system development phase is to build a system that meets the requirements set forth in the previous phases. The new system is developed in accordance with the design and analysis documents. These "blueprints" are used to construct a working system. The system may be purchased, or it may be developed in-house. New procedures may be designed so that people will know how to use the system.

Purchasing Hardware and Software

In many cases it is best to purchase a new inventory system, database management package, or vertical application package. A component of the new system may be purchased, for example, a second computer to decrease the time it takes to do the current work, or the entire system might be purchased as a *turn-key* package including hardware, software, and training—a system ready to operate once you plug it in and "turn the key." Buying a new system is likely to cost less than developing one, and it will almost always be available sooner. A purchased system can also be tested and evaluated before a commitment to the system is made.

In some cases the decision of whether to buy or to build is complicated. If the new system is an enhancement to the existing system, in-house programmers may understand the existing system well enough to modify it easily. An intermediate solution is to hire a consulting company to come into the organization to develop the enhancement. This has the advantage of allowing in-house control over the outcome without the disadvantage of requiring the company to hire people for a short-term job.

Compatibility is an important issue with purchased systems because they are usually more difficult to modify than systems developed in-house. A purchased system must "plug in" to the existing system at various levels: procedural, hardware, software, and strategic. At the procedural level you should ask how the new system will change the way things are done. Are the reports different? Can paychecks be drawn on demand as in the old system? Is the sales report as thorough as before?

Hardware compatibility means being able to connect machines together, obtain common maintenance, run software from the old machine on the new machine, transfer data between the old and new machines, and minimize the amount of training required to operate the new machinery.

Software compatibility means being able to use existing programs with the new program. It must be possible to exchange data between the old and new programs. If the new software is incompatible with the existing software, converting from one data file format to another may be a larger job than writing a new system from scratch.

Strategic compatibility is a management issue. A new computer or program may be compatible with existing systems, but if it takes the company in the wrong direction, strategically, then all other considerations do not matter. For example, a decision to buy small computers that do the job today may lock the company into inadequate computing power in the future.

Software Development

If the new system is to be developed instead of purchased, there must be a **software development process.** In this process user needs are translated into software requirements; software requirements are transformed into design; the design is implemented in code; and the code is tested, documented, and certified for use.

The software development phase begins with the decision to develop a program or set of programs, and ends when the product is no longer being enhanced by the developer. In general, this phase consists of organizing a team of developers, adopting a social process to guide the team's development efforts, equipping the team with software development tools, and then managing the process until completion. Thus, the success of the team depends on: (1) team structure, (2) organizational process, (3) software development tools, and (4) management.

Team Structure

Programmers work in teams to perform tasks that they could not accomplish individually. Teams allow large projects to be completed quickly. Because software development is not well understood and is thought of as an art, software development teams are more like groups of temperamental writers collaborating on a novel than the groups of people who built the pyramids.

One well-known team structure is called the **chief programmer team** because one programmer is assigned overall responsibility for the entire software project; all other programmers report directly to the chief programmer. Associate programmers are assigned tasks like building small libraries of programs that can be used by the chief, finding errors in the programs written by the chief, writing documentation, preparing test data, and so forth.

Another team structure, sometimes called the **democratic team,** is more egalitarian than the chief programmer team. In this structure, everyone is assigned duties that fit their individual strengths. If you are especially well versed in programming languages, you might be responsible for writing most of the software; if you are good at finding errors in other people's programs, you might be assigned to testing and debugging. Democratic teams also discuss the details of design and implementation as a group—arriving at a consensus before reaching a decision.

A third type of structure has grown up in the personal computer era. It does not involve a team at all; instead there is a single programmer, called a **hacker.** Most hackers use other people's work by purchasing libraries of reusable programs, downloading programs from computer networks, and exchanging code with other hackers. Some of the most successful software has come from hackers—including games, music synthesizers, spreadsheets, software development aids, and graphics.

In large organizations the first step in development is to adopt a team structure and staff the team with people who work well in the chosen structure. Hackers do not perform well in chief programmer teams, and democratic programmers may not be comfortable as hackers. Once the team is organized, the next step is to formalize the operation of the team.

Organizational Process

The team operates according to an *organizational process*—rules and regulations governing the behavior of the team members. An example is the **egoless programmer** process, one of the earliest processes used by teams. As the name indicates, **egoless programming** separates the programmer's ego from the program being developed. If an error is found in the program, the entire team, not the individual programmer, accepts responsibility for it. This reduces resistance to finding errors in the program, and leads to greater productivity. Egoless programming has had such an effect on software development that it has been given a technical definition by several standards committees. According to one,

> Egoless programming is an approach to software development based upon the concept of team responsibility for program development. Its purpose is to prevent the programmer from identifying so closely with his or her output that objective evaluation is impaired.[3]

The organizational process also includes a method of inspecting software as it is being manufactured. **Program inspection** is a formal evaluation technique in which software requirements, design, or code are examined in detail by a person or group other than the author to detect faults, violations of standards, and other problems. Inspection is the single most important step in developing highly reliable software.

One method of program inspection is an outgrowth of egoless programming; it is called a **structured walkthrough.** This is a review process in which a designer or programmer leads one or more other members of the development team through a segment of design or code that he or she has written, while the other members ask questions and make comments about technique, style, possible errors, violations of development standards, and other problems.

[3]ANSI/IEEE Standard 729-1983.

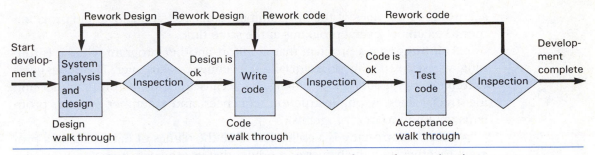

Figure 14.12 *The organizational process for a software development team.*

Structured code walkthroughs and egoless programming establish an organizational process within the team. This process is shown in Figure 14.12. It has often been compared to a "software factory" or "program assembly line." The design may be reworked after each inspection. The software is accepted only after the final walkthrough approves it.

The process shown in Figure 14.12 is only part of the inspection and testing process, however. The final walkthrough completes the preliminary or **alpha test** portion of software development. The software is not certified or approved for routine use until it has survived a beta test. **Beta testing** is done by users who accept the pioneer status associated with being first-time users. During beta testing the shortcomings and errors found in the system are logged and reported back to be fixed by the development team.

Software Development Tools

After the organizational process is established, the next major step in the development phase is to select the tools to be used by the team. A **software tool** is a program that helps a programmer write another program. The ultimate software tool would automate programming by converting the design specifications into a working system, but for most applications such a tool does not yet exist. Many less capable tools do exist, however, and they decrease the time and cost of development. They offer one of the best ways for a team of programmers to improve both productivity and quality. Because labor costs account for most of the cost of programming, improving productivity by 10 to 20 percent is very worthwhile. Much greater improvements are possible; for many programming tasks, tools have been invented that increase a programmer's productivity by a factor of 10 or more. We discuss only a few software tools here; several others are discussed in Chapter 10 on database management systems and Chapter 15 on programming.

An **editor** is a word processor specially designed for programmers. A programmer uses an editor to write, correct, and sometimes check the correctness of a program while it is being written. A sophisticated program editor, for example, automatically formats the program, checks for grammatical errors according to the rules of the programming language, and allows the programmer to examine several programs at the same time.

A **debugger** is a program that monitors another program while it is running; when the running program fails, the debugger takes over. The debugger is extremely useful during program testing because it helps the programmer find incorrect values, wrong instruction sequences, and a number of other problems common to new programs.

A **data dictionary** is a collection of all the names of data items in a program together with the names of modules that use the data item and a description of each data item's attributes (data type, length, representation, and so on). If one programmer changes a name in the dictionary, the change is made known to the other programmers. This prevents subtle inconsistencies in two modules of a program that share the same data item.

A **test-data generator** is a program for producing test data for another program. A test-data generator is used to test a module prior to acceptance. For example, if the module is supposed to sort a file, the test-data generator might be used to produce a file containing 10,000 records.

A **program analyzer** is a program that analyzes another program to determine if it has anomalies. A program analyzer may check a program for poor structure, violations in programming standards, or missing segments of code. Some software developers claim that their analyzers can judge the quality of a program written by a human programmer.

Management

The final ingredient in a software development team is proper management. A software development manager must understand the team, the organizational process, the tools, and the methodology used by programmers. Most managers are ex-programmers.

A manager oversees the process and guides development through a **software plan,** which is a collection of documents that describe the design and implementation methodology used by the team. In addition, the plan incorporates the blueprint of the system as described by data flow diagrams, hierarchy charts, and program structure charts. A **program structure chart** is used to define the most detailed level of a program prior to writing the program in a programming language. It documents the logic, and hence the essence, of a program module.

Several commonly used structure charts are flowcharts, Nassi-Schneiderman charts, HIPO charts (hierarchy + input/processing/output charts), and Warnier-Orr Charts. Figure 14.13 compares a flowchart and a Nassi-Schneiderman chart for the same segment of program logic.

In a flowchart rectangles represent a processing step such as a calculation. A diamond represents a decision point such as a choice between two alternatives. A parallelogram represents an input or output operation. The arrows

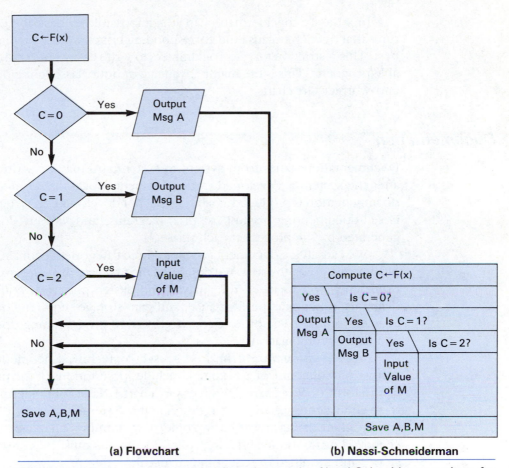

Figure 14.13 *A comparison of a flowchart and a Nassi-Schneiderman chart for representing the logic of a program module.*

connect the diamonds and boxes in exactly the way the program is supposed to evaluate the decisions and calculations.

A flowchart is easy to draw, but it has a major drawback: the lack of structure in a flowchart often leads to convoluted programs that are difficult to modify and maintain. Flowcharts are still used by many programmers, but they are gradually being replaced by "safer" methods of documenting the logic of a program module.

A Nassi-Schneiderman chart is a nested structure; that is, as Figure 14.13(b) illustrates, it is made up of boxes inside boxes. Each box represents a control construct such as making a yes or no decision, displaying a value, or computing a formula. In Figure 14.13(b) the decision construct "Is C = 0?" contains other decision constructs, and so on.

In a Nassi-Schneiderman chart it is impossible to describe control structures that overlap because the corresponding boxes would overlap rather than nest. This restriction forces programmers to write easily understood, maintainable programs. This is the major advantage of both Nassi-Schneiderman charts and Warnier-Orr charts.

Documentation

Documentation varies from system to system and may be written during or after the system is developed. A development process is *self-documenting* if documentation is produced as a by-product of development. Structured design is self-documenting because reports, diagrams, and various documents are generated by the process at each phase.

We can divide documentation into three categories according to the people who are going to use it. We described the first category, *design documentation,* when we discussed the analysis and design phases. It consists of flow diagrams; functional, performance, and data storage requirements; and management reports. The other two categories are programming documentation and user documentation.

Programming documentation is used by technical people to define the software architecture of a system. It includes descriptions of the program logic in the form of flowcharts, Warnier-Orr charts, Nassi-Schneiderman charts or their equivalent; narratives that describe the system; hierarchy diagrams; and the program listings (written in some programming language). Whenever a change is made in the software, these documents must be consulted, understood, and modified to reflect the change.

User documentation consists of training manuals, operations manuals, and reference manuals that describe how to use the system. Often this documentation is on-line—that is, users can temporarily interrupt their work and display help screens that instruct them in what to do.

Documentation has one major goal: to inform and instruct. Therefore, it must be clearly written, easily referenced, and complete. Unfortunately, most documentation is inadequate because it describes complex systems, the systems change quickly, and the people who build the systems are usually the ones who write the documentation—and designers, developers, and managers are not especially fond of writing documentation.

■ Installation, Maintenance, and Retirement

Installation is the phase in the system life cycle during which a system is integrated into its operational environment and is tested to ensure that it performs as required. This is the most precarious phase for an organization because it can jeopardize the entire operation. For example, a bank jeopardizes its entire cash-flow operation during the installation of a new check-cashing system.

During the installation phase the new hardware and software must be checked under real conditions. This means putting the system into use by the people who must run and maintain it. People must be trained, new procedures instituted, and the system thoroughly "shaken down" to eliminate any errors or deficiencies. Because of the risk of failure during this phase, various methods of conversion are employed.

- *Direct*. This is the most dangerous method of conversion because the organization switches immediately from the old to the new system. If the new system fails, it could hurt the entire organization; but if it succeeds, the cost of conversion is minimized. Most people will avoid the direct method unless there is no alternative or the new system is small and simple.

- *Parallel*. This method runs both the new and old systems side by side for a time. When the new system has been checked completely, the old system is retired. Although the parallel method ensures that the work gets done even if the new system fails, it is expensive because of the equipment, people, and time involved.

- *Pilot*. This method minimizes the risk by assigning a small pilot group of users to convert directly to the new system. If the new system fails, the damage is minimized because only a small part of the company is affected. Additionally, those in the pilot group become experts who can help the other users switch. This approach takes longer than direct or parallel conversions.

- *Phased*. With this method the new system is gradually phased in by introducing portions of the overall system over time. It takes longer than most other methods, but is less risky. For example, a new accounting system might be phased in over a year by starting with the general ledger, then converting accounts payable, accounts receivable, and finally payroll.

Which method of conversion is best depends on the circumstances. In fact, the best method may be a combination of parallel and phased, or pilot and direct methods. The idea is to minimize cost and risk.

After installation is complete, the maintenance phase begins. Its purpose is to modify the system after it is installed to correct faults, improve performance, or adapt the system to a changed environment. For example, an incorrect calculation of withholding taxes would be considered a fault in the payroll subsystem; an untimely or delayed report would be considered a performance problem.

Program maintenance is a major cost. Industry estimates say that more than half of all software development costs are related to the maintenance of existing programs.

The retirement phase is the period in the life cycle when support of the system is terminated. Retirement of the old system is typically carried out in conjunction with the installation of a new system.

■ Summary

Modern computer systems are too complicated to be designed by haphazard methods. Organizations turn to system analysts when new systems need to be developed or existing systems need to be modified. A system analyst uses many documentation techniques and review procedures to organize development of large computer systems.

A fundamental procedure of system analysis is stepwise refinement whereby a complex system is broken down layer by layer into subsystems of an understandable size. Much of the skill of a system analyst is wrapped up in the ability to choose appropriate subsystems and to document the linkages among subsystems effectively.

System analysis and design is keyed to the system life cycle. Identifying the phases of the life cycle encourages the orderly development of the system and provides management with verifiable checkpoints at which progress can be reviewed.

Each phase in the life cycle calls for the completion of specific documents. The documents created in each phase become the starting point for the next phase. For example, the system analysis report determines the requirements that the system design must meet, and the design documents become the blueprint that guides the development phase.

Key Terms

actigram	editor
alpha test	egoless programming
beta test	environment
boundary	feedback
chief programmer team	functional decomposition
data decomposition	hacker
data dictionary	hierarchical decomposition
data flow diagram	installation
datagram	interface
debugger	modular decomposition
democratic team	modules
design walkthrough	processor activity
documentation	program analyzer

program inspection
program structure chart
prototype
software development process
software plan
software tool
structured design methodology
structured walkthrough

subsystems
system analyst
system life cycle
systems approach
test-data generator
top-down analysis and design
top-down software design

Discussion Questions

1. What is a system? Compare an information system with a general system.

2. What is top-down design? How does it relate to the systems approach? What tools and techniques are used in top-down design?

3. Describe some ways of documenting the logic of a computer program module. Which way is likely to be most understandable to the layperson? Which way is likely to be preferred by a system analyst?

4. Consider the different ways to convert from an old system to a new one. Which method is likely to be used in each of the following situations:
   a. Introducing an "off-the-shelf" payroll program in a Fortune 500 firm.
   b. Introducing a new word processing package in a law office with five typists.
   c. Developing an on-line tracking and control system for production in a paper mill.
   d. Developing a new control program for a hard disk that will function as a file server on a local area network.
   e. Replacing a manual system of registration in a major university with a computer-based system.

5. Why would anyone build a new system when they could purchase a turn-key system? What are the factors that determine whether a new system is done in-house or purchased?

6. How does an analyst know whether a design is correct? What about the software? Describe what happens at each phase of a system life cycle to verify that the system is being constructed properly.

7. How are data flow, user interface, and hierarchy diagrams related? How is the data flow diagram transformed into a hierarchy diagram?

8. What is a chief programmer? A hacker? Describe how these two kinds of software developers create programs.

9. What is the purpose of a walkthrough? What happens during a code walkthrough?

10. Give some reasons for enhancing an existing system. How do these reasons compare with the reasons for considering a new system?

11. What is egoless programming? How does it affect programmers' ability to test their own programs? How does the code walkthrough contribute to productivity?

Exercises

1. Draw a data flow diagram of the "system" used by your instructor to lecture, test, grade, and report grades. Be sure to identify data storage, datagram, and actigram elements in your diagram.

2. Draw a flowchart and a Nassi-Schneiderman chart of the logic to determine letter grades from numerical test scores.

Score	Letter grade
100–87	A
86–79	B
78–55	C
54–41	D
40–0	F

3. Suppose it costs $36,000 per year for one clerk to process paychecks for a small company manually. The company expects to grow 50 percent per year and currently has 120 employees. One payroll clerk can process the current load; but when the number of employees per payroll clerk reaches 300, an additional payroll clerk is needed. Assume the one-time cost of installing a computer is $150,000, and the computer is capable of processing from 20 to 20,000 checks per month for an annual cost of $45,000. When should the company convert to the computer system? When will the break-even point be reached? Prepare a cost/benefit analysis of this system.

4. Using the data flow diagram shown in Figure 14.8, derive a different user interface and hierarchy diagram than the ones given in Figure 14.10. In other words, change the partitions or the method of selecting menus.

5. Give an example of design incompleteness, program incorrectness, and operational inconsistency.

15

programming

15

Near the end of World War II a German soldier named Konrad Zuse escaped the oncoming Soviet army by secretly driving a truck through southern Germany into Switzerland. Zuse hoped to be captured by the U.S. Army, rather than the Soviets, because he had in his possession one of the first electronic digital computers ever constructed. Perhaps, he reasoned, the British or Americans would allow him to complete his work in peace. But more important than the computer was Zuse's fundamental work on a new mathematical notation for programming the machine. Zuse had already worked out the details of a notation for communicating ideas to a machine, details that would permeate all of computing for the next forty years.

The basic concepts of modern programming are refinements of Zuse's programming language. These concepts are put to work every day by contemporary programmers who convey ideas called algorithms to computers in a notation called a programming language. An **algorithm** is a step-by-step list of instructions for solving a problem. For example, an algorithm could be designed to do a calculation, move data, or control a monitor. Algorithms are expressed in a **programming language,** a formalized notation that allows algorithms to be represented in a rigorous and precise way. There is little room for an ambiguous or imprecise idea in an algorithm. Therefore, most programming languages differ significantly from natural languages like English.

The word processing and spreadsheet software discussed in previous chapters are elaborate algorithms written in a language that a computer "understands." But occasionally a problem crops up that cannot be solved efficiently with a prepackaged program. When this occurs, the only alternative is to write a new program that solves the problem. Even if you have someone else write the program, you should know something about programming in order to discuss the program.

In this chapter you will see examples of programs written in several languages, and you will learn about programming languages, translators, and the technique called structured programming.

■ The Computer Tower of Babel

Machine Language Versus Programming Languages

There is only one language that a computer can run without modification: machine language. *Machine language programs* are nothing more than long sequences of binary numbers that have meaning for the computer. Programs written in other languages must be translated into machine language before they can be used to control a computer.

Machine language programs are the most elemental, or low-level, form of encoded algorithms. They are seldom used to program computers directly. To understand why, consider the following example of low-level programming. Suppose you tell a friend how to go to a nearby store and get a quart of milk. Here is a list of the low-level instructions that you might use.

1. Lean forward in your chair.

2. Push up with your hands and legs.

3. Raise up into a standing position.

4. Move your left foot forward.

5. Move your right foot forward.

. . .

100. Grasp the door knob with your right hand.

101. Turn the handle clockwise.

As you can see, these are extremely meticulous and tedious instructions. They certainly accomplish the task, but they are too detailed to repeat every time you want milk. To get around the need for such detailed instructions, you might compress the same meaning into fewer, more powerful words, as follows:

1. Stand up and walk out the door.

2. Get into your car and drive to the store.

3. Go into the store and get a quart of milk.

4. Pay for the milk and leave the store.

. . . .

12. Get out of your car and come back into the house.

13. Give me the milk and sit down.

Similarly, if you use a programming language instead of machine language, you can express the same meaning with fewer instructions. For this reason programming languages, rather than machine languages, are used by contemporary programmers.

Translation of Programs

People learn early in life how to translate the command ''go to the store'' into the numerous instructions to lean forward, stand up, walk, and so forth. A computer cannot learn a language by itself (at least not yet); so it must be programmed to translate all programs except machines language programs into machine language instructions before they can be processed by a computer.

A **translator** is a program for converting other programs from one language to another language. A translator reads an input program called the **source program** and converts the lines in the source program one by one into another language. The converted program is called the **target program.** Both the source and the target programs do exactly the same thing, but they are encoded in different languages.

A translator is a powerful tool for increasing the productivity of a programmer. Instead of giving detailed instructions in machine language, the programmer can give general directions at a higher level of abstraction, in a programming language, let a translator fill in the details, and obtain the proper results in a shorter time.

Compilers and Interpreters

Translation can be done in two radically different ways. A **compiler** is a translator that separates the translation process into stages. An **interpreter** is a translator that translates and executes your program in only one stage.

To understand the difference between compiling a program and interpreting it, consider two ways for an American to translate a document in French into an English speech. Using the compiler method, the American speaker converts the entire French document into an English document *before* giving the speech. Using the interpreting method, the American converts the French document into English *while* giving the speech (see Figure 15.1). This removes the need for creating an intermediate English document, but the speaker must convert the French document into English each time it is presented.

A computer program written in some programming language can be either interpreted or compiled. If it is interpreted, no translated document is produced; each time the program is executed, it must be translated. If it is compiled, an output document is produced so that the translation need never be done again. The compiler program takes the following steps:

1. Translate the source program into an equivalent **object program,** which is an incomplete, intermediate program that must be linked with other programs before it is run.

2. Link the object program with other support programs, producing an equivalent **target program** of machine language code.

3. Execute the target program.

In the second step the object program is read by a **linker program,** which converts the object program into machine language and combines it with operating system programs for writing lines of text on the screen, multiplying numbers, controlling the disks, and so forth. This linking ties the program to a

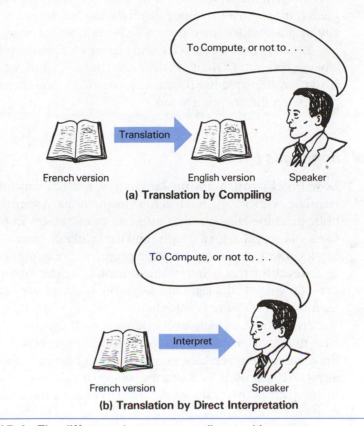

Figure 15.1 *The difference between compilers and interpreters.*

particular operating system, which is why application programs written for one operating system will not run on an identical computer that uses a different operating system.

Compilers produce fast, compact, and efficient machine language programs. They are the translators most frequently used by professional programmers. However, the three steps (compile, link, and execute) interfere with programming productivity because they take extra time and attention. Compiled programs run much faster than interpreted programs because there is no translation—that is done before the program is run.

Interpreters are good for novice programmers and for professionals testing new programs. In fact, running a BASIC program via an interpreter is a good way to learn how to write simple programs because the response is instantaneous: the results of your program are produced without inconvenient stages. Errors can be corrected and the program reinterpreted again and again until the program is correct. However, because interpreters repeatedly translate and execute statements one at a time, they are slow. In addition, the source program must coexist in memory with the interpreter while it is running. This usually means that less memory space is available for long programs.

BASIC, Lisp, APL, LOGO, and many other programming languages are usually interpreted. COBOL, FORTRAN, Pascal, C, and Ada are usually compiled. However, there are BASIC and Lisp compilers, and there are Pascal and C interpreters. So the choice is yours.

High-Level Languages (HLL)

Low-level programming languages, such as various assembler languages, translate one for one into machine instructions. **Assembly language** is a symbolic machine language that uses mnemonic codes in place of numbers (ADD for addition, MUL for multiply) and uses variable names instead of binary memory locations. Assembly language programs are compiled by a translator called an **assembler** that converts the mnemonic codes into machine language numbers. Low-level languages like assembly language are cryptic and require extra training and effort to comprehend.

In contrast, in high-level languages each "sentence" in the language translates into two or more machine language instructions. A high-level programming language resembles a combination of English and mathematics. English keywords are used to make the language readable, and a certain amount of mathematical formalism is employed to remove the ambiguity found in natural language. For example, the following sentence in English makes perfect sense to most people, but lacks the rigor required by a computer:

> Profit equals the number of units sold times the price per unit minus the cost per unit.

The computer might interpret this sentence to mean the mathematical formula

$$E = U * P - C$$

where

E = profit
U = units sold
P = price per unit
C = cost per unit
$*$ means multiplication

Unfortunately for those who speak English, the original sentence could also mean

$$E = U * (P - C)$$

This is the correct interpretation; but until we used the mathematical notation of $(P - C)$, the meaning was unclear. If the English version had been written as follows, the ambiguity would not have occurred:

PROFIT equals UNITS__SOLD times (PRICE minus COST)

Suppose we substitute + , − , * , /, and = for add, subtract, multiply, divide, and equals, respectively.

PROFIT = UNITS__SOLD * (PRICE − COST)

This formalized version could be used directly in most high-level languages. Indeed, a **high-level language (HLL)** is a restricted, formalized, and abbreviated version of a natural language. Its purpose is to express algorithms in a concise and unambiguous manner. Most programming languages are high-level languages.

A Sample BASIC Program

Many computers come equipped with a BASIC interpreter as part of their system software. For this reason we will first use BASIC to illustrate a simple high-level language program. Suppose you want to compute the formula $E = U * (P - C)$. Figure 15.2 shows a program for doing so, written in BASIC. You can type the program into your computer after first loading the BASIC interpreter. When you type NEW, the BASIC interpreter is told to begin a new program. It then allows you to enter commands as a list of numbered statements. After you have entered the program, typing RUN causes the interpreter to execute each statement one at a time.

Figure 15.2 *A BASIC program to compute PROFIT.*

```
NEW
10 INPUT "Enter number units sold", UNITS_SOLD
20 INPUT "Enter price per unit", PRICE
30 INPUT "Enter cost per unit", COST
40 PROFIT = UNITS_SOLD * (PRICE - COST)
50 PRINT "Profit $", PROFIT
60 STOP
RUN
```

When the program is executed, line 10 sends the prompt ENTER NUMBER UNITS SOLD to the screen and waits for your response. Whatever number you type is stored in the memory location identified by the name UNITS__SOLD. Lines 20 and 30 do the same thing for PRICE and COST. PROFIT is calculated in line 40; the PRINT statement in line 50 tells the computer to display the answer on the screen.

A Sample Pascal Program

Pascal is a good language to illustrate the nature of languages that are normally compiled, such as C, Ada, Modula-2, and PL/I. Pascal programs are divided into two sections: data definition and instruction processing. The *data definition section* is designated by the keyword VAR. All of the variables to be used must be declared at the beginning of the program inside the VAR section. A **variable** is a memory location that has been given a name. The *processing section* contains all of the actions to be carried out, and the order in which to carry them out. It begins with the keyword BEGIN and ends with the keyword END. Figure 15.3 shows a simple program to compute profit. The VAR section tells the compiler to make PROFIT, UNITS__SOLD, PRICE, and COST variables. The VAR section also declares that these variables are real numbers (signed numbers with decimal points); so they can store dollars and cents. The processing section follows. As in BASIC, the first statement is done, then the next statement, and so on. Although the syntax for the Pascal processing section of Figure 15.3 is slightly more complicated than that for the BASIC state-

Figure 15.3 *A Pascal program to compute PROFIT.*

```
PROGRAM PROFIT;

    VAR PROFIT     :  REAL;
        UNITS_SOLD :  REAL;
        PRICE      :  REAL;
        COST       :  REAL;

    BEGIN
        WRITE ('Enter number units sold');
        READLN (UNITS_SOLD);
        WRITE  ('Enter price per unit');
        READLN (PRICE);
        WRITE  ('Enter cost per unit');
        READLN (COST);
        PROFIT := UNITS_SOLD * (PRICE - COST);
        WRITELN ('Profit $', PROFIT)
    END.
```

ments in Figure 15.2, both programs accomplish the same task in the same basic way.

Because Pascal programs are compiled rather than interpreted, you must compile, link, and execute this program before any answer can be obtained. First, the source program PROFIT is read by the Pascal compiler program and converted into an object program that can be thought of as halfway to machine language. Then the linker program converts the object program into a machine language file that can be run by typing its name. The sample program in Figure 15.3 produces the following results (your inputs are shown in color):

```
Enter number units sold   5
Enter price per unit      1.50
Enter cost per unit       .75
Profit $3.750000
```

■ Structured Programming

Knowledge of a programming language is only one of the skills required of a programmer. The most important skill is knowing when and how to apply the right techniques. In a sense, the language is a paintbrush, the computer a canvas, and the programmer an artist. Knowing how to mix colorful paints does not guarantee a work of art. Similarly, knowing about computers and a programming language is no assurance that you can produce a high-quality program.

Steps in Programming

A programmer takes a written list of specifications for a program and uses them to write a program that solves a specified problem. The programmer first takes the following steps:

- Design an algorithm.
- Code it in a programming language.

The next steps are done by the computer.

- Translate the source program into the target program.
- Execute the target program.

The programmer takes the final steps.

- Debug the program. Program errors are called *bugs,* and the process of removing errors is called **debugging.**
- Redesign, correcting for major errors, and recode.

This cycle is repeated until all errors have been removed and the program works as it should, meeting the original specifications. In some cases the program is tested more than a hundred times before all errors are removed.

A large percentage of a programmer's time is spent debugging. This can be avoided, to some extent, by proper selection of a programming language. A high-level language is a good tool for minimizing the things that can go wrong in the programming process. But a high-level language is not enough; a programming methodology is also needed. To minimize the time spent debugging and increase the availability of high-quality software, professional programmers have developed a methodology called structured programming.

Structured Programs

In most disciplines a "divide and conquer" approach is used to divide a large and complex project into many simpler projects. Large programs are difficult to write, and so programmers employ their own version of "divide and conquer" called structured programming. **Structured programming** is a programming methodology that involves the systematic design of software. It includes the use of the structured design techniques described in Chapter 14.

A fundamental principle of structured programming is **software reductionism,** which is the idea that complex programs can be reduced to a collection of simple programs. This simple idea is very effective for reducing errors in programs and lowering the cost of developing new software. When a programmer uses reductionism to design and write a program, the result is called a **structured program.**

Structured programs can be reduced to elementary building blocks that are called control structures. **Control structures** are statements that control the order in which other program statements are executed. Every program can be constructed from the following three control structures:

1. *Sequence.* This control structure causes a program to execute statements placed one after the other in that sequence. Figure 15.4(a) shows the order of statement execution in a sequence of three statements (S_1, S_2, S_3).

2. *Choice.* When this control structure is used, statements in a program may or may not be executed depending on a decision made during program execution. If the decision results in a true condition, one path is taken; otherwise, the other path is taken. Both paths finally merge at a single point, where program execution continues. Figure 15.4(b) shows an example. If D is true, then statement S_1 is executed; otherwise, statement S_2 is executed. IF is used to designate the decision; THEN designates the path to be followed if the condition is TRUE; and ELSE designates the path to be followed if the condition is FALSE.

3. *Iteration.* This control structure is often called a *loop.* It causes statements to be executed repeatedly until some termination condition is reached.

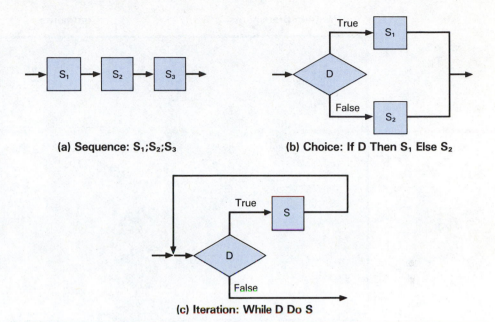

(a) Sequence: S₁;S₂;S₃

(b) Choice: If D Then S₁ Else S₂

(c) Iteration: While D Do S

Figure 15.4 *The fundamental control structures of structured programming.*

Figure 15.4(c) shows a loop. As long as D remains true, the program repeatedly executes statement S. As soon as D becomes false, the loop terminates, and the program executes the next statement following the loop. WHILE is used to designate the condition that is checked each time the loop is repeated; DO marks the statement to be repeated. The loop in Figure 15.4(c) is read, "While D is TRUE, do statement S."

A typical program is composed of hundreds of these fundamental components put together like Lego Blocks or Tinker Toys.

In a structured program these three control structures are the only ones used. When completed, a structured program has two major advantages over a nonstructured program. First, it is more likely to work correctly because it is simple. Second, it can be easily understood by someone else, modified, and enhanced.

A Sample Structured BASIC Program

Consider Figure 15.5, which shows a program that uses two of the three fundamental control structures—a loop and sequence statements. The loop begins with the keyword WHILE and ends with WEND. Indentations in the program indicate that the preceding statement contains the indented sequence of statements. Thus within the loop there is a sequence of three statements—the statements in lines 130, 140, and 150.

Program Statements   **Comments**

```
100 SUM  = 0                    'SEQUENCE OF 3 STATEMENTS...
110 COUNT= 0                    'COUNT HOW MANY INPUTS
120 INPUT "Enter # of NUMBERs "; N
125 WHILE N > COUNT             'ITERATION...
130    INPUT NUMBER             'SEQUENCE INSIDE ITERATION...
140    SUM = SUM + NUMBER
150    COUNT = COUNT + 1
160 WEND                        'LOOP ENDS
170 AVG = SUM / COUNT
180 PRINT AVG
190 END
```

Figure 15.5 *A structured BASIC program that computes an average of* N *numbers.*

This program accepts a list of numbers from the keyboard, computes their average value, and prints the average value. But it contains a bug. It does compute an average value if there is at least one input. However, if no input is entered at the keyboard, COUNT remains at zero, and the division by zero in line 170 causes the program to crash.

We can fix this bug by using the choice structure to test for a zero value of COUNT. To do so, we change line 170 to read

```
170 IF COUNT > 0 THEN AVG = SUM / COUNT ELSE AVG = 0
```

This is called an IF-THEN-ELSE statement. Figure 15.6 compares the two versions of the program.

We could have written the program in an unstructured manner. For example, instead of the IF statement we added to line 170, we could have used a GOTO statement—a command to go to a specified line, thereby skipping over other statements.

```
170 IF COUNT > 0 GOTO 175
172 AVG = 0
173 GOTO 180
175 AVG = SUM / COUNT
```

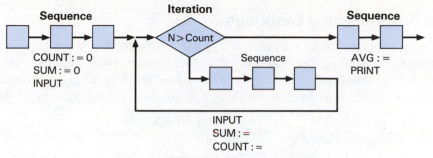

(a) First Version: Sequence and Iteration

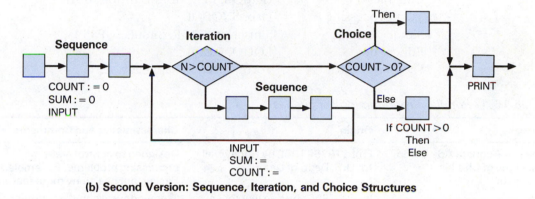

(b) Second Version: Sequence, Iteration, and Choice Structures

Figure 15.6 *Two versions of a program to compute an average of N numbers. The first version (a) is the program given in Figure 15.5. In (b) a choice structure has been added.*

But in structured programming GOTO statements are forbidden because they violate the restriction to use only sequence, choice, and iteration control structures. An illustration of the effect of using numerous GOTO statements in a BASIC program is shown in Figure 15.7. Programs without GOTO statements are easier to understand, and as a consequence, normally have fewer bugs.

Figure 15.7 *Effect of GOTOs on program structure.*

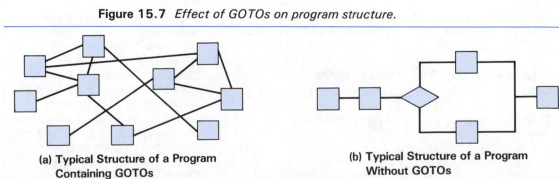

(a) Typical Structure of a Program Containing GOTOs

(b) Typical Structure of a Program Without GOTOs

■ Selecting a Programming Language

Every programming language has its loyal followers, but there is no one programming language that is best for all applications. Instead, families of languages exist to make certain problems easier to solve. The following list shows a small sample of the more than four hundred programming languages that exist:

Problem or application area	Some recommended languages
Numerical	BASIC, FORTRAN, APL, Pascal
Data files	COBOL, PL/I, dBASE II/dBASE III
Text processing	Lisp, SNOBOL
Simulation	Simscript, GASP, Simula, GPSS
Education	LOGO, Pascal
Factory control	Forth, machine language, APT

Table 15.1 *Popular Programming Languages*

Name	Origin	Characteristics and Comments
Ada (for Augusta Ada Byron, colleague of Charles Babbage)	From 1979–1982 by Honeywell for U.S. Dept. of Defense	Designed to control real-time processing problems. Resembles Pascal, but has many more features.
APL (A Programming Language)	In mid-1960s by Ken Iverson, a mathematician at IBM	Tremendously compact, powerful Language. Highly interactive; interpreted.
BASIC (Beginners All-Purpose Symbolic Instruction Code)	In mid-1960s by John Kemeny and Thomas Kurts at Dartmouth	Easily Learned Language. Widely used on small computers. Many incompatible versions exist.
C	In 1972 by Dennis Ritchie at Bell Laboratories	Originally designed to write system software. Very portable; generates fast compact code.
COBOL (COmmon Business Oriented Language)	In 1960 by a group of users and manufacturers.	By far the most popular language for commercial applications. Creates verbose, English-like, understandable code.
FORTRAN (FORmula TRANslator)	In 1957 by IBM	Used for scientific and mathematical programming.
Pascal (for Blaise Pascal, French mathematician)	From 1968–1971 by Professor Niklaus Wirth of Switzerland	Originally designed as a teaching vehicle to encourage structured programming. Small, memory-efficient compilers. Limited I/O features.
PL/I (Programming Language 1)	In 1966 by IBM	Designed to combine the best features of COBOL and FORTRAN. Used primarily on large computers.
RPG (Report Program Generator)	In mid-1960s by IBM	Allows reports to be created quickly and easily. Uses specification forms rather than programming statements. Popular on business minicomputers.

Making the Pieces: From Silicon Crystals to Computers

Computers are constructed from electrical parts — mainly transistors, capacitors, resistors, and wires. It takes millions of these parts to build even a small personal computer. Because of intense competition, successful firms must use low-cost methods to build and connect electrical components. The fruit of this competition has been a number of fascinating and exotic manufacturing techniques. As you study this photo essay, you will gain insight into how these techniques work.

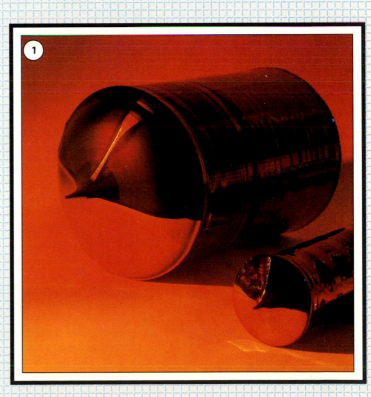

1. Large silicon crystals are the raw material from which most integrated circuit chips are manufactured. The crystals are grown in a furnace containing an exceptionally pure bath of molten silicon. Usually they are from 3 to 5 inches in diameter; often they are several feet long.

PREPARING THE SILICON SURFACE

2. Each silicon crystal is sliced with a diamond-edged saw into round wafers that are less than one-half millimeter thick. Because silicon crystals are harder than most metals, cutting them is expensive and slow.

3. The first step in removing damage caused by cutting the crystals is called lapping. Wafers are placed in carriers between two rotating plates that remove a prescribed amount of damage. Later the wafers are polished to a mirror finish.

4. Wafers are inspected many times during the manufacturing process.

5. A finished wafer contains many integrated circuit chips organized like postage stamps on a piece of paper. These wafers range from 1 to 5 inches. The trend has been toward larger wafers.

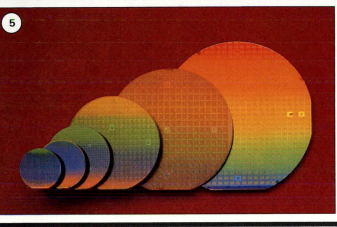

6. An IBM engineer inspects an experimental eight-inch silicon wafer that can accommodate more than 2,000 chips.

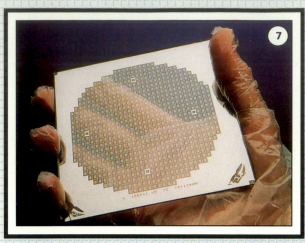

7

Photographic methods are used to transfer an image of circuit patterns into numerous copies on the silicon surface.

7. This photomask contains one layer of circuitry. The mask is created by an electron-beam exposure system that etches tiny images on a metal-coated glass plate; the glass is transparent to ultraviolet rays, but the metal isn't. Before the mask can be used to create circuits, the wafers are dipped in a bath of ultraviolet-sensitive photoresist (a photographic-type emulsion). Then each wafer is exposed by shining ultraviolet light through the mask. Finally, the wafer is washed in a developing solution, leaving a pattern on the surface. This process deposits an image of one circuit layer on the surface of the chip. A completed chip may require from 5 to 18 circuit layers.

8

9. A rack of wafers enters the furnace.

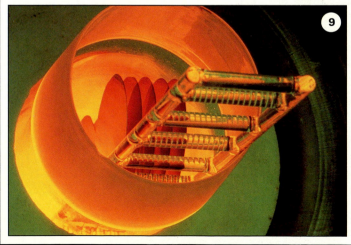

9

8. During some processing steps wafers are heated in ovens to produce an insulating layer of glass oxide on exposed silicon surfaces. Other steps use ovens to "dope" unoxidized surfaces with a thin layer of impurities, such as boron or phosphorus. The impurities create conductive and resistive regions in the silicon that form electronic circuits.

10. Peter Ferlita inserts a program card into an automatically controlled furnace at RCA's Solid State Division in Somerville, New Jersey. The card contains instructions for processing during a one-hour trip at temperatures of 1500° F. After more than 500 manufacturing operations, these wafers will be used in guidance control systems for missiles.

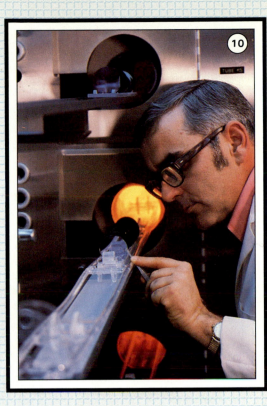

11. An Intel Corporation technician positions wafers to receive a thin coating of aluminum from an evaporator. Later most of the aluminum will be etched away, leaving trace lines that connect the circuits.

12. A wafer is washed after etching. This is a wafer of transducers to be used in read/write heads for hard disk drives.

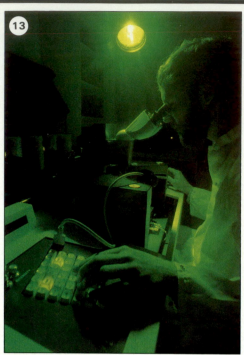

14. Microscopes are also necessary to align photo-masks with the circuits on a partially completed wafer.

13. Periodic inspections by microscope are necessary to ensure that the circuits are being constructed satisfactorily.

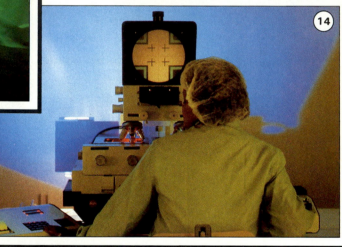

15. Even minute particles of dust in the air can land on the surface of the silicon and result in malfunctioning circuits. Manufacturing is done in highly controlled ''clean rooms'' where workers wear protective gloves and hats and the air is constantly filtered. This room is lit with yellow light to keep out extraneous ultraviolet rays.

TESTING AND CUTTING THE FINISHED WAFER

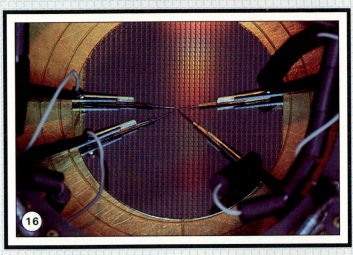

16. After the wafer is completed, each chip is tested to see if it functions correctly. The tests are conducted by placing probes on tiny electrical contact pads around the outside of the chip.

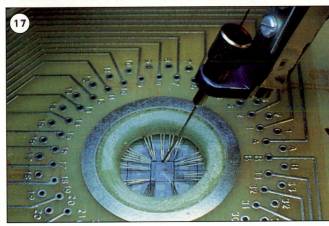

17. This testing machine at the National Semiconductor Corporation lowers 29 wires onto a chip and then runs it through a series of electrical tests. If the chip fails a test, a small ink spot is dropped on it to mark it as a reject.

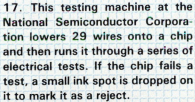

18. Eventually the wafer is ready to be diced into separate chips. Here a diamond-edged tool scribes lines along the wafer's surface.

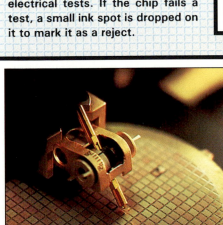

PACKING MEMORY CHIPS

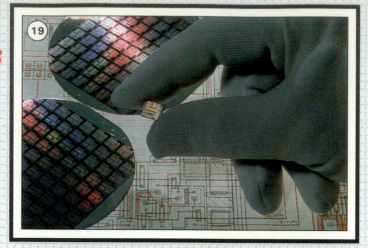

19. A composite drawing of circuit layers, two finished wafers, and a gloved hand holding an unmounted integrated circuit chip.

21. A packaged memory chip sits on top of a wafer of similar memory chips. Each chip can store 64K bits (65,536 bits) of digital data. Memory chips capable of storing more than one megabit are being developed in research labs.

20. Chips are mounted inside protective carrier packages to make them easier to handle and to help them dissipate heat. To mount the chip, tiny wires are soldered from pads on the chip's outside edges to contact areas on the carrier.

22. Very-large-scale-integrated (VLSI) chips require many input and output pins. Instead of having leads poked into holes in a circuit board, these chips have been mounted in leadless carriers that sit on the surface of a circuit board. This method produces smaller chips, which results in more densely populated circuit boards and, consequently, smaller and faster computers.

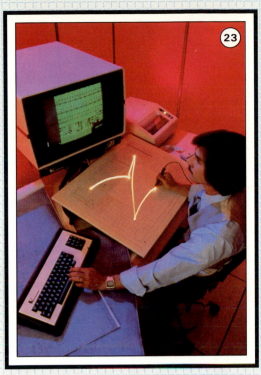

23.

DESIGNING THE CIRCUITS

Chips can have well over 100,000 circuit elements. Creating and testing the circuit design require extensive use of computers.

24.

23. This computer-aided design system supports a wide range of design, drafting, and manufacturing operations on large-scale integrated (LSI) chips. The user enters data from either the keyboard or the graphics tablet.

24. Once a design is stored in memory, it receives thorough computerized testing. The circuit's functions are simulated by programs that check for problems with the speed, timing, logic, and voltage. Modifications to the chip's design can be entered from the keyboard.

25.

25. Composite drawings of the various circuit layers are 400 times larger than actual size.

DESIGNING CIRCUIT BOARDS

The most common way of linking chips electrically is to mount them on printed circuit boards made of fiberglass.

26. High-quality graphics terminals help lay out the design of circuit boards quickly and accurately.

27. After the position of chips has been entered, straight lines can be drawn on the screen to point out how the chips' pins are to be connected.

28. Once the connections among pins have been specified, computer programs help determine where the copper traces (wires) should run along the circuit board's surfaces.

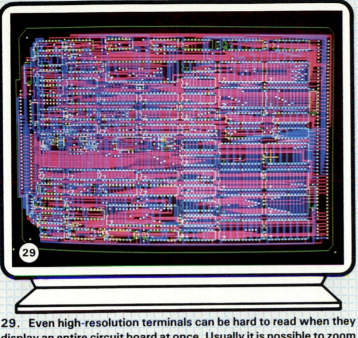

29. Even high-resolution terminals can be hard to read when they display an entire circuit board at once. Usually it is possible to zoom in to look at one portion more closely, or to scroll from one region of the board to another.

30. In minutes a color electrostatic plotter can produce a full-color plot of an entire circuit board so that designs can be previewed quickly.

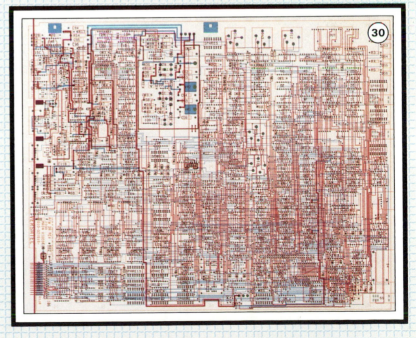

window 8

COMPUTER-AIDED MANUFACTURING

31. Computers do more than speed up the design process; they produce the media needed to manufacture printed circuit boards. Among these media are artwork and silkscreen masters, component drawings, and tapes that direct drilling and insertion operations.

32. Artwork masters can be extracted directly from a computerized circuit board design aided by a computer-controlled photoplotter.

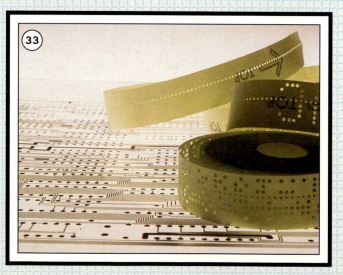

33. Punched tape is often used to load numerically controlled (N/C) manufacturing machines with control sequences. Many processes for manufacturing rely heavily on N/C machines.

BUILDING THE
BARE BOARD

34. An internal layer of a 16-layer printed circuit board is scanned by a programmable inspection machine to ensure high reliability. This circuit board will become part of an electronic system to protect military aircraft from radar-directed weapons.

35. A Cray Research technician coats a printed circuit board with copper. This step follows an operation that masks areas of the board so that only the unmasked areas are plated with copper.

36. Integrated circuit chips have been installed in this completed supercomputer circuit board manufactured by Cray Research.

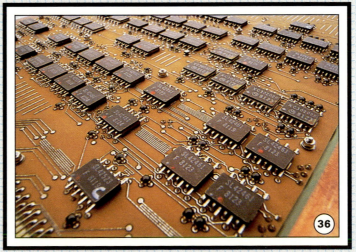

DRILLING, STUFFING, SOLDERING, AND INSPECTING THE BOARDS

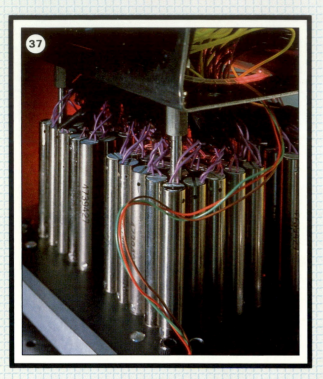

37. In one second this IBM-designed tool punches 1,440 precisely placed holes with the diameter of an eyelash; then it automatically inspects its own work. The holes are punched in ceramic substrates that serve as chip carriers in IBM's large-scale computers. As many as 40,000 holes in each of up to 33 sheets of ceramic substrate are punched with great accuracy in order to ensure the integrity of electrical connections.

38. An engineer completes the installation of a robotic system on an automated assembly line for IBM 3178 display terminals.

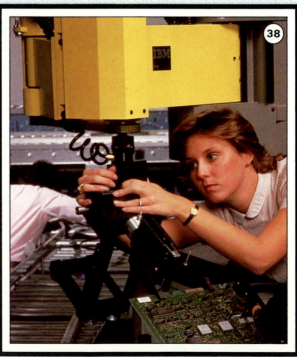

39. For low-volume manufacturing operations, electrical components are ''stuffed'' into a circuit board by hand. All of the components are mounted on one side of the board, leaving the back side bare. When the components have been added, the bare side of the board is passed over a flowing stream that solders all the pins in place in one operation.

40. Paradyne has several manufacturing and assembly lines that produce printed circuit boards. They have a high ratio of inspectors to assemblers so that possible problems can be identified early in the manufacturing cycle.

41. At Tandem's circuit board assembly facility in Watsonville, California, computer-controlled production includes a variety of bar code readers.

ASSEMBLING AND TESTING THE FINAL PRODUCT

42. As sales of personal computers climbed, the manufacturers required high-volume, assembly line production methods.

43. As many as one Macintosh every 27 seconds is built at Apple's highly automated factory in Fremont, California.

44. In Greenrock, Scotland, a technician monitors tests of the IBM PC/AT.

window 8

Table 15.1 presents a more detailed view of some of the most popular programming languages. The choices can be overwhelming, but here are a few guidelines to help you choose. First, decide what type of problem is to be solved. Using a text-processing language to solve a numerical problem will end in disaster. Next, consider compatibility with your machine, operating system, other programs, and other files. This is called *system compatibility* and is very important if you want the language to fit in with an existing system of hardware and software. Finally, consider such technical features of each programming language as the readability and maintainability of programs written in the language and the language's input/output abilities, its text-processing features, control structures, processing efficiency, and portability. In the following sections we take a closer look at these guidelines.

System Compatibility

An obvious first step in selecting a programming language is to make sure your computer has enough RAM to run the compiler or interpreter. Many compilers require large amounts of disk space as well. They may occupy several floppy disks and can make several passes over the source program during conversion to machine language. If this is the case, it can be very inconvenient or impossible to use floppy disk drives—a hard disk may be required.

You should choose the operating system you want to use before you choose a programming language. Most computers support more than one operating system; for example, an IBM PC can run programs for MS-DOS, UNIX, CP/M, and several other operating systems. But a certain programming language may work under only one operating system. Although the language translator may work with the desired operating system, it may or may not be compatible with other programs that work under the same operating system. A FORTRAN program under MS-DOS, for example, may not be compatible with a Pascal program also under MS-DOS.

Lack of compatibility can happen at several other levels. For example, the data files created by a Pascal program may not be readable by a BASIC program. Similarly, a program written in Pascal and translated into machine language may not be usable by a BASIC program that has also been translated into machine language. However, if the two are compatible, then considerable time might be saved by using the previously written Pascal program as part of the new BASIC program.

One major advantage of translation by compiling is the ability to combine programs from different languages into larger, more powerful programs through linking. When programs are written so that they can be used over again they are called **routines** or **subroutines;** a routine is reused by *calling* it. The linker program combines previously written routines with operating system routines to complete the translation of your program into a machine-level program that will run on a particular computer. If you plan to use a variety of programming languages on one machine, it may be worthwhile to purchase all of the translators from one company to ensure compatibility among them.

Readability and Maintainability

Readability and maintainability are important in the business world because some programs "live" for twenty years—far beyond the time when the original programmers are likely to be around. Thus, a readable and understandable program is a necessity for large banks, insurance companies, and corporations. If a million-dollar program cannot be maintained, then it becomes worthless.

A programming language affects readability and maintainability in several ways.

- *Syntax* determines the grammar of the language.
- *Modularity* affects the degree to which the program can be divided into easily comprehended parts.
- *Familiarity* refers to how similar the language is to natural languages.
- *Consistency* determines whether the language is predictable and lacks unexpected features.
- *Structured-ness* refers to whether the language provides structured programming control constructs.

Syntax

The *syntax* of a language determines its parts of speech and keywords. For example, the syntax of a COBOL program is very verbose and English-like so that with a little practice anyone can understand it. COBOL uses familiar English keywords like SUBTRACT, MOVE, TO, FROM, and PERFORM. The following fragment from a program that prints a mailing list illustrates COBOL's syntax:

```
PROCEDURE DIVISION.
MAIN-ROUTINE.
    OPEN OUTPUT MAIL-LABELS-FILE
        INPUT ADDRESS-FILE.
    READ ADDRESS-FILE
        AT END
            MOVE "NO" TO MORE-INPUT.
    PERFORM PRINT-ADDRESS-LOOP
        UNTIL MORE-INPUT IS EQUAL TO "NO".
    CLOSE MAIL-LABELS-FILE
        ADDRESS-FILE.
    STOP RUN.
```

COBOL programs are self-documenting, portable, and very good at handling files and reports; but they are weak at processing mathematical data. COBOL is used more than any other language for developing large business data processing programs.

FORTRAN, in contrast, uses a syntax that is more mathematical. For example,

```
DO 100 I=1,10
IF ( NUM-99 ) 2,3,3
X = SQRT( B**2 - 4.0 * A * C )
```

To a mathematician or engineer, FORTRAN's algebraic notation is familiar.

Modularity

Modularity is important because it helps make large programs understandable. Each module can be understood as a "chunk" or box, and then larger modules can be composed of smaller modules, and so forth. One feature of a modular language is the requirement to state explicitly where a module gets incoming data; this helps guarantee that the linkages among modules are well understood.

Modula-2 is an example of a highly modular programming language. For example, the following is a simple Modula-2 module that imports Read, Write, Sqrt, Sin, and Cos functions from two other modules:

```
MODULE Main;
FROM InOut IMPORT Read, Write;
FROM Math IMPORT Sqrt, Sin, Cos;
BEGIN
  .
  .                          ◄— The module's processing statements belong here.
  .
END.
```

BASIC is a counterexample; it provides little support for cleanly separating a large program into independent modules.

Both Modula-2 and its predecessor, Pascal, were invented to be implemented efficiently on computers. Pascal was designed by Niklaus Wirth in order to create a programming language that would teach students "the correct way" to program. It was one of the first languages to be designed with a familiar, consistent, and structured syntax. However, Pascal lacked the modularity of other languages; so Niklaus Wirth went back to the drawing board to design Modula-2 to incorporate modularity, greater consistency, and extensive structured-ness. Many other languages have been patterned after Pascal because of its clarity and elegance.

Consistency

If a language is *consistent,* it handles similar situations in a similar way, thus making programs easy to comprehend. Consider the formulas

Radius * Pi + Square
Strength − Stress * Factor

Several rules might be used to determine in what order to perform the arithmetic operations in these formulas. But if a language is consistent, the same order will be used for both of them. In APL all expressions are evaluated from right to left; so the meaning of the two expressions would be

Radius * (Pi + Square)
Strength − (Stress * Factor)

But in BASIC, because of an inconsistency in the grammar, the formulas would be interpreted as

(Radius * Pi) + Square
Strength − (Stress * Factor)

Structured-ness

Structured-ness is the degree to which a language conforms to the structured programming idea that all modules and all program statements should have a single entry point and a single exit point. For example, there is only one entry point and one exit point for the statements in the following fragment of Pascal:

```
IF A=0 THEN
     B:=100
ELSE
     B:=200;
WHILE B<200 DO
     BEGIN
     WriteLn( B );
     ReadLn( B )
END;
CASE B OF
10: A:= 0;
20: A:=10;
END;
```

Each of these statements has a single starting and ending point within the program. The IF-THEN-ELSE statement flows into the WHILE-DO statement; the BEGIN-END statement is nested within the WHILE-DO statement, and they both terminate in the same place; the CASE-OF-END statement executes either 10: or 20:, but not both, and then terminates at the END statement.

In contrast, BASIC and FORTRAN have no way to enforce structured programming. Here is an example using BASIC.

```
FOR I=1 TO 10
 IF I=J THEN GOTO 100
NEXT I
    ....
100 PRINT I
```

The IF-THEN-GOTO statement violates the requirement that there should be only one exit point because there are two paths out of the FOR-NEXT loop: one path leads out the bottom of the loop and would be taken after the loop has executed 10 times; the other path jumps from the middle of the loop to line 100 if the value in variable I is the same as the value in J.

FORTRAN, BASIC, and COBOL were all invented before the idea of structured programming; so they make it easy to write very convoluted programs that lack structured-ness. ALGOL (ALGOrithmic Language) was the earliest language developed with good structure. It was created in the early 1960s in Europe and used extensively there until Pascal replaced it. PL/I borrowed many of ALGOL's structured features. Pascal, C, Modula-2, and Ada are also derivatives of ALGOL.

Input/Output Abilities

I/O processing is very important because it determines how programs deal with printers, keyboards, screens, and other peripheral devices.

A good I/O-handling language must be able to read and write sequential, direct, and indexed files. Recall that a *direct file* is one in which each record of the file can be directly accessed; an *indexed file* can be accessed through a (sorted) index key. COBOL and PL/I incorporate these file types into the language, which makes it reasonably simple to store and retrieve data from large data files with these languages. In addition, COBOL and PL/I are often extended to allow them to communicate with a database management system.

Most BASIC interpreters provide special verbs for creating graphics, but writing to the graphics screen from FORTRAN, Pascal, and C is difficult unless these languages are augmented with special graphics routines.

Pascal, C, and most other languages can print a report on the printer; but COBOL and PL/I are especially good for formatting and printing reports. If your needs are limited to creating business reports, then RPG might be an even better choice. It is a special-purpose report-generating programming language. RPG allows a programmer to write a reporting program by filling out several forms that describe the way the report will appear on the printed page. An RPG compiler takes this sample report and turns it into a program.

Arithmetic Computation

COBOL and FORTRAN represent two extremes in their ability to perform arithmetic calculations. FORTRAN was designed to do mathematical calculations like exponentiation, logarithms, transcendental functions, and so on. COBOL is limited to simple expressions. Compare this statement in COBOL

```
COMPUTE INVENTORY = YEAR-TO-DATE-INVENTORY + ( ORDERED * PRICE ).
```

with the FORTRAN statement

```
HYPOT = SQRT ( A**2 + B**2 )
```

The differences may seem inconsequential until you attempt to do a calculation that does not exist in the language. For example, Pascal has no exponentiation operator; so our sample FORTRAN calculation cannot be done directly in Pascal.

Text Processing

Pascal, FORTRAN, COBOL, and most other widely used programming languages have difficulty processing characters and strings of text. Therefore, special-purpose symbol-processing languages like Lisp and SNOBOL were invented. These languages were developed in the 1960s to handle non-numeric data.

Instead of adding, subtracting, and multiplying numbers, a text-processing language joins together, separates, inserts characters of text, searches for patterns of characters, and performs other related operations. For example, in Lisp the CONS and CDR operators retrieve the first character and trailing characters of an alphanumeric list. These operators might be used, for example, to separate the first and last names of a full name.

Lisp has become the premier language of artificial intelligence because of its ability to handle lists and make associations, and because of its familiarity to the artificial intelligence community. SNOBOL (invented by Griswald while at Bell Labs) is used to process and analyze text.

Control Structures

Recall that a *control structure* is any statement in a programming language that controls the order in which other statements are to be executed. We have given examples of several control statements, including IF-THEN-ELSE (for making two-way decisions), FOR (for repeating or looping), and CASE (for multiple-way decisions). In theory, every conceivable program can be written with only three control structures: sequence (one statement following another), iteration (loops), and choice (IF-THEN-ELSE). In practice, additional control statements are added to a language to make it more convenient for a programmer to use. For example, in Pascal derivatives the CASE statement expands the IF-THEN-ELSE statement into a multiple-branching statement, and the CALL or PERFORM statements of FORTRAN and COBOL permit modules to be invoked from a main program, thus allowing modularity.

The control structures used in Ada are particularly interesting. Ada was created by the Department of Defense to reduce the huge expense of developing real-time systems—ones that could keep up with events happening in the real world. An Ada program can be divided into modules that run at the same time on multiple processors. Each module runs in parallel with the others. But when one module needs information computed by another parallel module, it exchanges this information through a control structure called a **rendez-vous statement.** It forces one module to wait while the other module catches up, thus synchronizing the two modules.

Other control structures include special statements for catching errors or unusual occurrences such as bad input data, a missing file, or an error in the program. These are called **exception statements** because they handle exceptions. In PL/I, for example, the ON ERROR GOTO statement takes care of I/O exceptions, attempts to divide by zero, and any other unusual circumstances that might arise when the program is executed. Some versions of BASIC have ON ERROR GOTO control statements, as do many extended versions of Pascal.

Data Structures

A **data structure** is a collection of values and associated information that provides a way to manipulate many values together as a unit. A simple example of a data structure is an **array,** an organized collection of data in a row-and-column format. The structure of an array makes it easy to update or retrieve any item in the array by referencing its position within the array. For example, in FORTRAN, a DIMENSION statement reserves an area of memory, as in:

```
DIMENSION SCORES(100)
```

This DIMENSION statement establishes SCORES as the name of a one-dimensional numerical array with the ability to store 100 values. You can think of this array as a single column of memory cells with 100 rows; each row can store one number. This array might be used to store up to 100 test scores in a manner that they can be manipulated easily to accomplish a task, such as finding the highest test score in a list. To reference the number in the third row of SCORES, for example, the FORTRAN syntax says to enclose the index 3 inside parentheses, as in X(3) = 3.14159. This stores 3.14159 in the third memory cell of array X.

The following data structure in Pascal demonstrates how to express a list of names along with the street address and telephone number of each person:

```
VAR
      People : ARRAY[1..MAX] OF
                  RECORD
                        Name : string;
                        Street: string;
                        Tele: PhoneNumber
                  END;
```

Data structures are also used to format external disk files. Again, in Pascal, the contents of a file can be clearly written as follows:

```
VAR
      DECK : FILE OF
                  RECORD
                    Name : PersonName;
                    Age  : 0..99;
                    Bal  : Dollars;
                    Sex  : ( Male, Female )
                  END;
```

Here, the contents of the file are clearly designated and can be referenced later on in the program by these same names.

FORTRAN and BASIC are especially deficient in data structures whereas Pascal, Modula-2, Ada, Lisp, and most modern programming languages allow the programmer to define new types of data structures. The syntax of Pascal data-structure declarations can be quite striking in its familiarity, consistency, and elegance. The readability and understandability of Pascal data structures have been copied by nearly every new programming language developed over the past decade.

Intrinsic Functions

An **intrinsic function** is a module that is supplied along with the programming language translator to make using the language easier. FORTRAN has many predefined intrinsic functions for doing arithmetic, transcendental functions (sine, cosine), and special-purpose mathematics (matrix multiply). Pascal does all of its I/O through intrinsic functions.

Much of the power and flexibility of a programming language comes from its intrinsic functions (or lack of them). BASIC would be uninteresting if it were not for the intrinsic functions for handling strings, mathematics, and graphics found in most dialects of BASIC. C is little more than a set of control statements plus a large number of functions.

The following is a list of the intrinsic functions you should look for when considering a programming language:

- *Arithmetic/logic.* Bit manipulation, string manipulation, and so on.
- *External device control.* Control of modems, mouse, joy stick, and so on.
- *Graphics and sound control.* Display, music, and voice output.
- *Conversion of data.* Character-to-numerical and vice versa, and so on.
- *Screen I/O.* Forms handling, report formats, and so on.

These functions can significantly reduce the amount of programming time and effort needed to build a new program from scratch.

Processing Efficiency and Program Size

A program written in a high-level language trades speed for maintainability (ease of modification and improvement). It must be translated, and the translated program is larger and runs more slowly than if the program had been written initially in machine language. The good news is that a program written in a high-level language is easier to understand and modify. If you expect to modify a program frequently, it is worthwhile to sacrifice speed and small size for maintainability and use a high-level language.

Most computer programs with wide appeal—such as 1-2-3, Symphony, Frameworks, WordStar, and AppleWriter II—are written in assembly language to achieve the greatest speed possible. Unless you are an expert programmer and are going to sell a million copies of your program, however, it is probably better to use a high-level language.

The machine language version of a programming language may vary in size and speed, depending on how clever the compiler writers were. A "fast" compiler produces fast-running programs; a "compact" compiler produces small-sized programs. Depending on the compiler, the target programs compiled from typical Pascal or C programs may differ in size and speed by a factor of 10 or more. One translator may produce very fast code, but require twice the amount of memory as another translator.

Benchmark programs are usually employed to measure the effectiveness of a compiler or interpreter. One well-known benchmark program, the sieve of Eratosthenes, computes prime numbers; it is commonly used to compare the computational speed and memory requirements of programs.

Portability

Portability refers to the ease with which a program can be moved from one machine to another—without modifications. The main method of achieving portability is to use a compiler for the other machine to recompile the source program. Suppose a Pascal program exists on an Apple computer, and you buy an IBM PC. If the source program is written in a portable version of Pascal, it can be copied onto an IBM PC disk (probably via communications), compiled by the IBM PC Pascal compiler, and then run on the IBM computer.

Few programs are 100 percent portable; instead they must be modified before being recompiled for the new computer. If portability is important, plan for it in advance. Avoid machine-dependent features of programming languages and consider purchasing compatible compilers for use on all the machines.

COBOL is probably the most portable programming language around because it has been standardized by the American National Standards committee. FORTRAN 77 is a 1977 standardized dialect of FORTRAN; BASIC, Pascal, and many other languages have also been standardized. Manufacturers of programming language compilers frequently add features to standardized languages, thus creating nonstandard dialects.

Pascal is a classic example of a language that suffers from too many nonstandard dialects. Rarely can a Pascal program written on one machine be compiled and run on another machine without extensive modifications. This situation exists because Pascal was originally designed to teach programmers rather than to be a commercial programming language. Because of its elegance, Pascal was adapted to the real world of software through a variety of extensions. The most notable extension was done by the University of California at San Diego—called UCSD Pascal. This dialect became one of the most widely used languages in the world, but it reduced the portability of Pascal programs from one version of Pascal to another because it greatly extended the original language.

C has become almost a standard language because there are no dialects that extend the language. The K & R standard (which was defined in a book by Brian Kernighan and Dennis Richey), is almost universally accepted as the definition of C. In addition, it is easy to write a C compiler for a new machine because C is very close to machine language yet similar to Pascal and other ALGOL derivatives. For this reason, many software developers use C to write programs for all sizes and brands of computers. In contrast, COBOL compilers are difficult to write and often take years to develop for a new machine.

■ Beyond High-level Languages

Very High-Level Languages (VHLL)

Clearly the best way to tell your friend to go to the store to get milk is to use an abstract notation such as English. In English the algorithm for getting a quart of milk might look like the following:

1. Go to the store and buy 1 quart of milk

2. Bring the quart of milk to me.

This "program" tells your friend *what* you want done, but not *how* to do it. The difference between a **very high-level language** (**VHLL**) and the programming languages we have discussed until now is the difference between saying *what* to do and giving detailed directions of *how* to do it. A very high-level language (sometimes called a *fourth-generation language*) is a **nonprocedural language** because it describes what processing is to be done without specifying the particular procedures to be used to complete the processing.

The database query languages and report generator languages described in Chapter 10 are examples of restricted VHLLs. Only a few VHLL translators exist because software designers are just beginning to solve the difficult problems associated with machine translation of nonprocedural programs. The few that do exist are limited to special purposes, such as creating a report, controlling the dialog in a learning module, or answering complex queries for information. But VHLLs are the computer languages of the future because they simplify programming, increase a programmer's productivity, are easy to modify and maintain, and can be understood by most anyone. We will discuss only two broad categories of VHLLs: application generators and program generators.

Application Generators

An **application generator** (**AG**) gives a detailed explanation of what data is to be processed, rather than how to process the data in an application. It is similar to a report generator, but it expresses processing steps in a notation similar to a high-level language. Hence, programs written for an application generator appear to be slightly procedural, as illustrated by Figure 15.8. Typically (but not always), application generators are extensions to the query facility of a database management system. As such, they assume the DBMS model of data. The example shown here is closely related to the dBASE II model of data.

Most AG translators are interpreters, not compilers; hence the AG program is directly interpreted. To run the application, you enter its name after the command DO. It is read into the AG translator and executed one statement at a time. In the case of Figure 15.8, the application finds all CUSTOMER_FILE records whose value stored in the field named YTD is greater than a value supplied by the user (YTD > MIN). It prints these records according to the report format stored in F1.

The following list explains the meaning of each command word in Figure 15.8:

■ ERASE. Erase the monitor screen.

■ STORE ' ' TO MIN. Store a blank in MIN (no value).

```
BEGIN
     ERASE
     STORE '     ' TO MIN
     @ 10,5 SAY ' Enter minimum search condition'
     @ 10,35 GET MIN
     READ
     ? ' Printing in progress...'
     USE CUSTOMER_FILE
     INDEX ON YTD TO ORDERED_FILE
     REPORT FORM F1 FOR YTD > MIN TO PRINT
     RELEASE MIN
     RETURN
END.
```

Figure 15.8 *Example of an application generator program.*

- @ 10,5 SAY. Prompt the user with the message ENTER MINIMUM SEARCH CONDITION. The prompt begins in line 10, column 5 of the screen.

- @ 10,35 GET MIN. Wait for the user to enter a value for MIN.

- READ. This forces the AG to read the previous two @ commands and save them for use later.

- ? Display the message PRINTING IN PROGRESS . . .

- USE. Select the file named CUSTOMER__FILE.

- INDEX ON YTD. Build a separate index file in ORDERED__FILE that is in order by YTD field values. Use this index file to retrieve records from the ORDERED__FILE in ascending order by YTD.

- REPORT. Use a previously defined report form stored in F1 to print a report. The report selects only those records from the database that satisfy the search conditions YTD > MIN.

- RELEASE. No longer use MIN as a storage variable; release the memory space used by MIN.

- RETURN. Return to whatever you were doing before you began this application.

The STORE, @, and RELEASE commands are procedural statements because they describe processing steps. In contrast, the USE, INDEX, and REPORT commands do not describe how their processing is to be done; they are nonprocedural. For the most part, MIN__PRINT tells the computer what to do, and not how to do it.

Program Generators

A **program generator (PG)** is a translator that converts nonprocedural information into a procedural program. Instead of using very high-level language statements, a PG usually employs a question-and-answer dialog to determine what processing is to be done. Then it takes this nonprocedural information and uses it to write a program in some programming language, often BASIC or COBOL, which in turn must be translated into machine language or directly interpreted. Most PGs allow you to display and modify the program they produce.

To use a PG, simply answer its questions. Figure 15.9 provides an example. The program generated from the dialog in Figure 15.9 does the same thing as the AG program in Figure 15.8.

Sophisticated PGs usually ask many questions. You might be asked for information concerning menus, file organization, printer configuration, the color and dimensions of the screen, and so forth. The questions asked by a PG are nonprocedural, as you can see in Figure 15.9. However, PGs are restricted in what they do. For applications requiring a lot of formulas, interaction with a user, or sophisticated data processing, you will probably need to use another method. But for uncomplicated tasks, program generators are excellent.

Figure 15.9 *Sample dialog with a program generator.*

```
BEGIN
      What is the name of the input variable? MIN
      What prompt is to be used? Enter minimum search condition
      What is the name of the input file?  CUSTOMER_FILE
      Is the input file sorted?  No
      Do you want to sort it?  No
      Is the input file indexed?  No
      Do you want to index it?  Yes
      Index what field?  YTD
      Index what field?
      Do you want to calculate?  No
      Do you want a report?  Yes
      What is the report format file?  F1
      Do you want to print in order?  Yes
      Enter index or sort key name:  YTD
      Do you want to limit retrieval?  Yes
      Enter limit or search condition:  YTD > MIN
      Enter limit or search condition:
      Do you want a disk copy of print?  No
      Are you done?  Yes
END.
```

■ Summary

Programming is a challenging intellectual activity that some people do exceptionally well and enjoy. For most of us, however, it is a chore requiring dedication and skill. Most people who use computers will not become programmers because of the specialized knowledge required to do so.

Low-level machine language is good for the expert programmer who wants to get the very last bit of performance from a computer. Most application programs that require fast responses are written in the symbolic form of machine language called assembly language (although this is slowly changing as computers become faster). Machine language is not the appropriate tool for the computer user who is simply trying to solve a problem.

High-level languages (HLLs) are, by far, the tools used most often in programming. They allow you to write any program with a reasonable amount of clarity and maintainability.

Selecting the right HLL involves many decisions concerning the translator. Should it be an interpreter or a compiler? Does it work with the other programs and the operating system on your computer? Is it portable, maintainable, and free from licensing restrictions?

Very high-level languages (VHLLs) broaden the range of people who can program. The goal of VHLL design is to emphasize *what* you want to do rather than *how* to do it. Most VHLLs fail to accomplish this 100 percent of the time, but they all use some sort of nonprocedural notation to avoid excess programming detail. A VHLL may be restrictive, but it will increase productivity, often a hundredfold. Report generators can be used by anyone with a modest amount of training. More practice is required to use very high-level application or program generators.

Knowing the syntax of a programming language is only a small part of knowing how to program. Good programmers have a storehouse of knowledge about control structures, algorithms, and techniques of design. Many of these techniques are based on the methodology known as structured programming. It is the programming counterpart to scientific reductionism. In chemistry, for example, reductionism states that matter can be broken down into molecules, atoms, and atomic particles. In computing, software reductionism states that every program can be broken down into fundamental control structures. Consequently, a program can be designed as a collection of fundamental control structures; sequence, choice, and iteration are the most basic of these.

Key Terms

algorithm	assembler
application generator (AG)	assembly languages
array	benchmark programs

compiler	program generator
control structures	programming language
data structure	rendezvous statement
debugging	routine
exception statement	software reductionism
high-level language (HLL)	source program
interpreter	structured program
intrinsic function	structured programming
linker program	subroutines
low-level programming language	target program
nonprocedural language	translator
object program	variable
portability	very high-level language (VHLL)

Discussion Questions

1. Why can't a computer "understand" English instead of a programming language like BASIC?

2. Compare a translator who works for the United Nations with a computer program that translates HLL programs. Is the human translator more like a program compiler or an interpreter?

3. If you were going to select and use a programming language, what would be your criteria?

4. List and describe the steps in programming. Why are there so many steps?

5. What is structured design and what does it accomplish?

6. What is the difference between an application generator and a program generator?

Exercises

1. What is the purpose of the linker program? Describe the steps needed to run a new program using the compiling approach to translation.

2. What are the three fundamental building blocks of all structured programs?

3. Use the three building blocks of structured programming and the notation of Figure 15.6 to describe an algorithm for computing the following two values:

   A = PAY / 10

   B = PAY / $(A - 5)$

   Assume that PAY is entered by the user and that A and B are printed out. What happens if $(A - 5)$ is zero?

4. Modify the application generator program in Figure 15.8 so that only YTD values equal to zero are printed in the report.

5. Modify the BASIC program in Figure 15.5 so that only values greater than or equal to zero are allowed for N. (Use only the basic building blocks of IF-THEN-ELSE, WHILE, and sequence.)

6. Is it possible for two programs written for the same computer to be incompatible? How?

7. Give both low-level and high-level instructions (in English) for brushing your teeth. How might you characterize the difference between the two algorithms?

8. What is a program bug? How are bugs typically removed from a program?

9. Go to the library and read about the history of the following languages, including who invented them. (You may not be able to find them all—do the best you can.)
   a. FORTRAN
   b. COBOL
   c. Pascal
   d. Ada
   e. Modula-2
   f. SNOBOL
   g. BASIC

10. Compare the functions in a spreadsheet such as Lotus 1-2-3 with the functions in a programming language such as BASIC, FORTRAN, or Pascal.

buying personal computers

16

- ■ **Deciding to Buy**
  Obtaining Information
  Assessing Your Needs

- ■ **Issues Affecting What to Buy**
  Ensuring Compatibility
  Planning for Expansion

Decisions to buy computer systems are made in very different ways. Selecting a mainframe system is quite different from buying a personal computer. As a general rule the acquisition of a large and complicated computer system requires a much more formal and careful process than the purchase of a small, stand-alone system. Large systems are normally acquired to handle the relatively well defined needs of organizations. Also, as the size and importance of the system grow, the effects of an inappropriate purchase can become catastrophic. As a result, these systems are almost always purchased in the context of a system analysis and design study, as described in Chapter 14.

In contrast, the cost of personal computer systems has fallen so low that the decision to buy one may not require much (or any) application of formal system analysis and design. Often people justify their purchase of a personal computer with nebulous arguments related to the benefits of learning more about computers, trying out new applications, or improving the productivity of a single worker. Frequently the personal computer ends up being used for tasks that weren't even considered when it was bought. Most concepts of system analysis and design apply to the purchase of a personal computer, but they are likely to be used in a haphazard way.

If you are going to buy a personal computer, a reasonable set of steps to follow is to

- learn about the technology and how it may help you.
- search for reliable and understandable information.
- choose software that matches your needs.
- select hardware capabilities (memory, monitor, drives, and so forth).
- evaluate as many products as you can, comparing their features and performance.
- consider long lists of questions about compatibility and the possibilities for expansion.
- decide where to buy everything.

Although this list seems logical enough—and is recommended by many computer professionals—it is unusual to find anyone who has followed these steps in sequence. Buying a personal computer is often an emotional decision, prompted by such frivolous factors as an advertisement or concern for status. One product may seem more attractive than another because it has additional features you don't really need. You may feel a strong but irrational attraction to a brand name or want to be the first among your acquaintances to buy a particular model. Perhaps most insidious is the appeal of getting a "good deal." Finally, there is the fatigue factor. What starts out as a logical, rational process may become overwhelming, causing you to settle on an easily acquired but not necessarily appropriate system.

- **Assessing Needs**
  Budget
  Software applications
    learning ease
    features and performance
    error handling
    customer support
  Hardware requirements
    capacity and performance
    service support
    installation
  Training and education

- **Obtaining Information**
  Cost
  Hands-on experience
  Product reviews
  User groups, club newsletters
  Sales personnel, trade shows
  Academic classes
  Professional training seminars
  Professional meetings and journals
  Advertisements
  Books, magazines, catalogs
  Demonstration disks

(a) **Deciding to buy**

- **Ensuring Compatibility**
  Hardware compatibility
    peripherals
    other members of the product
      family
    networking
  Software compatibility
    operating system
    data file
    hardware capabilities
  Social compatibility
    vendor presence in marketplace
    personal computers at work
    friends' personal computers

- **Planning for Expansion**
  Number of I/O ports
  Board slots
  External busses
  Product-upgrading policies
  Portability versus expansion
  Networking possibilities

(b) **Two issues affecting what to buy**

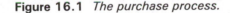

Figure 16.1 *The purchase process.*

This chapter discusses purchasing in two major sections, as shown in the two parts of Figure 16.1. The first section covers the steps leading to the decision to buy. The second section discusses two issues that should affect your decision: compatibility among components and future expansion needs.

■ Deciding to Buy

When most people begin thinking about purchasing a personal computer, they are unsure about what personal computers can do and what type of computer they need. Collecting information about the current capabilities of hardware and software will help you learn what personal computers can do. Carefully listing what you plan to do with a computer will help you define the requirements for the system. But these questions are related, and you should work at answering them at the same time. Your knowledge of what you want to do should guide the process of collecting information, and the information you collect will color your thoughts about how to use a personal computer.

Obtaining Information

Computers are virtually useless without software, so your search for information should focus first on the capabilities and limitations of high-quality programs. Numerous resources are available to help with this search.

- *Local computer clubs.* Computer clubs are an excellent source of help for beginners and advanced users. The members have wrestled with similar decisions, and they are eager to attract new people into the computer community. Their meetings usually include demonstrations of hardware and software. Many clubs have librarians who collect and distribute software that is in the public domain.

- *Hands-on experience.* Borrowing or renting equipment is another good source of ideas. With hands-on experience the practical uses of a computer quickly become more evident.

- *Computer magazines.* Independent reviews in computer magazines are reliable and increase your knowledge of features to look for. A six-month subscription to *InfoWorld* will provide current information. In contrast to general-purpose computer magazines such as *Byte, InfoWorld,* and *Popular Computing,* many magazines cover only specific brands of computers. For example, *PC World* is for the IBM PC and compatibles, *inCider* for Apple IIs, and *80 Micro* for TRS-80s.

- *Computer newsletters and indexes.* These publications can be found in many libraries and include *DP Directory, Microcomputer Software Newsletter, Microcomputer Index,* and *PC News Watch.* They are full of new product reviews, summaries of articles, and references to reviews. On-line databases such as CompuServe and The Source as well as services such as *SOFSEARCH,* which locates software, also include references to reviews.

- *Software catalogs and directories.* These provide helpful listings of programs. For each entry the lists include the name of the program, address of the vendor, hardware and operating system required, price, and either a brief description of the program or a list of its features, as shown in Figure 16.2. Some catalogs are devoted to a particular brand of computer or a particular application area such as games, business, or education. For example, the *Agricultural Computing Source Book* (Doane Publishing, St. Louis, Missouri) lists agricultural programs by area such as farmer and agribusiness systems. Unfortunately, catalogs and directories become out of date as soon as they are published, but some (such as *Datapro Directory of Microcomputer Software*) publish monthly updates.

- *Professional associations.* Anyone who faced problems and decided to solve them with a personal computer has learned something in the process. Ask your professional associates what problems they had and how they solved them.

TICKLER
Hardware Supported: IBM Personal Computer; Apple II/II Plus;
Radio Shack; North Star; Xerox 820; Vector Graphic MZ; Osborne
OSBORNE I; TeleVideo; Intertec Superbrain; Victor 9000; Morrow
Decision 1
Operating Systems: MP/M, CP/M
Languages: PASCAL
Number of Clients/Users: Not Specified
Narrative: TICKLER is a computerized appointment and re-
minder system. TICKLER will keep track of your appointments and
remind you of the various dates and events that are important to
your business and social life. TICKLER automatically gives ad-
vance warning of upcoming events, reschedules recurring events,
resets reminder dates for deadlines you did not meet, and selectively prints out portions of your schedule (so TICKLER can be
used by more than one person and you can separate your business and personal dates).
Special Configuration Requirements: 48K RAM, Micropolis
MOD II, IBM Display Writer

Contact Data:	**Pricing**
Digital Marketing Corporation	$250.00
2670 Cherry Lane	
Walnut Creek, CA 94596	
Tele. 415-938-2880	
Telex 17-1852 (DIGMKTG WNCK)	

Figure 16.2 *A typical listing from the* ICP Software Directory. *(Reproduced with permission from* ICP Software Directory. *Copyright © 1983, International Computer Programs, Inc. Indianapolis, IN.)*

■ *Retail outlets.* It may be necessary to visit retail outlets to see products work, but beware of misinformation. Salespeople will emphasize products' strong points; it would be a coincidence if these are the features you need.

Assessing Your Needs

It is hard to develop reasonable specifications for a computer system if you don't know what you want the system to do. To help find the answer you should list all the ways you expect to use the new computer. Do you want it to post accounting entries, store and retrieve business records, "talk" to a mainframe computer, draw graphs and charts, or print a mailing list? Be specif-ic. Begin by listing the activities you currently perform manually—especially those that are tedious, repetitive, or time consuming. Don't be limited by your lack of information about equipment or software. You can add to the list as you read product reviews and learn about the software available.

Once you have completed a first draft of the list, you are ready to begin learning about programs for those application areas. Almost at once you will face the perplexing problem of comparing similar programs that have hundreds of useful features. One spreadsheet might have better on-screen formatting than another, but perhaps it lacks a context-sensitive help system. Which is more important? A quantitative list of features similar to the one in Table 16.1 can help you determine how well each program meets your needs.

Table 16.1 *A partially completed software comparison chart*

Feature	Weighting Points	Product A	Product B	Product C
Ease of installation	10	10	5	
Time for program to load and begin execution	15	15	5	
Ease of learning	20	15	10	
Ease of operation	40	30	20	
Consistency of command structure	10	10	5	
Commands easy to remember	15	15	5	
Average response time	30	10	30	
Range of functions	40	10	40	
Ease of data entry	30	20	25	
Error handling	40	15	35	
On-screen help	20	20	20	
Customer support	30	15	15	___
Total possible points	300	185	215	

Begin by writing down which features you think would be useful. Then to each feature assign a weight that reflects its relative importance for the tasks you expect the product to perform. After you have created the chart and ranked the features, it is time to determine the quality of each feature in each program you are considering. If a program handles errors very well, then it earns full credit for that category. Average performance in a category might be worth half credit. When all the numbers have been filled in, the totals will provide a guide to which product to buy. Never trust your decision to a simple numerical ranking, however. You shouldn't buy a word processor that consistently crashes the computer system no matter how many other useful features it provides.

Many software reviews place their criteria in five major categories, as given in Figure 16.3.

1. *General criteria* include such items as the program's cost, its hardware and software requirements, and reviewers' comments.

2. *Learning aids* affect the level of technical knowledge and effort required to install and use the program. Does the program structure make it easy to learn and remember the commands? Do the manuals have both a simple, step-by-step "how to" section and a thoroughly indexed reference section? Are interactive disks with examples of the commands available? Are help screens available? Ease of use must be balanced against the features of the program. An easy-to-learn program may have limited features, and a hard-to-learn program may have powerful features.

Tutorials on disk have become a major selling point for professional-level software. They provide an interactive demonstration of how to use the software, guiding the user through examples of the commands and giving immediate feedback on the screen. Sample data files may also be provided so that you can test the program without entering information from scratch.

3. *Error-handling* capabilities determine how the program reacts to an improper command or other unusual conditions. Is the user asked to confirm a command that deletes a substantial amount of information? What message does the program display when a command is incorrect? How does the program react to unexpected events, such as a full disk?

4. *Performance and versatility* are critical to the program's overall usefulness. Evaluating a program's performance is best done with a hands-on trial period, but often this is impossible. Because of software piracy, vendors are understandably reluctant to allow customers to borrow a program to test it. This makes it difficult to verify marketing claims that a product is "user friendly" or offers "high performance" or a "wide range of convenient features." In-store demonstrations, even with actual data, don't provide enough experience with a program for you to make an informed decision. But they do show such things as how long it takes the program to load and begin running, whether the program keeps pace with keyboard instructions, and whether the program takes advantage of the computer's function keys and other keyboard features.

- **General**
  - Cost
  - Supplier reputation
  - User recommendations
  - Published reviews
  - Hardware required
  - Software required
  - Copy-protected disk?
  - Number of installations

- **Learning Aids**
  - Quality of the manual's
    - tutorial section
    - reference section
    - index
  - Availability of
    - a pocket reference guide
    - on-line help screens
    - a tutorial disk
    - sample data files

- **Error Handling**
  - No unexpected destructive procedures
  - No bugs that cause the program to crash
  - Appropriate recovery from incorrect commands

- **Performance and Versatility**
  - Feature comparison chart
  - Speed on benchmark tests
  - Range of features

- **Customer Support**
  - Included in price?
  - Telephone support?
  - Quality of warranties
  - Update policy
  - Newsletter?
  - User groups?

Figure 16.3 *Check list for comparing software.*

5. *Customer support* is the assistance that the manufacturer or dealer provides before and after the sale. This is an often overlooked but important consideration in the purchasing decision. A toll-free customer service number can be very important: occasions arise when neither the user manuals, salespeople, nor friends can solve a problem. You might try making a call before buying to evaluate the manufacturer's support.

Carefully read warranties. They describe policies for back-up copies, refunds, and updates. A policy of replacing lost or destroyed program disks is a major feature of customer support for copy-protected programs. Although two program disks are usually included in copy-protected products, there is always the possibility that one or both may become damaged. Software manufacturers do not have a standard policy for providing updated programs to their existing customers. When an improved version of a program is created, manufacturers may offer the new product to existing customers for the full price or a small fee.

It is much easier to select hardware once you have picked the software you want to use. For example, a program's documentation almost always lists the minimum resources the program needs. Avoid buying a computer that barely meets the minimum requirements; this is especially important for internal and external memory. Extra memory provides room for growth that is rarely wasted for long.

You may find it useful to create a chart similar to Figure 16.4 to compare the hardware features of various systems. Figure 16.4 is similar to the lists used

	Weighting Points	System A	System B
■ **Mandatory Requirements**			
256KB internal RAM		___	___
Typewriter-style keyboard with full-travel keys		___	___
9-inch diagonal display with 24 lines by 80 columns		___	___
2 floppy disk drives with at least 300KB each		___	___
1 serial port, 1 parallel port		___	___
. . .		___	___
Points for meeting mandatory requirements	600	___	___
■ **Desirable Features**			
1MB internal RAM	20	___	___
Detached keyboard	15	___	___
12-inch diagonal display with improved resolution	25	___	___
. . .			
Total points for desirable features	400	___	___
Total points	1,000	___	___

Figure 16.4 *An abbreviated list comparing hardware requirements.*

by data processing professionals when they create a *request for proposal (RFP)* for computer vendors. For a system to be considered for purchase it must meet all the mandatory requirements of the RFP. In addition to the points a system earns by meeting the mandatory requirements, points can be earned if the system has desirable features listed in the proposal. If an RFP is well constructed, the best system to buy is the one that provides the most points earned per dollar spent purchasing the system.

■ Issues Affecting What to Buy

Before you make the final purchase decision, you should consider numerous questions about compatibility and expansion. Many of these issues are outlined in Figure 16.1. Eventually you may decide to buy a notebook-size computer that is incompatible with the rest of the computer world and cannot be expanded; but if you make this decision, you should be well aware of the consequences.

Ensuring Compatibility

Compatibility issues fall into three categories: hardware, software, and social.

Hardware compatibility determines whether hardware components will interface correctly. The most basic level of hardware compatibility is whether the electrical plugs on two devices fit together or whether the disks from two machines are the same size. But the fact that the plugs fit is no reason to assume two devices will communicate successfully. For example, they might use different voltage levels, different control codes, or different transmission speeds.

Software compatibility refers to the ability of the programs in a computer system to work together successfully. The most basic levels of software compatibility determine whether a program will execute on a given processor or will work with a particular operating system. Other software compatibility questions include: Are data files transferable among programs? Can the program be modified to meet your particular needs? These issues are discussed more fully in Chapter 15 on programming.

One of the more frequent compatibility problems occurs when a program doesn't take advantage of the hardware's capabilities. For example, most printers can print proportionally spaced documents, but many word processing programs cannot send the necessary control signals to use this feature. This type of incompatibility can be infuriating. It is worse than useless to have a [HELP] key on the keyboard if none of your software responds when the key is pressed.

Social compatibility refers to the value of having a computer that is compatible with the other computers in your environment. Buying the same type of personal computer to use at home that you use at work eliminates the need to retrain yourself to operate a new computer. The advantages of sharing software among friends are obvious, though much of the sharing done today clearly violates copyright laws.

On a national scale social compatibility has created a tremendous bandwagon effect that attracts nearly all buyers to a few popular models. Both software developers and purchasers want ''on'' the bandwagon. Software manufacturers want to develop programs for popular models so that they have a large pool of potential users for their product. Purchasers in turn want the popular models so that they are assured of access to the best programs. The result is a more stable environment for the development of applications—at the cost of postponing the introduction of hardware innovations.

Planning for Expansion

If you purchase a computer without considering expansion, you limit the system's long-term usefulness. Most new users are amazed at how quickly they find new applications that require expansion of their first system. This situation occurs in part because manufacturers tend to sell some essential components as ''options'' in an effort to arrive at a low price.

Hardware expansion is accomplished in many ways. One of the simplest is to plug a new peripheral into an input-output (I/O) port on the back of the system unit. Many systems have unused, plug-in expansion slots hidden inside that allow additional circuit boards to be plugged into the computer. A more expensive expansion path is to upgrade from one computer in a *computer family* to a more powerful computer in the same family. For example, you might upgrade from a standard IBM PC to an IBM PC/AT. Other methods of expansion use external busses or cables to link large numbers of electrical devices in networks, as discussed in Chapter 11.

■ Summary

In 1985 there were more than 40,000 software packages for sale and over 60 manufacturers of personal computers. With such an array of choices, finding the right combination of hardware and software to suit your needs is not easy.

To prepare for the purchase you need to collect information about the current capabilities of personal computer systems and determine the likely tasks for your own computer. Most people find that the activities of assessing their needs and obtaining information are closely related and should proceed in parallel. Usually it is best to begin by identifying your software requirements, because they help determine the necessary hardware.

The final decision should carefully balance many issues relating to hardware, software, and social compatibility as well as the need to plan ahead for the inevitable expansion and upgrading of the system. Often it is easiest to weigh these options with the help of comparison charts and check lists. In a formal purchase decision, this work leads to the development of a request for proposal (RFP) listing both the mandatory and desirable features of the new system.

Discussion Questions

1. How are the steps in buying a personal computer likely to differ from those followed when a mainframe computer system is purchased?

2. Pretend you are the controller of a construction company with 1,000 employees and a division manager says, "I can't cost-justify the purchase of these personal computers—we won't be able to do that until we've had a chance to try them for a while to see what tasks they are good for." To what extent would you accept this argument?

3. Discuss what you feel would be the best sources of information for each of the following purchase decisions:
   a. Adding a memory board to an existing personal computer.
   b. Selecting a payroll program compatible with an existing personal computer for a business with 50 employees.
   c. Choosing whether to purchase several low-speed letter-quality line printers or one page printer for a real estate office with eight personal computers.
   d. Purchasing both the hardware and software for an integrated inventory-tracking, accounting, and billing system to be used in a retail pharmacy.
   e. Selecting a computer system for intensive spreadsheet analysis and fore-casting of financial information.
   f. Buying a personal computer for a family interested in increasing their computer literacy.

4. What kinds of product support would you want for each of the items to be purchased in question 3? How much would you be willing to pay for these services?

5. How important are hardware compatibility, software compatibility, and social compatibility for each of the items in question 3?

Exercises

1. You have been given the task of selecting a word processing system for a law office with four attorneys. Prepare a report that describes the likely word processing needs of the office, includes a requirements list for the purchase, and evaluates several software and hardware systems that satisfy the requirements list.

2. Locate and read an RFP that has been used in the past two years to purchase equipment. Many schools and government organizations treat their RFPs and the responses provided by vendors as public documents.

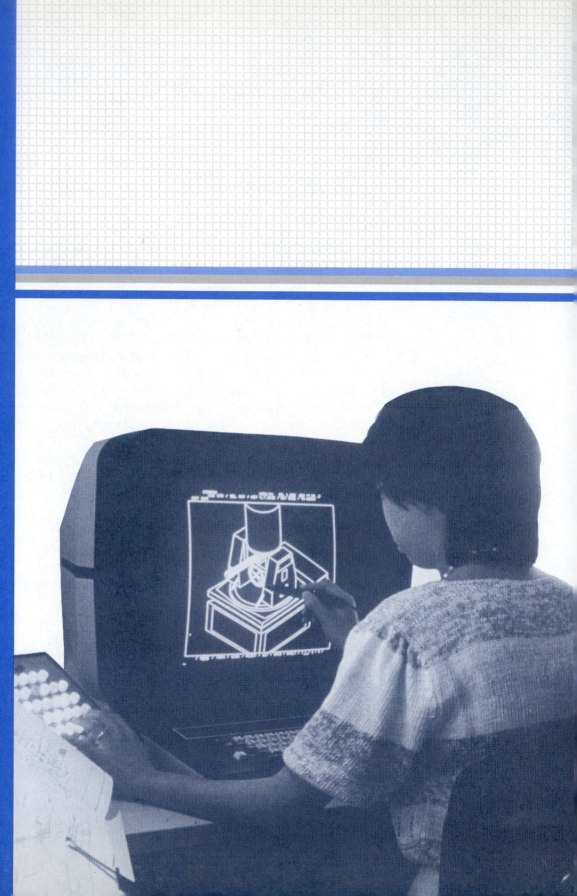

PART SEVEN

computers and us

Prior to World War II a ''computer'' was a person who performed lengthy calculations. An entire room of human computers was needed to complete the design of a skyscraper, bridge, or airplane; some calculations went on for months. Today, productivity packages like the ones discussed in this book have put the computational power of thousands of human computers into a single desktop computer. A trained accountant, engineer, or scientist can calculate complex formulas, manipulate large databases of facts, and plot graphs at the touch of a few keys. Modern methods of computing and the low cost of electronic computers have changed the way people work.

Many interesting events contributed to the transition from human to electronic information processing. In Chapter 17 we review some of these events, from the early history of computing to the present day. In addition, we make some informed predictions about the technical and social changes the future will bring.

Computers are admittedly powerful, but what about their social and legal ramifications? Are they invading your privacy by recording too many facts about your life in easily queried databases? Have you inadvertently become one of the new breed of "outlaws" because you copied a friend's recently purchased program disk? How can software authors protect their works from theft? In Chapter 18 we discuss the important issues of an evolving "computer morality."

the evolution 17
of computing

- **Early History of Computing**
  Charles Babbage (1791–1871)
  Herman Hollerith (1860–1926)
  First Electronic Computers
  Stored Program Concept

- **Mainframe Computer Generations**
  The First Generation: Vacuum Tube Systems (1951–1958)
  The Second Generation: Transistor Systems (1958–1964)
  The Third Generation: Integrated Circuits (1964–1971)
  The Fourth Generation: Large-Scale Integration (1971–1990)

- **Evolution of Personal Computers**
  Microprocessors
  Developmental Stage (1974–1977)
  Early Adopter Stage (1977–1981)
  Corporate Stage (1981–1984)
  Integrated Systems Stage (1984–1987)

- **Future of Computing**
  Microcomputer Chips
  Semiconductor Memory (RAM)
  Fifth-Generation Mainframes (1990–?)
  Future Personal Computers (1987–?)

- **Dawn of the Information Age**

17

The history of the computer field is not about people who have been dead for centuries or about events that only historians remember. Many of the key people are still alive and at work. Most of the significant technical developments have occurred so recently that our social systems are still adjusting to them.

Even if you assumed that no new technical breakthroughs would occur, it would be difficult to make accurate predictions about the ultimate effects of today's computer technology. But new technical breakthroughs are inevitable; research advances are occurring at an ever-increasing rate. Businesses find it is difficult to make useful long-range plans for computing because in five years the computing environment will be very different and in ten years it is likely to be totally unrecognizable. All of this makes studying the evolution of computers exciting and worthwhile.

Figure 17.1 *Time line for the history of computing.*

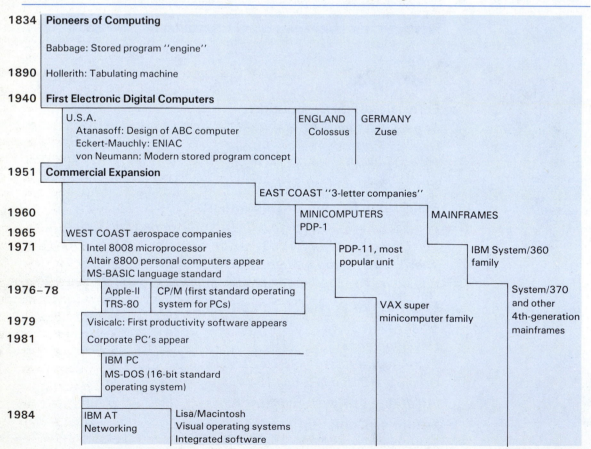

In this chapter we trace the 150-year process that led to the computer systems we use today. The major events we discuss are shown in the time line of Figure 17.1. In the first section we describe a few pioneers who laid the foundation for practical electronic computers. Then we describe the four generations of mainframe computers—from early vacuum tube systems to those of the present day. The next section follows the development of personal computers. The final two sections make some predictions about the future of computing and its effect on our society.

■ Early History of Computing

The computer was not invented by just one person. It was the product of a long sequence of contributions by a host of people. We will not attempt to discuss each innovation or every person. Instead, we will highlight some critical events in the development of modern computer systems.

Charles Babbage (1791–1871)

Charles Babbage is called the "father of computing" because he developed the concepts that underlie all modern computers. But he did not set out to build a computer. A respected British mathematician, Babbage wanted to correct the errors in astronomical tables used for navigation by the British navy. Creating accurate tables was extremely important but difficult because hundreds of error-prone human computers performed the calculations. Babbage thought that a mechanical engine could do the calculations without error; so he designed a machine called a *difference engine.* It was to be steam-powered and have thousands of gears, wheels, and barrels (see Figure 17.2). After spending some of his own funds on the initial design, Babbage persuaded the British government in 1822 to fund his difference engine. This was one of the earliest recorded instances of government-funded research.

Babbage never completed the difference engine—in part because the technology of his day could not produce the gears and wheels with the precision required. But Babbage also abandoned the difference engine because he decided to build a different computer, which he called the *analytical engine.* The difference engine was designed for specific computations, but the analytical engine was to be capable of performing *any* computation. Babbage planned to use instructions on punched cards to control his analytical engine so that if he wanted the computer to do a different task, he would simply change the deck of punched cards. He wrote,

Figure 17.2 *Babbage's difference engine.*

This day I had a general but only indistinct conception of the possibility of making an engine work out *algebraic* developments. . . . I mean without *any* reference to the *value* of the letters. . . . My notion is that as the [instructions on] cards of the calculating engine direct a series of operations and then recommence with the first so it might perhaps be possible to cause some cards to punch others equivalent to any given number of repetitions.[1]

Thus Babbage came up with the concept of a *stored program.* He also designed a control mechanism that could choose which card (instruction) to execute next, based on the results of a test. This made it possible for the machine to make decisions without human intervention. Thus Babbage laid the basis for modern programming.

After sinking £17,000 into the project, the British government cut off funding in 1842.

Babbage's analytical engine incorporated most of the ideas behind modern computers, but it was never completed.

[1]Anthony Hyman, *Charles Babbage: Pioneer of the Computer* (Princeton: Princeton University Press, 1982) page 244.

Herman Hollerith (1860–1926)

Herman Hollerith is credited with providing the impetus for automated data processing. His invention came in response to a problem: by the late 1800s it was taking the U.S. Census Bureau more than five years to complete each nationwide census, and the amount of time increased each decade. While working for the Census Bureau, Hollerith developed machines to help process census data more quickly. He designed and built a sorting and tabulating machine that processed data punched on dollar bill–sized, 80-column cards (see Figure 17.3). Using Hollerith's machines, the Census Bureau processed data for the 1890 census in less than two years.

Hollerith soon resigned from the Census Bureau. He formed his own company to market punched-card tabulating equipment. Then he sold the company to the Computing-Tabulating-Recording-Company, which later became International Business Machines Corporation—IBM.

First Electronic Computers

Unlike Babbage's engines, Hollerith's machine used electricity. Unlike modern computers, it was mostly mechanical and did not have a stored program. It was an electromechanical sorting and tabulating device. In contrast, an **electronic**

Figure 17.3 *Hollerith's machines for sorting and tabulating.*

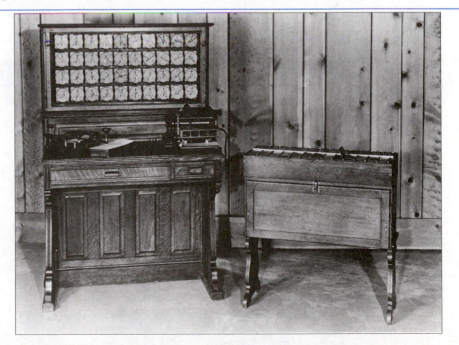

digital computer is an electromechanical device with circuits for storing and processing digitally encoded information by means of a self-contained program.

The complicated computations needed to solve scientific problems and World War II led to the development of the electronic digital computer. However, controversy surrounds who should receive credit for the invention of the first electronic computer.

Konrad Zuse, a German engineer recruited into the German army, is supposed to have had a program-controlled electronic computer working in 1941, but it was destroyed in an Allied bombing raid. A British computer, Colossus, was used as early as 1943 to break German cipher codes. Its work is still classified as secret, and scant information about it is available. **John V. Atanasoff,** a physics professor at Iowa State College, designed—but did not complete—the ABC electronic computer from 1939 to 1942. Atanasoff urged Iowa State to patent his computer, but they failed to act. From 1943 to 1946 **John W. Mauchly** and **J. Presper Eckert** of the University of Pennsylvania developed **ENIAC** (**E**lectronic **N**umerical **I**ntegrator **a**nd **C**alculator) (see Figure 17.4). Its development was funded by the United States Army to compute ballistics tables for artillery shells.

ENIAC is usually considered to be the first operational electronic digital computer. Unlike Babbage's analytical engine or other early devices, it was totally electronic and had no mechanical counters. But John Mauchly had visited

Figure 17.4 *ENIAC computer.*

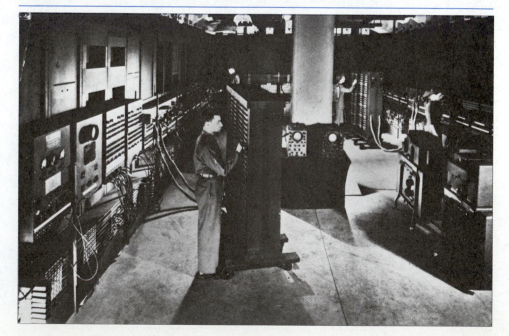

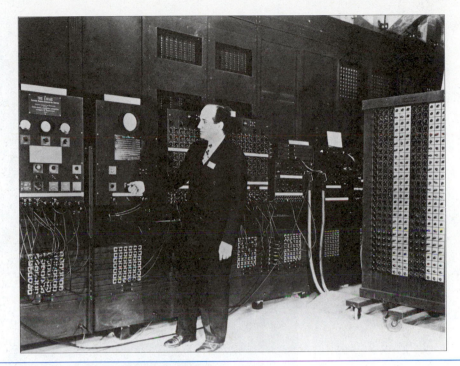

Figure 17.5 *Plug-board of the ENIAC.*

Atanasoff in 1940 and 1941 and based some of ENIAC on Atanasoff's work. In 1973 a U.S. federal court invalidated the Eckert and Mauchly patent for the electronic digital computer and declared Atanasoff the inventor.

ENIAC contained 18,000 vacuum tubes, 70,000 resistors, and 500,000 hand-soldered connections. It weighed 30 tons, used 100 kilowatts of electricity, and occupied a 20-by-40 foot room. Supposedly, all the lights in a section of Philadelphia dimmed when it was turned on. It had a limited amount of storage and was unreliable because the vacuum tubes frequently burned out. These problems were tolerable because ENIAC could perform arithmetic at the unheard-of rate of 5,000 additions or 300 multiplications per second.

ENIAC was limited in another way. It was programmed by plugging wires into three walls of plug-boards containing over 6,000 switches. To change the program required resetting switches by replugging the plug-board (see Figure 17.5).

Stored Program Concept

The last step in the development of the electronic computer was the revival of Babbage's idea of storing the instructions that control the computer in the internal memory of the computer. In retrospect, the advantage of storing a program electronically in computer memory is obvious: the program can be changed simply by reading another program into memory.

Figure 17.6 *UNIVAC I, the first commercial computer.*

John von Neumann, a famous mathematician at the Institute for Advanced Study at Princeton University, is credited with developing the modern concept of the stored program. But it is not clear that von Neumann should receive all the credit. Babbage, Zuse, and several others had some notion of the stored program before von Neumann. Still, without von Neumann's promotion of the concept, it might have been many years before the idea was revived. Today the use of a stored program separates calculators from computers. With stored programs computers possess their own control and thus can "run" without human intervention.

Von Neumann developed the concept of the stored program in conjunction with the design of **EDVAC** (**E**lectronic **D**iscrete **V**ariable **A**utomatic **C**omputer) at the University of Pennsylvania. EDVAC was the second computer developed by Mauchly and Eckert. When Mauchly and Eckert's computer company was in financial difficulty, Remington-Rand acquired it and produced the first commercial computer, the **UNIVAC I** (**Univ**ersal **A**utomatic **C**omputer), in 1951. Ironically, the UNIVAC I was purchased by Herman Hollerith's first employer, the U.S. Census Bureau (see Figure 17.6).

Remington-Rand's production of UNIVAC I signaled the entry of large corporations—GE, National Cash Register, Burroughs, Honeywell, RCA, and IBM—into the commercial computer field. These are the manufacturers who pioneered the next step in the development of the modern computer.

■ Mainframe Computer Generations

We can divide the second major stage of computing history into two paths followed by two groups: the "East Coast companies" and the "West Coast companies." Generally, the East Coast companies have three-letter names—IBM, NCR, RCA, DEC, and so on. The West Coast companies tend to be associated with the aerospace industry and the military.

The East Coast companies pursued data processing in government and large financial, manufacturing, and retail businesses. Data processing in these organizations requires powerful mainframe computers with huge memories and a professional staff. Today the financial community would collapse under tons of paper without large-scale, central mainframe computers. Never before have so many aspects of business depended on the infallibility of machines. The idea of a small personal computer would never occur to this group.

The West Coast companies pursued the scientific and engineering uses of computers, in particular for the military and for the space program. Controlling a missile requires a small, lightweight computer that can rapidly calculate trajectories, adjust engines, and communicate with earth stations. The scientists and engineers who design such computers typically work alone or in small groups—a combination ideal for nurturing small, individualized personal computers.

Thus the history of computing takes two separate paths from 1951 to 1980. The East Coast companies evolved large data processing machines through four generations, as shown in Table 17.1. The West Coast companies developed microelectronic computer systems for the manned space program

Table 17.1 *Generations of Mainframe Computers*

	First Generation (Vacuum tubes)	*Second Generation (Transistors)*	*Third Generation (Integrated circuits)*	*Fourth Generation (Large-scale integration)*
Speed (instructions per second)	Up to 10,000	Up to 1 million	Up to 10 million	Up to 1 billion
Memory capacity (in characters)	1,000 to 8,000	4,000 to 64,000	32,000 to 4 million	512,000 to 32 million
Failure rate	Minutes	Days	Days to weeks	Weeks
Relative cost (per operation)	$10.00	$1.00	$0.10	Less than $0.01
External storage	Cards	Tape	Disk	Mass storage
Operating system	Single user Jobs scheduled manually	Single user Jobs scheduled automatically	Multiple user Timesharing	Multiple user Networks and distributed systems

and ultimately turned space technology into down-to-earth products for commercial consumption—products such as pocket calculators, video games, and personal computers. To take a closer look at these two paths, we will first discuss the development of mainframe computers by the East Coast companies.

The First Generation: Vacuum Tube Systems (1951–1958)

First-generation computers used vacuum tubes to provide electronic circuits. For memory these computers used a magnetic drum, a rotating cylinder whose outer surface could be magnetized. Punched cards were used for input of both data and programs. Program instructions were given in machine language. These computers were slow, unreliable, expensive, and tedious to program.

The Second Generation: Transistor Systems (1958–1964)

The second generation of computers began when transistors replaced vacuum tubes. The transistors were 1/200th the size of a vacuum tube, generated less heat, were faster, and failed less often. The internal memory of these computers was composed of tiny, doughnut-shaped magnetic cores strung on thin intersecting wires. (This is the origin of the term *core memory,* which refers to internal memory.) Magnetic tape largely replaced punched cards for input and output. Printers with speeds up to 600 lines per minute were developed.

The second generation also brought improvements in software. One important development was the invention of high-level programming languages in the mid-to-late 1950s, including FORTRAN for engineers and COBOL for business programmers. These languages represented a giant step forward because they are less detailed and easier to learn and use than machine language. Thus a person with little or no technical knowledge of the computer could write programs to solve problems. Meanwhile, the task of starting and scheduling the execution of programs had become too complex and time-sensitive to leave to a computer operator. This problem was solved by the invention of the operating system.

The Third Generation: Integrated Circuits (1964–1971)

Integrated circuits replaced transistors in third-generation computers. An *integrated circuit* is a complex electronic circuit etched on a tiny silicon chip about one-fourth inch square. It is smaller, faster, and more reliable than separate transistors wired together.

Major improvements also occurred in the capabilities of peripheral devices. Magnetic disks replaced magnetic tapes for storing information when rapid access to data was required. Faster printers were developed; they could print nearly three thousand lines per minute. Cathode ray tubes (CRT) were used to display input and output.

Operating systems capable of timesharing also began to appear during the third generation. This allowed many users to use a single computer simultaneously, thereby permitting them also to share the enormous cost of third-generation computers. The BASIC programming language was developed at Dartmouth under a grant from the National Science Foundation. It was designed to make programming as easy as possible.

In the early 1960s IBM made a significant commitment to develop an entire family of computers that could run the same operating system and application programs. Five thousand people were assigned to develop the system software for this project on a two-year schedule. Then, on April 7, 1964, IBM announced the **System/360** family of computers. The family consisted of six computers with memory sizes ranging from 16KB to over 1 megabyte. These computers were enormously successful because customers could upgrade from one member of the family to another without changing their application software. Most of the computers IBM has introduced since 1965 are upwardly compatible with the original System/360 computers.

IBM captured and has held a 60 to 75 percent share of the mainframe computer market. The success of its System/360 computers drove several major competitors from the computer business. For example, General Electric quit the computer business in 1970, RCA in 1972, and Xerox in 1975. Other companies tried to survive by moving into defensible market niches.

One of these market niches was the small computer market. In 1960 the three-year-old Digital Equipment Corporation (DEC) brought out the first minicomputer, the PDP-1. It cost less than mainframe computers and had a much smaller instruction set. The PDP product line grew until the **PDP-11,** introduced in 1969, became the best-selling general-purpose minicomputer ever. DEC grew at a phenomenal rate to become the second-largest computer manufacturer in the United States.

The Fourth Generation: Large-Scale Integration (1971–1990)

The beginning of fourth-generation computers is not as clear as that of the first three generations. Usually it is said to coincide with the development of the *large-scale integrated (LSI) circuit*—a single chip that contains thousands of transistors. LSI puts many more circuits on each silicon chip than earlier integrated circuits.

Large fourth-generation computers can support extensive timesharing; up to several thousand users may use the computer at the same time. The computer allocates its resources so that each user feels he or she is the only one using it. In addition, programs and peripheral devices such as disks and printers have grown by leaps and bounds in variety, capability, and sophistication.

■ Evolution of Personal Computers

While the East Coast companies continued to develop mainframe and mini-computers, the West Coast companies were busy applying LSI to products for the aerospace industry and the military. The main center for this work was in a string of small towns located between San Jose and San Francisco—the famous Silicon Valley. It was here that two engineers working after hours in their bedrooms invented the first commercially successful personal computer.

Personal computers have gone through remarkable changes since they were introduced in the mid-1970s. The first personal computers were crude machines that could be used only by programmers. Today, the average person can learn to use a state-of-the-art personal computer for productive tasks in a few hours. One way of viewing the evolution of personal computers is shown in Table 17.2, which divides the process into six three-year stages: three stages in the past, the stage we are currently passing through, and two stages predicted for the future. The first three stages in Table 17.2 are loosely based on a presentation given in 1983 by David House, Vice-President of Intel, in which he predicted that new generations of microprocessor systems will continue to be introduced on roughly a three-year cycle. We will discuss each stage, but first it is appropriate to look at the development of the heart of every personal computer, the microprocessor.

Microprocessors

On November 1, 1956, William Shockley, John Bardeen, and Walter Brattain received word that they had been awarded the Nobel Prize in Physics for invention of the transistor. It was a student of Shockley's, **Robert Noyce,** who was to become the father of the integrated circuit—the basis of the microprocessor ''chip.'' (Recall that a *microprocessor* is a circuit built on a single silicon chip that can execute a program.) Noyce founded Intel Corporation, which in turn developed large-scale integrated (LSI) circuits used in personal computers.

The first microprocessor, the Intel 4004, was announced in 1971 by the Intel Corporation. It had been designed by a small group of engineers led by Ted Hoff. The 4004 had the equivalent of 2,250 transistors, making it an exceedingly limited processor. It could process only four bits of information at a time.

Table 17.2 *Evolution of Personal Computers: Past, Present, and Future*

Developmental Stage (1974–1977)   Example: the MITS Altair
- Sold in kits to hobbyists, mail-order distribution
- Main memory from 4KB to 32KB; crude 8-bit processor
- Computer and peripherals (keyboard, CRT, storage) purchased separately
- Programmed in machine language or BASIC
- Cassette tape storage
- Complete system cost about $2,500 in 1975 dollars

Early Adopter Stage (1977–1981)   Example: early Apple II models
- Sold as a fully assembled computer through retail computer stores
- Main memory from 16KB to 64KB; simple 8-bit processor
- 8-inch or small-capacity 5 1/4-inch floppy disk storage
- Standardized, simple operating system; first end-user applications
- Complete system cost about $3,000 in 1978 dollars

Corporate Stage (1981–1984)   Example: IBM PC
- Sold as a computer system by major corporations
- Main memory from 64KB to 256KB; early 16-bit processor
- Larger capacity 5 1/4-inch disk storage; expensive small hard disks
- Enhanced operating systems; well-developed application packages
- Strong industry standards for both hardware and software
- Complete system cost about $3,500 in 1981 dollars

Integrated Systems Stage (1984–1987)   Examples: Apple Macintosh, IBM AT
- Sold as a personal productivity tool for knowledge workers
- Main memory from 512KB to 1 megabyte (MB); early 32-bit processor
- 3 1/2-inch microfloppy, 5 1/4-inch minifloppy, and hard disk storage
- Visual-based operating system, integrated application packages
- Complete system cost about $3,000 in 1984 dollars

Networked Systems Stage (1987–1990) Examples: IBM AT, AT&T Unix
- Sold as a node to local area networks
- Main memory from 512KB to 4MB; advanced 32-bit processor
- Large internal hard disk, network access to huge hard disks
- Built-in conventional phone; local area network interface
- Multitasking operating system; integrated office automation systems
- Complete system cost about $2,500 in 1987 dollars

Information Age Stage (1990–?)   Example: Compuphone
- Sold as a commodity item for ''reaching out to touch the world''
- Main memory from 2MB to 16MB; several 32-bit processors
- Large hard disk; optical disk; network access to the world
- Built-in digital phone; several high-speed network interfaces
- Voice/visual-based operating system
- Complete system cost about $2,000 in 1990 dollars

A computer based on the 4004 contained two important chips: the 4004 microprocessor chip and another chip, called a *fixed program chip,* that could permanently store the instructions for controlling an electrical device. Other chips could be added as needed. Millions of 4-bit microprocessors have been used in appliances, hand-held calculators, cars, toys, and digital watches. For these applications the 4004 made a good special-purpose computer, but it was too slow and limited to be the processor for a personal computer.

Several 8-bit microprocessors were developed before 1974, but the 8-bit Intel 8008 (and its immediate successor, the 8080) was the first one with the speed and power needed for a personal computer. The 16-bit generation (1978–1981) began with the Intel 8086. The 32-bit generation began in 1981 with the Intel iAPX 432. Texas Instruments, NCR, Motorola, Hewlett-Packard, and other companies have also developed 32-bit microprocessors.

Developmental Stage (1974–1977)

The first personal computer, the Micro Instrumentation and Telemetry Systems **(MITS) Altair 8800,** was based on the Intel 8008 microprocessor. In 1974 the company was facing bankruptcy and decided to try to sell an inexpensive computer in kit form. In a smart move they sent one to *Popular Electronics* magazine, which published a feature article on it. Soon MITS was overwhelmed by orders. The Altair sold in kit form (unassembled) for $395 or fully assembled for $621. Most buyers were technically knowledgeable hobbyists. The Altair did not include a keyboard, CRT monitor, disk, or printer. These items were purchased separately much like the components of a stereo system.

Initially the Altair was programmed by hobbyists in machine language, but this method was arduous and error-prone. **Bill Gates** dropped out of Harvard to remedy the situation. Together with Paul Allen, Gates developed the first high-level language for a microprocessor. His version of BASIC on the MITS Altair soon became the standard programming language for personal computers. In 1974 Gates and Allen founded Microsoft Corporation.

In 1973 **Gary Kildall** was working as a consultant for Intel. His job was to implement a programming language for the 8080 microprocessor. To make it easier for him to use the microprocessor, he developed a program called *CP/M* (*C*ontrol *P*rogram for *M*icrocomputers) for controlling a keyboard, CRT screen, and disks. Kildall first offered the program to Intel, but Intel declined the offer, so Kildall sold CP/M by mail to hobbyists. In 1975 he set up Digital Research to sell CP/M. In no time at all CP/M was being used on more than a million systems.

Kildall's CP/M had a dramatic effect on the development of personal computers. Computer manufacturers no longer had to develop an individual operating system for each different computer, and programmers could use the same commands for a variety of computers. CP/M remains the most widely used operating system for 8-bit computers.

Figure 17.7 *On the left is Bill Gates, chairman of the board and executive vice president of Microsoft. On the right is Gary Kildall, chairman of the board for Digital Research.*

The success of these early entrepreneurs led others to manufacture and sell personal computers and accessories. Within two years there were stores, clubs, and magazines devoted entirely to the personal computer. By 1977 there were more than fifty brands of computers, and by the end of 1978 over seven hundred computer stores. Computer clubs provided members an opportunity to show off their computers, share experiences, and learn about new products. The Southern California Club had over three thousand members in 1977. Computer magazines such as *BYTE, Creative Computing,* and *Dr. Dobbs' Journal of Computer Calisthenics and Orthodontics* publish advertisements and articles about personal computers, programs, and applications.

Together, CP/M and Microsoft BASIC constituted a powerful force in determining the direction of personal computer programs. They established both a standard language for programmers and a standard vehicle for disseminating programs. But the trouble with both of them was that you had to be a programmer to use them.

Early Adopter Stage (1977–1981)

Steve Wozniack and Steve Jobs began business by selling the Apple I microcomputer in kit form out of a garage in California. They realized the shortcomings of kits and developed the **Apple II** personal computer. It was wildly successful because they sold it preassembled and included a disk drive and simple operating system. Consumers could buy a ready-to-use computer and a disk drive to store information in a form that could be quickly accessed. The Apple II soon set the standard for commercially successful personal computer manufacturers.

The Radio Shack division of Tandy Corporation introduced the first personal computer in their **TRS-80** line in 1977. The TRS-80 Model I was sold fully assembled and included a keyboard, cassette tape or disk, printer, and various sizes of memory. A true baby computer, the Model I was sold in Radio Shack's nationwide chain of retail stores for $500 to $1,500, depending on options. It also included the Microsoft BASIC language. The theory was that a person could write BASIC programs to solve his or her problems. Typical buyers were hobbyists, educators, and small businesses. Commodore Business Machines, a large adding machine company, introduced the **Commodore PET** in 1977. It was an assembled, complete computer with a keyboard, screen, and cassette tape drive that sold for $650.

A new idea in software soon expanded the usefulness of these machines. While taking a business course at Harvard University **Dan Bricklin** got the idea for a program that anybody could use—Visicalc. Its history is traced in Table 17.3. Visicalc turned a personal computer like the Apple II into a familiar spreadsheet that would total numbers in rows and columns. It was important for many reasons: it made people realize that anybody could use a computer; it caused Apple II sales to soar; and it promoted the idea of a computer *paradigm*. That is, Visicalc was more than a program; it was a metaphor, which many others soon copied. Even today the best software emulates some familiar model such as a spreadsheet, desktop, file drawer, or library.

At about the same time, word processing software on personal computers became popular as an alternative to expensive systems designed solely for word processing. AppleWriter by Paul Lutus and WordStar by Rob Barnaby were among the first best sellers. More than a half-million copies of each program were sold during the late 1970s.

Corporate Stage (1981–1984)

The large computer manufacturers such as IBM and DEC did not enter the personal computer field until the 1980s. This is quite surprising, especially since DEC specialized in minicomputers, which are only a step above microcomputers in size and power. Probably these companies delayed entering the personal computer market because they felt the marketplace was too volatile or because they did not realize its size and potential. When IBM and other large computer manufacturers did enter the market, they established a standard of excellence for personal computers and gave them legitimacy and credibility.

Table 17.3 *The Birth, Development, and Death of Visicalc.*

Spring 1970: At the Massachusetts Institute of Technology Laboratory for Computer Science, students Daniel Bricklin and Robert Frankston become good friends and discuss going into business together.

1973–1978: Frankston is a computer consultant. Bricklin works for Digital Equipment Corp. (1973–76) and Fasfax Corp. (1976–77).

Spring 1978: Bricklin, now an MBA student at Harvard Business School, envisions an electronic spreadsheet program that would eliminate the drudgery of the calculations for his business homework.

Fall 1978: Bricklin takes a prototype to Frankston, who agrees to help develop a workable version of the program.

Winter 1978: Fellow Harvard MBA Dan Fylstra agrees to market the new software for Bricklin and Frankston through his own young company, Personal Software.

January 2, 1979: Software Arts is incorporated by Bricklin and Frankston. They work out of Frankston's attic in Arlington, Massachusetts.

Spring 1979: The first electronic spreadsheet gets its name, Visicalc, which stands for Visible Calculator.

May 1979: Personal Software moves from Massachusetts to California's Silicon Valley.

June 4, 1979: Visicalc is shown to the public at the National Computer Conference in New York.

October 1979: Visicalc for the Apple II is shipped to the public.

August to December 1980: Visicalc becomes available for other major machines, including the Commodore PET, Atari, Hewlett-Packard, and Tandy Model I computers.

May 1981: Visicalc sales exceed 100,000, the best-selling computer program to date.

October 1981: Visicalc is the spreadsheet that is shown at the first product introduction of the IBM PC.

February 1982: Personal Software changes its name to Visicorp.

March 1982: Software Arts wins International Computer Programs' ''$10 Million Award'' as creator of Visicalc.

October 25, 1982: Lotus introduces 1-2-3.

February 1983: Visicalc sales exceed 500,000.

September 1983: Visicorp sues Software Arts for breach of contract, claiming Software Arts failed to upgrade the product to keep it competitive.

February 7, 1984: Software Arts files a countersuit, claiming Visicorp failed to promote the product adequately.

September 17, 1984: Software Arts and Visicorp settle the lawsuit out of court. The legal battle has crippled both companies.

November 1984: Visicorp, having sold most of its remaining products to raise cash, merges with start-up Paladin.

May 1985: The assets of Software Arts, including Visicalc, are acquired by Lotus Development Corp.

May 31, 1985: The last version of Visicalc ships.

Source: InfoWorld, June 24, 1985.

Figure 17.8 *The IBM Personal Computer, announced in 1981.*

This corporate phase began with the introduction of the IBM Personal Computer, or PC, in 1981 (see Figure 17.8). It legitimized personal computing for Fortune 500 companies, began the era of the 16-bit personal computer, and established Microsoft's MS-DOS as the standard 16-bit operating system.

Corporations began to realize that the personal computer could increase the productivity of office workers. Spreadsheet, word processing, and database management programs were used so extensively that they became known as *productivity software*. Productivity software invaded noncomputer companies, bringing change at a rate that rarely has been seen in the history of corporations.

Integrated Systems Stage (1984–1987)

The personal computer revolution is currently undergoing a period of consolidation in terms of hardware, software, and suppliers. Personal computers are being "integrated" with other personal computers and with mainframes to form computer networks. Programs are being "integrated" with other programs to form integrated packages. And the industry is going through a mid-life crisis that many of the smaller manufacturers will not survive. Some causes for this crisis are rapidly falling hardware prices, a downturn in the growth rate of personal computer sales, and an increased emphasis on standards for hardware and software.

An interesting trend during this period has been a rapid drop in the cost of personal computers designed specifically around a visual operating system. The Apple Lisa became the first member of this category of computers; it was introduced in early 1983 at $9,995. Then came the Apple Macintosh (introduced in early 1984 at $2,495), the Commodore Amiga (introduced in mid-1985 at $1,295), and finally the Atari 520 ST (introduced in late 1985 at $799). All of these machines use the same processor (the Motorola 68000), but the latter two machines also have a sound generation chip that can generate three or four simultaneous audio voices, a graphics coprocessor that provides superior graphics manipulation capabilities, and support for color monitors.

In 1984 IBM added an important new member to its family of personal computers with the announcement of the IBM PC/AT (the AT stands for "advanced technology"). The AT is about four times faster than an IBM PC and is far more expandable. Because its processor supports virtual memory, it can address up to one gigabyte (a *billion* bytes) of virtual memory. The processor also is designed for multitasking; that is, it can support multiple users or concurrent applications. In 1985 a flood of "AT-compatible" computers were introduced by competitors, including Compaq, Texas Instruments, Kaypro, Sperry, and AT&T.

Figure 17.9 *The Apple Macintosh, announced in 1984.*

The IBM PC family has taken a dominant role in corporate personal computing. For example, in 1985 the Dun & Bradstreet Corporation surveyed the buying plans of businesses that already have personal computers. Seventy-two percent of the planned purchases were for IBM personal computers; only 7 percent were for Apple computers, and most of the rest were for IBM PC-compatible computers.

■ Future of Computing

A major difficulty in predicting the future of computing is the rapidity with which research developments have moved from the laboratory to the marketplace. For example, Intel began planning the model 8088 microprocessor in 1976. Production of the chip began in 1979. By 1981 several operating systems, programming languages, and application programs had been written for the chip. In fourteen months IBM designed a new personal computer that exploited the microprocessor's capabilities, announced the product in August 1981, and began selling it in quantity. By the end of 1983 the IBM PC had single-handedly given IBM the largest share of the personal computer market.

The speed of technological innovation in the electronics industry is not decreasing. Scientists report that fundamental physical limitations, such as the speed of light or properties of chemical reactions, will not preclude building cheaper, faster, and smaller components and peripherals between now and the year 2000. And as automation in electronic manufacturing increases, the time between proving technical feasibility and widespread commercial use should continue to shorten.

Two hardware devices have had a dominant role in recent electronic advances: the microprocessor chip and the semiconductor memory chip. Successive improvements in these devices will lie behind the development of new generations of mainframe and personal computers.

Microcomputer Chips

The computational engines embedded on flecks of silicon continue to incorporate more functions and to increase in speed. Bernard T. Murphy, head of microprocessor design at Bell Telephone Laboratories, predicted in 1983 that "the 32-bit microprocessors will greatly change the world of computing. By the end of the decade, for example, the equivalent of the processor in today's $20,000 VAX should be available on a chip selling for less than $1" (*Wall Street Journal,* September 9, 1983). Equally important, according to Portia Isaacson of Future Computing, will be the use of coprocessor chips designed to handle specific functions such as graphics, spoken input and output, high-speed floating-point arithmetic, and interfaces for telecommunications and local area networks.

Recently introduced microprocessors include low-power versions of most popular microprocessors, suitable for extended battery operation; other microprocessor chips include the circuitry (clocks, timers, and input/output functions) that is normally placed on ten to thirty support chips.

Semiconductor Memory (RAM)

Gary L. Tooker, vice president and general manager of semiconductor products at Motorola, wrote in the August 1983 issue of *High Technology:*

> Every three to five years a new generation of RAMs has been unveiled, featuring four times the storage density of its predecessor. Each year, the cost per bit has fallen by 30 percent and semiconductor memory utilization has increased by 100 percent. Few, if any, other industries can claim a market where demand doubles annually.... Obviously, the cycle cannot go on forever, but the end is not in sight.

So far these predictions have been correct. Since August 1983 the market for 64-kilobit memory chips has been decimated by shipments of 256-kilobit chips; engineering samples of 1-megabit chips are being shipped; and 4-megabit chips are likely to be introduced by the end of the decade. To put this in perspective, a 4-megabit chip will occupy no more space than your thumbnail but will store the equivalent of 200 typed pages of double-spaced text. A single 4-megabit chip will contain more memory than all of the memory chips in most personal computers sold today.

Fifth-Generation Mainframes (1990–?)

In cooperation with the Japanese government, a consortium of Japanese computer manufacturers has embarked on a decade-long ambitious effort to develop a fifth generation of computers. The group hopes to leapfrog today's computers by pioneering the hardware and software necessary to create tomorrow's artificial intelligence systems. The initial funding comes from over $400 million dollars from the government plus matching funds from industry. If the project continues to look promising, much higher funding levels are expected.

The ultimate goal of the project is to develop computers that can understand natural language and apply common sense to everyday problems. Such machines will need the ability to accumulate knowledge and make inferences from facts stored in "knowledge bases." They are likely to

- use parallel processing methods to improve their response time.
- employ relational databases to store information.
- require new programming languages to express logic clearly.
- use special circuitry to form hypotheses and make inferences.

Their speed will be measured in MLIPS (millions of logical inferences per second) rather than MFLOPS (millions of floating-point operations per second), the measure used for more conventional computers.

An engineering model of this type of knowledge-based processor is currently under construction. The construction of a working prototype system is tentatively planned for 1990 to 1993.

Future Personal Computers (1987–?)

Table 17.2 predicts that personal computers will continue to evolve in three-year stages through 1990. The future characteristics listed in the table are informed guesses based on past trends and the predictions of industry analysts.

If Table 17.2 is correct, the Networked Systems Stage (1987–1990) will bring an increased emphasis on linking personal computers with local area networks. Customers will no longer need to purchase a network interface to attach a personal computer to a network. Instead, the interface will be standard equipment, just as I/O ports are standard on most personal computers today. An advanced 32-bit processor and larger memory capacities will allow several applications to be executed at the same time in different windows of the visual operating system. Mass production and expanding markets will lower the cost of a complete working system to about $2,500.

The characteristics listed for the Information Age Stage (1990–?) are entirely conjectural. As personal computers become commonplace and incorporate more communications ability, they may be called "compuphones." They may even tap into a worldwide communications network. Rather than using keyboard input, they may accept voice commands and visual cues.

■ Dawn of the Information Age

In many ways it is easier to predict technical developments than to predict their economic and social effects. It is difficult to tell in advance how effectively a new technical ability will be exploited or how radically it will alter individual behavior. According to Robert Noyce, Vice-Chairman of Intel,

> The usual futurist projections are too optimistic in the short term and too pessimistic in the long term. . . . Where we went wrong in our over-expectations [was the computer industry's inward focus and its inability to] project itself out to the plumber and what he does.[1]

Looked at from a broad perspective, our society seems to be moving from the Industrial Age to the Information Age. Table 17.4 compares the character-

[1] *Wall Street Journal,* September 16, 1985.

Table 17.4 *Characteristics of the Industrial Age and the Information Age*

Industrial Age	Information Age
Primarily mechanical tools that augmented our physical capabilities	Primarily electronic tools that augment our mental capabilities
Slowly changing technology	Rapid technical innovation
Output rated in physical terms: units sold, tons produced, and so on	Output judged by intangibles: value added, timeliness, accuracy, service, flexibility, usefulness
Rapid growth in domestic markets for goods	A world economy with mature markets for most goods
Simple tools designed for specific tasks	Complex tools supporting numerous tasks
Tools used on a stand-alone basis	Tools form highly integrated and sophisticated networks
Inventions built by entrepreneurs using custom tools	Innovations occur in research environments providing ample access to machine intelligence

istics of these eras. The differences are dramatic. The Industrial Age was characterized by the construction of mechanical machines for cutting, stamping, moving, and producing. These machines made farmers and blue-collar workers far more productive. Today our economy is being driven by electronic instead of mechanical innovations. The Information Age is characterized by the development of electronic systems to help us think, communicate, manage, and control. These new tools promise to make office workers, managers, educators, architects, scientists, lawyers, and other "knowledge workers" far more productive. They also provide us with entirely new challenges.

Assessing the value of inventions was easier during the Industrial Age. The benefits tended to be objective and physical: faster production, better yields, lower costs, and so forth. Innovations in the Information Age frequently produce intangible benefits and are harder to justify with static economic analysis. What is the value of more timely information or a more thorough analysis? What is the value of a more informed mind? Such questions don't usually yield dollars-and-cents answers.

■ Summary

We can find the origins of the modern computer in Charles Babbage's designs and Herman Hollerith's tabulating machines. But the need to solve large scientific problems involving tedious calculations provided the motivation for development of the electronic general-purpose computer. ENIAC, completed in

1946, was the first operational computer that was totally electronic. UNIVAC I, produced by Remington-Rand Corporation in 1951, was the first commercial computer. It marked the start of the first generation of mainframe computers.

The second, third, and fourth generations of mainframe computers were marked by technological improvements—transistors, integrated circuits, and large-scale integrated circuits, respectively. These led to faster operation, decreased size, and increased memory. Because of their cost, large computers were timeshared among many users.

The development of the microprocessor in 1971 spawned a new breed of computers designed to be used by one person. Thus in 1975 the first personal computers appeared. A new stage in the development of personal computers has evolved every three years since 1975. Current personal computers have the processing power of third-generation mainframe computers and are being integrated into computer networks.

The prospects for technical improvements in the computer field are so positive that accurate predictions are likely to seem unbelievable to the average person. The fields of computing and communicating are merging, causing the development of larger and more complex distributed processing systems. All of these trends can collectively be described as a shift from the Industrial Age to the Information Age—a shift from physical tools to mental-support tools.

Key Terms

Apple II	MITS Altair 8800
Commodore PET	PDP-11
EDVAC	System/360
electronic digital computer	TRS-80
ENIAC	UNIVAC I

Key People

John Atanasoff	Gary Kildall
Charles Babbage	John Mauchly
Dan Bricklin	John von Neumann
J. Presper Eckert	Robert Noyce
Bill Gates	Konrad Zuse
Herman Hollerith	

Discussion Questions

1. Who do you think should be given credit for inventing the electronic computer?

2. The phenomenal development of the computer has occurred in a very short time—less than fifty years. Can you think of anything else with a similarly rapid development? Consider the automobile, airplane, and television. If they had developed as far and as fast as the computer, what would they be like?

3. If a fifth generation of computers is successfully developed, what do you think they will be like? How will they be used?

4. As the speed and capability of personal computers increase, do you think the distinction between mainframe and personal computers will disappear?

5. Which social institutions are likely to adapt quickly to the Information Age? Which are most likely to resist change? Will resistance be successful?

Exercises

1. Match the persons in the left-hand column with the event in the right-hand column.

   1. John Atanasoff
   2. Charles Babbage
   3. Dan Bricklin
   4. Bill Gates
   5. Herman Hollerith
   6. Gary Kildall
   7. J. Presper Eckert
   8. John Mauchly
   9. John von Neumann
   10. Robert Noyce

   a. Developed CP/M
   b. ENIAC computer
   c. Father of computing
   d. Developed Visicalc
   e. Developed BASIC for personal computers
   f. Data processing
   g. Developed FORTRAN
   h. Apple II
   i. Developed COBOL
   j. ABC computer
   k. Stored program concept
   l. MITS Altair 8800

2. Charles Babbage was quite a character with an unusual collection of friends, including Countess Augusta Ada Lovelace, the first programmer. Read more about him and his inventions.

3. List some tasks that can be done on a large mainframe computer but not on a personal computer.

4. Choose an organization and write a report on how it is likely to be affected by changes in the computer field over the next five years.

ethics and computing

18

18

The computer has spearheaded the Information Revolution by making it possible to collect and manipulate more information and to do so with ever-increasing speed and efficiency. But the Information Revolution in turn has raised new concerns about the balance between an individual's privacy and society's "need to know." What type of personal information should be collected? Who should be allowed access to the information? How are we to balance such fundamental values as freedom of speech, the right to engage in new forms of commercial endeavor, and the spirit of an open society against the right of each individual to privacy?

Other concerns are caused by the growing importance of computer security. Are adequate safeguards in place to prevent unauthorized access to computer systems? Is it wrong to "look around" another computer system? How can computer systems be made less vulnerable?

Software piracy is a serious problem for software developers because software for personal computers is distributed on easy-to-copy floppy disks. How many back-up copies may you make? May you use the same program on several computers? Certainly selling an unauthorized copy of a program is illegal, but is it illegal to give a copy of a program to a friend or relative for demonstration purposes?

These questions are unlikely to yield to simple answers. Guidelines, procedures, technical safeguards, regulations, and laws to address these issues are being discussed by lawyers, computer manufacturers, computer center directors, software publishers, and legislators. Their deliberations have been confused by continual and rapid technological developments. What actions they take will greatly influence the future of computing.

Privacy, computer security, and software piracy are the major social issues considered in this chapter. We will describe some of the problems these issues raise as well as some solutions and safeguards.

■ Computers and Privacy

Privacy is the right of individuals to control information about themselves. The right to privacy is a cornerstone of democratic societies. In the United States the right to privacy has been upheld by interpretations of the Constitution, recognized by common law, and protected by laws enacted by Congress. However, certain personal information is required by government agencies such as the Internal Revenue Service and by other organizations such as schools and financial institutions. An important privacy issue is the proper balance between the information needs of these organizations and the right of an individual to control personal information. The ability of computers to collect, process, and share information affects this balance in many ways.

514

Threats to Privacy

Most people willingly provide information about themselves when the purpose for gathering the information is known, the benefits to be derived from it are clear, and they are given assurances that the information will be used in the intended way. State and federal tax returns, census data, and applications for employment and credit are common examples.

For some people the computer has shaken this confidence that personal information will be used properly. In manual record-keeping systems the amount of information that can be collected and processed is severely limited, and little information is shared among systems. Computers have changed this. They have allowed the inclusion of more personal data on census forms, tax returns, school applications, marketing surveys, and credit applications. Computers have also made it possible to collect detailed information, much of it without your knowledge, about your everyday activities. Each long distance phone call, credit card transaction, and check you write is recorded. At the same time technology has made it possible to access any one of the millions of records in a database within seconds.

Information may be gathered or shared without your knowledge or consent. In one instance American Telephone and Telegraph used billing information obtained from a secret survey of telephone use for marketing purposes. The intent of this survey was not malicious, and none of the survey's results about individual customers was made publicly available. Nevertheless, the sanctity of telephone conversations is so important that many people found the mere existence of the survey disquieting.

The electronic highways connecting computers make the sharing of massive amounts of information fast and simple. Computerized lists of magazine subscribers and membership lists of organizations and clubs are sold, given away, and traded. (That's why you receive so much junk mail.) Computers are capable of searching and combining information in several databases. Recently the Department of Health and Human Services used the computer systems of three federal agencies—the Justice Department, the Department of Defense, and the Office of Personnel Management—to find federal employees who were illegally receiving welfare benefits. It compared the social security numbers of welfare recipients with the social security numbers of employees in the computer systems of the other three agencies. Few people would argue against the intent of this particular search, but for some people it raises fears about the possible effects of less well intentioned searches.

Even if you "have nothing to hide," the information contained in computer files may cause embarrassment or inconvenience or modify your behavior. Computers greatly increase the potential for misuse of information. Your control over personal medical information provides a good example. A national medical database could save your life; but it could also contain information about an abortion, psychiatric treatment, alcoholism, or drug treatment. If given access to this information, a prospective employer might decide not to hire a woman who has had an abortion or a man receiving drug treatments. Similarly, a financial institution might not approve a loan application, and an insurance company might refuse to issue a policy.

In short, here are some reasons for concern that the use of electronic information threatens your right to privacy.

- Increasing amounts of personal information are being collected and stored in computer files. This is encouraged by the rapidly falling cost of disk space and the ease of maintaining and sharing computer files. In many instances irrelevant data is collected, and information is easily shared.

- Just as in a manual system, computerized data may not be correct, complete, or current. Once inaccurate information is shared, it is very difficult to track down and correct all occurrences of the error.

- Important decisions about individuals are often based largely on the interpretation of data in computer files. These decisions frequently include whom to hire, whether to approve a loan or grant credit, and whether to admit a student to college.

- Computerized telephone marketing campaigns can invade your privacy by pestering you with unwanted phone calls. Automatic dialing machines can be coupled with tape-recorded messages and voice synthesizers to dial numbers and dispense messages with merciless persistence.

Computer-aided Social Systems

If personal privacy were the only issue to consider about computer databases, the collection of personal information in computer systems would have been outlawed years ago. But computerized information systems can be a powerful instrument for improving and maintaining social systems and for encouraging the growth of new business services.

The most obvious examples of computer-aided social systems are in the field of law enforcement. Police information systems keep track of many personal facts about citizens with the goal of maintaining law and order. Much of this personal information is not immediately useful to the cases being investigated and is stored for future reference. For example, the fingerprints of a large portion of Americans are on file—even though most of these people have never been arrested for a serious crime and are not considered active suspects in unsolved crimes. Recent advances in the computerized access and retrieval of fingerprint information have led to the arrest and conviction of numerous criminals. Law enforcement agencies could be stripped of the right to store such "irrelevant" information, but this might lead to an increase in the amount of violent crime. Similarly, most people support (or at least tolerate) the collection of financial information by the Internal Revenue Service because they want to make sure that it's not just the honest citizens who pay taxes.

Our free-market system of business depends on the accurate transmission and storage of personal information. For example, automatic teller machines deduct money from your account before they dispense cash. Retail businesses use remote computer systems to obtain authorizations for large credit card purchases. Other business uses of personal information produce less immediate results but can be just as important. For example, computer-generated marketing information helps companies target their sales efforts directly at qualified customers.

Safeguards and Laws

Several principles for safeguarding the privacy of information about individuals have been proposed by people who advocate more regulation and control of computer files.

1. There must be no record-keeping system for personal data whose existence is a secret.

2. An individual should be able to
   a. learn what information about them is in a database and how it is used.
   b. prevent information that was obtained for one purpose from being used or made available for other purposes.
   c. correct or amend inaccurate information.

3. Any organization creating, maintaining, or using records of personal data should
   a. be responsible for the reliability of the data.
   b. take reasonable precautions to prevent unauthorized access or misuse of the data.
   c. discard the information after a certain period of time.
   d. record every access to an individual's file and make the access records available to the individual on request.

4. There should be regulations and laws for enforcing these principles and for auditing compliance with the law.

Many of these recommendations have not been implemented for a variety of reasons. Two major reasons are cost and inertia. Another reason is the chilling and often unintended effects that laws and regulations have on the development of improved services. For example, because any major change in the communications or banking industries must contend with stringent federal regulation, most proposed changes don't get off the drawing board.

Today the most common privacy safeguards are company policies and procedures and professional ethics. Policies and procedures are not failproof, but they seem to work reasonably well for organizations such as financial institutions, insurance companies, and health organizations. Employees who fail to follow confidentiality guidelines may be transferred to another position or fired. The ethics codes of societies of computer professionals urge members who work with personal information to respect privacy rights by minimizing the data collected, developing appropriate access controls, and ensuring the accuracy and proper disposal of data.

Since the early 1970s the federal government has passed several laws to limit the indiscriminate use of computer data banks. These laws have ranged from the Fair Credit Reporting Act of 1971 to the Right to Financial Privacy Act of 1979.

The *Fair Credit Reporting Act* (1971) is designed to protect the quality of personal credit information by giving individuals the right to examine and, if necessary, make corrections. Credit agencies are allowed to provide credit reports only to organizations that have received an application for credit from the individual. This law also requires credit agencies to notify a person if it intends to contact neighbors or friends about the individual's character or lifestyle.

The *Privacy Act* (1974) applies only to the records of federal agencies. It requires agencies to publish an annual notice of their databases and, upon request, to notify an individual about the personal information contained in each database. It gives an individual the right to examine and correct information in the database and requires the agency to obtain written consent from the individual or court approval before releasing information.

The *Right to Financial Privacy Act* (1979) pertains to the type of personal information federal agencies can obtain from financial institutions. It outlines the legal procedures the agency must follow to obtain the information if it does not have the individual's consent and spells out the rights of the individual in the process.

A law recently enacted in Great Britain may be a harbinger of things to come. The *Data Protection Act* (1984) requires anyone who maintains a database containing personal data to register the database with a government office. The act provides a few limited exceptions; for example, payroll files do not need to be registered. The registration must describe the name of the installation, the purpose for which the data is being held, a description of the source of the data, the names of everyone to whom the data may be disclosed, a list of the countries to which the data may be transferred, and the name of the person responsible for handling requests for access. About 400,000 applications for registration are expected. Starting in 1987 the act gives individuals the right to request a copy of their file.

■ Computer Security

Computer security procedures help protect both computer hardware and the information contained in the computer system from misuse or damage.

The procedures for protecting computer hardware are similar to the procedures for protecting any valuable equipment. Access to the computer room is controlled by guards, alarms, special door locks, and badges for personnel. Fire, burglar, and smoke alarms in the computer room along with back-up tapes and disks stored in fireproof safes help guard against deliberate and accidental damage. For personal computer owners the major hardware security problems are theft and accidental damage to disks.

Protecting software and limiting access solely to authorized users are more difficult. The two major problems are to prevent access to the computer system by unauthorized users masquerading as legitimate users and to limit rightful users to those parts of the system they are authorized to access.

Computer-abetted Crime

The Information Revolution has fostered the creation of a new breed of criminal who uses the computer to commit crimes. Accurate data on computer crimes is lacking, but from what has been reported the average loss is large—perhaps as high as several hundred thousand dollars. Most often the criminals are individuals who are authorized to use the system and have enough technical knowledge to exploit weaknesses in the system. Computer-perpetrated crimes are difficult to detect (many crimes are discovered by accident), and some are not reported because doing so would undermine the confidence of the public or investors.

Electronic funds transfer (EFT) systems are especially vulnerable to computer crime because of the high potential payoff. EFT systems execute financial transactions electronically; the value or money that is being exchanged is represented by electronic messages. Embezzlers with inside knowledge can transfer money from one account—usually an inactive account—to their personal account. For example, Stanley Rifkin was able to transfer $10.8 million dollars to a Swiss bank account by using his knowledge of a bank's procedures, a telephone, and an authorization code. Eventually he was caught.

Auditors have a difficult time detecting smart embezzlers because computer-generated reports and listings can be doctored to seem correct. For example, in a *salami attack* a payroll program is modified to round down all fractions of a penny in salary calculations and to add these amounts to the criminal's computer account or paycheck. These ''slices'' may not seem like very much, but they can add up to a surprisingly large sum in a company with several thousand employees. A salami attack is difficult to detect because the salary totals balance.

In a *Trojan horse* scheme an unauthorized program is hidden within a legitimate program such as a telecommunications control program. The hidden program scans the data that passes through the legitimate program to discover passwords. The criminal then uses the passwords to transfer money or discover valuable information.

One of the largest and most notorious schemes was the Equity Funding fraud. To inflate the stock of the Equity Funding Corporation, the corporation's top executives established a second data processing department, ostensibly for research and development. In actuality this department was used to program the company's computers to generate over 60,000 fictitious life insurance policies worth $2.1 billion. These fictitious policies were then sold to other insurance companies. Equity Funding received a commission on each fictitious policy sold, paid premiums on these policies to the reinsurers, and then generated fake medical records to show that some of the policy holders had died. Besides the profits from the sale of shares of Equity Funding stock, the executives also collected over $1 million as beneficiaries of the fake policies. They were caught when a disgruntled former employee revealed the fraud.

Hackers

Not all security breaches have serious consequences, and in some cases it is not clear a crime has been committed. Are the young computer hackers who access and look around computer systems committing a crime? Their activities have created a new definition of the term *hacker*. Initially, a **hacker** referred to a person with computer expertise who was obsessed with writing and rewriting programs and exploring the capabilities of computer systems. But most people today use *hacker* to refer to someone who gains access to a computer system without authorization. This has upset "old definition" hackers. They would prefer that the term **crackers** (short for "security crackers") be used to described computer trespassers.

The personal computer has been largely responsible for this new breed of hackers. Years ago mainframe computers were well protected from trespassers by user names, passwords, trustworthy employees, and a secure computer room. Then the development of dial-up timesharing created new security problems. Anyone with a valid password, modem, and terminal could gain access by dialing the system's telephone number and supplying a valid user name–password combination. Today the total investment needed is the cost of a microcomputer and modem—as little as $150. And the personal computer can be programmed to penetrate computer security. The movie *WarGames* realistically depicted the steps: the computer can dial telephone numbers until it detects a computer-generated answer; then the user can try guessing the

Computers and Us: Living in a High-Tech World

For several decades the cost of computing equipment has fallen between 20 and 40 percent each year. During the same time salaries have risen about 4 percent each year. These trends seem likely to continue, and they imply dramatic changes in how we live and work. How you will fit into this new world will depend on how well prepared you are and on what you want to do. This photo essay gives you a glimpse into the professional opportunities you may find after leaving school.

1. Equipment and software vendors often run training classes describing their products and how to use them. Here, an instructor assists customers in a classroom designed for on-line, hands-on training.

EDUCATION AND TRAINING PROGRAMS

Education is a continuing necessity in a world where today's technical skills soon become tomorrow's antiquated knowledge.

2. Colleges and universities offer degree programs in computer science and allied fields, such as management information systems. Academic programs tend to emphasize the theoretical rather than the practical aspects of computer science, and they frequently use obsolete equipment and software because of budgetary limitations.

3. Students at the University of Oklahoma are developing their skills on equipment donated by the Telex Corporation.

4. Most firms run in-house training classes to keep their employees up to date. New employees may be given special training programs lasting up to six months.

5. Computer professionals find they need to do much of their learning on the job, using publications like these IBM reference manuals.

COMPUTER USERS

Being a competent computer user has become a prerequisite to success in most professional fields. The most important skill is knowing how to select and use application software.

6–9. Whether you want to conduct banking transactions, prepare marketing plans, design mechanical parts, or manage a production line, you are likely to use a computer.

10,11. A computer operator's job is to keep the computer system running smoothly. Operators load paper in printers, mount disks and tapes, run computer programs at scheduled times, and call systems programmers or maintenance technicians when something major goes wrong.

12,13. Other employees in computer operations include clerks who enter vast quantities of data from input forms, the operations manager who schedules shifts and supervises employees, and librarians who catalog and maintain the installation's program listings and operational data.

PROGRAMMERS AND ANALYSTS

14. An analyst helps users determine how data processing can be applied to their problems. Together with the users, the analyst gathers facts about the current system and helps establish specifications for the new system. Then the analyst designs a system that meets the users' information-processing needs.

15. An application programmer takes the design specifications created by the analyst and converts them into programs containing the detailed instructions needed by computers.

16. Systems programmers select and maintain system software. They establish the software environment in which application programmers function. Because systems programming is more technically demanding than application programming, systems programmers usually receive higher salaries.

ENGINEERING AND DESIGN

17,18. The rising use of complex digital circuits is merging the fields of electrical design and software engineering. Designs are tested with software and then built into circuits.

19. A draftsman performs layout and design work on an integrated circuit. Drafting and design require good visual understanding and a willingness to pay close attention to detail.

20. Arranging computer systems so that they are convenient to use involves *ergonomics,* the study of how human beings relate to their environment.

MANUFACTURING, SERVICE, AND SUPPORT

21,22. Manufacturing jobs in the computer field require dexterity and patience. Work is done in a clean—and sometimes an ultraclean—environment.

23. Many organizations purchase service contracts that promise quick on-site repairs. Here, IBM service coordinators in Atlanta use a computer-based system to assign representatives to handle calls for service.

24. Maintenance and repair technicians need a background in electronics along with some common sense. Because computers are designed with expansion and maintenance in mind, generally hardware can be upgraded and repaired simply by adding or exchanging circuit boards. Fixing faulty circuit boards often requires special testing equipment; so faulty boards usually are sent back to the factory for repair.

window 9

25. Widespread use of personal computers has created numerous opportunities in retail sales. Success in retail sales requires a desire to work with people and the technical ability to find and demonstrate solutions to their problems.

26. Selling computers to businesses and government agencies is a team effort that requires more than demonstrating hardware and software. Most organizations won't decide to purchase until they have received responses to a formal Request for Proposal (RFP), tested a working system, talked with prior customers, and negotiated a maintenance agreement. Here, IBM instructors train U.S. Department of Agriculture employees as part of a contract that includes the installation of almost 2,900 computers.

account numbers and passwords, or the computer can be programmed to generate guesses. However, discovering passwords and accessing files are not as easy as *WarGames* suggested. Nevertheless, anyone with a personal computer and modem has a fair chance of "cracking" most computer systems.

Is a hacker a criminal or a prankster? In one case an ex-employee of a software company used his personal computer equipped with a modem to access his former employer's confidential records of product data and customers. Even though his files had been removed from the computer system, he penetrated the security system by guessing the passwords of other employees. He then used this information to develop similar products and to offer them to his former employer's customers at attractive discounts. Clearly this individual committed a crime.

Classifying the activities of hackers such as the "Milwaukee 414" group (414 is the telephone area code in Milwaukee) is not as straightforward. Twelve teenagers in Milwaukee used national packet-switching networks, such as GTE Telenet, to gain illegal access to over sixty government and business computer systems. Getting into the GTE Telenet system required only a local telephone number and a two-digit access number. Once on the network, the teenagers were able to gain access to the computers at the Sloan-Kettering Cancer Institute, the nuclear weapons laboratory at Los Alamos, New Mexico, and a Los Angeles bank. They only looked around these computer systems and did not change any files. Was this an innocent prank or was a crime committed?

Those who believe that it is not wrong just to look around a computer system often argue that inadequate security encourages hackers and is partly to blame. Some believe that a hacker should be able to access a computer system when it is not being used (late at night or on weekends) because this is a good way to learn about programming and computers. To encourage this type of activity, some hackers exchange telephone numbers and passwords by electronic bulletin boards and other schemes.

Those who think computer trespassing is a crime do not see any difference between invading a computer system and breaking into an office to snoop in the file cabinets. That the intruder only browsed and did not steal anything is immaterial. Information is a valuable resource, and the temptation to alter or misuse it is great. Unauthorized changes to the records of medical or financial institutions or of governments could be catastrophic. They could endanger life and greatly undermine public confidence. Trade secrets, product information, and marketing data also must be protected; they provide businesses with a crucial competitive edge.

Victims are in a bind. They don't want publicity because publicity might inspire others to attempt similar schemes, and because they depend on public trust. A bank certainly would not want to publicize a million-dollar embezzlement by personal computer. Businesses are reluctant to prosecute a hacker who just browses around their files, but they have prosecuted hackers who change or destroy information.

Stories about the activities of hackers have heightened public apprehension about the vulnerability of computer systems and lax security. But surprisingly, less than half of the states have enacted laws that make computer break-in a crime.

Security Safeguards

There is no perfectly secure computer system. Safeguards against intentional or accidental damage to computer hardware were discussed earlier. Other types of safeguards are administrative controls and software safeguards.

Administrative controls discourage computer crime by making it more difficult for the crime to remain undetected. Some administrative controls are to

- share the assignment of sensitive duties among several employees. In particular, separate the tasks of developing programs, operating the computer system, and generating data for the system into separate departments.
- establish audit controls to monitor program changes, access to data files, and the submission of data.
- shred sensitive documents before discarding them.
- limit employee access to the computer facilities essential to their job.
- thoroughly investigate the trustworthiness of individuals in sensitive positions.

Software safeguards that prevent unauthorized access are the most difficult to develop. After revelations about hackers, computer networks and facilities were urged to take some immediate steps, including the following:

- Change passwords frequently and avoid using common words as passwords (such as *test, system,* or the names of persons). Passwords should include both digits and letters to make guessing more difficult.
- Remove invalid user names and passwords.
- Watch for unusual activity such as a user who repeatedly gives an incorrect password when attempting to connect with the computer system.
- Use an unlisted telephone number and change it frequently.

These measures are only a first line of defense. Underground newspapers and some electronic bulletin boards undermine them by publishing phone numbers and passwords. Several technical schemes can stop this threat, including port protection devices, callback port protection devices, access-monitoring, and data encryption.

Port protection devices (PPD) are black boxes between the computer system and the incoming telephone lines. They are independent of the dial-in access ports and transparent to the computer system. When potential users dial the computer system, they are connected to the PPD and must enter a password. If the password matches one in the PPD's memory, the user is connected with the computer system. If it does not match, the call is terminated and the user is not connected with the computer system. Some PPDs offer additional protection by generating a synthesized voice to answer calls instead of the tell-tale high-pitched tone of a modem. This prevents auto-dialing modems from detecting a computer answer.

In a **callback PPD** all calls are screened before they reach the computer. Each user has an identification number and an authorized telephone number. A user dials in, enters the identification number via a push-button telephone, and hangs up. The callback system verifies the identification number, searches its directory for the authorized telephone number, dials the number, and waits for a one-digit connection code. If all the information is correct, the user is given access to the computer. Otherwise the information is saved as part of an audit trail. This scheme normally adds about thirty seconds to the time needed to access the computer.

Access-monitoring allows a user only a certain number (say, five) attempts to give the correct password to access the computer system. Once that number is exceeded, the user's account is frozen until the manager of the computer system receives a valid explanation of the problem.

Data encryption scrambles both the data in files and the data transmitted over the communication lines so that they cannot be read without knowledge of the encryption scheme. The disadvantage of this scheme is the cost of the special equipment needed.

As technology improves, computers might be protected by devices that recognize voice and fingerprints. For now, these schemes are expensive and unproven.

■ Software Piracy

Software piracy is the unauthorized duplication of software. Pirates discourage the creation of new and innovative software because the revenues from sales support the development and marketing of new products.

Very few instances of piracy involve software for mainframe computers. Typically, this software is specially tailored for a particular computer facility, and it is written by relatively few companies. A negotiated contract spells out what programs are to be developed, the performance conditions they must satisfy, and maintenance and support responsibilities. Vendors can easily monitor the use and distribution of this software. Furthermore, business customers are accustomed to abiding by contracts. For the most part they are honest and fair, if only because unhappy employees serve as watchdogs. They may make a few more copies for back-up than their contract allows, but they are not likely to engage in large-scale piracy.

The same cannot be said of the consumer market. The personal computer completely changed the development and sale of software. Many companies and individuals develop software for personal computers. Millions of these programs are sold by dealers, computer stores, and mail-order outlets. For example, over a million copies of Lotus 1-2-3 have been sold. It would be impractical if not impossible to monitor each program sold.

The prime targets of software pirates are games and popular application programs, such as word processing and spreadsheet programs. Games are easy to use and require no support from the seller, making them perfect targets for a pirate.

No one knows exactly how much piracy costs software companies. According to some estimates, there may be as many as ten stolen copies for each legitimate copy. Probably a majority of personal computer owners possess or have used illegal copies. No one knows how many people would have purchased the software if they could not steal copies. At least one recent survey discovered that many users purchase software after a trial with an unauthorized version of the software. Users said they had made costly mistakes in the past and did not want to risk money on a program without trying it first.

Legal Protection for Software

There are three forms of legal protection for software: copyright, trade secret, and patent.

Copyright is the easiest and least expensive form of protection to obtain. In the United States copyright protection is automatic once the work is published, although to be safe (in the case of legal action) the work should be registered with the Copyright Office. Copyrights were originally developed for literary works. The Federal Copyright Law was amended by the Software Protection Act in 1980 to allow a user to make only archival copies of a software package. In the United States (and many other countries) a copyright gives an individual exclusive use of the work for life plus fifty years. For corporations a copyright is generally effective for seventy-five years. But a copyright protects only the tangible form in which an idea is expressed, not the idea itself. Thus it is only the actual program code that is protected, and it is permissible to write a new program that does the same thing as a copyrighted program.

In contrast, if a program can be designated a **trade secret,** even the idea embodied in the program is protected. This is the most popular and successful form of software protection. A program can be protected as a trade secret if the program has some secret information or formula that gives it an advantage over its competitors. However, there are two shortcomings. First, once the secret is out, protection is lost. Thus a software developer must guard the secret by limiting access and enforcing nondisclosure agreements. Second, trade secrets are based on state rather than federal laws; the extent of protection varies from state to state.

Patent protection is the most difficult protection to obtain because of the paperwork, the time the Patent Office takes to grant a patent (several years), and the reluctance of the Patent Office to give patent protection to programs. A patent gives exclusive rights to the concepts embodied in the program for seventeen years, which is more than sufficient in view of recent computer developments. But a patent is granted by the Patent Office only if the applicant convincingly demonstrates that the concepts have not appeared in other programs, a mighty tall order for the applicant.

Software License Agreements

Personal computer software usually comes in a shrink-wrapped box, or the disks are packaged in a sealed plastic bag. A notice warns the purchaser not to open the package before reading and agreeing to the license agreement. For most programs the license agreement is quite one-sided. It states that the software company is not liable for any losses resulting from use of the program, and it warns the purchasers that they will be in big trouble if they make copies (other than back-up copies, if allowed) or run the program on more than one machine.

Many personal computer users are unsure of what is software piracy and what is legal. Copyright law includes some **fair-use provisions,** which designate some copying of copyrighted material as "fair use" and legal. But what is fair use is not clear. Selling copies of the program is not fair use. Making a back-up copy certainly is fair use. But does fair use override an implied agreement to limit the number of back-up copies? Many users would like a copy of their business software for use on their home machines. This is not considered fair use because the copy is not for back-up use only.

For companies that have a large number of personal computers, preventing unauthorized copies is difficult. One solution is to negotiate a *site license agreement* with the vendor that allows the company to make an unlimited number of copies as long as they are all used at designated locations.

Thwarting Software Piracy

Software publishers have tried to combat software pirates by educational programs and a variety of technical schemes. Technical schemes use hardware, software, or a combination of the two; but they have not been completely successful. Ideally the scheme should be transparent to the legitimate user or at worst be a slight inconvenience.

The most common technical scheme is to **copy-protect** a disk by placing an error on the disk (such as an improperly formatted or improperly labeled sector) that does not interfere with the running of the program but does cause a standard disk-copy routine to report an error. This is not a permanent solution, because for each new copy-protection scheme a way will be found to defeat it. In fact, there is an active market for programs designed to defeat copy-protection schemes.

Copy-protected disks are a nuisance, especially when used with a hard disk. One common copy-protection scheme requires that the copy-protected system disk be inserted into the floppy disk drive each time the program is started. Programs that defeat this sort of copy-protection scheme usually cost between $25 and $50, but they make an exact duplicate of the original disk on another floppy disk. Thus it is reasonably easy for a pirate to make an illegal copy of the floppy disk, but it is not convenient for a legitimate user to use the software on a hard disk.

With copy-protected software there is always the risk of damaging or destroying the original disk, in which case the program no longer functions. So some copy-protected programs allow a specific number of back-up copies to be made by encoding a count on the original disk that is decreased by one each time a copy is made. When the count reaches zero, no more copies can be made.

Two other protection schemes involve passwords and codes. In a password scheme the user must remember a secret password to gain access to the program on the disk. In a code scheme a different serial number is encoded in each personal computer's ROM by the manufacturer. The number is read by the program the first time it is run and is used thereafter to initialize the program. The program must read this number to run. As a result, it cannot be used on a different computer. Although this scheme would probably be popular among software companies, very few personal computer manufacturers have decided to take the first step by electronically numbering their personal computers (an exception was the Apple Corporation's Lisa).

There is no simple solution to the problem of software piracy. An ideal solution would make it impossible to copy a program illegally but would not inconvenience legitimate users. Thus far, copy protection has made it harder for casual users to copy a program at the cost of inconveniencing all users.

Software publishers have not come up with a solution to stop software piracy. It is doubtful they will. Taking a combination of steps seems to be a reasonable approach. Some suggestions are to

- make it more difficult for pirates to copy programs and thereby discourage all but the most technically sophisticated pirates.
- develop protection schemes that minimally inconvenience legitimate users. Inconvenient schemes encourage piracy.
- educate users about the rights of software distributors and the rights of purchasers. Licensing agreements should be reasonable and should clearly state the rights and responsibilities of each party.

■ Summary

This chapter has presented three thorny social issues directly related to the use of computers: individual privacy, computer security, and software piracy. No simple solution or policy has been developed that deals adequately with them. One step is to make hardware and software developers and computer users aware of these issues. Another step is to encourage them to incorporate this awareness in their work.

Any new computer development is likely to involve social issues. For example, several questions about electronic mail systems are unresolved. What security measures should be taken to protect the information in these systems? Who is responsible if information is divulged? Technological advances occur so rapidly it is difficult to develop laws, safeguards, or guidelines against their misuse or to adequately study and address their social impact.

It is all but impossible to prevent an expert user from copying a program or to prevent a user with inside information from accessing a computer system. But safeguards will discourage the casual user from attempting piracy or trespassing, and will make success more difficult for the technically competent user.

Key Terms

access-monitoring	fair-use provisions
callback PPD	hacker
copy-protect	patent
copyright	port protection devices (PPD)
cracker	privacy
data encryption	software piracy
Electronic funds transfer (EFT) systems	trade secret

Discussion Questions

1. What rights should people have regarding information about them in computer databases? How might these rights interfere with the efficiency of a free-market economy?

2. Do you support the establishment of a universal identifier card that would serve as a driver's license, credit card, and health record? What long-term benefits might this system have?

3. What information (if any) should owners of private databases be required to make publicly available?

4. Social security numbers are often used as a key in accessing personal information contained in several databases. Should some restrictions be placed on the use of a person's social security number?

5. Do you think the government's matching of computer files to find welfare cheaters was unethical or illegal? What portion of fraud and tax evasion do you think might be prevented if government agencies were allowed unlimited access to the records of financial institutions?

6. Authorities have raided several electronic bulletin boards used by "crackers" and seized their computing equipment and disks. They said they hoped to "scare the kids." Should the person running the bulletin board be responsible for what callers write in the bulletin board?

7. Do you think a hacker should be able to access a computer system when it is not busy? Is a computer system with inadequate security an attractive nuisance?

8. Would lowering the price of software reduce piracy?

9. Is allowing computer software to be used on just one machine too restrictive? Can you suggest a more reasonable rule?

Exercises

1. Find a reported case of computer crime. What type of security safeguards would have prevented the crime?

2. Interview the director of a computer center about security safeguards.

3. List some reasons a bank might not prosecute a computer-aided embezzler. List some reasons why they should prosecute.

4. Read several software license agreements for personal computer software. What restrictions are included? If the programs come from different companies, list the differences.

5. Investigate the history of patents for computer programs.

6. Determine what if any laws your state has enacted concerning computer trespass.

7. List some tasks a computer should not perform. Justify your choices. Because a computer cannot be convicted of a crime, who is responsible when a computer commits a criminal action? The programmer who wrote the program? The computer operator? The computer user? The computer's manufacturer?

how computers process information

A

The basic building block of computers is the transistor. A **transistor** is an electronic device for controlling the flow of electrons in an electrical circuit. Think of a transistorized circuit as a switch like a light switch at home: the switch is either on or off and stays that way until it is flipped again. If electrons are allowed to flow, the circuit is on; if electrons are not allowed to flow, the circuit is off. The on-off flow of electrons in these small circuits is used to encode information as binary 1s and 0s.

A modern electronic computer is often called a *binary* computer because its most basic circuits can remember either one of the binary digits 0 and 1. These digits are called *bits*. Both the internal and external memory of a computer are nothing more than storehouses for bits. RAM (random-access memory), ROM (read-only memory), disk, and tape all store 1s and 0s. No other form of information is stored in a computer—not numbers, keyboard characters, programs, or word processing documents. How, then, does a computer store and process decimal numbers, business letters, and other forms of information? The binary number system and computer codes provide the answer.

■ Representing Information

Binary Versus Decimal

The key to understanding computers is the binary number system. Whereas the decimal number system has ten digits, 0 to 9; the binary number system has only two digits, 0 and 1. To understand how these digits are used, recall that decimal numbers represent powers of 10. For example, the decimal number 537 is really the sum of powers of 10.

$$537 \text{ decimal} = (5 \times 10^2) + (3 \times 10^1) + (7 \times 10^0)$$
$$= (5 \times 100) + (3 \times 10) + (7 \times 1)$$
$$= 500 + 30 + 7$$

Notice that the decimal number 1 is 10 raised to the 0 power; and 10, 100, 1,000, and so on are all 10 raised to some power.

Binary numbers are the sums of powers of 2 in the same way that decimal numbers are sums of powers of 10. The following list shows the decimal numbers that are represented by some powers of 2.

$2^{-2} =$	0.25
$2^{-1} =$	0.5
$2^0 \ \ =$	1.
$2^1 \ \ =$	2.
$2^2 \ \ =$	4.

$$
\begin{aligned}
2^3 &= 8. \\
2^4 &= 16. \\
2^8 &= 256. \\
2^{16} &= 65{,}536. \\
2^{20} &= 1{,}048{,}576. \\
2^{24} &= 16{,}777{,}216. \\
2^{32} &= 4{,}294{,}967{,}296.
\end{aligned}
$$

A binary number is a string of 1s and 0s, each indicating the presence or absence of a power of 2. For example, consider the binary number 101. This number is converted to its decimal equivalents as follows:

Binary number	0	0	0	0	0	1	0	1
Power of two	7	6	5	4	3	2	1	0
Decimal number	0	0	0	0	0	4	0	1

$$
\begin{aligned}
101 \text{ binary} &= (1 \times 2^2) + (0 \times 2^1) + (1 \times 2^0) \\
&= (1 \times 4) + (0 \times 2) + (1 \times 1) \\
&= 4 + 0 + 1 = 5 \text{ decimal}
\end{aligned}
$$

Thus 101 is the binary number representation of the decimal number 5.

The fractional part of a binary number such as 101.1 is a sum of *negative* powers of two. For example, 101.1 binary is converted to its decimal equivalent as follows:

$$
\begin{aligned}
101.1 \text{ binary} &= (1 \times 2^2) + (0 \times 2^1) + (1 \times 2^0) + (1 \times 2^{-1}) \\
&= (1 \times 4) + (0 \times 2) + (1 \times 1) + (1 \times 1/2) \\
&= 4 + 0 + 1 + 1/2 = 5.5 \text{ decimal}
\end{aligned}
$$

Here are some other examples.

$$
\begin{aligned}
4 \text{ decimal} &= 100 \text{ binary} \\
16 \text{ decimal} &= 10000 \text{ binary} \\
31 \text{ decimal} &= 111111 \text{ binary} \\
6.25 \text{ decimal} &= 110.01 \text{ binary} \\
145.625 \text{ decimal} &= 10010001.101 \text{ binary}
\end{aligned}
$$

Keep in mind that computers work exclusively with binary numbers because they can store only a 1 or a 0. To do arithmetic and word processing they must convert from binary to decimal and back again. We see only the result of this conversion and not the binary numbers themselves. It is not necessary to know anything about binary arithmetic to use a computer. But if you want to know what happens inside a computer, then it is essential that you learn the "secret code" of binary numbers.

Characters and Strings of Text

How does a binary computer process textual information? Individual keystrokes generate letters, numbers, and other symbols called *characters*. Groups of characters treated as a unit are called *strings*. Because characters and strings cannot be processed directly by a machine that "understands" only binary numbers, they must be encoded in some kind of binary code. One of these codes is ASCII (American Standard Code for Information Interchange), which associates a unique 7-bit binary number with each character.

In ASCII the letter *A* is associated with 1000001 binary. The numeral (not its value) 1 is associated with 0110001 binary. However, because binary numbers are tedious to remember, people usually convert binary codes to their decimal equivalents when they refer to them. Hence, *A* is represented by the decimal number 65, and the numeral 1 is represented by decimal number 49.

Keyboard character	Binary code	Decimal code
A	1000001	65
a	1100001	97
Z	1011010	90
z	1111010	122
0 (zero)	0110000	48
9	0111001	57
+	0101011	43
(carriage return)	0001101	13

Suppose you want to store a line of text in the computer's memory. You enter the string of characters "Hello C3 PO" into the computer through the keyboard. The keyboard converts each keystroke (including the spaces) into ASCII binary code.

Character (keyboard)	ASCII (decimal)
H	72
e	101
l	108
l	108
o	111
(space)	32
C	67
3	51
(space)	32
P	80
O	79

When the computer displays this line of text on its screen, the reverse process occurs: circuits in the screen display convert the ASCII binary code in memory into visible characters.

A 7-bit coding system like ASCII can represent only a limited number of different characters. The largest decimal number we can express in a 7-bit binary number is the equivalent of the binary number 1111111, which is

1111111 binary = 64 + 32 + 16 + 8 + 4 + 2 + 1 decimal
= 255 decimal

Everything is exactingly stored in the computer as binary numbers: letters of the alphabet, numerals, punctuation marks, and special characters ($, #, %, and so on). Each character has its own 7-bit code. Because the memory of a computer can record binary digits and nothing else, all kinds of information must be encoded. The power of a computer to manipulate symbols is hidden in the simplicity of a coding scheme.

Numeric Codes

Values of numbers can be encoded in many ways; we will discuss the two most common ways. Natural or counting numbers are encoded as binary **integers** (whole numbers). Signed numbers with decimal points are called **real numbers** and must be encoded using **floating-point representation.** For example, a whole number like 35 is an integer, but a number with a decimal point in it—say, 35.0—is a real number and must be encoded in the floating-point format.

Integers

A computer stores binary numbers in groups of bits called *bytes* (8 bits = 1 byte) and *words* (which may be 8, 16, 32, or more bits depending on the computer). An 8-bit byte can encode only 256 different integers—say, from −128 to +127 decimal value. A 16-bit word can encode binary integers from −32,768 to +32,767 decimal. The size in bits of a computer word affects the power of a computer because it limits the size of the numbers that a computer can represent conveniently. Our examples assume a 16-bit word length.

Computers perform addition, subtraction, multiplication, and division on the binary code, not on decimal integers. After the arithmetic is carried out in binary, a program converts the result from a binary number into a decimal number. Conversely, when a decimal integer is entered into a computer, it must be converted into a binary integer before any arithmetic can be performed.

The correspondence between decimal and binary integers is straightforward. The first bit of a binary integer is called a *sign bit;* it is a 0 if the number is positive and a 1 if the number is negative. All binary numbers from zero through 0111111111111111 (16 bits with a leading 0 bit) are equivalent to the decimal numbers 0 to 32,767. The binary numbers 1111111111111111 (16 bits, all set to 1) through 1000000000000000 (16 bits with a leading 1) are equivalent to decimal numbers −1 to −32767. Negative numbers count backward to make subtraction simple for electronic circuits.

Integer representation results in fast arithmetic, but it also has disadvantages. Only whole numbers can be manipulated, and the size of each number is restricted. To get around these limitations, computers also use floating-point representation.

Floating-Point Numbers

Floating-point representation is based on scientific notation, which expresses each number as a magnitude times a power of 10. For example, in scientific notation 120 is written as 1.2×10^2. Similarly, floating-point representation separates a number into three parts.

1. The sign. This is either plus or minus.

2. The magnitude. This is expressed as a decimal fraction between 0 and 1.

3. The exponent. This is a power of 10 (or a power of 2). It reflects the location of the decimal point within the decimal (or binary) number.

In the computer field, floating-point numbers are often written in *scientific notation* as follows:

```
0.50 E +01
```

Exponent or power of 10

Separator

Fractional part

Sign of entire number (either +, −, or left blank for positive numbers)

To convert a decimal floating-point number to an ordinary decimal number you simply move the decimal point right or left (depending on the sign of the exponent) the number of digits specified by the exponent. For example, to obtain the value of 0.50 E +01, move the decimal point one digit to the right of its original position, because the exponent is 1 and its sign is positive.

$$0.50 \text{ E } +01 = 0.50 \times 10 = 5.0$$

The sign of the number is always the sign shown in front of the floating-point representation. Here are several other examples.

0.55	E −01	is	0.055
0.123	E +03	is	123.0
−0.95	E +00	is	−0.95
−0.95	E +01	is	−9.5
−0.95	E +05	is	−95,000.00

There is a limit to the size of number that can be encoded in this fashion. If two digits are allowed in the fraction and in the exponent, then the largest number that can be encoded is $+0.99$ E $+99$, and the smallest number is -0.99 E $+99$. The numbers nearest zero would be $+0.01$ E -99 and -0.01 E -99. Zero is a special case, usually represented by $+0.00$ E $+00$.

■ Processing Information

How Electronic Circuits Compute

The brain of a computer is its central processing unit, which contains the arithmetic logic unit (ALU). The brain of a personal computer is a microprocessor. Inside the ALU or microprocessor is a collection of circuits that add, multiply, transfer, compare, and so on. It is instructive to examine how these circuits work—for example, how an addition takes place.

Because all numbers, characters, and instructions are stored as binary numbers, addition of two numbers reduces to the addition of bits.

$$
\begin{array}{ll}
1010 & \text{binary} \\
+\ 1101 & \text{binary} \\
\hline
10111 & \text{binary}
\end{array}
$$

The addition circuit must do just two things in order to perform this addition: add two bits together to get a sum, and produce a carry bit (0 or 1). The ability to perform these simple operations is wired into the computer by building circuits that obey two rules.

1. If only one of the addend bits is a 1, then the resulting bit is a 1; otherwise the result is a 0. This is the rule for adding two bits.

2. If one or both of the addend bits is a 0, then the resulting bit is a 0; otherwise the result is a 1 bit. This is the rule for obtaining the carry bit.

These rules are represented in the following **truth tables:**

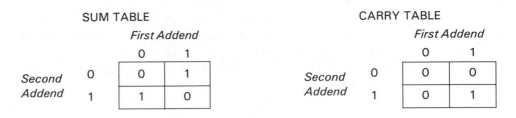

SUM TABLE					CARRY TABLE		
		First Addend					First Addend
		0	1				0	1
Second Addend	0	0	1		Second Addend	0	0	0
	1	1	0			1	0	1

These two truth tables summarize how to perform binary addition one bit at a time. For instance, if a 0 is added (first addend) to a 1 (second addend), the result is 1, as shown in the corresponding entry of the sum table. Similarly, if a 1 is added to another 1, the result is 0 according to the sum table and a 1 according to the carry table.

If the sum and carry tables are used repeatedly, any binary numbers can be added. Suppose the computer is asked to add 1101 to 0111. The sum for each column is noted, and the carry bit is shifted one place to the left of the column just added and placed below the sum.

$$
\begin{array}{lll}
 & 1101 \text{ binary} & (13 \text{ decimal}) \\
+ & 0111 \text{ binary} & (\ 7 \text{ decimal}) \\
\hline
\text{Sum} = & 1010 \text{ binary} & \\
\text{Carry} = & 0101 & (\text{shifted left 1 place})
\end{array}
$$

This sum and the carry bit are then added in the same way. These steps are repeated until there are no carry bits to be added (000), leaving the final answer. Thus

$$
\begin{array}{lll}
 & 1101 \text{ binary} & (13 \text{ decimal}) \\
+ & 0111 \text{ binary} & (\ 7 \text{ decimal}) \\
\hline
\text{Sum} = & 1010 \text{ binary} & \\
\text{Carry} = & \underline{0101} & (\text{shifted left one place}) \\
\text{Sum} = & 0000 & \\
\text{Carry} = & \underline{1010} & (\text{shifted}) \\
\text{Sum} = & 10100 & \\
\text{Carry} = & \underline{0000} & \\
\text{Answer} = & 10100 \text{ binary} & (20 \text{ decimal})
\end{array}
$$

In short, the computer adds two numbers by performing sum, carry, and shift operations through repetitive steps. The operations are very simple; but when combined in just the right way, they can do powerful things.

We have just shown that computers work by simulating operations on binary numbers through electronic circuits that perform elementary functions. Addition, for example, is nothing more than a sequence of simple summation, carry, and shift operations. Higher-order operations are nothing more than lengthy sequences of elementary operations. This, combined with binary encoding of information, is the secret to how computers work.

Computers do not know how to think. They merely perform millions of simple truth table operations. To show how computers can blindly compute wrong answers, in the next section we consider the problems associated with arithmetic on real numbers.

Numeric Precision

Sometimes the computer prints a value that is not quite what you expect. For instance, it might print 1.9999 instead of 2.0, or a calculation may be off by a few cents—yielding an answer of $12,235.20 instead of $12,235.24. Both of these results reflect the fact that the computer does not provide infinite precision. In particular, some information is lost during calculation because the encoding of floating-point numbers is approximate.

To understand this lack of precision, consider the following addition:

$$
\begin{array}{r}
3000.0001 \\
+ \quad 3000.0001 \\
\hline
6000.0002
\end{array}
$$

The computer must convert 3000.0001 to binary code; add the two binary-encoded numbers; convert the result back to 6000.0002 decimal; and display the result. When the floating-point number is stored in 32 bits, the encoded value of 3000.0001 is approximated as 0.3000000 E +01. Thus, when the computer adds these numbers, it comes up with a sum of 6000.0000 instead of 6000.0002.

Whenever computers calculate with floating-point numbers, they round off the numbers, which creates errors. For this reason, you should always ask yourself, To how many digits is this number reasonable and accurate? Typically, floating-point numbers are accurate to about the first six or seven digits. So unless the program uses double-precision arithmetic (which stores each number in twice as much storage space), you should use only the first six or seven digits in the answer even if the computer prints more than seven digits.

careers in computing B

Growth in Data Processing Employment
Programmers
System Analysts
Operations Personnel
Management Positions
Database and Communications Specialists
Jobs with Computer and Software Firms
Computer Educators

Jobs in the computer field vary considerably. Some computer professionals are paid exorbitant salaries, receive many job offers, and work in attractive surroundings. Others have low-prestige jobs that require repetitive work for low pay. Where you will fit in—should you decide to embark on a computer-related career—will depend largely on the skills you have and the steps you take to prepare yourself.

In this appendix we present an overview of the types of jobs in the computer field. For each job category we describe the usual activities and responsibilities, the necessary background and skills, and an approximate salary range. Before you read this appendix you may want to review Window 9; it presents a pictorial survey of careers in computing.

A few comments about the usefulness of job categories are appropriate. Even if two people may have the same job title, their duties, backgrounds, and compensation may be markedly different. For example, a programmer in a payroll department and a programmer in a scientific laboratory are likely to have different educational backgrounds and use different programming tools. There are also differences between jobs in large and small organizations. A large firm may hire many employees for each job category, whereas in a small business one person may perform tasks from several job categories.

Growth in Data Processing Employment

The computer field is an exciting and rapidly growing area with outstanding opportunities. Table B.1 illustrates the growth in traditional data processing jobs; total employment doubled during the 1970s and is expected to double again by 1990.

Table B.1 also shows that the growth rates for different jobs vary considerably. The average annual growth rate for jobs in programming has declined from 7.2 percent per year during the 1970s to 5.0 percent in the 1980s. This decline has been caused by the development of software tools that improve the productivity of programmers. Meanwhile the need for system analysts is growing in response to the backlog of application development requests in large institutions and the expansion of distributed computing in small organizations. Jobs for data entry operators are increasing only at a slow rate, despite the tremendous increase in the amount of data acquired and processed by computers. This apparent conflict is explained by technological advances that allow computers to acquire data without the help of professional typists.

Job opportunities in data processing are increasing at the fastest rate for computer operators. Most of this growth is occurring because clerical workers are switching to computerized methods of work—thereby becoming computer operators. Surprisingly, large computer installations are hiring few new oper-

Table B.1 *Growth in Data Processing Employment from 1970 to 1990.*

	Number of Jobs			Annual Average Growth Rates	
	1970[a]	*1980*[a]	*1990*[b]	*1970–1980*	*1980–1990*
Programmers	160,000	320,000	520,000	7.2%	5.0%
System analysts	80,000	220,000	520,000	10.6%	9.0%
Computer operators	120,000	420,000	1,305,000	13.3%	12.0%
Data entry operators	255,000	395,000	480,000	4.5%	2.0%
Total	615,000	1,355,000	2,825,000	8.1%	7.6%

[a]Adapted from data published by the Bureau of the Census of the U.S. Commerce Department.
[b]Estimated figures.

ators. These installations can add processing capacity without expanding their personnel by purchasing peripherals that require less attention from operators, by moving input and output devices into user areas, and by using software that performs monitoring and maintenance tasks previously done by computer operators.

The growth in data processing employment has created a shortage of experienced people and intense competition for their services. This has encouraged people to shift from one job to another. Estimates place the annual turnover rate in the industry between 20 and 25 percent—much higher than in other fields. Not all of the job hopping is motivated by salary considerations; people also look for new jobs to develop new skills, gain access to current technology, and advance to more challenging work.

Programmers

A *computer programmer* translates the specifications established by analysts, managers, and users into reliable computer programs. Programmers tend to be creative problem solvers who can think in logical steps and concentrate on details. A programmer needs good communication skills, proficiency with the programming tools to be used, and a thorough understanding of modern programming and documentation techniques. Most programmers work in teams, but some work individually. There are two major types of programmers: application and systems programmers.

Application programmers write programs that solve specific problems for users. Business application programmers need a business background and will most likely write their programs in COBOL, RPG, or PL/I. Scientific application programmers need a strong mathematics or statistics background and knowledge of a particular scientific area. They usually write their programs in FORTRAN, APL, or Pascal.

Systems programmers maintain and develop enhancements to system software. They modify system software and develop utility programs that improve performance or make the operating system easier to use. A systems programmer needs the technical background that a computer science program provides, or equivalent professional training. Systems programmers tend to be paid more than application programmers. Most systems programmers write programs in assembly language or C.

Programming is the most common entry-level position for a person with a two- or four-year college degree. There are several levels within this category, based on experience and responsibility.

Job title	Experience and responsibilities	Typical salary[1]
Trainee or junior programmer	Two- or four-year college degree; little or no experience. Directly supervised.	$16,000 to $25,000
Programmer	Two years of experience. Works on a limited number of tasks at one time.	$19,000 to $30,000
Senior programmer	Three or more years of experience. Supervises other programmers.	$24,000 to $36,000
Lead programmer	Four or more years of experience. Two or more years of supervision experience. Manages a group of programmers.	$28,000 to $40,000

System Analyst

A *system analyst* interacts with users, managers, and programmers and analyzes, designs, implements, and evaluates computer-based information systems. Most system analysts are ex-programmers. A system analyst usually has

- a four-year college degree in computer science, business, or mathematics.
- up-to-date knowledge about the capabilities and limitations of computer hardware and software.
- knowledge of the organization's objectives and goals.
- good problem-solving, organizational, and planning skills.
- good communication skills and the ability to work well with people.

[1]The salaries listed are based on industry averages for 1985. If you want more current figures, you should look at *Datamation* magazine's annual survey, which is published in each September issue.

Even though a system analyst may not write a single line of code, programming experience is strongly recommended and is often required. Programmers aspiring to a position in management often choose a job as system analyst as a step toward that goal. In some companies, especially small ones, the positions of programmer and analyst are combined into one position with the title programmer/analyst.

Just as for programmers, there are several levels of system analysts based on background and experience.

Job title	Experience and responsibilities	Typical salary
System analyst trainee	Limited, if any, system analysis experience. Directly supervised.	$18,000 to $26,000
System analyst	Two years of experience. Requires limited supervision.	$23,000 to $32,000
Senior system analyst	Three or more years of experience; some supervising experience.	$28,000 to $40,000
Lead system analyst	Four or more years of experience; two years of supervising experience. Responsible for managing a project.	$32,000 to $49,000

Operations Personnel

Operations personnel are concerned with the smooth functioning of the computer facility.

Job title	Experience and responsibilities	Typical salary
Computer operator	Junior college degree or on-the-job training. Prepares peripherals with paper, disks, and so on; monitors the operation of the computer; runs programs and enters some data.	$13,000 to $18,000
Production control clerks	On-the-job training. Schedules jobs for processing; distributes computer output.	$12,000 to $16,000
Data entry operator	High school diploma; excellent typing skills.	$12,000 to $18,000
Word processing operator	High school diploma; secretarial skills; excellent typing ability.	$15,000 to $23,000
Librarian	Basic data processing and record-keeping skills. Catalogs and maintains files of data, programs, tapes, and documentation.	$12,000 to $16,000

Management Positions

Management positions vary considerably depending on the management level within the organization and the size of the organization. In these jobs technical expertise is not as important as the ability to organize, motivate, communicate, plan, and budget. Frequently an advanced degree, such as an MBA degree, is required.

Traditionally, if you wanted to be a manager, you worked your way up through the ranks. However, companies are beginning to place more importance on managerial skill by providing employees with the opportunity to take management training courses and by hiring professional managers.

Job title	Responsibilities	Typical salary
Programmer/analyst manager	Supervises a group of programmers and analysts.	$31,000 to $52,000
Data entry supervisor	Supervises a group of data entry operators.	$15,000 to $21,000
Data processing operations manager	Responsible for computer operations, data entry, production control.	$23,000 to $41,000
Director of information systems	Supervises all data processing personnel.	$36,000 to $57,000
Vice president of information systems	Sets long-range planning and policy; supervises all data processing.	$43,000 to $85,000

Database and Communications Specialists

Advances in database systems and communications have created the need for specialists in these fields. The demand for experienced people in these areas is currently much greater than the supply, so salaries for these jobs have risen rapidly over the last few years.

Database specialists design and control the use of an organization's data. They analyze the interrelationships of data usage, define physical data structures and logical views of data, recommend new database systems or changes in existing systems, and eliminate data redundancy. This position requires a college degree in computer science and knowledge of programming, methodologies of system analysis, and database design. The salaries for database specialists range from $25,000 to $58,000.

A *data communications specialist* is responsible for analyzing the need for voice and data communications and designing systems that fit these needs. This position requires a degree in electrical engineering, communications, or computer science. The salary range is from $24,000 to $52,000.

Jobs with Computer and Software Firms

Computer firms design, manufacture, and sell computers; after a sale they also provide product support to customers, answering questions and analyzing problems. Software firms create programs and documentation, and offer support services to satisfy the specific processing needs of their customers.

Electrical, industrial, and mechanical engineers and technicians design and manufacture new computers or improve existing computers. These engineering positions require at least a four-year engineering degree and in some cases an advanced degree. Salaries for engineers range from $21,000 to $90,000. Technicians need training from a junior college or technical school. Their starting salary is about $18,000.

Sales representatives determine their customers' needs, work closely with technical experts to develop plans that fit those needs, and make sales presentations. Sales representatives must be knowledgeable about the company's products, deal effectively with people, and possess excellent written and oral communications skills. A beginning sales representative earns between $20,000 and $25,000; an experienced representative may earn two to four times that amount. Most sales representatives are given quotas to meet and are paid commissions on sales.

Product support representatives provide training for the use and care of equipment as well as maintenance and repair. *Software support representatives* maintain programs by fixing errors and adding new features; they also answer questions and educate customers about the software. This work is usually performed by programmers or people with an equivalent background. *Customer engineers* install and test the equipment, provide routine maintenance, and perform repairs at computer installations. Customer engineers should have two years of technical training after high school, but many employers require an engineering or computer science degree. New employees in these positions are usually given special training by their firm. The typical salary range is from $22,000 to $35,000.

Computer Educators

As the demand for computer-trained personnel continues to escalate, the need for educators has grown as well. There is a critical shortage of qualified teachers for computer and data processing programs at community colleges, four-year colleges, and universities. Community college instructors need a master's degree in business or computer science, or a bachelor's degree combined with some work experience. Salaries range from $15,000 to $28,000. Four-year colleges and universities require instructors to have at least a master's degree—and in many cases a Ph.D.—in computer science or a related field. Average salaries range from $16,000 to $40,000, depending on background and experience.

Computers are also in widespread use in elementary, junior high, and high schools for administrative as well as instructional tasks. Programming, word processing, and computer literacy classes are offered in junior high and high schools. Teachers may obtain a background in computing while earning their college degree or by taking in-service courses in computing. The salaries of teachers in public education range from $14,000 to over $20,000.

Summary

This appendix has presented a brief introduction to the variety of challenging and rewarding careers in the computer field. The future seems equally attractive as all predictions point to continued advances in computer technology, more computer applications, and the need for additional people who are knowledgeable about computers.

programming in BASIC

C

BASIC (*B*eginner's *A*ll-purpose *S*ymbolic *I*nstruction *C*ode) was developed in the 1960s at Dartmouth College by John Kemeny and Thomas Kurtz. Since then, BASIC has become the most standard programming language for personal computers and can be found on nearly every mini and mainframe computer as well. It is a simple language, and simple programs can be written in the first few hours of practice.

The BASIC language has many *dialects*—versions that are unique to a certain computer. For example, Apple BASIC is different from the Microsoft BASIC used on an IBM PC. In fact, there are several incompatible versions of BASIC available for almost every machine. These dialects are so far removed from the original BASIC language that the inventors have since designed and implemented TRUE BASIC—another dialect that is incompatible with all others.

The proliferation of different versions of BASIC has created a problem. Programs written on one machine probably will not run on another machine. In this chapter we describe how to write BASIC programs on an IBM PC or IBM compatible computer. You should be aware that some of the commands we discuss—particularly those dealing with loading and saving programs—will not work on other machines.

First, we describe how to run an existing program that is written in BASIC. Then we explain some of the commands, statements, and ways of organizing data that you might use to write simple programs of your own.

This supplement should be used in combination with the system analysis and programming chapters. Many important concepts relating to the design of programs are covered in these chapters.

■ Interacting with BASIC

The BASIC programs that you write are formally called *source programs,* because they are interpreted by another program called BASIC. That is, the program you write in the BASIC language is data to the BASIC interpreter program. Hereafter we will shorten the phrase "the BASIC interpreter" and just call it BASIC.

There are three versions of Microsoft BASIC on an IBM PC: Cassette BASIC, Disk BASIC, and Advanced BASIC. Advanced BASIC can execute any Disk BASIC program, and Disk BASIC can execute any Cassette BASIC program.

Cassette BASIC is provided as part of the computer and is stored in 32KB of ROM at the factory. This version of BASIC is missing many useful features; for example, the only storage device that Cassette BASIC allows you to use is a cassette tape recorder.

You can add features to Cassette BASIC by loading Disk BASIC or Advanced BASIC into memory. The most important additional feature of Disk BASIC is its support for floppy and hard disk drives. Advanced BASIC includes all the features of Disk BASIC and offers additional graphic commands, music commands, and other features useful to experienced programmers. Although this chapter will not describe Advanced BASIC commands in detail, occasionally you may want to use Advanced BASIC to execute programs written by others that require its features.

The Disk and Advanced BASIC programs are stored in files on the Disk Operating System (DOS) disk. Disk BASIC is stored in the file BASIC.COM; Advanced BASIC is stored in BASICA.COM. You must load one of these files into memory before you can use any of their extended BASIC features. To do this, you insert the DOS disk in drive A and turn on the computer. When DOS prompts you for a command, type BASIC to use Disk BASIC (or type BASICA if you need any of the features of Advanced BASIC).

To load, erase, save, or run a program, you type commands to BASIC. *Commands* are executed immediately; tell BASIC what to do with your program statements. *Program statements* accept input and generate output, perform calculations, make decisions, and repeat other statements. In addition to statements, a program contains data. Each piece of data is given a name. There are strict rules for naming data; we will learn some of these rules in this chapter.

Thus a program is a collection of data and statements that operate on the data. Programs are executed by the BASIC program resident in ROM or RAM: each statement instructs BASIC, which in turn controls what the computer does.

Starting BASIC

This section describes how to use BASIC to execute an existing program on disk. To begin using BASIC you insert a DOS disk in drive A and "boot" the machine by turning it on. Depending on how the DOS disk is configured, the operating system may ask you to set the date and time of the computer's clock. If it does this, the following dialog shows you how to set the clock to May 5, 1986 at 2:15 p.m.:

```
Current date is Tue 1-01-1980
Enter new date (mm-dd-yy): 5-21-86

Current time is 00:01:05.43
Enter new time: 14:15:00
```

The commands that you type, in this and the following examples, are shown in color; the other messages are prompts displayed by the computer.

```
A>BASIC
Ok
LOAD "MYPROG"
Ok
RUN
?5
      5 SQUARED IS     25
Ok
SYSTEM
A>
```

Figure C.1 *This short session with BASIC runs an existing program.*

After the operating system is loaded in memory (and you have set the clock if necessary), the operating system prints a prompt on the screen. In Figure C.1 the operating system provides the prompt A > ; then you load Disk BASIC into memory by typing its name. From this point on, BASIC is in charge. Figure C.1 shows two other prompts: Ok and ?. The Ok prompt means that BASIC has completed what it was last told to do and is waiting for you to enter the next command or program statement from the keyboard. BASIC generates a question-mark prompt whenever the program it is executing makes a request for data to be entered from the keyboard. Thus the question mark tells you that BASIC is waiting for input to a program whereas Ok indicates that BASIC is waiting for input itself.

After you have loaded BASIC, it generates an Ok prompt. Then you must load the desired source program into memory. In Figure C.1 the program is called MYPROG, so you load it into memory by typing the command LOAD "MYPROG". Then to tell BASIC to begin executing the program, you type RUN. As Figure C.1 shows, a question mark then appears, indicating that MYPROG is waiting for you to enter data. BASIC will wait until you enter a value followed by a [RETURN] (which appears on the keyboard as [↵]). The source program in Figure C.1 computes the square of whatever number is typed on the keyboard (in this case, the number is 5) and displays the result (5 SQUARED IS 25).

Occasionally you may want to stop execution of the source program in midstream. To do so you press [CTRL]-[C] or [CTRL]-[BREAK]. This causes BASIC to stop executing the source program, display the Ok prompt, and wait for a command.

When BASIC has finished executing the source program, it displays the Ok prompt again, indicating that it is waiting for you to enter another command. You can quit BASIC and return control to the operating system by typing the command SYSTEM. Anything left in main memory when you exit BASIC is lost; so if you made changes to your program since the last time it was saved, be sure to save your program before typing SYSTEM.

BASIC Commands

Figure C.1 shows how to run an existing program, but you will also want to enter programs of your own design. To do this you must know how to direct BASIC by entering commands. Once BASIC is loaded in memory, you can enter commands to load a program from a disk into memory, display the program in memory on the screen, begin executing a program, or perform other actions. We will be concerned mainly with the following commands:

- NEW erases any existing program in memory in preparation for starting a new one.
- LOAD copies a program from a disk into memory.
- RUN begins execution of the current program in memory.
- SAVE copies the current program from memory to a disk.
- LIST displays statements of the current program on the screen.
- DELETE removes statements from the current program.
- RENUM renumbers existing statements in the current program.

In addition to these essential commands, Disk BASIC includes commands to list the names of files on the disk (FILES), help debug your program (TRON/TROFF), clear the screen (CLS), and perform other useful functions. These extra commands are worth learning after you have mastered the basics of BASIC.

NEW

A new program can be entered by simply typing a list of statements to be carried out by BASIC. If a program already exists in memory and you want to remove it to make room for the new one, you should use the NEW command to erase the old program.

For example, the following dialog erases any old program in memory and then enters a program that makes the computer display HELLO on the screen:

```
NEW
Ok
100 PRINT "HELLO"
Ok
999 END
Ok
```

The word HELLO in line 100 is enclosed in quotation marks to identify it as text (data to be processed) instead of a statement keyword or variable name.

Notice the numbers at the beginnings of the third and fifth lines. In BASIC the first part of each statement is a number; these numbers help BASIC determine the order in which to execute statements. Program statements are numbered in the order they are to be interpreted. The statement numbers can be any integer from 1 to 65,529 or from 1 to 99,999, depending on the version of BASIC. It is a good idea to choose statement numbers that are not consecutive; for example, 10, 20, 30, and so on. That way, if you need to add statements to the middle of the program, there will be unused numbers available.

RUN

The statements you type are stored in memory so that they can be interpreted later. After you have entered all the statements in the source program, enter the RUN command to tell BASIC to execute the numbered statements—one at a time, and in numerical order.

When RUN is entered, BASIC starts interpreting the statements beginning with the statement with the lowest line number. In our sample program, statement 100 tells BASIC to print HELLO on the screen, and statement 999 tells BASIC to stop executing the program.

LIST

Suppose that after entering our sample program you want to see what is in memory. The current program in memory will be displayed on the screen if you enter the command LIST.

```
Ok
LIST
100 PRINT "HELLO"
999 END
Ok
```

The LIST command displays the entire program on the screen. If the program is many pages long, the listing will simply fly past your eyes. To list a portion of the program you can include line numbers as arguments to the LIST command. For example, the command LIST 100 lists just one line—line number 100. The command LIST 100-200 lists all lines between 100 and 200, inclusive. The general format for the LIST command is

LIST *start – last*

where *start* and *last* are line numbers.

Also, a modified form of the LIST command can be used to print the BASIC program currently in memory on the printer. The syntax of this form of the LIST command is: LLIST start-last. For example, LLIST 150- prints all lines from 150 through the end of the program.

SAVE

The current program in memory is lost when you exit from BASIC or turn the computer off, but you can make a permanent copy on the disk by using the SAVE command. For example, the command SAVE "MYPROG" will save the current program as a file named MYPROG. The general format of the SAVE command is

SAVE "*filename*"

where *filename* is any valid name of a disk file. The *filename* may incorporate a disk drive designation when your computer has multiple disk drives. For example, SAVE "B:MYFILE" would cause the memory resident BASIC program to be copied to the disk in drive B. If a file with *filename* already exists, BASIC throws the old version of *filename* away when it saves the current program in its place.

LOAD

When you want to retrieve a program saved on the disk, use the LOAD command. The general format of the LOAD command is

LOAD "*filename*"

where *filename* is the name of the file containing a BASIC source program. For example, LOAD "PROG5" causes the file named PROG5 to be copied from the disk to memory.

The LOAD command does not erase an existing program in memory; it merely merges the program from the disk into the program in memory. Usually you will not want to merge the lines of two programs; so it is a good idea to use the NEW command before loading a program from a disk. If you use the LOAD command to merge the text of two or more BASIC programs together, be sure each program has different line numbers. The LOAD command can be very useful for quickly and easily combining pieces of BASIC programs into larger and more useful programs.

DELETE

You can delete a statement by typing its line number followed by [RETURN]. But if you want to remove many lines at once, you should use the DELETE command. For example, the command DELETE 100-120 deletes any lines numbered 100 through 120. The general format of the DELETE command is

DELETE *start – last*

where *start* and *last* are line numbers. All lines from *start* to *last* are removed, inclusively.

General Editing

You can add a new statement or modify an existing one simply by typing it. Suppose, for example, the following program is in memory:

```
Ok
LIST
100 PRINT "HELLO"
110 PRINT "HOW ARE YOU?"
120 END
Ok
RUN
HELLO
HOW ARE YOU?
Ok
```

To add a statement with the line number 115 (so that it will be executed after statement 110 but before statement 120), you might type

```
115 PRINT "TODAY"
```

If you give the LIST command, you can see how the program has been changed.

```
LIST
100 PRINT "HELLO"
110 PRINT "HOW ARE YOU?"
115 PRINT "TODAY"
120 END
Ok
```

BASIC automatically inserts new lines in their proper numerical sequence in the program.

Now suppose you want to modify statement 100. You could delete it and then enter the revised version, but this is not necessary. Instead, you can change a statement by typing a new statement with the same line number as the statement you wish to change. This procedure replaces the first version of the line with the new one.

You can also edit statements with the help of a built-in screen editor. The screen editor allows you to change any statement displayed on the screen. Usually this is a faster way to modify an existing statement than to retype it from scratch. To use the screen editor, press the up-arrow key to move the cursor up the screen to the statement you want to edit; then modify the parts you want to change and skip over the other parts. When you are through editing the line, press [RETURN] to tell BASIC to store the modified line in the program. While you are editing a line, you may perform the following editing operations on it:

- Replacing characters. Use the left- and right-cursor keys to position the cursor at the beginning of the characters you want to change, then type the correct letters to replace the incorrect ones.

- Deleting characters. Position the cursor where you want to begin deleting characters, then press [DEL] to delete characters one at a time.

- Inserting characters. Position the cursor where you want to begin inserting characters, press the [INS] key to get into Insert Mode, and type the characters you want to insert. You can tell when you are in Insert Mode because the cursor changes to look like a small box. You can toggle in and out of Insert Mode by pressing [INS] repeatedly.

A more complicated way to edit your programs is to use an external editor. An external editor works like a word processor and produces text that can be loaded into BASIC with the LOAD command. External editors offer powerful editing features such as the ability to move groups of statements from one spot in a program to another or to change the name of a variable throughout a program.

Renumbering Lines

After extensive additions and deletions, the line numbers in your program are likely to become messy. A more serious problem occurs if you want to add a new statement between statements with consecutive line numbers, such as between lines 356 and 357. You cannot solve this problem by adding a statement with the number 356.5, because line numbers must be integers.

All of these problems can be solved by renumbering the lines in your program with the RENUM command. For example, if you type RENUM to renumber the lines in our sample program and then give the LIST command to display the program, the following appears:

```
RENUM
Ok
LIST
10 PRINT "HELLO"
20 PRINT "HOW ARE YOU?"
30 PRINT "TODAY"
40 END
Ok
```

Notice that the RENUM command has renumbered all the lines in the program with a constant increment of 10 between lines. The general form is

RENUM *newstart, oldstart, increment*

With this command you can renumber just the end (the highest line numbers) of the existing program; *oldstart* is the first line number in the existing program that is to be renumbered. If you do not specify values for *newstart, oldstart,* and *increment,* default values are used, as they were in our example. The default value for *oldstart* is the lowest line number of the existing program. *Newstart* becomes the first line number in the sequence of renumbered lines; its default value was 10 in our example. *Increment* determines how far apart the new numbers are spaced out; its default is also 10. For example, suppose that immediately after our last example you type a second RENUM command—RENUM 100,30,25—and then give the LIST command. On the screen you will see

```
RENUM 100,30,25
Ok
LIST
10 PRINT "HELLO"
20 PRINT "HOW ARE YOU?"
100 PRINT "TODAY"
125 END
```

Only the last two lines have been renumbered, and they were renumbered with an increment of 25.

Exercises

1. What does the NEW command do when you already have a program in memory?

   a. Experiment with the NEW command by entering

   ```
   NEW
   100 PRINT "HELLO"
   RUN
   NEW
   RUN
   ```

   What caution should be used with the NEW command?

   b. Create an experiment to determine what happens if you load a program from a disk without first using the NEW command to erase the old program from memory.

2. Suppose the following program is already in memory:

   ```
   100 PRINT "HELLO"
   200 PRINT "GOOD BYE"
   300 END
   ```

   a. How do you insert 250 PRINT ''INBETWEEN'' between lines 200 and 300?

b. What is the easiest way to change line 200 to 200 PRINT "ADIOS"?

c. What is the easiest way to modify the program so that the statement that is now on line 100 will execute after statement 200?

3. Give a RENUM command to change the line numbers on the following program to 500, 550, 600, 650.

```
10 REM Start
11 PRINT "HI"
15 PRINT "HOW ARE YOU?"
17 END
```

4. Give a command to delete lines 550 through 810 of a program.

■ Components of BASIC Programs

Every program must accept inputs and generate outputs; copy, move, and calculate new values based on data stored in memory; and make decisions by comparing results from previous steps and then performing one group of instructions while skipping another group. These components of all programs are also components of BASIC programs. The building blocks of these components are called constants, variables, and statements. We will give special treatment to input and output statements because these statements are particularly important and because they are more difficult to understand than other statements in BASIC.

Constants, Variables, and Statements

In BASIC programs *constants* store values that cannot change while the program is being interpreted, *variables* hold values that can change during interpretation. Constants and variables can be combined into arithmetic and logic expressions such as A + B and A = B. The result obtained from evaluating an expression can be assigned to another variable, and so forth. *Reserved words* are words that have been assigned a unique meaning such as PRINT or END. The reserved words in BASIC statements explain what type of processing to do.

There are strict rules in BASIC for forming constants, variables, and statements. These rules are similar to the rules for spelling and sentence structure in English; therefore, we call them *syntax* rules. Similar rules for meaning or *semantics* define how each statement in BASIC is interpreted.

Constants

There are many types of data. A *data type* is a collection of constants and the operations that are permitted on the collection. In this section we discuss two numeric data types (integers and real numbers) and one data type that stores text.

An *integer* is a whole number like 0, 1, 2, or -100. Integers can be added, compared, and printed on the screen. Integers range in value from $-32,768$ to $+32,767$.

A *real number* is a number like -1.5 or 3.14159—any number containing a decimal point. Like integers, real numbers can be added, compared, and printed on the screen. When mathematical operations are performed on real numbers, the resulting real numbers tend to become very small or very large. Rather than display a 20-digit real number, BASIC will print very large or small real numbers in *scientific notation*. Some examples of the way BASIC prints numbers in scientific notation are

$1.5E+03$, which means $(1.5)(1000) = 1,500$
$-0.25E-02$, which means $(-0.25)(0.01) = -0.0025$

Appendix A discusses how to read scientific notation. You will see scientific notation frequently when running BASIC. In fact, the displayed numbers may not be exactly what you expect. For example, 500,001 might be displayed as $0.5E+06$ instead. In this case a small rounding error has occurred during interpretation. Rounding errors may not be harmful for the type of programs you write, but you should be aware that they happen.

Some versions of BASIC allow two types of real numbers to be used: single- and double-precision. Double-precision numbers take twice the storage space of single-precision numbers, but they are more accurate in calculations.

BASIC can also process limited kinds of textual constants. A *string constant* is data that consists of a series of characters. BASIC can tell the difference between a string and other parts of a program because strings are enclosed inside quotation marks. We used a string to display the word HELLO on the screen. It is important to emphasize that any series of characters enclosed in quotation marks is a string and is treated as data. For example, although the string "LIST 100-200" looks very much like a command, BASIC would treat this string as data because of the quotation marks and would not analyze the characters in the string for semantic sense. String constants are useful for communicating with the user.

There is a big difference between numbers and strings. Numbers can be added and multiplied; a string can be connected to another string, or characters removed from a string. The operations that work on a number may be meaningless when applied to strings. For this reason it is important to remember to put quotation marks around string constants.

BASIC cannot mix strings and numbers together when performing calculations. If a program attempts to add a string to a number, BASIC will stop executing the program and display an error message. This sort of error is an example of a *syntax error,* because the program is syntactically incorrect.

Variables

A word that is not a reserved word is treated as a *variable name*. A *variable name* is a symbolic code for a storage location that contains data. Thus, in the statement 50 PRINT HELLO the word HELLO is the name of a memory cell. This PRINT statement is radically different from the statement 50 PRINT "HELLO", which prints the word HELLO. In contrast, when BASIC executes the statement 50 PRINT HELLO, it interprets HELLO as a variable name and therefore copies the current contents of cell HELLO onto the screen. If the number stored in the variable HELLO is 10.5, then the value 10.5 is displayed on the screen (see Figure C.2).

The first character of a variable's name must be a letter of the alphabet. The second and subsequent characters of a name can be either letters or numerals, as in BUCKET17 and X15. Names can also include the decimal point character, as in NEW.TAX or OLD.PAY.RATE. Here are some examples of valid and invalid names.

Valid variable names		Invalid variable names	
A	PAYRATE	10T	(Begins with a number)
BOX	HOURS	P@	(Contains an illegal character)
B29	TAX1	$TAX	(Contains an illegal character)

Figure C.2 *The PRINT statement takes the value of HELLO from memory and displays it on the screen.*

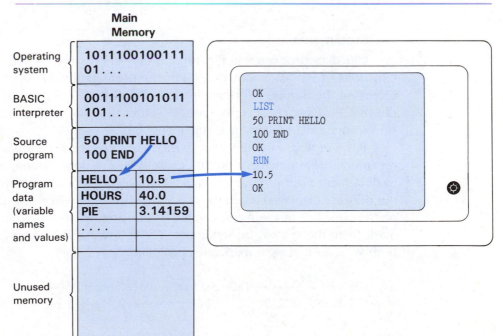

Names can be any length, but only the first 40 characters are significant. This lets you choose meaningful names such as PAYRATE or TRUCKS. There are two major types of variables: *numeric variables,* which store numbers, and *string variables,* which store strings of text. The last character of a variable's name indicates which type of variable it is. If the last character is a letter or a number, then it is a numeric variable that stores a single-precision real number. String variables end with a $.

The Microsoft BASIC used by an IBM PC has three types of numeric variables; they store integers, single-, and double-precision real numbers. These variable types present a trade-off between the precision of computations and the storage space and time required to perform computations. It takes only 2 bytes to store an integer, and calculations run faster with integer variables. But single- and double-precision numbers may be necessary to obtain a sufficiently accurate answer. The following rules apply to naming variables:

Suffix	Meaning	Sample names	Sample contents	Storage space for the variable's value
%	Integer	I%, COUNT%	53, −238	2 bytes
!	7-digit number	R!, CIRCLE!	3.14159, −238.	4 bytes
#	16-digit number	SALES#	81,358,257,010.18	8 bytes
$	String	JOB$	''JANITOR''	Length of the string

Statements

Like data, program statements come in a variety of types. Originally, BASIC consisted of ten statement types, but the proliferation of BASIC dialects has increased the number. For example, Microsoft BASIC as it is implemented on the IBM PC has over seventy types of statements. We will restrict our discussion to the most fundamental statements.

The simplest statement type is the REM statement; it allows you to insert remarks. A REM statement doesn't cause BASIC to do anything, but it is useful to document your program. Characters following REM are ignored by BASIC; but they are displayed when the program is listed. You may also place remarks on the same line as another statement by using a single quote to separate the remark from the rest of the statement. The following two statements illustrate both ways of placing remarks in a program:

```
100 REM     ------ This Statement Does Nothing --------
100 PRINT "HELLO"        'This remark is tagged onto PRINT
```

In either case the remark is useful to the programmer but is ignored by BASIC. Remark statements should be used liberally to explain what your program does and perhaps to describe a little about how it does it.

Some statements declare what kind of data is to be processed, and others are devoted to doing the processing. Processing statements either control the order of events, or they perform certain operations. In all cases statements begin with a line number that is followed by a *keyword*. The keyword is a reserved word that identifies which type of statement it is. The keyword is usually a verb or verb phrase that describes what is to be done.

Here are some types of statements and a brief explanation of what they do. Notice that the ordinary English meaning of each keyword is only loosely related to the keyword's meaning in BASIC.

- PRINT. Display data on the screen or send output to the disk or other output device.
- LET. Let a variable be a certain value; calculate the value.
- INPUT. Get input from the keyboard, disk, or other input device.
- FOR. Repeat statements for certain values of a variable; repeat a group of statements.
- STOP. Whoa! Stop executing statements.
- IF. Decide what to do next based on the result of testing a condition in the IF statement.
- END. Whoa! An END statement is similar to a STOP statement except that it should be the last statement (that is, the statement with the highest line number) in a program.

These statement types account for 90 percent of the statements used in a typical BASIC program. How they are combined to create a program is the most difficult skill to learn when starting to program. We will illustrate each statement type by using it to create real programs.

Keyboard Input and Output

The first step in writing BASIC programs is to master the statements that input and output. PRINT statements are used to copy numbers and strings from memory to a screen, printer, or disk file. INPUT statements do the reverse; they copy numbers and strings from the keyboard, disk file, or serial input adapter to memory.

The general form of the simplest variety of INPUT and PRINT statements is

INPUT *variable list*
PRINT *expression list*

The *variable list* in an INPUT statement can be a single variable name, such as WORK2, or it can be a series of variables separated by commas. The *expression list* in a PRINT statement can contain variables, constants, and formulas that are separated by either commas or semicolons.

We will use the ECHO1.BAS program in Figure C.3 to illustrate PRINT and INPUT statements. The first four statements of ECHO1.BAS are remarks that identify the program and tell what it does. Line 130 displays a string constant—a prompt to the user. Line 170 halts the program. The interesting parts of ECHO1.BAS are lines 150 and 160.

The INPUT statement in line 150 instructs BASIC to display a question mark, wait until you type a string and press [RETURN], and store the string in L$. Recall that L$ is a string variable because it ends with a dollar sign. String variables can hold anything that can be typed at the keyboard. Thus if you type ABC, the string constant "ABC" is stored inside L$ by line 150. Or if you type 10.5, the string constant "10.5" is stored in L$. It is important to emphasize that because L$ is a string variable, BASIC stores "10.5" as a series of four characters, not as a number. You cannot perform arithmetic on the contents of a string variable—even if the string it contains happens to look like a number.

Line 150 copies keyboard characters into memory and stores them in the location named L$. Line 160 displays the value stored in L$. This is how ECHO1.BAS got its name; line 160 echoes to the screen whatever was entered from the keyboard. If GOODBY is typed into line 150, the output will appear as shown in Figure C.3.

INPUT Statements

Figure C.4 illustrates a program that accepts two numbers, performs a simple calculation on them, and displays the result of the calculation. The INPUT statement on line 140 has two variables as its argument; it tells BASIC to read

Figure C.3 *Loading, listing, and running ECHO1.BAS.*

```
LOAD "ECHO1.BAS"
Ok
LIST
100 REM --------------------- ECHO1.BAS ----------------------------
110 REM    This program parrots back whatever is typed in.
120 REM ============================================================
125 REM                                      'Instructions
130 PRINT "Enter a line followed by pressing [RETURN]."          .
150 INPUT L$                                 'Read from keyboard
160 PRINT L$                                 'Display on screen
170 END
RUN
Enter a line followed by pressing [RETURN].
?GOODBY
GOODBY
Ok
```

```
Ok
LIST
100 REM --------------------- AREA.BAS ---------------------
110 REM    Computes the area of a rectangle of length X and width Y
120 REM ----------------------------------------------------
130 REM
140 INPUT X, Y                              'get length and width
150 A = X * Y                               'compute the area
170 PRINT "The area of a", X, " by ", Y, " rectangle is", A
999 END '---------------------------------------------------
RUN
? 3.2, 4.5
The area of a  3.2           by            4.5           rectangle is
 14.4
Ok
```

Figure C.4 *Computing the area of a rectangle.*

two numbers from the keyboard and store them in variables X and Y. The numbers should be entered on the same line and should be separated by a comma. For example, if you type

    12.4, 8

and press [RETURN], BASIC stores the number 12.4 in X and stores 8.0 in Y. In this example the integer 8 is automatically converted by BASIC into the real number 8.0 because Y is a real-number variable.

Suppose you type BUZZ OFF and press [RETURN] when BASIC is expecting data for line 140 in Figure C.4. This presents BASIC with a problem. Although a number can be stored as a series of characters in a string variable, ordinary text cannot be stored as a number in a numeric variable. BASIC responds to this problem by displaying the error message REDO FROM START followed by another question mark. This is called an *execution error* because it occurs while the program is executing. A *fatal execution error*—such as attempting to divide a number by zero—forces BASIC to display an error message and stop executing the program entirely.

PRINT statements

Line 170 of Figure C.4 illustrates a PRINT statement that contains several constants and three variables. Each item in the list is printed on one line of the screen until the edge of the screen is reached; then BASIC continues printing on the next line. The punctuation that separates items determines the spacing between them when they appear on the screen. BASIC divides the screen into 5 print zones; each zone is 14 characters wide. When commas are used to separate items, each item is printed at the beginning of the next print zone. Thus, commas provide an easy way to line up the output of several PRINT statements in vertical columns. For example,

```
40 PRINT 12.5, 15, .845
50 PRINT 3, 563.2, 9452
RUN
 12.5          15            .845
 3             563.2         9452
```

The commas in line 170 of Figure C.4 don't work well, however. They cause too much of a gap between items for a pleasing appearance. You can avoid these gaps by using semicolons instead of commas. When semicolons are used, strings are printed without intervening spaces. For example, 100 PRINT ''HI'';''THERE'' prints HITHERE as one word. However, even when semicolons are used, numbers are not printed next to each other. All numbers are followed by a space, and positive numbers are preceded by a space. For example, if line 170 is replaced with

```
170 PRINT "The area of a"; X; "by"; Y; "rectangle is"; A
```

then the output becomes

```
The area of a 3.2 by 4.5 rectangle is 14.4
```

You can control where items are displayed by printing blank lines and by printing spaces. A PRINT statement without an argument (an empty PRINT statement) prints a blank line. Spaces can be printed just like any other character by enclosing them inside quotation marks, thereby making them string constants. Spaces that are not enclosed in quotation marks have no effect on the output. For example,

```
40 PRINT "        NAME              AGE   WEIGHT"
50 PRINT "---------------------     ---   ------"
60 PRINT
70 PRINT "THOMAS                ";45;"   ";213
80 PRINT "JENNIFER              ";    13;  "   ";    87
RUN
        NAME              AGE   WEIGHT
---------------------     ---   ------

THOMAS                    45    213
JENNIFER                  13    87
```

Another way to control vertical spacing is to place a comma or semicolon at the end of a PRINT statement. This causes the next PRINT statement to begin printing where the last PRINT statement left off—instead of starting at the beginning of the next line. This strategy is useful if you need to print a long line. For example,

```
40 PRINT "This sentence is too long to fit conveniently in one ";
50 PRINT "print statement."
RUN
This sentence is too long to fit conveniently in one print statement.
```

As another example, compare these three ways of printing two numbers.

```
100 PRINT 5.2    100 PRINT 5.2;    100 PRINT 5.2,
110 PRINT 4.8    110 PRINT 4.8     110 PRINT 4.8
RUN              RUN               RUN
 5.2              5.2  4.8          5.2              4.8
 4.8
```

PRINT USING

In the PRINT statements we have discussed two types of information are merged in each statement's argument: the data to be printed (strings and numbers) and formatting information (such as commas, semicolons, and spaces). The commas, semicolons, and spaces provide convenient formatting tricks that make it easy to print items quickly, but they do not let you control the exact placement and format of the printed items. For example, decimal places are not likely to line up in a column when printed, and strings cannot be right-justified in a field of a specific width.

PRINT USING statements give you precise control over the appearance of output by separating the argument into two parts. One part specifies what data is to be printed. The other part determines the placement and format of the data and answers such questions as, How many digits of each number should appear? Where should the first character of a string begin? Exactly how wide should each field be in the output line?

In some dialects of BASIC these two parts are placed in separate statements: a PRINT USING statement contains the data to be printed, and an IMAGE statement determines the appearance of the output line. Microsoft BASIC uses a simpler method that avoids a separate IMAGE statement. Instead, it places the description of the output line's layout in a *format string*. The simplest general form of this type of PRINT USING statement is

PRINT USING "*format string*"; *expression list*

The *format string* contains fields that specify the format of the numbers and strings given in the expression list. The first item in the expression list is printed in the first field of the format string, the second item in the second field, and so on.

    Number fields are constructed from number-sign characters; they look like *####* or *####.##*. The length of the field determines the largest number that will fit in the field and specifies how many digit positions to print. In the following examples, assume that variable PAY stores 5.75:

```
40 PRINT USING " ###.## ### "; PAY, PAY * 2
50 PRINT USING " ###.## ### "; PAY * 2, PAY
RUN
    5.75    12
   11.50     6
```

If BASIC cannot print the full precision of a number, it rounds the number appropriately. Thus, in the preceding example 11.50 was rounded to 12 before it was printed in the *###* field.

    String fields begin and end with backslash characters; they look like \ \ . The number of characters between the backslash characters determines the length of the field. If a string is longer than its field description, its extra characters are ignored. In the following examples assume that JOB$ stores ''JANITOR'':

```
60 PRINT USING "\ \"; JOB$
70 PRINT USING " \              \"; JOB$
RUN
JAN
 JANITOR
```

It is also possible to embed constants in the format string of a PRINT USING statement. For example, if line 170 in Figure C.4 is replaced with

```
170 PRINT USING "The area of a ##.# by ##.# rectangle is ##.##"; X; Y; A
```

then the output becomes

```
The area of a 3.2 by 4.5 rectangle is 14.40
```

Microsoft BASIC has many additional features for controlling the appearance of output. It can float dollar signs to the immediate left of formatted numbers and provides commands that position the cursor on a specified row or column of the screen as well as commands that set the display attributes of characters on the screen (blinking, inverse video, and so on).

Assignment Statements

Input and output consumes much of a programmer's time, but assignment statements are the most frequently used statements in a typical BASIC program. An *assignment statement* assigns a value to a variable. Assignment statements can move values from one variable to another or calculate a variable's value from a formula. The general forms for assignment statements are

[LET] *numeric variable name = arithmetic expression*
[LET] *string variable name = string expression*

Both types of assignment statement may begin with the optional verb LET. The important part of the assignment statement begins with the name of the variable to receive a value; it must be followed by an equal sign, which must be followed by an expression.

The expression may contain constants, variables, and operators. An *operator* is a symbol (such as + or /) that indicates an action to be performed on the constants and variables. An assignment statement evaluates the expression to obtain a single value (either a number or a string) and stores the value in the variable named on the left side of the equal sign. For example, 150 LET AREA = LENGTH * DEPTH assigns the result of the arithmetic expression LENGTH * DEPTH to the variable AREA. Because multiplication is indicated by an asterisk, the formula LENGTH * DEPTH multiplies the value stored in LENGTH by the value stored in DEPTH to obtain the value to be stored in AREA. The new value in AREA replaces the previous value, which is permanently lost.

Assignment statements are not equations. They *copy values* rather than state a mathematical fact. For instance, the following assignment statement is common in BASIC:

```
100 LET I = I + 1
```

This means: add 1 to the current value of I and store the result back in I. Thus, I is increased by 1.

Here are some examples of assignment statements

```
100 LET COUNT5 = 0            'copy zero into COUNT5
135 LET PAY = SALARY          'copy contents of SALARY into PAY
195 LET JOB$ = "JANITOR"      'store the value "JANITOR" in JOB$
220 LET MATH = 14/2           'store the value 7 in MATH
250 LET DENOM = (A+B)/(A-B)   'quotient of sum and difference in DENOM
```

The last example illustrates how to use parentheses to group subexpressions together when ambiguity might otherwise result. Without the parentheses,

(A + B) / (A − B) would become A + B / A − B, which is interpreted as A + (B / A) − B. The operators used in assignment statements include

- ■ * for multiplication
- ■ / for division
- ■ + for addition
- ■ − for subtraction
- ■ ^ for exponentiation

Exponentiation means "raising to a power," as in 3^2.

The order in which operations are performed often influences the value of an expression. BASIC unravels arithmetic expressions by performing operations in the following order:

1. Expressions inside parentheses
2. Negation
3. Exponentiation
4. Multiplication and division
5. Addition and subtraction

Parentheses may be nested, in which case the innermost expression is evaluated first. If two or more operators in an expression are at the same level of the hierarchy (for example, B/C/2), then the operators are evaluated from left to right. The following expressions illustrate these rules:

```
100 LET X = (A + 2 / (2 * B))   'first 2*B, then 2/(2*B), then add A
200 LET M = A * B - C           'first A*B, then subtract C
300 LET Z = 1 + A^2             'first A^2, then add 1
400 LET A = A / B / 2 * D       'first A/B, then /2, then multiply by D
```

Here are some assignment statements with comments explaining what they do:

```
100 LET C = 5 * (F - 32) / 9   'convert from F to C degrees.
200 LET Y = M * X + B          'compute the height of a straight line.
300 LET A = (B * H) / 2        'find the area of a triangle
```

Figure C.5 illustrates the use of assignment statements in a complete program. The program computes the length of the hypotenuse (the longest side) of a right triangle. The mathematical formula for computing the hypotenuse requires squaring the lengths of the two shorter sides, adding these two numbers, and taking the square root of the result. The exponentiation operator is used to calculate both the square and the square root.

```
LIST
100 REM ------------------- TRIANGLE.BAS ---------------------------
110 REM        Computes the hypotenuse of a right triangle
120 REM =====================================================================
130 REM
140 INPUT "A = "; A            'Prompt user for A; get A from keyboard
150 INPUT "B = "; B            'Prompt user for B; get B from keyboard
160 C = (B^2 + A^2) ^ (.5)     'Compute the length of the hypotenuse
170 PRINT "C = "; C            'Display the answer on the screen
999 END '-------------------------------------------------------------
Ok
RUN
A = 3
B = 4
C = 5
Ok
```

Figure C.5 *Calculating the length of the hypotenuse of a right triangle.*

Notice that instead of using both a PRINT and an INPUT statement, we have used an extended version of the INPUT statement in Figure C.5.

```
Standard method      Extended short cut
PRINT "A = ";        INPUT "A = "; A
INPUT A
```

An extended INPUT statement allows a prompt to be printed and data to be collected from the keyboard—all in one statement.

Library Functions

BASIC provides several library functions to help with mathematical calculations and to manipulate strings. A *function* is a prewritten routine that accepts one or more input values, performs some operations on them, and returns a single value. We will discuss only arithmetic functions in detail, but you should know that string functions can extract portions of a string (truncate the string), search a string for a specific pattern of characters, and perform other types of text processing.

Table C.1 lists some of the standard arithmetic functions of BASIC. Arithmetic functions take only one input value. To call a function, you use its name in an assignment expression or a PRINT statement in the same way you would use a variable's name. The function's name is followed by the function's input value, which is enclosed in parentheses. For example, if you want to

Table C.1 *Mathematical Functions of BASIC*

Function	Returned Value	Example	Value
ABS(X)	Absolute value of X	ABS(−4.6)	4
COS(X)	Cosine of X; X is in radians	COS(0.0)	1
EXP(X)	E raised to the Xth power	EXP(1)	2.718282
INT(X)	Largest integer in X	INT(4.6)	4
RND(X)	A random number between 0 and 1	RND(5)	.5119751
SIN(X)	Sine of X; X is in radians	SIN(3.14159/2)	1
SQR(X)	Square root of X	SQR(4)	2

calculate the square root of the value in P, you type SQR(P). Thus we could have simplified the calculation of the hypotenuse in Figure C.5 by replacing line 160 with

```
160 C = SQR(B^2 + A^2)     'Compute the length of the hypotenuse.
```

Here is another example of the square root function.

```
40   LET TURTLES = 64
50   PRINT "THE SQUARE ROOT OF TURTLES IS:"; SQR(TURTLES)
60   LET TURTLEFOOD = SQR(TURTLES) * 3
70   PRINT "THE AMOUNT OF TURTLE FOOD TO BUY IS:"; TURTLEFOOD
RUN
THE SQUARE ROOT OF TURTLES IS: 8
THE AMOUNT OF TURTLE FOOD TO BUY IS: 24
```

The INT function is used to throw away the fractional part of a number and retain only the integer part. The following program fragment uses the INT function to determine how many quarters should be dispensed from a vending machine to make change.

```
1010  INPUT "PLEASE ENTER THE AMOUNT OF CHANGE NEEDED: "; CHANGE
1015  QUARTERS = INT(CHANGE / 25)
1020  PRINT "THEN DISPENSE";QUARTERS;"QUARTERS"
RUN
PLEASE ENTER THE AMOUNT OF CHANGE NEEDED: ? 95
THEN DISPENSE 3 QUARTERS
```

The calculation in line 1015 divides the amount of change to be dispensed (in this example, 95 cents) by 25; this intermediate result (3.8) is truncated by the

INT function to determine the number of quarters to dispense. To be useful, this fragment would need to be followed by similar statements that would calculate the number of dimes, nickels, and pennies remaining to be dispensed.

Exercises

1. Determine the value of A after each of the following assignment statements is executed. Assume that each part is done independently and that the starting values are A = 4, B = 3, C = 25, and CAT = 2.
   a. LET A = −1
   b. LET A = B + C − 2.5
   c. LET A = B * C / CAT
   d. LET A = A^2 * B^2 / C
   e. LET A = (A − 1) * (B + 2)

2. Which of the following are *invalid* variable names in BASIC?
   a. X15   **e.** M2M2
   b. 15X   **f.** M2_M2
   c. X$ **g.** PER%
   d. $X   **h.** PERSON2-AND-A-1/2

3. Write a program that computes the cost of traveling M miles in a car that gets R miles per gallon. Assume that gasoline costs C dollars per gallon. Include prompts that ask the user to provide the values of M, R, and C. Test your program on a 135-mile round trip that took 12.4 gallons of gasoline purchased for $1.38 per gallon.

4. Write a program that requests three data items from the user: a description of an inventory part, the part's price, and the quantity sold. Assume that the values entered by the user are "PENS", .24, and 16. Make your program calculate and print the following report:

```
PART DESCRIPTION  QUANTITY   PRICE   INVOICE
----------------  --------  -------  -------
     PENS            16     $  .24   $ 3.84
```

5. The payments on a mortgage are calculated as follows:

```
P = i * A * V / ( V - 1 )
```

where

   i = monthly interest rate
   A = amount borrowed
   V = $(1 + i)^M$
   M = number of months to repay loan

Write a BASIC program to compute the monthly payments on a loan of $90,000 for 29 years at 10 percent annual interest rate. Your answer should be approximately $794.23.

6. Write a statement that uses the INT function to round the value in HOURS to the nearest tenth. HINT: This statement rounds HOURS to the nearest integer: 50 HOURS = INT(HOURS + .5).

7. Complete the fragment of the vending-machine program given earlier so that it calculates the number of dimes, nickels, and pennies to be dispensed.

■ Program Control

Most programs make decisions based on the data they receive from a user or on calculations made by the program. When a decision is made, the program branches to one of several optional statements and then resumes executing each statement in the order encountered. A *branch* is a point in a program where the next statement to be executed is determined by the running program—not just by the statement numbers. Branching statements provide a way to skip one part of a program in favor of another part, depending on the input data. BASIC's branching statements include the IF, GOTO, and ON GOTO statements.

Loops provide another way of altering the sequence of a program. A *loop* is a group of statements that are executed repeatedly. The FOR and NEXT statements are used to set up a loop that will be repeated a certain number of times. Loops can also be constructed from IF and GOTO statements. IF-GOTO loops are normally used when the loop is to be executed until a particular condition becomes true. Both methods of looping shorten programs. If you use a loop, you do not need to write the same statements over again; the loop directs BASIC to execute the statements repeatedly.

GOTO Statements

The simplest branching statement in BASIC is the GOTO statement. It begins with the verb GOTO followed by a line number.

GOTO *destination line number*

When this statement is interpreted by BASIC, the *destination line number* becomes the next statement to be interpreted rather than the statement following the GOTO statement. The intervening statements are skipped, as shown by the following example:

```
100  A = 0
200  GOTO 300
240  A = 1
300  PRINT A
```

This program fragment prints 0 as the value of A because the GOTO at line 200 forces BASIC to skip statement 240 and go to line 300.

The GOTO statement is not particularly useful by itself, because it does not make decisions. GOTO statements are most helpful when used with IF statements.

IF Statements

The IF statement sets up a test that determines how BASIC will branch. If the result of the test is true, one path is taken; if false, another path is taken.

There are two kinds of IF statements. The IF-THEN statement has one potential branch; the IF-THEN-ELSE statement has two potential branches.

IF *test* THEN *statement-1*
IF *test* THEN *statement-1* ELSE *statement-2*

If *test* is true, then *statement-1* is interpreted. If *test* is false, *statement-1* is skipped. In the case of an IF-THEN-ELSE statement, *statement-2* is interpreted if the *test* is false.

Consider the following IF-THEN-ELSE statement:

```
100 IF ITEM$ = "PENCIL" THEN PRINT "ERASE IT"
110 PRINT "DONE"
```

The test, ITEM$ = "PENCIL", is true if the string stored in ITEM$ is equal to "PENCIL"; it is false if the string in ITEM$ is anything other than "PENCIL". If the test is true, the message ERASE IT is printed. Otherwise, the PRINT "ERASE IT" statement is skipped. In either case, DONE is printed.

Compare the previous example with the following IF-THEN-ELSE statement:

```
100  IF ITEM$ = "PENCIL" THEN PRINT "ERASE IT" ELSE PRINT "CUT IT OUT"
110  PRINT "DONE"
```

If the test is true, ERASE IT is printed; otherwise CUT IT OUT is printed. In either case, DONE is also printed.

Frequently you will want to interpret several statements in the THEN or the ELSE parts of an IF statement. To do this you must use a different form of IF statement, one that contains line numbers. The line numbers cause BASIC to branch to a new part of the program.

IF *test* THEN *line-number-1* [ELSE *line-number-2*]

If *test* is true, the next statement to be interpreted is *line-number-1*. The ELSE keyword is optional; that is why its portion of the IF statement is shown in brackets. If the ELSE clause is omitted and the *test* is false, then the next statement to be interpreted is the statement following the IF statement. If there is an ELSE clause and *test* is false, then the next statement to be interpreted is *line-number-2*.

IF statements are often used in conjunction with GOTO statements. For example,

```
100  IF HOURS = 0 THEN 110 ELSE 200
110    LET PAY = 0              'begin THEN clause
120    LET DEDUCTIONS = 0
130  GOTO 250                   'skip over ELSE clause
200    REM                      'begin ELSE clause
210    LET PAY = HOURS * RATE
250  REM                        'end of IF-THEN-ELSE
```

First, the expression HOURS = 0 is tested. If it is true, the next statement to be interpreted is at line 110. Otherwise, BASIC skips to the statement at line 200. Lines 200 and 210 are called the *ELSE clause* because they are reached by interpreting the ELSE portion of the IF statement.

Lines 110 through 130 are interpreted in sequence if HOURS = 0 is true. At line 130 BASIC is directed to skip to line 250. Lines 110 through 130 are called the *THEN clause* because they are interpreted only when the THEN portion of the IF statement is interpreted. Both THEN and ELSE clauses can be much longer than our examples. It is considered good form to place the THEN clause before the ELSE clause.

If the ELSE keyword is dropped, it is still possible to have an implicit ELSE clause in your program. For example,

```
100  IF HOURS = 0 THEN 200
110    LET PAY = HOURS * RATE
120    LET TAXES = .32 * PAY
200  REM  --  End of implicit ELSE clause.
```

In this example, statements 110–120 are skipped unless the test HOURS = 0 is false.

Comparison Operators

The test expression in an IF statement must be either true or false. Expressions that are either true or false are called *boolean expressions* or *conditional expressions.* Conditional expressions are constructed with *comparison operators,* as shown in Table C.2. Parentheses can be used to avoid ambiguities. Here are some samples.

Table C.2 *Comparison Operators in BASIC*

Conditional Operator	Example	Meaning
=	A = 0	Equal
< >	A < > 0	Not equal
>	A > 0	Greater than
<	A < 0	Less than
> =	A >= 0	Greater than or equal
<=	A <= 0	Less than or equal
AND	(A = 0) AND (B = 1)	Both subparts true?
OR	(A = 0) OR (B = 1)	Either subpart true?
NOT	NOT (A = 0)	Same as A < > 0

```
(0 < A) AND (A < 10)        Is 0 < A < 10?
(0 < A) OR (A < 10)         Is A > 0 or is A < 10?
(A <> 0) OR (NOT (B = 0))   Is A not equal to zero or is B not equal
                            to zero?
```

In an AND comparison both of the expression's subparts must be true in order for the whole expression to be true. In contrast, an OR comparison is true if *either* subpart is true.

To illustrate an OR comparison, consider the problem of checking data entered from the keyboard to make sure it is reasonable. For example, suppose the ages of potential customers are to be entered, and reasonable values for the age are considered to be 10 through 110. The following program fragment will force a correct input:

```
100 INPUT AGE
110    IF (AGE < 10) OR (AGE > 110) THEN 120 ELSE 140
120    PRINT "Please enter an age between 10 and 110. Try again."
130    GOTO 100
140 REM
```

The IF-THEN-ELSE statement tests the value of AGE each time it is entered. Unacceptable values of AGE cause an error message to be displayed and force BASIC to return to the INPUT statement in line 100. This cycle is repeated until the value entered for AGE is acceptable; then the ELSE clause is interpreted.

Nested IF Statements

It is a good idea to indent the THEN and ELSE clauses of an IF statement to make them readable, especially when IF statements are part of other IF statements. A *nested IF statement* is any IF statement that is part of a THEN or ELSE clause. Here is a simple example in which indentation is used to clarify the nested statements.

```
100 IF WEIGHT < 40 THEN 110 ELSE 200
110    IF BIG < 15 THEN 120 ELSE 150    'Nested inside THEN clause...
120        LET SHIP$ = "CARRY IT"       'Innermost THEN clause
130        GOTO 190                      'End of inner THEN clause
150        LET SHIP$ = "DRAG IT"         'Innermost ELSE clause
190        REM                           'End of inner IF Statement
199    GOTO 220                          'End of outermost THEN clause
200    LET SHIP$ = "HAND-TRUCK IT"       'Outermost ELSE clause
210    REM                               'End of outermost ELSE clause
220 REM                                  'End of outermost IF statement
```

Indentation shows which statements belong to the outer IF statement and which ones belong to the inner IF statement. Lines 110 through 190 are all part of the innermost IF statement, which in turn is part of the THEN clause of the IF statement that starts in line 100. Lines 199 through 210 are part of the outer IF statement, so they are only indented once.

A Complete Example

Now let's put IF statements to work in a longer example. Consider the equation $AX^2 + BX + C = 0$, where A, B, and C are constants and X is a variable. You may recall from algebra that this equation is called a *quadratic equation* and can be solved to find the values of X that cause the equation to be true. These values are called *roots* of the equation. Most quadratic equations have two roots that in BASIC notation are given by the following:

$$X = \frac{-B + SQR(B\hat{~}2 + 4 * A * C)}{2 * A} \text{ and } X = \frac{-B - SQR(B\hat{~}2 + 4 * A * C)}{2 * A}$$

The formulas seem quite straightforward, but it is not simple to write a BASIC program to find the roots. Here is a list of what can go wrong.

1. If the values of both A and B are zero, the equation has no roots.

2. If A is zero and B is not equal to zero, then the formula is undefined. In this case there is only one root, and it is given by the formula X = −C / B.

3. The argument of the square root function (called the *discriminant*) could be less than zero, in which case the equation has no roots.

We can take all of these possibilities into account by using IF statements and GOTOs to check the values of A, B, and C. This is why the resulting program in Figure C.6 is rather imposing. QUADRAD.BAS asks the user for the values of A, B, and C in lines 140 through 155. Next, the value of A is tested in line 160 to see if it is zero.

```
100 REM ---------------------- QUADRAD.BAS ----------------------
110 REM     Compute the roots of the equation AX^2 + BX + C = 0
120 REM ==============================================================
130 REM
135 REM           Input Values of A,B,C
136 REM
140 INPUT "A = "; A              'Prompt user for A; get A from keyboard
150 INPUT "B = "; B              'Prompt user for B; get B from keyboard
155 INPUT "C = "; C              'Prompt user for C; get C from keyboard
156 REM
157 REM           Logic Section & Calculations
158 REM
160 IF A = 0 THEN 165 ELSE 200            'Decide if A = 0
165    IF B = 0 THEN 170 ELSE 180         'Both A = 0 and B = 0 ?
170      PRINT "***ERROR**** Bad Inputs"
172      GOTO 300                         'Bad inputs, so quit
180    PRINT "The one root is:"; (-C)/B   'Solve BX + C = 0
181    GOTO 300                           'One root, then quit
182 REM                                   'End of inner IF statement
200 REM ELSE
205 REM
210    DISC = B^2 - 4 * A * C             'Discriminant could be negative
220    IF DISC < 0 THEN 230 ELSE 250
230      PRINT "There are no real roots"  'There are only imaginary roots
240      GOTO 290                         'End of Disc < 0 clause
250    REM
252    REM ELSE                           'ELSE within an ELSE
255    REM
260      PRINT "Real Roots = ";(-B - SQR(DISC)) / (2*A)
270      PRINT "           = ";(-B + SQR(DISC)) / (2*A)
280    REM                               'End of inner ELSE
290 REM                                  'End of outer ELSE
300 REM                                  'End of outer IF statement
999 END '--------------------------------------------------------------
RUN
A = ? 4
B = ? 0
C = ? -4
Real Roots = -1
           =  1
Ok
```

Figure C.6 *Solving the equation AX^2 + BX + C = 0.*

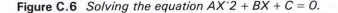

If the value of A is zero, the value of B is tested in line 165 to see if the equation has one root, or if it has no solutions. If both A and B store zero, then the quadratic equation is degenerate and has no solutions. In this case the program prints an error message in line 170 and skips to the end of the program. Alternatively, if the value of A is zero and the value B is not zero, the program calculates the equation's one root in line 180 and skips to the end of the program.

When the value of A is not zero, either the equation has two roots, or the discriminant is negative and the equation has only "imaginary" roots. Thus the final IF statement is in line 220, where the program decides if real roots exist by testing the discriminant.

This program illustrates the use of IF and GOTO statements, but more importantly, it shows how to properly structure a program that contains many paths. All paths in the program lead to the same ending. And the inner IF statements are terminated before the outer IF statements, as shown in lines 280 through 300. These features are characteristics of a structured program. In a *structured program* all branches must converge at some later point in the program in a way that guarantees nonoverlapping paths through the program. Careful placement of GOTOs can guarantee proper structure, but careless placement can make a program much more difficult to understand. For more details about structured programming, see Chapter 15.

ON GOTO Statements

The IF statement is used to decide between two alternatives, but sometimes you will want to decide among many alternatives. The ON GOTO statement is used to direct the program down one of many possible paths. Its general form is

ON *variable* GOTO *list of line numbers*

The value of the variable determines which of the line numbers in the list is interpreted next. For example, if the value of the variable is 3, then the third line number in the list becomes the next statement to be interpreted.

```
200   INPUT J                  'Get a number
210   ON J GOTO 220,230,240    'Branch
220      PRINT "FIRST"
225      GOTO 250               'Skip the rest
230      PRINT "SECOND"
240      PRINT "LAST"
250 REM                        'End of ON GOTO
```

In this example, the value of J is obtained from the keyboard and is used to determine which statement to branch to. First, if necessary, the value of J is truncated to an integer. Then, depending on whether the value of J is 1, 2, or 3, the next statement to be interpreted is 220, 230, or 240, respectively. For example, if the value of J is 2, then lines 230 through 250 are interpreted because the ON GOTO branches to line 230 and continues from there. If the truncated value of J is less than 1 or greater than 3, then the ON GOTO at line 210 has no effect at all and line 220 is interpreted next.

```
100   REM --------------------- MENU.BAS -----------------------
110   REM        Illustrate a simple menu-selection system
120   REM ===============================================================
130   PRINT "        THE WHIZ-BANG PAYROLL SYSTEM'S MASTER MENU"
140   PRINT
150   PRINT "1 -- Enter payroll transactions"
160   PRINT "2 -- Print paychecks or reports"
170   PRINT "3 -- Perform maintenance functions (back-up files, etc.)"
180   PRINT "4 -- QUIT by returning to the operating system"
190   INPUT "        Enter your choice:"; CHOICE
200   ON CHOICE GOTO 1000, 2300, 4000, 7000
210   PRINT "Please enter a value between 1 and 4"
220   GOTO 130
1000  REM -- The statements for entering payroll transactions follow.
  ...
2140  REM -- End of data entry section.
2300  REM -- The statements for printing reports follow.
  ...
3860  REM -- End of reports section.
4000  REM -- The statements that perform maintenance functions follow.
  ...
6280  REM -- End of maintenance section.
7000  REM -- Return to operating system.
  ...
9999  END
```

Figure C.7 *A menu-selection system.*

A more practical example of ON GOTO statements is given in Figure C.7. It illustrates how an ON GOTO statement can form the basis of a menu-selection system.

FOR/NEXT Loops

One of the most powerful features of computers is their ability to repeat monotonous operations over and over again without error or complaint. Repetitious calculations are done in BASIC programs by using FOR/NEXT loops. Their general format is

FOR *loop counter* = *start* TO *stop* [STEP *step size*]
  body of the loop
NEXT *loop counter*

The statements bracketed between the FOR and NEXT statements are called the *body of the loop.* The number of times that the body of the loop is repeated is determined by the *start, stop,* and *step-size* values. These values can be constants, variables, or expressions. The *loop counter* is a numeric variable that keeps track of the number of times the loop has been repeated. The loop starts with the FOR statement and ends at the NEXT statement. The STEP clause is optional. If it is omitted, the default value for the step size is 1.

When the FOR statement is first interpreted, BASIC assigns the start value to the loop counter. With each pass through the loop, the loop counter is increased by 1 (or by the optional step-size value). When the loop counter becomes greater than the stopping value, the statement that follows the NEXT statement is interpreted. For example,

```
100 FOR I = 1 TO 8
120 PRINT I * 2,
130 NEXT I
140 END
RUN
 2              4              6              8              10
 12             14             16
Ok
```

The starting value of I is 1. Each time the segment is repeated, the value of I is automatically increased by 1 until it exceeds 8. When the value of I is 9, the loop ceases, and the statement following 130 NEXT I is interpreted.

The preceding FOR/NEXT loop is equivalent to the following program that uses IF and GOTO statements. In this example the FOR/NEXT loop is preferable to a loop constructed from IF and GOTO statements because it provides a shorter, clearer solution.

```
100 LET I=1                     'Starting value of loop counter
110 IF I <= 8 THEN 120 ELSE 140 'Test the loop counter
120   PRINT I * 2,              'Body of the loop
125 LET I = I + 1               'Increase the loop counter
130 GOTO 110                    'Repeat it all
140 END
```

Notice that the loop counter is tested *before* the body of the loop is interpreted. (Some older versions of BASIC test the loop *after* the body is interpreted—this means the loop is always interpreted at least once). In this example the test seems unnecessary, but in general it is needed because the loop may be done *zero* or more times. Suppose, for example, the initial and final values of the loop counter are variables.

```
100 FOR MONTHS = PRESENT TO FUTURE
```

Here, it is possible that the value of PRESENT is already greater than the value of FUTURE. If so, the loop is skipped altogether.

The body of the loop may contain other FOR/NEXT loops, IF-GOTO loops, and many other statements. Because these statements easily become confusing, it is good to indent the body of a loop to identify what is being repeated.

Computing a Total

Adding numbers to determine their total is one major use of loops. This is done by assigning to a variable the task of storing the sum of all the numbers that have been added so far. The initial value of this variable is zero, because no numbers have been added to it. While the loop is being interpreted, numbers are added to the variable, and it maintains a running total. For example, this loop calculates the sum of three numbers.

```
100 YARDAGE = 0                  'Store an initial value of zero
150 FOR DOWNS = 1 TO 4           'Start at DOWNS = 1, stop at 4
200   INPUT "Enter yards:"; YARDS  'User enters a number
250   YARDAGE = YARDAGE + YARDS  'Add YARDS to the running total
300 NEXT DOWNS                   'End of loop
350 PRINT 'The total yardage is:'; YARDAGE
```

The value of YARDAGE is increased from zero to the final total by adding YARDS to it each time the body of the loop is repeated. YARDS takes on a different value each time it is entered from the keyboard. Suppose the numbers entered from the keyboard are 3, 5, 1, and 35. The following table shows the values of DOWNS, YARDS, and YARDAGE after each time through the loop:

DOWNS (Counter)	YARDS (Input)	YARDAGE (Calculated)
1	3	3
2	5	8
3	1	9
4	35	44

When DOWNS reaches 5, the loop is terminated because 5 is greater than the stopping value of 4.

In the preceding example the loop is designed to add exactly four numbers. The following example relaxes this restriction by asking the user to enter how many numbers are to be added. This example also computes the average of the numbers.

```
1000 TOTAL = 0                             'TOTAL is initially zero
1010 INPUT "How many numbers are there"; N
1020 FOR COUNT = 1 TO N                    'Perform the loop N times
1030   INPUT "Enter a number"; X           'X changes each pass
1040   TOTAL = TOTAL + X                   'Repeatedly add X to TOTAL
1050 NEXT COUNT                            'Increment COUNT by 1. Done?
2000 PRINT "The average is:"; TOTAL/N
RUN
How many numbers are there? 2
Enter a number? 12
Enter a number? 6
The average is: 9
```

A Payroll Example

Figure C.8 illustrates the basic idea of summing within a FOR loop, but in a more sophisticated application. Although this program is more complicated than our previous examples, it retains the basic pattern of looping for the purpose of computing a sum.

Like most long programs, PAYDAY.BAS begins with an initialization section. This section (lines 140–190) sets the values of the six total variables to zero. The repeated part of the summation is enclosed in a single FOR loop from lines 230 to 410. Each pass through the loop represents one day's worth of wages. In the body of the loop, line 280 decides whether the employee worked more than eight hours and should be paid overtime. After the loop does the totaling, the totals are printed in a formatted table, as specified by lines 440 through 470.

The Loop's Step Size

The optional step size in a FOR/NEXT loop tells BASIC how much to add to or subtract from the loop counter each time through the loop. For example, the statement 100 FOR FEET = 1 TO WALLSIZE STEP 3 causes the loop counter to take on the values of 1, 4, 7, and so on until the value in FEET exceeds the stop value in WALLSIZE.

The main reason for choosing a step size other than 1 is to use the loop counter conveniently within the body of the loop. For example, if you wanted to print the even numbers from 1 to 15, you would set the step size to 2, and then have the value of the loop counter printed each time through the loop.

```
100 FOR I = 1 TO 16 STEP 2
120 PRINT I,
130 NEXT I
RUN
 1              3              5              7              9
 11             13             15
```

```
100 REM ------------------------ PAYDAY.BAS ------------------------
110 REM                Compute 5 days' worth of pay
120 REM -----------------------------------------------------------
130 REM
140 LET REGPAY = 0              'total regular pay
150 LET OVRPAY = 0              'total overtime pay
160 LET BIGBUCKS = 0           'total dollars earned
170 LET REGTIME = 0            'total regular hours
180 LET OTIME = 0              'total overtime hours
190 LET TIME = 0              'total hours worked
200 REM
210 INPUT "Enter $/hr rate of pay"; RATE
220 REM
230 REM <+++++ LOOP ++++++++++++++++++++++++++++++++++++++++++++++++++<
240 FOR I = 1 TO 5              'repeat for each day of week    |
250   INPUT "Enter hours worked :"; HRS                        '|
270   LET OVRTIME = HRS - 8     'anything over 8 hrs is overtime |
280   IF OVRTIME > 0 THEN 290 ELSE 340   'overtime pay? -------->|
290     LET OTIME = OTIME + OVRTIME                            '|
295     LET REGTIME = REGTIME + 8                              '|
300     LET PAY = RATE * 8                                     '|
310     LET BONUS = RATE * OVRTIME * 1.5                       '|
320     LET OVRPAY = OVRPAY + BONUS                            '|
325     LET BUCKS = PAY + BONUS                                '|
330     GOTO 380                                               '|
340     REM ----------else clause ----------------------------<| |
345     LET REGTIME = REGTIME + HRS                            '|
347     LET PAY = RATE * HRS                                   '|
350     LET BUCKS = PAY                                        '|
370     REM ----------end of IF ----------------------------- | |
380     LET BIGBUCKS=BIGBUCKS + BUCKS  'total $ earned for the week |
390     LET TIME = TIME + HRS           'add up total hours worked  |
400     LET REGPAY = REGPAY + PAY       'add up total regular pay   |
410 NEXT I                                                     '|
420 REM >++++++++++++++++++++++++++++++++++++++++++++++++++++++++++++>
430 REM
440 PRINT USING "Regular : ### hrs.   $###.##"; REGTIME; REGPAY
450 PRINT USING "Overtime  ### hrs.   $###.##"; OTIME; OVRPAY
460 PRINT "            ------------------"
470 PRINT USING "Totals    ### hrs.   $###.##"; TIME; BIGBUCKS
480 REM
490 END '-----------------------------------------------------------------
RUN
Enter $/hr rate of pay? 5
Enter hours worked :? 7
Enter hours worked :? 4
Enter hours worked :? 9
Enter hours worked :? 6
Enter hours worked :? 9
Regular :  33 hrs.    $165.00
Overtime    2 hrs.    $ 15.00
           ------------------
Totals     35 hrs.    $180.00
Ok
```

Figure C.8 *A program to compute a paycheck for one week.*

FOR loop counters can run "backwards" as well. If the step size is a negative number, the loop counter is decreased. Each time through the loop, the negative step value is added to the loop counter. Suppose you want to print all numbers from 100 down to 49, in steps of 9.

```
500 FOR I = 100 TO 49 STEP -9  'Start with 100, stop at 49, step -9
510   PRINT I                  'Print 100, 91, 82, 73, 64, 55
520 NEXT I                     'Add (-9) to I
```

Observe that the last value of I to be printed is 55 rather than 49. The next value of I would be 46—a number outside the range of acceptable counter values from 100 to 49.

Limitations of FOR Loops

The FOR loop saves time and effort when you know exactly how many times you want to repeat the body of the loop. Unfortunately, there are many instances in programming when you do not know in advance the number of times to execute the body of a loop. In these circumstances, the FOR loop is of little value.

As an illustration, suppose you want to repeat a loop until the number entered from the keyboard is zero. You might attempt to do this with the FOR loop as follows:

```
200 FOR TIMES = 1 TO 100
210   INPUT X
220   IF X = 0 THEN 300
230   REM the rest of the body
299 NEXT TIMES
300 REM outside the loop
```

There are several things wrong with this approach. First, you can never be sure that the termination value 100 is large enough. What if the user wants to enter 101 numbers? The second reason to avoid this approach is even more important. The IF statement at line 220 violates structured programming practice because it causes an exit from the middle of the loop. Recall from Chapter 15 that a structured program contains only single-entry and single-exit control constructs. Allowing an additional exit point from the middle of the FOR loop results in a multiple-exit construct.

The FOR loop fails to serve your needs in this case. Instead, you might use an IF statement, as in the following:

```
200 REM Repeat until X = 0
210   INPUT X
220   IF X = 0 THEN 300
230   REM the rest of the body
299   GOTO 200
300 REM outside the loop
```

This more accurately mirrors the intended operations, but the structure is still weak because of the convoluted IF-THEN clause. (Try to identify the THEN clause as a separate grouping from the body of the loop.) You can use the WHILE statement to overcome this problem.

WHILE/WEND Loops

The WHILE statement repeats a loop body until the test portion of the WHILE is satisfied.

> WHILE *test*
>   *body of loop*
> WEND

The WHILE statement is actually two statements: the beginning of the loop is marked by the WHILE statement, and the end is marked by the WEND statement. (WEND is short for "WHILE end".) If *test* is true, the body of the loop is interpreted until the WEND statement is encountered. BASIC then returns to the WHILE statement and checks the *test* condition again. If *test* is false, interpretation resumes with the statement that follows WEND. Otherwise, the loop is repeated again.

We can write our example problem in a structured fashion by first asking for an initial input value from the keyboard and then entering the WHILE loop.

```
200 INPUT X                          'Initialize input value
205 WHILE X <> 0                     'Test looping condition
230   REM the rest of the body
299 INPUT X
300 WEND                             'End of loop
```

This version maintains the single-exit feature we are looking for. Each time the loop is repeated, a new value of X is entered into the running program. When line 300 is interpreted, control is passed to line 205, where the value of X is tested. When X is zero, the loop is skipped, and the statement following line 300 is interpreted.

Exercises

1. For each example, tell which statement is interpreted next. Assume that A is 3 and B is 10.
   a. 100 IF (NOT (A=0) AND (B=10)) THEN 110 ELSE 150
   b. 200 IF (A=0) OR (A=3) OR (B=9) THEN 220 ELSE 290
   c. 100 IF (A=3) AND (B<20) THEN 150 ELSE 300
   d. 100 IF ((A=3) AND (B=10)) AND (B>20) THEN 150 ELSE 400
   e. 150 IF (A*B > 30) THEN 180 ELSE 200

2. In each of the following pieces of code, how many times will statement 110 be repeated?

a.
```
100 FOR I = 3 TO 85
110    PRINT I
120 NEXT I
```

d.
```
FOR I = 3 TO -40 STEP -2
110    PRINT I
120 NEXT I
```

b.
```
100 FOR I = -1 TO 99
110    PRINT I
120 NEXT I
```

e.
```
100 FOR J = 2 TO 5
105 FOR I = J TO 5
110    PRINT I,J
115 NEXT I
120 NEXT J
```

c.
```
100 FOR I = 2 TO 39 STEP 2
110    PRINT I
120 NEXT I
```

3. Assume that A is 5 and B is 10. What do the following program fragments print?

a.
```
100 IF A = 3 THEN 150 ELSE 110
110    PRINT A
120    GOTO 200
150    PRINT B
200 REM
```

b.
```
100 IF (A=3) AND (B=10) THEN 150 ELSE 110
110    PRINT A
120    GOTO 200
150    PRINT B
200 REM
```

c.
```
100 IF (A=3) OR (B=10) THEN 150 ELSE 110
110    PRINT A
120    GOTO 200
150    PRINT B
200 REM
```

d.
```
100 IF ((A=3) OR (B=10)) AND (B<5) THEN 150 ELSE 110
110    PRINT A
120    GOTO 200
150    PRINT B
200 REM
```

4. Modify the sample program for summing input values so that it also finds and displays the smallest value entered.

5. Write an ON GOTO statement that prints the day of the week, given that a number between 1 and 7 is entered.

6. Write a program to compute the average value, variance, minimum, and maximum values of a list of numbers entered from the keyboard. Your program should begin by asking the user how many numbers are in the list.

■ Data Structures

Until now we have not discussed how data is organized inside programs that manipulate substantial quantities of data. A *data structure* is a collection of values and the information needed to organize these values into a coherent whole. For example, a card file is a data structure that is used in some manual systems to store names and addresses. BASIC is a difficult language to use for large projects and commercial programs because it is notoriously devoid of elegant data structures. Arrays and simple files are the only structures found in BASIC programs. We will discuss only the array structure, and leave the discussion of file structures to an advanced text on BASIC.

One-Dimensional Arrays

An *array* is a variable that can contain more than one value. Because each value takes up memory space, you should tell BASIC the size of array variables before using them. The DIM (dimension) statement is used to declare the name and size of an array; it tells BASIC how much memory to reserve for the array's values. The general form of a DIM statement is

DIM *variable*(*size*)

where *variable* is the name of an array, and *size* specifies how many values are in the array. For example, suppose you want ITEM$ to be an array containing up to 50 strings. You would put the following DIM statement at the beginning of your program:

```
10 DIM ITEM$(50)          'ITEM$ is a string array of 50 values
```

If the name of an array variable is used without a DIM statement, the size of the array is assumed to be 10.

A list of variables separated by commas can be placed in a single DIM statement. For example, if CARS and TRUCKS are both arrays, you can declare them in a single DIM statement, as follows:

```
50 DIM CARS(50), TRUCKS(100)
```

Each value stored in an array is called an *element* of the array. In the previous example, array CARS can hold up to 50 elements and no more. Because CARS is a numeric variable name, each element of CARS must be a number.

The elements of an array are numbered as shown in Figure C.9. The numbers are called *subscripts* and are used to refer to a particular element in the array. The subscript must be an integer, and it is always enclosed in parentheses

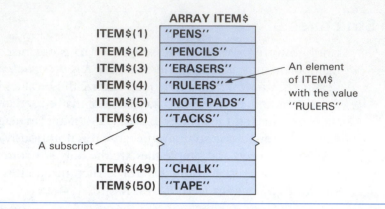

Figure C.9 *Arrays, subscripts, and elements.*

after the name of the array. For example, to refer to the third element in the array ITEM$, you would type ITEM$(3).

The following example shows how the data shown in Figure C.9 might be placed in the array ITEM$:

```
200 DIM ITEM$(50)
250 ITEM$(1) = "PENS"          'Store PENS in element 1
300 ITEM$(2) = "PENCILS"       'Store PENCILS in element 2
350 ITEM$(3) = "ERASERS"       'Store ERASERS in element 3
```

In this example the array is made of string variables. In one way numeric variables are trickier than string variables: with numeric variables it is easy to confuse the subscript with the value of the element itself. For example,

```
40 LET X(3) = -5      'Store the value -5 in element 3
50 LET X(5) = 8       'Store the value 8 in element 5
60 LET X(1) = X(3)    'Move the value in element 3 into element 1
70 PRINT X(1); X(2); X(3)
RUN
-5 -5  8
```

Using Arrays

The power of arrays is tied to the manipulation of array elements in loops. FOR loops are frequently used to store, retrieve, and search arrays. Suppose you want to load an array of numbers from the keyboard. You might repeat the INPUT statement for each array element, but that would be a tedious method. A better way is to use a FOR/NEXT loop.

```
500 FOR I = 1 TO 11     'Get all 11 elements...
550    INPUT X(I)       'I is a counter and a subscript!
600 NEXT I
```

Here we have used I as both a loop counter and a subscript. The FOR loop increases I from 1 to 11, and the INPUT statement uses I as a subscript of X. The first pass through the loop causes a value to be entered into element X(1); the second pass enters a value into X(2); and so forth until the value of X(11) is entered and stored in X(11).

One common task is to search an array to find a particular value. For example, we might want to know if the string "NOTE PADS" is in array ITEM$, and if it is, which element it is in. The FOR/NEXT loop and its counter can be used to search an array. The simplest method is to examine each array element one at a time and compare it with a *search key* (the value to be found); if they match, the search is successful. If all elements are compared with the search key and none match, then the search fails.

The LOOKUP.BAS program in Figure C.10 shows only one of many ways to search an array for a particular value. It does this by brute force—comparing each of the elements of X with the search key. When a match is found, the subscript of that element is remembered.

The first notable feature of LOOKUP.BAS is the DIM statement in line 140. This statement tells BASIC to reserve space to store 100 elements in array X. All 100 elements may never be used, but the memory is reserved in case they are

Figure C.10 *Searching array X for the value K.*

```
100 REM ------------------- LOOKUP.BAS ----------------------
110 REM            Search array X for the value K
120 REM -------------------------------------------------------
130 REM
140 DIM X(100)               'Reserve memory for the array
150 REM
160 FOR I = 1 TO 5           'Read five values into the array
170   PRINT USING "X(##) = ";I;  '...from keyboard...
180   INPUT X(I)            'one at a time
190 NEXT I
200 REM
210 J = 0                   'J is used as a flag: J = 0 means NOT FOUND
220 INPUT "Enter the search key="; K
230 REM
240 FOR I = 1 TO 5               'Search all values....
250   IF X(I) = K THEN 260 ELSE 270  'for possible match.
260     J = I                   'Store the location of the match in J.
270 NEXT I                      '
280 IF J = 0 THEN 290 ELSE 310  'Was a match FOUND or NOT FOUND?
290   PRINT "NOT FOUND"
300   GOTO 320
310   PRINT USING "FOUND AT ##";J  'show where
320 REM
330 END '-------------------------------------------------------
```

needed. Lines 160 through 190 are used to load the values for the elements of array X from the keyboard. Because the counter of the FOR/NEXT loop runs from 1 to 5 and is also used as the subscript for array X, only 5 elements of the 100 available are used. To increase the number actually used, you would raise the loop's stopping value in line 160 from 5 to a higher number. Note, however, that you must also change the DIM statement if more than 100 elements are to be used.

Line 210 sets the initial value of J to zero. This program uses J to store the subscript of the element that matches the key. If no element matches the key, the value of J stays at zero. Thus J becomes a flag indicating that no match was found. A *flag* is any variable that indicates a certain condition in a program.

Lines 240 through 270 perform the search by comparing elements in X with the key stored in K. If an element matches the key, the value of I is saved in J. Thus, if line 260 is interpreted, a match is found, and the location of the matching element is "remembered" in variable J.

When the FOR/NEXT loop terminates, line 280 tests to see if a matching element was found. It does this by checking to see if the value of J is still zero.

LOOKUP.BAS can easily be modified to perform many other kinds of searches. For example, you can find the largest or smallest element in an array by making minor changes in LOOKUP.BAS without affecting its basic structure. To find the largest element of an array X, you might begin by assuming that the first element is the largest. Its subscript will become the initial value of J. The FOR/NEXT loop then will compare the value of the element pointed to by J with the other elements one at a time. If a larger value is discovered, its subscript can replace the value in J. After all elements have been compared, J will store the subscript of the largest element in the array.

Using this strategy, you can convert LOOKUP.BAS into a program that finds the largest element of array X by (1) removing the INPUT statement for K, (2) removing the IF statement at the end, and (3) changing the following lines:

```
210 J = 1                    'J = 1 means assume X(1) is largest
250  IF X(I) > X(J) THEN 260 ELSE 270
310  PRINT USING "MAXIMUM FOUND AT ##";J
```

Of course, you should also change the comments appropriately.

Two-Dimensional Arrays

A two-dimensional array stores values in a table format instead of in columns. It is declared in the same way as a one-dimensional array, except that it has two subscripts instead of one.

DIM *variable(size1, size2)*

Size1 specifies the maximum number of elements in each column; *size2* tells the maximum number of elements in each row.

For example, suppose you want to store the height, weight, and IQ of five people. The organization of these numbers will be much clearer if you use a table with three columns and five rows instead of a column with fifteen elements. A DIM statement for this example is

```
DIM STATS(3,5)
```

where STATS is a two-dimensional array containing 3 * 5 = 15 elements, as in the following:

Column 1	Column 2	Column 3
STATS(1,1)	STATS(2,1)	STATS(3,1)
STATS(1,2)	STATS(2,2)	STATS(3,2)
STATS(1,3)	STATS(2,3)	STATS(3,3)
STATS(1,4)	STATS(2,4)	STATS(3,4)
STATS(1,5)	STATS(2,5)	STATS(3,5)

You must use two subscripts to refer to an element in a two-dimensional array. The first subscript indicates the column, and the second subscript designates the row. For example,

```
100 LET STATS(2,3) = 100          'Store 100 in column 2, row 3
110 LET X = STATS(1,1) + STATS(2,3)  'Access (1,1) and (2,3)-th elements
```

Each element is processed individually like a simple variable, but in addition, the entire array can be processed with the aid of a FOR/NEXT loop. For example, to enter the entire array into memory, you might use two nested FOR/NEXT loops.

```
100 FOR ROW = 1 TO 5
150    FOR COL = 1 TO 3
160      INPUT STATS(COL, ROW)
170    NEXT COL
180 NEXT ROW
```

The inner FOR/NEXT loop is always executed more rapidly than the outer loop. Thus, this fragment of code reads the entire two-dimensional array in the following sequence:

STATS(1,1)
STATS(2,1)
STATS(3,1)
STATS(1,2)
STATS(2,2)
STATS(3,2)
STATS(1,3)
. . . .
STATS(3,5)

If you reverse the loops, the order of input changes.

Exercises

1. Assume that array T is declared as T(3,2). Write a segment of a BASIC program that reads values into it in the following order:

T(1,1)
T(2,1)
T(3,1)
T(1,2)
T(2,2)
T(3,2)

2. What does each of the following program fragments print?

a.
```
100 DIM A(100)
110 A(1) = 2
115 A(2) = 3
120 FOR I = 3 TO 100
130   A(I) = A(I - 1) * 2 - A(I - 2)
140 NEXT I
150 PRINT A(99)
```

b.
```
100 DIM A(2,2)
110 A(1,2) = 5
120 A(2,1) = 7
130 I = 2
140 J = 1
150 PRINT A(J,I)
```

3. Write a program that accepts numbers into two arrays (UNITCOST and QUANTITY), computes values for a third array (COST), and completes the following report. Your program should print totals for all three columns at the bottom of the report.

Unit cost	Quantity	Cost
12.96	5	
6.80	3	
9.99	9	
52.50	2	
19.35	7	

4. Rewrite the program in problem 3 using a two-dimensional array to store all three columns of numbers. Which way is easier?

5. Write a BASIC program that will read a list of ten numbers into an array and then find the number of numbers in the array that exceed the average value.

using TriPac

TriPac is an integrated program with three components: a word processor, a spreadsheet, and a record manager. The word processor lets you write and edit letters, reports, and other documents. With the spreadsheet component you can calculate and analyze the relationships among numbers in a worksheet. The record manager lets you enter, sort, and query data that is stored as records in a file. These components are tied together under a supervisory program called the *desktop manager;* it provides access to each component.

Each component of TriPac is easy to use and incorporates the most important features of commercial software. But instead of burdening you with the complexity of full-featured commercial software packages, the components of TriPac are restricted. They illustrate the concepts in this book but are not intended to be real-world implementations.

Each component can be used productively by itself without reference to the others. Therefore, we have divided this appendix into an introductory section and three stand-alone sections—one for each component—so you can choose to learn the applications in any order. We first discuss the TriPac desktop manager and how to use menus to operate each component.

■ Invitation to TriPac

The three application components and the desktop manager all fit on one 5 1/4-inch disk. If the TriPac disk is configured appropriately, all you need to do to begin using TriPac is to slip the disk into the disk drive, turn on the computer, and wait for the desktop manager to appear on the screen, as shown in Figure D.1.[1] If there are several disk drives, put the TriPac disk into drive A, which is usually the one on the left.

Once the desktop manager appears, the line at the top of the screen will read: File, Setup, and Info. This line is called a *menu bar;* the words on the menu bar are the titles of subsidiary *pull-down menus.* For example, if you select the File option from the menu bar, a pull-down menu will appear below the word *File* on the menu bar.

Beneath the menu bar are three columns that list the names of the TriPac data files on the disk. The word processing files are listed in the DOCUMENTS column, worksheet files are in the SPREADSHEETS column, and record management files are in the DATABASE column.

---

[1]The TriPac disk provided to instructors does not contain a copy of DOS, so it cannot be used to boot the computer. We recommend that the instructor configure this disk for classroom use by copying DOS onto it. TriPac is not copy-protected and is distributed on double-sided MS-DOS disks.

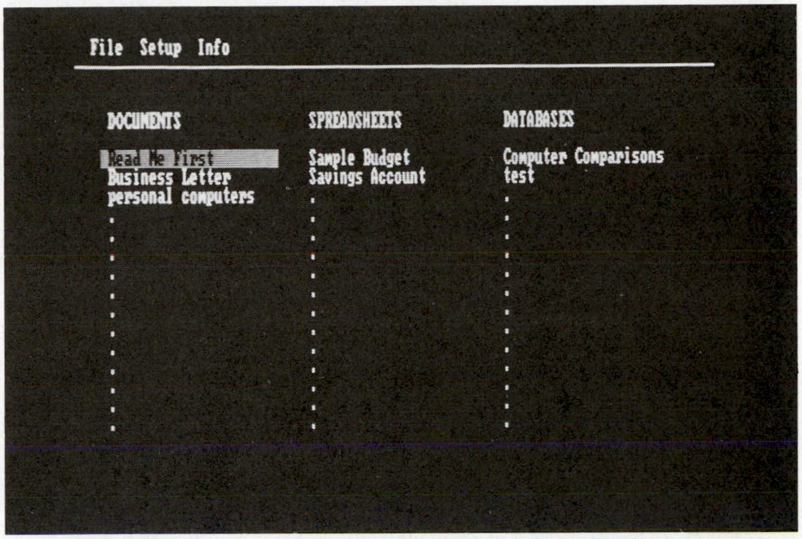

Figure D.1 *The TriPac desktop as it appears when the program is started. The menu bar is shown at the top of the screen. Files belonging to each of the three applications are shown in three columns: word processing DOCUMENTS, spreadsheet SPREADSHEETS, and record management DATABASES.*

At any given time, the name of one file is shown in inverse video—that is, in black letters on a white background. In Figure D.1, the file READ ME FIRST in the DOCUMENTS column is highlighted in this manner. You can highlight different files by using the cursor-movement keys. The highlighted file is the one that will be affected if you use the menu bar to open a file, rename a file, or perform other file operations. Soon we will discuss how this is done, but first you should become familiar with the keys that are used to control TriPac.

Keyboard Layout

Figure D.2 shows the layout of an IBM PC keyboard. Nearly all operations in TriPac are activated by the following keys:

■ *[ESC].* The escape key is used to toggle back and forth between the application and the menu bar. If the cursor is in the desktop or an application, you can press [ESC] to activate the menu bar. If an item on the menu bar is highlighted, you can press [ESC] to go back to the desktop or an application.

The [ESC] key is also used to escape from a mode of operation or to cancel an uncompleted command. For example, if you give a command to erase a file, TriPac will warn you of the dangers of erasing a file and allow you to cancel the operation by pressing [ESC].

■ *[ENTER].* The [ENTER] key is used to enter commands. For example, if you have highlighted an item on a menu, pressing [ENTER] acknowledges that you want to select and use the highlighted item. When you are using the word processor, the [ENTER] key is also used to create new paragraphs.

■ *Cursor-movement keys.* To the right of the [ENTER] key is a dual-purpose keypad that can act as either a cursor-movement keypad or a numeric keypad. Each key has two symbols on it (for example, the number 8 and an up-arrow symbol). When the keypad is in its number mode, the keys generate numbers. When the keypad is in its cursor-movement mode, the keys move the cursor or change which item on the screen is highlighted. You can toggle between the two modes by pressing the [NumLock] key immediately above the keypad.

When you are using the menu bar, the cursor-movement keys are used to select which word in the menu bar is highlighted. For example, to select Setup from the menu bar in Figure D.1, press [ESC] to move from the desktop to the menu bar, and then use the right-arrow key to move the highlighting from File to Setup.

The down-arrow key is also used to pull down a menu from the menu bar, and the up- and down-arrow keys move the highlighting from one

Figure D.2 *The layout of an IBM PC keyboard.*

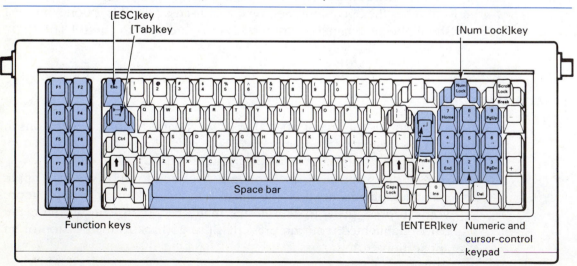

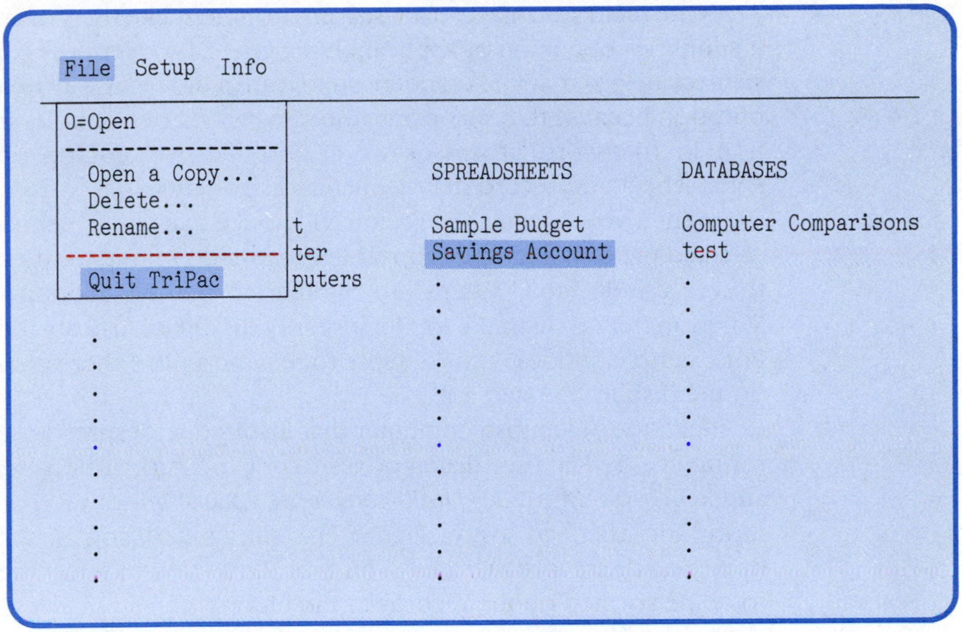

```
  File  Setup  Info

 ┌─────────────────┐
 │ O=Open          │
 │ --------------- │
 │  Open a Copy... │       SPREADSHEETS        DATABASES
 │  Delete...      │
 │  Rename...      │  t    Sample Budget       Computer Comparisons
 │ --------------- │  ter  Savings Account     test
 │  Quit TriPac    │  puters  .                  .
 └─────────────────┘
            .              .                  .
            .              .                  .
            .              .                  .
            .              .                  .
            .              .                  .
            .              .                  .
            .              .                  .
            .              .                  .
            .              .                  .
```

Figure D.3 *Using a pull-down menu to exit from TriPac to the operating system.*

item to another of a pull-down menu. The term *pull-down* is appropriate, because this is exactly what happens: the menu extends down over the application or desktop. In Figure D.3, for example, the last item of the File menu is highlighted. Pressing [ENTER] activates the highlighted item, erases the menu, and tells TriPac to perform the operation.

■ *[TAB].* The [TAB] key is used to move from one field to another. For example, in the record manager you can skip from one field of a record to another by pressing [TAB]. You can tab backward (from right to left) by pressing [SHIFT] and [TAB].

The Desktop Manager

The desktop manager is a program that controls the operation of the TriPac applications. It organizes all the data files used by TriPac and provides access to the applications. Like the Macintosh desktop (described in Chapter 4) TriPac uses pull-down menus and dialog boxes. The names in the middle of the screen organize word processing, spreadsheet, and record management files. The words on the menu bar represent the categories of commands that you can give. These names and other words are visual hints that constitute the *visual environment* of TriPac.

One main advantage of a visual environment like the TriPac desktop is that it simplifies operation of application programs by relentless consistency. *Consistency* means that you do not need to learn a different way to operate each application because they all operate the same way. For example, an editing operation in the word processor works just like the editing operation in the spreadsheet and record management components.

When you operate TriPac you will notice that some menu items cannot be selected even though they appear in the pull-down menu. If you look closely, these "unselectable" items are dimmer than their accessible companions. When an item is dimmed, it is temporarily disabled—usually for a good reason. For example, it doesn't make sense to rename a file if there aren't any data files on the disk to be renamed.

Like the Macintosh computer that inspired widespread use of visual environments, TriPac uses dialog boxes to ask for information, warn of dangers, and keep you informed. *Dialog boxes* are special windows that appear temporarily and then go away. Figure D.4 shows a dialog box obtained while operating the record manager. This box allows you to select the sort operation to be performed on the records in the file.

Figure D.4 *This screen shows the dialog box for a sort operation in the record management application. The sort operation can be canceled by pressing [ESC] or accepted by pressing [RETURN].*

File Edit Search Layout				Database: Computer Comparisons	

Make   Any Order
Model   Any Order
Type   Any Order
Memory Size Any Order
Price   Any Order
Remarks   Any Order

Press Esc to cancel   Press Enter to Sort

Compaq	286	Personal	640000	6299	Transportabl
IBM	3031	Mainframe	8000000	1338000	Medium-sized
Apollo	Domain	Minicomputer	3500000	80000	High-end min
IBM	S-370/158	Mainframe	2000000	488000	Older mainfr
Prime	9995	Minicomputer	16000000	400000	Supermini 4
Apple	Macintosh	Personal	512000	2495	User friendl
IBM	3090	Mainframe	64000000	5000000	IBMs Top of
Amdahl	5840	Mainframe	16000000	2500000	Large-scale
Digital	PDP 11-70	Minicomputer	4000000	89500	Traditional
Honeywell	DPS6/96	Minicomputer	16000000	130000	High-end min
IBM	PC	Personal	640000	1995	Defacto PC s

Some dialog boxes require you to "push" *buttons* in order to control the application. The [ESC] key is a button for canceling the operation—exiting it without side effects. The [ENTER] key is a button for proceeding with the settings shown in the dialog box. For example, the [ESC] and [ENTER] buttons at the bottom of the dialog box in Figure D.4 permit you to cancel the sorting operation or to perform the sort with the conditions shown in the dialog box.

Entering the Application Components

Creating a new data file and using an existing file require basically the same procedure. You can edit or modify an existing file by selecting it from the list displayed on the desktop screen. First you use the cursor-movement keys to select the file you want to work with, then press [ESC] to move to the menu bar, press the down-arrow key to pull down the File menu, and press [ENTER] to select the Open item from the menu. When [ENTER] is pressed, TriPac will load the appropriate application component and open the file so that you can work on it.

To create a new file, you first use the left- or right-arrow keys to select the appropriate column of the desktop for the application you want. Then press the down-arrow key until it highlights a file named "untitled". Now press [ESC] to activate the menu bar, press the down-arrow key to pull down the File menu, and press [ENTER] to select Open. When [ENTER] is pressed, TriPac will display a dialog box that asks for the name of the new file. After the file is named, TriPac will load the application component and open the new file.

The Clipboard File

The desktop manager also manages a hidden file called the *clipboard*. This file temporarily holds text that is cut or copied from an application file. The clipboard holds only the most recent piece of text cut or copied; subsequent cut or copy operations replace the previous contents of the clipboard.

The clipboard provides a good illustration of the value of a consistent user interface. You can use the clipboard to delete a paragraph from a word processing file, copy a group of cells in a spreadsheet file, or move records from a record management file into a word processing file. Although your reasons for using the clipboard will vary, the method of using it is always the same.

The procedure for using the clipboard involves the following steps:

- Open a file (either word processing, spreadsheet, or record management) and move the cursor to the beginning of the text you want to transfer to the clipboard.
- Press [ESC] to activate the menu bar. Then use the right-arrow key to highlight Edit on the menu bar and press the down-arrow key to pull down the Edit menu and highlight the item S = Start Selecting. Figure D.5 shows how the menu would look at this point.

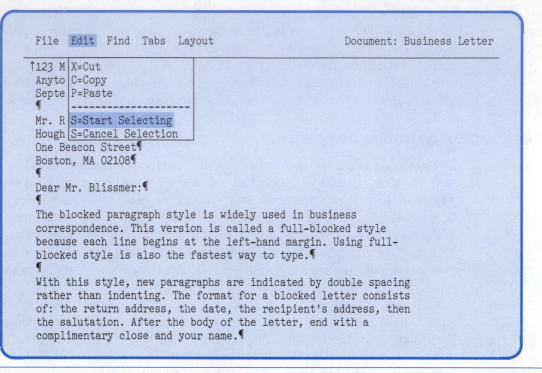

```
    File  Edit  Find  Tabs  Layout              Document: Business Letter

 ↑123 M │X=Cut
 Anyto  │C=Copy
 Septe  │P=Paste
 ¶      │--------------------
 Mr. R  │S=Start Selecting
 Hough  │S=Cancel Selection
 One Beacon Street¶
 Boston, MA 02108¶
 ¶
 Dear Mr. Blissmer:¶
 ¶
 The blocked paragraph style is widely used in business
 correspondence. This version is called a full-blocked style
 because each line begins at the left-hand margin. Using full-
 blocked style is also the fastest way to type.¶
 ¶
 With this style, new paragraphs are indicated by double spacing
 rather than indenting. The format for a blocked letter consists
 of: the return address, the date, the recipient's address, then
 the salutation. After the body of the letter, end with a
 complimentary close and your name.¶
```

Figure D.5 *Using a pull-down menu to select text in a word processing document.*

- Press [ENTER] to tell TriPac to erase the pull-down menu and start the selection procedure. At this point TriPac expects you to use the cursor-movement keys to point out the text to be selected. As you use the cursor-movement keys, TriPac will highlight the text between the cursor's initial location and its current location (see Figure D.6).

- When the desired block of text is highlighted, return to the Edit menu and select either the X = Cut or the C = Copy item and press [ENTER]. If you select X = Cut, the text disappears from its original location and is placed in the clipboard file. C = Copy merely copies the highlighted text to the clipboard without removing it from its original location.

- Move the cursor to the position where you want the text to be inserted. Then select the P = Paste item from the Edit menu to insert the contents of the clipboard at that location. The paste operation makes a copy of the contents of the clipboard. If you want to make several copies of the same data, you can paste several times in a row.

You can always paste text into the same file, or the same type of file, that it was cut or copied from (such as copying a paragraph from a business letter into a memo). However, there are restrictions on pasting material into a different

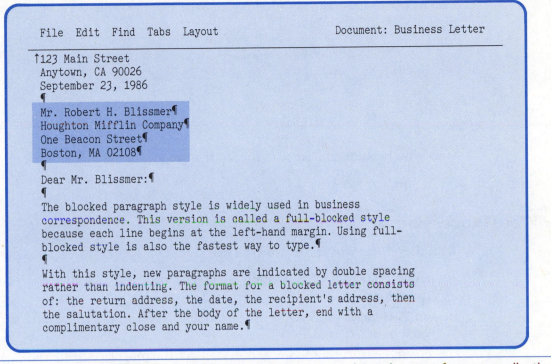

Figure D.6 *The cursor-movement keys are used to select text from an application file. The selected text is highlighted to show what part of the document is to be manipulated.*

type of file. You cannot move text from a word processing file into a spreadsheet or record management file. Nor can you move data between spreadsheet and record management files. But you can transfer any type of data into a word processing document.

Desktop Shortcuts

The desktop control keys such as [ESC], [ENTER], and [TAB] are easy to use, but using them requires several keystrokes. For this reason, short cuts are provided, using the [CTRL] key in combination with another key.

In Figure D.5 several shortcut keys are listed inside the pull-down menu, to the left of an equal sign. For example, the Cut operation is shown as

    X=Cut

which means that holding down the [CTRL] key while pressing the [X] key is a shortcut method of telling TriPac to cut the selected text from the file and place it in the clipboard. Shortcuts accomplish in one keystroke what the desktop manager does in several keystrokes. Compare these two methods of performing the Cut operation:

Shortcut	*Desktop*
[CTRL]-[X]	[ESC]
	Right-arrow
	Down-arrow
	[ENTER]

Once you become familiar with the shortcut sequences, they save time.

■ Word Processing

With the TriPac word processor you can

- enter, edit, and print a written document that is up to 15 double-spaced pages long.

- undo changes to the current version and revert to the previously saved version of a document.

- cut and paste text or copy and paste text from one place to another, even into a different document. Text from the spreadsheet and record manager components can be pasted into a word processing document from the clipboard.

- find and replace patterns of text (letters, words, and phrases).

- set tabs for convenience in indenting.

- specify how the document should look when it is printed. You can insert page breaks, choose either single- or double-spacing, and enter text to be printed at the top or bottom of each page.

To open an existing word processing document, use the cursor-movement keys to highlight the name of that file in the DOCUMENTS column of the desktop. Then you can press [CTRL]-[O] to use the shortcut method to open the document and start the word processor. The desktop menu bar will be replaced by the word processing menu bar as shown in Figure D.6. The body of the screen will show the beginning of the file being edited, but you can use the cursor-movement keys and the [PgDn] and [PgUp] keys to scroll through the document.

Entering a Sample Letter

In this section we describe how to enter, edit, format, and print a sample letter. For example, assume that you want to enter the letter shown in Figure 5.1 into a new document called JOHN DOE. To create a new document, you follow the same basic procedure that you use to edit an existing document, except you begin by highlighting a blank line in the DOCUMENTS column of the desktop. In Figure D.1 these lines appear below the "Personal Computers" file; they represent "untitled" or empty documents. Thus, you begin by using the left-arrow key to select the DOCUMENTS column and then press the down-arrow key until an "untitled" document is highlighted on the screen. Now press [ESC] to toggle to the menu bar from the desktop. The File option on the menu bar should be highlighted, indicating that it is selected. To create the document, press the down-arrow key to pull down the File menu and press [ENTER] to select the O=Open item. (As described earlier, these steps can be performed more quickly with the [CTRL]-[O] short cut.) After you press [ENTER], a dialog box will appear so that you can name the new document.

```
Name of new document: JOHN DOE [ENTER]
```

There will be a noticeable pause while the new file is created on the disk. The word processing menu bar will appear at the top of the screen, but the body of the screen will be blank because the document is empty. A blinking cursor indicates where text will appear when you begin to type.

Next, type the letter shown in Figure 5.1. Use the [ENTER] key to begin new paragraphs. There is no need to press [ENTER] each time the cursor approaches the end of a line because TriPac automatically moves to the beginning of a new line when a word is too long to fit at the end of the old line. TriPac does not allow you to adjust the margins. As a result, the format of your version of the letter may be different from that shown in Figure 5.1.

You can use the backspace key (located immediately above the [ENTER] key) to correct errors. To insert text, simply move the cursor to where the text should be inserted and type the text. You can delete text in two ways: with the [DEL] key or with the backspace key, which is located immediately above the [ENTER] key. The backspace key deletes the character to the left of the cursor and the [DEL] key deletes the character at the cursor's current position.

Feel free to experiment with the menu items. For example, to set a tab stop 10 spaces from the left margin, move the cursor to column 10, and press [CTRL]-[T], the short cut for setting a tab. Tab stops in TriPac work the same as on a typewriter except that you can tab backward (from right to left) by pressing [SHIFT]-[TAB].

When you have finished entering the letter, press [ESC] to toggle to the menu bar. Pull down the File menu and select the Save Document item to save the letter on the disk. If you wish, select the Print Document item to print the letter. When you are finished, select the Quit Word Processor item from the File menu to return control to the TriPac desktop manager.

In the following sections we summarize all operations possible with the word processing component of TriPac. Try each one, and then practice by doing exercises 1 and 8 provided at the end of this appendix.

File Menu

The File menu shown in Figure D.7 is used to save a document on the disk, print the document, copy the disk version of a document into memory, and exit from the word processor to the desktop manager. Use the [ESC] key to activate the menu bar, then use the up- and down-arrow keys to highlight the particular item you want. Pressing the [ENTER] key selects the highlighted item. Pressing the [ESC] key a second time cancels the selection and returns the cursor to the body of the document.

- *Save Document.* While you are editing a document, it resides in memory. When you want to make your changes permanent, use the Save item to copy the version of the document in memory to the disk file shown in the upper-right corner of the screen.
- *Print Document.* This item prints the current document on the printer. The document will not look the same on paper as it does on the screen because it is formatted according to instructions given in the Layout menu.
- *Revert to Last Version.* This item causes the version of a document in memory to be erased and replaced by the earlier version on the disk. Use this item if you want to throw away editing changes made since the last time the document was saved.
- *Quit Word Processor.* This item saves the document in memory on the disk and then exits from the word processor to the desktop manager.

Edit Menu

The Edit menu is used to select text to be deleted, duplicated, or relocated. First, you select the text to be manipulated. Then you either use the backspace or [DEL] key to delete the text, or you return to the Edit menu to Cut, Copy, or

Figure D.7 *The File menu is used to save, print, or abandon the document as well as to exit from the word processor to the desktop manager.*

```
File  Edit  Find  Tabs  Layout

  Save Document
  Print Document...
------------------------------
  Revert to Last Version...
------------------------------
  Quit Word Processor
```

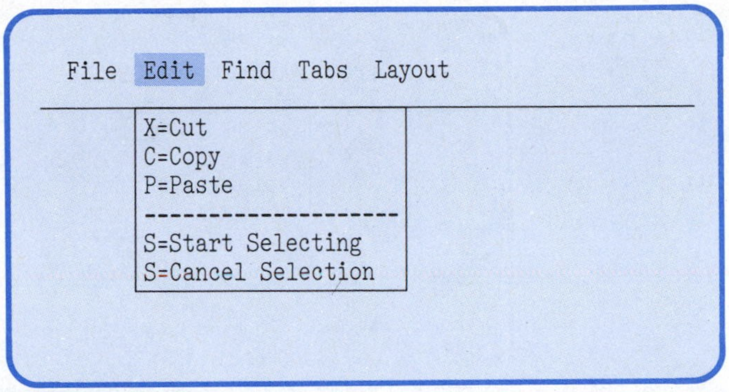

```
   File  Edit  Find  Tabs  Layout
  ┌─────────────────────────┐
  │ X=Cut                   │
  │ C=Copy                  │
  │ P=Paste                 │
  │ ----------------------- │
  │ S=Start Selecting       │
  │ S=Cancel Selection      │
  └─────────────────────────┘
```

Figure D.8 *The Edit menu is used to control the operation of the clipboard.*

Paste the text. Here are the options listed in the menu, which is shown in Figure D.8.

- *X=Cut.* The selected text is removed from the document in memory and written on the clipboard so that it can be pasted elsewhere.
- *C=Copy.* The selected text is copied onto the clipboard. This item allows you to duplicate portions of the document.
- *P=Paste.* The text in the clipboard is pasted into the document at the cursor's current position.
- *S=Start Selecting.* This item causes the word processor to shift into a selection mode that allows you to highlight the block of text to be deleted or transferred to the clipboard. You do this with the cursor-movement keys: the highlighted block of text is bounded by the cursor's initial location and its current location. When the desired block of text is highlighted, you leave the selection mode by using the CUT or COPY, or by pressing the backspace or [DEL] key.
- *S=Cancel Selection.* This item cancels the selection mode and allows you to continue editing the document.

The shortcut [CTRL]-[S] is a toggle that alternates between starting and canceling the selection mode.

Because Cut and Copy operations destroy the previous contents of the clipboard, do not attempt to cut or copy more than one section at a time. Only the most recently cut or copied section of text is remembered.

Find Menu

To locate a particular pattern of text and (optionally) to replace it with another pattern of text, you use the Find menu. First, you must tell TriPac the *search phrase,* which is the pattern of text to be located, and the *replacement phrase,*

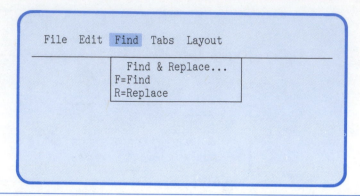

Figure D.9 *The Find menu is used to search for a word or phrase and, optionally, to replace it with another word or phrase.*

which is the replacement for the search phrase. Then you can repeatedly use the FIND command to locate and highlight occurrences of the search phrase. Finally, the REPLACE command allows you to substitute the replacement phrase for a highlighted occurrence of the search phrase.

As Figure D.9 shows, the options in the Find menu are

- *Find & Replace.* Choosing this item causes a dialog box to appear, in which you can enter the search phrase and the replacement phrase.

- *F=Find.* Each time this item is selected, the next occurrence of the search phrase is located and highlighted in the document. The search proceeds from the cursor's position to the end of the document; then it automatically resumes at the beginning of the document and continues until it reaches the cursor's original position.

- *R=Replace.* This item removes the highlighted occurrence of the search phrase and replaces it with the replacement phrase.

Suppose you want to find all occurrences of ''John'' and replace them with ''Jon'' in the letter written by Mary Smith in Figure 5.1. First, select Find & Replace by pulling down the Find menu. In the dialog box that appears, enter the search phrase ''John'' and the replacement phrase ''Jon.''

```
Find what text? John [TAB]
Replace text: Jon [ENTER]
```

Notice that the [TAB] key is used to move from field to field of the dialog box. The [ENTER] key is used to signal that you are finished with the dialog box.

After you have entered the search and replacement phrases, you must give separate commands for each find operation and each replace operation. The best way to do this is with the shortcut commands [CTRL]-[F] and [CTRL]-[R].

[CTRL]-[F] locates and highlights the first occurrence of "John," and [CTRL]-[R] causes "John" to be replaced with "Jon." To replace "John" with "Jon" throughout the letter, you must give these two commands repeatedly.

Tabs Menu

Setting tabs enables you to use the [TAB] key while typing to skip to a predetermined column. You can set as many tab stops as you want. As Figure D.10 shows, there are just two options in the Tabs menu.

■ *T=Set*. This item sets a tab stop at the cursor's current column position. The tab setting is shown as a small tick mark immediately under the menu-bar line. Thus, to set a tab stop, you should first place the cursor in the column where you want the tab, then press [CTRL]-[T].

■ *T=Clear*. To clear a tab setting, you can either select this item from the menu or press [CTRL]-[T] a second time. The cursor must be at the column to be "untabbed."

Layout Menu

Figure D.11 shows the Layout menu. It controls the layout of a printed document; it does not affect the layout of the document on the screen. You can use it to insert page breaks, or to choose single- or double-spacing, or to enter text for headers and footers, which are lines of text at the top and bottom of each printed page.

■ *Single Spaced/Double Spaced*. These two items control whether the document will be single- or double-spaced when it is printed. Regardless of your choice, the document will be single-spaced on the screen.

Figure D.10 *The Tabs menu is used to set and clear tab stops that mark where the cursor will stop when the [TAB] key is pressed.*

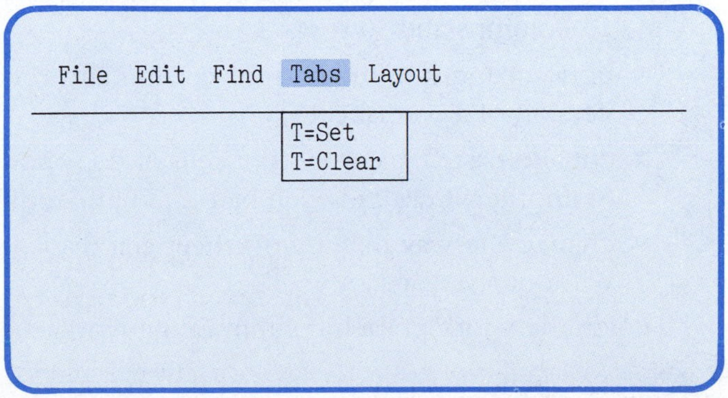

```
  File   Edit   Find   Tabs   Layout
                      ┌─────────┐
                      │ T=Set   │
                      │ T=Clear │
                      └─────────┘
```

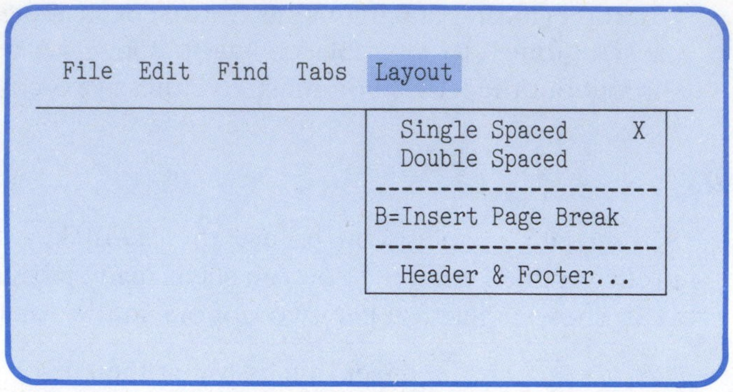

```
  File  Edit  Find  Tabs  Layout

                       ┌────────────────────────┐
                       │  Single Spaced      X   │
                       │  Double Spaced          │
                       │  ──────────────────     │
                       │  B=Insert Page Break    │
                       │  ──────────────────     │
                       │  Header & Footer...     │
                       └────────────────────────┘
```

Figure D.11 *The Layout menu is used to control the appearance of the printed document.*

- *B=Insert Page Break.* This item is used to insert a page break where one would not otherwise occur. The page break is inserted at the position where the cursor is located when the command is given.

- *Header & Footer.* When you select this item from the Layout menu, a dialog box appears requesting the text of the header and footer lines. Although you enter the text for the header and footer lines only once, the word processor will print them on each page. To include page numbers in headers and footers, you place the "#" symbol in the header or footer line where you want the page number to appear. For example, if you want the footers to read "Page 1," "Page 2," and so on, type "Page #" into the dialog box for the footer.

■ Spreadsheet Analysis

With the TriPac spreadsheet program you can

- enter labels, numbers, and arithmetic formulas into a worksheet that has 14 columns and 30 rows.

- undo changes to the current version and revert to the previously saved version of a worksheet.

- cut and paste the contents of cells or copy and paste them from one place to another. Cells can even be pasted into a different worksheet.

- change the way that a worksheet cell displays its value, such as with or without a dollar sign.

- set the width of each column in the worksheet.

To open a worksheet, you use the cursor-movement keys to highlight the worksheet's file name in the SPREADSHEETS column of the desktop. Then you can use the shortcut [CTRL]-[O] method to open the worksheet and start the spreadsheet program. The desktop menu bar will be replaced by the spreadsheet program's menu bar as shown in Figure D.12. The body of the screen will show the upper-left corner of the worksheet; you can use the cursor-movement keys to scroll to other parts of the worksheet.

Entering a Sample Worksheet

In this section we describe how to enter, edit, format, and print a sample worksheet. For example, assume you want to enter the worksheet shown in Figure 7.2 into a new file called SALES. To create a new worksheet, you will begin by opening an "untitled" or empty worksheet file. Select the SPREADSHEETS column, and then press the down-arrow key until an "untitled" worksheet file is highlighted on the screen. Now press [ESC] to toggle to the menu bar from the desktop. The File option on the menu bar should be highlighted, indicating that it is selected. To create the worksheet, press the down-arrow key to pull down the File menu and press [ENTER] to select the

Figure D.12 *A typical screen from the spreadsheet application. At the top of the screen is the spreadsheet menu bar. The body of the screen shows a portion of the worksheet in memory.*

```
  File  Edit  Layout                        Spreadsheet: Sample Budget

 A1        Budget for:                                          Text
              A            B         C         D        E
  1        Budget for:
  2
  3                     One-time   Monthly    Annual
  4        --------------------------------------------------
  5     Monthly Expenses
  6
  7            Rent      600.00    600.00    7800.00
  8        Utilities     200.00    200.00    2600.00
  9        Telephone      60.00     60.00     780.00
 10             Food                200.00    2400.00
 11             Car      425.00    215.00    3005.00
 12             Gas                  50.00     600.00
 13        --------------------------------------------------
 14        Total Expense 1285.00   1325.00   17185.00
 15        --------------------------------------------------
 16        Net Income    1000.00   1250.00   16000.00
 17        --------------------------------------------------
 18     Savings or -Loss -285.00    -75.00   -1185.00
 19        --------------------------------------------------
 20
```

O = Open item. After you press [ENTER], a dialog box will appear asking you to name the new worksheet.

```
Name for new spreadsheet: SALES [ENTER]
```

After a pause while a new file is created on the disk, a blank worksheet will appear on the screen. Initially cell A1 is the *active cell;* that is, it is the highlighted cell available for immediate use or modification. At the top of the screen is the spreadsheet program's menu bar; immediately below it is the *edit line.* The left side of the edit line tells you the coordinates of the active cell; it currently says A1. The right side of the edit line tells you whether the active cell is a label, number, or formula; at present, it says *empty.* The edit line allows you to enter data into the worksheet.

You can move the active-cell marker around the worksheet with the cursor-movement keys. If you try to move the active-cell marker off the edge of the screen, the screen will scroll to another portion of the worksheet. Because the worksheet is relatively small, it does not take long to scroll to its edges. The columns are labeled from A through N; the rows range from 1 to 30.

To enter a label, number, or formula into the active cell, you simply type the entry into the edit line and press [ENTER]. When [ENTER] is pressed, the entry is transferred from the edit line and replaces the previous contents of the active cell (if any). With this description you should be able to enter the labels shown in column A and row 1 of Figure 7.2.

Some labels may not be lined up in their cells the way you want. For example, all entries are right-justified by default, but the labels for column A are supposed to be left-justified. Later in this chapter we describe how you can change the way the active cell is justified by using the Layout menu. Notice that the Layout menu affects the active cell. If you want to change the format of a region of cells, you should use the Edit menu to highlight the region, and then use the Layout menu to specify the region's format rule. Cells can be formatted before or after they are given entries.

Both column B and column C of Figure 7.2 contain numeric data, but column D contains formulas. A formula is entered by typing an equal sign followed by an expression involving numbers and cell names. The equal sign tells the spreadsheet that the cell is going to contain a formula rather than a label or a number. For example, the formulas for computing Sales in cells D2, D3, and D4 are

```
=B2 * C2
=B3 * C3
=B4 * C4
```

The value that appears in each cell is the result of using the formula (a number), not the formula itself. You must enter the formula for each cell individually. If you were using a commercial spreadsheet program, you could use a copy-and-paste operation to replicate the formula from cell D2 into cells D3 and D4. This would save you the time and effort of entering three formulas.

The total sales can be calculated by either of two formulas: $=D2+D3+D4$ or $=D2:D4$. The second method adds a range of cells.

Formulas in the TriPac spreadsheet are limited to simple arithmetic operators: + for addition, – for subtraction, / for division, and * for multiplication. The spreadsheet does not have built-in functions for calculating logarithms, standard deviations, or other functions typical of commercial spreadsheet programs.

When you have finished entering the worksheet, use the items on the File menu to print and save the worksheet. The item Quit Spreadsheet automatically saves the worksheet to the disk before it returns control to the desktop manager. When the desktop reappears, your new worksheet will be listed as SALES. In the following sections we provide more details on the operation of each menu item in the spreadsheet.

File Menu

The File menu shown in Figure D.13 is used to save the worksheet on the disk, print it, copy the disk version of the worksheet into memory, and exit from the spreadsheet to the desktop manager. Use the [ESC] key to activate the menu bar; then use the up- and down-arrow keys to highlight the particular menu item you want. Pressing the [ENTER] key selects the highlighted item. Pressing the [ESC] key a second time cancels the selection and returns the cursor to the body of the document.

■ *Save Spreadsheet.* While you are editing a worksheet, it resides in memory where you can view it and make changes. When you want to make these changes permanent, use the Save item to copy the version in memory to the disk file named in the upper-right corner of the screen.

Figure D.13 *The File menu is used to save, print, or abandon the worksheet as well as to exit from the spreadsheet to the desktop manager.*

```
File  Edit  Layout
  ┌─────────────────────────────┐
  │  Save Spreadsheet            │
  │  Print Spreadsheet...        │
  │ --------------------------   │
  │  Revert to Last Version...   │
  │ --------------------------   │
  │  Quit Spreadsheet            │
  └─────────────────────────────┘
```

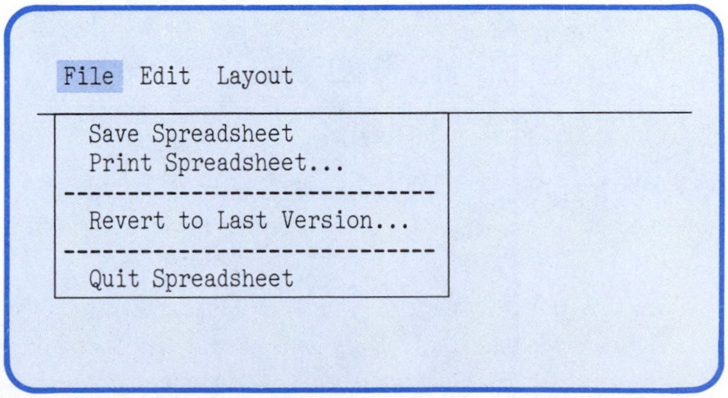

■ *Print Spreadsheet.* This item prints the worksheet on the printer.

■ *Revert to Last Version.* This item causes the version of the worksheet in memory to be erased and replaced by the earlier version on the disk. Use this item if you want to throw away changes made since the last time the worksheet was saved.

■ *Quit Spreadsheet.* This item saves the worksheet in memory on the disk and then exits from the spreadsheet to the desktop manager.

Edit Menu

The Edit menu is used to select cells to be removed, duplicated, relocated, or reformatted (see Figure D.14). First, you select the cells to be manipulated; then you either Cut, Copy, or Paste them, or use commands in the Layout menu to change their format. Keep in mind that cell references are absolute, not relative. This means that the cell references in a formula are not adjusted when the formula is copied from one location in the worksheet to another. If they need to be adjusted, you must do so manually.

■ *X=Cut.* The selected cell or cells are removed from the worksheet in memory and written on the clipboard so that they can be pasted elsewhere.

■ *C=Copy.* The selected cell or cells are copied onto the clipboard. This item allows you to duplicate portions of your worksheet or to move a copy of cells to another application.

■ *P=Paste.* The cells in the clipboard are pasted into the worksheet beginning at the current active cell.

■ *S=Start Selecting.* This item causes the spreadsheet to shift into a selection mode that allows you to highlight a block of cells to be transferred to the clipboard. You do this with the cursor-movement keys: the highlighted block of text is bounded by the current active cell and the location of the

Figure D.14 *The Edit menu is used to control the operation of the clipboard.*

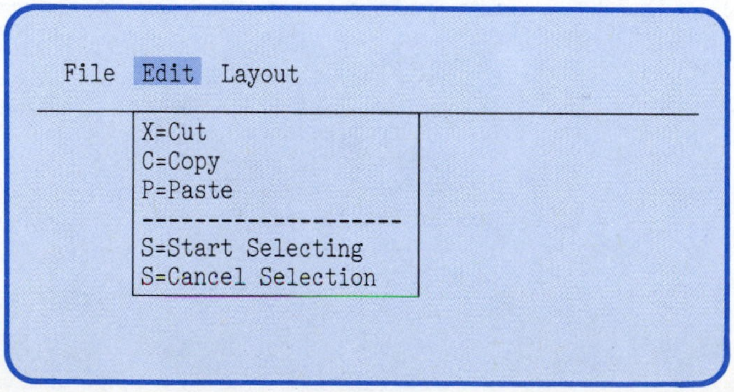

```
File  Edit  Layout

     X=Cut
     C=Copy
     P=Paste
     --------------------
     S=Start Selecting
     S=Cancel Selection
```

active cell when the selection mode began. When the desired block of cells is highlighted, you leave the selection mode by using the Cut or Copy operation to transfer the contents of the cells to the clipboard.

- *S = Cancel Selection*. This item cancels the selection mode and allows you to continue editing the worksheet.

The shortcut [CTRL]-[S] is a toggle that alternates between starting and canceling the selection mode.

Because Cut and Copy operations destroy the previous contents of the clipboard, do not attempt to cut or copy multiple sections. Only the most recently cut or copied section of text is remembered.

Layout Menu

The Layout menu lets you adjust the format rules that determine how the values in cells will appear on the screen. It is also used to change the width of the columns in the worksheet. As Figure D.15 shows, the options in the menu are

- *Decimal Place* and *No Decimal Place*. These menu items allow you to specify the number of digits that should appear to the right of a decimal point. If No Decimal Place is selected, the cell displays a whole number.
- *Dollar Sign*. This item determines whether a number will be preceded by a dollar sign. If it is not selected, numbers are displayed without dollar signs. You must select this item for all cells you want to contain dollar signs. This item is a toggle; that is, if you select it a second time, the dollar sign will disappear.
- *L = Left Align, M = Middle Align,* and *R = Right Align*. These menu items determine whether the contents of the cell will be aligned at the left, the right, or the center of a cell. The shortcut method allows you to format the active cell more quickly by typing [CTRL]-[L], [CTRL]-[M], or [CTRL]-[R].

Figure D.15 *The Layout menu is used to control the appearance of a single cell.*

```
 File  Edit  Layout

              Decimal Place...
              No Decimal Place
              Dollar Sign
              -------------------
              L=Left Align
              M=Middle Align
              R=Right Align
              -------------------
              Column Width...
```

■ *Column Width.* Each column of the worksheet can be made wider or narrower. Selecting this item will cause a dialog box to appear asking how many characters wide the column should be.

As an example, look again at Figure 7.2. The second column includes the numbers 12,500, 6,700, and 9,000. To enter these numbers into the worksheet, you should type them without commas, as in 12500, 6700, and 9000. They will be displayed with two zeros after the decimal place, as in 12500.00, 6700.00, and 9000.00. You can adjust the appearance of numbers by using the Layout menu. If you choose the No Decimal Place item from the Layout menu, the numbers appear as 12500, 6700, and 9000. There is no way to format numbers to have embedded commas, such as 12,500.

■ Record Management

With the TriPac record manager you can

- enter, edit, and print records stored in a database.[2] Each database may have about 50 records; each record may have 10 fields; and each field may have up to 20 characters.
- undo changes to the current version of the database and revert to the previously saved version.
- cut and paste records from the database or copy and paste records in order to move them into a word processing document. Text from the other two applications cannot be pasted into a database from the clipboard.
- add new records to the database and modify the contents of existing records.
- find records matching certain criteria such as being equal to, not equal to, or less than a specified value in a field.
- sort records in ascending or descending order on any of the fields in the database.
- set up and view the structure of each record.

To open an existing database, you use the cursor-movement keys to highlight the name of a file in the DATABASES column of the desktop. Then you can use the shortcut [CTRL]-[O] method to open the database and start the record manager. The desktop menu bar will be replaced by the record manager's menu bar as shown in Figure D.16. The body of the screen will show the first records in the database being edited; you can use the cursor-movement keys and the [PgDn] and [PgUp] keys to scroll through the database.

[2]Although *database* is more commonly defined as a collection of data files, in this section we will use the term *database* to refer to a single record management file. This usage has been adopted by vendors of record management programs in order to give their programs more stature.

```
  File  Edit  Search  Layout                    Database: Computer Comparisons
  _____

   |Make        |Model       |Type        |Memory Size|Price    |Remarks
 → |Digital     |8600        |Minicomputer|  32000000 |  970000 |Supermini 4.
   |HP          |3000        |Minicomputer|   8000000 |  166100 |Traditional
   |IBM         |3081K       |Mainframe   |  32000000 | 4260000 |Large-scale
   |Apple       |IIe         |Personal    |    128000 |     995 |Transportabl
   |IBM         |System 38   |Minicomputer|   8000000 |  252900 |High-end min
   |Grid        |Gridcase 3  |Personal    |    512000 |    4350 |Portable
   |Sperry      |1100/90     |Mainframe   |  16000000 | 3135660 |Large-scale
   |Tandy       |Model 200   |Personal    |     72000 |    1500 |Portable
   |Prime       |9950        |Minicomputer|  16000000 |  320000 |Supermini 2.
   |HP          |Touchscreen |Personal    |    640000 |    6000 |IBM Compatib
   |Compaq      |286         |Personal    |    640000 |    6299 |Transportabl
   |IBM         |3031        |Mainframe   |   8000000 | 1338000 |Medium-sized
   |Apollo      |Domain      |Minicomputer|   3500000 |   80000 |High-end min
   |IBM         |S-370/158   |Mainframe   |   2000000 |  488000 |Older mainfr
   |Prime       |9995        |Minicomputer|  16000000 |  400000 |Supermini 4
   |Apple       |Macintosh   |Personal    |    512000 |    2495 |User friendl
   |IBM         |3090        |Mainframe   |  64000000 | 5000000 |IBMs Top of
   |Amdahl      |5840        |Mainframe   |  16000000 | 2500000 |Large-scale
```

Figure D.16 *A typical screen from the record management application. At the top of the screen is the record management menu bar. The body of the screen shows a portion of the "database" (the file of records) in memory.*

Entering a Sample Database

In this section we describe how to enter, edit, format, and print a sample database. For example, assume that you want to create a database called SUBSCRIBERS that contains the magazine subscription list described in Chapter 9. To create a new database, you follow the same basic procedure that you use to edit an existing database, except that you begin by highlighting an "untitled" database. Then press [ESC] to toggle to the menu bar from the desktop. The File option on the menu bar should be highlighted. To create the database, press the down-arrow key to pull down the File menu and press [ENTER] to select the O = Open item. After you press [ENTER], a dialog box will appear asking you to enter the name of the new database.

```
        Name for new database: Subscribers [ENTER]
```

There will be a noticeable pause while a new file is created on the disk and the record manager is copied into memory. The record manager's menu bar will appear at the top of the screen, and the body of the screen will go blank.

Before you can enter data into a new database, you must specify what the structure of each record looks like—in other words, the number of fields in each record and the name and type of each field. Thus, whenever you create a new database, you must use the Layout menu to describe the structure of the database's records before you can use the Edit menu to add records to the database.

Because your first task is to describe how each record will look, you should select the Define Record Structure item from the Layout menu. A dialog box will appear with the following prompts:

```
Field 1 Name:          Type: Text 20
Field 2 Name:          Type: Text 20
Field 3 Name:          Type: Text 20
Field 4 Name:          Type: Text 20
        .                      .
        .                      .
        .                      .
Field 10 Name:         Type: Text 20
```

As these prompts indicate, each record in the database can contain up to 10 fields and each field can be up to 20 characters long.

At this point you enter the names of the fields into the dialog box, using the [TAB] key to move from one prompt in the dialog box to another. For each field you must also select the *field type,* which determines the field's size and whether the field holds textual or numeric information. For example, the following choices would be appropriate for the subscription list:

```
Field 1 Name: NAME [TAB]        Type: Text 20 [TAB]
Field 2 Name: ADDRESS [TAB]     Type: Text 20 [TAB]
Field 3 Name: ZIP [TAB]         Type: Text 8 [TAB]
Field 4 Name: BALANCE [TAB]     Type: ####.## [TAB]
Field 5 Name: [ENTER]
```

The field types for the ZIP and BALANCE fields are different from the default type of "Text 20." When the cursor is tabbed to the "Type: " prompt for ZIP, you can view all the options for the field type by pressing the space bar. Each time you press the space bar, the option for the field type will change: in order of appearance, the options are Text 20, ####.##, ###.###, #######, Text 2, Text 4, Text 8, and Text 12. Then the series will repeat itself. Keep pressing the space bar until the field type you want appears; then press [TAB] to select it and move to the next prompt in the dialog box.

To acknowledge that you have entered all of the field names and types, press the [ENTER] key. The dialog box then disappears, and the field names are shown as column headings immediately below the menu bar. Before you press the [ENTER] key, you should check the record structure carefully. If you discover an error, you can use the [SHIFT]-[TAB] combination to move back to the item in error and then edit it.

You can return to the Define Record Structure item of the Layout menu to change the structure of the database at any time. But after data is entered into the database, changing the record structure erases all the data in the database.

To enter records into the database, you will use the Add a New Record item of the Edit menu. Suppose, for example, you want to add Adams, 123 Main, 86501, and 10.00 to the first row. Selecting the Add a New Record item causes a dialog box to appear containing prompts for each field.

```
NAME: Adams [TAB]
ADDRESS: 123 Main [TAB]
ZIP: 86501 [TAB]
BALANCE: 10.00 [ENTER]
```

After you type an entry, press [TAB] to move to the next prompt. Use [SHIFT]-[TAB] to back up to a previously entered field. When you are through entering data into the record, you press [ENTER]. This causes the newly entered record to be added to the end of the database. The new record will also appear on the screen.

After you have entered a few records, you will notice an arrow-shaped pointer on the left-hand side of the screen; this arrow points to the current record in the file. The up- and down-arrow keys are used to scroll this pointer vertically; they move the cursor from one record to another. If the database's records are too wide to fit on the screen, you can use the left- and right-arrow keys to scroll horizontally.

Now, suppose you want to sort the file into ascending order by the ZIP field. To do so, select Sort Records from the Layout menu. A dialog box appears asking you to define which field is to control the sort operation, as well as which order to use—any order, ascending order, or descending order. The space bar is used to scroll through these options. For example, the dialog

```
NAME:     any order
ADDRESS:  any order
ZIP:      Ascending Order
BALANCE:  any order
```

causes the records to be sorted with the smallest zip code first and the largest zip code last.

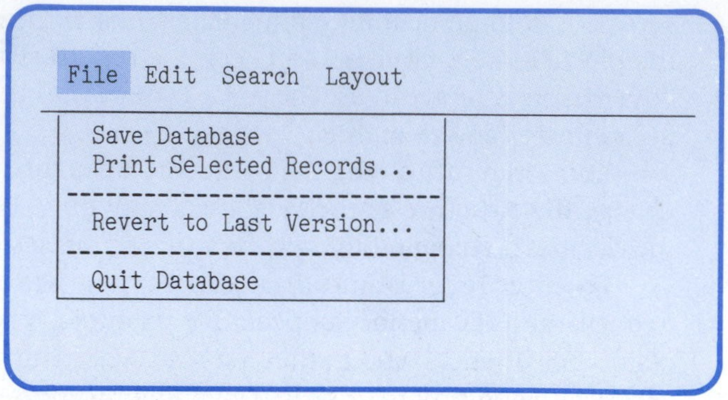

```
  File  Edit  Search  Layout

   Save Database
   Print Selected Records...
   ----------------------------
   Revert to Last Version...
   ----------------------------
   Quit Database
```

Figure D.17 *The File menu is used to save, print, or abandon the database as well as to exit from the record manager to the desktop manager.*

File Menu

The File menu shown in Figure D.17 is used to save the database in memory on the disk, print records, copy the disk version of the database into memory, and exit from the record manager to the desktop manager. Use the [ESC] key to activate the menu bar; then use the up- and down-arrow keys to highlight the particular menu item you want. Pressing the [ENTER] key selects the high-lighted item. Pressing the [ESC] key a second time cancels the selection and returns the cursor to the body of the document.

- *Save Database.* While you are editing a database, it resides in memory where you can view it and make changes. When you want to make these changes permanent, use the Save item to copy the version in memory to the disk file named in the upper-right corner of the screen.

- *Print Selected Records.* This item prints the selected records in the database in the order that they appear on the screen.

- *Revert to Last Version.* This item causes the version of the database in memory to be erased and replaced by the earlier version on the disk. Use this item if you want to throw away the editing changes you have made since the last time the database was saved.

- *Quit Database.* This item saves the database in memory on the disk and then exits from the record manager to the desktop manager.

Edit Menu

The Edit menu controls cut and paste operations and the operations that add a new record on the end of the database and modify an existing record. To perform cut-and-paste operations, the Edit menu works in conjunction with the Search menu. The Search menu is used to select the records to be removed or relocated; then you use the Edit menu to copy or move the selected records to the clipboard. Data cannot be pasted into another database from the clipboard, but the clipboard can be used to copy or move records from a database to a word processing document. Because the cut and copy operations destroy the previous contents of the clipboard, you should not try to cut or copy records repeatedly from the database. Instead, select all records you want to cut or copy, and then collectively copy them to the clipboard. Only the most recently cut or copied records are remembered.

Figure D.18 shows the options in the Edit menu. They are

- *X=Cut.* This item removes the highlighted records from the database and writes them on the clipboard so that they can be pasted into a word processing document. X=Cut removes records permanently; there is no Paste command.

- *C=Copy.* This item copies the selected records into the clipboard.

- *N=Add a New Record.* With this item you can add a new record to the end of the database. Selecting it brings a dialog box to the screen; the box contains a data entry form that shows the field names, followed by blanks for you to fill in with each field's entry. You use the [TAB] key to move from one prompt to the other. When the data entry form is completely filled in, press [ENTER] to add the new record to the end of the database. To add several records to the database, you must select N=Add a New Record repeatedly.

- *E=Edit Current Record.* This item allows you to edit the record pointed at by the arrow in the left-hand margin. Selecting this item activates the same dialog box that is used by the Add a New Record item, but it is already filled out with the current record's data. You use the [TAB] key to move to the fields you want to modify. When all the modifications have been made, press [ENTER] to return the modified record to its place in the database.

Figure D.18 *The Edit menu is used to move records to the clipboard and to add or edit records.*

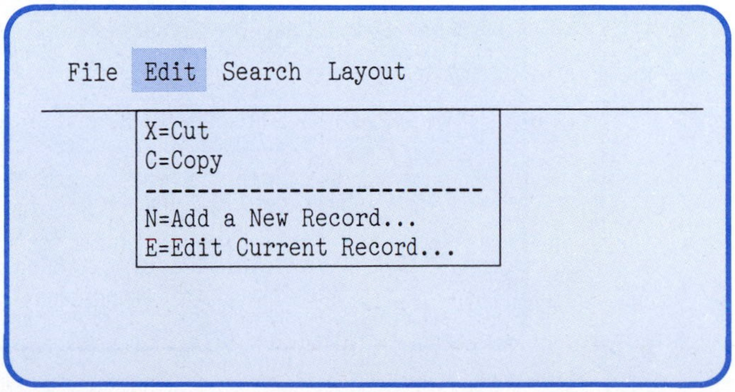

```
   File   Edit   Search   Layout
 _____
 | X=Cut                           |
 | C=Copy                          |
 | ------------------------------- |
 | N=Add a New Record...           |
 | E=Edit Current Record...        |
```

Search Menu

The Search menu is shown in Figure D.19; it lets you select only those records that match certain search conditions. You establish the search conditions by answering the prompts in a dialog box that shows field names on the left-hand side and a list of conditions in the middle. The dialog box for our subscription list database would initially look like

```
NAME          any
ADDRESS       any
ZIP           any
BALANCE       any
```

Pressing the space bar causes the search conditions to scroll through a hidden list of options. The search conditions and their meanings are as follows:

any	Any value in the field matches the search condition.
>=	The field's value matches the search condition if it is greater than or equal to the search value provided by the user.
<=	The field's value matches if it is less than or equal to the search value.
=	The field's value matches if it is equal to the search value.
NOT=	The field's value matches if it is not equal to the search value.
>	The field's value matches if it is greater than the search value.
<	The field's value matches if it is less than the search value.

Suppose you want to print a list of all the subscribers living in areas with zip codes greater than 68000. You begin by choosing the Search & Select item

Figure D.19 *The Search menu is used to select specific records from the data file.*

```
File  Edit  Search  Layout
--------------------------------------
             Search & Select...
             Search & Unselect...
            ---------------------------
             Select Every Record
             Unselect Every Record
            ---------------------------
            S=Select Current Record
            S=Unselect Current Record
```

from the Search menu; this causes the dialog box to appear. Then you tab down to the ZIP field, press the space bar until the > option appears opposite the ZIP field, press [TAB] again to accept the > search condition, and type in 68000 as the search value. The dialog box would now look like

```
NAME          any
ADDRESS       any
ZIP           >        68000
BALANCE       any
```

When you press the [ENTER] key, the dialog box disappears, and then all records that match the criterion ZIP > 68000 will be highlighted. You could print this list by choosing the Print Selected Records item from the File menu.

- *Search & Select*. This operation allows search conditions to be entered into a dialog box, and then selects all records in the database that match the search conditions. The selected records appear on the screen as highlighted rows.

- *Search & Unselect*. This operation works the same as the Search & Select operation except that records that match the search conditions are "unselected"; that is, if the matching records were previously highlighted, they are un-highlighted.

- *Select Every Record*. This operation causes all records in the database to be selected (highlighted). It is useful if you want to select and print all records in the database.

- *Unselect Every Record*. This "unselects" all records in the database, leaving no records highlighted.

- *S = Select Current Record* and *S = Unselect Current Record*. This operation is used to select or unselect the record pointed at by the current-record arrow in the left-hand margin. The shortcut command [CTRL]-[S] toggles between Select and Unselect.

Layout Menu

The Layout menu contains items that specify the layout of the database. It is also used to sort the records into ascending or descending order and to view a list of the field names and field types in the database. The options in the menu are shown in Figure D.20.

- *Sort Records*. Selecting this menu item causes a dialog box to appear asking you to select the sort key (the field that will be used to sort the database) and to choose whether to sort the file in ascending or descending order. When the dialog box appears, press [TAB] until the pointer highlights the

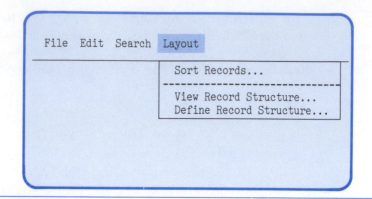

Figure D.20 *The Layout menu is used to sort records and to view or define the names and width of fields in the file.*

sort criterion for the field you want to specify as the sort key. Then press the space bar to cycle through the following options:

■ *Any.* This option should be used for all the fields that are not sort keys.

■ *Ascending.* This field's values are placed in ascending order.

■ *Descending.* This field's values are placed in descending order.

When you press [ENTER], the dialog box disappears and the database is displayed in the order you specified.

■ *View Record Structure.* This item displays a dialog box listing the field names and field types of the database.

■ *Define Record Structure.* When you create a new database, you must first use this item to define the record structure. The name and type of each field is entered into a dialog box. Each record can have up to ten fields, and each field can be given a name and type. The type is obtained by cycling through the following textual and numeric options:

■ *Text fields* can be 2, 4, 8, 12, or 20 characters wide.

■ *Numeric fields* are 7 characters wide and use one of these three field formats: *######*, *####.##*, and *###.###*.

Changing the structure of an existing TriPac database causes the record manager to erase all information previously stored in the database. In effect, a TriPac database cannot be restructured after it contains data.

Exercises

1. Create a document file called JOHN and enter the letter shown in Figure 5.1 into the document. Can you format the letter so that it appears as shown in Figure 5.1? Is it possible to insert paragraph markers after the letter has been entered? How would you duplicate the first paragraph of this letter?

2. Create a worksheet document like the one shown in Figure 7.2.

   a. Add a column of formulas that project next year's sales by multiplying the sales in column D by 1.1.

   b. Add a new row to the worksheet with the following data:

        Shoes   8500   49.95

   Insert the formulas for the Sales and Projection columns and modify the formula for computing the Total Sales.

   c. Use the Layout menu to add two decimal places to all cells containing dollars and cents. Decrease the width of column A. What happens when the width is decreased to four characters?

3. Use the record manager component of TriPac to create the subscriptions file shown in Figure 9.1.

   a. Enter the seven records shown in Chapter 9, and then sort these records into ascending order by NAME. Print the database.

   b. Use the Search menu to locate all records in the database that contain a zip code greater than 55000. What is displayed on the screen?

   c. Sort the records into ascending order by the zip code. Save the database. Now sort the database in ascending order by BALANCE. What happens when you choose the Revert to Last Version item from the File menu? What happens if you simply choose the Quit Database item from the File menu and then open the same database a second time? Have the records been reordered in either case?

4. Copy the database described in problem 3 into the document described in problem 1 and print the resulting document.

5. Copy the worksheet described in problem 2 into the document described in problem 1 and print the resulting document.

6. Use the spreadsheet to build a grade book as follows:

   > Column A: Student Name
   > Column B: First Midterm Grade (as a percentage)
   > Column C: Second Midterm Grade
   > Column D: Final Exam Grade
   > Column E: Total Scores
   > Cell F10: Average Class Score

   Leave room for nine students in the worksheet. Use your worksheet to compute the class average for an imaginary class of nine students.

7. Use the record manager to build a "Gradebook" database containing the following fields in each record:

```
Name   :          Text 20
Mid1   :          ######
Mid2   :          ######
Final  :          ######
```

Discuss the difficulty of computing a class average from the contents of this file (assuming the file contains the scores for a single class). How might a database management system be used to compute the class average? How is a record manager different from a database management system in terms of the ability to calculate new values from values stored in different records?

8. Use the word processor to write a letter to the admissions department of your school. Print the letter, sign it, and give it to your instructor.

9. Construct an experiment to determine the maximum size of a document.

bibliography

Along with the Information Age has come an explosion of printed literature. Most of the writing in the computer field is hastily completed in a legitimate effort to publish ideas before they become obsolete. Much of it is poor; some is excellent. Even the excellent writing will often cover something you already know, don't care about, or don't yet have the background to understand. Your best defense is to approach everything with skepticism. Begin more articles and books than you finish.

■ Magazines

Business Software (monthly). P.O. Box 27975, San Diego, CA 92128.
"The Computer Magazine for Power Users."

Byte (monthly). 70 Main St., Peterborough, NH 03458.
"The Small Systems Journal." Best-selling microcomputer journal; technical emphasis.

ComputerWorld (weekly). 375 Cochituate Road, Box 880, Framingham, MA 01701.
"The Newsweekly for the Computer Community." Emphasizes large computer systems.

Datamation (twice monthly). 875 Third Ave., New York, NY 10022.
Written for data processing professionals. Sent free to qualified subscribers.

inCider (monthly). P.O. Box 911, Farmingdale, NY 11737.
>   "The Apple II Journal."

InfoWorld (weekly). 1060 Marsh Road, Suite C-200, Menlo Park, CA 94025.
>   "The Newsweekly for Microcomputer Users." Hardware and software reviews.

LOTUS: Computing for Managers and Professionals (monthly). One Broadway, Cambridge, MA 02142.
>   Emphasizes spreadsheet processing.

MICRO Communications (monthly). 500 Howard St., San Francisco, CA 94105.
>   "The Personal Computer Communications Magazine." Sent free to qualified subscribers.

PC: The Independent Guide to IBM Personal Computers (twice monthly). PC Communications Corp., One Park Ave., New York, NY 10016.
>   The same company also publishes *PC Tech Journal* for more technical issues and *PC Disk Magazine,* which distributes programs on disk each month.

PC World (monthly). PC World Communications, Inc., 555 De Haro St., San Francisco, CA 94107.
>   "The Personal Computer Magazine for IBM PCs and Compatibles." The same company also publishes *Macworld* for Macintosh users.

Popular Computing (monthly). P.O. Box 328, Hancock, NH 03449.
>   Introductory, general articles on personal computing.

■ Information Utilities/Database Services

CompuServe. 5000 Arlington Centre Boulevard, Columbus, OH 43220. (800) 848-8990, or in Ohio (614) 457-8650.
>   A general-purpose information utility, available from 6 P.M. to 5 A.M. weekdays, all day Saturday and Sunday.

Dow Jones News/Retrieval. P.O. Box 300, Princeton, NJ 08540. (800) 257-5114, or in New Jersey or Canada (609) 452-1511.
>   News includes the *Wall Street Journal;* good financial and investment coverage.

Knowledge-Index. Dialog Information Services, Inc., 3460 Hillview Ave., Palo Alto, CA 94304. (800) 227-5510; in California (415) 858-3796.
>   Computerized searching of over 4 million descriptions of articles, reports, and books. Over 10,000 journals indexed.

MCI Mail. Box 1001, 1900 M St. N.W., Washington, DC 20036. (800) MCI-2255.
>   "The Nation's New Postal System." An electronic mail system; allows access to the Dow Jones News/Retrieval.

The Source. 1616 Anderson Road, McLean, VA 22102. (800) 336-3366.
>   "America's Information Utility."

Western Union's EasyLink Service. Western Union Telegraph Company, One Lake St., Upper Saddle River, NJ 07458. (800) 527-5184, or in Texas (800) 442-4803.
>   An electronic mail system. Allows convenient access to the Telex network and letters delivered by the United States Postal Service.

■ Part I   World of Computing

General sources about computing, hardware, and software.

Datapro on Microcomputers. Datapro Research Corporation, Delran, N.J.
> An expensive, two-volume collection aimed at corporate and professional personal computer users. Comprehensive and constantly updated. Includes surveys and users' reactions to microcomputer products.

Dravnieks, Dzintar E., ed. *IBM Personal Computer Handbook.* And/Or Press, Berkeley, Calif., 1983.
> Periodically updated. A collection of essays on the basics of using an IBM PC followed by a survey of hardware and software available for the machine.

Kroenke, David. *Business Computer Systems: An Introduction.* Mitchell Publishing, Santa Cruz, Calif., 1984.

Lu, Cary. *The Apple Macintosh Book.* Microsoft Press, Bellevue, Wash., 1984.
> General introduction to Apple's innovative personal computer.

Sanders, Donald. *Computers Today.* McGraw-Hill, New York, 1985.
> A popular introduction to data processing textbook.

Stern, Nancy, and Robert A. Stern. *Computers in Society.* Prentice-Hall, Englewood Cliffs, N.J., 1983.

■ Part II   Word Processing

Arca, Julie. *Practical WordStar Uses.* Sybex, Berkeley, Calif., 1983.
> Much clearer than the manuals published by MicroPro.

Fluegelman, Andrew, and Jeremy Hewes. *Writing in the Computer Age.* Anchor Press/Doubleday, Garden City, N.Y., 1983.
> Good advice from two well-known authors for adapting your writing style to word processing.

Stern, Fred. *Word Processing and Beyond.* John Muir Publications, Santa Fe, N.M., 1984.
> A general introduction to word processing.

Waite, Mitchell, and Julie Arca. *Word Processing Primer.* Byte Books, Peterborough, N.H., 1982.

■ Part III   Electronic Spreadsheets

Anderson, Dick, and Douglas Cobb. *1-2-3 Tips, Tricks, and Traps.* Que Corporation, Indianapolis, Minn., 1984.
> Advanced topics in using Lotus 1-2-3.

LeBlond, Geoffrey, and Douglas Cobb. *Using 1-2-3.* Que Corporation, Indianapolis, Minn., 1983.
> In-depth, understandable coverage of how to use Lotus 1-2-3.

Trost, Stanley, and Charles Pomernacki. *VisiCalc for Science and Engineering*. Sybex, Berkeley, Calif., 1983.

> Complete templates for sixty-two scientific problems—from determining the characteristics of coaxial cables in communications to calculating the image distance and magnification of a compound set of two thin lenses.

Williams, Andrew. *What If? A User's Guide to Spreadsheets on the IBM PC*. Wiley Press, New York, 1984.

> An excellent introduction based on Context MBA, Lotus 1-2-3, Multiplan, SuperCalc, and VisiCalc.

Wolverton, Van. *VisiCalc Advanced Version: Worksheets for Business*. VisiPress, San Jose, Calif., 1983.

> Numerous good examples of spreadsheet applications for business.

■ Part IV   Data Management

Codd, E. F. "Relational Database: A Practical Foundation for Productivity." *Communications of the ACM,* 25 (February 1982), 109–117.

Date, Chris. *An Introduction to Database Systems*. Addison-Wesley, Reading, Mass., 1981.

Kroenke, David. *Database Processing: Fundamentals, Design, Implementation*. SRA, Chicago, 1983.

> Traditional textbook coverage of database processing with an emphasis on relational models.

Kruglinski, David. *Data Base Management Systems*. Osborne/McGraw-Hill, Berkeley, Calif., 1983.

■ Part V   Application Areas

Sources of information on miscellaneous applications including communications, graphics, and vertical market software.

Artwick, Bruce. *Applied Concepts in Microcomputer Graphics*. Prentice-Hall, Englewood Cliffs, N.J., 1984.

> A well-written, comprehensive book that focuses on the technical information needed to work with and design graphic systems.

Cane, Mike. *The Computer Phone Book*. New American Library, New York, 1983.

> A guide to the public access bulletin boards; descriptions of 450 of them.

Glossbrenner, Alfred. *The Complete Handbook of Personal Computer Communications*. St. Martin's Press, New York, 1983.

> Primarily a "how-to" book for using telecommunications; emphasis on using information utilities.

Lambert, Steve. *Online: A Guide to America's Leading Information Services*. Microsoft Press, Bellevue, Wash., 1985.

> Explains the basics of using information utilities.

Nilles, Jack. *Micros and Modems: Telecommunicating with Personal Computers*. Reston Publishing, Reston, Va., 1983.
> Emphasizes the nuts and bolts of communications hardware and software.

Shapiro, Neil. *The Small Computer Connection: Telecommunications for the Home and Office*. A Micro Text/McGraw-Hill Copublication, New York, 1983.
> Emphasizes hardware and how the data is moved electrically.

The Source: User's Manual, 1985. Source Telecomputing Corporation, McLean, Va.
> Published annually. Well-written guide to The Source. Comes free with a new membership to The Source; can also be purchased separately.

Stanton, Jeffrey, et al. *The Addison-Wesley Book of Apple Software 1984*. The Book Company, Los Angeles, 1984.
> Published annually; full of one- to two-page reviews written by a large group of reviewers. Books like this one are a good first place to look when buying software. Even the "just-curious" will find them worth a quick perusal.

Tanenbaum, Andrew. *Computer Networks*. Prentice-Hall, Englewood Cliffs, N.J., 1981.

Wells, Robert, et al. *The Addison-Wesley Book of IBM Software 1984*. The Book Company, Los Angeles, 1984.

■ Part VI Developing New Systems

Sources on designing, programming, and purchasing computer systems.

Ackoff, Russell L. "Management Misinformation Systems." *Management Science*, 14, No. 4, 147–156.
> A classic statement of the ways a computerized information system can go awry.

Boehm, Barry W. *Software Engineering Economics*. Prentice-Hall, Englewood Cliffs, N.J., 1981.
> A careful analysis of the factors that affect the costs of developing computer programs.

Brooks, Fredrick P., Jr. *The Mythical Man-Month*. Addison-Wesley, Reading, Mass., 1975.
> An in-depth treatment of the problems associated with developing complex computer programs.

Dijkstra, Edsger. *A Discipline of Programming*. Prentice-Hall, Englewood Cliffs, N.J., 1976.
> An important book by the father of structured programming.

Glossbrenner, Alfred. *How to Buy Software*. St. Martin's Press, New York, 1984.
> Description of all steps in purchasing software—locating programs and software reviews, putting a program through its paces, and so forth.

Knuth, Donald. *The Art of Computer Programming*. Addison-Wesley, Reading, Mass., 1973.
> A classical reference that presented the first comprehensive treatment of data structures and introduced the analysis of algorithms.

Kruse, Robert. *Data Structures and Program Design*. Prentice-Hall, Englewood Cliffs, N.J., 1984.
> Assumes that the reader has an elementary knowledge of Pascal.

Lucas, Henry. *The Analysis, Design and Implementation of Information Systems*. McGraw-Hill, New York, 1981.

Martin, James. *Application Development without Programmers*. Prentice-Hall, Englewood Cliffs, N.J., 1982.

　　Makes a persuasive argument for the use of nonprocedural languages.

Martin, James, and Bonnie Walker. *Diagramming Techniques for Analysts and Programmers*. Prentice-Hall, Englewood Cliffs, N.J., 1985.

　　In-depth and oriented toward the practicing professional.

Yourdon, Edward, and Larry Constantine. *Structured Design*. Yourdon Press, New York, 1978.

■ Part VII　Computers and Us

Sources on piracy, privacy, and social issues of personal computing.

Baker, Richard. *Scuttle the Computer Pirates Software Protection Schemes*. Tab Books, Bule Ridge Summit, Pa., 1984.

　　Discussion of software piracy and what legal steps can be taken to thwart pirates. Valuable appendix with proposed regulations, software laws, patents, rights, and license agreements.

Bauer, F. L., and H. Wossner. "The Plankalkul of Konrad Zuse: A Forerunner of Today's Programming Languages." *Communications of the Association for Computing Machinery,* 15 (July 1972), 678–685.

　　Description of the notational system developed by Konrad Zuse in 1945 for expressing data processing problems. His system contained many features that are standard in modern programming languages.

Computer Crime: Electronic Fund Transfer Systems and Crime. Bureau of Justice Statistics, U.S. Department of Justice, U.S. Government Printing Office, Washington, D.C., 1982.

　　Identifies the types of EFT crimes and how they relate to EFT technologies.

Denning, Peter. "Moral Clarity in the Computer Age." *Communications of the Association for Computing Machinery,* 26 (October 1983), 709–710.

　　Condemnation of the actions of computer hackers and the lack of response from the computing profession.

DiNucci, Darcy. "Copying Software: Who's Right?" *PC World,* September 1985, pp. 126–141.

　　Presents both the viewpoints of vendors and purchasers.

Fishman, Katherine Davis. *The Computer Establishment*. McGraw-Hill, New York, 1981.

　　Entertaining account of the history of the major large computer manufacturers, focusing on IBM.

Freiberger, Paul, and Michael Swaine. *Fire in the Valley: The Making of the Personal Computer*. Osborne/McGraw-Hill, Berkeley, 1984.

　　An entertaining treatment of the people and events in the early days of personal computers.

Gillard, Collen, and Jim Smith. "Computer Crime: A Growing Threat." *Byte,* October 1983, pp. 398–424.

　　Background information on cases of personal computer trespass and discussion of technological devices and other steps to prevent trespass.

Graham, Robert L. "The Legal Protection of Computer Systems." *Communications of the Association for Computing Machinery,* 27 (May 1984), 422–426.
> General description of copyright, trade secret, and patent protection of software.

Levering, Robert; Michael Katz; and Milton Moskowitz. *The Computer Entrepreneurs: Who's Making it Big and How in America's Upstart Industry*. New American Library, New York, 1984.
> Entertaining biographical sketches of 65 men and women.

Osborne, Adam. *Running Wild: The Next Industrial Revolution*. Osborne/McGraw-Hill, Berkeley, Calif., 1979.

Papert, Seymour. *Mindstorms: Children, Computers, and Powerful Ideas*. Basic Books, New York, 1981.
> The impact of personal computers on education and thinking; Logo.

Parker, Donn. *Crime by Computer*. Scribner's, New York, 1976.
> A classic discussion of computer crime, including the massive Equity Funding Corporation embezzlement.

Randell, Brian. *The Origins of Digital Computers: Selected Papers*. Springer-Verlag, Berlin, 1973.
> History of computers from Babbage to UNIVAC I; includes papers by computer pioneers such as Babbage, Hollerith, Zuse, von Neumann, and others.

Sprague, R. "A Western View of Computer History." *Communications of the Association for Computing Machinery,* 15 (July 1972), 686–692.
> West Coast companies' account of computer development from 1945 to 1955.

Staines, Anne. "The Data Protection Racquet." *Practical Computing,* September 1985, pp. 70–71.
> A very readable description of the British Data Protection Act of 1984.

Tekla, Perry, and Paul Wallich. "Can Computer Crime be Stopped?" *IEEE Spectrum,* May 1984, pp. 34–45.
> Survey of categories of computer crime. Cites cases and what steps should have been taken to prevent the crime.

credit
lines

C-1

Figures 8–10 Courtesy of Shared Medical System Corporation

Figures 11–13 Courtesy of Apple Computer, Inc.

Figure 14 Courtesy of Commodore Electronics Ltd.

Figures 15, 16 Courtesy of International Business Machines Corporation

Figure 17 Courtesy NCR Corporation

Figure 18 Courtesy of ROLM, an IBM Company

Figure 19 Courtesy of Hewlett-Packard Company

Figure 20 Courtesy of Compugraphic Corporation, Wilmington, Massachusetts

Figure 21 Courtesy of ROLM, an IBM Company

Figures 22–26 Photos courtesy of Atex, Inc., a Kodak Company, of Bedford, Massachusetts

Figures 27–30 Photos courtesy of Intergraph Corporation, Huntsville, Alabama

Figure 31 Pathfinder® printer by Monarch Marking Systems, a subsidiary of Pitney Bowes

Figure 32 Courtesy NCR Corporation

Figure 33 Photograph courtesy of Scope Incorporated, Reston, Virginia

Figures 34, 35 Photos courtesy of Gerber Scientific, Inc.

Figures 36–42 Courtesy of International Business Machines Corporation

Figures 43–47 Photos courtesy of Gerber Scientific, Inc.

Figure 48 Photo: Loral Corporation

Figure 49 Courtesy of Sanders Associates

Figure 50 Photo: Loral Corporation

Figure 51 Courtesy of Sanders Associates

Figure 52 Courtesy of Hewlett-Packard Company

Figure 53 Commodore Electronics Ltd.

Window 2

Figure 1 Photo courtesy of Intergraph Corporation, Huntsville, Alabama

Figures 2–18 Courtesy of International Business Machines Corporation

Figure 19 Courtesy of Memorex Corporation, a Burroughs subsidiary

Figure 20 Photo courtesy Seagate

Figure 21 Courtesy of Memorex Corporation, a Burroughs subsidiary

Figure 22 Courtesy of Storage Technology Corporation © 1984

Figure 23 Photo courtesy Seagate

Figure 24 Courtesy of International Business Machines Corporation

Figure 25 Courtesy of Comdisco, Inc.

Figure 26 Courtesy of Northern Telecom Inc.

Figure 27 Courtesy of Ampex Corporation, one of The Signal Companies, Inc.

Figure 28 Courtesy of Storage Technology Corporation © 1984

Figure 29 Courtesy of TRW Inc.

Window 3

Figure 1 Photo courtesy of C. Itoh Electronics, Inc.

Figure 2 Courtesy of Apple Computer, Inc.

Figure 3 Word Star® is a trademark of MicroPro International Corporation®

Figure 4 Compugraphic Corporation, Wilmington, Massachusetts

Figure 5 Courtesy of International Business Machines Corporation

Figure 6 Courtesy of Hewlett-Packard Company

Figure 7 Courtesy of Texas Instruments

Figure 8 Courtesy of Apple Computer, Inc.

Figure 9 Courtesy of Okidata

Figure 10 Courtesy of Qume Corporation, a subsidiary of ITT

Figure 11 Courtesy Martin Marietta Data Systems

Figures 12, 13 Courtesy of Apple Computer, Inc.

Figure 14 Sweet-P Plotters by Enter Computer, Inc., 6867 Nancy Ridge Drive, San Diego, California 92121. (619) 450-0601

Figure 15 Courtesy of Sanders Associates

Figure 16 Photograph courtesy of Gerber Scientific, Inc.

Figure 17 Courtesy of Versatec, a Xerox Company

Figures 18–20 Photos courtesy of Gerber Scientific, Inc.

Figure 21 Photo courtesy of GTCO Corporation, Rockville, Maryland

Figure 22 Courtesy of International Business Machines Corporation

Figure 23 Pathfinder® printer by Monarch Marking Systems, a subsidiary of Pitney Bowes

Figure 24 Courtesy of National Semiconductor Corporation

Window 4

Figure 1 Courtesy of Caere Corporation

Figure 2 Courtesy of International Business Machines Corporation

Figure 3 Courtesy of Commodore Electronics Ltd.

Figure 4 Courtesy of Electronic Data Systems, Dallas, Texas

Figure 5 Courtesy of Apple Computer, Inc.

Figure 6 Courtesy of Radio Shack, a division of Tandy Corporation

Figure 7 Courtesy of International Business Machines Corporation

Figure 8 Courtesy Martin Marietta Data Systems

Figure 9 Compugraphic Corporation, Wilmington, Massachusetts

Figures 10, 11 Courtesy of Hewlett-Packard Company

Figures 12, 13 Courtesy of Apple Computer, Inc.

Figures 14, 15 Photos courtesy of Gerber Scientific, Inc.

Figure 16 Courtesy of TRW Inc.

Figure 17 Courtesy of Docutel/Olivette Corporation

Figure 18 Courtesy MSI Data Corporation

Figure 19 Photograph courtesy of Scope Incorporated, Reston, Virginia

Figure 20 Courtesy NCR Corporation

Figure 21 Courtesy of Caere Corporation

Figure 22 Courtesy NCR Corporation

Figure 23 Courtesy of Texas Instruments

Figure 24 Courtesy of Hewlett-Packard Company

Figure 25 Courtesy of Sperry Corporation

Window 5

Figure 1 Photo from Xerox Corporation

Figure 2 Courtesy of Apple Computer, Inc.

Figure 3 SuperCalc is a registered trademark of Computer Associates International, Inc. Micro Products Division.

Figures 5, 6 © Lotus Development Corporation 1985. Used with permission. "1-2-3" is a registered trademark of Lotus Development Corporation

Figure 8 Courtesy of International Business Machines Corporation

Figure 13 Wordstar® 2000 is a trademark of MicroPro International Corporation®

Figure 14 Wordstar® 2000 is a trademark of MicroPro International Corporation®

Figure 15 Courtesy Martin Marietta Data Systems

Figure 16 © Lotus Development Corporation 1985. Used with permission. "Symphony" is a registered trademark of Lotus Development Corporation

Figure 17 Courtesy Cullinet

Figure 18 Courtesy of Apple Computer, Inc.

Figure 19 Copyright © Ashton-Tate 1984. All Rights Reserved. Framework, dBase III and Ashton-Tate are trademarks of Ashton-Tate. Used by permission. 10150 W. Jefferson Boulevard, Culver City, California 90230. (213)204-5570

Figure 20 Courtesy of International Business Machines Corporation

Window 6

Figure 1 Courtesy of Northern Telecom Inc.

Figures 2, 3 Courtesy of RCA

Figures 4, 5 Courtesy of Electronic Data Systems, Dallas, Texas

Figures 6, 7 Courtesy of Northern Telecom Inc.

Figure 8 Courtesy of TRW Inc.

Figure 9 Photograph provided by Tandem Computer Incorporated

Figure 10 Courtesy of General Electric Company

Figure 11 Courtesy of TRW Inc.

Figure 12 Photo courtesy of Telex Computer Products, Inc., Tulsa, Oklahoma

Figure 13 Courtesy of Electronic Data Systems, Dallas, Texas

Figure 14 Vitro Corporation, Silver Spring, Maryland

Figures 15, 16 Courtesy of Northern Telecom Inc.

Figures 17, 18 Courtesy of MICOM Systems, Inc.

Figure 19 Courtesy of Hewlett-Packard Company

Figures 20, 21 Courtesy of ROLM, an IBM Company

Figure 22 Photo courtesy of National Data Corporation

Figure 23 Courtesy of International Business Machines Corporation

Figure 24 Courtesy MSI Data Corporation

Figure 25 Courtesy of General Electric Company

Figure 26 Courtesy of RCA

Window 7

Figure 1 Photo courtesy of Intergraph Corporation, Huntsville, Alabama

Figures 2, 3 Courtesy of Apple Computer, Inc.

Figures 4–7 Courtesy of International Business Machines Corporation

Figure 8 Courtesy of Graphic Communications, Inc.

Figures 11–13 Courtesy Design Resources, Inc.

Figure 15 Courtesy of Sanders Associates

Figures 16–25 Photos courtesy of Intergraph Corporation, Huntsville, Alabama

Window 8

Figures 1–4 Photos courtesy of Monsanto

Figure 5 Courtesy of National Semiconductor Corporation

Figure 6 Courtesy of International Business Machines Corporation

Figure 7 Courtesy of National Semiconductor Corporation

Figure 8 Courtesy of Commodore Electronics Ltd.

Figure 9 Courtesy of TRW Inc.

Figure 10 Courtesy of RCA

Figure 11 Photograph courtesy Intel Corporation

Figure 12 Courtesy of Memorex Corporation, a Burroughs subsidiary

Figure 13 Courtesy of National Semiconductor Corporation

Figure 14 Courtesy of Commodore Electronics Ltd.

Figure 15 Courtesy of Motorola, Inc.

Figure 16 Photo: Loral Corporation/Ovak Arslanian

Figure 17 Courtesy of National Semiconductor Corporation

Figure 18 Photograph courtesy of Intel Corporation

Figure 19 Courtesy of TRW Inc.

Figure 20 Courtesy Commodore Electronics Ltd.

Figure 21 Courtesy of Texas Instruments

Figure 22 Courtesy of TRW Inc.

Figure 23 Courtesy of Paradyne Corporation, Largo, Florida

Figures 24, 25 Courtesy of National Semiconductor Corporation

Figure 26 Photo courtesy of Gerber Scientific, Inc.

Figures 27, 28 Photos courtesy of Intergraph Corporation, Huntsville, Alabama

Figure 29 Photo courtesy of Gerber Scientific, Inc.

Figure 30 Courtesy of Versatec, Inc.

Figures 31–33 Photos courtesy of Gerber Scientific, Inc.

Figure 34 Courtesy of Sanders Associates

Figures 35, 36 Courtesy of Cray Research, Inc.

Figures 37, 38 Courtesy of International Business Machines Corporation

Figure 39 Courtesy of Hewlett-Packard Company

Figure 40 Courtesy of Paradyne Corporation, Largo, Florida

Figure 41 Photograph provided by Tandem Computer Incorporated

Figures 42, 43 Courtesy of Apple Computer, Inc.

Figure 44 Courtesy of International Business Machines Corporation

Window 9

Figure 1 Courtesy of Management Science America, Inc.

Figure 2 Photo courtesy of Hewlett-Packard Company

Figures 3, 4 Courtesy of Telex Computer Products, Inc.

Figure 5 Courtesy of Comdisco, Inc.

Figure 6 Courtesy Docutel/Olivette Corporation

Figure 7 Courtesy of Apple Computer, Inc.

Figure 8 Vitro Corporation, Silver Spring, Maryland

Figure 9 Photo courtesy of Gerber Scientific, Inc.

Figure 10 Courtesy of Electronic Data Systems, Dallas, Texas

Figure 11 Courtesy of Pertec Computer Corporation

Figures 12–14 Courtesy of Electronic Data Systems, Dallas, Texas

Figure 15 Courtesy of TRW, Inc.

Figure 16 Courtesy of Comdisco, Inc.

Figures 17, 18 Courtesy of Rockwell International Semiconductor Products Division

Figure 19 Courtesy of RCA

Figure 20 Courtesy of TRW Inc.

Figure 21 Courtesy of Commodore Electronics Ltd.

Figure 22 Photograph courtesy Intel Corporation

Figure 23 Courtesy of International Business Machines Corporation

Figure 24 Courtesy of TRW Inc.

Figure 25 Photo courtesy of C. Itoh Electronics, Inc.

Figure 26 Courtesy of International Business Machines Corporation

glossary

Absolute cell reference In spreadsheet processing, a reference to a cell location in the worksheet that is to remain unchanged if the formula that contains the reference is moved to a new location. Contrast with *relative cell reference*.

Access time The time it takes to locate and begin transferring information from an external storage device.

Accumulator A general-purpose register inside a CPU that holds temporary results of computations.

Acoustic coupler A low-speed modem that is attached to the telephone system by jamming a telephone handset into two rubber cups on top of the coupler. Contrast with *direct-connect modem*.

Active cell In spreadsheet processing, the worksheet cell currently available for use. It is pointed to by the cursor.

Address A number identifying a location in memory. Data in internal memory is organized into words, and each word is given its own numeric address.

Algorithm A step-by-step list of instructions for solving a problem.

Alphanumeric A set of characters that includes letters and digits and often includes punctuation characters as well.

Analog A way of representing data as a continuous, smoothly varying signal wave. Contrast with *digital*.

Application generator A very high-level language that allows the programmer to give a detailed explanation of what data is to be processed, rather than how to process the data.

Application software Programs written to perform specific tasks for computer users rather than computer programmers. Examples include accounting programs, word processing, and graphics programs. Contrast with *system software*.

Argument See *parameter*.

G-1

Arithmetic/logic unit (ALU) The part of the CPU that has circuits to perform arithmetic and logical operations such as adding, multiplying, comparing, jumping, and shifting.

Array An organized collection of data in a column or table format. An array associates many pieces of data with a single variable name. It is an important type of *data structure*.

Artificial intelligence A research area concerned with developing computer systems capable of simulating human reasoning and intelligence.

ASCII Short for the *American Standard Code for Information Interchange*. A code for representing letters, numerals, and special characters as a pattern of seven bits. ASCII is used in virtually all personal computers to store and manipulate textual information.

Assembler A program to translate assembly language instructions into machine language.

Assembly language A programming language in which each instruction in the program corresponds to an instruction that the circuits of the computer can perform. Assembly language allows the programmer to write programs with words like MOVE, ADD, or JUMP instead of coding the binary numbers of machine language.

Asynchronous protocol A communications protocol that transmits data one character at a time without any prior arrangement as to how many characters are to be sent. Contrast with *synchronous protocol*.

Audit trail The footprints left by a transaction as it is processed through an accounting or computer system.

Auto-answer A feature that allows a modem to answer a telephone and establish a connection with another computer without assistance from a computer operator.

Back-up copy An extra copy of a file or disk, stored in case something happens to the original.

BASIC *Beginner's All-purpose Symbolic Instruction Code*. A popular programming language that was originally developed for timesharing and interactive problem solving.

Batch processing A processing technique that collects and processes data in groups.

Baud rate A measure of transmission speed. Technically, the baud rate is the number of times the communication line changes state each second. Most people use *baud rate* and *bits per second* interchangeably.

Benchmark program A program that is used as a standard of comparison to test the relative capabilities of computer systems.

Binary The number system with two possible states for each digit: 0 or 1. This system is important to computers because their circuits have only two states: on or off.

Bit An abbreviation for *binary digit*. A bit is the smallest unit of computer memory.

Bit-mapped display A method of generating screen images by creating a one-for-one correspondence between bits in memory and pixels on the screen. In color graphics, three or more bits are required in the bit map to represent the red, green, and blue values of an individual pixel. Contrast with *character-oriented display*.

Boilerplate Passages of text that are used over and over without modification.

Boldface An attribute of characters that are darker and slightly wider than normal.

Boot To start a computer by loading part of the operating system. Usually a computer is booted by inserting a system disk and turning on the computer or by pressing the computer's reset button. *Boot* is short for *bootstrap* as in "pulling yourself up by your bootstraps."

Buffer A temporary storage area used to compensate for a difference in data transfer rates between two devices.

Bug An error in a program.

Bulletin board system A personal computer with an auto-answer modem that answers incoming telephone calls. Nearly all bulletin board systems allow the caller to read and leave messages; many allow the caller to send or receive programs as well. Also called a *public access message system (PAMS)*.

Bus A cable or a set of electrical conductors that carry signals among the devices in a computer or network. Only one device at a time is allowed to send data on the bus, but each device continually listens to the bus for messages addressed to it. Because devices can be attached to any point along the bus, a computer network that uses a bus can be expanded easily.

Byte Eight adjacent bits of memory treated as a unit of information.

Cache A small high-speed memory that acts as a buffer between the CPU and the slower main memory.

CAD Short for *computer-aided design*—drawing with the aid of your computer.

CAI Short for *computer-aided instruction*—using computers for individual and classroom instruction.

CAM Short for *computer-aided manufacturing*—automated production.

Cathode ray tube (CRT) A display device that generates images by bombarding a phosphor-coated glass tube with a beam of electrons.

Cell In spreadsheet processing, the intersection of a row and a column on a worksheet.

Central processing unit (CPU) The brain of a computer. The central processing unit contains circuits that execute instructions and control the other units.

Character-oriented display A method of generating screen images that breaks the screen into many boxes arranged in rows and columns. Each box can display one character. Contrast with *bit-mapped display*.

Characters per second (CPS) A measure of the rate at which data is transferred.

Clock rate The speed at which the central processing unit performs operations; usually measured in megahertz.

Coaxial cable A cable that consists of a wire that is encircled by a metallic tubular sleeve. Coaxial cable is used in cable television networks and in high-speed computer networks.

Command An instruction given to the computer to perform a specified task.

Command-line operating system A system of giving instructions to the computer by typing full-word keywords, which are often followed by arguments.

Command processor The part of an operating system that accepts commands from the user for operating system tasks. Also called a *shell*.

Compiler A program that translates programs written in a high-level language into machine language. A compiler is dedicated to a single programming language, such as

BASIC or Pascal, and translates the entire program before execution begins. Contrast with *interpreter*.

Context-sensitive help A system that displays information about the function currently being used when the [HELP] key is pressed.

Control key A special key on the keyboard, usually labeled [CTRL]. Like a shift key, a control key is used in combination with other keys; unlike the shift key, it generates different character codes and is used to give commands.

Control panel A portion of the screen reserved for status and help information.

Control structure Any statement that determines the order in which other statements are executed. Common control structures include FOR statements (for repeating or looping), IF-THEN-ELSE statements (for making two-way decisions), and CASE statements (for multiple-way decisions).

Control unit (1) The part of the CPU that interprets instructions and coordinates their execution. (2) A peripheral device that controls other peripheral devices. For example, a disk control unit might supervise the operation of several disk drives.

Copy-protect To prevent a disk from being copied by a standard disk-copying routine.

Copyright The exclusive right to publish or sell a creative work. Copyrights are the most common legal method of protecting computer programs from unauthorized distribution.

CP/M Short for *Control Program for Microcomputers*. CP/M is a popular operating system for personal computers.

CPU See *central processing unit*.

CRT See *cathode ray tube*.

Cursor An indicator on the screen that shows where things will happen next. The cursor can be an underline (blinking or nonblinking), a rectangle, or even an arrow.

Cursor-movement key A key that when pressed moves the cursor in a designated direction. Cursor-movement keys generally have directional arrows on their keytops, as in [↑], [↓], [←], and [→].

Daisy wheel The print element of a letter-quality printer. Daisy wheels are made from metal or plastic and have spokes radiating from the center. Each spoke contains a letter, number, or symbol at the end.

Data Information in code, text, or numerical form. (Usage note: In everyday usage, *data* is a singular collective: *This data is in error*. Most dictionaries list *datum* as the singular form of *data* and note that *data* is plural in formal usage. In this book we have adopted the more common singular usage.)

Database A logically connected collection of data.

Database management system (DBMS) A set of programs that provide for the input, retrieval, formatting, modification, output, transfer, and maintenance of information in a database.

Data dictionary A list of all the files, fields, attributes, formats, and access rights in a database.

Data flow diagram A visual representation of how data moves through a system.

Data structure A method of organizing data. Some common data structures are arrays, lists, files, and stacks.

Data transfer rate The rate at which data is transferred from external storage to computer memory or from computer memory to external storage.

DBMS See *database management system*.

Debugger A program that aids a programmer in locating and removing the errors in a program.

Default The value or setting that a program uses if the user does not specify a value.

Delimiter A symbol that indicates the end of a command, argument, or parameter. In the command TYPE LETTER.JIM, a space is the delimiter between the command keyword TYPE and its argument, LETTER.JIM.

Demodulate To convert an analog signal into a digital signal.

Device independence The ability to add an input, output, or storage device to a computer system by modifying only the I/O manager of the operating system, without altering other software.

Dialing directory A file containing telephone numbers and communication parameters. In conjunction with smart modems, a dialing directory can be used to dial a telephone number and log onto a remote computer almost automatically.

Dialog box A temporary window on the screen that contains a prompt in the form of a question whenever the executing program needs an answer from the user.

Digital A way of processing information by storing it as binary numbers. A digital circuit is either on or off; a digital signal is either present or absent. Contrast with *analog*.

Digitize To register a visual image or real object in a format that can be processed by the computer. Digitized data is read into the system with graphics input devices, such as a puck or stylus.

Direct-access A file organization in which records can be read directly, without reading all intervening records. As a result, the time required to retrieve a record is independent of its location.

Direct-connect modem A modem that plugs directly into a telephone jack to make a direct electrical connection with the telephone system. Contrast with *acoustic coupler*.

Directory A system file that lists the names and locations of all other files on a disk.

Distributed computing The simultaneous use of independent computers that are linked in a network to work on a common problem. Contrasts with *centralized computing*, in which all jobs are fed into a central mainframe.

Documentation Any written information that describes hardware or software, including tutorial lessons, reference manuals, pocket reference guides, and so forth.

Document chaining The merging and sequential printing of information from several files.

Dot matrix printer An impact printer that forms characters by printing a series of dots. Dot matrix printers are very popular and inexpensive, but unlike letter-quality printers, they do not create characters with smooth, fully formed edges.

Downloading To send information from a large computer to a smaller one.

Dumb terminal A terminal that has no processing capabilities of its own.

Editor A program used to write, enter, and edit programs. The major difference between an editor and a word processor is that word processors tend to have more features for fancy printing.

Electronic dictionary A program that compares words in a document with its own list of correctly spelled words and displays the words that do not match. It is also called a *spelling checker*.

Electronic thesaurus A program that lists synonyms for a given word.

Expert system A computer program that simulates the reasoning process used by a human expert in a particular subject.

External storage Long-term nonvolatile storage that is not part of the central processing unit. Tapes and disks are the most common forms of external storage. It is also called *secondary storage* or *auxiliary storage*.

Fiber optics cable A cable made from strands of glass that carries data in the form of pulses of light.

Field The part of a record reserved for a particular item or type of data.

File (1) A collection of related records. (2) A named collection of bytes on a disk.

File conversion program A utility program that translates a file from one format to another.

File server A device in a computer network that controls the hard disk and connects it to the network.

Fixed disk A hard disk in which the disk platter is mounted permanently inside an airtight, factory-sealed unit.

Floating-point number A number represented in scientific form. A floating-point number is broken into two parts: the fractional part and the exponent.

Floppy disk A flexible, flat, circular piece of magnetic material for storing information. It is the most common medium for external storage for personal computers.

Footing A line or lines of text printed in the bottom margin of a page.

Form A template that indicates both the items of data and where they are to be placed. Forms assist in the process of collecting and storing data.

Format (1) The arrangement of data. (2) To prepare a blank disk so that it can be used to store information. Also known as *initializing*.

Free-form windows A method of presenting windows on the screen that allows them to overlap one another, like objects stacked on top of a desk. Contrast with *tiled windows*.

Frequency modulation A method of analog signaling that encodes data as changes in the frequency of the signal. Frequency modulation is used in FM radio and in some low-speed methods of data transmission over telephone lines.

Front end computer A small computer that is located between a host computer and the terminals and other devices needing access to the host computer. The front-end computer handles communications and error-checking tasks related to routing messages in and out of the host computer.

Full-duplex A method of transmitting data that allows the simultaneous sending and receiving of data. Contrast with *half-duplex*.

Function keys Extra keyboard keys that are used for specific purposes, which depend on the program being executed. The keytops of function keys are frequently labeled with [F1], [F2], and so forth.

Gantt chart A visual representation of a project schedule; the columns are time intervals and the rows correspond to activities.

Gigabyte A unit of storage—roughly one billion characters.

Global search and replace A search-and-replace operation that is performed repeatedly throughout an entire document.

Graphics editor A program for editing pictures. Typical operations include drawing, moving, rotating, and enlarging items on the screen.

Hacker A person with computer expertise who is obsessed with learning about programming and exploring the capabilities of computer systems.

Half-duplex A method of transmitting data that does not allow data to travel in both directions at once. Contrast with *full-duplex*.

Handshaking The exchange of signals that control the flow of information between two electrical devices.

Hard disk An external storage device that stores data on a quickly spinning rigid disk with a magnetic surface. Hard disks offer a much greater storage capacity and faster access time than floppy disks.

Hardware The physical equipment in a computer system.

Hashing function A procedure for transforming a record key into the position of the record in a random-access file.

Heading A line or lines printed in the top margin of a page.

Hierarchical model A method of organizing a database that establishes a top-to-bottom relationship among the records, much like the members of a family on a family tree. Each item has a unique parent or owner but can have many items below it. Contrast with *network model* and *relational model*.

High-level language (HLL) A programming language with English-like constructs or mathematical notation that is used to describe a procedure for solving a problem. High-level languages require little or no knowledge of the computer being used.

Home The upper-left position on the screen.

Horizontal software Programs designed to serve a wide range of users who must tailor the programs to their own needs. Examples include word processors and database management systems.

Icon A picture of an object such as a printer, trash can, or pad of paper.

Indexed file A collection of two or more closely related files, one of which contains the data; each of the other files contains an index to the data file.

Information utility A timeshared computer that provides a wide range of processing and information retrieval services to customers who access the utility through telecommunications.

Initialize See *format*.

Instruction register The register in the CPU that holds the instruction currently being carried out by the computer.

Instruction set The set of elemental operations that the circuits of a central processing unit are capable of performing directly.

Integrated circuit An electronic circuit etched on a tiny silicon chip. Integrated circuits replaced transistors in third-generation computers.

Integrated program A collection of related programs combined in a package that provides a means of transferring data between the programs.

Interface The connection between two data processing elements. For example, the central processing unit is connected to peripheral devices through hardware interfaces, and the control of an accounting program might be governed by a full-screen menu interface.

Interpreter A program that translates and executes a program written in a high-level language. An interpreter translates one line of the source program, then executes that line, then translates the next line, and so on. In contrast, a *compiler* translates the entire source program before execution begins.

I/O device A peripheral that accepts input or provides output.

I/O port A standard interface between the computer and external devices.

Job control language (JCL) A special programming language used to give instructions to the operating system and to control when programs run.

Justify To align text. Text that is flush with both the left and right margins is often said to be *justified*.

Key A piece of information that is used to identify a record in a data file.

Keyboard macro A series of keystrokes that is associated with a single key on the keyboard. Whenever the macro's key is pressed, the keystrokes in the macro are played back just as if they had all been typed.

Keywords Words with a special meaning or function in a command.

Kilobit A measure of storage capacity equal to 1,024 bits.

Kilobyte A measure of storage equal to 1,024 bytes (or characters). Kilobyte is often abbreviated *K* or *KB*.

LAN See *local area network*.

LCD Stands for *l*iquid *c*rystal *d*isplay. LCD displays are used in many portable computers because they are small, flat, and require little power.

Letter-quality printer A printer that produces output indistinguishable from that of a good typewriter.

License agreement A document that spells out the legal and authorized uses of a program.

Light pen A pencil-shaped, light-sensitive device used to select a location on the screen or to read bar codes on paper.

Line printer A printer that prints an entire line of characters almost simultaneously rather than one character at a time.

Liquid crystal display See *LCD*.

Local area network (LAN) A system of interconnected data processing equipment in a limited physical area.

Logging off The process of telling the computer you are through using it.

Logging on The process of identifying yourself to a multiuser computer system—by typing an account number and a password—for billing and security purposes.

Logical schema The description of the files, records, fields, and relationships among the data in a database. Contrast with *physical schema*.

Machine independence The ability to move software from one type of computer system to another without reprogramming.

Machine language program A program written in the binary code that can be executed directly by the control unit of a CPU. All programs written in high-level languages are translated into machine language before they are executed.

Macro A single instruction or command that invokes a previously stored sequence of commands.

Mainframe A large multiuser computer. The term refers to the racks and cabinet used to house the central processing unit of a large computer.

Megabyte A measure of storage roughly equal to one million characters, although technically a megabyte is equal to a kilobyte squared, or $2^{20} = 1,045,576$ bytes. Megabyte is often abbreviated *M, MB,* or in slang, as *meg.*

Megahertz One million cycles per second. Megahertz is used to measure a CPU's clock rate.

Memory A portion of the computer where programs and data are stored while being used by the computer system. Memory is also called *main memory, primary memory, RAM,* or *internal memory.*

Menu bar A one- or two-line list of commands displayed on the screen. *Keyword menu bars* list the entire word for each available command. *One-letter menu bars* list only the first letter of each command.

MFLOP Short for *m*illions of *f*loating-point *op*erations per second. Used as a rough measure of a computer's processing speed.

MICR Short for *m*agnetic *i*nk *c*haracter *r*ecognition. MICR devices are used mainly to read the characters on the bottom of bank checks.

Microcomputer Any small computer based on a microprocessor.

Microprocessor A programmable processing circuit built on a single silicon chip.

Microsecond One-millionth of a second.

Microspacing A form of printing that inserts tiny spaces between letters and words to give text an even, professional appearance. Each character is assigned the same fixed-width field regardless of its shape; only the space between characters is adjusted. See *proportional spacing.*

Millisecond One-thousandth of a second.

Minicomputer A medium-sized computer that is usually capable of timesharing. The distinctions among micro, mini, and mainframe computers are blurring, and there are no clear-cut dividing lines between them.

Mode A program state in which only a restricted set of operations can be performed. For example, in the entry mode of spreadsheet processing it is not possible to do anything other than enter or edit the contents of the active cell.

Modem A communications device that converts (modulates) the digital pulses gen-erated by computer equipment into analog signals that can be sent over voice-grade telephone lines. When receiving data, it demodulates the incoming telephone signal to recreate the original digital signal.

Modulate To convert a digital signal into an analog signal.

Module An identifiable part of a program. Writing programs in modules enables programmers to focus attention on one part of the programming problem at a time. Many large programs are left in modules so that only part of the program needs to be in memory at once (see *program overlay*).

Monitor A CRT-based visual display unit. Basically, a monitor is a high-resolution television set without a speaker, channel selector, or radio-frequency receiver. In a *monochrome monitor* each pixel can glow in only one color; in a *color monitor* each pixel is three dots: red, green, and blue.

Mouse A hand-operated pointing device that senses movements as it is dragged across a flat surface and conveys this information to the computer. Most mice also have buttons that can be clicked to signal to the computer.

Multiplexer A communications device that interleaves messages from low-speed transmission lines and sends the composite signal on a single high-speed transmission channel.

Multitasking The ability of a computer to execute two or more programs simultaneously. For example, a multitasking computer might allow the user to edit a document with a word processing program while it uses a communications program to receive a file from another computer.

Nanosecond One-billionth of a second.

Network A system of machines that are connected electrically and can communicate with each other.

Network database model A method of organizing a database that establishes a many-to-many relationship among records. Contrast with *hierarchical model* and *relational model*.

Nonprocedural language A very high-level programming language in which the programmer describes *what* the desired results are, but does not need to be concerned about the details of *how* the work is done.

Object program The machine language version of a source program that is created when the source program is compiled or assembled.

OCR Stands for *optical character recognition*. Optical character recognition devices allow computers to read printed information (usually in a special typeface) more reliably and faster than it can be typed.

Off-line Not connected directly to the computer.

On-line Any device that is under the direct control of the computer.

Operating system The master set of programs that manage the computer. Among other things, an operating system controls input and output to and from the keyboard, screen, disks, and other peripheral devices; loads and begins the execution of other programs; and manages the storage of data on disks.

Option switch A parameter that can be included in a command to override a default value. For example, an option switch might be added to the command to execute a program in order to tell the program to send its output to a file rather than to the printer.

Packet-switching network A telecommunications network that sends information through the network in the form of units of data called *packets*.

Page design The process of specifying the boundaries of text on a page. Includes choosing margins, headings, footings, and page length.

Paragraph reforming In word processing, to rearrange the text in a paragraph so that it fits neatly between the margins.

Parameter A piece of information that regulates the behavior of a program. For example, the command that tells the operating system how to communicate with a printer might include a parameter specifying the speed at which data is to be transferred.

Parity bit An extra bit that is added to a computer word to detect errors.

Patent The legal protection granted by the Patent Office for exclusive use of an original idea or invention. Patents are rarely granted for programs.

Peripherals External equipment connected to the computer such as input and output devices and external storage units.

Personal computer A small, inexpensive, single-user computer based on a microprocessor.

Physical schema The description of how data is physically stored on a disk. Contrast with *logical schema*.

Pixel An acronym for *pic*ture *el*ement. A pixel is the smallest display element on the screen. See *monitor*.

Plotter An output device that produces a hard copy of pictures, drawings, or other graphical information.

Presentation graphics An easy-to-understand, high-quality display of numerical information, such as a bar chart, pie chart, or line graph.

Print server A device in a local area network that shares a printer among all users connected to the network.

Print spooler A program that enables a computer to print a file and execute another program at the same time.

Program A set of instructions that directs a computer for solving a problem.

Program generator A translator program that converts nonprocedural information into a procedural program. Program generators often use a question-and-answer dialog to determine what processing is to be done and are limited in type of application that they can produce.

Program overlay A program module that is moved from external storage into computer memory when it is needed for processing.

Prompt A signal from the computer that it expects the user to enter information.

Proportional spacing A form of printing that allocates room for characters based on their width. With proportional spacing an *M* is printed in a wider field than an *i*. Typeset documents are normally proportionally spaced, and an increasing portion of computer printers are capable of proportional spacing.

Protocol A set of rules that controls the interchange of data between independent devices.

Prototype A trial system that simulates the behavior of the real system in order to let users try the system before it is constructed.

Puck A very precise hand-held pointing device with cross hairs and a magnifying glass; it is used to enter the coordinates of graphical data.

Pull-down menu A list of commands that appears from the top of the screen when a command needs to be given and then disappears when the selection has been made.

Query language A programming language for giving commands that search or modify a database.

Race condition A condition where two concurrent processing activities interact to cause a processing error.

RAM An acronym for *random-access memory*. RAM is memory built from silicon chips that is used to store programs and data temporarily while they are being processed.

RAM disk An area of memory that mimics the operations of a very high-speed disk drive in order to speed up file processing.

Random access The ability to read or write each piece of information in a storage device in approximately the same length of time, regardless of its location. Internal memory and disks are random-access devices.

Range of cells In spreadsheet processing, a rectangular group of worksheet cells treated as one unit.

Raster scan A method of creating a CRT image in which an electron beam moves horizontally across each line of the screen fifteen or more times each second, turning pixels on and off.

Read/write head The part of the tape or disk drive that reads or writes information on magnetic media.

Real-time processing A type of on-line processing that acts on information quickly enough to keep up with events occurring in the outside world.

Record A collection of related data items treated as a unit. Often a line in a data file is thought of as a record.

Record management system A set of programs for managing data in a single file.

Register A special high-speed memory location within the CPU where information is held temporarily and is manipulated according to program instructions.

Relational model A method of organizing a database that arranges the information as tables. A *relation* is a table whose columns and rows correspond to fields and records, respectively.

Relative cell reference In spreadsheet processing, a reference to a location in the worksheet that is interpreted with respect to the formula's current cell location. Contrast with *absolute cell reference*.

Repeating key A keyboard key that generates a constant stream of characters when depressed. The keys on most computer keyboards will repeat after being held down for about a half second.

Report break A position in a report where one or more fields change value according to some rule. For example, in a sales report a report break might occur after the list of sales made by each salesperson.

Report generator A program that extracts information from one or more files, manipulates it, and then prints it in a formatted form.

Resident routines The parts of the operating system that are loaded into memory when the computer is turned on and remain there during processing. The opposite of a *transient routine*.

Resolution A measure of the accuracy or fineness of detail in a picture or display device.

RF modulator A device that converts a video signal from a computer into the radio frequency of a television channel. RF modulators are used to attach television sets to home computers to serve as visual display units.

Right-justified Text aligned flush with the right margin.

ROM An abbreviation for *read-only memory*. ROM is a form of internal memory that stores information permanently. Thus, the information in ROM can be read but cannot be changed.

Routine Any program or set of instructions that has general or frequent use.

RS-232 A standard that specifies the voltages and signals used to transmit data across an interface cable. The RS-232 standard is used to connect a wide range of peripheral devices to the I/O ports on computers.

Schema A model or description of the structure of a database.

Scrolling The horizontal or vertical movement of information on a screen in order to display additional information.

Sector A pie-shaped wedge of one track of a disk. On most computers a sector is the smallest unit of information sent between the disk drive and CPU.

Sequential storage The storage of information so that items must be read or written one after the other; thus, jumping from one item to another is not permitted. Tape is the most common type of sequential storage. Contrast with *direct-access*.

Shell See *command processor*.

Soft spaces Spaces added by a word processor between the words in a line so that the line ends flush with the right margin.

Software The generic term for any program or programs.

Software piracy The illegal copying of a computer program.

Software portability The ability to move programs from one type of computer to another without reprogramming.

Sort key The field or fields on which a file is sorted. There are both *primary* and *secondary* sort keys. For example, a sales report might be sorted on the customer-name field, which becomes the primary sort key; and all the sales transactions with the same customer name might be sorted by the sales-amount field, which then is the secondary sort key.

Source program A program written in a high-level language. Source programs must be compiled or interpreted before they can be executed by the computer.

Spelling checker See *electronic dictionary*.

Spreadsheet program An application program that manipulates numbers in an electronic worksheet containing a grid of cells.

Status line In spreadsheet processing, a line in the control panel that displays the co-ordinates and contents of the active cell.

Streaming tape drive A cartridge tape system designed to back-up and restore information on hard disks.

Structured programming A disciplined approach to the design and coding of programs that leads to easily understood and maintainable program code. Structured programs use a restricted set of control structures and fit within a top-down design.

Structured walkthrough A formal review process in which a designer or programmer leads one or more members of the development team through a segment of design or code.

Subroutine A set of instructions that has been taken out and made into a subprogram which can be executed from any point in a main program.

Subschema A description of the part of the logical schema that is relevant to a particular user or program. The subschema may also contain a description of how data should be formatted for presentation to the user.

Supervisor The part of the operating system that controls the execution of other programs.

Synchronous protocol A communications protocol that sends data in packets that do not contain timing signals. Contrast with *asynchronous protocol*.

System analyst An information-processing specialist who studies systems in an organization. A system analyst defines the problem to be solved, analyzes the problem, and recommends solutions.

System disk A disk containing operating system programs.

System software Any program that controls the computer system or helps programmers develop new programs. System software includes the operating system, programming languages, utilities, debuggers, editors, and so forth.

Template In spreadsheet processing, a formatted worksheet that contains all the labels and formulas for an application but does not contain the user's data. For example, an income tax template might contain labels describing how to fill in the template and formulas for calculating the income tax due, but it would not contain the amount of income and expenses.

Terminal Any device that allows a person to communicate with a computer. A terminal usually includes a keyboard and either a video screen or a printing mechanism.

Terminal emulator A communications program that makes a personal computer act like a terminal for the purpose of interacting with a remote computer.

Tiled window A screen display divided into nonoverlapping windows. The opposite of a *free-form window*.

Timesharing The simultaneous sharing of a computer's resources by many users.

Toggle switch A switch with two settings. Each time the switch is thrown, it maintains its new setting until it is thrown back again.

Top-down design A system analysis methodology in which the overall structure of the solution is developed first; each succeeding phase of the analysis is more detailed. Top-down design is one of the chief concepts underlying structured programming.

Touch screen A display unit that can sense where a finger or other object touches its screen.

Touch-tablet A touch-sensitive flat electrical device that transmits to the computer the location of a stylus or pen touching its surface.

Track A concentric circle of a disk on which information is stored.

Trade secret The legal protection of an idea, formula, or other valuable business information because it provides the basis for a competitive advantage in the marketplace.

Transient utility A program that is loaded from a disk into memory only when it is needed. The opposite of a *resident routine*.

Transparency Word used to describe a program action that occurs automatically and usually without the user's being aware of it. For example, the details of how a file is stored on tracks and sectors are transparent to the user.

T-switch An electrical switch that allows the user to change the connections between computing equipment just by turning a knob on the switch. T-switches are useful for sharing infrequently used peripheral devices such as a letter-quality printer.

Tuple A row of a relation (file) in a relational database.

UNDO command A command that reverses the effect of the previous command and thus is useful for correcting mistakes.

Uploading To transfer a file from a small computer to a larger computer.

Utility program A system program that performs an operating system function or helps in the development or maintenance of programs.

Variable An area of memory that has been given a name. The term has the same meaning in programming as in mathematics.

Vector graphics A method of generating pictures by drawing numerous straight-line segments (vectors) on the screen.

Vertical software Specialized application software that is designed for a particular discipline or activity. Examples include software that tracks the stock market and medical billing systems.

Very high-level language See *nonprocedural language*.

Virtual memory A method of simulating a very large main memory by automatically moving parts of a running program from internal to external memory as the program runs. Thus, if a program needs 10 megabytes of memory to execute, it might be run on a virtual memory computer that has only 2 megabytes of main memory and 100 megabytes of disk storage. Also called *virtual storage*.

Visual display unit Any televisionlike display unit, such as a CRT or a liquid crystal display.

Visual operating system An operating system that relies on icons for giving commands to the computer.

Volatile Term used to describe memory devices that lose information if electrical power to the device is interrupted. The internal memory of almost all general-purpose computers is volatile, but special-purpose computers such as portable computers sometimes use nonvolatile memory. Memory devices relying on magnetic media (tapes and disks) are nonvolatile.

Window A region of a screen through which part of a file or some data in memory can be viewed. Some programs allow windows to be split into several parts, called *window panes*.

Word size The number of bits in each memory location or *word* of memory. Also called *word length*. Early personal computers had a word length of 8 bits, minicomputers typically have 16- or 32-bit words, and mainframe computers have 32 or more bits per word.

Word processor A program to help create written documents.

Word wrap A common and convenient word processing feature that automatically begins a new line of text whenever the word being entered does not fit within the margins of the current line.

Worksheet The grid of rows and columns used by a spreadsheet program.

Write-protect To prevent magnetic media from being written on by a program. Sometimes this is done physically by removing a tab from a tape case or by covering a notch on a floppy disk jacket. At other times various software methods are used to protect individual files.

index